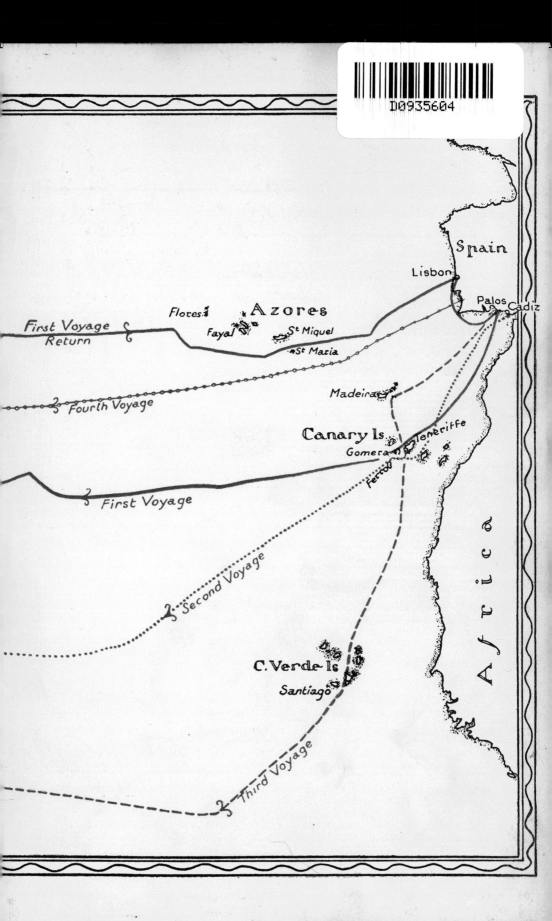

CHRISTOPHER COLUMBUS

THE MACMILLAN COMPANY
NEW YORK · BOSTON · CHICAGO
DALLAS · ATLANTA · SAN FRANCISCO

The oldest known portrait
of the Very Magnificent Lord
Don Cristóbal Colón

SALVADOR DE MADARIAGA

CHRISTOPHER COLUMBUS

Being the Life of

The Very Magnificent Lord

DON CRISTÓBAL COLÓN

1940

THE MACMILLAN COMPANY

NEW YORK

— PRINTED IN THE UNITED STATES OF AMERICA —

To

THOMAS JONES, C.H.

59294

La verdad no se casa con nadie.
(Truth marries no one.)

Spanish proverb.

TABLE OF CONTENTS

PROLOGUE

PART I

CHRISTOFORO COLOMBO GOES TO SEA

PART II

CHRISTOVÃO COLOMBO, A STUDENT IN PORTUGAL

PART III

CRISTÓBAL COLOMO, AN ADVENTURER IN CASTILLE

PART IV

THE VERY MAGNIFICENT LORD DON CRISTÓBAL COLÓN

PART V

THE GRAND ADMIRAL OF THE OCEAN SEA

PART VI

FALL, DEATH AND TRANSFIGURATION

NOTES

Notes to the Chapters—(*continued*)

ILLUSTRATIONS

PROLOGUE

CHAPTER I

THE BANNER AND THE CROSS

ON the second day of January 1492, (1) King Ferdinand rode in the clear sun of Andalucía towards that city of Granada, the last jewel of his crown still in the hands of the infidels, (2) which had been for over a century the obsession and the dream of his ancestors. Dressed in bright-coloured rich clothes, on a horse caparisoned with gold and covered with red brocade, he rode at the head of as brilliant a squadron of knights as had ever been seen in those days in Spain or anywhere else; the Dukes and Maestres, Marquises and Counts who for over ten years had helped him, day in day out, to conquer step by step, castle by castle, city by city, the rich kingdom of Granada, whose capital he was now going to receive from the trembling hands of Boabdil the Young. There were the Cardinal of Spain, Pedro González de Mendoza, one of the leading spirits of that austere age; and the powerful Master of the military order of St. James, and the Dukes of Medina-Sidonia and of Cádiz, and Don Alonso de Aguilar, and the Marquis of Villena, the Count of Ureña, the ever-active and ubiquitous Count of Cabra, terror of the Moors, and many more prelates and knights—a living mass of purple, silk and brocade, glittering with silver and gold, moving on at the gracious rhythm of Andalusian and Arabian horse, under the shadow of a forest of pennants, banners and standards, over all of which there rose in triumph the golden Cross and the Royal Banner of Castille.

The capitulation had been signed on December 30th. The Moors, after an eight-month siege, had surrendered to hunger and agreed to give up the fortresses held by Boabdil on condition that their faith and property should be respected. These were the usual conditions under which Moorish towns, with some grim exceptions such as Málaga, had surrendered to King Ferdinand during the campaign, for he was of those shrewd spirits who prefer a fair treaty to a good fight. The surrender of the town was due to take place on January 6th, but King Boabdil, in fear of the progress made by an agitator who was arousing the crowd

3

against him and the Christians, sent word to Ferdinand to advance the date of his entry into Granada.

Queen Isabel, with Prince Don Juan, then fourteen years of age, and the Infanta Juana, whose son, the future Charles V, not Juan her brother, was to be the heir of all that splendour and much more to come, were watching the sight from a hill close to the town; at their feet, the Genil wound its way towards the Vega, still scarred by the terrible devastations of the ten-year war; Santa Fé, the brick-and-mortar town built instead of the royal camp destroyed by fire only six months earlier, looked like a chessboard of dusty red on muddy brown, gaily decorated with flags, thronged with mules, asses and horses, choked with the carts of the ordnance and victualling services; towering above the wooded slopes, the walls of the Alhambra, "the Red," bristled with the crowd of the trembling, dejected garrison and its women-folk, waiting with mixed feelings for a sad defeat which was withal a comfortable deliverance and, despite the gravity of the occasion, enthralled like good Orientals by the splendour of the pageantry which they were beholding.

A less bright pageant was riding down from the red-walled town towards the Genil. Boabdil the Young, with a scanty desolate suite, came to close an era of over seven centuries of Moorish sway. Their white burnooses, which in the days of their glory rose like wings over their beturbaned heads as they galloped yelling defiance and death towards the Christians, hung dispiritedly by their sides like the shrouds of their soulless bodies. They rode in silence. Boabdil sighed, heavy with re-sponsibility, remembering perhaps the civil wars in which he had consumed whatever strength remained in the last years of the Moorish rule.

As Ferdinand waited, he would observe on Boabdil's face the traces of nine years of wars, dangers and privations. For it was nine years earlier, in 1483, that the powerful Christian King had held Boabdil at his mercy in Córdoba and set him at liberty again, thinking him more dangerous to his own kith and kin as one of the leaders in their civil strife than to the Christians as the leader of the Infidels. It was then that, to those of his courtiers and captains who pressed him to make the vassal king kiss his hand, Ferdinand gave the noble answer: *I certainly would, were he free in his kingdom; yet I will not while he is a prisoner in mine.* (3) Both men were perhaps reminded of this episode when Boabdil stopped with all his suite in front of the brilliant battalion of the Christians and made a move to alight and kiss Ferdinand's hands. But

Ferdinand would have none of it, and Boabdil, without dismounting, bowed low, kissed Ferdinand's arm and delivered up to him the keys of Granada.

All those who have seen Velázquez's masterpiece "The Surrender of Breda" can imagine the courtly, generous gesture with which King Ferdinand received those keys—not the keys of just another town taken from the enemy, after Baza, Málaga, Loja and so many others which had surrendered to him, but the keys of that bejewelled brooch which clasped the many kingdoms, seigneuries and allegiances of the peninsula into one only Spain.

Ferdinand handed them to the Count of Tendilla, a scion of that house of Mendoza to which Spain already owed many of her best soldiers and churchmen, and one of her best poets of all times. Thereupon, Tendilla, with the Commander-General of Leon, Don Gutierre de Cardona, followed by a motley crowd of knights and preceded by the Cross and Banner, rode up towards the Alhambra. A moment of intense emotion for Moor and Christian alike; thousands of eyes, in a tense silence, following this final ascent of the Cross and Banner to the last fortress of Islam. And presently, while the Kings at Arms proclaimed aloud, "Granada, Granada for King Ferdinand and Queen Isabel," the Cross first, the Royal Banner afterwards, rose against the sky over the tower of Comares. No trumpets, no drums, none of that courtly and gay music of which the Queen was so fond. But in the silence the Queen's chapel of singers, who surrounded her, began to chant the solemn tune of the church hymn of thanks— *Te Deum Laudamus;* and the Queen fell on her knees and wept.

* *

She was nearly forty-one years of age. We may form an idea of her looks and character from the pen-picture left us by her confidential secretary and chronicler, Hernando del Pulgar: (4)

"This Queen was of middle height, well made in her person and in the proportion of her limbs, very white and fair; her eyes between green and blue, her glance graceful and modest, the features of her face well set, her face very beautiful and gay. She was well measured in the countenance and movements of her person; she drank no wine; she was a very good woman and liked to have old women of good lineage and character beside her. She kept in her Palace noble maids, daughters of the Great of her kingdoms, a custom which we have read of no other Queen in any chronicle. She loved much the King her husband and was jealous about him beyond all measure. She was both clever and sensible, which is rarely to be seen together in one person; she spoke very well and was of so excellent a mind that along with so much and arduous work as the government of her kingdoms exacted from her, she took on that of learning Latin letters and within a year attained so much knowledge of them that she was able to understand any Latin speech or writing. She was catholic and devout; she used to leave secret alms in adequate places; she honoured houses of prayer, she would visit monasteries and houses of religion, particularly those which to her knowledge lived an honest life, and endowed them generously. She abhorred sorcerers and soothsayers and all persons of similar arts and inventions. She took pleasure in the conversation of religious persons who lived a clean life, with whom she often had private councils; though she heard their opinions and that of the other learned men who were at her call, she nevertheless handled most things according to her own mind. She came out well in all that she began. She was very much given to rendering justice, so much that it was said of her that she followed the way of rigour rather than that of ruth; and this she did to arrest the great corruption of crimes which she found in the kingdom when she acceded to it. She wished her letters and orders to be diligently carried out. This was the Queen who extirpated and uprooted the heresy which was rampant in the kingdoms of Castille and Aragon, due to some Christians of Jewish lineage who went back to Judaism, and who made them live as good Christians. In the provision of sees which fell vacant in her time, she had so strict a rule, that, putting off all personal leaning, she always applied to the Pope for generous, learned and clean-living men; which we do not read of any other past King to have done so diligently. She honoured the Prelates and the Great of her kingdoms in the way of addressing them and of seating them, and respected the precedence due to each of them according to his person and dignity. She was a big-hearted woman; she hid her temper and dissimulated it; and owing to this feature of hers which was well known, the Great of the Kingdom as well as all other persons dreaded to fall under her indignation. By natural bent she was truthful and given to keeping her word; though, owing to the great changes due to the wars and other great happenings of her kingdom as well as to the shifting attitude of certain persons, she did at times swerve. She was a hard worker, as will appear in this Chronicle. She was firm in her decisions, from which she receded but with great difficulty. It was said of her that she was not liberal because she did not give away vassals of the royal patrimony to those who served her in those days. True, she kept the royal patrimony so carefully that we saw her give away but few towns and lands, for she had found that many had been alienated. But strict as she was in the husbanding of her lands, she was liberal and lavish in the distribution of constant expenses and presents of great value which she made. She used to say that kings must hold to their lands because by giving them away they lose the rent which enables them to favour their loved ones and they reduce their power to be feared. She was a ceremonious woman in her dress and attire and in the service of her person, and she would be served by men of greatness and nobility with much respect and humiliation. We do not read of any past king who had men of so much greatness at his service as she had. And while on this account she was held to be at fault on the ground of excessive ostentation, we understand that no ceremony in this life is so extreme as not to remain below what is owed to the royal state, since such a state is unique and the highest in the realm and must be held in highest honour and splendour over all the states as having a divine authority on the earth. Owing to this Queen's solicitude was begun, and owing to her diligence was continued, the war against the Moors, until the whole kingdom of Granada was conquered. And we tell the truth before God, that we knew some great lords and captains of her kingdoms who, tired out, had lost all hope of winning it, considering the great difficulty in waging it further; and by the great constancy of this Queen and by her labour and diligence which she put in the matter of provisions, and by other forces which with much strain on her spirit she harnessed to this endeavour, she brought to its final success the conquest which seems to have begun moved by the divine will, as will be seen anon in this Chronicle."

When this high-spirited and high-minded woman was shedding tears of joy at the sight of the Cross on the Alhambra, she was living one of those culminating instants of existence in which all life seems to gather up its light and radiate it over the stretches of dusty drudgery which lie between them. She could remember then the long years spent in fighting against the unspeakable anarchy of the country as her unfortunate brother Henry IV, known as the Impotent, had left it; starting from a royal house dishonoured by the scandalous life of the King and by the excusable but just as scandalous adulteries of the Queen, the dry rot had eaten deep into the vitals of that kingdom, once so virile and so disciplined by the perpetual crusade in which it lived, so that nobles, bishops and upstart royal favourites carved territories and privileges for themselves, while brigands and all kinds of scum exploited and terrorised the countryside, ruined the merchants and despoiled the peasants. This shame had vanished, thanks to the close collaboration between the Queen and the King, which many a trouble-maker had tried to destroy without success.

The victorious King was then just short of forty. A contemporary chronicler, Bernáldez, records that King Ferdinand was born on a Friday, the second of March 1452, "at ten in the morning, while his planet or sign was on a very high triumph of good venture, according to astrologers." (5) Pulgar has left us a masterly portrait of this fortunate lord: (6)

"This King was a man of middle height, well proportioned in his limbs, his features well composed, his eyes merry, his hair dark and straight, and of good complexion. He had an even speech, neither hasty nor slow overmuch. He was of good understanding, and very temperate in food and drink and in the movements of his person, for neither ire nor pleasure could unbalance him. He rode very well; he jousted with ease and with so much skill that no one in his kingdom did it better. He was a keen sportsman and a man of good endeavour and of much activity at war. By natural bent, he liked to render justice, and he was also compassionate and felt sympathy for miserable people whom he saw in trouble. He had a singular grace, to wit, that all who spoke to him at once loved him and wished to serve him, for he had a friendly intercourse. He was also given to following advice, especially that of the Queen, for he knew her great competence. From childhood, he had been brought up in wars, in which he underwent much hardship and personal danger. And as he spent all his income in the war and was always short of money, we cannot say he was liberal. He was a truthful man, though the narrow situations in which wars often put him, made him at times swerve. He enjoyed all kinds of games such as ball, chess or royal tables, and he devoted to this pleasure more time than he ought to have done; while he loved the Queen his wife dearly, yet he gave himself to other women. He was a man kind and easy towards all, particularly towards his permanent servants. This King conquered and won the Kingdom of Granada, as will be seen in this Chronicle."

The happy blend and co-operation of these two master-minds

succeeded in raising the Crown to a position of moral authority which it had not known for over seven centuries, since the rebirth of the Christian kingdoms after the Moorish invasion of practically the whole peninsula.

In their childhood, both had been made to read and study that classical page written by their ancestor, the King—astronomer— poet, Alfonso X, on *the Praise of Spain and how she abounds in all good things*, the last words of which sound today so tragically contemporary: (7)

"And each land of the world and each province, God honoured in a different way and gave it gifts: but of all the lands the one He honoured most was the Spain of the West, for He provided her with all the things which man is wont to covet. For since the Goths wandered over all lands hither and thither, trying them by wars and battles and conquering many places and provinces in Asia and in Europe, trying many dwelling places everywhere and considering and choosing which was the most profitable, they found that Spain was the best of all, and they prized her much more than any other, for, of all the lands of the world, Spain excels in abundance and in good parts more than any other. . . .

"Spain is abundant in her harvests, delightful in her fruit, extravagant in her fish, savoury in her milk and in all the things which are made from milk; full of game, covered with cattle, happy in her houses, comfortable in her mules, safe and well provided with castles, merry with good wines, easy in her abundance of bread; rich in metals, lead, tin, quick-silver, iron, copper, silver, gold, precious stones, marble, sea salts and land salt-mines and salt-rock and many other mines, bluestone, clay, red ochre, alum and many more to be found in these lands; proud of her silk and all that is made of it; sweet with honey and sugar, lighted by her wax, plentiful in oil, gay with saffron.

"Spain is more than other lands ingenious, bold and valiant in a fight, light-hearted in her cares, loyal to her lord, persevering in her studies, courtly in her speech, rich in all good things. There is no land like her in abundance, nor her equal in fortresses, and few are in the world as great as she is. Spain is foremost in greatness and prized over all others in loyalty. Oh Spain, nor tongue, nor mind can tell your excellence. . . .

"This was the realm, so noble, so rich, so powerful, so honourable, which was overrun and wasted in one onslaught owing to discord among the sons of the land, who turned their swords against themselves, some against others, as if they lacked enemies, and they all lost, for all the cities of Spain fell to the Moors and were broken and destroyed at the hand of their enemies."

* *

Spain paid seven centuries of endeavour for this discord. And it fell to King Ferdinand and to Queen Isabel to crown this age-long struggle with the fall of Granada. They had fully deserved this honour from the hand of Fate, for both King and Queen had deliberately worked for it with the mind and will of statesmen. Their means had been the utmost firmness in the handling of high and low alike, justice scrupulously served, at times even by the very person of the King and Queen, the most watchful exactness in point of respect and devotion to the royal couple on the part of the magnates, and, last but not least, a relentless prosecution of the crusade against the infidel which kept their barons busy on a national, unifying endeavour.

"One of the advantages which the neighbouring Kings envy you," wrote Hernando del Pulgar to the Queen, (8) "is to have within your frontiers people against whom you can wage not merely just war but holy war, in which you may occupy and exercise the chivalry of your kingdoms; for Your Highness should not think it to be a small convenience." The Queen and the King were aware of this advantage and used it to the full. Yet, all these were but the means to their success. The mainspring of it was in the two human beings at the head of the nation; the wise and active King, the spirited and masterly Queen.

On that sunny winter morning, under the crystalline snows of Sierra Nevada, Ferdinand and Isabel, on the summit of a hill in the landscape of their life, could contemplate their past with pride and their future with hope. This glorious minute had cost them ten years. Ten years during which he had been under harness over six months a year, the indispensable, ever-present Commander-in-Chief; and she had been personally responsible for the commissariat and hospitals of her troops. Her presence, nay, her very existence, put courage, faith, reassurance into the heart of high and low. Her chronicler Hernando del Pulgar (9) tells us how, when discontent and ill-humour were rife during the siege of Baza, all desired the Queen to come and see "the constant fights, and deaths and wounds [. . .], adventures and dangers [. . .], and the scanty results." And he adds that "it was a case worthy of admiration to see the sudden change [. . .] for as we were there and saw it, we witness true before God who knows it and before the men who saw it, that after this Queen entered the camp it seemed as if all the hardship of the fighting, all the lowered spirits, all inimical and contrary intentions were tired out and ceased."

Bernáldez has left us a delightful description of her arrival at the camp after the conquest of Illora: (10)

"On the Friday when the Moors left Illora for Granada, the Marquis-Duke of Cádiz and the Adelantado of Andalucía rode forth from the royal camp to the Lovers' Rock to receive the Queen Doña Isabel who was coming to visit the camp and to see part of the victory and good fortune of the King her husband; the Queen had a suite of as many as forty riding persons, not counting those who had gone to meet her, and it included as many as ten women; the reception made to her was very notable; for there went out a league and a half to receive her on the road the Duke of the Infantadgo, who had come to the war in person, very powerful and ostentatious, and the Pennant of Seville with its troops, and the Prior of St. John; and a battalion was aligned on the left of the way, all ready as if for a fight; and as the Queen appeared, she bowed to the Pennant of Seville and ordered it to be passed over to her right, and all ran forward with great joy to receive her, which gave Her Highness much pleasure; and there came then all the battalions and banners of the camp to receive her, and all the banners dipped as the Queen passed; and then the King arrived with many grandees of Castille, and before embracing each other, they bowed three times, at which the Queen uncovered her head and she was seen with just a coif on, her face exposed, and the King approached, embraced her and kissed her face; then he went towards the Infanta his daughter and embraced her and kissed her on the mouth and blessed her: the Queen rode a chestnut mule on a rail-saddle set with silver-gilt, the mule covered with a cloth of crimson velvet, and the reins and harness were flat, made of silk with gold lettering and the edges embroidered with gold; and she wore a velvet bodice and brocade skirts and a hood-cloak, and her dress was adorned in the Moorish style and she had a black hat trimmed with brocade round the crown and rim; the Infanta also rode a chestnut mule harnessed with white silver, the hem of gold; and she was wearing a black brocade bodice and a headdress trimmed like the Queen's.

"The King wore a doublet of velvety damask, and a *quisote* of yellow silk cloth, and over it a coat of brocade and a brocade-covered cuirass, with a rich Moorish sword and a toque under a hat, and he rode a chestnut horse beautifully harnessed; while the apparel of the Grandees there present was marvellous and rich and varied, some in war style, some in festive style, which it would be too long to describe."

There was an Englishman in the pageant, a "Conde de las Escalas" mentioned in more than one chronicle of the day. He was the Lord Scales, Earl of Rivers; his name has suffered less in translation than that of "milor Tamerlant," who is very much in evidence in another of the great chronicles of the age, and who turns out to be Lord Stanley. (11)

This Conde de las Escalas fought well, so well indeed that he was singled out for special praise by Hernando del Pulgar, (12) who relates how, as he lay in his tent to recover from his wounds, and in particular from the loss of two teeth, King Ferdinand honoured him with a visit, during which the royal visitor was good enough to say that the Earl should feel happy since his virtue had knocked out his two teeth, which age or any illness might have done, and that, bearing in mind how and where he had lost them, they made him rather beautiful than deformed. To which the Earl courteously answered that he thanked the Lord and the glorious Virgin His mother for this visit of the most powerful King in Christendom, and that he did not think much of the loss of two teeth in the service of Him who had given to him all those he had. He could prance on a horse as well as speak, this good Count:

"Presently," Bernáldez says, "the Count of England came after the King to greet the Queen and the Infanta, in great pomp, in a strange manner, coming after all the others, armed in white, riding a white horse caparisoned with cloth which reached the ground, all of blue silk with a white silk band as wide as a hand and all starred with gold and lined with purple Ceuta cloth; and over his armour he wore a French doublet of black flat brocade, and a white French hat with plumes, and on the left arm a small round shield with gold bands, and a very striking helmet made in such a new style that it was generally admired; and he was followed by five horses caparisoned, with their pages on them, all dressed in silk and brocades, and there came with him a number of his gentlemen in lovely apparel, in which guise he came to pay homage to the King and for a while rode here and there on his horse greeting all and sundry, and jumping this way and that with much measure and control while the grandees and all the others looked at him and thought well of it, and of all this did Their Highnesses derive much pleasure and all came back to the royal camp where the King and Queen with their daughter were well lodged, as well as the ladies and gentlemen which accompanied them in this visit."

* *

But the Queen was not a woman to dwell on memories of silks and bright array while the ·dream of her life was being enacted under her eyes on that sunny Andalucian morning. She was of a stern fibre and of an austere nature. Her mind was then probably dwelling on the terrible sights which her eyes had beheld in those ten years of never-relaxing activity. The war campaigns were cruel, and the stretches of precarious peace were no less cruel. The times were stern and hard, in Spain no less than elsewhere. The Christian captives left in the hands of the Moors underwent terrible hardships. The Queen no doubt would remember the grief and emotion which she had felt at the sight of the Christians delivered from long captivity by her armies when Málaga had surrendered after a stubborn siege.

"And then," says Bernáldez, (13) [the King] "summoned the Christian captives who were in Málaga and he had a tent set up at Granada Gate, in which he and the Queen and their daughter the Infanta received them, and the Moors brought them there, no less than six hundred men and women; [. . .] And as they came up to where their Highnesses were, they all humbled themselves and fell on the ground and wished to kiss their feet, but their Highnesses would not consent, but gave them their hands, and all who saw them praised God and wept for joy with the captives who came out so thin and yellow with great hunger that they would fain perish all, and with iron manacles on their hands and necks and iron balls at their feet, all hairy and with long beards. [. . .] And thereupon the King had them fed and unfettered and dressed and given alms to meet their expenses for their journey home, which was all done and accomplished. And there were amongst them persons for whom great ransoms had already been paid; and persons who had been ten, fifteen and twenty years in captivity, and others less."

That nightmare was over. The country was at last united behind the two monarchs. The world had never seen a transformation such as that which in seventeen years had raised Castille from the corruption and anarchy of the previous reign to the order, power and splendour of 1492.

When in 1485 Ferdinand and Isabel sent the Count of Tendilla as a special ambassador to the Pope, while the Holy See and Naples were at war, this Castillian nobleman expected, and obtained from the two parties then at war, that a truce should be arranged while he acquitted himself of his embassy—a truce, by the way, which by his skill and authority he transformed into a permanent peace. (14)

The Queen could feel confident about the future. The strength was there, exercised by a permanent war against a permanent enemy. The arts and crafts of war were there, as she, the Quartermaster, Ordnance, Commissariat and Health Chief of the armed forces for ten years knew well; and she could depend on the artificers, carpenters, wheelwrights and ironmasters who had stood her in good stead during all those long campaigns; the Commander-in-Chief was there, in her husband, a good leader, who could learn if necessary from a defeat and from his experienced captains and experts, spirited men who were not in the least afraid of speaking their minds, as she well knew that the Marquis of Cádiz and Diego de Valera had done after the first disastrous siege of Loja. (15) The tradition was there, seven centuries old. The aim was as clear as the blue skies over the snows of the Sierra, and had already been defined by the same Diego de Valera in the course of the correspondence in which he endeavoured to induce King Ferdinand to put some method and some strategy into what was still too much of a medieval, glorious, devil-may-care, chivalrous adventure. "It is clear," he writes to the King in 1485, "that our Lord intends to carry out what has been prophesied for centuries [. . .] to wit, that you shall not merely put these Spains under your royal sceptre, but that you will also subjugate the territories [partes] beyond the sea . . ." (16) a statement in which we meet with this fact, too often forgotten or unknown, that the word *Spain* meant still in those days, as it often did in antiquity, not merely the Peninsula, but the North of Africa as well. The command of the sea was there, for, under the watchful eye of the Queen, the Straits of Gibraltar had been continuously held open for Spain and closed for the Moors by her armed sea forces which had often co-operated with the inland cavalry, as in the siege of Málaga. The same Diego de Valera with his son Charles had organised the Fleet and often written to the King about it; he had even commanded it in partnership with his son.

All historical trends then converged towards Africa. Gathered up by the masterful leadership of Ferdinand and Isabel, the Spanish forces would cross the Straits and pour their energy over the African shores of the Mediterranean. While watching that Cross and that Banner raised by their endeavours to the summit of European Spain, Ferdinand and Isabel could dream, they certainly dreamt, of carrying both symbols, Christ and Empire, over to the Spain beyond the sea which was Africa: there, the captains and the seed of captains which flourished so easily in Spain would plant the religion of their ancestors and the language of Spain, that language which in or about that very year, one century before Shakespeare, had created in *Melibea* a masterpiece of Shakespearian excellence. Round the Latin Sea their armies and fleets would prolong the victories of the last ten years, and by the African coast, round Asia Minor, the Castillian drive would meet the drive of Aragon, already victorious in Sicily and Naples, making the King and Queen predominant partners in Italy, and, even beyond, holders, in far distant Greece, of the Catalan Duchy of Neopatria which was one of the titles on their blazon. . . . And so with the march of time new Spains would flourish in Morocco, in Tunis, in Algeria, which would make of the Mediterranean a Spanish sea for centuries to come. . . .

But it was not to be. For, lost in the crowd, his person wrapped in mystery, his head lost in an ecstasy of dreams, an obscure man had fastened his magnetic eyes on that Cross and that Banner, and, by a miracle of his unshakable faith, he was to take hold of that Banner and of that Cross and to carry them beyond the seas —not South, but West.

CHAPTER II

CRISTÓBAL—THE CROSS. COLÓN—THE BANNER

WHO was this mysterious man whose single spirit changed the course of history, deflected a mighty nation from its natural path, doubled the size of man's physical world, widened his mental horizon beyond the wildest expectations of the age, created, in fact, the setting for that bold, humanistic conception, lured by which man, the super-monkey, has since then dreamt himself to be an undergod?

Three features stand out from the glimpses of him which his contemporaries have let us catch in the faint, possibly distorted reflection of their writings. Mystery surrounds him. Pride stiffens him up. A sense of a mission entrusted to him from on high drives and illumines him. No one knows who he is, where he comes from, what he actually wishes to do. No one can browbeat him, pin him down, make him accept one inch less than the whole of what he demands. No one can fail to feel that he is possessed of an idea, bent on an action, bearer of a message, entrusted with a mission. Can we then wonder at his success?

Here is his portrait by the Bishop Bartolomé de las Casas, who knew him and had access to his papers:

"As the time had come [. . .] when in these parts of the earth (sown the seed or word of life), the fruit was ripe to be gathered, [. . .] the divine and supreme Master chose from amongst the sons of Adam who dwelt in these our days on the earth that illustrious and great Colón, i.e. by name and works, first coloniser, to trust to his virtue, mind, zeal, labours, knowledge and wisdom, one of the mightiest divine exploits which in our century He wished to achieve in His world, and as the supreme divine Providence usually sees to each thing according to its natural condition [. . .] and as this enterprise was to be so high, arduous and divine, [. . .] hence it is to be believed that God endowed His minister and first apostle of these Indies with such natural and acquired qualities [. . .]. This chosen man was of Genoese extraction, of some place in the province of Genoa; which place

16

it was, where he was born, what was the name of such place, there is no standing information as to the truth of it, save that, before reaching the status which he reached, he called himself Cristóbal Columbo de Terra-rubia, and so did his brother Bartolomé Colón [. . .]. A Portuguese history written by one Juan de Barros, under the name of *Asia*, in Book III, Chapter 2, of its first decade, on mentioning the discovery, says no more than that, as everybody says, this Cristóbal was of Genoese extraction. His parents were notable persons, one time rich, whose way of living must have been sea-trade, as he himself suggests in one of his letters; at other times they must have been poor, owing to the wars and strife which are always occurring in Lombardy. His lineage is said to be generous and very old, descending from that Colón of whom Cornelius Tacitus says in Book XII that he brought Mithridates a prisoner to Rome, owing to which he was granted Consular insignia and other privileges by a grateful Roman people. And it must be known that of old the first name of this lineage was, they say, Colón, then, as time went by, the successors of this Colón, Roman or Captain of Romans, styled themselves Colombos; and these Colombos are mentioned by Antonio Sabellico in Book VIII of Decade 10, folio 168, in which he speaks of two illustrious Genoese men named Colombos, as later will be seen. But this illustrious man, giving up the name set by custom, wished to call himself Colón, going back to the old word less perhaps [because it was his original name] than, as we may rather believe, moved by that divine will which had elected him to work out that which his Christian name and surname implied. Divine Providence usually ordains that persons It designates to serve be given names and surnames in accordance with the task they are meant to perform, as may be seen in many places of Scripture and in the Philosopher in Chapter IV of his *Metaphysics*, where he says: 'that names must fit the qualities and uses of things.' He was therefore named Cristóbal, i.e. *Christum ferens*, which means bringer or bearer of Christ, and so he often signed his name; for in truth he was the first to open the gates of this Ocean sea by which he brought our Saviour, Jesus Christ, to these remote lands and realms, until then unknown [. . .]. His surname was Colón, which means *repopulator*, a name befitting one thanks to whose labour so many souls, through the preaching of the Gospel [. . .], have gone and are going to repopulate the glorious city of Heaven. It also befits him inasmuch as he was the first to bring over people from Spain (albeit not as they should have been) to found *colonies* or new populations which, settling among the original inhabitants [. . .], should constitute a new [. . .] Christian and happy republic.

"As for his outward person and bodily disposition, (1) he was tall more than average; his face long and of a noble bearing; his nose aquiline; his eyes blue; his complexion white, and somewhat fiery red; his beard and hair fair in his youth, though they soon turned white through hardships borne; he was quick-witted and gay in his speech and, as the aforesaid Portuguese history says, eloquent and high-sounding in his business; he was moderately grave; affable towards strangers; sweet and good-humoured with those of his house, [. . .] of a discreet conversation and thus able to draw love from all who saw him. Finally, his person and venerable mien revealed a person of great state and authority and worthy of all reverence; he was sober and moderate in his food, drink, garments and shoes; he was wont to say, whether in merriment or in wrath: *As between you and God, don't you think this or that?*, or *Why didst thou do this or that?* In matters of Christian religion no doubt he was a Catholic and of great devotion; in almost every case, before saying or doing something, he always began with: *Jesus cum Maria sit nobis in via;* [. . .] His oath was at times: *I swear by St. Ferdinand;* when he wished to assert something of great importance in his letters, particularly when writing to the King and Queen, he said: *I swear that this is true.* He fasted with the utmost strictness when ordained by the Church; he confessed often and took Communion; he prayed at all canonical hours as do Churchmen and friars; most averse to blasphemies and oaths; a very devout worshipper of Our Lady and of the Seraphic Father St. Francis; he seemed to be very grateful to God for the benefits received at the Divine Hand, and so it was almost a proverb with him, which he quoted every hour, that God had shown him great favour, as to David. When gold or [other] precious objects were brought to him, he entered his chapel and said: *Let us thank our Lord who made us worthy of discovering so much wealth.* He was a most jealous keeper of the honour of God; eager to convert the peoples and to see the seed and faith of Jesus Christ spread everywhere, and especially devoted to the hope that God would make him worthy of helping in winning back the holy Sepulchre; and in this devotion and the confidence which he had that God would help him in the discovery of this World which he promised, he begged Queen Isabel to make a vow that she should spend all the wealth gained by the Crown as a result of the discovery in winning back the land and holy house of Jerusalem, which the Queen did, as hereafter will be said. He was a man of a great and valorous heart, of a high mind, naturally given—as one may infer from his life and doings, and writings and conversation—to initiate great and famous enterprises; patient and very long-suffering (as will be seen anon); who would forgive insults, wishing no more, as it is said of him, than that those who offended him should realise their errors and that the guilty parties should be reconciled with him; most steadfast and patient in adversity and hardship which constantly recurred and were unbelievable and untold; always trusting in divine providence, and truly, from what I heard of him and from my own father who accompanied him when he went back to populate this Island Española in 1493, and from other persons who accompanied him and served him, he always was most faithful and devoted to the King and Queen." (2)

The good bishop was a younger man, and did not know Colón till after the discoverer had vindicated his faith and justified his pride—though not clarified his mystery, which he never did. Las Casas was, however, hot-hearted, easily swayed by the emotions of the moment, so that his views on Colón are apt to change with the occasion which prompts them. Yet, in this somewhat verbose and grandiloquent chapter of his *History of the Indies*, the discoverer stands out already as the man mysterious in his origin, high-minded in his conceptions, unshakable in his faith; as Christoferens—the Cross and Colón—the Banner, the man who knew that he had been chosen to expand the boundaries of civilisation in both its aspects—the spiritual and the material.

There is an old Spanish story of two young peasants one of whom was extolling the quality of his paramour to the other in such glowing terms that the listener's interest was raised to the point of asking: "Where does she live?", whereupon the other answered: "She has moved." This story of worldly wisdom comes often to mind when reading the life-records and above all the words of Colón, for, like the squid, he oozes out a cloud of ink round every hard square fact of his life. This ink, multiplied by the industry of his historians, has made but blacker and thicker the mystery which attaches to him.

When was he born? Where was he born? What was his name? Where did he study? Where had he travelled? What did he know? What was his plan? How much did he know of it when he proposed it to the King of Portugal first, then to the King of Spain? All points on which, after over four hundred years of time and over four hundred volumes of research, there is genuine ground for disagreement.

Bernáldez, (3) the historian of the reign, who knew Colón well and was his host, described him "as a man from the land of Genoa, a merchant of books of print who traded in them, named Cristóbal Colón, a man of high mind, of no great knowledge, very well versed in the art of Cosmography and of the lie of the world"; Garcia Fernández, the doctor of La Rábida, where Colón sought hospitality on his arrival in Spain with his little son Diego, describes how Fray Juan Pérez, a friar of the monastery, "seeing he looked like a man of another country or kingdom and alien in language, asked him who he was and whence he came, and the said Cristóbal Colón told him he came from the Court of His Highness" (i.e. "he had moved"). (4)

His contemporaries, immersed in the last stage of the war of reconquest, might well ask themselves, probably did ask themselves, a host of questions about this foreigner in their midst. First his age. Why this white hair to these young, eager eyes? Then, if, as his Genoese friends would say, he was a common weaver of Genoa, the son of a poor weaver who had to keep a tavern in order to help his loom, how was he so dignified? And again, if he was a Genoese, as others said, why did he keep so silent about it and why did he never speak Italian, nor write it even when addressing his countrymen, and why did he speak Spanish with a Portuguese accent? And if, as he often would say, he had spent all his life at sea, when had he learnt his Latin, and his cosmography? And if he was as good a Christian as he was keen to show himself in his devotions, why was he so fond of the company of Moors and of Jews, (5) and why had he become entangled in a love-affair with a Córdoban girl, of whom he had a bastard, just as if he were a Castillian Grandee or a Portuguese Archbishop? And if he knew so much, why did all learned men smile, nay laugh at his theory on the narrowness of the ocean or the smallness of the earth, and on the existence of islands which he made bold to discover, "just as if he had them in his room locked up with his own key"? (6) And if all this was so laughable, why did the King and Queen, busy as they were, keep him hanging on at Court and in their camps under besieged Moorish cities instead of just giving him up as the saintly Prior of the Prado advised them to do? And if he was just an adventurer, how was he in a position to show a letter from the King of Portugal calling him "my special friend"? (7) And if he was the King of Portugal's special friend, how was it that he had to offer his grandiose scheme to the Queen of Castille when Portugal was then the nursery of all great discoveries? And above all, how could an upstart Genoese bookseller and map-scribbler, who went about down at heel and wrapped in a cloak of many holes, demand beforehand as the price of his discovery-to-be such exorbitant privileges and titles as that of Admiral, till then reserved to the greatest of the great, to men closely related to the royal family by ties of blood? And, strangest of all, why did the King and Queen ever consent to listen to such wild demands?

Now, the story of the discovery of America by Colón, or Columbus, as he is misnamed against his determined will, with the dogged determination of Fate to thwart him in his most cherished designs, does not begin till his arrival in Castille. But the story of great Cristóbal Colón himself, and of the true shape and line and impulse of this singular soul, requires as good a knowledge of his origin and early years as is possible in the circumstances, for it is surely in the years of his formation, and particularly in the circumstances of his birth, race, nature and social environment, that we may hope to find the key to one of the most singular characters of human history.

It so happens that circumstances in this case have conspired to surround Colón's life with as much mystery as he himself seems to have wished. Not that, as is the case with Shakespeare, the data at our disposal are but scanty and unimportant; but on the contrary, that the data we possess do not tally. No amount of ingenuity can solve the crossword puzzle of Colón, if we accept in their literal sense on the one hand all his statements and on the other all the documents which have been so industriously put together by the Italian Government and by the City of Genoa to prove his Genoese birth and to provide him with a family. Nor can we accept the solutions based on the rejection of the Genoese documents as forgeries; (8) amongst other reasons because, leaving aside the fact that a great nation and a great city would never consent to such a thing, if the documents had been forged, they would tally with whatever facts of Colón's life were known already at the time of the forgery; a dismissal of the whole Genoese conception—such as is recommended by one or two contemporaries —seems no more acceptable, for while there are still unbridged gaps and unexplained difficulties, the number of clues which the Genoese family satisfies is far too high to be accounted for by mere coincidence. On the other hand, there are biographers and specialists of Colón who solve the difficulty by merely declaring him a wholesale liar. (9) That he would, when necessary or suitable, keep his counsel, there is little doubt. But there is surely a singular lack of subtlety as to Colón's own character and even as to human nature in general in attributing to any man, let alone the discoverer of America, a predisposition to lie, when the natural tendency to economy of action makes most human beings find it easier in most cases to speak the truth. So that the gaps remain unbridged and the difficulties unexplained.

Let us then first establish the points of agreement between the discoveries made by scholars and the facts or statements made by him; then examine the differences; finally, try to solve what still remains the fundamental enigma of Colón's life—who was Colón?

PART I

CHRISTOFORO COLOMBO GOES TO SEA

CHAPTER III

THE COLOMBOS OF GENOA

TOWARDS the beginning of the fifteenth century, one Giovanni Colombo lived perhaps a lusty, happy, prosperous, perhaps a gloomy, difficult, sad sort of life, coming and going, between business and pleasure, eating and drinking and cracking jokes in that Genoese riviera so sunny and full of the joy of existence. But that human butterfly, fluttering about in the sunlight of by-gone days, has vanished for ever, and all that remains of it are two or three shadows which it cast on dusty papers saved by sheer oblivion from the death in which all life must end. The dusty papers tell us that he placed his son Domenico as an apprentice-weaver in 1429 and that he died in 1444. Little else is known of him. Trades in those days, however, were more fixed and traditional than in our time; we may therefore safely assume that he was a weaver himself. He came from the village of Moconesi, in the valley of Fontanabuona, and had settled in Quinto, a few miles to the east of the town of Genoa, which has now swallowed it. He had two sons, Antonio and Domenico, and one daughter, Battistina. Nothing is known of Battistina, who need not be disturbed from the peace of oblivion. Antonio was the father of four sons, all weavers, or tailors, of whom more will be heard anon. Domenico had four sons and one daughter—and the eldest of them discovered America.

This Domenico, when "about eleven years of age," was the object of the notarial deed to which we owe our knowledge of his father's existence and of his own birthdate, for, on February 21st, 1429, Johannes *de Columbo* (note de Columbo in Latin)(1) promised and solemnly agreed with Guglielmo de Brabante, of Germany, a Flemish clothweaver, that his son Domenico remain and continue as apprentice and pupil in order to learn the trade. As all we have to go upon are the rare glimpses of his life which the dusty papers have caught and kept for us, the next thing we know is that the young apprentice of 1429, already grown to a full mastery of his trade and to manhood, leased a house and land in Vico dell'Olivella,(2) a lane which the City of Genoa has since

25

devoured in its growth and transfiguration, but which, Genoese authorities tell us, was then a lively thoroughfare in the neighbourhood of the Palazzo di Pammatone, in the Portoria district, leading up to the eastern gate of the city, known as the Gate of Sant'Andrea. The landlords were the monks of the Monastery of Santo Stefano, who, the deeds tell us, *capitulariter congregati sono campanule*, i.e. were gathered in the chapter house at the sound of bells, for the purpose of granting the lease. Seven years later, exactly on February 4th, 1447, i.e. when Domenico the weaver was twenty-nine years of age, (3) the illustrious and excellent Lord Giano Campofregoso, Doge of the Genoese, or, as they would say nowadays, their Duce, by the grace of God (or so he believed or wanted the Genoese to believe), "elected his beloved Domenico *de* Columbo to the wardership of the Tower and Gate dell'Olivella, during the pleasure of the said illustrious Doge, with the customary pay and rights without any exception."

Neither the pay nor the pleasure of the illustrious Doge amounted to much, for we read that every three months, Domenico the weaver-gatekeeper was paid twenty-one Genoese pounds, (4) at the rate, therefore, of seven a month, "for him and his companions"; while we know that new letters of appointment had to be given him on November 10th, 1450, this time wisely limited to thirteen months, which seems to have been the illustrious Doge's own estimation of his constancy towards "his beloved Domenico de Columbo." And so, on September 25th, 1451, the same excellent and fickle lord granted to an equally beloved Agostino of Bogliasco, for a "pleasure" equally estimated at thirteen months, the keepership of the Tower dell'Olivella "immediately on the completion of the thirteen months already conceded to Domenico Columbo."

At about the same time, in 1449, his brother Antonio, (5) who seems also to have possessed Domenico's combined ability to weave cloth and to keep towers, obtained from the Doge the keepership of the Tower of Capo di Faro, or Lighthouse Cape, at the other end of the city, so that during three years, 49-51, the City of Genoa was kept at the sea-end by Antonio and at the land-end by Domenico Colombo. It was then, when the two weaver-watchmen were keeping both towers, that Christoforo was born to Genoa. But, though his realm was to be the sea, he was not born of Antonio, the sea-tower watchman, but of Domenico, the keeper of the Tower of Sant'Andrea, which, as we know, was the gate opening towards the East. There, some time in 1451, was born the greatest weaver of dreams and the greatest keeper of towers that the world of men has ever known.

His mother was Susanna Fontanarossa, (6) of whom little is known, except that in August 1473, when she agrees to let her husband sell the lease of the house in the Gate dell'Olivella, she has two sons old enough to have their consent registered in the deed; these two sons are Christoforo and one Giovanni Pellegrino, who, utterly indifferent to the glory which Fate offered him by making him a member of this illustrious family, departed from this world without ever waiting for the discovery of America. The deed, further, reveals that she was the daughter of a Giacomo Fontanarossa of Bisagno.

While this deed proves that Domenico the weaver-towerkeeper retained the lease of his house in Vico dell'Olivella till 1473, another dusty paper dated 1455 shows that he leased another house from the same monks of Santo Stefano, (7) who seem to have possessed the usual clerical knack for combining contempt for worldly goods with ownership of houses. This second house was built on the ground of the Monastery, in Vico Dritto di Ponticello. Whether the step was for the better or for the worse is not clear, but it may be surmised that this change of abode, like the previous and the coming changes of occupation, was due to financial difficulties and lack of success in the business which, through all his vicissitudes, remained at least officially the profession of Christoforo's father—woolweaving. He seems, however, to have been an influential and trusted member of the trade, for in 1470 he was sent by his fellow-weavers to negotiate with the trade in the neighbouring city of Savona, (8) with a view to establishing a common tariff and, finding the place to his taste, he settled there—not, however, without having known the jail of his native city, where he spent a period of enforced rest in the same year, on his return from his successful embassy to Savona. This mishap would appear to be due to a lawsuit between Domenico Colombo and Gerolamo del Porto, (9) in the course of which Domenico, *and his son Christoforo*, are sentenced to pay del Porto a sum of thirty Genoese pounds. For the first time Christoforo appears associated with his father in so responsible a situation, and considering the boy was only nineteen, this fact should have been given a little more weight than it seems to have received on the part of biographers and critics. Domenico, then fifty-two years of age, was extricated from his difficulties by his youthful son, and the next time the dusty papers allow us to see him, the old weaver-towerkeeper is living up in Savona, still a weaver but a publican (10) as well—for, much as some light-fingered biographers may wish to disguise his occupation as "innkeeper," or as that of a nice, don't you know? sort of weaver who received paying-guests, the deed of March 2nd, 1470, described Domenico as a *tabernarius*, i.e. as the owner of a public-house.

This same year, another dusty paper, (11) and the most important of the lot, gives the age of Christoforo as "over 19." It is dated Wednesday, the last day of October 1470. So far, it is the most direct document we possess to ascertain the date of the discoverer's birth.

The family is now settled in Savona, a small town within the borders of the Genoese Republic, to the west of Genoa, on the coast. Its fortunes do not seem to have become any the brighter for its exile, since now and then we find Christoforo having to endorse responsibility, either to pay or promise to pay for wine (as in the above-quoted deed in which Christoforo is declared to be over nineteen years of age), (12) or to guarantee the payment of cloth.

More children come. In 1461, Bartolomeo, who was to act as his brother's brilliant second, comes to enrich the family, in life and honour if not in material wealth. No papers vouch for his actual date, none, at any rate, within the Colombo-Genoa file. But more than one of the deeds of the Genoese family show that there was a son by this name, and the age of such a Bartolomeo would not conflict with, rather would it fit, the choice of 1461 made on other than Genoese grounds. In 1484 we find a "Giacomo Colombo," son of Domenico, citizen of Genoa, "voluntarily pledging and binding himself as apprentice . . . in order to learn the craft of clothweaver." (13)

By this time, the family had returned to Vico Dritto in Genoa, (14) none the richer, since on January 27th, 1483, Domenico signs a deed letting the shop on the ground floor to Giovanni Battista Vella, a shoemaker, and confining his now more numerous family to the top floor, garden and first floor, save the kitchen, which the shoemaker retains. This hardly suggests prosperity, and fully explains the loans which Domenico obtained from his eldest son.

As for the class and rank of life in which the family moved, the peculiar inclination which all the Colombos—save Bartolomeo—seem to have had towards witnessing documents, has provided a number of fairly definite clues. Giacomo, the future Diego, witnessed a deed in 1487, "as a clothweaver in Genoa, son of

Domenico." The future Admiral of the Indies, as a "woolmaker of Genoa," in company with a tailor named Domenico Vigna, both "citizens of Savona," witnessed a will in March 1472. (15) In 1479, Christoforo Colombo is mentioned in a notarial deed registered in Genoa (16) as having been sent to Madeira to buy sugar on behalf of Paolo Dinegro. He is stated to be present, and declares on oath that the previous year in the month of July he and Paolo were at Lisbon. He also states that the next day he must leave for Lisbon, and that he is about twenty-seven years of age. The authenticity of this document has been much disputed. If genuine, in connection with a previously mentioned deed in which Christoforo is described as "over 19," it narrows down the possible dates of his birth to the period August 26th to October 31st, 1451. Though there is something to be said for the doubting Thomases, one feature of this document seems to stamp it with the seal of truth. "Asked . . . which of the two parties he desires to see victorious, he replies . . . that he desires that party to win that is in the right." That surely is Colón's voice. "He had moved." His father witnessed the will of one of his neighbours, living in the Gate of the Arch, near the Vico Dritto, on September 30th, 1494. (17) His co-witness was a shoemaker. By this time Christoforo was an Admiral and Viceroy of the Islands and Mainland and was officially addressed as "the Very Magnificent Lord Don Cristóbal."

This transmigration of Christoforo and of his two brothers from the looms, tailor-shops and public-houses of Genoa and Savona to the Eldorados of Spain is quietly and coolly registered in the dusty papers—first in 1489, when, on the occasion of some litigation with a cheesemonger over the price of his house, (18) Domenico, already a widower, styles himself as legitimate administrator of his three sons, Christoforo, Bartolomeo and Giacomo; and then in 1501, when several Genoese citizens swear on oath that Christoforo, Bartolomeo and Giacomo de Colombo, sons and heirs of the late Domenico, "have been absent from this city and from the jurisdiction of Savona for a long time, beyond Pisa and Nice in Provence, and that they are living in the country of Spain as was and is well known." (19)

Whatever the greatness of their castles in Spain which they erected thanks to the genius of the eldest of them, the three Spanish Colóns, Admiral, Adelantado and Governor, came, therefore, from a family of weavers and were the cousins of tailors, the neighbours of cheesemakers and shoemakers, and the sons of a publican with little financial success, more than average mobility of residence and occupation, and a taste for watching over gates and towers.

* *

So much for the glimpses of Colón which the notarial files of Genoa and of Savona allow us to catch through the thick walls of time. They are confirmed by all the mentions of him found in the works of his Genoese contemporaries, the most important of whom, Antonio Gallo, was Chancellor of the Bank of San Georgio, an institution which was the financial backbone of the republic. Gallo was, moreover, official chronicler of Genoa from 1477 till his death. His account of the discovery and of the discoverer is particularly weighty because it was the basis for the work of two subsequent chroniclers of Colón's adventures, who, taking advantage of the fact that the good Chancellor's record had remained unpublished (it was not printed until 1723 in Milan), lifted his narrative almost verbatim. Here is the relevant part of Gallo's record: (20)

"Christopher and Bartholomeo Colombo, brothers, Ligurian by nation, sprung from Genoese plebeian parents, and who supported themselves from the wages of woolmaking (for the father was a weaver and the sons were at times carders), then acquired great fame throughout the whole of Europe by a deed of the greatest daring and of remarkable novelty in human affairs. Even though they had small learning in their childhood, when they reached the age of puberty they gave themselves to navigation after the manner of their race. But at length Bartholomeo, the younger, settled in Lisbon in Portugal, where, for his livelihood, he undertook the production of painted maps adapted to the use of mariners, on which, in correct drawings, seas, harbours, coasts, bays and islands are represented in their true proportions. Every year, for the last forty years, expeditions went forth from Lisbon and returned by the sea to and from the western coasts of Africa, and revealed continental lands and peoples unknown to past ages. But Bartholomeo, influenced by his study of maps and familiar with the tales of those who in some manner returned from distant parts of the world, communicated their arguments and thoughts to his brother, more skilled in maritime matters, disclosing how, as a matter of necessity, if any one leaving behind him the southern shores of Africa should direct his course in the open sea to his right hand, towards the west, he would come somewhere on his way upon continental lands."

In 1499, Seranega, a contemporary of Gallo, and his colleague as Genoese Ambassador to Milan, then in the power of Louis XII, also wrote on Colombo. (21) He adds nothing to Gallo's account, save that, more specifically, he speaks of Christoforo Colombo, *Genoese*, but for the rest, his record is a hardly touched-up copy of Gallo's narrative.

Nor is Giustiniani's a much more original work. This learned bishop published at Genoa in 1516 a *Polyglot Psalter*, in Latin, Greek, Hebrew, Arabic and Chaldaic. (22) In this rare book, as a marginal comment on a line of Psalm xix.—*et in fines mundi verba eorum*—Giustiniani prints what amounts to a summary transcription of Gallo's story. He also says definitely that Colombo was "a native of Genoa" (*patria genuensis*), and also that he was "of plebeian extraction" (*vilibus ortus parentibus*).

These authorities, the more to be respected as, with the exception of the last, their manuscripts remained unknown till the middle of the eighteenth century, establish, therefore, not only that towards 1450-80 there was in Genoa a family of Colombos whose Christian names coincide with those of the discoverer of America, but that it was a plebeian family of woolweavers, carders and tailors, and that two young boys of this family went to sea at the age of puberty, settled in Lisbon and discovered America, so that "their words have gone abroad to the ends of the earth."

* *
*

How is it, then, that so much resistance is opposed to the acceptance of a historical fact so well substantiated by contemporary documents, both legal and literary?

First, no doubt, because national pride and prejudices come to cloud the issue and to prevent a cool interpretation of the facts. No time need be wasted in elaborating this all too obvious point. Moreover, as if the national foibles of some Spaniards, Portuguese and Italians did not suffice, the early—as well as the late— history of Colón is further complicated by those religious and historical prejudices which seem to have smothered the history of Spain with their rank overgrowth to an even worse extent than that of any other nation. Protestant, Catholic, Jewish, reactionary and revolutionary prepossessions have flourished on this fertile historical soil—the discovery of America—until the mere statement of simple, plain facts sounds like unheard of heresy or wild lucubration. Here, again, examples would swarm if they were worth the space. But when all this is granted, there still remains that the history of Christoforo Colombo and that of Cristóbal

Colón differ at so many points and in so many ways that such differences explain, if they do not altogether justify, the numerous "solutions," "keys," and alternative identities which have been suggested. Now, while most of the difficulties raised can be explained away, one at any rate has not been satisfactorily answered by the "Genoese" school—in fact, it has not been answered at all, and it is so crucial that, were it to remain unanswered, it would make nonsense of all the documents of Genoa.

CHAPTER IV

COLOMBO *VERSUS* COLÓN

THE first difficulty comes from the fact that, though he wrote much and often about himself, in none of the papers which are indisputably of his hand does Colón actually say that he is a Genoese. (1) It is true that he often referred to himself as a foreigner ("un extranjero"), but this word, in such days, in a Castillian context, did not exclude people such as the Catalans and the Aragonese. In 1485 the See of Seville was vacant. The Pope appointed Cardinal Don Rodrigo de Borja, the future Alexander VI Borgia—who was a Spaniard, but of Valencia, and therefore a subject of the Kingdom of Aragon. But though the King of Aragon was Ferdinand, Isabel's husband, the King and Queen told the Papal Nuncio in Seville, and wrote to the Pope as well, "that such a See was one of the most important in their kingdoms and covered territories close to lands held by the Moors, so that it was not wise to appoint to it a foreign person, not born in Castille." (2) Numerous examples might be here added to show that the notion of *foreigners* was in those days far less rigidly connected with our contemporary perspective, dominated as it is by the idea of the Nation-State, while the State itself was in people's minds little more than an extension of the idea of *estate*, and the King little more than a feudal lord. When, therefore, Colón described himself as a foreigner, far from giving himself away as a Genoese, he was cautiously sheltering behind his usual veil of vagueness and reserve.

A similar vagueness is to be observed in the first chroniclers who deal with Colón, particularly those who knew him directly. Peter Martyr, the prolific Italian letter-writer, gossip-monger and, at times, ambassador of the King and Queen, always speaks of him as *Colonus Ligur*, Colón (not Columbus nor Colombo), Ligurian. (3) Trivigiano, who translated Peter Martyr's letters into Venetian and, much to his annoyance, rushed them into print in 1504, begins his book with the words: "Cristophoro Colôbo, Zenouese." Trivigiano knew Colón, who had allowed him to copy some of the correspondence which crossed between the discoverer and the royal couple, so that this testimony which, of his own accord, the young Venetian adds to his translation of Peter Martyr's epistles, is not to be passed over lightly. But, after him, we come back to vagueness. Las Casas, in his general portrait given above, seems to go out of his way to throw doubt over his own assertion that Colón was "of Genoese extraction," even to the point of providing a quite unnecessary quotation from the Portuguese Barros, since this quotation, instead of adding to our information, seems only to confirm our reasons for doubt. Oviedo, one of the earliest historians of the Indies, says that Cristóbal Colón, "as I am informed by men of his nation, was of the province of Liguria, which is in Italy," (4) and adds that he may be of Savona or of Nervi or of Cugureo. As for Don Fernando Colón, his ingenuity to cover with a dust of doubt the ray of light which he consents to give us on the birthplace of his illustrious father is unrivalled by any other historian of the period. "Some," he says, revealing the subconscious preoccupation which, at any rate in part, explains the mystery, "who in a certain manner intend to obscure his fame, say that he was from Nervi, others that he was from Cugureo, and others that he was from Bugiasco, which are all small places near the city of Genoa, and on the same coast; and others, who wish to make him more exalted, say that he was a Savonese, and others a Genoese; and still others, who are more given to inexactness, say that he was from Piacenza, in which city there are some honoured persons of his family and sepulchres with the arms and inscriptions of the Colombos." (5) This is a strange passage coming from the son of the man whose birthplace is so variously discussed. Fernando Colón puts a finishing touch to his curious reticence when, commenting on what he calls Giustiniani's errors, he says he does not wonder at them "in this matter which is occult." Moreover, he actually travelled over to Genoa and its neighbourhood and found no trace of his father's family.

This would appear to make up a formidable case againstGenoa; it has, at any rate, provided the stock argument for those who would make Colón a Catalan, a Gallegan or a Portuguese. Yet a detached examination of the problem should surely lead to the conclusion that, on this point, the birthplace, the accumulated testimony of Colón and of his contemporary chroniclers writing at the Spanish end do not conflict with, rather do they confirm, the evidence supplied by the documents on the Colombo, weaver-publican family.

What does this "Colón" evidence say? First impression:

reticence and vagueness. Second impression: this cloud of reticence and vagueness does not cover the whole world, nor the whole of Italy; it settles on or about Genoa. Therefore, the reasonable conclusion is that, since Colón came from a family which was certainly an obstacle to his ambitions in Spain—ambitions which were most exalted—he had to hedge and ward off questions about it; yet, since he did come from Genoa and truth will out and one cannot very well wander very widely from it, his reticence and vagueness did nevertheless hover round Genoa. In actual fact, the vagueness and the variety of suggestions to be found in his historians must come from him. Colón, when asked, must have given one name here and another one there, so as to keep the matter, so to speak, in the air.

The first difficulty, therefore, vanishes.

The second difficulty comes from the comparison of the ages of the three Colombos and of the three Colóns. Christoforo Colombo was born between August 26th and October 31st, 1451. We do not know for certain when Cristóbal Colón was born. If we were to take Bernáldez at his word, he died in 1506 at seventy "more or less," (6) and would have been born in 1436. It is generally believed that Bernáldez, who knew Colón, must have meant sixty, which in Spanish may easily be misprinted into seventy (*sesenta—setenta*). This would give 1446 for his birth date. Now, as it happens, 1446 would fit several other clues provided by Colón himself. Without going into a tedious discussion of these details, it may be safely asserted that, in the absence of "Christoforo Colombo," i.e. had we no Genoese papers, general agreement would have been achieved round 1446-48. Yet, Christoforo Colombo was born in 1451, and the question now to be discussed is whether 1451 is compatible with the data we possess on the discoverer's side, i.e. whether Christoforo Colombo is compatible with Cristóbal Colón.

On December 21st, 1492, Colón writes in his Diary that he has "been at sea twenty-three years without being away from it for any time worth counting." (7) Leaving aside for further discussion the question of his real profession and activity in his early years which this quotation raises, the fact emerges that Colón was twenty-three years at sea. He can hardly count the seven or eight he spent in Spain, so that, taking 1484 as the date of his arrival in Spain, he went to sea in 1461.

In 1501, Colón says that he went to sea at an early age, and he adds a sentence often misunderstood and mistranslated by the students of his life: (8) "At a small age, I went to sea, and have sailed since to this date; his very craft incites the man who devotes himself to it to want to know the secrets of this world; I have been in this habit for over forty years. I have sailed over all that is nowadays navigated." He does not *necessarily* mean that he has been forty years at sea, but that he has been forty years in the habit of trying to penetrate the secrets of this world. Still, there are three statements here which we must retain:

He was of a small age when he went to sea; his craft had been that of a seaman for the past forty years; and he had sailed all there was to be sailed. This tallies with his first assertion: he began to navigate in 1461.

But the most disputed statement of Colón's is that in which he declares explicitly that he was twenty-eight when he came to serve. This statement is to be found in his famous letter to the King and Queen, written on July 7th, 1503, in great anguish of mind, while in Jamaica. (9) But when did he come to serve? Human beings are not machines. They are apt to be vague and to call different things by the same names and the same things by different names. "Come to serve" may mean many things in Colón's mind, and in some papers he may refer to one date and in other papers to another date. He has given a definite, clear statement of the date which he considered as the official beginning of his service to the Castillian State. "After I came to serve them [Ferdinand and Isabel], that is, seven years ago from the 20th of this very month of January . . ." (10) he says, on January 14th, 1493. Officially, therefore, he began to serve on January 20th, 1486. But he "came to serve" earlier, for in 1500 he says: "It is now seventeen years since I came to serve these princes with the enterprise of the Indies," (11) that is to say, seventeen years ago I rendered these princes the service of offering them—and not some other prince—the discovery of the Indies. Now, seventeen years from 1500 is 1483. It matters little that he may have made a mistake on this. The fact is that he was apt to think of 1483 as the year of his arrival in Spain. Now, may we for once leave the dusty papers and come back to flesh and spirit. There is this man, pen in hand, writing his letter to the royal couple, writing freely, flowingly, as one impelled by a strong gust of the wind which blows over the soul in stormy days. And when he comes to imagine the bygone events which will enable him to fill up that blank under his pen—"I came to serve when I was—blank—years"—he of course thinks backwards; he is writing in 1503; he first thinks of the year he came to serve, and naturally his mind rests on that 1483, which gives him a round figure; then, another step backwards, also of a round figure, say 30, and that brings him back to 1453; "but," he thinks, "I was born in 1451"; then there is a difference of two years. His swift, mental reckoning, while the pen waits, is over; but, as he is counting backwards, he makes a mistake and, instead of adding two years to his thirty, he subtracts them. He was thirty-two when he came to serve; he writes twenty-eight. Here again it is enough to imagine the man alive and to assume that he was human, and the difficulty vanishes.

A similar difficulty has been raised because in a letter quoted by his son Fernando, Colón says that he began to navigate when he was fourteen. (12) This has been attacked on two points. First, because Gallo says that the brothers Colón went to sea at the age of puberty, as if fourteen were not the age of puberty for Genoese boys, or as if fourteen were not Juliet's age in *Romeo and Juliet*; then because if Colón went to sea at fourteen and had twenty-three years of sea-life in 1484, he was not born in 1451 but in 1447. Yet, are we not here again taking him too much at his word? What does he mean by "navigate," by "go to sea"? If at ten he is taken on sailing-boats here and there on short trips, "to learn the ropes," and at fourteen he begins a sailor's life, why should he not date his sea-days now in 1461, now in 1465? There is nothing here to justify drastic conclusions going as far as the rejection of the whole Genoa case. (13)

Two other difficulties are raised at this point, both by those who reject the Genoa case on the ground that it conflicts with Colón's word, and by those who throw over Colón as a liar on the ground that his story does not tally with the Genoa papers. These cases refer to Colón's life at sea, and cannot be discussed without considering his attitude towards Genoa. Leaving them in abeyance for the present, we may then conclude that on the whole, and without taking undue liberties with the texts, Christoforo Colombo and Cristóbal Colón may have been born in the same year.

After hovering over a choice of no less than sixteen dates ranging from 1430 to 1456 for Cólon's birthdate, the general consensus of his biographers settles, therefore, on a date between August 26th and October 31st, 1451, which makes Colón be born midway between Queen Isabel (April 22nd, 1451) and

King Ferdinand (March 2nd, 1452). Those who keep—as did Colón himself—an open mind as to the influence of the stars on human affairs may find food for meditation in this curious fact.

Nothing in the Genoa papers, somewhat reticent about Bartolomeo Colombo, (14) stands in the way of the only clear statement we possess about the age of Bartolomé Colón: in 1512, as a witness in a lawsuit between his brother's heirs and the Crown, Bartolomé says he is "fifty years or more." He was, then, born in or before 1462. The very silence of the Genoese documents suggests early absence from Genoa, which would again tally with the two statements made by Gallo about Bartolomeo: that he went to sea early in life, and that he settled in Lisbon before his elder brother. Cristóbal Colón landed in Lisbon in 1476. Bartolomé Colón, if Gallo is correct, which Fernando Colón denies, (15) must therefore have been there at the latest in 1475. It follows that in all probability Bartolomé was born before 1462. At any rate, Bartolomé's "fifty years or *more*" provide a margin of at least five years which would suffice to account for the arrival of Bartolomeo Colombo in Lisbon at a not too early age (thirteen to eighteen).

In any case, an emigration, at so early an age, suggests that a previous link existed between the Colombo family and Lisbon. In those days, however, men matured earlier than in our own. They grew older sooner also: boys of fifteen were men; men of forty were old men. When the Spanish dramatists of the great epoch (1550-1650) write *Don Pedro, viejo* (Don Pedro, an old man), in the list of their *dramatis personae*, they mean that Don Pedro was about forty, i.e. a yellow-skinned, wrinkled-faced, toothless ruin of a man, with about twenty-five years of fast living behind him.

This should be borne in mind when coming to the next difficulty raised by some authors against the Genoa case. (16) Giacomo Colombo was born in 1468. On July 21st, 1512, Don Diego Colón writes to King Ferdinand complaining that an order signed by the King will deprive him of three hundred Indians, while he, the brother of the Admiral who had so well served the King, is "old, poor and sick." Since Giacomo would then be forty-four, he was not old, say the critics. Here again, though Don Diego was no doubt appealing to the King's feelings by stressing his age, he was not using that word "old" in an unusual sense for a man of forty-four. Don Diego Colón's age is not, therefore, an obstacle which should prevent us from identifying the Colombos and the Colóns.

* *
*

The third difficulty comes from the apparent incompatibility between Christoforo Colombo's trade—woolcarding—and Cristóbal Colón's profession—navigating. There are students of Colón who, on the strength of the Genoa papers, reject all Colón's claims to have sailed the seas as pure invention, (17) and consider that he did not move from Genoa or Savona till after he was twenty-two years of age, and that till that date he was a woolweaver and a publican in partnership with his father.

Now, this way of writing down a man's life in the teeth of everything he himself said about it would make nonsense of all history. The fact that Colón never used the Italian language at all—the importance of which requires separate treatment—would suffice to refute the puerile view of a Christoforo Colombo who stuck to his father's looms and wine-jars in Genoa till the ripe age of twenty-two. Moreover, Gallo himself, that very Gallo whose records add so much authority to the Genoese school, tells us that both Christoforo and Bartolomeo went to sea at the age of puberty. And, better still, we claim that the Genoese documents, on the strength of which we are told that Colombo was continuously a woolweaver and a publican, say nothing of the kind, and on the whole rather strengthen than weaken the view that he was a sailor from a very early age.

To begin with, these documents say nowhere that Christoforo Colombo was a wool*weaver*. The only son of Domenico who became a wool*weaver* was Giacomo. Christoforo's name is given either without any mention of his trade at all or as a wool*worker*. The above-mentioned deed of August 1472 is most eloquent in this respect, for it excludes Christoforo from the two qualifications which cover his father: *Dominicus Columbus lanerius, habitator Saone et Christoforus, eius filius*, (18) i.e. Christoforo is at the time neither a woolworker nor a citizen of Savona. It is true that in March 1472 Christoforo witnessed a will as "a woolworker of Genoa" (not a woolweaver), but we all know that if a scribe is intent on writing down a man's trade and that man has or has had several trades, some of which are easier to define than others, any one of them, even if no longer professed, will fill up the gap, for, after all, most legal documents are paid by the word and "woolworker" is just as long as or longer than "sailor" or "seaman," let alone "corsair" or "pirate."

On examination of the Genoese notarial documents we find, therefore, that: (*a*) Christoforo was never a woolweaver, and is at times mentioned in a way that allows us to think that he was no longer in the wool trade at all, nor a constant resident in the Republic; (*b*) Bartolomeo never was in the wool trade and is never or hardly ever in Genoa or Savona; (*c*) Giacomo, the youngest son, is the only one who became a weaver like his father: therefore, Giacomo was the only one of the three brothers to be engaged in the trade long enough and *continuously* enough to rise to the top of the ladder and become a weaver.

Our first conclusion will therefore be that the Genoese notarial documents confirm

> (*a*) Gallo's statements to the effect that Domenico was a weaver but his elder sons only carders, that the two sons went out to sea at an early age, and that Bartolomeo settled in Lisbon;
>
> (*b*) Colón's own assertions to the effect that he went early to sea.

Nor have we yet exhausted the wealth which these most looked-at documents may still yield. How is it that this Christoforo, who is supposed to be continuously in Genoa and in Savona, by his father's side, as a woolweaver and a publican, presumably running the same commercial risks, buying and selling the same cloth and the same wine, how is it that this younger partner of nineteen can save his father from debt and stand caution for him in his purchases of wine and cloth? For that is what the documents say. The obvious answer is that, *since Christoforo had better credit than his father, he had other and better sources of livelihood, i.e. that he had another profession.* Moreover, this profession was not one to boast about, for when it came to writing it down on notarial deeds, either nothing was said about it, or a return to the old paternal trade allowed the matter to be passed over without difficulty. Let us look a little more closely into the dates on the strength of which we are asked to believe in a sedentary woolweaving Colombo till he was twenty-two years of age.

September	22nd, 1470	Genoa.
October	31st, 1470	Genoa
March	20th, 1472	Savona.
August	26th, 1472	Savona.
August	7th, 1473	Savona.

What these documents prove is that in twenty-two years Colón was certainly at home five periods of time, which may have been short or long, but which, in view of our first well-established conclusion, did certainly not imply a permanent residence.

It follows that the notarial documents, if reasonably read and interpreted, lead to the conclusion that Christoforo Colombo did spend most of his time at sea during a period of time which began in 1461, and that on or about 1470 the profession—whatever it was—which he pursued, was lucrative enough to enable him to help his father out of financial difficulties.

* *
*

Now this fits in most beautifully with Cristóbal Colón's own assertions, despite what erudite, though rash, scholars may have thought, and, as we may still see more than once, Colón's veracity comes tolerably well out of this severe test. May we not, then, hesitate again before following the same rash critics in dismissing as a pure invention the main adventure of Colón the seaman as he tells it himself in a letter to the King and Queen?

"It happened to me that King Reynel, who is now with God, sent me to Tunis to seize the galleas *Fernandina*, and when I was already on the island of St. Peter in Sardinia, a settee informed me that the galleas was accompanied by two other ships and a carack, whereupon there was some agitation among the men and they refused to sail on unless we returned first to Marseilles to pick up another ship and more men. Seeing that I could not force their hand without some artifice, I agreed to what they asked me, but, changing the bait of the magnetic needle, I spread sails at sunset, and the next morning, at dawn, we were within the cape of Carthagine while all had been certain that we were going to Marseilles." (19).

This episode refers to René of Anjou, one of the princes chosen in succession as king by the Catalans in their struggle with their King Juan II, father of the Ferdinand of Aragon to whom Colón wrote the letter. (20) The history of that struggle shows that the episode told by Colón can only have happened in 1472-73. Colombo was then twenty-one. "Therefore he is not Colón," say those who want him for Spain; "therefore Colón is a boastful liar," say, in more polite terms, those who are determined to make him a woolweaver-publican. But if Colón had been navigating since 1461, and if he was, as he certainly was, a man of an exceptionally compelling and commanding personality, why should he not be the captain of a ship at twenty-one?

History is full of cases of youthful captains, and if Napoleon could be a commander-in-chief at twenty-five, Colón could certainly be the captain of a modest ship at twenty-one.

Moreover, though the action which he relates has been considered as impossible by some of his more severe critics, (21) the proof of its impossibility has not been provided. On the contrary, this action evinces that peculiar combination of daring in the aim and of caution, and even of guile, in the means which is one of the constant features of Colón's psychology. There is a line in his own letter which carries conviction with it, for it betrays one of the keys of his behaviour in future years—*seeing that I could not force their hand without some artifice* . . . That is Colón all over.

Finally, this window which Colón suddenly opens out for us over his pre-Spanish days shows him in his true light as a leader of seamen and as a corsair. For, obviously, Colón was then a corsair in the temporary service of René Anjou.

Now it so happens that the next time we hear of him he turns up as a corsair, fighting under a French admiral bearing his name— and against the Genoese.

CHAPTER V

THE KEY TO THE MYSTERY

WE may then imagine Christoforo Colombo as a young man born in a family of needy woolweavers and tailors, who felt in him that hunger for space which is the mark of ambition and the sense of inner greatness. Unknown to him—for the innermost facts of our life are so close to us that they are the last to be revealed to our consciousness—this sense of space led him to the Boundless One, to that blue sea ever lapping on the shores of his native Genoa, and from the age of ten he began to desert the paternal looms for the fishing-boats of the harbour. His childhood hummed with the rumours, alarums and excursions which over-ran his native Genoa during the protracted duel between René d'Anjou and Alfonso of Aragon and Sicily over the crown of Naples. The small republic, no doubt an unwilling character in this drama, was unable by sheer geographical reasons to follow Sancho Panza's advice: *between two millstones never put your thumbs*, and fell now this way, now that, as the fortunes of war and the relative weight of partisanship in internal politics dictated. At the time of Christoforo's birth, Genoa was veering back to Alfonso, after having backed René. But when the boy was seven years old, his little country went back to French allegiance and actually accepted from Charles VII no less a governor than Jean d'Anjou, René's own son and heir. We may well see the child drinking in all these dramatic changes, accompanied as they always were by brilliant pageantry in which now the French, now the Aragonese swaggered in bright array through the Gate of Sant'Andrea, which his father had kept, and rode and marched through the Vico dell'Olivella, while their ships filled the lovely bay with their bright colours and elegant lines and with the noise of their joyous artillery.

On the death of Alfonso, Charles VII of France and his lieutenant, Jean d'Anjou, tried again to wrench the crown of Naples from Alfonso's bastard son and heir, Ferdinand. Feelings in Genoa were divided, and there must have been some excitement in young Christoforo's home (he was then nine) when the victory of Savona was announced, for on that day the French beat the Aragonese. Yet the elation of the Angevine party in Genoa was not to last long, for their adversaries won over public opinion and both Jean and René had to rush to the city—without, however, being able to prevent a massacre of Frenchmen by the Genoese. This happened when Christoforo was ten. During four more years Jean d'Anjou kept the war going, or, at any rate, off and on, so that our youngster, who was then already beginning his sea experiences, can hardly have escaped participating in some land or sea skirmishes, almost certainly on the Angevine side.

Such was the real school of young Christoforo: the seas, a war almost endemic in its persistence, the example of high endeavour, risk, danger and adventure—a picture quite different from the plebeian looms and taverns which a too literal reading of dusty papers has led some of his biographers to set up before us.

After four or five years as apprentice he would, at fourteen, definitely cast in his lot with the sea-folk and embark in one of the corsair boats which King René and his son Jean needed for their relentless war. In this capacity he would, after the manner of the day, combine trade with war, and possibly a pinch of piracy now and then, if the price were worth the risk, and if the owner were an infidel, or even an adversary. Hence the knowledge of Chio, which has been noted in his diaries (1) and letters, and that experience of the sea which, together with his inherent mastery over men and things, made of him a sea-captain at the early age of twenty-one.

Here we are confronted with another difficulty. If that be so, we are asked, where did he learn his mathematics, his astronomy and his Latin? Ah yes, where indeed? For, if we reject as pious filial imagination or illusion his son Ferdinand's assertion that he studied in Pavia University, (2) how on earth could he know anything, since he had not been at college? This is a naïve question to be sure, yet it is to be found expressed or assumed in some biographies of Colón, as if no learning could be had outside universities and as if there were any lack of evidence that Colón was a self-taught man.

Colón, who was certainly one of the wiliest men that ever lived, was also one of the most candid. No contradiction in this; candid by nature, wily by pressure. There is a singular charm in the way in which he describes his knowledge and his parts, which is worth tons of notarial documents, for any one whose mental ear is attuned to truth: "To this my wish"—that of finding out the secrets of the world—"I found Our Lord most propitious, and to this end I received from Him a spirit of intelligence. In seamanship He made me abundant, of astrology He gave me enough, as well as of geometry and arithmetic, and of ingenuity in mind and hands to draw this sphere and on it the cities, rivers and mountains, islands and harbours, everything in its right place. In this time I have seen and studied all writings, cosmography, histories, chronicles and philosophy and other arts . . ." These are Colón's own words, as quoted by Las Casas from a letter to the King and Queen. The good bishop adds a rider which increases their value as a first-hand document on Colón's education: "He says 'enough' [of astrology] because by intercourse with men well versed in astrology he learnt enough of it to perfect what he knew of seamanship; not because he had studied astrology himself . . ." (3)

Bearing in mind that by "astrology" both Colón and Las Casas mean astronomy (no doubt with a good deal of astrology thrown in, for the two notions had not yet been separated), this statement gives a candid and truthful account of the great sailor's education which fits all we know of him on the "Colombo" as well as on the "Colón" side. The small boy who began sailing at ten and navigating at fourteen picked up his astronomical notions while at the ropes. He does not claim to be a Ptolemy; he says God gave him as much astronomy as he needed and no more; and we have it from his friend and confidant that he picked up his astronomical lore by intercourse with the learned. Let us never forget, when dealing with men whose life-story is worth telling, that they are men out of the common and therefore quicker to learn in the particular direction of nature in which their mental interests lie. Surely there is no problem here. Sailing is not always made up of storms and, in the sunny Mediterranean, a sailor has many hours of leisure. There, under the blue sky and over the blue sea, must we recognise Colombo's university. Almanacks and books of Astrology may have lain about in the captain's berth; if not, we may rely on that eager soul to have sought them on land from those Moors and Jews he loved to frequent. This point, as well as that of his Latin, will repay further study; for the present it may suffice to say that nothing in Colón's education stands in the way of identifying the Admiral of the Ocean Sea with the son of the Genoa woolweaver—rather the reverse. As in preceding cases, things become clear as soon as we agree to attach to Colón's own words the faith which they no doubt deserve.

*
* *

For they do deserve faith, even if, as Ruy de Pina, the Portuguese chronicler, roundly says of him, "the said Admiral always went beyond the bounds of truth when reporting his own affairs." (4)

This is a common and an excusable failure with men of "high fancy," of "muy alto ingenio" as Bernáldez says of Colón. If read with a sympathetic insight into the character they are trying to depict, all these chroniclers who met the discoverer manage to reveal a true, consistent, living personality. He had a "high fancy"; his feet did stand on truth, yet his imagination made him go "beyond the bounds of truth in reporting his own affairs." This is a constant feature of the discoverer—a kind of bouncing energy which made him use truth as the springboard from which to fly up to high fact. Shelley was made that way. Most great discoverers of continents, whether on earth or in heaven, are bound to be made that way. But oh the pitiful comments and interpretations when their winged sayings fall petrified by age under the power of bookworms!

Here is, for instance, the story of Colón's dramatic arrival in Portugal. It has come down to us through the first two chroniclers of the discoverer's exploits, the two intimate historiographers, considered, not without reason, as having had the advantage not only of private papers but of private confidences from the great man himself—his son Fernando and Bishop Las Casas. According to the good bishop, the time was coming when America had to be discovered, and so it was necessary for the Lord to bring Colón over to Spain. He therefore proceeds to inform us of the way in which the Lord set about to achieve this end. It so happened that "as Colón was so much given to the affairs and exercise of the sea and in those days there sailed a famous man, the greatest of the corsairs of those times, [who was] of his name and lineage, by name Colombo Junior, to distinguish him from another one who had been known and famous earlier, and this Junior brought a great fleet against the infidels and Venetians and the enemies of his nation, Cristóbal Colón determined to go and sail with him, and he sailed in his company a long time. This Colombo Junior, having news that four Venetian galleases had passed over to Flanders, waited for them on the way back between Lisbon and Cape St. Vincent to fall on them." The good bishop describes the battle at some length, then shows how Colón's ship and a galleas to which it had been chained in an embrace as close as the embrace of love were set on fire together by war, as is also the way of love, and how most men "preferred to die by water than by fire," but "Cristóbal Colón was a great swimmer and was able to seize hold of an oar which at times held him afloat while he rested, and so he made progress till he reached land, a little over two leagues from the spot to which the ship had drifted during their senseless battle." (5)

Las Casas gives chapter and verse for all this story by quoting an Italian chronicler named Sabellico. But Sabellico's narrative differs from his and from that of Don Fernando Colón in several important respects: in Sabellico's there was no fire, no grappling, no disaster, but a victorious arrival of Colombo Junior in Lisbon with the captured Venetian galleases; and the fight he describes took place in 1485, when Colón was already in Spain. What a magnificent occasion for showing up Colón's lack of veracity, and for explaining that the reference to that "Colombo, of his name and lineage" was one more boastful invention of his vainglorious mind! Scholars, moreover, discovered that Colombo Junior was no such Colombo at all, but one George Byssipat or George the Greek, a corsair in the service of France. From this observation it was an easy step to throw over the whole story, including the battle, the fire, the swimming and the oar.

Further study, however, led scholars to the discovery of another battle of St. Vincent which fitted the facts as given by Las Casas and by Don Fernando. Two contemporary authors, Ruy de Pina, the Portuguese chronicler, and Alonso de Palencia, a Spanish historian of the period, (6) both tell of a battle fought on August 13th, 1476, when Colón was still sailing the seas and in which a French corsair-admiral, Guillaume de Casenove-Coullon, known in Italy as Colombo and in Spain as Colón, engaged some Genoese ships in battle in exactly the same circumstances as related by Colón's biographers.

Poor Cristóbal Colón! How difficult he finds it to be believed over four centuries after his death! Even when the very dusty papers which so often seemed to testify against him are good enough to turn up a trump card in his favour, scholars will refuse to believe what the discoverer said, because they have made up their minds that things "must" have happened otherwise.

Though the date fits, though the admiral fits, though the events of the battle fit, Colón, we are told, could not have fought as he says, namely on the side of Coullon, because Coullon fought against the Genoese, and as Christoforo Colombo was such a good patriot he must have fought on the Genoese side, i.e. against Coullon.

Now, this is very well reasoned out, but it does not tally with what actually occurred at the battle. It so happens that this, the first battle of St. Vincent, is also told by Diego de Valera in a passage which has so far escaped attention. (7) In the chronicle of this historian-sailor-statesman, Chapter XXI bears precisely the following title:

Of the case which befell the Captain of the French fleet called Colon in the Cape of St. Mary, which is thirty-six leagues from the city of Cadiz.

This is, we may point out, the first Admiral Colón we find in a Spanish chronicle; and, moreover, King Ferdinand himself, answering a letter of Diego de Valera in which his loyal *Maestresala* informs him of the battle in terms almost identical with this chapter and, incidentally, with Las Casas' narrative, the King's own pen writes *Colón* for the first time, applying that name, in its Spanish form, to the French corsair whom Cristóbal Colón considered as of his name and lineage; this, be it noticed, in 1476, when Cristóbal Colón was still Christoforo Colombo, and had not yet "returned" to his name of Colón nor written: "I am not the first admiral in my family." (8)

Leaving for later discussion his name and possible connection with Colón the Frenchman, the narrative of Diego de Valera, an expert, be it remembered, on naval things in southern Spain, and the official watchman of the Straits at the time, is more than enough to dismiss as extravagant nonsense the view of those who would put Colón on board the Genoese ships; for these ships, says de Valera, returned to Cádiz, while it is evident that, since Colón swam towards Portugal, he was on the Portuguese side, which was that of the other Colón, i.e. *the side on which he said he was.* Therefore, the discoverer's story, once purged of the errors committed by his chroniclers, is vindicated. He did fight on the side of an admiral of his name; his ship did take fire when grappled together with the Genoese ships; and he did swim over to the Portuguese coast with the help of an oar in which he was entitled to see the helping hand of Providence. (9)

But in the steps of this mysterious man enigmas flourish. How is it that we find this Genoese fighting against the Genoese? No wonder the opinion which refuses to identify Colón with Colombo dies hard. Yet die it must. If Colón was not Colombo, when had he a better opportunity to show it than at this time, when he was arriving in Portugal after a battle against the Genoese? It is known, nevertheless, that the name *Colombo*, which makes a Genoese of him, was the first name under which he was known in

Lisbon. The chapter in which Ruy de Pina, a contemporary observer, narrates the discovery of America is entitled: *Discovery of the Islands of Castille by Collombo*, (10) who is described in the text as "Christovam Colombo Italiano." History, being life, is apt to gambol out of logic, particularly of *our* logic; we cannot write down beforehand the rules to which lives such as Colón's are to adjust themselves. Our method must be the very reverse; first, let us have the fact; then, if we can, we will find out its explanation. Therefore, all we can say for the present is that Christoforo Colombo, a corsair of Genoa, fought against the Genoese in 1476, at Cape St. Vincent. As to his love—or no love —for Genoa, it will take care of itself.

The conclusion, nevertheless, is of the utmost importance, for, on the strength of unimpeachable documents fitting in perfectly with the discoverer's own assertions, we find that *Cristóbal Colón, though a Genoese, was not a patriotic Genoese*. It is imperative that this fact should be now established beyond dispute. Let no "dusty paper" stand in the way. There is no direct, *undisputed* utterance of loyalty to Genoa on the part of Colón. Even the disputed—and perhaps apocryphal—letter to the Bank of San Georgio does not go beyond a guarded and general statement with no explicit reference to Genoa. "Though the body be here, the heart is there continuously"; (11) that is all, and in Spanish!

Moreover, this man who has found a continent and is as sure of it as if he had it under lock and key, this man who is born in one of the world's greatest sailing-centres of the time, never even thinks of offering his discovery to his fatherland (12) and to that Bank of San Georgio which might have given him the couple of million Castillian *maravedis* he needed for the discovery without the quiver of an eyelash. And, once the continent had been found, and he had at last climbed to the summit of worldly glory and power, and was addressed as *The Very Magnificent Lord*, did he ever think of going to Genoa to visit his family and his country-men so that they might say of him: *There goes Christoforo, the son of the woolweaver and tavernkeeper who used to be the watchman at the Gate dell'Olivella?* Did his brothers, the Adelantado Don Bartolomé and that pale and loitering Giacomo-Diego, (13) wandering in the shadow of his mighty brothers, unable to fish out of the lucky pot of destiny, in spite of its continental dimen-sions, the paltriest episcopal see? What Genoese are these who, hardly arrived in Spain, drop the Colombo, become Colón and, turning their backs on Genoa for good and all, pretend to forget about it until, their bodies laid to rest, the dusty papers rise from their own sepulchres, scholarly libraries and notarial files to pull them back to their native looms? What Genoese is this who goes to sea at an early age and, instead of serving Genoa, fights against her at St. Vincent and hands over the greatest glory of the sea to the King and Queen of Castille?

* *

One thing is certain. This Genoese wrote and spoke Spanish. With the rashness which his own intemperate, passionate and easily roused nature seems to impart to his critics, it has been said that he knew no Italian. True, not one single word by him remains which may be said to be in Italian—since the one note which is quoted in this connection (14) is but a comic concoction of Italian, Castillian and Portuguese, in which Italian or pseudo-Italian words are not even in the majority. This curious text, fifty-seven words in all, is so exceptional, nay so unique, that, unless it be apocryphal, it can only be the outcome of some passing moment of mental aberration. It is the twenty-third marginal note to his copy of the *Natural History of Pliny.* (15) Again a tantalising enigma. This book is an Italian translation (so much for those who say Colón knew no Italian); yet, save for the last note but one, which is in that ridiculous jargon, and for a purely devotional inscription in Latin, all the marginal notes written in this Italian book by its Italian reader are in Spanish.

If the letters to the Bank of San Georgio and to Nicolo Oderigo, Genoese Ambassador in Castille, are genuine, they present the same enigma under a new form: a Genoese, writing to Genoese persons, writes to them in Spanish. True, he is by now a great personage in Spain and considers himself a Spaniard. But it seems only natural that in sending the Genoese Bank a letter in which he declares that his heart is in Genoa, he should have selected the language of the place where his heart was supposed to be.

Furthermore, the correspondence between Colón and his right-hand man, Father Gorricio, (16) is in Spanish—i.e. not merely Colón's letters, for Father Gorricio writes to Colón in Spanish. Now, this monk was an Italian, and therefore the fact that he wrote to Colón in Spanish shows conclusively that this was the language of Colón for all practical purposes. And finally, Colón writes in Spanish not only to his son Diego but to his brother Bartolomé, who was as Genoese as he. (17)

This is no doubt the most serious obstacle against the Genoese conception, and of itself suffices to justify the existence of several alternative solutions for the enigma of Colón; nor can it be said that, so far, the advocates of the Genoese solution have met the difficulty at all. (18) Most of them let it lie after a passing puzzled comment; (19) others vaguely suggest that Colón may have forgotten his native language in foreign lands, an explanation which, inconsistently enough, they ask us to accept along with an uncompromising view of a Christoforo Colombo at his weaving-loom and tavern till twenty-three years of age—as if a language spoken till twenty-three could be wiped out of one's memory and habits for practical purposes at thirty-three. Matters as they stand are therefore intriguing enough. But there are two more features in the situation which make it still more enigmatic.

The first is that *Colón spoke and wrote Spanish before he came to Spain*; nay, before he came to Spain he used Spanish as the language in which he couched his own thoughts for his personal, intimate use. This is proved from a marginal note by his own hand in a book which he crammed with notes, the *Historia rerum ubique gestarum*, of the scholarly Pope Pius II. In this note Colón reckons the age of the world according to the Jews, i.e. by adding the successive ages of the patriarchs from Adam down and other periods of Jewish history to—and this is what matters—"the present moment, which is the year of our Lord 1481," a year which he repeats when recapitulating, and finds therefore that "from the beginning of the world down to this time of 1481 it makes 5241 years." (20) Whatever we may think of Colón's views as to the age of the world, this note does reveal that Colón wrote Spanish for his personal use three years before he came to Spain. And that is a fact which cannot be easily disposed of.

Nor is it the only one of its kind, for his Latin is no less mysterious than his Spanish or his lack of Italian. When did he learn it? It is not very good, we are told. Granted. But it is fairly good and familiar enough to him to be the only language which he wrote for his personal use as frequently at least as Spanish. Many of his marginal notes, some almost as long as essays, are in Latin. Moreover, he was an assiduous reader of books of science, which in those days were practically always written in Latin. As if further to complicate the issue, when his Latin went wrong, it did so precisely in a Spanish way. One of the best Italian Colombists, the Pontifex Maximus of the Genoa school, (21) has commented on this fact, which he was the first to observe, with as much candour as confusion, and has pointed out an amusing example of solecism which could only come from a Spanish-speaking man.

The conclusion would appear to be obvious. "Colón learned his Latin in Spain." It is, of course, that which all the opponents of the Genoese Colombo eagerly adopt. Nor can we blame them for it until we are in a position to explain how a Christoforo Colombo born and bred in Genoa as a woolweaver never wrote in Italian even to Italians, spoke and wrote in Spanish, even to Italians, and even to himself, and wrote Latin with characteristic Spanish mistakes.

Let us dismiss the only explanation which has been so far attempted: "Colón's Spanish and Spanish-Latin were acquired in Portugal, where, in those days, Spanish was a language of great prestige and of general use." (22) Castillian, it is true, did occupy an exceptionally strong position in the whole Peninsula in the days of Colón; but that a man coming from Italy to settle in Portugal would learn it *rather* than Portuguese, and use it to the exclusion of the languages both of his land of origin and of his land of residence and marriage (for he married a Portuguese lady in Lisbon), raises more problems than it lays to rest. We must look for something else.

As for his Latin, it was, despite its faults, far too good and fluent to have been acquired late in life. No amount of juggling will date some of his elaborate texts later than 1480 or 1481. Now, he was sailing almost continuously till 1479, if the latest Genoese document is genuine. Therefore he must have learnt Latin at sea. To be sure, the thought is revolting to those scholars who remember how they went to sea for a rest from their declensions and Latin proses; but may we look again at that soul burning with ambition, looking at the stars during the long nights in the Mediterranean, brewing problems in his unlettered mind, wondering how to steer a ship on cloudy days, how to reckon distances, how to penetrate the secrets of nature, on which he tells us he was bent from his early days? And may we not guess what the reaction of this iron-willed young boy would be on finding that the key to it all was in books written in Latin? Had he a teacher? Did he work alone? Who cares? On land or at sea, spending a few days or weeks or months at home in Genoa, or sailing to Chio for mastic, or to Tunis for a galleas for King René, we may be certain that Christoforo Colombo learnt his Latin furiously.

But then, why a Spanish-Latin?

Let us sum up the position. Christoforo Colombo was a young self-taught woolworker of Genoa, turned sailor, who

    (1) Read Italian but did not write it;

(2) Spoke and wrote Spanish for his personal use before he came to Spain;

(3) Knew Latin as a Spanish-speaking person would, though he learned it before he came to Spain.

From which premises the conclusion is obvious:

Christoforo Colombo was a young Genoese whose Italian was not presentable, and whose culture-language was Spanish.

Now there is only one reasonable way of explaining this fact: the Colombo family were Spanish Jews settled in Genoa, who, following the traditions of their race, had remained faithful to the language of their country of origin. (23)

CHAPTER VI

COLOMBO—COLOMO—COLOM—COLÓN

CHRISTOFORO COLOMBO was a Genoese of Spanish-Jewish origin. This conclusion has been reached as the only possible explanation for a group of facts which, so far, have been found too awkward for explanation. Confronted with such facts, the host of students of Colón's life has split into two irreconcilable sets—those who say he was a Genoese and those who say he was a Spaniard; but though they hold opposite views, their methods are identical; for both maintain their case by throwing over half the facts, either openly condemning them as untrue, or quietly and unobtrusively dropping them out of sight. It is difficult to see how *all* the facts can be reconciled and given their adequate weight otherwise than by adopting the view put forward in these pages. Born in Genoa, Colombo was of Spanish-Jewish origin, bilingual from the first, speaking a popular and uneducated sort of Genoese dialect and brought up by his family in a Spanish atmosphere; therefore, a Spanish Jew.

Two tests remain to be met by this view of the discoverer:

(1) How does it fit the facts we already know about him?
(2) How does it fit the remaining facts of his life?

As for the first, not only does it fit the facts, but the facts will not fit without its help; as for the second, we shall often have occasion to show that, if the Jewish hypothesis had not forced itself upon us on grounds of language, Colón's ways, character and writings would have brought home to any impartial observer the fact that he was a Jew.

When discussing his birthplace, we pointed out that the modesty of his family circumstances and occupation might explain—at least in part—his curious reticence on this important point. But we took care to say "at least in part." For, as a matter of fact, Colón never hid that he was of humble extraction. This is a point which is often overlooked, and on which serious mistakes have been made by those who would make him a Spaniard. Capital is made of the fact that on his passport the King and

54

Queen describe him as a nobleman, *nobilem virum*, while in the royal letter of May 24th, 1493, his arms were "increased," which, of course, implies that he already had some blazon. Much ink might have been saved by reading what the Admiral himself has to say. In his letter to the Aya of Prince Don Juan, speaking of the King and Queen, he writes: " who from nothing have raised me to so much honour." (1) Moreover, on the very first page of his first report on the discovery, Colón writes with his usual candour: "So that [. . .] in the same month of January, Your Highnesses ordered me to go to the said parts of India with a sufficient navy; and to that end, they bestowed great favours on me and ennobled me, allowing me thenceforward to style myself Don," a fact which is documentarily proved by the royal letter appointing him Admiral, Viceroy and Governor, for in it the discoverer is mentioned as plain *"Cristóbal Colón"* and is later explicitly authorised to call himself *Don Cristóbal Colón.*

It follows that if the humble origin of his family may explain in part Colón's reticence as to Genoa (for men's actions are many-rooted like trees, and like trees many-branched), it cannot be accepted as the only cause of it, since he was not so reticent on his having risen "from nothing" as he was on his having come from Genoa.

But if his family were not only poor and humble but Jewish as well, at a time when the Jewish race was passing in Spain through a crisis never equalled in history till the days of Nazi Germany, his reticence as to the actual spot where they lived and on the actual people they were, becomes immediately explicable.

And so does his curious un-Genoese behaviour. We have seen him somewhat indifferent to the ties of patriotism—in a passive way right through his whole life, in an active way on two occasions: when he fought for King René at a time when this prince was considered as an enemy by Genoa; and when in the battle of St. Vincent he attacked a Genoese fleet while serving under the banner of Casenove-Coullon. Here, again, the *Genoites* wriggle out of the facts by pronouncing Colón a liar and declaring he served the Genoese; while the *Hispanites* triumph over the Genoites by declaring that the Genoa case is thereby proved wrong. But we know that Colombo–Colón was born in Genoa, and we know that at St. Vincent he attacked the Genoese, rather dastardly, as a matter of fact. Is it not obvious, then, that Colón was indifferent to Genoa, that he was an unassimilated Genoese, not a genuine Genoese citizen rooted in the soil, but a bird of passage, ready to make his nest anywhere, even in those undiscovered continents which he felt beyond the seas of his dreams?

A Jewish Colón solves the problem. Note his extreme mobility, and that of his brother Bartolomé. This in itself is no more than a hint of Jewishness. Spain and Portugal were then overrun with Genoese; but who remained Genoese. Colón was Portuguese in Portugal and Castillian in Castille. "Colom had become a natural vassal of that land [Portugal] by his marriage," (2) says Oviedo; and Fernando Colón: "Holding himself to be a subject of these realms, which were the fatherland of his sons . . ." Bartolomé will show a similar adaptability. Note their special indifference to Genoa, their readiness to change the soil on which their lives were to be built and the banner under which they were to serve, even against Genoa; and then the Jewish explanation is forced upon the mind.

For it is worth observing that this explanation does not merely fit the facts; it is needed in order to make them fit with each other. Neither the linguistic difficulty, nor Colón's reticence over Genoa, nor his attitude while a corsair towards his fatherland, have ever been satisfactorily explained. They do not become intelligible until Colón is seen as a Genoese-born Spanish Jew.

Two possible objections may be raised:

(1) The doctor of La Rábida, in his statement describing the arrival of Colón at the Monastery, says that Fray Juan Pérez "seeing that he looked like a man of another country or Kingdom and alien in language . . ."

(2) Las Casas says of him: "He seems to be a native of another language, for he does not fully grasp the meaning of the words of the Castillian language nor of its way of speaking." (3)

These two objections are easily met. Colón came from abroad and did give an impression of foreignness. His language was not the Spanish of the fifteenth century, but that of the fourteenth; it had remained unevolved in that lopped-off branch transplanted to Genoa towards 1390, and had undoubtedly absorbed many Italianisms.

The quotation from Las Casas, moreover, should be carefully read. "He *seems* to be a native of another language," says this intimate friend of the discoverer, who has told us definitely that Colón was a Genoese. Then, why he *seems*? As usual, Las Casas cannot hide the fact that he is not quite sure that there is not a mystery somewhere about Colón. That this is no empty suspicion on a casual oddity of style may be shown not only by the similar attitude of the good bishop with regard to Colón's birthplace, but by his strange remarks on Colón's religion, so strange indeed as to require further discussion:

"In the matters of the Christian religion, *no doubt* ["sin duda"], he was a Catholic and of much devotion." Why "no doubt"? And again: "Having said all about the origin and fatherland and lineage and parents and even appearance and ways [. . .] and also of *what was known of* Christianity in Cristobal Colón . . ." And again: "Who realising he was so feeble, as a Christian, *which certainly he was*, he received the Sacraments with great devotion," a phrase which in Spanish is even more curious than in translation. Why this reticence, which I have italicised in every case, suddenly, on referring to his Christianity? And on the part of the man who knew him best? All, however, becomes clear on the hypothesis that Colón was a Jew.

*
* *

A similar conclusion will be reached when we come to examine the problem of his name. Not in vain does his son Fernando write: "To conform it with the fatherland where he went to live and to take a new state, he filed down the word to make it conform with the old, (4) and thus called himself *Colón*; this leads me to believe that just as most of his things were worked out by some kind of mystery, so in what pertains to the variation in his name and surname there is sure to be some mystery." This is a fairly transparent mystery! Colón, says his own son, came to the fatherland, when he came to Spain, and took again the name of Colón to conform his name to the old name of his family.

What would a plain Genoese *Colombo* do with his name on coming to serve in Spain? Nothing whatever. *Colombo* is a perfectly good Spanish form, and there are to this day thousands of Spaniards with names not unlike it, such as *Pombo*. There are nowadays in South America thousands of *Colombos* who have not thought it necessary to tamper with their name, since its sonority fits into the Castillian language as to the manner born; and even in Spain the name *Colombo* has been known to exist, at any rate since the seventeenth century. Even if Colombo had been an un-Spanish, Italian name, Spain was at the time full of Italians, including many Genoese, who continued to call themselves by their Italian names, even those who, like Juanoto Berardi, had frequent transactions with the Crown.

Why then should Colombo have to change his name to *Colón*? The Hispanites answer, "Because he never was 'Colombo.'" We cannot take this view, amongst other reasons, because documentary proof can be provided for all the phases of the evolution Colombo—Colomo—Colom—Colón. (5) Now this evolution is neither necessary nor linguistically inevitable; *Colón* is by no means the phonetic or somatic translation of *Colombo* from Italian into Spanish. Just as *Palumbus* gives *Palomo*, a well-known Spanish patronymic, so *Columbus* should have given *Colomo*. Therefore, the evolution *Colombo—Colón* must have been guided by some preconceived notion. A psychological force must have existed somewhere strong enough to produce these two results: (*a*) a change of name which in itself was not in the least necessary; (*b*) the attraction of another idea, foreign to the original meaning, which determined in reality not an adaptation but actually a change into something quite different. May we point out how Jewish this all is? The men of the wandering race are so often bound to shift the conditions of their existence that, with them, change of name has become a habit, practically unknown though it is to the rest of mankind. We are all familiar with the *Friedmann* who becomes *Freeman*, and the *Levy* who becomes *Lewis* by a kind of conscious play of words which gives an intelligent meaning to what otherwise would be a mere adaptation. The number of name-transformations amongst Spanish Jews in the fifteenth century is too great for quotation. The mere fact that, of all the Genoese we hear of in Spain at the time, Colón is the only one who makes his name undergo four swift transformations, from *Colombo* to *Colón*, should have sufficed to put students on the track of his real race. Having come to the conclusion, on entirely different grounds, that Colón was a Jew, we are entitled to consider the tendency to change his name as a striking confirmation of our Jewish hypothesis.

But why *Colón*? Let us look back at the explanations given on this subject by his two historiographers. Three statements stand out in the portrait of the Admiral left us by Las Casas:

(1) "His parents were notable persons, one time rich [. . .], at other times they must have been poor, owing to the wars and strife which are always occurring in Lombardy."

(2) "Of old, the first name of this lineage was [. . .] Colón, then, as time went by, the successors of this Colón [. . .] styled themselves Colombos; [. . .] but this illustrious man, giving up the name set by custom, wished to call

himself Colón, going back to the old word, less perhaps because it was his original name . . .

(3) ". . . than moved by that divine will which had elected him to work out that which his Christian name and his surname implied. [. . .] His surname means repopulator [. . .] he was the first [. . .] to found colonies."

True, Las Casas engrafts on all this a couple of delusions born of Don Fernando's megalomania: a Roman consul and the two admirals of Sabellico. But again, when imaginative people invent legends they do not invent them out of nothing. There is always a root of fact to the flower of fancy. It seems only fair to retain from the narrative of the worthy bishop that in all probability:

(1) The Colón family had been richer than it was, and fell on worse days, whether owing to the civil strife in Lombardy or not is another matter.

(2) Colón's name had been *Colón* before it became *Colombo*, and he merely returned to it when he came to Spain. Moreover, the tradition that the Colombos had been Colóns before they became Colombos existed in the family.

(3) Colón took this old form of his name for mixed reasons; one of them being the family tradition about it, and the other the attraction of its significant meaning.

These conclusions, which naturally flow from the statements made by the two men closest to his intimate thoughts, admirably fit the facts.

Nothing is known or has been found in Italy about the family beyond Giovanni Colombo, Christoforo's grandfather. Now, for reasons which will become clear later, the family emigration to Italy must have taken place towards 1390, i.e. about the time of Giovanni's birth.

A higher social status before they came down to weaving fits in perfectly with the dignified bearing, high stature and commanding personality which contemporaries agree in attributing to Colón.

But what was exactly the family tradition about Colón's old name, or, in other words, what was the original Spanish form of *Colombo*? The disappearance of the last syllable, what Fernando Colón calls the "filing of the word," can *only* have occurred through the Catalan form *Colom*. The influence of the idea of colonisation on this evolution of Colón's name is known to us, thanks to Las Casas. *But the fact that this evolution existed at all shows unmistakably that the family traditional name was Colom;* in confirmation of which we may point out two facts:

(1) That a *Colón* emigrating to Italy might have turned his name into *Colono* or *Colonna*, or even have left it unchanged, *Colón*, but that there is no reason why he should have made it *Colombo*.

(2) That two historians, one Oviedo, a Spanish contemporary, the other Barros, a Portuguese writing soon after, always call the discoverer *Colom*, which would be utterly inexplicable in non-Catalan writers unless there were sound reasons for this spelling.

From this traditional *Colom* the transition to Colón was easy, led as it was by two psychological forces:

(1) the *colonising* connotation of the word;

(2) advantage of the Castillian over the Catalan form, at a time when Castille was already the leading kingdom in the Peninsula.

The Colombo family would then be Catalan Jews. Colom was and is a frequent name in all Catalan-speaking Spain, including Majorca. And at this stage two more facts come to insert themselves into the picture. The first is, that in the forest of Coloms to be found in Catalonia at that time many families were Jewish; an Aaron Colom and his family are known in Zaragoza in the fourteenth century, and in 1479, four or five years before Colom settles in Spain, one Andreu Colom, a Catalan Jew, was burnt as a heretic by the Inquisition in Tarragona. (Note that one Vincenzo Colombo was hanged as a pirate in Genoa in 1492, the very year of the discovery, so that Christoforo, Genoese corsair in Genoa, Catalan Jew in Spain, had to steer a difficult course between the stake and the scaffold.) In 1461, when Christoforo Colombo (or Colom) was ten, the Inquisition of Valencia (a much older institution than the Castillian Inquisition) prosecuted one Thomé Colom and his wife Leonor, their son Joam Colom, and daughter-in-law Aldonza, for having buried Thomé's mother-in-law with Jewish rites. (6) They were all *Conversos* (*neofiti*). In 1489, when Colón was already negotiating with the King and Queen of Castille, Andrés Colom, Blanca Colom and Francisca Colom, *Conversos*, were condemned by the Inquisition of Tarragona for having observed Jewish rites. In later days there is a family of Sephardi Jews in Amsterdam by the name of Colom.

But Catalan scholars make yet another claim, (7) this time in the heraldic field. When the King and Queen ennobled Colón, they showed themselves truly magnanimous with him in the matter of his arms; for the first and second quarter of his blazon they granted him nothing less than the royal arms of Castille and Leon, the castle and the lion; his third quarter was to be "a few islands and sea-waves," and the last "your arms which you used to wear." *Used to wear*, of course, is a rather elastic phrase, and we need not conclude from it, as it has rashly been concluded by hot-hearted partisans of the Colón-was-a-Spaniard school, that King Ferdinand, who knew his Italy well and had one whole hand in the Genoese pie, was not aware of the degrees of nobility of the "nobilis vir" he was sending to Cipango. The point will be discussed anon. But, though Colón's family was one of manual workers, it does not follow that he could not put forward a more or less real or fanciful claim to a blazon-bearing family, and, as a matter of fact, an examination of his full arms as an admiral reveals that he did entertain such a claim.

In circumstances which are not fully explained, he altered the royal instructions to the extent of filling the fourth quarter, not with the arms which "he used to wear," but with the five anchors which were characteristic of the blazon of the Admiral of Castille. The royal instructions had put "his" arms last, in the fourth quarter; he relegated them to a fifth division, in itself a significant hint of the purely formal character of his claim to them. Some arms, nevertheless, there were, of course: to wit, a field of gold with a band azure on a chief gules, which in plain un-heraldic English means a blue band across a background of gold surmounted by a splash of red. Catalan specialists are able to quote several families whose arms are similar, if not identical, with these. This fact, if established, would confirm the view that Colón's family had come to Genoa from some Catalan region in which Castillian was the predominant language. (8) This would, moreover, account for the Catalanisms observed in his language by several authors.

There were several of these regions in Catalonia in those days. Two of them deserve special attention: the region of Tortosa and Majorca. In both these regions the name Colom is frequently found, and both were at the time centres of sea-activity, of that ill-defined type of spirited navigation which was in later days to develop into three diverging and definite forms: royal navies, corsairs and piracy.

* *
*

This, again, brings in two more facts which, again, insert themselves into the picture. The first is the claim to have had another admiral in his family which Colón made, referring, no doubt, to Casenove-Coullon. True, Don Fernando, and Las Casas after him, led into error by Sabellico, drag in two admirals, including a rather shadowy and ill-defined Colombo Junior. But when we come back to what the discoverer himself actually said, all we are told is that he was not the first admiral of his family. Now, our examination of the facts about the battle of 1476 has shown that, through the mass of errors in Las Casas and in Don Fernando, the truth of what Colón himself had evidently narrated to them was fully vindicated by contemporary chroniclers unknown to either Las Casas or Don Fernando, in all but what concerned the family connection with Casenove-Coullon, which, on the other hand, though not proved, remained possible.

Now, having by entirely independent methods traced Colombo back through Colón to Colom on the Mediterranean shores, we are entitled to ask whether, after all, the burden of the proof is not on those who deny, rather than on Colón himself who asserted, the connection between a Catalan family of Coloms and a family of southern-Frenchmen, Casenove-Coullon, whose first name, Casenove, is obviously in close alliance with the Casanovas and Casenoves of Catalonia.

Moreover, the evident relation between our Genoese Colombo and the Catalan-Jewish Coloms fits in perfectly with another of Colón's disputed assertions, his campaign for King René; it is well known that a number of Coloms of Catalonia fought for King René against John II of Aragon (King Ferdinand's father), and that Casenove-Coullon himself, as Admiral-corsair-pirate for Louis XI, King René's ally, also took part in this protracted struggle. The Consuls of Barcelona sent a circular letter to the port authorities pointing out to them the danger arising from the presence off their shores of the corsair Colom. (9) This corsair was Casenove-Coullon, and the circular is dated October 1473. While, therefore, no documentary proofs can be said to exist to prove an actual family relation between the two Colóns, the general weight of historical evidence comes at every turn to vindicate Colón's veracity.

Moreover, when we are led by an examination of facts such as the changes in his name to confirm his own statements and to accept as certain that he served at sea in the Mediterranean, we find that this solution, so natural in many ways, makes him spend his eager and ardent youth in the very centre of sea-expedition, at the very spring of the enquiring spirit which sent forth navigators anxious to "penetrate the secrets of the world."   Much as the Portuguese may vindicate priority in this for Prince Henry the Navigator, we are in a position to establish Catalonia and Majorca as the oldest and most active centres of discovery, on the authority of the prince of geographers, Alexandre de Humboldt: "We must not forget that the enterprises of Catalan sailors have been for Western Africa what those of the Norman-Scandinavian sailors were for the Northern part of the New World.   They have preceded the discoveries of Prince Henry [of Portugal] and of Queen Isabel of Castille.   The Island of Majorca had become from the thirteenth century the hearth of scientific knowledge in the difficult art of navigation.   We know from the *Fenix de las Maravillas del Orbe* of Ramón Lull that the Majorcans and the Catalans used navigating charts (*cartas de marear*) long before 1286;   that instruments, no doubt rudimentary, were made in Majorca for measuring time and the height of the pole on board ships.   From there, knowledge originally borrowed from the Arabs spread to the whole Mediterranean. The royal ordinances of Aragon prescribed in 1359 that each galley should be provided with not one but two sea-charts.   A Catalan navigator, Don Jayme Ferrer, had arrived in August 1346 at the mouth of the Rio de Oro, five degrees south of that Cape of No which, Prince Henry claimed, Portuguese ships had turned for the first time in 1419." (10)

This was the tradition, this the environment in which Colón moved and lived during his Mediterranean days.   That he was in it and not weaving or selling wine is obvious now as the harmonious conclusion of a number of converging clues.   Here is a further document which should be final:

In a letter to the King and Queen, dated February 6th, 1502, which is a masterpiece of seafaring experience, and of that spirit of observation for which Humboldt admired Colón as much as some contemporary critics, quite unscientific, despise him, the Admiral writes the following significant passage: "In summer and in winter, those who come and go ["andan continuo"] between Cádiz and Naples know well the wind they are going to find on the coast of Catalonia according to the season, and also when passing through the Gulf of Narbonne;   those who have to go from Cádiz to Naples, if it is winter time, sail within sight of the Cape of Creus in Catalonia along the Gulf of Narbonne;   at that time there is a very strong wind there, and at times it is best for the ships to obey it and run under it until Berbery, and that is why they sail closer to the cape, so as to keep longer to the bowline and attain the Pomeges of Marseilles or the islands of Hyeres, and thereafter they never steer away from the coast till they reach the aim of their voyage. If from Cádiz they have to go to Naples in summer time, they sail along the coast of Berbery until Sardinia, as has been said, on the other side of the north wind. For these navigations, there are well-known men who have given themselves to this so much that they know all these roads and which kind of weather they may expect according to the time of the year. These men are generally known as *pilots*, which amounts to *leader* on land, who, well as he may know the road to lead an army from here to Fuenterrabía, he will not know it from here to Lisbon; the same happens at sea, where some are pilots for Flanders and others for the Levant, each for the country he has frequented most." (11)

The accent is that of the true sailor; the experience is concrete; it refers to the Mediterranean. When could Colón have acquired it if not in those days of his sailing youth of which he speaks with so much candour? His own words come true and, despite his critics, place him in that Mediterranean-Catalan environment on which so many of his clues converge.

But let us now look more closely into this environment of Majorcan and Catalan sea-life. The leader of this scientific centre of geographers, whose knowledge was then sought by sailors and cosmographers all over the world, had been "Master Jaime," i.e. Jehuda Cresques, a prominent member of a Jewish family which had given a doctor to the King of Aragon. (12) The pogrom of 1391 transformed him into "Jaime Ribes"; he settled in Barcelona till 1438 when, being already sixty years old, he was invited by Henry the Navigator to preside over the famous Academy of Sagres, a Portuguese house of cosmographical learning. Nor is he an isolated case, for it is well known that the focus of cosmographical activity in Majorca was mostly Jewish. This Master James incarnates for us the cultural centre of Majorca— typically Jewish—the Mediterranean-Catalan nautical activity and the connection with Lisbon, traditions which, despite the pogroms of 1391 and of 1425, so far as the Jewish centre of Majorca is concerned, had remained alive down to the time of Colón. When Cristóbal settled in Lisbon, and when his younger brother Bartolomé went to settle there before him, they found, therefore, a connection ready-made both by their profession and by their race. All their biographers tell us, Spaniards such as Las Casas, Italians such as Gallo, that both were skilful in the art of drawing maps; both found in Lisbon the tradition of the Majorcan-Jewish first Director of the Academy of Sagres, "Mestre Jacome, a man very skilled in the art of navigation, who made charts and instruments."

This was, then, the environment in which young Colombo began to open out his soul to the secrets of the world. And in this environment of Catalan-Jewish cosmographers a map, a famous map, had been drawn towards 1374, in which, on the Indian Sea, are shown to exist no less than 7548 islands "rich in precious stones and valuable metals."

In later years, his son Don Fernando, at the summit of wealth and fame, was to write, as a conclusion of a chapter on Colón's mystery and on what he calls the "occult case" of the family name, the following significant words: "Let us end this chapter with the words [the Admiral] writes in a letter to the Aya of Prince Don Juan, 'I am not the first Admiral of my family—let them give me the name they will, for, after all, David, a very wise King, kept ewes and later was made a King of Jerusalem, and I am the servant of that same Lord who raised David to that state.'" (13)

PART II

CHRISTOVÃO COLOMBO,
A STUDENT IN PORTUGAL

CHAPTER VII

THE TEST BY FIRE AND WATER

ON August 13th, 1476, Christoforo Colombo, then just under twenty-five years of age, was in danger of death. He was near enough to death to be able to say that on that day he was reborn. From all we know of his tense, imaginative and highly religious soul, we may safely assume that on that day he is sure to have heard that Voice which in later years was at times to call him back to duty or to requicken his dying hopes with its severe admonitions. His imagination still aglow with the glamour of the burning ships and the bloody scenes of the struggle, and astir with the boom and rattle of the guns and musketry, Christoforo, swimming on, fighting with the billows, resting his weary body now and then on the floating oar, listened no doubt to that awe-inspiring Voice which said: "*What have you done with your youth? Do you think that I freed you from your dark looms in Vico dell'Olivella, or from the public-house in Savona, for a mere life of sea-loafing and piracy, to make money by attacking innocent merchantmen just because it suits the King of France or the King of Portugal? Did I give you that abundance of seamanship and that ability of hand and mind for depicting the world with its lands and seas, and that understanding of cosmography and astrology for you to waste it all in a life just like any other life? When are you to rise to the top of your soul and find out how high it is—higher than any tower or lighthouse which your father ever kept? Awake, Christoforo, awake and serve Me.*" And young Christoforo would then swim on with a new courage until he touched the pebbles of the shore with his weary knees, let go the oar from his weary arm and, exhausted in body but refreshed in mind, would fall on his knees, raise his eyes to the lovely blue skies where the sun would by then be setting, and promise that he would serve the Lord.

For he was obviously born with that inner hunger for high endeavour which is the mark of great souls. No one can read his great letters, the outpourings of his heart, to the King and Queen without feeling that spacious simplicity which we call greatness. Twenty-five is a good age for a great soul to be reborn

69

on the edge of the abyss of death. Youth is over; ripe age is at hand. Stocktaking of the madcap years and of the first gains of experience comes in as a natural mood. If at that moment the whole being has to pass through a life-and-death ordeal, dull must be the man who will not feel shaken to the very foundations. Christoforo Colombo was not dull. He was keen as steel and ardent as a flame. And so we may be certain to remain within the bounds of psychological truth when we say that on that 13th of August of his 25th year Christoforo Colombo was reborn.

* *

For a man hungry for high endeavour, what land better than Portugal in 1476? Why Portugal? Look at the map and wipe out America, the *inexistent* continent at the time. Portugal was the end of the world, Land's End, the window over the Unknown. And this was the first cause. The Unknown wishing to be known, calling out for man to come and save it from the hell of nothingness, to open it to the light of mankind's reason and awareness. This deep call of the forgotten limb of life to the Whole of life acted on Portugal more than on any other human land, because on Portugal its impact was more direct, and the contrast more violent between the void of the Unknown Deep and the fulness of the known land which stared at it and which every evening saw the sun set over a horizon still closed to man.

When Portuguese painters, poets, sailors, beheld the sunset, the rays of their dream-glance did not fall on Italy, as did those of the Greeks, nor on Spain as did those of the Italians, but on —nothingness, infiniteness, the sea ever again and again; and all these dreams sank into the soul of Portugal and gradually turned into springs of action.

Oh yes. There was the spice-trade and all that. And have we not heard how the fall of Constantinople to the Grand Turc closed the usual channels of communication for that trade, and thereby determined the effort to open up new ways of access by sea round the African Continent? This is no doubt correct so far as it goes, but it does not account for the fact that Constantinople fell in 1453, while in 1419 the Portuguese ventured out into the unknown and discovered Madeira and in 1434 Gil Eanes turned the terrifying Cape Bojador while Afonso Gonçalves Baldaia reached the Tropic of Cancer, the edge of that torrid zone the habitability or otherwise of which was one of the conundrums of medieval cosmographers. It is easy to smile now, but when the general consensus of learned opinion was on the whole against the possibility of human life in that zone, the idea of just "go and see" reveals no uncommon courage—and without the added zest of the fall of Constantinople, too! And in 1445, without in the least waiting for the fall of Constantinople, nor possibly even thinking of helping the spice-trade, Dinis Dias passed opposite the Senegal and reached Cabo Verde, to the astonishment of the natives, who wondered whether his ship was a fish, a bird or a ghost.

The driving spirit of this quest was Prince Henry the Navigator. He was the third son of King John I and of Philippa of Lancaster. On her death-bed Queen Philippa presented swords to her three sons who were leaving for the siege and final conquest of Ceuta. To Dom Duarte, the future King, she entrusted the defence of her peoples; to Prince Dom Pedro, that of ladies and girls; and then she turned to her third and favourite son Henry, and spoke thus:

"You have seen how I have distributed the other swords to your brothers, and this third one I give you, for as you are strong, so will it be. And because I entrusted the peoples to one of your brothers and the women and girls to another, to you I wish to entrust all the lords, knights gentlemen, and squires of these kingdoms, whom I recommend you to keep in your special charge.[. . .] And I give you this sword with my benediction, with which I pray and recommend you to become a knight." (1)

He did become a knight, but of the sea. The Moors were beaten, and though the fight was carried over to Africa and he fought continually in Ceuta, all these lords and knights whom his mother had entrusted to him needed new fields for their activity. He created the Knighthood of the sea.

This prince, somewhat taciturn, a deep and sombre flowing river within steep forbidding banks, sought a spot in harmony with his own proud and solitary but energetic soul to found his famous academy of seamanship—the Rock of Sagres, a prow of land, advancing towards the Unknown Deep with all its granitic might, close to that Cape St. Vincent where Colón was to land almost miraculously thirty-eight years later. Disdainful of political economy, he did not wait for the fall of Constantinople either; his nautical centre was founded in 1438. What was his aim? Diogo Gomes (2) said that it was twofold: the road to India round the African Continent; and the exploration of the West, in search of islands or terra firma, after Ptolemy. Why so much precision? His aim, did he know it? Do we have an aim in life, or are we not rather impelled by an inner spirit than drawn by an outer lure into doing something, incarnating some force which is at the time "in the air," and must work itself into history through a living man? Prince Henry came to incarnate the destiny of Portugal at the time, which was to satisfy the hunger of the Unknown Deep for the spirit of Knowledge, staring at it from the Balcony which was Portugal.

Lisbon was then becoming more and more important as the northern-European ports grew in wealth and power, for it was a welcome calling-port on the way from the Mediterranean to England, Flanders and the Hanseatic harbours. It was no doubt then, as it is now, one of the most attractive cities of Europe, though it had not yet brought over from its newly acquired possessions those palm-trees which add now to its charm a languorous feeling of leisure.

It was nobly built after the fashion of the day, stone and brick in happy alliance, happiest under the honey-coloured sun which washed its frontages, two, three and even four storeys high, and laid broad patches of yellow splendour over its well-paved streets. Narrow, no doubt, for our standards, but broad enough for the traffic needs of those days, the busy streets of Lisbon offered ample passage for the swift horse of the knight or traveller, the ox-cart of the peasant and general carrier, and the few sedan-chairs of the mighty. A town of seaport smells, in whose salt-laden air the cool, dark mouths of shop, store and bodega exhaled their breath, now of wine in the wood, now of salt fish, of tar, of tallow, of mastic, musk or cinnamon, not to speak of the animal smell of mule and ass and ox and horse, parked, as we do our cars today, just by the door, and even of Moor and Christian and Jew, living together in this cosmopolitan town where Easterners and Westerners, Mediterraneans and Atlantians met on common ground. A town of learning too. One generation later, no less than fifty-four booksellers were registered, in whose shops could be found books in all the ancient and in all the contemporary Latin languages; in 1476 it was already an important centre of culture, and particularly in the arts in which Colón was most eager to learn—cosmography and astronomy.

It was probably in one of these bookshops that he found his brother Bartolomeo, (3) a bookshop in which no doubt were to be found also astrolabes and compasses, and *ampolletas* as the sand-clocks were then called in Spanish, with a significantly Catalan diminutive form of the word. There is abundant evidence to show that Bartolomeo had a better chance than his elder brother to develop the theoretical side of the art of seamanship. "To judge by the books and sea-charts annotated and commented upon in his handwriting which must have been his or the Admiral's," says Las Casas, "I believe he was so skilled in that art that the Admiral did not exceed him by much. [. . .] He had a very good hand at writing, better than the Admiral's, for I possess many papers in the handwriting of both of them." (4) This would suggest more time spent at the desk. Since, when Christoforo arrived in Lisbon in 1476, Bartolomeo was still in his teens, it is probable that the youngster, even though with some experience of the sea behind him, was being educated, earning his living as well, perhaps thanks to those Jewish learned connections which we have noticed as traditional between Majorca, Barcelona, Genoa and Lisbon. And since it is well known that Christoforo engaged in the trade of map-drawing and book-dealing while in Lisbon, we may surmise that this was the learned trade which had given hospitality to young Bartolomeo.

Cosmography, map-drawing, astronomy were then, we know, if not exclusively, predominantly Jewish occupations. A greater freedom of thought, a more natural disposition to learn Oriental languages, and the continuous hold over roads, caravans, distances, and reports from distant towns which they needed for their commercial activity, and which they obtained through the universality of their race, were all favourable circumstances for the pursuit of a noble task which in those days was rapidly coming to the forefront: the study of the earth and the sky and their true size and shape. In Lisbon there had always been a numerous, rich and active Jewish colony. Its prestige, both social and intellectual, had been increased by the strong proportion of Jewish master-cosmographers amongst the men of science whom Prince Henry had of old gathered at Sagres. At the time of Colón's arrival in Lisbon, the leader of these learned Jews was Mestre Joseph Vizinho, the King's physician, a pupil of the celebrated Spanish-Jewish astronomer, Abraham Zacuto.

The young corsair whom the Lord had tested by fire and water, eager to find his path to service, fell in the midst of a city throbbing with the fever of discovery. Prince Henry's initial impulse was by no means spent. In fact, it had conquered the opposition which his uncompromising faith and his purpose—possibly too high for second-rate captains—had at first raised amongst his less-spirited countrymen. He persisted, says old Barros, "against the opinion of many; though no sign had been found to satisfy those who held this business to be a fruitless one and very dangerous to all who ventured on it, for [the reason expressed in] this proverb well-known amongst seafolk: *He who sails beyond the Cape of No may return or not*. And the fear of this passage [beyond Cape Nâo] was so deep set in everybody's heart, for they had inherited this opinion from their ancestors, that the Prince could find but with the utmost difficulty persons who would agree to serve him in this, though the discovery of the Island of Madeira had put some heart into seamen. For many said: how is it possible to sail beyond a Cape which the navigators of Spain had set as the terminus and end of all navigation in those parts, as men who knew that the sea beyond was not navigable, not only because of the strong currents, but because it was very broken with so much boiling over of its waters that it sucked up all the ships. [. . .] We do not know what result he expects from this discovery, save the loss of all those who go in the ships, leaving many orphans and widows in the Kingdom. [. . .] For there always were Kings and Princes in Spain eager to achieve great things [. . .] and we do not see nor read in their chronicles that they directed this land to be discovered, though it was so near at hand." (5)

All this was over. Now, Portuga was well launched on her career as a nation of sea-explorers. Concessions were granted by the Crown to go, see and conquer any stray island or forbidding cape which might stand in the way of a Portuguese ship: João Vogado in 1462, Prince Ferdinand in 1451, 1462, 1473, Rui Gonçalves da Camara in 1473; in 1474 Fernão Telles is granted a concession (6) for "any unpopulated island or land," and in November 1475 the concession is extended to islands or lands already populated. New concessions are granted almost continuously at the time of Colón's arrival and during all his stay in Portugal.

* *

So that was to be his work? The idea must have sunk into his mind at once, for if the harbour and the Street of Merchants and the Court were full of it, what else could be discussed amongst the cosmographers, Christians, Moors and Jews, whom, he tells us, he was wont to frequent, led by his enquiring mind? With what eager eyes would those cosmographers and chart-drawing draftsmen listen to the story of captains and pilots, telling them of the new coast seen and measured, the unsuspected island, the great river, the trails of the caravans, possibly the measurement of a concrete distance on the map, the correction shown to be necessary to the profile of such a coast. So this was to be his work, and this was the reason why he had been thrown out from a corsair ship like Jonah from the whale?

And, of course, there was money in it. Prince Henry, who was the master of the Order of Christ, had started this wave of discoveries as a sea-crusade, "so that," says Barros, "his name should remain amongst men as that of the first conqueror and discoverer of the idolatrous nations." (7) But as Constantinople had fallen in 1453, shutting out completely the direct way to the land of spices, which had been none too easy since Saladdin had conquered Egypt in 1171, Christians were now entitled to drink the wine of glory and to eat the bread of virtue with the spice of gain. On its watery shoulders the old spacious Tagus carried bulging galleys, prouder and prouder as the length of their cruises became more and more impressive in the eyes of breezy seamen and studious cartographers. Everyone in Lisbon was thinking of Guinea, the hot seas, blacks and parrots, and the lands of Prester John. Travellers' stories, sacred books, charts and documents, old wives' tales, every form of lore contributed to the discussions, the beliefs, the plans, the hopes with which the streets and quays of Lisbon hummed, to the accompaniment of the hammers and the saws which in the shipyards of Ribeira Nova erected the wooden skeletons of imposing galleons and elegant caravels for the discoverers.

Three strains were predominant: the patristic or biblical; the scientific, and what we would nowadays call the touristic, i.e. the stories of such travellers as the Jew Benjamin de Tudela, the Knight Tafur, that magnificent chatterbox John of Mandeville, and, most famous of all, Marco Polo. Life carried all these strains in an inextricable mixture, so that it is nearly always impossible to disentangle them even within the same brain. Here is an amusing example. Cardinal Filliastre or Philastre stands high in the history of geographic progress because he was the first to use the division of the degree into minutes and seconds instead of in arithmetical fractions, a considerable step in geodesy. He has, moreover, another title to scientific consideration bearing specially on Colón's discovery: in an atlas of twenty-six maps which he had prepared in 1427 a Welsh cartographer, Claudius Cymbricus, included a map of Greenland, along with a note to the effect that "it lies towards the island of Thule [Iceland] which is to the East of it. Thus this map includes all the northern region still an unknown land. Ptolemy does not mention it, and it is believed he did not know of it." This scientific statement is decorated by the charming further intimation that "In these Northern lands there are diverse nations, including the Unipedes and the Pygmies. As to the Griffins, they are in the Orient, as may be seen in the map." (8)

This is a fair example of a scientific mind in those days. Round a kernel of direct observation there spread a circle of authority, classical and biblical, and beyond it an aura of hearsay, and still further afield a world of imagination. Those sailors and merchants who thronged the quays of Lisbon, fingered the books in the shops, swarmed in the anterooms of royal princes and Jewish financiers, and now sailed out into the Unknown Deep, leaving behind a trail of sighing hearts, now returned battered and crestfallen in defeat, or in the pride and splendour of islands discovered and capes conquered, came to add both legend and fact to this world of speculation.

Was all the earth inhabitable? Did the Southern Seas boil? Were there men with one eye, one foot, a tail? Was there an island governed by women (I mean openly so)? How much of the earth was covered with water and how much with land? What was the exact *land* distance between the Western coasts of Europe and the Eastern coasts of Asia? What was the girth of the earth's equator? And by way of consequence, what was the distance between Europe and Asia through the Atlantic? (9)

These were the questions which occupied that lively world. In 1470 Affonso V, King of Portugal, had put his son and heir John, the future John II, in charge of expeditions and discoveries; in fact, had made him the King's First Lord of the Admiralty and Secretary of State for the Colonies. The young Prince's hand is seen at once in the two concessions to Fernão Telles; in the regulations of sea-traffic, and in the law of November 4th to foster shipbuilding. Prince John could not fail to notice the turmoil of ideas in which his seafaring countrymen then lived. One, above all, was in the mind of the leaders: East or West?

The great Portuguese navigators, faithful to the tradition of Prince Henry, pushed on year in, year out, along the coast of Africa, *Guiné* as they called it, in the hope of turning the Cape, which they did, and reaching the land of dreams and spices, India. But, since the earth was round, why not the West? The Prince was told that a Canon of Lisbon, one Fernão Martins, or Fernão de Roritz, had discussed the matter with a well-known mathematician and physicist of Florence, Paolo del Pozzo Toscanelli. He summoned the Canon and heard from him that Toscanelli held the way of the West perfectly possible, and certainly shorter and easier than the way of the East. Prince John bade him write to Toscanelli and ask for a definite statement of his scheme.

On June 25th, 1474, Toscanelli answered the Portuguese canon, sending him "a map made by my own hands, from which you should begin to make the journey ever towards the West, and the places which you should reach and how far from the Pole or from the equinoctial line you ought to turn, and how many leagues you will have to cross to reach those regions most fertile in all kinds of spices and jewels and precious stones; and think it not marvellous that I call West the land of spices, while it is usually said that spices come from the East, for whoever navigates Westward in the lower hemisphere shall always find the said paths West and whoever travels Eastward by land in the higher hemisphere shall always find the same land East." (10)

Toscanelli was a good physicist and mathematician, but had only begun to dabble in cosmography in later life, under the pressure of financial difficulties and the zest of a possibly unscientific interest in spices, in which his family had traded for long. This letter and map could not impress the Portuguese. The plan of the Florentine amateur-cosmographer rested on a number of ideas of which the scientific cosmographers and the seasoned captains who surrounded Prince John might say: "What is good is not new; what is new is not good," to wit:

(1) *The earth is round,* which everybody knew in those days.

(2) *The known continent from Lisbon to the Indian coast,* BY LAND, i.e. EASTWARDS, *covers 230 degrees of the circumference of the earth.* This was known in Lisbon to be a mistake of the old geographer Marinus of Tyr, which had been corrected by Ptolemy. Toscanelli took no notice of Ptolemy's correction and added insult to injury by increasing Marinus's mistake (220) to 230 degrees.

(3) *Therefore there remain only 130 degrees of sea to cross in order to get at the Indies by sailing dead West.* This was not true, since the previous conclusion was false. The distance in degrees was greater, though by how much, opinions varied.

(4) *The length of a degree being about $62\frac{1}{2}$ miles, the total distance from coast to coast was only $62\frac{1}{2} \times 130 = 8125$ miles.* The Portuguese could afford to smile at this, because most of them held $62\frac{1}{2}$ to be far too short a figure and they inclined to think the degree was at least 70 miles long.

(5) *From Cabo Verde to the Coast of Asia the distance is about one-third of the sphere,* i.e. 116 degrees.

(6) *Moreover, there is Antilia on the way, between which and Cipango there are 10 "spaces,"* i.e. 50 degrees.

This was the only point which might make the Portuguese ponder over the matter a bit. Antilia! Cipango! What did they know about them?

About Antilia, little that they could hold as serious. This ghost-island seemed to rise in men's imaginations at the call of three entirely different causes: the tradition of the lost continent which Plato describes under the name of Atlantis, easily transfigured into Antilia by the wear and tear of time; the optical illusion, or maybe the psychological obsession of the inhabitants of Madeira and of the Western Canaries, who under certain weather conditions saw a land West of them on the horizon; and an old tradition stubbornly held in all Spain (including Portugal) that during the Moorish invasion, in the eighth century, a mass emigration of Spanish Christians had taken place under seven bishops to the Island of the Seven Cities. Antilia, the name itself, seems like an evocation from the depths of the mind dreaming at sunset. There must be an Island opposite: Anti-island, Anti-Ilha, Antilia.

But the cosmographers of King John were no dreamers, and as a port of call on the way to India they would not consider this Antilia of the Seven Cities a great asset.

Cipango was another matter, for it was known as an existing part of this hard planet, at any rate since Marco Polo had not only extolled its wealth, but situated it on the map so to speak, by giving the distance which separated it from the Indian (i.e. Asiatic) continent—1500 miles. This name was the only valuable indication which the Prince and his advisers, eager to find a quick access to India, could find in the otherwise disappointing document of the Florentine.

Yet, though disappointing as a solution for the great problem of the day—the road to India—the letter of Toscanelli did leave a trace in the minds of some at any rate of the royal hangers-on. Those "Seven Cities!" They did sound glorious. Mestre Joseph Vizinho and Mestre Rodrigo, the two Jewish doctors, might smile incredulously, but suppose they did exist after all? Did not this Toscanelli know as much mathematics as the two clever Jews? Well-known maps, such as Becario's (11) or Andrea Bianco's, did give Antilia as an existing island.

So, on November 20th, 1475, Fernão Telles, governor, and chief steward of the King's beloved daughter, who had but a few months earlier (January 28th, 1474) obtained a concession to discover and overlord any unpopulated islands, "provided they be not in the region of Guinea" (i.e. provided they be out West), having easy access to events which occurred within the discreet palace walls, succeeded in obtaining an enlargement of his concession which bears obvious signs of the influence of Toscanelli's letter, at any rate on him: "And because in the said letter [the first concession] there is question of unpopulated islands, and which the said Fernão Telles might order to be populated [. . .], and it might well be that, while seeking them, his ships or men might find the Seven Cities or the populated islands, not at present navigated [. . .], I declare by this letter [. . .] that it is my pleasure that he have the same overlordships and superiority and power over their inhabitants [. . .] as over those of the other islands." (12)

Having thus given a Portuguese nobleman an imaginary kingdom over the Seven Cities, Toscanelli's letter and map, found wanting as a plan for sailing to the East through the West, were quietly shelved.

Yet not so hidden that Colombo's eyes could never find them.

CHAPTER VIII

THE LURE OF THE WESTERN SEA

WHEN young Colombo lands in Portugal, in 1476, at the very foot of that Rock of Sagres where Prince Henry had perched his nest of sea-birds of prey, we witness, to use a telling Spanish expression, the meeting of Hunger and Appetite. Colón's hunger for high endeavour meets the land longing for discovery. Barros was to say of him later on that he was "a skilled man, eloquent and a good Latin scholar, and very glorious in his affairs." (1) It is therefore fair to assume, and so have we assumed already on other grounds, that in 1476, at twenty-five years of age, his Latin was already fairly good, and that, therefore, keen as he was to learn and read, he had read many a classic. There is good reason for thinking that either before his arrival in Portugal or soon after, within the year 1476, he had read the *Medea* of Seneca, (2) for his mind, probably already full of his own star, saw a world of his own dreaming in a few lines of this tragedy of the Spanish-Latin poet, and he acted accordingly soon after. In Act II of this somewhat grim tragedy there occurs the following passage:

> venient annis
> Saecula seris quibus oceanus
> Vincula rerum laxet : et ingens
> Pateat tellus : Tiphysque novos
> Detegat orbes : nec sit terris
> Ultima Thyle.

Though somewhat free and explanatory, Colón's own translation, to be found in his Book of Prophecies, is correct:

"There will come a time in the long years of the world when the ocean sea will loosen the shackles that bind things together and a great part of the earth will be opened up and a new sailor such as the one who was Jason's guide, whose name was Thyphis, shall discover a new world, and then shall Thule be no longer the last of lands."

This passage of the Spanish-Roman poet struck him deeply. The prophetic sense, a tendency to find a hint of things to come

80

in all he read, was one of his most marked features. Are we to wonder, then, that in February 1477 Colón was in Thule, and even one hundred leagues beyond "the last of the lands"? All we know of his character suggests that Colón went there already smitten with this inner belief in his destiny, which was the real root of his indomitable strength. Why Thule? This voyage, on any other basis, is so devoid of meaning that his more matter-of-fact biographers simply deny that it ever took place. (3) And yet Colón himself says he went there. "In some notes he made," says Las Casas, "to show how all the five zones were inhabitable, proving it on the experience of his navigations, he says: 'In the month of February 1477 I sailed beyond the Island of Tile one hundred leagues, and its southern part is 73° north of the equinoctial and not 63° as some say, and it lies not within the line which contains the Occident, as Ptolemy says, but much further West, and to this Island, which is as big as England, the English go with goods, especially those of Bristol, and at the time I went the sea was not frozen, though there were great tides, so much that in some parts it rose and fell 25 braces twice a day.'" (4)

The geographical errors of this text, far from telling against Colón's veracity, speak in its favour, for if, as some of his modern critics claim he had boasted of this visit on the strength of a mere perusal of sea-charts or maps, one has to deprive him of intelligence as well as of honesty, since he would thus have ventured to correct from his study in Portugal figures admitted by cosmographers and inscribed in maps. The objection is childish. He *did* go there. The proof is that he made bold to correct what others wrote about it before, whether competent to do it or not matters nothing for the argument.

He went there because it was still Ultima Thule—not for long —and because he felt that the time had come when it should cease to be so. He went there to see for himself what Thule was like, and one hundred leagues beyond—of course, West. And that when he went he was already "possessed" can be proved, curiously enough, again by making use of another of his errors. A note in his hand, to the *History* of Pope Pius II, reads as follows: "Men have come eastward from Cathay. We have seen many a remarkable thing [of this kind], and particularly in Galway, in Ireland, two persons hanging on to two wreck planks, a man and a woman, a beautiful creature." (5) It is evident that the arrival of Chinese shipwrecked people in Galway was in those days utterly impossible. The combination of circumstances which gave rise to this misapprehension on the part of Colón is, however, easy to imagine. Any Northern ship wrecked—Russian or even Norwegian—having on board persons of Finnish or Lap features —high-cheeked and somewhat un-European-looking—would suffice, by means of a few misinterpretations between Irish-English-Gaelic-Latin and Genoese-Spanish-Jewish-Portuguese-Latin, with the possible help of an Irish wag, to induce the highly imaginative Colón to see his ever-present Cathay in the strangers saved from the waves. But the main point is that Colón shows by this error of his not only that he did go North in 1477, but also that in 1477 he was already brewing his design to reach Cathay through the West.

This is, unfortunately, all we know of his voyage to Iceland. But, though it does not shed much light on his actual physical movements, it helps to outline the history of his inner thoughts. We know that by now Colón's corsair and possible commercial years are over, and that henceforward he is intent on the mighty problem of the day. It matters little that in 1479, if the "Assereto" document be genuine, he was sent to buy sugar in Madeira by a Lisbon Genoese called di Negro. No one in his senses will imagine that because Colón became passionately devoted to the Westward quest in 1476-77 he thereupon ceased to eat and drink or to pay for his food and lodging. The Assereto document may be genuine; we have seen that one of the statements which it attributes to Colón is singularly in keeping with the discoverer's character. If it be genuine, all it shows is that Colón sought to make some money, which he had every right to do. But that Colón was in Genoa in April 1479 is neither here nor there, and that he declares he had gone to buy sugar for di Negro, a Lisbon "Genoese," matters little more, except that *Negro* (6) was the name of a most powerful Jewish financier of Lisbon who may or may not have been related to the di Negro of the Assereto document.

That letter of Toscanelli and that map were meanwhile shelved away in the King's library, and though we do not know for certain when Colón set eyes on them, it is reasonable to assume that by a convergence of mutual interests, let alone racial ties, Vizinho and Rodrigo, the King's doctors and keepers of his astronomic conscience, would some time or other bring it, wittingly or unwittingly, materially or by mere reference, to the knowledge of the eager young sailor smitten with the fever of discovery. At any rate, from the middle of 1477 Colón is back in Lisbon, and we are going to see him gradually ascend the slope of his high destiny—inwardly, by educating his mind and developing his information through travel and consultation with mariners; outwardly, by seeking a social position in his adoptive country.

* *

Las Casas tells how Colón used to go often to attend divine service in a convent known as "the Saints," in which there lived certain commander-ladies ("comendadoras"). (7) In Lisbon, towards 1478, every street corner and main square was sure to offer a house of prayer for the earnest-minded to attend religious services. All we know of the calculating and purposeful character of the discoverer goes to warrant the assumption that in his choice of that particular convent he was guided by ulterior motives, not necessarily religious in character. *Pray God and hammer on* is a good and sound old Spanish proverb, and much as Colón may already have been convinced of his providential destinies, there was nothing to prevent him from co-operating with Providence in bringing Its plans to a satisfactory conclusion.

For it so happened that the convent in question belonged to the Nuns of the Military Order of St. James (8) and had been founded to provide a home for the wives and daughters of the Knights of St. James while the said Knights fought against the Infidels. The ladies therein received were supposed to make a vow of conjugal chastity, of poverty and of obedience. It was a house renowned no less for its virtue than for its high social standing, as was soon to be shown when King John II appointed as its Mother Superior the very mother of his own natural son, Don'Ana de Mendoça.

This convent was therefore as good a nursery of young noble ladies as an ambitious sailor should wish; and when a young sailor is twenty-seven, and has had a considerable experience of the sea, and maybe a few Jewish friends at Court; and when, moreover, he is "of a good size and looks, taller than the average and of sturdy limbs; the eyes lively and the other features of the face in good proportion; the hair very red; and the complexion somewhat flushed and freckled; a good speaker, cautious and of great talent and an elegant latinist and a most learned cosmographer, graceful when he wished, irate when he was crossed"; (9) when a young sailor with all these parts comes in now and then from the breezy out-of-doors air into the confined, shut-in air of a convent, even if only to pray, there is sure to be a pair of eyes indoors longing for liberty and life and ready to give their youth and noble name for a tale about a basket of islands left derelict on the wide seas.

And so Christovão Colombo married Filipa Moniz Perestrello. She was noble on both sides. On her mother's side she came from the powerful family of Moniz, in close touch with the Crown, since in the twelfth century its founder, Egas Moniz, had been Governor under Affonso Henriquez, first king of Portugal. On her father's side she came from the Italian Palestrellos or Pallastrellis of Piacenza, one of whom had settled in Portugal under King John I, and successfully proved his noble blood by refusing to pay for the expenses of the war in Africa on the ground of his clean ancestry. This nobleman had four children, Richarte, Isabel, Branca and Bartholomeu.

Richarte soon gave a lead of sorts to his sisters and brother by combining holy orders—he became prior of Santa Marinha in Lisbon—with unholy disorders—he became the father of two boys. (One of these young Perestrellos was to command a ship in Vasco de Gama's second voyage to the Indies.) Thus encouraged by their elder brother's example, Isabel and Branca became intimate friends with the most magnificent churchman of the times, Don Pedro de Noronha, Archbishop of Lisbon, whose doubly royal blood (for he was related to the reigning families of both Castille and Portugal) proved too much for the restraints of ecclesiastical chastity. This magnificent prince of the Church was no light-hearted lover. He seems to have paid homage simultaneously to both Branca and Isabel, if one is to judge by the ages of Dom Joâo, Isabel's son, and of Doña Isabel, Dom Diogo and Dom Pedro, Branca's children. Moreover, he was a loving father, and, despite his position as head of the Portuguese Church, he had all his offspring officially legitimised in 1444 and saw to it that the girl married into the royal house of Braganza and that the three boys rapidly reached the highest posts in the State and in the Church.

Colón's father-in-law was, then, well, not precisely the *brother-in-law* of the Archbishop, but let us say his *brother-in-love*. On the basis of Colón's two earliest biographies, the view has been traditionally held that this Perestrello (Bartholomeu) had been given the hereditary captaincy of the Island of Porto Santo owing to his seamanship and valorous deeds. Upon which, both Fernando Colón and Las Casas build up a story of papers and instruments and hints on islands to be discovered and what not, which Perestrello's widow gave her son-in-law. But let us read it in Las Casas, since it is worth having at first hand, the better to enjoy the distance between high-sounding legend and ludicrous reality: "As days went by, the mother-in-law realised how bent on the things of the sea and of cosmography was Cristóbal Colón [. . .] so that [. . .] she told him how her husband Perestrello had also been a person leaning to sea-affairs, and how, by order of Prince Henry, he had gone in company with two other gentlemen to the Island of Porto Santo, recently discovered, and soon after he was alone entrusted with the task of populating it, and the Prince granted him properties in it, and as in those days there was a great boiling over of the practice and exercise of discoveries on the coast of Guinea and on the islands of the Ocean sea and the said Bartolomé Perestrello had the hope of discovering other islands from his, as indeed they were discovered [. . .], he probably had instruments and papers and pictures on navigation which the mother-in-law gave Colón, from the view and reading of which he received much pleasure." (10)

It is plain that this story is a mixture of fact and of conjecture. For instance, Las Casas himself suggests that the existence of instruments, papers and pictures of Perestrello is a mere conjecture of his. But, unfortunately for the reputation of Perestrello as a discoverer, and particularly as a populator, the good bishop provides the key to the crucial text in which the whole fabric is seen to fall to the ground. Let us now read Barros on "how Joam Gonçalvez & Tristam Vaz discovered the island of Porto Sancto, owing to a tempest which took them there."

"There sprang on them such a storm with strength of contrary winds that they lost all hope for their lives. [. . .] And as, in those days, sailors were not in the habit of going out at sea and always sailed [. . .] within sight of land, [. . .] they were all [. . .] so much out of their judgment that they could not tell where they were. But [. . .] the storm ceased, and though the wind made them lose the purpose which the Prince had in sending them forth, it did not take them astray from their good fortune, for they discovered the Island we now call Porto Sancto [. . .]. With which news, without further voyaging they returned to the kingdom, which gave the Prince great pleasure [. . .], and he had this pleasure increased when these two knights, one of whom was named Joam Gonçalvez Zarco dalcunha and the other Tristam Vaz, told him they came very happy about the air, emplacement and freshness of the land and wished to return to populate it [. . .], and not only they and those of their crew, who had seen it, but many more, owing to what they heard and also to please the Prince, offered themselves to populate it, amongst them a notable person named Bartholomeu Perestrello who was a gentleman in the household of Prince John his [Prince Henry's] brother. [. . .] Then with great diligence [the Prince] had three ships armed, one of which he gave to Bartholomeu Perestrello and the two others to Joam Gonçalvez and Tristam Vaz, first discoverers, who went forth well provided with all the seeds and plants and other things with which they hoped to populate the land and settle in it. Amongst which, there was a rabbit which Bartholomeu Perestrello took with him, pregnant, in a cage, and, at sea, she happened to bring forth, which gave all great pleasure and they held it in good omen, since even on the way their seeds began to fructify and that rabbit gave them hope of the great multiplication which would accrue to them in that land. And to be sure in this hope of great multiplication the rabbit did not disappoint them, yet was it more to their sorrow than to their pleasure: for, when they arrived in the island and let the rabbit free with her offspring, within a short time she multiplied to such an extent that they could not sow or plant anything that was not instantly eaten. And this grew to be such a plague in the two years which they remained there that they began to hate the work and way of life they had there and Bartholomeu Perestrello decided to return to the Kingdom, or perhaps for other reasons he had for doing so."(11)

The ironical, almost mocking intention of this text is in keeping with its substance. The knights who discovered the island, even if much against their wish and will, were Gonçalvez and Vaz; Perestrello was a hanger-on of Prince John who came to the scent of profit and was given a ship through sheer favouritism; and his efforts towards that population of the island which his widow, in Las Casas' version, says was entrusted to him alone, were limited to the rabbit species. Nevertheless, he tried again, for his pull at Court was strong, and in 1425 Prince Henry entrusted him with another populating expedition to Porto Santo, this time, we hope, with no pregnant rabbits on board. His success, however, does not seem to have warranted a long stay, for in 1431 he is given a house in Lisbon, where in 1437 he is registered as a municipal councillor.

So that when in 1446, over twenty years after his two unsuccessful attempts, but only two years after the legitimisation of his *brother-in-love's* bastards had shown the blatant power of Don Pedro de Noronha, Perestrello is granted by Prince Henry the captaincy of Porto Santo, we are entitled to the conclusion that such an honour was due less to his sea-adventures than to the love-adventures of his gifted sisters.

Whatever its origin, there was power and social standing in

that family, and, moreover, a well-known, permanent connection with the Island of Porto Santo, for that captaincy was hereditary. And now that we know the sea-talents and competence of Perestrello to have been inexistent, it is obvious to us, though it was not to Las Casas, that his "papers and instruments" could not have been the cause or inspiration of Colón's design; which fact goes to confirm that the scheme or "urge" towards discovery was active in Colón's mind before he ever entered his Portuguese family, and therefore that he probably entered that family because it was so powerful in Porto Santo, an admirable base for exploring the Western sea.

Bartholomeu I of rabbit memory had died in 1457, or at the beginning of 1458, when his widow, Colón's mother-in-law, ceded the captaincy of the island to his brother; her son, Bartholomeu II, took it over in 1473, and was actually the captain of Porto Santo when his sister Filipa (perhaps so named in honour of the princess of Lancaster who had been Prince Henry's mother) married Christovão Colombo, as he then no doubt had himself called. The marriage must have taken place in 1478 or 1479, probably in Lisbon, where Diego Colón, who was to be the second hereditary admiral of the ocean sea, was born towards 1479 or 1480. We see, by the way, whence Colón may have got into his head the idea of founding a lineage of hereditary Island-Captains.

Incredible as it may seem, students of Colón's life have been found, and not the least painstaking, to throw doubt on Las Casas' positive assertion that the discoverer lived in Porto Santo. (12) But is it not fairly obvious that the main reason why he married into that family was precisely because of their connection with the foremost base of discovery at the time? As Las Casas puts it: "and so he went to live in the Island of Porto Santo [. . .] very likely owing to that only reason that he wanted to navigate, leaving there his wife, and because in that island as well as in that of Madeira, close to it, and recently discovered then, there was then beginning to be a great concourse of ships to populate and settle it, and there was frequent news every day of the fresh discoveries that were being made." (13)

We may be certain that Colón, who by 1479 was sure to have heard of—if not yet actually read and even copied—Toscanelli's letter, that Colón, who was to do what he did, was not going to stay in Lisbon, wistfully looking at the galleys and caravels on the Tagus, while his brother-in-law was the actual lord of the most ideal base for discovery which his time and adoptive country could boast of. That he settled in Porto Santo is therefore not merely a fact provided by Las Casas on the authority of the Admiral's son, Diego, who told him so in Barcelona in 1519, but a psychological necessity of the first order.

We may imagine his life there, and indeed we may be certain, again, that he navigated during his Porto Santo days. This flows from the conjunction of men and circumstances before us. What did people go to Porto Santo for if not to navigate—or do Colombist students imagine that he indulged in rabbit-breeding like his illustrious father-in-law Perestrello? As for those strange human beings who believe that psychological necessities do not exist and may just be literary fancies, we are in a position to satisfy their matter-of-fact minds. It so happens that competent geographers hold Colón's science as a cosmographer and navigator in higher esteem than critics not so well trained in science. A contemporary American geographer has studied "The Geographical Conceptions of Columbus" (14) in a small but substantial book, in which it is shown that Columbus had equipped himself with the best and most scientific information on winds, currents and general navigating conditions west of the Madeira group of islands. In short, subsequent events proved him to be so skilful a navigator and so excellent an Atlantic pilot, that a wide sailing experience at this time and in these seas becomes of necessity an indispensable part of his life-story. This, moreover, tallies perfectly with his assertion that he had sailed for twenty-three years, (15) which, assuming he began in 1461, can only end in 1484, i.e. when he went to Spain. He, therefore, counts his Portuguese years as a period of sea-life. And, once again, the general weight of evidence is on his side and against those who throw doubt on his word.

All these years, therefore, did this obsessed man seek and navigate, for by then navigation was a perpetual quest to him. And as he was growingly possessed of his sense of a mission, of his conviction that he was elected—a peculiarly Jewish prepossession—he thought the Lord sent him all the signs and warnings which in fact he solicited out of the Lord's reality by his own restless and tireless activity. "From all sides and in many ways did God give Colón motives and causes that he should not doubt to undertake so great a deed." (16)

Colón himself tells how he sought seamen who navigated the Western seas in order to interrogate them. Once a pilot of the King of Portugal, one Martin Vicente, told him how, while about 450 leagues west of Cape St. Vincent, he saw and picked up a piece of wood (17) "carved by craft and, so far as he could judge, not with iron tools," from which he thought that as the wind had been blowing from the West, this wood was sure to come from some Western island. A brother-in-law of his, Pero Correa, told him of a similar piece of cut wood he, Correa, had seen in Porto Santo, as well as of big canes every section of which "could hold over a gallon of water or wine"; (18) a fact which was confirmed to Colón by the King of Portugal in person, who had had these canes shown to him. Colón heard from the inhabitants of the Azores that in time of stormy western and north-western winds the sea carried pine-trees which it threw on to the coast, especially on to Graciosa and Fayal Islands, while nowhere in those lands could any pine be found. Colón again was told, and all these stories he heard show how eagerly he sought them, that in the Island of Flowers, in the Azores, the sea had thrown up two bodies of persons "who seemed to have very wide faces and of a different shape from the Christians." And so the tale of all this sea-gossip goes on and on, including Antilia and the Seven Cities and St. Brandan. The call of the empty sea wishing to be populated, the lure of Unknown America sending imaginary decoys to this highly imaginative and ambitious man, never ceased, so that "all these things were certainly enough to make him, who lived already so bent on this affair, hug it close to himself, and they were signals whereby God seemed to move him on by constant pushes." (19)

CHAPTER IX

LESSONS AND DREAMS

A MAN chosen by God and to whom God gives no respite cannot but prepare himself for his task. Christovão Colombo worked hard. If we are to judge by the books he has left, (1) he was a painstaking reader and an active scribbler of marginal notes. The dates of some of the notes and the dates of publication of the books themselves enable us to place the beginning of this intellectual activity at 1477, i.e. the year of his journey north, and, more likely, at 1478-79, the year of his marriage.

These notes are first-hand documents which reveal the inner workings of his mind, and even at times of his character. Thus, they evince a keen attraction for gems and for gold, which is in keeping with his Jewish race. The Jews have always experienced a curious fascination for gold and precious stones, forms of nature which, quite apart from their commercial value, are in deep harmony with the soul of Israel—like gold, unconquerable through its vicissitudes in its innermost Sancta Sanctorum, and somewhat glittering and glossy like diamonds, jet and rubies, and the eyes and hair and lips of the daughters of Sion.

The Jew in Colón, usually shy and out of the way, hardly discernible in a discreet hint for the initiated only, comes to the surface, irresistibly attracted as soon as there is a mention of gold or gems in the books he reads. "The land is rich and thickly populated with ferocious men. It produces crystals and some gems," says d'Ailly of Germany; and Colón, in the margin, dropping those ferocious men, merely notes: "In Germany one finds crystal and other gems." (2) "It [Italy] produces gems, syrtites, coral, turmelines. This country also contains boas, ferocious lynxes and herons," says d'Ailly. And Colón, in the margin: "Italy produces gems and coral." (3) "The country [Spain] is fertile; it produces all kinds of fruit: it abounds in precious metals and in stones," says d'Ailly. And Colón in the margin: "Spain very rich in gems and metals." (4) "In this country [Britain] there are a number of rivers, and big ones; one also finds hot-water springs and a great abundance of metals,

90

of agates and of pearls," says d'Ailly. And Colón, in the margin: "Abundance of metals, of agates and of pearls." (5)

Nor are these isolated or picked-out examples. It is safe to say that not once does Colón see precious stones in a text without singling out the fact in the margin, drawn by a kind of instinctive fascination.

Gold is his other lure. He cannot resist the attraction of the king of metals, and as he sees it gleam in a text, he promptly marks the fact for his own personal attention. He underlines that Thessaly is the place where gold coins were made for the first time; (6) and notes how Sicily is rich in gold lands; he notes the name of the Pactolus river, then adds: "Pactulus, river which carries golden sands." (7) Throughout his hundreds of marginal notes, gold is from the first with him a constant pre-occupation, rooted less in a definite acquisitive sense than in the sheer fascination of the lovely metal which called out from the depths of his soul a rich racial and personal resonance.

This metallic and glittering quality—so typically Jewish that it has led in the English language to the curious subconscious pun on *Jew* and *jewelry*, whereby *jewels* become the goods typically handled by *Jews*—is naturally connected in Colón, as in many men of his race (and of other races), with a sense for all goods having a commercial value. His notes often reveal that his eye is on all merchandise which may be translatable into wealth and power. This is particularly so in his notes to his much-read copy of Marco Polo. We see him underlining "perfumes, pearls, precious stones, gold cloth, ivory," or again "innumerable merchandise," or "pepper, nuts, muscat, clover and other spices in abundance."

Yet we would err in jumping to the conclusion that Colón was mainly interested in material goods. Hard, and even harsh, as we may see him in later years, disputing inch by inch with the Crown over his dues and incomes from the discovery, his heart is not in goods and coin but in the power and glory which goods and coin bring to a man big enough to handle them as they deserve, i.e. as instruments of the human spirit. That is why further study of his marginal notes will at once reveal other features which on a shallower view of his character would seem utterly incompatible with his sense for material values; and particularly a delightful poetical imagination, often, it is true, wandering into irresponsible or naïve fancy, which makes Colón's letters and diaries so full of light, of air and of space. His love for the fanciful and imagin-ative can even conquer the denser magnetism which draws him to gems, metals and spices. Thus, on reading a paragraph on Araby saying: "Myrrh and cinnamon grow in the meadows. It is there that the bird Phoenix is found. There one can find sardonyx, onyx, rock salt and iris," he forgets his gems and his spices for once to follow the flight of the imaginary bird, and notes down: "where the bird Phoenix was born." (8)

This tendency to yield to the lures of his imagination was the easier for his ignorance, partly due to his epoch, partly to his haphazard education. When cardinals such as Philastre could combine good mathematics with a sincere belief in Unipedes and Pygmies, why should not a self-taught sailor believe in the bird Phoenix and in men with tails? D'Ailly, moreover, a lesser mathematician and cosmographer than Philastre, put his immense authority as the head of the greatest university of that age (for he was chancellor of the Sorbonne) behind the most fantastic assertions, which Colón was bound to read, at any rate at first, with the greatest respect. Yet, though he is open to vast fields of credulity and imagination, what strikes the reader of his notes is less his easy acceptance of unknown facts than his cautious silence when marvels become too marvellous. Thus, when d'Ailly says, speaking of Arcady: "One finds there the stone called Asbestos which once kindled never goes out, and blackbirds of dazzling whiteness," Colón writes down: "Asbestos—stone, which once kindled never goes out" (9) but quietly drops those white blackbirds. And when, speaking of "the land of Scythes," the learned Cardinal is good enough to inform him that "a great part of this country remains uninhabitable, for, though it abounds in gold and precious stones, it is inaccessible to men owing to the presence of griffins," Colón in his marginal note puts down the gold and the precious stones (10) but takes no notice whatever of those griffins, even though vouched for by the eminent head of the Sorbonne. He is apparently willing to believe in a spring which freezes under the sun's heat and which becomes hot in the cool of night, and in the existence of dragons along with monkeys, ostriches and elephants in Ethiopia and Morocco respectively; (11) he registers without even the quiet protest of silence the fact that gems are found in the skulls of dragons. But when he is told that the Troglodytes feed on serpents and are deprived of speech, he merely comments: "multa miranda"—many astonishing things; (12) when he reads about the Gorgades Islands: "a legend says that there grows in them an evergreen vine which bears a fruit of gold," (13) not even his attraction for gold makes him depart from a cautious silence; and a silence no less cautious is his adequate comment on the too marvellous marvel of the following paragraph: "Chrysos and Argyros Islands are on the Indian Ocean. They are so rich in metals that it is said their surface is paved with gold and silver. Hence their names." (14)

This attitude of critical discrimination is the more remarkable for the humility with which he learns all kinds of facts—whether true or imaginary—on those "secrets of the world" which, as he tells us, he was so keen to penetrate. He notes the origin of the names given to the several winds and their respective characteristics, and singles out the "fact" that "Pestilence is caused by corrupted air; the Auster generates it and the Aquilon fights it back." (15) He registers that "tempests occur when we are neither at the height of summer nor in full winter," and that "Vegetius teaches which are the months when navigation is safest," (16) a note over which he places a + as if to single out its importance. Throughout, the tone and general attitude is that of the student learning and not of the argumentative master disputing with a rival in scientific knowledge. A good deal of Geography is absorbed under our eyes, not all of it worth the earnest, painstaking effort bestowed upon it. One of the worst cases occurs in connection with the rivers of Spain, a subject on which Cardinal d'Ailly already shows the traditional ignorance of Spanish affairs cultivated by his countrymen, and makes the most fantastic assertions without drawing the slightest protest from his docile pupil, who meekly copies in the margin: "The Tagus. Carthage of Spain, where it has its origin; rich in gold-bearing sands." (17) How many books trying to prove that Colón was a Spaniard would have been saved by this simple observation that no Spaniard born could ever have accepted the ludicrous error of d'Ailly on the river which flows past both Toledo and Lisbon!

On the other hand, a good number of his notes reveal how attentive he remains to all things Jewish. (18) "Jericho, a town which has become famous owing to Jeremiah," he notes in the margin of a paragraph on the prophet's birthplace; and on the next paragraph, in which are mentioned several places with familiar names, he writes: "many Jewish places mentioned." We can feel a tone of pride in a note in which he records: "All peoples received their astronomy from the Jews." (19) In Chapter X he discusses in the margin (20) the smallness of the country occupied by the Jews and notes the limits of the Promised Land as defined by the Cardinal, whose position in the Church gave him, no doubt, a certain assurance as to the Lord's real meaning and intentions in the matter. D'Ailly gives, as a matter of fact, a most reasonable and even rationalistic explanation of it all in his Chapter XIX, (21) where he says that Judea is so rich in various fruits, pure water and precious balms, that it is no wonder the Jews imagined it to be the land promised to their forefathers. And as Jerusalem is in the centre and "is as the navel of the whole country, that is why it has been said of Judea that redemption had taken place in the middle of the earth." Upon which, Colón comments: "How we must understand this saying: that redemption took place in the middle of the earth."

No more transparent window on to his mind could be desired than these revealing, honest and unadorned notes in which Colón is seen in the quiet solitude of his study, gradually building up his education and situating his mind in the universe, just as in later years he was to situate his ships on the ocean by seeking his bearings in the steady stars. We see a man by no means well informed and by no means original as a thinker; one who absorbs fact, fancy and fiction with an equal respect for authority, as do all the men of his time; for whom a verse of the Bible, a line of Aristotle and a direct observation seem still to have the same value; yet a mind by no means set in an illogical and confused middle zone where all these tendencies meet, but rather swaying between them—from authority to observation; from revelation to experience, as we are able to show with the most significant example that could be found in the whole range of Colón's opinions.

Chapter XII of d'Ailly's *Ymago Mundi* is devoted to the discussion of the parts of the world which are inhabitable. It is one of the chief conundrums of that age, and one which drew Colón's attention to a considerable degree. In the course of this chapter, d'Ailly raises another of the favourite themes of Colón's speculation: the actual site of Paradise on Earth. This is d'Ailly's text: "It follows that if the special conditions favourable to human life agreed with the general circumstances which make a land inhabitable, to wit, a fertile soil, a good exposition to the sun and a good aspect of the stars, the region would be of the best possible climate: it is likely that Paradise on Earth was a region of this kind and so is certainly the place which authors call Fortunate Islands." (22) Cardinal d'Ailly does not say that the Fortunate (i.e. the Canary) Islands were Paradise on Earth. Yet such is the rash conclusion which fiery Colón writes down in the margin: "Paradise on Earth is certainly the place which authors call the Fortunate Islands." But, later on, when in Chapter XLI the learned Cardinal discusses the Fortunate Islands themselves and, having extolled their fertility, again explains (as he had done in the case of the Promised Land) that "this fertility of the soil led the Gentiles to believe that Paradise was in these Islands," (23) Colón drops his conceit and merely records: "Error of the Gentiles who said that the Fortunate Islands were Paradise, owing to their fertility."

Nor is this all. For in Chapter LV, when dealing with rivers in general, d'Ailly very properly begins with the four rivers of Paradise (24)—on which he gives much information, if not all of the same value, nor even held with the same conviction. Thus, he declares that "There is a spring in Paradise which waters the Garden of Delights and which splays into four rivers . . ." "A fountain in Paradise" notes Colón in the margin. On the basis of several "authorities" the learned Cardinal explains then that: "The Paradise on Earth is a pleasant place, situated in certain regions of the Orient, at a long distance by land and by sea from our inhabited world," and Colón practically repeats this statement in the margin. Then d'Ailly enters warily on more controversial ground. "It rises so high that it touches the lunar sphere and the water of the Deluge could not reach it. This should not be understood to mean that in actual fact the Paradise on Earth reached the Circle of the Moon; for it is only a hyperbolic way of saying that its altitude over the low lands is incomparable and that it reaches the layers of calm air which lie on top of the zone of troubled air where the emanations and vapours which [. . .] form a flux and reflux towards the Lunar globe tend to gather." There is no marginal note on this, and none other than a list of the four rivers of Paradise opposite a curious phrase in which the Cardinal sets down in stark contradiction his "revealed" geography and the facts of observation: "From this lake, as from a main spring, there flow the four rivers of Paradise: Phison or Ganges: Gihon or Nile; Tigris and Euphrates, though their respective origins do seem to lie in different places." Colón's silence on this point of crucial divergence between fact and faith might be interpreted as an offshoot of his critical sense, particularly since in the margin of the following chapter of d'Ailly's book, "On the Rivers of Paradise," (25) he gives an unmistakable proof of his unwillingness to follow fancy (or faith) and of his attachment to fact. D'Ailly describes the Euphrates: "A river of Mesopotamia, whose spring is in Paradise; it is very rich in precious stones. . . ." And Colón notes in the margin: "Euphrates" and drops Paradise; then he reads about those precious stones, his blue eyes light up and he writes the name again: "Euphrates: the richest in precious stones." Withal, it is not easy to let Paradise go. D'Ailly is discussing whether the regions beyond the Tropic of Capricorn can be inhabitable. Pliny says they are, and so does Ptolemy, in spite of the heat prevailing in them. The Cardinal sums up, in one of his typical balanced sentences, trying to combine faith and disbelief: "Though certain regions beyond the Capricorn be inhabitable, as according to Aristotle and Averroes in his books on *Heaven* and on the *World*, they are the noblest parts of the earth, or, as some assert, the Paradise on Earth, it is a fact, nevertheless, that we cannot find a description of these regions in any author." (26) To which cautious text, Colón appends a most sanguine and affirmative note: "Beyond the tropic of Capricorn is the most beautiful dwelling, for there is the highest and noblest part of the world, namely, the Paradise on Earth."

In later years, these notes of Cardinal d'Ailly about the height of Paradise and the four rivers which flow from it will blossom out in Colón's tropical imagination into the most delirious construction of mystical geography known to history.

What strikes us most in his notes is the humility of the student before what he reads, and the elementary character of some of the facts he singles out from his text to memorise in the margins of his book. "A person moving from East to West passes to a different meridian." (27) "The half [of the sky above the horizon] is called hemisphere." "Mount Olympus where comets are formed." (28) "Each country has its own West and its own East related to its own horizon." (29) Almost a schoolboy's hand, one might think. On Chapter V of *Ymago Mundi*, d'Ailly explains how the dimensions of the Earth may be measured by travelling along a meridian and noting when the height of the Pole falls (or rises) by one degree. This lesson was important for Colón, and he was to benefit by it and to found on it the crucial error upon which he launched forth into the Unknown Deep. So he writes in the margin: "This is the way the earth has been measured." (30)

Now and then the student puts down an idea of his own: "The Toledan tables put the Occident further West than Ptolemy, on Cape St. Vincent"; (31) a note which shows that Colón, despite what some of his critics say, did go to original books for his ideas as well as to such compilations as d'Ailly, since in this note he refers to the Alfonsine Tables, the great Monument of astronomic science put together at Toledo, in the thirteenth century, by a Commission of Astronomers (most of them Jewish) under the

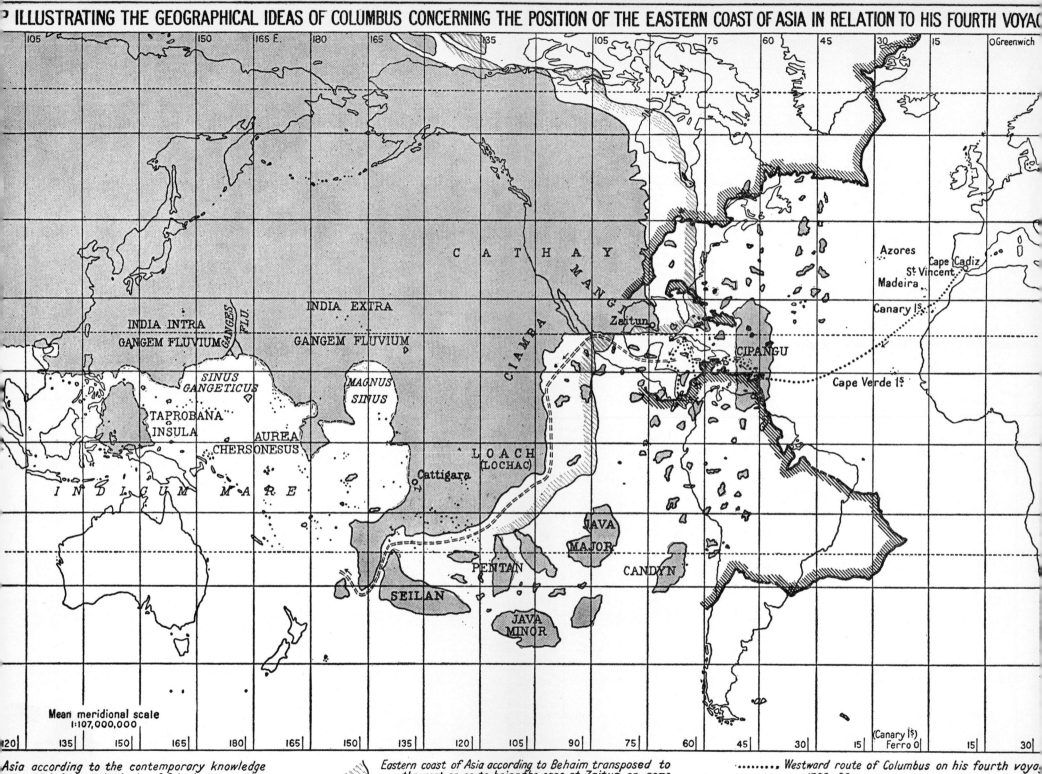

ILLUSTRATING THE GEOGRAPHICAL IDEAS OF COLUMBUS CONCERNING THE POSITION OF THE EASTERN COAST OF ASIA IN RELATION TO HIS FOURTH VOYAGE

Mean meridional scale 1:107,000,000

Asia according to the contemporary knowledge which formed the basis of Columbus' conception (southern coast ----- according to Ptolemy, printed edition of 1478, stretched in longitude to conform to Marinus of Tyre; continued beyond Cattigara by eastern coast ——— according to Behaim 1492).

Eastern coast of Asia according to Behaim transposed to the east so as to bring the cape at Zaitun on same meridian as eastern end of Cuba, which Columbus took for Asia.

Coast of America according to the world map of Juan de la Cosa 1500, incorporating the discoveries up to that date.

Coastal outlines in their true position according to modern maps.

.... *Westward route of Columbus on his fourth voyage, 1502-03.*

===== *Route Columbus believed he was following along the coast of Asia on his fourth voyage and continuation he had at one time considered following to reach India*

auspices of Alfonso the Learned of Castille. His assurance grows. Here and there we hear quite a different voice: Colón writes with authority. The explanation is easy. He read his book several times, a fact for which there is abundant evidence, and in later years, confident in his experience and in a knowledge which he had checked by travel, he sets down an opinion of his own as a fact. "Note that the town of Arbis is on the edge of the first climate, near the Island of Meroe. [. . .] The distance of this town to the equator is 18°, and to the Occident 62°. See Ptolemy and four of our maps." (32)

* *
*

Such is the man who, in those years, "boiling over with the practice and exercise of discovery," was eagerly trying to find out —what? Perhaps he did not know himself. Lands to discover? The way to the Indies? Why not both or a mixture of both? Here, again, his notes to d'Ailly are going to throw floods of light on the ideas, the guesses and even the fertile errors which guided his quest and shaped his plan.

The ideas which gradually emerge from his experience, from his travels, from his readings and from his dreams, bear a strong resemblance to those of Toscanelli. (33) They are, in fact, based on Toscanelli to an extent sufficient to justify the view that by 1480 Colón had read the letter and studied the map of 1474—an assumption, moreover, which the general weight of evidence renders almost inevitable. Yet his plan was very much his own and differed from Toscanelli's in one important respect—it was far more erroneous; and therefore it strengthened his determination to cross the Unknown Deep, since it made the cruising easier by all this added error. We are going to see him at work in the quiet of his study, checking up with his beloved books the ideas already formed in his mind, either originally, or on reading them in Toscanelli's letter, or, more likely, as a result of an agreement between his own personal meditations and the information found in Toscanelli which would come to strengthen his self-assurance.

(1) *The earth is round.* This was no news to well-trained minds, for by then it constituted the generally accepted doctrine for Christian, Jew and Moor alike, but it was a notion which a self-taught man like Colón would be glad to find confirmed in print. "The earth must be considered as spherical," writes d'Ailly, and his disciple underlines this with evident satisfaction: "The earth is round and spherical." (34) He sums up another of d'Ailly's

passages with the following words, which are rather in his own vision than in the actual text of the Cardinal—somewhat confused and unscientific for our views: "The water and the earth together make up a round body." And, no doubt, most satisfactory to him of all other proofs, he registers that "the eclipse of the moon is caused by the shadow cast by the earth." (35)

(2) *The distance by land between the edge of the West and the edge of the East is very long.* This is a point on which he returns again and again in his notes. He repeats, and indeed confirms and expands, d'Ailly's assertion to that effect in the following words: "From the end of the Occident [i.e. the Canary Islands] to the end of India by land, the distance is more than half the circle of the Earth, which is 180°"; (36) and below: "The extent ["*quantitas*"] of inhabitable earth is much bigger than the majority of philosophers reckon it to be." And again: "The distance by land between the end of the Occident, i.e. Portugal, and that of the Orient, i.e. India, is very long." (37)

This may be taken to have been his most fertile error. *India*, in those days, was a word commonly used for both what we nowadays call *India* and *Asia*. No one had an exact, and few had an approximate, notion of the length of land beyond our India, i.e. of the distance along parallels between our India and the Pacific Coast of China and Siberia; and that ignorance, allowing, as it did, ample room for opinion and therefore for error, explains the assurance with which Colón was to cross the Atlantic.

(3) *The distance between Spain and India by sea is therefore very small.* A venerable error, founded on the best authorities. Colón meets it in d'Ailly time and again, and underlines it always with evident relish. "The end of Spain and the beginning of India are not very far distant. [. . .] It is evident that this sea may be crossed in a few days with a good wind." (38) Once, the old error returns under a new guise which deserves quotation: "Note that if the Island of Taprobane is placed as herein stated, it would be 58° west of the true Occident, and we are right in saying that there is but a small sea between Spain and India." (39) He has drawn a square round this note, which shows the importance he attached to it. It does not repeat a text of d'Ailly's on the narrowness of that sea; it reveals that Colón was not merely picking up knowledge on this point from his authors, but rather that he came to seek confirmation and assurance for an opinion he had already formed.

(4) *The length of a degree is* 56⅔ *miles.* In this, Colón parted

company with Toscanelli, who, though the authorities differ on the point, (40) seems to have taken for his calculations and charts a degree of $62\frac{1}{2}$ miles at the equator. But there are few opinions to which he held with more energy. The view is set off in the margin of his book where it occurs, and, moreover, he has more than once left on record that he actually measured a degree and confirmed this figure. Now, this figure had been given first by an Arab cosmographer known as Alfraganus, or El Fargani, (41) who, on the strength of the measurements made by order of Khalif-Almamum (813-32), adopts $56\frac{2}{3}$ miles to the degree as the measurement of the earth. These are Arabic miles, worth 1,973·50 metres, and therefore the Arabic measurements, made in the ninth century, being only 251,880 metres in excess of the 40,007,520 metres we now believe the equator to measure, turn out to be by far the most accurate estimate ever made until modern days. Colón, at a first glance, seems to have had a flair for the best figure. (42) Unfortunately his miles were not Arabic but Italian, i.e. only 1,477·50 metres, which means that he made the world about one-fourth smaller than it actually is.

This did not merely reduce the width of the sea he was to cross to reach "the Indies," by reducing the length of each degree; it made that sea much narrower as a result of the roundabout calculations by which Colón estimated its dimensions. (43) Colón believed the land-distance between Spain and "India" to cover 282° of the earth's circumference; there remained only 360—282, or 78°, for the sea-distance between Lisbon and Cathay. And as these degrees were only of $56\frac{2}{3}$ miles at the equator, i.e. of about 50 miles at the Canary Islands, the distance in miles was a paltry 3900 miles, or 975 leagues.

This set of errors on Asia placed his "India" more or less where America actually is. And thus by indirections did he direction find. No wonder that when he found land at the point where he expected it, Colón remained convinced that he had landed in Asia.

(5) And yet, sure of himself as he was, particularly when in error, we would misread his character were we to imagine as simple and solid a mind which was essentially complex and fluid. The most reasonable conclusion to be drawn from his papers and actions is that while his will was single and set, his ideas were shifting and many-branched; this is so in particular with the main notion which is the basis of his plan—the length of sea to cross in order to reach the Indies. There is no doubt that his views on this point were influenced by Toscanelli's and also by his own error on the length of a degree. But there were other influences

as well, and notably that of "the prophet" Esdras, one of the authors of the *Apocrypha*, to whom, for some unknown reason, he attached an immense importance. He probably came across Esdras for the first time in d'Ailly. (44) But why he should single out this "authority" from the others (Aristotle and Pliny) mentioned in the same chapter, all of whom deserve more credit on these points of geography, can only be explained by some subconscious attraction of the Jewish missionary-visionary towards the Jewish prophet. Colón has many times invoked Esdras's authority in favour of his plan, both before and after the discovery. His note on Esdras, in the margin of d'Ailly, a characteristic piece of medieval writing, will repay study at a later stage. For our present purpose it is important to point out that in Colón's view the crucial contribution made by Esdras to his plan is the assertion that the world is six parts dry land and one part sea. (45)

Now, despite the insistence with which Colón declares Esdras to be *his* authority, no one seems to have taken the trouble to wonder whether the discoverer, instead of navigating by Marinus, Ptolemy or Toscanelli, actually navigated by Esdras. "I have said," he wrote to the King and Queen in 1502, "that in the carrying out of this enterprise of the Indies neither reason nor mathematics nor maps were any use to me: fully accomplished were the words of Isaiah." (46) Colombists have argued as to why Colón expected to find islands between 600 and 700 leagues from the Canary Islands, as we shall see when we come to accompany him on his first voyage; obviously, since he believed, with Esdras, that only one-seventh of the earth was under water, his expectation was but natural. For he might take this seventh to be one-seventh in degrees, or he might take it to be one-seventh of the surface. In the first case he was bound to reckon the sea between Spain and "India" at one-seventh of $360°$, i.e. about $51°$, which, at the rate of 50 miles at which he reckoned his degrees, amount to 2550 miles, or 637·50 leagues. If he took Esdras to mean the seventh in surface, his estimate of the width of the sea would depend on whether he thought there were seas in the Southern hemisphere. Now, in numerous notes to his d'Ailly, he is concerned with showing that the Southern hemisphere is populated, i.e. dry. "It is not true," he writes, as a comment to a similar assertion by d'Ailly, "that half the earth is covered by water. That fourth part of the earth which is under the equator opposite us is similar to ours, and therefore both must be above water and inhabitable." (47) And a few lines above he states the same belief, carrying it perhaps beyond the bounds of scientific credibility in more ways than one: "The earth is inhabited even to the regions in which are the cardinal extremities of the world, where days last six months. There live the happiest peoples, who only die of weariness of living." (48)

Having thus made up his mind that the Southern hemisphere was as dry as the Northern, he was sure to interpret Esdras in the sense that his seventh part of water was equally divided between the two halves of the world. This threw him back on to his first alternative, i.e. he was entitled to consider the distance between India and Spain by sea as one-seventh of the circumference, i.e. $51°$ of $56\frac{2}{3}$ miles. (49)

Such was his secret. Toscanelli, for Colón, was on the way to truth, but as he had not read Esdras his plan still required mariners, not used to losing sight of land, to navigate $130°$ of $62\frac{1}{2}$ miles, i.e. 8125 miles over unknown seas. Colón, through his study of Esdras, "knew" that the distance was only 2550 miles. This surely was a secret worth its weight in gold.

There, only a little over 600 leagues of sea away, lay India and Taprobane, and many more islands. His notes to d'Ailly are full of the splendour of these Oriental dreams: "The island of Taprobane, which contains ten cities, not counting a great number of islands as well . . ." "Between these mountains there are innumerable islands, amongst which many are full of pearls and precious stones . . ." (50) a note, this, which he singles out for attention by drawing a hand with a finger pointing at it. Then comes a note in which, mixing up what d'Ailly says of India and of Taprobane, he nevertheless selects the useful and rejects the fanciful. Says d'Ailly: "The country contains big elephants, licornes, parrots, ebony and various species of spices." To this Colón comments: "Taprobane contains gems and elephants." And d'Ailly—still on Taprobane: "It produces ivory and many precious stones. Moreover, it is there one finds mountains of gold which are inaccessible because of dragons, griffins and human monsters"; (51) whereupon Colón shifts this carload over to India, but drops some of it on the way: "India contains many things and aromatic spices, an abundance of precious stones and mountains of gold." Such a country is well worth seeking and studying. So he sets down some geographical information about it: "The frontier of India stretches down to the tropic of Capricorn"; and further: "It must be understood that the frontier of India, which is opposite us, i.e. opposite Spain, stretches from the boreal region to the tropic of Capricorn;'' (52) both of which notes are marked with a cross.

Now that we have seen his mind at work, in silence and solitude, far from the solicitations to dissembling which a nature as imaginative and as sensitive as his was bound to feel in the presence of men, we are perhaps in a better position to understand not only the set of ideas but, up to a point, the set of emotions, the driving forces of both mind and heart, which led him to put his scheme before King John of Portugal.

CHAPTER X

DON QUIXOTE COLÓN FAILS IN PORTUGAL

JOHN II, King of Portugal, impressed his subjects so deeply that he is known in Portuguese history as "the Perfect King." His historiographer and confidant, Ruy de Pina, has penned a vivid picture of this monarch: "The King Dom Joham was a man rather big than small in body, very well made, and well proportioned in all his limbs; his face was long rather than round, and suitably covered with a beard. The hair of his head was auburn and smooth; yet, at thirty-seven his head and beard were already grey, at which he showed much satisfaction, owing to the increase in authority which his Royal Divinity obtained from his white hairs; and his eyes were of perfect sight, and at times there appeared veins and spots of blood in the white of them, wherewith in matters which might raise his fury, if he happened to be touched by it, his countenance became very frightening. And yet, in matters of honour, pleasure or festivity, very gay and of a very Royal and excellent grace; his nose was somewhat full and overhanging though without ugliness. He was white all over, save his face, which was red in a good way. [. . .] He was a Prince with a marvellous mind and a sharp wit. [. . .] He had a quick and expert memory and his judgment was clear and profound, and therefore his sayings and opinions had more truth, wit and authority in their invention than sweetness or elegance in their wording, for his elocution was not clear, being somewhat nasal, which took away some of his grace. He was a King with a very brave and stout heart, which made him sigh for great and strange deeds; hence, though his body, personally, went about in his Realms to govern them well, as he did, his spirit was always roaming abroad, desirous of enlarging them." (1)

This was the Prince, so similar in many ways to Colón, to whom Colón for the first time submitted his scheme. What this scheme exactly was, and when it was put to King John, have been the subject of considerable argument and speculation, much of it idle; for in spite of their admirable industry and scholarship, these disputants have perhaps lost sight of the living element which makes all life vague, less set and clear, and far more dependent on individual caprice than we afterwards imagine when we try to label and date it.

Did Colón mean to go to the Indies, or did he only put before King John a plan of discovery of new islands? And when did Colón present his scheme? The first obstacle comes from a statement of Colón himself: (2) "The Lord," he writes to King Ferdinand in 1505, "sent me miraculously so that I could serve Your Highness; I say miraculously because I came ashore in Portugal, where the King of that country was engaged in discovery more than any other. He [the Lord] shut the King's eyes and ears and all his senses, for in fourteen years I was unable to make him understand what I said to him." Fourteen years! All Colombists fall on that figure and tear it to pieces. Why! He did not swim ashore till 1476, he discovered "the Indies" in 1492, and he left Portugal in 1484; so, how does he make that out? The ingenious say he meant fourteen months, and the impatient and matter-of-fact, as usual, dismiss him as an intolerable juggler with truth. (3)

Yet, he is quite honest about it. How transparently honest may be gathered from the fact that in writing those words to the King, who could break him on the wheel if he wished, he let out candidly that he had been in touch with King John on the discovery, even after he had gone over to the Court of his most dreaded rival in this field. And, as usual, his plain unadorned words give the key to what actually happened.

We, from a world of facts dead, docketed and classified, are apt to imagine that Colón prepared a scheme, drafted it, and presented it cut and dried on a set date, discoverable through our industry, to the King of Portugal, who in his turn applied to it a hard-and-fast procedure, sending it to his "Committee of Mathematicians," who considered it and advised the rejection of it; whereupon the King had Colón informed that his scheme had been duly considered and rejected.

Such a vision, which is in fact the background of the arguments for or against dates and actual contents of the plan, is utterly at variance with the nature of things, and even more so with the nature of men. Fourteen years from 1492 brings us to 1478. Colón is just back from Thule. He is full of it. He has seen the "last of the lands" and navigated beyond it. For all we know he may have heard there of the prediscovery made by Northern navigators, (4) or, at any rate, of various traditions on the relative vicinity of lands across the main. In any case, he is already "possessed" of his idea, even if he has not, as he certainly had not yet, evolved it fully in his mind. He is a man of strong passions and of strong imagination. He has friends who open for him the circles of the Court—else, how could he marry into the Perestrello-Moniz family the following year? All the weight of historical evidence is therefore again in his favour and confirms that he spoke to King John about discovery as early as 1478, for though King John did not begin to reign till 1481, we know he began to handle "discoveries" on behalf of his father in 1474 (5). Did Colón submit a plan? Certainly not, if by a plan is meant a complete proposal for definite action. He was not then fully aware of his ideas himself. But all we know of him, his impatient, opinionated, easily roused nature, his youth at the time, twenty-seven, the very nature of the enterprise, full of gold-in-dreams, of light-in-sunsets, of islands-in-imagination, forces us to the conclusion that he would not wait to mature his plans before proposing them to the King—to that King who had been for years granting everybody round him commissions to go, discover and people unknown lands.

The natural view is then to take Colón at his honest word and to see him coming and going from bookshop to Court, from Lisbon harbour to Porto Santo, or to La Mina in Guinea, to measure the length of a degree, and back to Court with a fresh load of stories about islands seen at sunset and pieces of wood carved in an unusual way, and new views on the length of a meridian, and now and then a hint about a prophecy which he would shyly bottle up on catching a twist of a smile round the royal lip, and back again to his Marco Polo and his d'Ailly, to the maps his brother was copying, to his pen and astrolabes and to his astronomical tables, again to emerge hotter and hotter about it.

For he was hot about it: "with this fire I came to Your Highnesses" (6) he was to write to Ferdinand and Isabel in 1503. And in this inner fire, rather than in any outer fact or fiction picked up in books or travels, must we see the true origin of his enterprise. On no feature of his personality are all his contemporaries more in agreement than on his imagination. "Alto ingenio," says Bernáldez; "de gran ingenio," says Oviedo; "com as quaes imaginaçoes . . ." writes Barros; (7) ". . . and as each day he dwelt more and more [on land discovered and to be discovered] and with greater vehemence of imagination . . ." says Las Casas. And Fernando Colón: "This authority and several others quoted by this author [d'Ailly] were those that moved the Admiral most to believe in his own imagination." (8)

* *

This language sounds familiar. It brings echoes of a well-known story, the one best known to all those who read the language of Castille. And once this idea has entered the mind, it sheds such floods of light on Colón's character that all his actions become clear and the glorious yet absurd adventure of the discovery of America is at last integrated into the truest and deepest life of Spain. Colón is a pre-incarnation of Don Quixote. (9)

He is predominantly a contemplative man. In the quiet of contemplation his imagination flares up. This lamp of inner fire soon outshines the light of outer fact. Reality takes a purely subjective value. No matter what "reason, or mathematics or maps" may say, he knows. Reality must adjust itself to what he says it is. "That an inn? Of course it is a castle!" "That Haiti? Of course it is Cipango!"

The first operation is therefore a pure creation of the mind. It rests, like all human creations, on two poles, the self and the world. Colón, like Don Quixote, feels that he is called to perform a deed, to fulfil a mission. Which? It matters little. When Colón had discovered America, he felt that his mission was the deliverance of Jerusalem, and in a letter to the King and Queen he transfers to this second enterprise the arguments he had already used to induce them to back him in the first. Don Quixote is ready to protect anyone who may need protection, and he sallies forth compelled by a sense of duty and by faith in this his mission. This sense of being elected for some high service is therefore the first quixotic feature of Colón. The other pole of their construction is in the world. For, subjective as their creation is, it rests, of course, on materials drawn from outside. Though the inn be not a castle, both inns and castles have walls and are human dwellings. Moreover, though both Colón and Don Quixote go off at the deep end as soon as there is a question of Cipango for Colón, of Dulcinea for Don Quixote, they are only mad north-north west, and for the rest of life they are sensible and even intelligent. Colón can impress even Humboldt, on matters such as magnetic needles and sea-currents; Don Quixote impressed even canons of Toledo and gentlemen farmers by the acumen and wisdom of his utterances. Colón may believe in Cipango and in Esdras, but he will have nothing to do with d'Ailly's dragons and griffins; Don Quixote may believe in giants and enchanters, but he stops at the speaking head in Barcelona. And both believe in islands.

Everybody, of course, in Colón's days and in Portugal, believed in islands. After all, every now and then one or more of them emerged beyond the veil of nothingness and became actually tangible, and livable, and enjoyable, offering their untrod meadows and their virgin forests of palm-trees with the lavishness of the innocent. And every now and then one heard that a seaman, or King's secretary, or rabbit-breeder had become hereditary captain of one of these new realms which the Ocean kept offering the King of Portugal on a tray of azure blue hemmed round with silvery foam, and covered with a veil of mist.

But there are several ways of wanting an island. And we guess that few island-hunters can have sought them as eagerly as Colón and Don Quixote. An island, for an ardent and contemplative mind, is, in truth, an ideal place. There, your Self holds sway, undisturbed by outsiders. The sea surrounds you, protects you in every direction, from every danger. Those cruel bumps and knocks from reality of which you are so much afraid, they are kept at bay. The sea prevents reality from approaching, and you, within your impassable, liquid frontiers, can keep a closer watch on things and people who may seek to reach you, that is, to hurt you. There contemplation can be a joy indeed, and the fire of your soul can burn in peace, burn you away so that your flame can rise undisturbed in the blue sky without being exposed to the impurities of action and to the ashes of criticism. That is why ardent contemplatives, such as Colón and Don Quixote, are so fond of islands.

* * *

We gather then that Colón began to air his views at Court from 1478 and, off and on, kept the idea alive until 1484, when he left in disgust for Castille; and that his plans were mostly the word-expression and the geographical image of an inner fire kindled in his dry imagination by the sun of discovery which was then at its zenith in Portugal.

We have in Colón's own words a perfect summary of the quixotic architecture of his construction: the personal inspiration; the minimum of outside material to give it a tangible support; and the ardent faith within: "In this time I have seen and endeavoured to see all kinds of writings, histories, chronicles and philosophy, and other arts, with which Our Lord opened my understanding with a palpable hand that it was feasible to navigate from here to the Indies and opened up my will for the execution of it, and with this fire I came to Your Highnesses." (10)

It is idle to discuss whether the Indies by way of the West or the discovery of new islands were alone or even foremost in his mind. Neither could be absent from that part of his imagination which rested on the object, since both the Western way to India and the islands beyond Madeira and Cabo Verde were then "in the air" in Lisbon. (11) But his imagination did not rest on the object as much as on the subject. He was mostly afire about his mission and his discovery, no matter which, and from this kind of highly imaginative and passionate soul, it is useless to expect precision on detail or steadiness of *outside* purpose. All the steadiness is in the inner drive.

We may be certain that, when challenged, he grew excited and hot—a fact for which we have ample evidence from the Portuguese chroniclers—and that he was apt to shift his argument, not only according to the particular yarn from Madeira, or calculation from Ptolemy, or prophecy from Esdras, which happened at the time to be uppermost in his mind, but even within the same hour, according to the trend of the conversation, the impression he made or thought he had made on his interlocutors, his hopes or his fears. For, with all his unbounding faith and courage, he was full of fear—just like Don Quixote. He lived in mortal dread lest his faith be shattered by a hard knock from reality, or lest his precious secret be stolen from the treasure-chest of his soul. And under the stress of this fear, his innate cautiousness turned sour and became suspiciousness, amounting almost to a persecution mania.

Moreover, it must be remembered, in extenuation of his vagueness, that his plan was rather difficult to put into words. It was probably like one of those inner melodies which we can sing in silence perfectly but which shock everybody, even ourselves, if we try to sing them out aloud. When hard pressed for concrete proposals, what could he say? He moved within a triangle: Toscanelli's letter and map, which he was not supposed to know and which therefore were taboo at Court; the stories about carved wood and fortunate pilots, which were then current talk on caravel decks and in harbour taverns, but which were certainly smiled at in higher circles; and . . . Esdras, whom he was probably alone in considering as an authority on the matter. What could he do but be vague? It must have been a torture for him to have to remain there before the King, fumbling about degrees and widths of water, when right within he was as clear and as determined—and as hot—as the sun. And we fancy we can see then his freckled white skin redden with his inner fire, his eyes flash lightning-lights and his voice burst out as in peals of thunder, more noisy than intelligible.

Yet, it was precisely this contrast which gave him so much assurance. The more difficult he found it to put his vision into words, the clearer it stood out as a vision before his mind's eye; the more doubts he raised round his faith, the brighter did his faith shine. Las Casas has often emphasised this extraordinary assurance of Don Quixote-Colón: he had "conceived in his heart the most certain confidence to find what he claimed he would, as if he had this [new] world locked up in his trunk"; (12) and this, again, even more positive: "for, as I understand, when he decided to seek a Christian Prince who should help and back him, he was already certain that he would discover lands and people in them, as if he had been there personally (of which I certainly do not doubt). . . ." (13) It is evident that the main asset he had was not Toscanelli, which he would not mention, nor the various sea-yarns, nor even Esdras, but his own unconquerable faith.

On the strength of these somewhat intriguing utterances of his historiographer, and of other documents not to be lightly dismissed, some Colombists have put forward the view that Colón did go "there" before 1492. This most fascinating of the problems of a life bristling with them will be discussed at a later stage. (14) For the present, it will suffice to point out that no such pre-discovery is necessary to explain Colón's firm conviction. On the contrary; for a nature such as the discoverer's, an actual visit to reality would have acted rather in a deterrent and a depressive way on his faith. All we know of him leads us to suspect that his conviction was far firmer when arguing with kings and astronomers in Lisbon or Granada than when, after 1492, he had to argue with himself and with . . . Haiti.

No, he had not been "there." That is why he was *both* so vague and so sure. Those who claim that he did not then think of the Indies, and only spoke of Antilia and Cipango, miss the main point. (15) Cipango was "the Indies"; and the "Indies" was Asia; round Asia, i.e. round the Indies, there was a dust of islands, all more or less golden, a golden halo of islands, one of which was Cipango; and, in any case, since Colón meant to sail West, he did mean in a general way to go to "India." Where else could he go westward?

Nor do we need to draw merely on our own ratiocinations to come to this evident conclusion. There is direct and unimpeachable evidence to show that such was actually the meaning which Colón attached to the word. Las Casas defends Colón against the Dean of Reina, one Maestre Rodrigo de Santaella, who objected to the use of the word *Indies* for the Antilles, and this is his argument: "Cristóbal Colón did not call them Indies because others had seen and discovered them, but because they were the Eastern part of India-beyond-the-Ganges, which, prolonged eastwards, became Western to us, since the world is round.[. . .] And since these lands were the Eastern unknown part of India and had no name of their own, he gave them the name of the nearest country and called them West Indies . . ." (16) True, he adds: ". . . particularly since he knew that the wealth and great fame of India was manifest to all, he sought to win over the King and Queen, who were hesitating on his enterprise, telling them he was going to seek and find the Indies by the Western way . . ."; but it is patent that the first argument applies with equal strength to his Portuguese days.

There seems, however, to be some confusion as to the words "discover" and "discovery." They often seem to be taken in so exclusive a sense as to suggest that when a sailor or cosmographer spoke of "discovering" a country, that country was bound to be savage and primitive. But was it actually so? What was exactly the mental vision which the fifteenth and sixteenth centuries called forth when they said "discovery"? For the men of those days it obviously meant "incorporation into the Western society of men and nations." They might not have put it that way, but that is what they meant. And there is nothing in this idea to prejudge that the countries thus discovered, i.e. recovered or salvaged from their isolation, and brought into the commonalty of Western men, were either civilised or savage. Colón himself speaks of "the great cities of the Grand Khan which will no doubt be discovered." (17) And in one of his notes to d'Ailly he says: "More than half of the fourth of the earth where we are is unknown to us, and there are cities still unknown to the learned." (18)

What if Colón purposed to take over "a number of chests with exchange goods such as mercer-wares from Flanders, bells, brass-basins, brass-leaf, strings of beads, glass of several colours, mirrors, scissors, knives, needles, pins, linen-shirts, rough cloth of several colours, coloured bonnets and similar things, all of low price and value, although greatly prized by the ignorant amongst them"? (19) All "India" was not civilised, nor paved with gold and bridged over with marble, and the dust of islands certainly contained "undiscovered" countries not merely for the West but for the East as well. There is therefore no reason whatever to differ from the opinion expressed by Las Casas, who admirably sums up the plan ultimately submitted by Colón to King John of Portugal in a typically hybrid and imaginative sentence: "He proposed his affair to the King of Portugal, and what he offered to do was as follows: that by way of the West towards the Auster or South he would discover great lands, islands and terra firma, most happy, most rich in gold and silver and pearls and precious stones and infinite peoples; and that, by that way, he intended to come upon lands of India, and the great island of Cipango and the kingdoms of the Grand Khan." (20)

* *
*

This, it will be owned, was a fair offer. What was the price which the King was to pay for it? Colón was by no means modest in his claims. But mark Las Casas' words: "First, that he should be honoured and armed a Knight with [the right to wear] golden spurs." (21) Oh *Ingenious* gentleman Don Quixote, how cordially would you have approved this first condition which your precursor put before the King of Portugal, you who on the eve of your very first day of Knight-errantry, weary of riding over the sun-baked plains of La Mancha, spent the night watching over your arms, to be armed at dawn by that scoundrel of an innkeeper whom you mistook for the Lord of the Castle! This Genoese sailor, eking out a meagre life by drawing maps, but carrying his head high as one in whose head high dreams are housed, wants as his first condition for discovering the Indies the right to wear golden spurs! Truly has it been said by a Portuguese author (22) that the host of discoverers made up a kind of sea-chivalry. Spices, indeed! What is the value of the right to wear golden spurs, in political economy? Here is Colón, asking to open up the short way to the land of spices, for a pair of golden spurs with which to hasten on the horses of Neptune. And then, "that he should have the right to call himself Don Cristóbal Colón, and his successors also." Here again we can see Don Quixote nod assent, for we know how carefully he pondered over what his name should be and how by his great deeds he made that title *Don* world-famous; so that he could not but have felt highly pleased when Don Cristóbal de Cipango demanded this condition as the most important after the concession of the golden spurs.

The next condition was that he should be granted the title of Grand Admiral of the Ocean Sea, which, to be sure, is a most magnificent title and one to be coveted by any man in his senses. Nor can it be doubted for a moment that he fully deserved this title, which he ultimately won, not from the King of Portugal, who was far too much of a rationalist and a Machiavellian to understand him, but from the Queen of Castille; for, Cipango or no Cipango, America or no America, he did sail the high seas for the first time, as Oviedo has justly said: "Cristóbal Colón was the first who in Spain taught how to navigate the vast ocean sea by the height of the degrees of the sun and of the north, and the first who put it into practice; for till he came, though such an art was read in the schools, few (or better said, none) ventured to try it actually at sea." (23)

As for the privileges which so exalted a position would entail, Colón was not taking any risks nor leaving anything to conjecture; he was to be granted "all the pre-eminences and prerogatives, privileges, rights, dues and immunities enjoyed by the Admiral of Castille." For it should be known that the Admiral of Castille was the most lavishly endowed lord who in those days rode the waves. Colón was, moreover, to be "perpetual Viceroy and governor of all the islands and terra firma which he might discover in person or which might come to be discovered through his industry."

Then, but only then, after his greatness and nobility had been well established, Colón took up material conditions. He was to have "the tenth of all the income accruing to the King from all things of gold, silver, pearls, precious stones, metals, spices and other profitable things, and from all kinds of goods bought, exchanged, found or conquered within the limits of his Admiralty." And, finally, he would have the right to contribute one-eighth to the expenses of every expedition to the new-discovered lands, and to derive one-eighth of the profit. These last conditions have made many worthy critics frown at him and accuse him of cupidity and avarice. Yet, how could a man go about in golden spurs and down at heel? That is not done. A knight with golden spurs must ride a thoroughbred, and on a thoroughbred a knight can only ride in gold and brocade clothes. Can a Grand Admiral of the Ocean Sea command his fleets wrapped in a threadbare cape? The criticism is simply silly. Colón was mainly a quixotic type, hungry for glory, splendour and renown, and his close watch on material gain was but the sign of the care with which he guarded his dignity against the low attacks of poverty. A magnificent lord must have a magnificent estate.

No one had ever put before the King of Portugal such extravagant claims. If, as it seems to be the case, this final form of the oft-repeated proposal was made in 1483 or 1484, Colón was then about thirty-two. He had, it is true, navigated "all that till our day is navigated," (24) as he himself was to say later. Still, he was socially a humble stranger, patronised by the King's Jewish doctor and married into a well-known family, much loved by the head of the Portuguese Church; and these circumstances did not warrant the proud claims made in advance for the delivery of somewhat nebulous if not fabulous lands. How can we explain this obvious lack of balance between what Colón "offered" and the exorbitant price which he exacted for it?

In a sense, the amount of this price is a measure of the exaltation to which Colón had been raised by his inner discovery. The quixotic certainty of his hallucination led him, no doubt, to imagine that the whole wealth of the Grand Khan was already in his pocket. Yet it is easy to surmise that, along with the fire of his ardent imagination, another fire, of a grim nature, was then also torturing his soul with a worse, unmixed torment. At the time he put his exorbitant proposals before King John of Portugal, his kith and kin, the converted Jews of Spain, were being hounded out of their homes, covered with shame and opprobrium, and burnt at the stake. He had to triumph for them, to rise the higher for the terrible depths of his brethren's fall. Nothing short of this sombre tragedy, which, as will be shown in due course, was ever present in his mind, can explain the almost diabolic intensity of his pride, which towers for the first time above common sense in these preposterous conditions demanded of King John of Portugal and was in later years to be the main cause of his downfall.

John II, of course, received his proposal with little sympathy. "The King," says Barros, "seeing that this Christovam Colom was a babbler and a vainglorious man in showing off his ability, and more fantastic and [full of] imaginations about his island of Cypango than accurate in what he said, gave him little credit. Yet," Barros adds, not without a certain superciliousness, "under the stress of his importunacies, [the King] sent him to Dom Diogo Ortiz, Bishop of Ceuta, and to Master Rodrigo and Master Josope, to whom the King usually referred these matters of cosmography and discovery, and they all held as vanity the words of Christovam Colom as it was all based on imaginations and things of the Island of Cypango of Marco Polo." (25)

The three men to whom Colón had been referred were fully qualified to judge. Two of them were the King's Jewish doctors and astrologers; the third, the Bishop of Ceuta, later of Vizeu, a Castillian, was not there as the representative of theology, for hardly anyone in those days, but Colón himself, mixed up theology with cosmography; he was there owing to his scientific competence. (26) Science therefore, taking the part of Sancho Panza as the representative of reality, cried to Don Quixote-Colón: "Do stop, Sir Don Quixote. There is no such Cipango, but a wide and impassable sea on which no king in his senses will ever risk his caravels." But Don Quixote would not be Don Quixote and he would not have conquered immortality if he had listened to the voice of mere reality, nor would reality ever rise above itself if a Don Quixote did not now and then appear on the stage of history determined to rouse it out of its sluggish forms and habits. So Colón made up his mind that King John was past praying for, and that the Lord had shut his eyes and ears and all his senses. Who knows? Perhaps he would profit by the "information" supplied him by the would-be discoverer to send a caravel (27) across the ocean and steal Cipango and all that lay behind it, including immortality, from the well-locked chest in which their legitimate owner—and inventor—had kept them till then and which he had unwisely half-opened? He decided to leave Portugal. But where was a discoverer to go? He must have a prince. Only a reigning prince can "help and back" the mighty enterprises of a discoverer. He would leave Portugal; and the Lord obviously agreed with him, since He had just taken to His bosom the discoverer's wife, "for," says Las Casas, always well-informed of the Lord's intentions, "it was meet that he should be unencumbered of the care and obligation of a wife for a business in which God was to occupy him all his life." True, his little boy remained, but he could more easily be disposed of. His Portuguese days were over. With typically Jewish adaptability he had become a Portuguese. "Colom had married into that Kingdom," (28) says Oviedo, "and had become a natural vassal of that country by his matrimony." With typically Jewish mobility he was ready to shift his allegiance again. What was his allegiance? The greatest Spanish genius of his race was but a few years later to coin that admirable answer which Calisto, the lover of Melibea, gives to the question: "Are you not a Christian?" "I am a Melibean," says Calisto. (29) Colón was neither Genoese nor Portuguese nor Castillian, nor even Jewish. He was Cipanguish. He belonged to the Ocean Sea. He had no other fatherland. For him a country was but the land behind a harbour where his three caravels awaited him. But—which land? Once Portugal was struck out of his map there were but three countries left big enough to grant him his golden spurs: France, England and

Castille-Aragon. He "knew," from d'Ailly, and had duly noted in his own hand, that "the French and the English are not skilled in astrology." (30) Yet France and England were kingdoms worth considering, with many harbours and not a few caravels. He would send his brother northward.

As for him, Castille was of course the obvious choice. It was the most important sea-power; it had the best tradition of cosmographical learning. And it was the country in which his brethren were suffering death and humiliation—therefore the country in which and *over* which he, a *Converso*, was to win his golden spurs.

So, to Castille. But, stay, who says that over there, when putting my case before astronomers and other learned men, I shall not be again defeated by my inability to provide a concrete argument, an authority, a map? That Toscanelli. . . . Here, in Portugal, it was a liability because I could not quote it: there, in Castille, it might be an asset. Why not? One day Colón went into the closet where he knew the precious map and letter lay forgotten under layers of dust. He had in his hand a book of his own, the *Historia Rerum Ubique Gestarum* of Pope Pius II. He drew the document out from its pigeon-hole, and on one of the blank pages of the volume he copied it. Cautious, as usual, he omitted the essential data, such as the point of departure from which the calculations of the length of the crossings had been made; then he took enough notes to copy the map at leisure; and, finally, having secured the treasure which he needed as scientific credentials for his Spanish quest, he left the room, knowing that, though the King of Portugal might consider him a traitor, he was safe with posterity. (31)

And so, his precious map and letter in his wallet, close to his heart, with his little Diego, then five years of age, for his only companion, Colón stole out of Portugal for the last, and this time the successful, stage of his quest. Brave as Don Quixote, he walked straight towards danger. In his heart he felt "the fire of his enterprise"; and over the hills and beyond the Guadiana River, the eyes of his mind could see the fires of religious fanaticism consuming his kith and kin, the flames through which he was to walk to victory: fire was meeting fire.

PART III

CRISTÓBAL COLOMO,
AN ADVENTURER IN CASTILLE

CHAPTER XI

JEWS, CHRISTIANS AND *CONVERSOS*

WHEN Colón turned his face East again and entered the lands of Castille, he was coming home in more ways than one. Spain had been a Jewish national home for centuries. No country—save Palestine—had come to be so closely identified with the Jewish race. This was partly due to the inherent Oriental nature of the Peninsula, which at all times makes it so attractive to Easterners; Spain as a geophysical environment enhances all things Eastern: three Oriental races—the gypsies, the Arabs and the Jews—have been raised to the highest pitch of creative activity in Spain.

But in the case of the Jews, the Iberian Peninsula was also a home for reasons of antiquity. Jewish tradition goes back as far as the days of Solomon for the first settlement of the Jews in Spain, and even credits them with the founding of Toledo, the name of which has been considered by some rabbis as a form of the Hebrew word *Tholedoth*, meaning *generations*. Though it is only natural to surmise that coast-settlements of sea-traders may have existed as early as 1000 B.C. (1) when the Phoenicians, close cousins of the Jews, were establishing a profitable trade with the rich and attractive Peninsula, historically ascertained immigration begins with the great exodus caused by the destruction of Jerusalem in A.D. 74 under the reign of Vespasian. From that date until their expulsion in 1492, the Jews enter so deeply into the life of the country that the history of Spain cannot be written without them. "It would be difficult," writes the best Spanish authority on the subject, "to open the history of the Iberian Peninsula, whether civil, political, religious, scientific or literary, without meeting on every page with some memorable fact or name relating to the Hebraic nation." (2) Finance, trade, industry, politics, law, scholarship, science, and especially medicine, letters, all the forms of civilised life, except perhaps the plastic arts, bear in Spain the stamp of this most active, industrious and creative people.

Their fortunes upon the Spanish soil, during the fourteen centuries in which they inhabited it, varied considerably, as they were bound to do, with the deep changes which the Peninsula had to undergo, first as a Roman province, then as a Visigothic kingdom, finally as a frontier-land between Christian Europe and Moslem Africa, during seven centuries of life in common, through peace and war between Moors and Romanised Celt-Iberians.

A detached survey of this period leads to a number of well-established conclusions: (3)

(1) After phases of anti-Semitism and of oppressive legislation, particularly at the beginning of the Visigothic period and after the Moorish invasion, the Jews found in Spain greater prosperity and greater freedom to organise their own religious and political life than in any other European nation.

(2) In no country and at no time in history did the Jewish race share in the financial administration of the royal and of the feudal States, and even in the economic life of the rich and powerful families, to the extent it did in Spain. (4)

(3) The Jews were a most useful factor in the development of the Iberian civilisation, owing to their important contribution to the industrial, agricultural and commercial life of medieval Spain and to the stimulating effect they had on the intellectual activity not merely of Spain but, through Spain, of the whole of Europe.

(4) The monarchs of Christian Spain held on the whole, with few exceptions, to a tradition which led them to consider themselves as the natural protectors of the Jews. Legally, the Jews "belonged" to the Crown. "My Jews" will write Ferdinand IV, when strongly putting down an attempt to persecute them. The greatest kings, Ferdinand III of Castille, Jaime I of Aragon, were definitely and actively pro-Semitic. On the death of Ferdinand III his son Alfonso X, who was to found in Toledo a famous centre of astronomic learning, mostly Jewish, built a mausoleum in Seville in honour of his father, on which he wrote the dead King's praises in Castillian, Latin, Arabic and Hebrew.

(5) Persecution rose mostly on waves of popular origin, usually at the instigation of some agitator. It was always frowned at by the King and by the great. In modern language, we would say that persecution was always a "democratic" feature. Its causes may be summed up as follows:

(a) The tradition that at the advent of the Moors, in 711-15, the Jews had opened towns and fortresses to the invaders and accepted the charge of the conquests made, thus enabling the Moors to march on to further victories. This fact, historically ascertained, was bound to leave a deep trace in the Spanish-Christian nation. (5)

(*b*) The envy produced in the poorer classes by the wealth and prosperity of the Jews. Exceptionally industrious and intelligent, the Jews rose easily up the social ladder of wealth. Those who were wise, generous and clean, rose one way; those who were unwise, mean and crafty, rose another way. But *all rose*.

(*c*) Usury. It is a well-established fact that usury was predominantly a Jewish speciality in medieval Spain. Throughout the fourteen centuries of their residence in the Peninsula the Jews seem to have been unable to realise the danger which they were allowing some of them to accumulate on all of them by letting usury be identified with Jewry in the imagination of the Spanish people. Church Councils and Royal *Cortes* bear a constant witness to this evil.

(*d*) The predominance of the Jews, almost to the exclusion of Christians, in the administration of taxes, which brought on them the odium of extracting the money from the unwilling payer. This feature is universal: in all the Spanish kingdoms and at all times the tax-gatherer is a Jew.

(*e*) A tendency to take part in internal feuds and "politics," which was usually resented and heavily paid for when the party they had chosen was defeated.

(*f*) A number of popular beliefs relating to the abominations which the Jews were supposed to commit, some based on tolerably reasonable fact, such as their tendency to proselytise (why shouldn't they?); some on wild generalisations based on criminal cases, famous precisely because they were so exceptional, such as the prevailing notion that on Good Friday they crucified young Christian boys; some simply absurd, such as the belief that Jewish doctors (most doctors were Jews) poisoned their Christian patients whenever they could.

It will be easily seen that all these "causes" are rooted in one only cause which explains them all: *difference*. There is an apologue in the Talmud which puts the matter in a nutshell. Three drops of oil asked to be allowed into a jar of water. The water refused, because, it said, if you come in you will not mix, you will come to the top, and whatever we do afterwards to clean the jar, it will for ever remain oily.

Difference is the only real cause of the century-old troubles which afflict Israel. Wherever it goes it is different; and therefore whatever it does is found wrong. Tax-gatherers, usurers, ostentatious persons and criminals are found everywhere: every nation abounds in and has to put up with them; but when they happen to be Jewish, every nation resents, as coming from a stranger, that which, coming from its own kith and kin, it has to swallow in silence. Nor is the negative side of the sheet compensated for by whatever distinction the Jews achieve in science, letters or other walks of life, for, it is felt, such a distinction honours Jewry rather than the nation in which the talented men happen to dwell.

Difference, however, was a universal feature in Spanish medieval life. The Peninsula was split into Moorish and Christian kingdoms; in the Moorish kingdoms there were a considerable population of Christians who had been converted to Islam or remained Christian under Moorish rule—and, of course, many Jews. In the Christian kingdoms there were many converted, as well as many unconverted, Moors and many communities of Jews. It is difficult for us to imagine the complexities of life in the Peninsula in those days. An oath before the law, for instance, had to be different according to the religion of the litigants, of which there were six combinations, assuming there were only two litigants.

But that is precisely why the Jewish question became acute by the end of the fourteenth century and finally led to a crisis in the fifteenth. Because by the end of the fourteenth century the Christian element in Spain had acquired such a predominance that the body politic could no longer tolerate the difference. A living body is given a piece of meat, i.e. a piece of "different" life. It digests it and *assimilates* it, i.e. it abolishes the difference. Two hours after an astronomer, a pianist and a cat have partaken of the same beef at dinner, that beef is no longer ruminating, but measuring the stars in the first, playing a nocturne in the second, and mewing at the moon in the third. Meat is life cut off from its source, and therefore inert. But the Jewish people, though cut off from its source, is not inert. It has kept intact its vigorous distinctive spirit through the centuries. The body politic of the Spanish nation, which was beginning to assert itself at the end of the fourteenth century, could not assimilate the Jews.

This is the reasonable, historical way of looking at it. The mistakes, oppression, crimes and misdemeanours of the Jews, and the fanaticism, cruelty and gullibility of the Christian anti-Semites of Spain, must be considered as mere forms; the substance of the Jewish tragedy in Spain comes from the fact of *difference*.

Hence the peculiar part played in this tragedy by the converted Jew, i.e. by the Jew who had *tried* to be assimilated. Spanish history shows that the *Converso* was often the worst scourge of his race. Many of them took upon themselves the task of attacking the "reprobate Jews" for their contumacious resistance to the Word of God, with a zeal far exceeding that of the old Christians. The persistence of the "different" Jews was bound to produce a deep irritation on those who had sacrificed their faith in order to rub out that "difference," a resentment against the obdurate ex-brethren who prevented them from achieving complete assimilation. This circumstance explains what at first sight might appear monstrous—the anti-Semitic tendency of the *Converso*. The tradition was old. It had begun, curiously enough, with a document to which Colón attached so much importance that he had it copied in his Book of Prophecies: (6) the letter written in Arabic in 1066 by Rabbi Samuel of Morocco to Rabbi Isahak of Sujulmenza, and which, translated into Castillian and Catalan, and later into Latin, won considerable fame in all Christendom; forty years later, Rabbi Mossé, baptised as Pero Alfonso, published his *Dialogues against the Impious Opinions of the Jews*; (7) in 1263 and 1264, friars of Jewish origin held public controversies with rabbis before the King of Aragon, and published anti-Jewish books, the title of one of which already reveals the rising cruelty of the passions under the mental sharpness of the controversy: *The Poignard of Faith*. (8) The name seems to have caught on, for in the late fourteenth century the Dominican Fray Pedro de Barcelona, also of Jewish descent, published his *Poignard of the Jews*.

This fourteenth century was fatal to the Jewish race all over Europe; the Black Death which desolated every European nation in turn raised a blind anger first in Germany, then in other peoples, against the Jews, whom they imagined to be the authors of the pest—a tragic but significant example of the dangerous effects of "difference." The efforts of Pope Clement VI to arrest this outburst of senseless fanaticism were of no avail. Spain, where the pestilence made many victims, also felt its anti-Semitic after-effects, which began with grim massacres in Barcelona and Gerona. Yet these events were but the forerunners of the wholesale persecution which began in Seville in 1391 under the leadership of the Archdean of Seville. This priest, Don Ferrán Martinez by name, stubborn to the point of rebellion, and relying on the popular favour, defied direct orders from the pro-Jewish King, Archbishop and Chapter, and led the crowd, against the royal arms, to a wholesale massacre and loot of the rich Jewish quarters of the town. Like a forest fire, the pogrom "caught" in many other towns, with similar terrible effects. The wealthy "juderías" of the towns of Spain were destroyed by loot, their inhabitants destroyed by murder. The great Chancellor, Pero Lopez de Ayala, was to write later in his dry, implacable style: "And it was all cupidity to rob rather than devotion." (9) The loss to Spain's economic life was incalculable. Under the pressure of events, many Jews left Spain. (It is very likely that Colón's ancestors fled to Genoa at about this date. Weaving was a peculiarly Jewish profession in Mediterranean Spain.) Many became Christian. Conversions on a small, individual scale had always occurred; but this was the first movement of wholesale conversion in the Peninsula. The leader was Fray Vicente Ferrer, who was to be canonised and become St. Vincent Ferrer. One of his most signal successes (10) was the conversion of Selemoh ha-Levi, a famous rabbi, known in all Spanish Jewry for his scholarship and talent, who became a no less famous prince of the Church as *Don Pablo de Santa María.*

This illustrious *Converso*, Don Pablo de Santa María, was the chief leader of Spanish anti-Semitism in the fifteenth century. Equally respected for his science and for his virtue, he rose rapidly in the Church and in the State and became Bishop of Burgos, tutor to Prince John (the future John II of Castille), and Chancellor of the Kingdom. A true father of the Church in more ways than one, Don Pablo de Santa María placed in the highest posts of Church and State his numerous, and, it would seem, gifted, family. By his own unrivalled authority over Church and State, and with the help and collaboration of his numerous and gifted sons, this man, no doubt upright and honest, but moved by a strong passion against his former brothers in religion, successfully organised and led a campaign of opinion and legislation which was to culminate not only in the expulsion of the Jews in 1492, but in the relentless persecution of the *Conversos* by the Inquisition which began towards 1483 and was to last for centuries.

Pablo de Santa María was the first to draw a distinction between *faithful*, i.e. converted, and *faithless*, i.e. unconverted, Jews. During all his life, which was very long, he remained an inveterate, intelligent and active enemy of his race. He began his official activities by drafting and promulgating the *Ordinance on the Enclosing of Jews and Moors* (January 2nd, 1412), (11) known as the *Ordinance of Doña Catalina*, by the name of the English Queen Regent of Castille who signed it. The twenty-four articles of this law aimed at the complete annihilation of the material and moral share which the Jewish people had carved for themselves in the land.

The influence of this anti-Jewish Jewish family throughout

the fifteenth century could hardly be exaggerated. The central figure of this century, (12) Don Alvaro de Luna, powerful Prime Minister of a weak king (John II, Queen Isabel's father), faithful to the Spanish royal tradition, was a protector of the Jews. But, despite his genuine efforts to win over to his side the Santa María family, these powerful *Conversos* remained his adversaries, and Alfonso de Santa María, son of Don Pablo and his heir in the see of Burgos, was instrumental in bringing about Don Alvaro's downfall. On his way to the scaffold, Don Alvaro received spiritual help from a friar of St. Francis, Alonso de Espina. This friar, also a converted Jew, was to carry one step further the anti-Semitic work led by Don Pablo de Santa María.

The next reign, that of Henry IV, is also governed by the *Conversos*. The rising favourite, Diego Arias Dávila, is a converted Jew. The favourite, whom he gradually displaces, Don Juan Pacheco, is a Christian son of a Jewish father. Arias Dávila was not, however, an anti-Jewish *Converso*, (13) and, despite the *Ordinance of Doña Catalina*, he allowed the Jews to recover control of State and feudal tax-gathering. The representatives of towns and cities in the Cortes of 1462 asked that the Jews should again be allowed to trade with the Christians and lend them money (without usury). This petition showed that intercourse, even though defective, is better than no intercourse. Public opinion seemed to be veering round in favour of the Jews.

But Fray Alonso de Espina was watching. He had risen rapidly and had become confessor of King Henry IV (it must have been an appalling task if the King did unburthen his soul) and Rector of the University of Salamanca. This man, of a lower stamp than Don Pablo de Santa María, published in 1459—when Colón was a boy of eight—his treatise *The Fortress of the Faith*, (14) a violent attack against all Jews—"faithful" as well as "faithless." Incredible as it may seem, such was the path which this Jew chose for himself and which he followed relentlessly. He rehashed the vilest tales which popular tradition had kept alive about the race whence he sprang; he decided in favour of compulsory baptism, against the official opinion of the Church; but worst of all, he roundly accused the *Conversos*, of whom he was one, of betraying their faith in secret; and, recalling the Visigothic laws which punished new Christians relapsing into Jewry with the death penalty, he wrote these words, pregnant with a dreadful future: "I believe that if in this our time a true *inquisition* were made, numberless would be those who would be given over to the fire amongst those who would really be found *judaising*; who, if they are not down here more cruelly punished than public Jews, will be burnt for ever in eternal fire." (15)

Nor was this a mere rhetorical outburst. The fiery Franciscan (Franciscan! the cruel irony of it!) invited the Jeromites (16) to petition the King jointly for an Inquisition and, straining at the leash, began agitation by means of the broadcasting of those days —sermons. The technique of false news was already at his dipsosal. One of his co-agitators declared in a sermon that he possessed material proof of one hundred circumcisions of sons of judaising Christians. He was convicted as a liar both by the King and by the General of the Jeromites, an enlightened order which withstood with admirable sense and charity the onslaught of the demagogic, anti-Jewish wave. Fray Alonso de Espina wrenched from the weak hands of Henry IV a decree ordering a "general inquisition," i.e. a general enquiry on "clandestine Jews," to be entrusted to the Bishops. The Archbishop of Toledo handed over the business to Fray Alonso de Oropesa, the General of the Jeromites, whose report impartially condemned old Christians and new Christians for their lack of charity; and the threat petered out.

Yet the militant attitude of the Franciscans led to a serious cleavage between old and new Christians, which gave rise to disastrous and sanguinary fights in several towns (Toledo 1467, Córdoba 1473, Segovia 1474, a singular case in which Don Juan Pacheco, a *Converso*, led the populace in a riot against the *Conversos*). Here again the movement was demagogic; the surging wave was popular; their leaders monks or artisans: while powerful lords such as the Count of Cabra and Don Luis Portocarrero wisely forestalled the pogroms in their townships; or, like Don Alfonso de Aguilar, in Córdoba, espoused the cause of the *Conversos*, fought for them and led them into exile; or, like the High Constable Don Miguel Lucas de Iranzo, paid with their lives, at the hands of an irate crowd, the crime of having lived up to the gospel by protecting the persecuted.

The reign of Ferdinand and Isabel begins, therefore, in the midst of this turmoil. Not two but three are the parties to the debate and to the riots and wars which it entails—the old Christians, the Jews, and the *Conversos*. From the religious point of view, the old Christians feel abhorrence for the "law of Moysén" and suspicion towards the possibly hypocritical *Converso*; the Jews keep a distant silence, perhaps a veiled contempt for the law of Christ, but their contempt for the *Converso* is deeper and hardly hidden; while the new Christians, anxious to rule out the distinction between "old" and "new" within Christianity, are equally keen to draw the line between faithful and faithless Jews. From the civil point of view, the old Christians are apt to realise that the Jews, after conversion, are just as able to come to the top of the ladder and to find out the lucrative spots as their unbaptised brothers used to be; the Jews brood over the fact that conversion is a weapon wherewith their baptised brethren beat them easily in the daily struggle; while the *Conversos*, benefiting in actual fact from the advantages of the two states, able as Jews, admitted to all posts as Christians, soon fill up the higher ranks of State and Church, and tend to become stiffer even than the old Christians had been, in closing the barriers of State and municipal posts to their rivals the "faithless Jews."

The influence of the Jews, faithless or faithful, on the events of the reign is greater than can be imagined. The very foundation of the reign, the marriage of Isabel, her choice of Ferdinand of Aragon instead of the King of Portugal or the Duke of Berry, brother of the King of France, was mostly a Jewish affair. Ferdinand of Aragon was then (1469) King of Sicily. His father, John II of Aragon, sent to Castille as negotiator one of his wealthy *Conversos*, Mosén Pedro de la Caballería the younger, the founder of a family of Aragonese *Conversos*, as powerful in Aragon as the Santa María family was in Castille, and author also of a violent anti-Jewish book, *Zeal of Christ against Jews and Saracens*, (17) in which he declared of the Jews that "on their ruin would be raised and built the true and universal Christian hope." The young negotiator found his task eased by two prominent old Jews, who had not taken the trouble to be baptised: Don Abraham Senior of Castille, who was to house the princely suitor and take him to meet his betrothed in a secret interview; and Don Selemoh of Aragon, who presented Isabel with a magnificent golden necklace, which Ferdinand had bought, of course, with Jewish money.

Both the King and the Queen were literally surrounded by *Conversos*. When John II had sent Ferdinand as King to Sicily, (18) he had given him a council composed for the greater part of new Christians; when the young Prince came back to take on the Crown of Aragon, he did but increase the power of the *Conversos* over his councils and household. Several members of the La Caballería family were made members of his council; his two secretaries were *Conversos*; five brothers Sánchez, sons of a baptised Jew, were given five high functions of State, including those of General Bailiff of Aragon, Grand Treasurer, and

Rational Master (a kind of Minister of Finance)—a mere choice in a long list of the new-Christian dignitaries who surrounded the King. In military affairs, Ferdinand entrusted *Conversos* with the three key posts of his kingdom: the places of Perpignan and Pamplona and the fleet off Majorca. The Church of Aragon was also to a considerable extent in the hands of new Christians. The private chamberlain (*Camarero*) of the King, Cabrero, was also one of them.

The administration and household of Queen Isabel—financial, military and ecclesiastic—was no less Jewish. Her three secretaries, one of them Hernando del Pulgar, often quoted in these pages, were all new Christians. The Marquesa de Moya, her inseparable friend, who closed her eyes at death, was the wife of Andrés Cabrera, a prominent *Converso*. And *Converso* also—at any rate on his mother's side—was the Queen's confessor, Hernando de Talavera, one of the saintliest and most high-minded men of that or of any other age.

Fray Hernando de Talavera was to take so important a share in the reign, and particularly in the life of Colón, that time must be taken to strike a closer acquaintance with him. He was no ordinary man. Endowed with a quick intelligence, which he stimulated by study, and with a quick temper, which he completely mastered by discipline, this gifted man seems to have achieved a perfect life of selflessness. He became Prior of that Prado Monastery, on the meadow (*prado*=meadow), on which the famous picture gallery was to be erected later. He acquired complete authority over the monks by taking on the most difficult and even the lowest and most repugnant tasks for himself. The Queen wanted a confessor. Her advisers unanimously said: "The Prior of the Prado." He was summoned. He disliked the worldly distinction but accepted the duty. The scene of her first confession with him has been left us by Fray José de Sigüenza, the historian of the Order of the Jeromites to which Fray Hernando de Talavera belonged.

"She used to kneel with her confessor by a seat or small bench; Fray Hernando arrived and sat on the bench to hear her confession; the Queen said to him: 'We must both kneel.' The new confessor answered: 'No, Madam, I must sit and Your Highness must kneel, for this is God's tribunal and I am here on His behalf.' The Queen kept silent and went through it like a saint, and they say she said later: 'This is the confessor I was looking for.'" (19)

He certainly acquired an unrivalled authority over the Queen and King (whom he also seems to have confessed), as shown in a letter from the Queen to him in which, with great humility, she excuses herself from accusations of frivolity made to her by him in a letter, evidently lost, but, to judge by the Queen's answer, of a severe character. The Queen explains that she had not danced on the occasion to which he referred, that she was wearing clothes bought the year before and had only bought one new dress. Through this correspondence (20) we gain so intimate a view of the interplay between these two leading spirits of that day that we are not entitled to rely on guesswork or on the caprice of passion for the interpretation of Isabel's intentions. Much as we may dislike some of the events of her reign, there is not the shadow of a doubt that this woman was transparently honest, that she had a conscience, and that she had chosen a saint as the keeper of it.

Fray Hernando de Talavera became the Queen's confessor in 1478. The Inquisition was first suggested to the King and Queen in 1477 by a Dominican, the Prior of St. Paul in Seville, strongly backed by the papal nuncio Nicolao Franco. The King and Queen yielded, reluctantly, but, as Henry IV had done before them, they asked the great Cardinal of Spain, the Archbishop of Seville, Pero González de Mendoza, to undertake an "inquisition," i.e. an enquiry. The aristocratic Cardinal applied evangelical methods—preaching, persuasion, schools. But the people, the monks, the lower clergy, were certainly of the opinion set down by Bernáldez: "In all this, two years were wasted and it was of no avail, for each did what he was used to do; and to change one's habits is a wrench as bad as death." (21) In 1479 the King and Queen yielded to popular pressure and founded the Inquisition.

Few institutions have raised hotter passions in the heart of men; few have darkened the light of reason in its critics with blacker smoke. A balanced and detached estimate of its principles and practices lies beyond the boundaries of this work. But this must be said: a condemnation, from our century, of deeds of another century may be a more or less pleasant self-indulgence: it is not understanding; therefore it is not history. The historian must try to live up to the maxim of Spinoza: "Do not weep; do not wax indignant. Understand."

And to begin with, the Inquisition was not meant to, nor did it actually, act against the Jews, i.e. against the "faithless" or "public" Jews; but only against those amongst the "faithful" Jews who were "secret" Jews, i.e. against the Christians who, to use a phrase of those days, "judaised." In trying to understand the motives of the King and Queen when they accepted an idea which ran so patently athwart the trend of all their policy—were they not almost completely served by new Christians?—we have therefore to consider:

(1) Whether they thought the movement too popular to be resisted.

(2) Whether, on a close study of the actual situation, they did not come to think that there was some substance in the popular complaint.

The sensible view is that both these reasons weighed on the decision of the King and Queen. That the movement was popular was obvious, and the cause of this also—we have met with it before: envy. It can be read between the lines of Bernáldez's history, when he explains that "this heresy" spread through "the great wealth and vainglory of many learned men and doctors and bishops and canons, and friars, and abbots, and accountants and secretaries and agents of Kings and of great Lords." There is the original passion, which leads the simple curate to abominate the *Conversos* because they avoided the ways of living of the Christians, "for you must know that before the Inquisition their ways were just those of the filthy Jews, owing to their constant intercourse with them: thus they were gluttons and big eaters, and never lost their Jewish tastes in eating [. . .] stews of onions and garlic, and fried in oil, and the meal cooked in oil [. . .] to avoid lard, and oil with meat is a thing which gives an ill smell to the breath; and their doors smelt foul owing to those stews and they themselves had the same smell as the Jews owing to their stews and to their not being baptised." (22)

The good curate gets somewhat mixed up in his arguments towards the end, and gives perhaps a too material sense to the phrase "odour of sanctity." But this page is worth quoting, for it shows how Jewish Spain has remained despite the Inquisition. Cooking in oil is no longer Jewish but Spanish cooking. Not in vain did the water in the jar say: "And, no matter how well we wash the jar, it will for ever remain oily."

This text reveals in a vivid way the main source of the trouble: *difference*. Even if they were sincere in their new faith, the new Christians ate differently; smelt differently; lived differently; worst of all, they *were* different. And as they rose, they gave offence.

Moreover, were they sincere? A general answer, either way, is out of the question. There are on record types of *Conversos* of a high moral standard—such as Pulgar—and men of *Converso* descent, such as the Prior of the Prado, Hernando de Talavera, who were saints, nearly perfect men. But the material inducements to become a Christian were so tempting for a Jew that it is only human to suspect that if some of the best Jews became Christians led by the spirit, many of the worst Jews became Christians led by the flesh. There can be no doubt that the accusation of secret Judaism corresponded to an all too frequent reality. Bernáldez is ludicrous in his bias, but his details often have a ring of genuine truth, such as when he asserts that the children were washed when they came back from being christened, to wash away the baptismal waters. And Jewish authorities have plainly given it as a fact that, *in general*, conversion was but feigned. Thus Kayserling: (23)

"The conversion was, however, only external, or feigned; at heart they adhered loyally to their ancestral religion. Though outwardly Christians, they secretly observed the tenets of the Jewish faith; this was not infrequently true even in the case of those who had become dignitaries of the Church. They celebrated the Sabbath and holidays, assembled in subterranean and other secret synagogues and practised Jewish rites in their homes."

A similar conclusion may be drawn from the chapter devoted to the question by Hernando del Pulgar, (24) himself a *Converso*, who quietly acquiesces in what was being done.

This, then, is the key to the painful and awkward facts which, otherwise, are so difficult to explain. We know that Talavera disliked the idea. "The Prior of the Prado," says Zurita, "was contrary to the said office of the Inquisition." (25) Yet he acquiesced in it. Weakness is out of the question. How could the saintly confessor of an upright queen countenance such a gross breach of the evangelical spirit in which all his life was steeped? Because the King and Queen were frightened by a state of affairs *partly existing*, partly exaggerated by fanatical bigotry and, worse still, by envy. The tradition that Spain was to become a Jewish-controlled land may or may not have existed amongst the Jews—it probably existed in the exalted and foolish ones and was smiled or frowned at by the wise ones; but the belief that it existed in them was entertained in Spain by the anti-Semitic *Conversos* themselves. It is a prominent argument in the two dialogues published by Don Pablo de Santa María when well over eighty, (26) and in which he recalls Jacob's prophecy *Non auferetur sceptrum de Ihuda*, which, he declared, the Jews applied to their dominance of Spain. This rash accusation against the "faithless Jews," coming from a prominent ex-Rabbi who ought to know what his kith and kin were thinking, recoiled on his own unfortunate class, the *Conversos*, who paid with their lives at the stake, fully ten years earlier than their "faithless" brethren with their exile, for the fears thus raised in the Christian people of Spain.

That there was fear is obvious, since there was cruelty. But let us try to understand. The King and Queen could not be accused of anti-Jewish bias. Practically the whole of their household was Jewish. There is an episode in their reign which aptly illustrates their independence from Rome, the earnestness of their statesmanship and their freedom from merely racial prejudice. It is the more eloquent as it occurs when the Inquisition is already in full swing. The see of Cuenca fell vacant in 1482. The Pope appointed his nephew, a Genoese. The King and Queen remonstrated (27) that they wanted their sees given to subjects of their kingdoms "presented" by them, amongst other reasons, because these sees were often close to Moorish territories and had to be entrusted to persons of the land. The Pope resisted. The King and Queen ordered all their subjects in Rome to leave, and threatened to call all the Princes of Christendom to a Council, to study this and other points relating to the Church. The Pope sent an ambassador to them. Not only was he not received, but he was requested to leave the dominions of the King and Queen. In the end, the King and Queen won; the Pope withdrew his previous appointment and the King and Queen secured that of their own trusted candidate, Don Alonso de Burgos, chief chaplain of the Queen. *Don Alonso de Burgos was of Jewish race.*

This concrete case, one out of many others, should suffice to show that the King and Queen were sincere in their respect for racial differences, once they were satisfied that conversion was genuine and that the faith was firmly held. But this is what they were told: "The Jews propose to get hold of Spain. Their great Rabbis, when converted, have let us know. Seeing they could not do it if they remained openly Jewish, they have been converted. But their conversion is only external and feigned. Some of them, such as Alonso de Espina, King Henry IV's confessor, have said so. Danger. Instant danger. See how they have coiled themselves like a serpent round your two Highnesses." And who shall say that the picture was altogether devoid of plausibility?

A legend which arose in Castille under the reign of Peter I may well be the plastic representation of this fear of the Jewish race coiling itself inextricably round the people of Spain. Peter used to wear a waistband given him by his wife Doña Blanca, who wanted to expel the Jews from the realm. His neglected mistress, Doña Maria de Padilla, secured the waistband with the help of an old Jew, very powerful at Court, Simuel Ha-Levi, and this Jew bewitched it so that the next time Peter wore it—it was during a Court ceremony, when he was in his regal attire—the waistband turned into a serpent which, to the horror of all those present, coiled itself round the King's neck. (28)

Of course there was a strong Jewish case. The terrible massacres of 1391 had driven underground their threatened faith, and a tradition of dissimulation had set in which was but too well justified; conversion was seldom followed by assimilation, at any rate in the lower ranks of society: the historian of the Jeromites, pro-Semitic like all his order, points out "the bad habit which Spain has of treating those who are converted from these sects (Jews and Moslems) worse than before their conversion, for they hardly ever called them by their names [i.e. the Christians insult them], whence it follows that many of them refuse to adopt a faith which shows so little charity in those that profess it." (29) Moreover, envy, the canker of the Spanish character, was certainly the most active motive behind the campaign, as was to be shown in the sixteenth and seventeenth centuries, when, all danger or shadow of danger burnt away by the Inquisition, clever, learned, and therefore prosperous *Converso* ecclesiastics were hounded out of their livings by the Inquisition under the demagogic pressure of ignorant monks. (30) The passionate and uncritical historians who have attributed the principle and policy of the Inquisition to royal or Church greed (31) miss both the obvious disinterestedness of the King and Queen and the real nature of the psychological fears which lead to the Inquisition. In the same chapter in which he records the birth of the Inquisition, Diego de Valera tells how King Ferdinand, having sentenced to death a local magistrate (*regidor*) of Toledo who had perpetrated many abuses and crimes, was offered a big sum of money for reprieving him, and how the King refused the money and had him executed, his wealth confiscated to compensate those he had injured for their losses, and the remainder given to the poor. (32) The money confiscated by the Inquisition was earmarked for the wars of Granada. It helped to pay for Colón's voyages.

The real motive which explains that the Inquisition attacked preferably the rich, was envy. It was the peculiar hatred of the neighbour's success which, like a rank weed, grows in the stagnant soul of the indolent. Here, again, Bernáldez is a faithful interpreter of the popular feeling when he complains of the protection extended to the Jews by the kings and the great, "owing to the great profit which they drew out of them." (33)

The reign of Henry IV produced a curious satirical document which may be taken as the literary expression of this form of anti-Semitism, fermenting in market-places, and monasteries of the mendicant orders: *Las Coplas del Provincial.* It is cast in the form of a swift series of questions and accusations addressed by the Provincial of the order to the "Monastery chapter," i.e. to the whole of Castille, the first "friar" castigated being the King himself. The wit is low and even coarse; the atmosphere distinctly that of a monastery parlour. The oft-recurring note is that the "friar" accused is of Jewish descent. (34)

Difference again. What else could raise such passions as fear and cruelty? And as fear and cruelty call out cruelty and fear, the *Conversos* fell a prey to the temptation: in Seville, they prepared an armed rising in the house of the most powerful of them, Diego Susan; but, denounced to the Inquisition by Susan's own daughter, they were given over to the flames.(35) In Zaragoza, the conspiracy took place in the house of a man whose family name is written large on the golden book of the discovery of America: Luis de Santángel; it led to the murder of an inquisitor, Pedro de Arbués, and, of course, to the stake and the flames for the conspirators.

By this time (September 1485) Colón was already in Castille. In his scanty luggage there was a book in which the envious and trained eye of an inquisitor would have spotted the *Converso* at once. Attitudes had become so set that they could easily be detected and interpreted. If a man's trend was to draw the borderline between old Christians and Jews (whether "faithful" or "faithless"), he was an old Christian; (36) if he put the frontier between Christians (whether "old" or "new") and faithless Jews, i.e. if he laid stress not on the difference between Christian and Christian, but on that between Christian Jew and Jewish Jew, he was a *Converso.* Now, in his d'Ailly, Colón had written in his own hand a revealing marginal note which seems to have attracted less attention than it deserves from the point of view of Colón's origin and race. It is a long note, in which Colón tries to prove that Esdras *was* a prophet (for otherwise, of course, Esdras's opinion on the width of the sea would not matter at all); and in this note there occurs the following passage: "But this prophecy is not accepted by the reprobate Jews ['Iudei reprobi'], yet it has been accepted by the innumerable ones amongst them who have believed in the Gospels. Israel has thus been split into two branches—a division predicted as inevitable by the Prophet Samuel to King Saul. The reprobate Jews themselves hold [. . .] Esdras as [a] canonical authority." (37)

Read in the context of that day, this document, so insistent on the distinction between the *reprobate* Jew and the faithful Jew, shows that Colón reacted as a *Converso* to the chief problem of the day.

CHAPTER XII

DUKES AND MONKS

BRAVE though he was, Colón was cautious, and he certainly knew that in Castille, amidst grandees and inquisitors, he would have to walk with wary steps. In this land, new and yet so old for him, the mental-moral soil was broken, crossed and recrossed by forbidding abysses which emanated all kinds of poisonous gases and murderous flames. Not till, in recent years, the desolation of class war and the abomination of totalitarianism have come to split up our own mental-moral soil in a similar fashion, has the West known a time when life was as dangerous and as worthless as it was becoming then in Spain. A man may be a dreamer without being a fool, and Colón was certainly no fool, though he was a dreamer.

Where did he stand? There is no doubt that in religion he was a sincere Christian. The curious non-committal expressions on the subject which we have noted in Las Casas (1) do nevertheless respond to some real *distance* between the religion of the discoverer and that of his chief biographer. One may be a Christian in so many ways! Leaving aside the *Conversos*, numerous as they certainly were, who had espoused the Christian faith under the pressure of fear (2) or under the stimulus of gain, a mere glance at the psychological situation is bound to show that the *Converso* must have held his faith with a difference. He came from another religious climate—no matter which. He was therefore bound not only to carry over into his new religious home the deeper-lying trends and tendencies which the old home had developed in him; but also to feel in himself the effects of the mere change, considered as a psychological experience in itself.

There are at least three features in the Jewish faith which Colón certainly transferred to his Christianity: the prophetic sense; the sense of having been selected by the Lord for a specific purpose; and, last but not least, the contractual sense, that attitude which sees every event of life as a transaction and expects and demands a definite *quid* for every *quo*. In those days these features were dangerous in Castille. To the trained and

136

tender nostrils of the Inquisitor they smelt Jewish as much as Bernáldez's oil-and-onion stews. The prophetic sense was no doubt very Christian, but it was not for a mere layman to go about interpreting sacred words: the missionary sense was a gross breach of Christian humility; and that contractual sense smacked too much of the hard bargains which poor old priests had to close with wealthy Jewish money-lenders, to make both ends meet.

Nor was this all. For the change of religion, the mere fact that the spirit of a man has passed from one religion to another, was bound to create another *difference* of its own with the old Christians, just as an engrafted plant differs from a seed-born plant. We have no reason for thinking that in Colón's case conversion took place in his lifetime. It is more natural to think that it happened when the family emigrated, probably during the pogroms at the close of the fourteenth century. But the effects of a graft of this kind do not vanish in two generations. Under his Christian orthodoxy Colón was bound to have kept the sense of the unity of all men which is the main lesson of religious change. We know, indeed, that this was the case, and that every time he felt free to speak, or even when he allowed his sincerity to overflow the brim of his safety, he expressed in unmistakable terms a fine human and universal sense.

Colón was probably unconscious of most of this. A *lived* psychological situation differs as much from the same situation analysed later as the same sea seen by a swimmer from under the water and seen by a loafer from the shore. Yet he cannot have failed to be aware of what was then happening in Spain, and his cautious mind must have carefully pondered over the best way to move in the new waters which he was to navigate.

The foremost enemies of the *Conversos* were then the Franciscan friars. This religious order was behind—and at times ahead of—the main drive which led to the Inquisition. The obvious move was therefore to enter Castille under a Franciscan cloak. And to be sure, the next time we hear of Colón—and the first time we hear of him in Castille—he is talking to a Franciscan friar in the monastery of La Rábida,(3) two and a half miles from that very Palos from which he was, eight years later, to start on his great voyage.

Why Palos? The district was an obvious choice for many reasons. We must not imagine that countries were then so neatly separated as they are now in our time. Relations *within* any country between the chief centre and the periphery were less easy and frequent; and, therefore, relations across the frontier between regions of two different countries close to the periphery were relatively more frequent and easier. The Condado de Niebla, as it was then known, i.e. all the region of the Guadiana mouth and Huelva, was then in the closest possible touch with Portugal (as a matter of fact, it still is). Colón himself had two brothers-in-law living there: Pedro Correa, Iseu Perestrello's husband, (4) and Miguel de Mulyart, the husband of Violante or Briolanja Muñiz; a circumstance which suffices to explain that Colón should have entered Castille that way to leave his little Diego with one of his aunts, as he himself said to the friar who questioned him. (5) The whole region lived in a close sea-comradeship and rivalry with Portugal, sailing to the Canary, Madeira and Cabo Verde Islands and trading with the coast of "Guinea" and "the Mine" in all kinds of commerce, including black slavery, for which they often contended with the Portuguese in the fourteenth and fifteenth centuries.

A man who is anxious to escape unnoticed is not likely to take the slow land way when a quiet sail will spirit him away from the harbour before anyone can realise he is thinking of going. Although there is little indirect and no direct evidence on the subject, it is, however, safe to say that in all probability Colón left Lisbon by sea and landed in Palos.

It is idle to speculate as to whether he knew or did not know people in Palos before he went there. He did in Huelva, anyhow, which is next door to Palos. But, on arriving in the town, he learned that a short distance away, up on the hill, amidst the umbrella-pines, there was a house of St. Francis. That—said Colón to himself—is the place for me. And he walked up the gentle slope leading to the monastery. He found there a genial monk, Fray Juan Pérez, (6) who listened with an open mind to his wonderful tale and called the monastery physician, who dabbled in astronomy, to listen to this newcomer also. Fray Antonio de Marchena, the real astronomer of the monastery, happened, unfortunately, to be away at the time. But Colón obtained two advantages from his happy inspiration: his boy found a home and a school; and he was able to strike new acquaintances and to gain a new assurance as to his enterprise, among the sea-folk of Palos.

This little harbour was then a miniature Lisbon, in close touch with it, and therefore haunted by the same yarns, legends, hopes and visions as the capital of discovery which Lisbon was then. Here, in the monastery of La Rábida, a Castillian pilot, Pedro de Velasco, told Colón of the Portuguese expedition led by Diego de

Teive, (7) in which he, Velasco, had served as a pilot, a significant proof of the close ties which united Lisbon and Palos in those days. Velasco must have been then retired from sea, and of a ripe age, for his tale refers to the times of Prince Henry, quite forty years earlier. They had left Fayal Island and sailed one hundred and fifty leagues under a north-west wind, and "on their way back they discovered the Island of Flowers, guided by many birds which they saw flying towards it, for they knew them to be land- and not sea-birds, and therefore they thought that all those birds were going to some land to sleep." We may imagine the eager eyes of the future discoverer of a whole world of flowers, drinking in this story and treasuring in his mind for further use the value of birds as harbingers of land. It is also possible to surmise that this was the period of his life when he heard from his brother-in-law, Correa, (8) the valuable information that in Porto Santo he had seen such traces of unknown land as a piece of carved wood and big canes holding gallons "of water or of wine" within each section. Correa was then captain of Porto Santo, having bought the captaincy from the heirs of Rabbit-Perestrello, which did not prevent him from living comfortably in Castille.

Much refreshed and confirmed in his faith, Colón left for the Court as soon as possible, with the added assurance of a Franciscan visa on his passport. The Court was then in Seville, where the King, pleased with the recent capture of Setenil from the Moors, came to spend the winter with his chief adviser and Quartermaster-General—the Queen. Colón, however, did not apply straight to the monarchs. He went first to the most powerful of Spanish magnates, the Duke of Medina-Sidonia. Don Enrique de Guzmán, second Duke of Medina-Sidonia, was the scion of a family which had carved for itself the most magnificent feudal domain in the whole Peninsula; he was the richest man in Spain, and practically reigned over the district which surrounded the harbour of Sanlúcar. Had he wished to do so, he might have financed the whole enterprise himself. But either he did not wish or he was not able to undertake the task, and he walks out of Colón's life-story with all the pomp and circumstance of so mighty a lord, but without the wreath of American laurel which his memory would be for ever wearing had he listened to the blue-eyed, red-haired, hot-tempered dreamer whom he sent away empty-handed.

There was no lack of mighty dukes in those days, and having failed with Medina-Sidonia, Colón applied to Medinaceli. Don Luis de la Cerda, fifth Count and first Duke of Medinaceli, had to yield to the Duke of Medina-Sidonia in point of wealth, but by no means in point of rank; for while Don Enrique was the bastard son of a noble father, Don Luis was the legitimate heir of the eldest branch of Castille: his direct ancestor was the first-born of Alfonso the Sage, whose sons had been dispossessed of the Crown by their uncle, Don Sancho. He might therefore have looked down even on Queen Isabel, but he did not, for he had learnt loyalty from his father, who, seeing his own father veer away from the loyalty due to the King, had preferred to remain loyal, and, says Pulgar, "served the King all his life with so much obedience that his perseverance in service was an example of loyalty to others." (9) In short, a knight without reproach, unless we count against him that "he was conquered by the love of women and was loved by them." The Duke had inherited the loyalty of his love-smitten father towards the royal Crown, and he gave a singular proof of it with regard to Colón; for, though he was certainly caught by the plan of this imaginative stranger, whom he housed and protected from want from the autumn of 1484 till the beginning of 1486, (10) he gave up to the Crown the honour of the undertaking.

The Duke resided then in El Puerto de Santa María, known in all southern Spain as El Puerto. He listened to Colón with evident sympathy, and, if we are to believe Las Casas, he went so far as to order the ships to be built in his own shipyards at El Puerto. Colón, whom the generous Duke had sheltered from want by providing for all his expenses out of the ducal household, must have then been nearer than ever to that state of exhilaration which precedes the contemplated achievement of a dream. It was then, while in El Puerto, coming down every day to the yards to cast a loving glance at his rising caravels, that a one-eyed sailor told him of a voyage he had made to Ireland when "he saw that land which the others believed to be over there and which they imagined to be Tartary, coming round by the West." (11) That was it! Don Quixote-Colón must have heard this tale with great elation. It was all true, no matter what sceptics might say. Was not the Duke made of flesh and blood, and as important a person as any in the kingdom but the King and Queen? And had he not granted him "three or four thousand ducats to make three ships or caravels"? Here they were, in the Duke's yards, (12) still in their stays, but soon no doubt floating, "furnished with food for a year or more"—he knew he would not need as much if Esdras were right, as he was sure to be, since he was a prophet—"and of exchange-goods and crews and all that might seem necessary"; and had not the Duke given orders "with the utmost solicitude that the ships should be laid in the yards in that very river of El Puerto de Santa María, and that work should proceed apace till they were finished"? Just as Don Quixote, on entering the Duke's castle and seeing himself treated as a knight-errant, "for the first time fully knew and believed himself to be a knight-errant, true and not fantastic, seeing himself treated in the same way as he had read that such knights were treated in bygone centuries," (13) so Colón, when the Duke "had him summoned and, treating him as he deserved, in keeping with his own noble and kind nature and with the weighty appearance and gracious presence of Colón, sought detailed information" on his plan, must have felt for the first time that he was fully a discoverer of new islands, true and not fantastic, beyond a real sea.

The year, however, was not favourable. Everybody's thoughts were on Granada, still held by the Moors. "In the name of Jesus Christ, Saviour and Redeemer of the World," says Bernáldez, "on the fifteenth day of the month of April of the year 1485 of our Redeemer's birth, the illustrious and famous King Don Fernando with his host very large and very marvellous and very beautiful, sallied forth from Castille to wage war on the Moors." (14)

The base, he says, was Córdoba. The King and Queen and their chancery had spent the winter in Seville and gone over to Córdoba in March, where on their summons the great leaders of their nobility—and therefore of their armed forces—had congregated to begin the spring campaign. The Duke of Medinaceli was there. (15) The campaign was exceptionally strenuous, but also exceptionally brilliant. Coín, Cártama, Benamaquex, Ronda and Marbella, these two last the two keys of Málaga, fell to the King's arms between the middle of April and Midsummer's Day when he returned to Córdoba. (16) There was more fighting later; so that the Duke, busy with the Moors, could hardly have lent much attention to Cipango and the caravels until the autumn. Unfortunately, in that autumn, Andalucía was afflicted by severe floods. Rain, says Bernáldez, began on November 11th and did not stop till Christmas, and "it rained so hard and so much water that never had those who were then alive seen so much water nor so much flood in so little time." (17) The monastery of Las Cuevas, which was soon to become a kind of home for Colón, was then under water "and the monks had to be taken out in boats."

In the end, however, it was not Nature but human nature which proved fatal to Colón. The loyal Duke felt scruples, whether spontaneous or due to some conversations he might have had in Córdoba during the year, no one knows. There is, moreover, a third possibility, perhaps the closest to reality: that the scruples felt by the loyal Duke may have been raised by Colón himself. For, after all, a duke has been known to appoint Sancho Governor of the Island Barataria, but no duke ever appointed anybody Admiral of the Ocean Sea, nor gave anybody the right to wear golden spurs; and it would be wholly in keeping with Colón's character—highly imaginative in his vision, cautious and secretive in his ways to attain it—if, having convinced the Duke and even converted him to his "enterprise" and carried him along by being, or pretending to be, enthusiastic about the caravels and the food for a year and what not, he should then have gradually led his powerful convert to back him at Court rather than take direct responsibility for the enterprise.

The story is told by the Duke's own hand in a letter written on March 19th, 1493, to the Cardinal of Spain (18) upon hearing of the arrival of Colón in Lisbon in the glorious aura of his discovery: "And as I saw that this enterprise was [so important that it should be left] for the Queen our Lady, I wrote about it to Her Highness from Rota and she answered that I was to send it to her. I sent it to her then. [. . .] Her Highness received it and passed it on to Alonso de Quintanilla."

This letter, read in conjunction with statements of Colón and of his earliest biographers, enables us to say with some confidence that the plan for the discovery of what was to be "America" was officially put before the Queen's Chancery on January 20th, 1486, the date from which Colón dates the beginning of his "service." It was put before the Chancery, but not before the Queen (save in so far as she had "accepted" the business on receipt of the Duke's letter). During that winter the King and Queen had gone North, "for," says Pulgar, "the land of Andalucía was tired out [and] the King and Queen decided to let it rest for the winter and go to the Kingdom of Toledo." (19) Ferdinand and Isabel were itinerant monarchs, and their Court, which was also a central administration and the military headquarters of their permanent army against the Moors, severely drained the resources of whatever part of their kingdoms they chose as their temporary residence.

On January 20th the King and Queen were in Madrid. (20) Colón went to Córdoba and, following no doubt his instructions, he applied to Alonso de Quintanilla, *Contador Mayor*, i.e. Chief Treasurer and Accountant of the King and Queen, "a remarkable man and a zealous servant of the King and Queen, for whose prosperity he was keen to work." (21) This man, we are told by a usually reliable chronicler, "gave orders that he should be given food and other necessary things, out of pity for his want," a circumstance which is bound to strengthen our suspicion that it was Colón who left Medinaceli rather than Medinaceli Colón, for, otherwise, it is not in keeping with so powerful a magnate that the man he had housed for over a year should have been dropped in want merely because he, the Duke, thought the scheme he advocated should be left to the royal initiative. Finally, after no doubt many long and wearisome hours spent in anterooms waiting to be received by many important persons who have left no trace in history, Colón, through Quintanilla, gained access to the Cardinal of Spain. (21)

Quintanilla was then sure to be deeply concerned with the state of the royal treasure. The weak spot of the Spanish monarchy—it remained so right through its splendour under Charles V and Philip II—was the lack of an adequate financial machinery for the State. The royal State was still far too much like a royal estate, and no adequate distinction was made, nor even seen, between the finances of the nation and those of the two persons at the head of it. Ferdinand and Isabel spent all they had in their crusade against the Moors, and they accepted as gifts, for which they felt grateful, any financial or military help which their magnates thought fit to put at their disposal. In the winter of 1486 the Treasury was bone-dry. "All that was collected from the crusade and from the subsidy of the clergy, and from the [money] sentences on those who had judaised and were reconciled with the Church and from their [the King and Queen's] ordinary income and from every part where money could be found, [the King and Queen] ordered it to be devoted to the war." (22) The King and Queen had to borrow from the private purse of "some singular persons" (23) amongst their subjects, an euphemism by which cautious Pulgar no doubt quietly suggests that the money came from the two great Jews Don Abraham Senior and Don Isahak Abarbanel, associate managers of the royal revenue. (24) It is therefore but natural to surmise that when Quintanilla heard the magnetic Colón put to him in so convincing and "hot" a language the marvellous possibilities of a voyage West for securing gold, silver and precious stones, the mouth of the loyal Treasurer must have watered. No wonder that he soon managed to open for the discoverer-to-be the well-guarded doors of the Cardinal of Spain.

Don Pero González de Mendoza, Archbishop of Toledo, Cardinal of Spain, was known as the "Third King," for he wielded the combined power of the first see of the Spanish Church (the first ecclesiastical and one of the main feudal lordships of those days) and that of his functions in the State—as what we would call today the Prime Minister. He was a man of first-rate intelligence, courage and virtue, and came from the Santillana house, one of the most illustrious in Spain. Having gained access to this powerful man, Colón was sure to be heard by the King and Queen.

The King and Queen came back to Córdoba towards the end of April or the beginning of May. (25) It was then, in the warm spring of 1486, in Córdoba, that Colón set eyes on the King and Queen for the first time. We know next to nothing about this interview. The three leading persons of the epoch, and in particular in the great design then taking shape, were of about the same age: Ferdinand, just over thirty-four; Colón, not quite thirty-five; the Queen, just thirty-five. The best impression, the most convincing, of what must have happened on that day, is that conveyed by Bernáldez in his brief narrative. It comes to confirm the essential, the living character of Colón's plan, as it has more than once been interpreted in these pages on the strength both of direct observations and of the records of those who wrote about it at the time.

"And so Colón came to the Court of King Don Fernando and of Queen Doña Isabel, and he related to them his imagination, to which they did not give much credit [. . .] and he talked to them and told them what he said was true and showed them the world map, so that he put them in desire to know about those lands . . ." (26)

CHAPTER XIII

THE SAINT AND THE HERO

WHEN Colón was exerting on the King and Queen that "singular grace which [the Lord] had granted him for his ministry" (1) and which made him capable of "inducing [others] to see him easily with love," he was fully aware of the value of his prospective prey. The King and Queen were then at the head of the most important naval power in the Western world.

The epoch-making marriage of Ferdinand and Isabel had united the forces of two of the three great naval nations of Spain. Earlier on, the Crown of Aragon had found in Catalonia one of the strongest and most creative traditions of seamanship then known in the Western world. The Catalans had shown themselves not only daring and enterprising mariners, but shrewd organisers and legislators of sea-affairs, as proved by the success achieved in the whole Mediterranean by their Consulate of the Sea and its written laws.

They had been pioneers in African discovery; (2) they had crossed the Mediterranean and settled in Greece; they had maintained in Majorca a brilliant centre of cosmopolitan studies; so that when, after their federation with the Crown of Aragon, an enterprising monarch, James the Great, raised the power and efficiency of the Catalan-Aragonese marine and navy to a level till then unknown in those seas, it came to be said that the fishes of the Mediterranean wore on their silver coats the red-and-gold bars of Aragon.

James the Great flourished in the same century as the great king who laid the foundations of the Castillian sea-power. Ferdinand III achieved his great victory, the conquest of Seville, with the effective collaboration of his sea-power. (3) This king, the same prince, famous for his pro-Semitic policy, whom the Church canonised as St. Ferdinand—the same St. Ferdinand whose name was constantly on Colón's lips—was the monarch who founded the high office of *Almirante Mayor*, or Chief Admiral of Castille, on which Colón explicitly modelled his own exalted title, and the same who, by a consistent policy of commercial liberalism and protection to harbours and sailors, established the supremacy of Seville as a trade capital and that of the Castillian marine as one of the chief sea-forces of the West.

While the vital impulse for all this sea-activity was, of course, born on the sea-coast, in the sturdy sailing-centres of the North, and later (as they were liberated from the Moorish sway) of the South, the institutional instincts which canalised it and turned it into an instrument of the State came from inland, for the chief town in sea-affairs and the birthplace of the Spanish admiralty was Burgos, a table-land city over three thousand feet above sea-level, where the "University of Merchants" laid the foundations of Castillian sea-laws as the *Consulat del Mar* had done in Barcelona for Aragon-Catalonia.

King Ferdinand granted the Genoese an exceptionally liberal charter in Seville. They were to have "a quarter, a granary, an oven and a bath" (4) of their own; while two "consuls" chosen by them and appointed by the King would judge all civil cases between them, and even cases in which the defendant was a Genoese and the plaintiff a Sevillian. This charter, which was successively confirmed by all Spanish monarchs, including Ferdinand and Isabel, was so liberal that when, in the following reign, the Catalans asked for privileges for their merchants in Seville, they referred to it as a model.

Commerce, luxury and the merchant marine grew apace under this enlightened royal attention, and even what we would nowadays call the *navy*, a less permanent institution than it became in later times, was of course bound to benefit by the added skill in shipbuilding and navigating which this progress implied. King Alfonso X armed several "fleets" during his reign, one of which, that which co-operated in the siege of Algeciras, (5) was composed of no less than eighty galleys, twenty-four vessels and a great number of smaller craft; he erected great shipyards in Seville and instituted the order of St. Mary of Spain to reward valiant deeds at sea.

Relations with the rising sea-power of the North were not always cordial. The Cortes of 1348 asked that the King should request the King of England to pay compensation for damages caused to Castillian ships by English corsairs in time of truce; and the cities of Ghent, Ypres and Bruges asked and obtained from King Edward II of England a safe-conduct for all Castillian, Catalan and Majorcan ships and merchants trading with Flanders; while, to make the story even, the King of England complained that the Castillians bid fair to gain control of all the sea, to judge by the assaults they made on his ships, and to put a remedy to this situation he made a treaty in London with delegates of the sea-towns of Castille and Biscay. (6)

Yet in 1371 twelve galleys of Castille, with the help of artillery, used for the first time at sea, (7) destroyed thirty-six English ships, captured their general, eight hundred men and a rich treasure which they were conveying, then terrorised the English coast in the same Christian way which Drake was later to reciprocate. By dint of perseverance in this spirited policy, the Spanish Crown conquered the heart of an English princess, Catherine, daughter of the Duke of Lancaster, who married the future Henry III. In 1398 Henry III promulgated a law (8) providing that any merchant, "Genoese, Placentine [from Piacenza] and Catalan, as well as French and English," should prefer Castillian to other ships on equal terms of freight to convey goods exported from his kingdoms. He waged a successful sea-war against Portugal, while a famous Castillian seaman, Don Pedro Nuño, beat off new English attacks in the Ocean, and carried the war against the English right into their harbours.

This reign saw the first expeditions to the Canary Islands organised by free-lance seamen, Andalucian and Basque, who looted five of the islands just to show the natives the headway which Christianity had made in Europe since the days of its Founder. This expedition, more lucrative than honourable, established the right of Spain over these islands which the Portuguese had discovered half a century earlier; their first real conqueror, however, was a Frenchman, Jean de Bethancourt, who acknowledged the suzerainty of the King of Castille. The rivalry between the two Spanish Crowns—that of Portugal and that of Castille—entered then on an acute phase, (9) Prince Henry, the Navigator, having tried to take possession of all or some of the islands, by diplomacy or by force or even by purchase, from the King of Castille.

By 1460, at the death of Prince Henry, Pope Martin V had "granted" the Portuguese all discoveries made or to be made beyond Cape Bojador up to the "Indies," i.e. to the Asiatic Continent. But the rivalry continued.

It was not merely political; it was popular. It was stimulated by the stories of wonderful wealth which circulated about "India," an elastic word in those days, covering Ethiopia and Guinea, and everything that is rich and far-off. It was raised to a fever by the discovery of La Mina, a region on the west coast of Africa, in which gold was freely offered by the natives for any trifle brought over from Spain, and particularly for big sea-shells which "were held in high esteem because in those parts there fall many lightning strokes from heaven and those barbarians believed that anyone who had on him a shell such as these was safe from lightning"; (10) some of these shells came to be worth as much as twenty reals of silver in the harbours of Andalucía.

The King and Queen tried to put some order and authority into this spontaneous, popular and profitable trade, for "it happened that one trip was worth ten thousand *pesos* of gold, each peso being worth ten florins of Aragon," and they bethought themselves of their "fifth," due to them as Lords of that land. The title was, to say the least, doubtful. But later events were to show that it had been put forward as an exchange pawn in a diplomatic game with Portugal, a game, moreover, which could not be fully played till Ferdinand and Isabel made good their more solid claim to the Canary Islands, which they definitely conquered and attached to their Crown in a campaign begun in 1479. (11)

The year was by no means propitious, for on July 29th, (12) at midday, "the sun made the most terrifying eclipse that those then alive had ever seen, for it covered itself wholly and remained black and the stars appeared in the sky as if it were night [. . .], and never again did the sun recover its colour, nor was the day ever clear as days used to be before, and so the weather turned very misty." No wonder that there were "schisms and deaths" between the two captains sent by Ferdinand to reduce the barbarous Canarians to Christian order and brotherhood. A second expedition, however, sent in 1480, under Pedro de Vera, free from the evil effects of the eclipse, was less "schismatic" and more successful. At about the same time, the King and Queen sent to La Mina a fleet of thirty-five caravels loaded with shells and brass goods and other boons of civilisation to relieve the blacks of their gold. This expedition was most successful, but on its way back the Castillian fleet was thoroughly beaten by the Portuguese, and so the gold, going down step by step from clever swindle to brave robbery, finally landed in the Treasury of the King of Portugal, no less Christian in his love of gold than the King and Queen of Castille. It so happened that the Portuguese had just been thoroughly beaten inland by the Castillians, so that the prisoners were exchanged, and that was about the only really Christian action which can be recorded in this whole affair.

It soon became patent that the King and Queen were playing more or less fortunately on both "Guinea" and the Canary

Islands, to get rid of the Portuguese claim on the Canaries in exchange for an equal surrender of their shadowy rights over Guinea. The treaty of Alcaçobas (1479-80) definitely leaves the Canary Islands for Spain and the Madeira, Azores and Cabo Verde Islands for Portugal, and reserves Guinea and the right of discovery "south of the Canaries and along Guinea" for the Portuguese. (13)

* *

It was at this point that an enthusiastic foreigner came from Portugal, precisely to put before the King and Queen a plan of discovery. This plan was clear and forcible while he was expounding it, vague and nebulous as soon as his warm voice had died out and his fiery blue eyes no longer illumined the room: for Colón was no clearer in Castille than he had been in Portugal. Still, for all his imaginative language and enthusiastic fire, he did speak degrees and meridians and he did display navigating charts. The King and Queen, tempted by his "singular grace," must have felt incompetent to judge the merits of the scheme he had put before them. While they went on with their pressing task, the war against the Moors, they decided to send Colón to a Commission of experts.

No dilatory measure, to be sure, but the most elementary step to be taken in the circumstances, and one which Colón should have interpreted as a singular success on his part—indeed the acme of achievement. (14) What more could he expect to obtain from a first interview on so vague a proposal (for it was vague, as every competent and detached student knows nowadays) than to see himself the subject of the labours and attentions of a Commission of experts especially appointed by the King and Queen for the purpose?

The Chairman of this Commission was no less a person than Fray Hernando de Talavera. He was not merely the Queen's confessor; he was a kind of universal minister to her, the jack-of-all-(difficult)-trades of the Crown, the man whose spirit of sacrifice, depth of human insight, experience and intelligence had been tried by the Queen again and again in the last eight years. Would the Queen have put yet another burden on so overworked a man (15) if she had not thought Colón's idea worth the very best attention, at least *prima facie*? The facts are here as patent as they can be, and should have—but have not—proved beyond cavil, misinterpretation or distortion, whether due to prejudice or to mere fancy: (16) the King and Queen attached enough importance to Colón's first statement to set up a competent Commission "in order that they should hear Cristóbal Colón with more detail and that they should see the quality of the proposal and the proof he gave that it was possible, that they should confer and discuss upon it, and then should report fully to their Highnesses." (17)

We know the exact day when King Ferdinand left Córdoba that year—on May 15th. (18) The decision to appoint the Commission must therefore have been taken towards the beginning of May. The King and Queen, who had visited Galicia in the later part of the year, spent in Salamanca the "hard of the winter," from November 30th to January 26th. (19) It is generally believed, though without indisputable proof, that the Commission worked in Salamanca, where it was relatively easy to find the necessary expert advice and reference books and maps. Either it was not in a hurry or it found great obstacles in its way, for, as a matter of fact, it did not report till 1490.

On the strength of Fernando Colón's and of Las Casas' versions (20) two errors have gained credence for a time about this Commission: that Talavera was hostile to Colón on narrow theological grounds; and that the Commission was incompetent. Las Casas' own competence may be judged from the very words in which he condemns the Commission: "The lack of mathematical sciences, and of knowledge of the old histories of those who had been entrusted with the business" (21) is for him the first cause of Colón's setback; so that he considered the knowledge of old histories to be on the same plane as mathematics for deciding on the merits of a plan for crossing the ocean! The verbose and irrelevant erudition wherewith he justifies the discoverer's plan after the event, shows that, even half a century later, he was still utterly unable to realise what the objective, reasonable, one might even say, scientific position had been. His testimony is of no value whatever to understand what actually happened in the Commission.

Spain was then one of the best centres of cosmographical learning in Europe, (22) and Salamanca University, far from being a nest of bigoted obscurantists, had amongst its staff one of the greatest Jewish astronomers of the day—Abraham Zacuto—and was one of the first homes of learning in all Christendom to adopt the Copernic system in its teaching. It had, moreover, undertaken the task of editing the Astronomical Tables of Alfonso the Sage. Las Casas himself, so biased in these matters, informs us that the Commission was composed of astronomers, cosmographers and mariners as well as of "philosophers." Dr. Maldonado, the Governor of Salamanca, who was a member of it, also says it contained "learned men and mariners." (23) So that this Commission, entrusted to a man as high-minded, disinterested and intelligent as Talavera, was bound to be competent.

As for Talavera himself, his feelings can be easily guessed. He was no less out of the common than Colón—but in such a different direction of the human compass that a thorough understanding was well-nigh impossible between them. Colón was a hero; Talavera was a saint. This is no literary fancy; it is a matter-of-fact description of the two types. Colón, with his fire to do something, to conquer, to reach the summit of glory, must have appealed to Fray Hernando as a poor man suffering from a monstrous swelling of the self, and the good prior's charitable soul must have ached for him. Those who have read any feeling below the best in Talavera's behaviour towards Colón would not have fallen into that error if they had known his exemplary life. His yearning did rise high, as did that of Colón—higher indeed, much higher, than the proud, after all self-seeking, ambition of the hero; only he sought to rise not by a stiff-necked exaltation of the self, but by a humbling of it, by being always ready to let it be trampled under the feet of the first beggar on the road. Issued from the same Jewish blood which, in Asia Minor, flourished under both Asiatic and European winds, Colón and Talavera incarnated the types of manhood which have stood for centuries as the models of high achievement respectively for East and West —the saint and the hero. Colón's motto might have been *Ad augusta per angosta*. Talavera, had he known it, would certainly have adopted as his that gem of St. John of the Cross:

> " Y abajéme tanto, tanto
> Que fuí tan alto, tan alto,
> Que le dí a la caza alcance."

> " And I abased myself so much, so much,— that I rose
> so high, so high,—that I overtook the game."

It is therefore safe to surmise, on the strength of these psychological tensions which were obviously at work, that, while Fernando Colón and Las Casas are correct on the fact of Talavera's opposition to Colón, they are in error as to their analysis of its motives and causes. The fact itself of the opposition must indeed be qualified. Talavera was utterly unable to throw his own self athwart any fellow-being in a deliberate and conscious fashion.

His biographer tells a delightful story to this effect. (Fray Hernando was by then Bishop of Avila, the Queen having obliged him to accept a see after many refusals: "How is that, Fray Hernando?" said the Queen. "Are you not going to obey me one single day when I obey you so many?" (24)) He had been given the arduous and unpleasant task of ferreting out some suspected leakages in a set of royal accounts, possibly more complicated than they should have been; and the two officials with whom he was discussing the matter met him with so formidable an array of figures that the good friar, who though a saint was by no means a fool, suspected the worst and became insistently concrete and inquisitive; the accountants tried to tire him out, but he was indefatigable, and when the whole afternoon and a good part of the night had been spent in this tiresome process, one of the accountants, either really in a temper or by way of changing his tactics, banged the table, upset the candlestick which fell, plunging them in darkness, and left in a fury. The good bishop stooped in silence, relit the candle and accompanied the boorish accountant to light the way for him down the dangerous steps. The man was moved and ashamed: "Sir, it is not meet for so saintly a prelate to light the way for a man as discourteous and wrongheaded as I am"; whereupon Fray Hernando: "On the contrary, it is the business of prelates to light the way for those who err, and you might fall down those steps." The man took the candlestick from the bishop's hands, returned to the papers, and "all was done as he [the bishop] wanted." (25)

No intrigue, no antagonism, no "opposition," in the current sense of the word, could ever come from such a man. But, when Fate put Talavera face to face with Colón, there was bound to result a lack of sympathetic understanding of this great hunger on the part of one who had killed all hunger in himself, of this great imagination on the part of one whose whole soul was centred in the spirit, and of this great urge to action on the part of one whose acts were so many sacrifices of the self on the altar of eternal being. In short, when the King and Queen entrusted Colón's plan to Talavera's guidance, they were unwittingly bringing together two mutually incomprehensible worlds, two uncompromising absolutes.

This deep-lying, subconscious discord between the hero and the saint is, no doubt, the chief cause of the delay of four long years—1486-90—inflicted on the impatient discoverer by the Spanish Court. He complained bitterly and frequently about it, and even after he had discovered "the Indies" and vindicated his faith, he came back again and again on "these six or seven years of grave grief"; (26) "seven years was I in your Royal Court during which everyone to whom I spoke of this enterprise thought it was a mere jest." Las Casas describes this period with unusual felicity: "He entered then into a terrible continuous, painful and tedious battle, for, to be sure, a material battle fought with weapons would not have been for him as hard and horrible as that of having to instruct so many persons who did not understand him, though they claimed they did, to answer and bear with many who neither knew him nor cared for him, while receiving many insults of words which afflicted his soul." (26)

Yet all was not bad in his situation, and much of the bad was inevitable in the circumstances, given his case, his character and the historical conjuncture in which he had to work.

At any rate, his stay in Salamanca brought him an invaluable friendship. We need not waste any time in the romantic fancies woven round the famous but certainly imaginary conferences in the University of Salamanca or in its College of San Esteban, in which Colón is shown eloquently expounding to large and enthusiastic audiences a plan of discovery which prejudice and intrigue constantly thwarted. Nothing could be further removed from his cautious, secretive mind, as well as from his aristocratic, exclusive instincts, than this ostentatious appeal to public opinion. His technique throughout was entirely the reverse: discreet work in direct touch with the powerful. The fact that remains when all these historical weeds (27) have been removed is that Colón was patronised by the College of San Esteban, and particularly by Fray Diego de Deza, professor of theology in the University, and if not actually head of the College, one of its prominent lights.

Now it so happens that, next to the Franciscans, the Dominicans were the most ardent champions of the anti-*Converso* drive and of the Inquisition which incarnated it. They were, in fact, a more efficient and dreaded instrument than the Franciscans, owing to their intellectual eminence. It is therefore in keeping with Colón's policy that, having secured a Franciscan cloak in La Rábida, he should have sought in Salamanca the patronage and hospitality of the chief Dominican house of learning of the chief university of Spain. And it is not less significant that the eminent professor of theology who patronised him, the one of whom he was to say in later years: "Since my arrival in Castille he has favoured me and wished me honour," (28) was a *Converso* himself.

Mark these words of Colón: Since his arrival in Castille this

Converso friar of St. Dominic was not merely one of those who considered his plan in an open-minded way; he favoured Colón and always wished him honour. Why should this have been so? Is not this a merely subjective link, not yet discernible in any of the Castillian personages so far met by Colón? Quintanilla and the Grand Cardinal pass him on to the King and Queen, a great service in fact, but an objective service; Talavera, for the reasons analysed above, actually gives Colón (if we are to believe his historiographers) an impression of antagonism; Fray Diego de Deza is the first who, *from the beginning*, wishes him honour and favours him, the first who definitely becomes a partisan on his side.

From this all-important meeting two sets of consequences are to be observed; one is that though Colón does not make much headway with the Commission, he is not dropped by the Crown; the other is that Colón's set of important friends at Court develops and, almost without exception, on the *Converso* side of it.

The Commission did sit collectively to hear Colón. Las Casas is quite positive about it. (29) A member of it, the only one besides Talavera whose name is known, says that "they"—the Commission—"discussed with the said Admiral on his [proposed] voyage to the said islands." He even adds that they "all agreed that it was impossible that what the Admiral said should be true." What did Colón say? We are nowadays in a better position to discuss this point than were Colón's first biographers and the sentimental-romantic historians who followed them. Colón can only have spoken "Marco Polo," "Toscanelli," "Esdras," or a mixture of the three. It is practically certain that he used all three sources, for he was impetuous; but equally so that he did not mention Toscanelli nor produce his map, for he was cautious. This flows from the necessities of the case; for even if he felt fairly safe in Spain, a letter and map secured as he had secured them had better be kept for a more discreet use than a Commission of astronomers and seamen who might wax inquisitive as to how he had come by them. Moreover, Las Casas is quite candid about Colón's reticence before the Commission, even if he is in error as to its cause. He describes Colón before the Commission "giving reasons and authorities to induce them to consider it [his proposal] as possible, though keeping silent about the most urgent ones, lest the same should befall him as with the King of Portugal." (29)

And this, it must be owned, was the second cause why Colón could not make much headway with the Commission. The clear, transparent soul of Talavera must have felt ill at ease listening to this opaque man; and the "learned men and mariners" (29) who made up the Commission must have felt impatient with a man who could be both so vague in argument and so obstinate in purpose, and who would not show a map. (Maps of fabulous islands could be shown to imaginative queens but not to expert cosmographers.) In these circumstances, the marvel was not that Colón was made to hang on and wait instead of being swiftly adopted as the discoverer of America, as so many historians have bewailed, but that he should have been made to hang on and wait instead of having been dismissed at once.

This, it is fair to surmise, he owed to Fray Diego de Deza. For, as luck would have it, this *Converso* friar became a Court power precisely in that year 1486, during the stay of the Court in Salamanca, when he was appointed tutor to Prince John, the heir to the throne. From that moment on, he began a career of swift ascent to prominence which was to culminate in the archiepiscopal see of Toledo and in the succession to Fray Tomás de Torquemada as Inquisitor-General. There is no other explanation than Deza's helping hand to account for the fact that Colón should have been repeatedly granted sums of money by the King and Queen during the year 1487. These sums were no doubt small, yet, given the state of the Treasury at the time, they reveal an exceptional benevolence towards a man who was after all a foreigner and would have had no claims whatever on the royal purse even if he had been a subject of the King and Queen. Colón (and Deza) had followed the Court to Córdoba, in which town, the military base for the Moorish wars, he received three thousand maravedís on May 5th, 1487, another three thousand on July 3rd and four thousand on August 27th, to defray the cost of his journey to the royal camp in Málaga, a town just taken from the Moors (August 18th). All these receipts are extended to *Cristóbal Colomo*, (30) which suggests that in 1487 the discoverer still had himself styled in that way, at any rate in official documents.

Nothing is known of this visit of Colón to Málaga, nor even if, though paid for, it took place. Neither Bernáldez nor Pulgar nor Valera mention Colón when relating the siege. It is, in fact, a significant feature of Colón's life that no one mentions him either in Castille or in Portugal, till after he has discovered "the Indies."

The siege of Málaga was long and stubborn on both sides. The brilliant intervention of the Duke of Medina-Sidonia, the arrival of a powerful fleet, are all duly noted by Pulgar; Bernáldez is most meticulous in his details, and so is Diego de Valera, but even this last chronicler, a specialist of sea-affairs and "discovery," remains entirely silent on the visit to Málaga of the still obscure man who within five years was to sail straight into a New World and to make all the glory of the siege of Málaga sink into insignificance.

CHAPTER XIV

COLÓN-THE-POET BETRAYS COLÓN-THE-KNIGHT

ONE thing we do know about Colón's visit to the camp before Málaga: it led to no result. The situation of Colón deteriorated. Time wears out even well-established positions built on the rock of power; how could it fail to undermine one so weak, resting only on the quicksands of favour? Colón knew the humiliation of having to beg, he whose dreams were a priceless treasure. Nor was the begging of material wealth the most galling: the three thousand maravedis (1) which he received from the royal purse in 1488 were but a trifle anyhow, and for him the more insulting; but the grief of his days, the anguish of his nights was surely that he, who dreamt he had so much to give, had to beg: beg for attention, when he should have granted it; beg for time, when his was the more precious; beg for imagination, when his was resplendent with marvels; beg for a little power, when he had a world of power in his dreams. Have we not been told about his poverty, his cape in holes, his want which had reduced him to resort to book-selling! But that was not the poverty which made him smart. For a man of his mental-moral build, poverty is but a token or measure of deeper needs unsatisfied. "All this delay," says Las Casas, "did not go without great anguish and grief for Cristóbal Colón, for [. . .] he saw his life was flowing past wasted, to judge by the days he would need for his sovereign and enduring work [. . .], and above all because he saw how distrusted his truth and person were, which for generous persons it is known to be as painful and detestable as death." (2) This time was for him a period of spiritual starvation.

No wonder that this is precisely the period of his life occupied by his one love-affair. It is fairly clear that his marriage had been no love-match. There is no trace in his hand or in that of his biographers, no act of his either, to suggest that his wife was ever for him anything more than a useful link with a powerful family. Young and ambitious, Colón was in Lisbon less susceptible to love than when, ten years later, in Córdoba, his dream somewhat sour and stale by repetition in two Courts, doubts began perhaps to cloud his mind and "the fire he brought to their Highnesses" began to carry too many ashes. A dryer soul—possibly a purely Castillian soul, or a harder nature such as his brother Bartolomé —would have gone through this ordeal without feminine help. But in Colón's being there was water as well as air and fire. His spirit had a strong poetic vein, which, though not at its best in his mediocre attempts at rhyming, (3) makes him soar with splendid grandeur in some of his unguarded utterances, and often inspires him with moods of a delicate, almost feminine sensibility. There is a tenderness almost maternal in the way he ends his letters to his son: "Your father who loves you more than himself."

In this year of trial, he met Beatriz Enríquez, who was to be the mother of his son and biographer Fernando. A cloud of mysteries surrounds her, as is the case with nearly everything and everybody concerning Colón. Prejudice and counter-prejudice have fed on this episode of the discoverer's life, much helped by lack of information. (4) Three sets of factors should be considered and, as far as possible, treated separately:—the facts; the systems put forward to explain them; their most reasonable explanation.

The facts are:

(1) Fernando Colón, son of Cristóbal Colón, was born on August 15th, 1488.

(2) He was the son of a Córdoban woman, Beatriz Enríquez, as openly admitted by Colón himself in his Codicil to his [now lost] 1502 testament. (5)

(3) Colón felt "an obligation" and even a "load on his conscience" with regard to Beatriz Enríquez. "For this weighs much on my soul."

(4) There was a mystery or secrecy about it. "The reason for this I am not at liberty to disclose here."

(5) Diego Colón is equally discreet, for in his own testament, while, following his father's precedent, he might have mentioned that Beatriz was his half-brother's mother, he is content to say that "the Admiral my lord left Beatriz Enríquez recommended to me owing to certain obligations he had towards her." (6)

(6) Fernando Colón never mentions his mother.

(7) Colón loved her and esteemed her. This flows from his language and from his acts. On leaving for his fourth voyage he writes to his son Diego: "Take care of Beatriz Enríquez, for the love of me, as much as you would of your mother." (7) He

leaves her a pension at the time, he passes on to her the prize of 10,000 maravedis granted him for having been the first to see land, as soon as he comes back, and carefully provides for her in his will. He entrusts her with the care of both Diego and Fernando when he leaves for his first and most hazardous voyage. He gives important posts to a cousin of hers, Diego, whom he made *Alguazil Mayor* of his first voyage fleet, a post of the utmost responsibility which, for a distrustful man like Colón, implied blind confidence; and to a brother of hers, Pedro, whom he made captain of one of the ships for his third voyage.

(8) He did not marry her.

Such are the facts. The fancies are many: from the romantic twaddle about Colón having saved Beatriz's brother from a dangerous night brawl, to the charitable and decorous twaddle about a secret marriage. (8) The more cynical view that Beatriz was not married because she was, so to speak, unmarriageable, has also been suggested, regardless of the set of facts given above, which unmistakably show that Colón loved and esteemed the mother of his second son.

A more reasonable view might be put forward. Colón did not marry for the reason suggested by Las Casas when he was good enough to let us know the Lord's intentions in taking Colón's wife; he was, above all, to be free to discover his world.

But Colón *needed* a woman's tenderness, because he was a poet as well as a knight, and of a lesser continence than the chaste knight of La Mancha.

Hence the "obligation" and the "load on his conscience." As Colón-the-knight he had sinned. When one needs a woman one is not free to claim freedom from women. Beatriz Enríquez was for him his weakness incarnate.

But who was she? Here more twaddle. Some good people have endeavoured to show that she was of "noble" birth. She was nothing of the kind. Others, on the strength of her love-affair, have gone to the other extreme and made her an inn-servant of easy disposition—as if Colón could have loved that way! Yet, this view rests on a right appreciation of the value of sexual morality in Christian Spain. A girl who gave herself without marriage, *in those layers* of society, i.e. in the lower gentry or middle class, was bound to be disreputable, not merely in an apparent and social way, but in her inward being. Then?

Beatriz Enríquez may have been a Jewess. The sexual morality of the Jews was of course different from that of the Christians. It was no worse, though the Christians thought it so. "They (the *Conversos*) did not believe that God rewards virginity and chastity," (9) says old Bernáldez, always sure to echo the popular view, like an honest, uncritical soul. But we possess a beautiful document of Spanish-Jewish sexual morality in the *Tragi-comedy of Calisto and Melibea* (*circa* 1490-1500) of a *Converso* genius, Fernando de Rojas. In this masterpiece, second only to *Don Quixote* in the annals of Spanish letters, Melibea loves Calisto and gives herself to him, and then faces the tragic consequences of her impulsive and imprudent action. The point is, that while in those days a Christian young woman who gave herself without marriage was almost certainly a good-for-nothing, a Jewish girl who gave herself without marriage might very possibly be a thoroughly decent soul, as Beatriz Enríquez seems to have been. It should be added that her father's name was not Enríquez, but Torquemada. Yes, Torquemada. Now, that was the name of a famous *Converso* family, that of Don Juan de Torquemada, Cardinal of St. Sixt, (10) to which it would appear the famous Inquisitor-General belonged also; and while this is no argument for thinking that Beatriz's father was of the same family, it is one more suggestion added to other features in this episode, all tending to establish the *Converso* environment in which it took place. The last and most significant symptom is the obvious *suppression* of the name of the father by both Beatriz and her brother. It was not unusual in those days that one or other of a man's children should take another family name than the paternal one; but most unusual that *all* should do so. Does not this suggest the disinclination of a *Converso* family to display a name so hated in their midst?

The picture then becomes clear. Colón lives in Córdoba, dejected. He feels the need of a feminine hand. He is thirty-six years of age. She is eighteen to twenty. The idyll is easily woven round his distress, her beauty, his fine looks, "his singular grace" for "inducing others to see him with love," and a common origin, a common fear, a common shame at what is going on under their eyes—the stakes, the flames. Then comes the obstacle in him. Colón-the-knight stiffens up Colón-the-poet; Colón-the-poet betrays Colón-the-knight. And one day, seeing all this suffering added to so much suffering accumulated in that sensitive soul, young Beatriz does what an "old-Christian" woman would not have done—she generously gives herself. (11)

**

She was the only flower on a thorny path. That year, in March, Colón was in Murcia. This is a surmise, but a fair one, for Murcia is a town he visited and in May the King and Queen were there, (12) and why should Colón go to Murcia at all when there is no sea there and his lady-love is expecting a child, if it be not to see or accompany the King and Queen? We know that he was in Murcia because Las Casas records that "a gallegan seaman, Pedro de Velasco by name, told Cristóbal Colón in Murcia that voyaging towards Ireland they went sailing on and advancing so much towards the north-west that they saw land on the West of Ibernia. . . ." (13) How constant in his quest, how sure of what he wants, how keen, however, to find outside witnesses to buttress up his passionately held yet quivering faith!

This was the year 1488. His great design had shone in his inner world for fully ten years. Lisbon, Palos, La Rábida, Seville, Sanlúcar, El Puerto, Córdoba, Salamanca, Córdoba and Seville again, and Murcia now; King John, the two Dukes, the Grand Cardinal, the King and the Queen, a row of cities, a sequence of great potentates, dead memories dragging behind his weary soul. Should he begin all over again? His thoughts went back to Lisbon. In a moment of despair he had written to the King of Portugal. (14) He assured him of his goodwill and affection and of his desire to serve. He suggested returning, possibly to explain what he had done and to try to convert the King to his views. The King's answer, being dated March 20th, 1488, must have reached him while in Murcia, for in those days postal communications were fitful and slow. It was singularly cordial, so cordial indeed that many scholars had come to think it apocryphal. It is, however, genuine, and reveals how anxious King John was to recover Colón. The King addresses him as "Christouon Collon, our special friend," and, having expressed his pleasure at Colón's letter and the feelings it conveyed, he adds these significant words: "And as you might perhaps harbour a certain distrust towards our justices owing to obligations which you may have, We by this letter, guarantee you that during your coming stay and return, you shall not be arrested, held up, accused, remanded or made to answer for any thing, whether civil or criminal, of any kind."

Several explanations have been attempted for these words, including a possible implication in one of the conspiracies of the day. The most natural has not yet been given. Do we not possess an actual material proof that Colón stole Toscanelli's letter? Who would copy a whole letter on a blank sheet of a book if he were performing an open, fair, legitimate operation? Is it not obvious that this most unusual way of securing a text savours of a surreptitious trick? Do we not possess abundant proof of the secretive character of the Portuguese policy in matters of discovery? And do we not know that Colón left Portugal secretly? It is evident that Colón was not the man to get entangled in conspiracies and other incidents of local interest for which he could feel no interest whatsoever, and that his mind and soul were all centred in discovery. His "crime" was a "discovery" crime. He stole, yes, but what he stole was the way to the New World.

And that is why King John called him back with honeyed words. No one can say what would have happened to Colón had he accepted this invitation which he himself had solicited. King John was somewhat sudden in his acts of justice. Having heard that his young brother-in-law, the Duke of Viseu, was conspiring against him, (15) he summoned the young prince and with a few words, which presumably in their irate eloquence summarised an accusation and a death-sentence, he thrust his dagger into the culprit's heart. This had happened but four years before Colón read the King's professions of friendship. Whether Colón thought about it or not, we cannot tell. But he did not go to Portugal. (16)

His situation in Castille, however, was none too good. It is difficult to form an exact opinion about this period of his life, for the documents available are scanty and may not accurately reflect the real position. This is no doubt the time of want to which some of his chroniclers refer: "He went about for a time in great need and poverty, without being understood by those who heard him," says Oviedo; "And they took all he said to be hollow. And this importunation lasted for seven years, [during which] he made many offers of great wealth and estates for the Royal Crown of Castille. But as he wore a threadbare (or poor) cape, they held him to be fantastic and a dreamer of all he said and spoke about, both because he was an unknown foreigner and lacked friends who would favour him and because the things he proposed to give and achieve were so great and unheard of." (17)

On one point, however, this accurate and human description can be questioned. By 1489 it is impossible to say that Colón was unknown and that he lacked friends at Court. Later events are to show so imposing an array of powerful officials and members of the royal household on his side that it is difficult to see how Colón could be utterly devoid of some kind of a link with most

of them just three years earlier. These friendships could not all
have sprung up by a miracle just at the last moment. It is therefore reasonable to surmise that the black side of this period has
been somewhat overstressed, owing mostly to Colón's own
sensibility, which led him to exaggerate it in subsequent years.
True, he receives little or no help from the Crown at this time,
but this fact may be read both ways, as a sign of dire poverty,
but also as a sign that he did not need such help. A glance at
the list of the persons whom we know for certain to have been
his friends will suffice to show that the reasonable view is the
second of these two alternatives.

***

Leaving aside Quintanilla, the Cardinal of Spain and Diego de
Deza, the next protectors of Colón recorded by tradition are
Andrés Cabrera and his wife Beatriz Fernández de Bobadilla,
Marquess and Marchioness of Moya. Both enjoyed the closest
possible friendship of the Queen. He had been one of the first
partisans in the protracted fight for the succession to the throne,
and the Queen had rewarded his loyalty with a marquisate. She
was the Queen's intimate friend, the more beloved since that famous
night during the siege of Málaga when a Moor nearly killed
her in the royal tent, believing he was murdering the Queen. (18)
Cabrera was a *Converso* and on that account is favoured with a
special "copla" in the famous *Coplas del Provincial*: "He is said
to have eyes like a goat (*cabra*=goat), and to be the son of Pedro
López de Madrid, in Cuenca, Rabbi David." (19)
Colón was no less befriended in the King's household than in
the Queen's. As later events are to show, he was able to benefit
by the efficient help of Juan Cabrero, the *Camarero* or Private
Chamberlain of King Ferdinand. Cabrero was more than a
mere servant to the King; he certainly had been able to win his
confidence and respect, for his name is to be found amongst the
executors of the King's will. He belonged to a family which had
been for some time in close touch with the house of Aragon, and
was also of well-known *Converso* stock. (20)
Two high officials of Aragon are known to have befriended the
discoverer: Gabriel Sánchez, General Treasurer, and Luis de
Santángel, "Escribano de Ración," a kind of Minister of Finance.
Both were Jews. Both belonged to prominent *Converso* families
of Aragon. Both saw several members of their family (for they
were related) perish at the stake; one of them, Santángel, was the
cousin of that Luis de Santángel in whose house the murder of

the Inquisitor Arbués had been planned and for which crime he went to the stake; these two powerful personages, wealthy and highly esteemed at Court, successfully beat off the repeated attempts made to dislodge them by the envious denouncers who served the Inquisitor; both were friendly to Colón, and Santángel may well have been the determining factor in the final decision which was taken in favour of the expedition. (20)

A man who had met Deza in 1486 and was to see his scheme refloated (after he himself had made it sink) by men as powerful as Santángel and Cabrero, could not be entirely derelict in Castillian official circles. We know that he travelled about: "this illustrious man," says Zúñiga, "was in Castille and Andalucía, mostly in Seville," (21) which does not suggest utter misery. In 1489 he was granted a special privilege by the King and Queen, who, on May 12th, inform the "Councils, Justices, aldermen, knights, squires, officers and good men of all the cities, boroughs and villages" (22) of all their kingdoms and dominions that "Cristóbal Colomo is coming to this our Court, to deal with some things concerning [their] service," and they order them to lodge "him and his" without payment and to feed them at the local price. This royal letter is instructive in more ways than one. It shows that the King and Queen had by no means dropped Colón; that Colón had friends at Court who gave thought to the material details of his life; and that he was not so badly off when the order, presumably drafted by someone who knew him, provided not merely for him but for "his"; and since he was not then with his family, this can only mean his servants.

* *

Colón benefited by this document to go to Baza, which the King had besieged. We need not waste any time in admiring his military exploits against the Moors during the siege, for these exploits seem only to have existed in the imagination of the "historians," (23) who, in thus admiring them, admired nothing but their own inventive fancy. His stay in Baza was nevertheless to be for Colón a revealing experience and one which was to strike deep echoes in his sonorous soul.

While he wandered about amidst the still medieval chivalry of the siege, not in the least out of it, for he was very much a medieval knight himself, two friars of St. Francis appeared in the camp. No unusual sight, to be sure. But these two Franciscans were certainly out of the common, for they were treated with exceptional deference and attention and they were closeted for long and repeated interviews with the King and Queen. (24) The two friars came from the "Great Sultan" (of Egypt). One of them, Fray Antonio Millán, was prior of the monastery of the Holy Sepulchre in Jerusalem. They had been in Rome to report to the Pope—Innocent VIII—the dangerous state of mind of the great Islamic potentate, and the Pope had bid them put the matter before the King and Queen, along with his own letters thereon.

The Spanish Moors, seeing that the campaign begun in 1482 was rapidly eating up the territory they still held in Spain, had appealed to the Great Sultan, who thereupon wrote to the Pope to demand a cessation of the war under threat of "treating the Christians under his sway as the King and Queen of Castille treated the Moors who were of the Sultan's Law, and lived under his protection." Ferdinand and Isabel answered that there was no parity; that Spain had been unjustly overrun by the Moors and therefore the war against them was legitimate; that the Moors were not content to possess Granada, but constantly attacked the neighbouring territories; and that the Moors left in the reconquered kingdoms were left in peace "and their persons are in liberty, and they are free to possess their property, and they are allowed to live within their own law without outside pressure." (25) In short, the King and Queen, having pondered over this matter, no doubt serious for them and for all Christendom, decided to take the risk and carry on the war.

But this incident struck a deep chord in Colón, whose emotive religion had a strong Old Testament background. Jerusalem was a word full of resonance for him. These two friars came from Jerusalem. The Holy Places were in the hands of infidels. Here was a goal worthy of a great Christian knight, particularly a Christian knight born of the house of that David whose name was often on his lips. (26) "David, a very wise king, kept ewe lambs, and later was made King of Jerusalem; and I am a servant of the same Lord who put David in that state." Those proud words reveal how deep was his subconscious link with the house of David—a typical feature, by the way, of Spanish high-class Conversos. (27) His mind must have then felt that the "mission," that call to service which in all probability he felt on the day he swam his way to Portugal and which had been gradually becoming clearer and clearer, was at last completely revealed to him by this "providential" arrival of the great Sultan's embassy precisely when he, Colón, was at the camp. Discovery—Cipango—the new races to christianise—gold, pearls and spices—yes. But why, after all? Was his own transfiguration from an obscure sailor into a Grand Admiral of the Ocean Sea a sufficient event in itself to mobilise Providence? A doubt might remain in his mind as to the full meaning of the mission for which the Lord had chosen him. Now the Lord had removed that doubt. By calling him to Baza just when the friars from the Holy Sepulchre were due to arrive, the Lord said to him: "*This is your ultimate goal. The West is only a step to the East, the high means to a still higher end. Go. Conquer. Bring back the wealth of the Indies which Marco Polo has described to you and which I have shown you through Esdras, my prophet, to be closer to Spain than most people think— and with that wealth, free from the infidel the Holy Sepulchre of my Son and the House of Sion in which David, the King of your people, sang my praises. And by this service to both Jewry and Christianity, rise in triumph above Torquemada's flames.*"

This voice, no doubt, resounded in his mind, this vision shone in his imagination, when one day, we do not know where, but probably in Baza, he assured the King and Queen that all the gain that would be made out of his enterprise would be spent in the conquest of Jerusalem. Their Highnesses laughed and said they were content, and that even without that condition they would willingly help him. (28)

CHAPTER XV

AD AUGUSTA PER ANGOSTA

THE year 1490 was one of joy and festivity for the Castillian Court. The King of Portugal had sent special ambassadors to Ferdinand and Isabel, asking the hand of their eldest daughter for his son and heir Alfonso. The betrothal was celebrated in May, with unusual splendour and with that passion for gold cloth, silk and pearls which Spain received from the Orient and poured over Europe along with a host of ideas on algebra, medicine and astronomy. (1) A fresh wave of gorgeous Oriental ceremonies and rejoicings passed over the two countries in November, when the Infanta arrived in Lisbon at the head of an imposing retinue and was married to the Portuguese prince. The description of her wedding trousseau reads like a fairy-tale.

Wandering in the midst of all this joy and splendour like a desolate ghost, Colón awaited the final decision of the Commission appointed four years earlier to report on his great venture. It was unfavourable. How could it be otherwise? Colón would not reveal any concrete data enabling men of common sense and general experience, such as Talavera and the sea and sky experts he had gathered together, to form an opinion on what this imaginative and secretive stranger actually wanted. It is unnecessary to assume that the main reason for this setback was the exorbitant character of his demands, (2) for there is no proof that he did submit his demands at so early a stage in the proceedings, while all the psychological probabilities point in the opposite direction. It goes without saying that Colón's proposal would be first: "I offer to discover 'the Indies' for the Crown of Castille," and that not till the Commission had answered, "We are ready to let you have a try; what are your conditions?" would he dare to utter his inner thoughts. For he was keenly sensitive and had often felt the acid of satire and the salt of insult bite on the tender skin of his soul, and he was not the man to expose himself unnecessarily to injuries of so lasting a character.

So, towards the end of 1490 or the beginning of 1491, Colón had every reason to feel that his quest in Castille was finally lost.

167

"His promises and offers had been judged by the King and Queen to be impossible and vain and worthy of all rejection," (3) since "it was not in the interest of the authority of their royal persons that they should give their support to a business so weakly founded and which was bound to seem uncertain and impossible to any well-educated person, however lacking in expert knowledge, for they would lose their money invested in it as well as their royal authority without reaping any advantage." Even then, the King and Queen do not seem to have taken a final and irrevocable decision. (4) Whether because they wished to be courteous and euphemistic, or because they did sincerely think what they said, Ferdinand and Isabel "directed that an answer should be given Cristóbal Colón to the effect that he was sent away for the time being, though without taking away all hope to return to the matter when their Highnesses should be less occupied [with the Granada wars], and that later on a better opportunity might occur." Whatever the royal intentions, however, this decision was fatal to him. His situation was desperate. He had a small son, in La Rábida, aged eleven; his last-born, Fernando, just over a year old, was in Córdoba, with his mother; he lacked even "the necessaries of life," and, worst of all, he had "lost all hope of finding a remedy in Castille." (5) Where was he to go?

He went to La Rábida. (6) To fetch his son Diego? Possibly, but not necessarily so. The sensitive, emotional and imaginative Colón need not have gone to La Rábida for any reason at all connected with action. He may have gone there merely moved by some obscure affinity, some magnetic intuition, or the thought that the monastery might be for him a quiet, hospitable home while he thought things over, and that, in any case, Palos and its sailors were close by and he would be able to feed and strengthen his starved design amidst their simple but vehement faith in Antilles, Cipangos, carved pieces of wood and ghostly pilots.

He went to La Rábida. Fray Juan Pérez, who had shown so much interest in him and in his ideas when he first came to the monastery, was there, as open-minded and as friendly as ever. But Colón met in La Rábida two other men who were to contribute powerfully to his success: Fray Antonio de Marchena and Martín Alonso Pinzón.

Fray Antonio de Marchena was an "astrologer." Little is known of him, and what is known cannot all be accurate, for the rare glimpses of him which records and quotations allow us to catch, mixed up with equally rare glimpses of Fray Juan Pérez, have given rise to a composite figure registered by some Colombists as Fray Juan Pérez de Marchena. (7) The King and Queen had a high opinion of his science, for on September 5th, 1493, between the first and the second voyage, they wrote to Colón advising him to take a good astronomer with him for his second expedition; "and it seems to us," they added, "that Fray Antonio de Marchena might be a good choice, for he is a good astronomer and we always thought that he was of your way of thinking." (8) This was also Colón's opinion, who wrote to the King and Queen from Española: "Your Highnesses know well that I stayed for seven years in your Court, pestering you with this: never was there in this time a pilot, a seaman, a philosopher or any other learned man but who said one and all that my plan was meaningless, and I never found any help from anyone, save from Fray Antonio de Marchena, after that of the Lord." (9) No wonder that, remembering what Fray Juan Pérez had also done for him, he should have recorded his gratitude to the "two friars who always were constant to him" when "all those who had had anything to do with it or heard it, held it as mockery."

Nor was this their only service to the homeless stranger. For during those days of doubt and misery they housed him in the monastery, where his son Diego had found a home for the last six years, and they provided for him the company which he needed most—that of the men tanned by the sea and opened by the sea to all kinds of hopes and imaginations.

One such man came to the monastery more than once. Martín Alonso Pinzón (10) was no mere ignorant sailor or weather-worn pilot. In his little birthplace of Palos he was something of a potentate, for he had a caravel of his own and some small seacraft. He lived with his wife, María Alvarez, in the Street of Our Lady of La Rábida, and went to sea from his early days till he became a recognised pilot and sea-captain in the expert community to which he belonged. He had sailed the old seas to Italy and the new seas to Guinea and the Canary Islands. The long war with Portugal had tested his naval and military talents, and shown that he could be as brave in war as skilful in the more pleasant and lucrative activities of peace; for he was prosperous, a circumstance which, combined with his straightforward character and clean life, had won for him a situation of great moral authority in the harbour and district of Palos.

Pinzón was, like everybody else in those days, smitten by the fever of discovery. About a year before he met Colón, he had gone to Rome, probably on commercial business, with one of his sons, Arias Pérez Pinzón, to whom we owe the story. (11) Pinzón

Senior had a friend who served in the household of Pope Innocent VIII and who was a good cosmographer. The rest may be guessed, for it seems to have been an almost universal obsession in Europe in those days. The papal cosmographer informed both Pinzóns, father and son, of "those lands which were still undiscovered," which immediately made Pinzón the elder conceive a plan "to fit out two ships and go to discover those lands."

This was precisely the state of mind of Martín Alonso Pinzón when Cristóbal Colón arrived in Palos, beaten and sad but by no means crestfallen. The meeting of these two men under the hospitable roof of the monastery was no doubt one of the decisive moments in the discovery of America. Don Cristóbal de Cipango was returning from his second sally. All the Sanchos of the world had told him that his castle beyond the sea was nothing more than a cloud in his own mind, "impossible and vain and worthy of all rejection." But lo, here in this saintly house, clean and fragrant with the scent of pines and fresh with the salt-laden breeze of the sea, a renowned captain, a man before whom everyone in Palos bowed with respect, not merely for his wealth but for his bravery, an acknowledged chief of prudent and cautious Sanchos, listened to him, smiled, not at last in irony and derision, but in sympathy, and actually confirmed Colón's opinions, plans, hopes, with a map of lands to be discovered given him by an astronomer of the Pope's household. His words must have fallen like a soothing balm on the wounds which the long-suffering discoverer-to-be carried open and raw in his sensitive soul. "And when the said Admiral saw this," said Pinzón Junior, to the Law Court, "he became so close a friend of the witness's father that he came to an agreement with him and asked him to sail in his company." (12)

An accession of strength of this quality was bound to raise the hopes of Colón. The idea of making a new attempt to triumph over the resistance of the Queen's advisers must have originated as the result of this conjunction of two seafaring men. Yet Pinzón was only a local power. He had no influence at Court, indeed was probably unknown in it. His opinions, even backed by a more or less skilful copy of a more or less imaginative map, could hardly alter a decision taken after four or five years of procrastination on the considered opinion of an authoritative royal Commission. Some new fact of bigger weight than Pinzón's approval of the scheme must have occurred at this juncture to determine a dramatic change such as that which took place then in Colón's fortunes. One night, after a conversation with Colón,

Fray Juan Pérez sent a man to the Court with a letter for the Queen. (13) About a fortnight later the Queen sent for the friar, instructing him to leave Colón "in security of hope till she should write to him." Presently, one Diego Prieto, a citizen of Palos, arrived in La Rábida from the Court with a letter from the Queen for Colón and "twenty thousand ˙maravedis in florins so that Colón might dress decently and buy a beast and present himself before Her Highness." (14)

What had happened? Obviously, the letter of Fray Juan Pérez had revealed a new fact, important enough to change the course of events; obviously, also, the Queen thought it best to discuss the revelation with the friar before calling back Colón. It is important to stress two points: the first is that the fact was bound to be new, for no reiteration of a story repeated *ad nauseam* for over five years would have made the King and Queen change their minds; the second, that the only documents we possess tend to show that either Colón was not required to appear before another Commission at all (15)—which is the most reasonable conclusion to be drawn from the evidence—or, if there was a Commission, that it was not one of experts but one of grandees.

It follows that Fray Juan Pérez's revelation was of such a nature that it settled once and for all the cosmographical aspect of Colón's scheme—his "offer"—in the minds of the King and Queen; they accepted it. Nothing remained but the discussion of Colón's demands. This is the conclusion to be drawn from the facts. Until Fray Juan Pérez's letter, Colón has been struggling to make himself heard on the geographical issues of his scheme. After the letter of Juan Pérez to the Queen and his interview with her, Colón has settled that problem and his only struggle is to gain acceptance for his exorbitant demands.

In these conditions, the key to the mystery is not far to seek. What was Colón's chief obstacle before statesmen and cosmographers? His lack of documentary proofs. He was heard by virtue of his "grace," of his magnetic power. But a proof, a document, a map? When confronted with whatever map Pinzón showed him, Colón must have reacted inwardly in two simultaneous ways: "That map of Toscanelli's is perhaps right, and even perhaps safer than Esdras"; and "I had better show my map before Pinzón shows his and I am deprived of my priority." With this idea in his mind, Colón went to Fray Juan Pérez and "opened his heart to him in secret." (16)

This is, then, what Fray Juan Pérez must have revealed to the King and Queen: Colón had in his possession a map and a letter sent by Toscanelli to one of the advisers of the King of Portugal. Colón knew he had no right to possess that map and that letter, which were both the property of the Portuguese Crown. He had tried hard to convince King John to act upon the advice of the great Florentine "astrologer," but had failed. To his great grief, the King and Queen of Castille had not listened to his advice either, but this might be because he had been, so far, unable, for obvious reasons, to mention those two documents. Colón had revealed their existence to Fray Juan Pérez and to Fray Antonio de Marchena. Fray Antonio, who was an astrologer, believed them worthy of consideration. The two friars thought that Colón was entitled to have his secret respected by the King and Queen, and advised them to put the matter to the test of experience.

This explanation satisfies all the clues we have: (17) the King and Queen ask first to see Fray Juan, whose letter, presumably, imparted the mere existence of an important secret fact; they then decide to accept in principle the cosmographical aspect of the matter, in view of the high-sounding authority of the Florentine (of whom very likely they had never heard), of the blessing of Fray Antonio de Marchena, "a good astronomer," and of the impossibility to consult other experts since the matter was secret. Moreover, the secret belongs to the King of Portugal; now, if it fails, little has been lost; if it succeeds, they have reached the Indies by *their* way, independent of the way of the Portuguese. The zest of rivalry must have compensated in their minds any doubts they might have had, particularly in view of the fact that the King of Portugal had not thought fit to follow Toscanelli's advice. The importance attached by Colón to both friars becomes clear. Clearer still, these words of Las Casas on Fray Antonio de Marchena: "Neither could I ever know when, nor on what, nor how he [Marchena] favoured him" [Colón]; (18) for how could Las Casas, in possession of all the papers and of many confidences of Colón and of his brother Bartolomé, remain in ignorance of so important a point if Colón had not made a secret of it? (19)

⁎
⁎ ⁎

All this coming and going, the high-falutin plans of the importunate stranger, Cipango, Jerusalem, must have appeared somewhat unreal and almost irrelevant to the overworked King and Queen. For them there were at the time two great questions of State: the Moors and the Jews.

They were entering the ninth yearly campaign of the war for the conquest of Granada. The whole of Christendom had its eyes on them. They had gradually conquered all the strongholds which the Moors had possessed for so long—Málaga, for instance, which had been under Moorish sway—had indeed *been* Moorish for seven hundred and seventy years. And now they were girding themselves for their last effort—the conquest of Granada itself. On April 11th, 1491, the King, the Queen and Prince Don Juan left Seville for the campaign. (20) Leaving his wife and young son in Alcalá la Real, Don Fernando advanced with his armies into Moorish territory and spent the spring and part of the summer in unceasing raids and skirmishes preparatory to the siege. In August, well satisfied with this preliminary phase of his plan of campaign, King Ferdinand chose a site in the rich Vega or Plain of Granada, and there built his camp. He built it with brick and mortar, as a city, to signify to the Moors that he had come to stay, and he "called it Santa Fé because his desire and that of the Queen his wife always pointed to the increase and favour of the Holy Catholic Faith of Jesus Christ." (21)

This faith, however, was then threatened by what, in their eyes, was a most dreadful pestilence. To their consternation, the Inquisition had revealed the shallow character of the wholesale conversions made towards the end of the fourteenth century by fear, and throughout the fifteenth century mostly by design and ambition, in the vast Jewish populations of the Peninsula. It is difficult for us, born and bred in times of agnosticism and of variety of creeds and opinions, to realise what life was like in a period of orthodoxy and unassailable belief. That thousands of persons "washed" in the purifying waters of baptism, and "enlightened" by the light of faith, should have relapsed into the "black night of heresy" must have had terrifying effects beyond anything we can imagine, on a world of sincere, wholesale-believing Christians. We know enough about the character of the King and Queen to realise that when the Inquisition showed how widespread was the "heretical depravity" in the ranks of the *Conversos*, they must have been appalled at the magnitude of the disaster. It is indeed difficult to evade the conclusion that they must have felt personally touched by the "pestilence." The names dearest to them, closest to their daily life, were compromised: members of the families associated in their administration, glittering in their Courts—La Caballería, Santángel, Sánchez—had to don the penitent's "holy sack" and even to ascend the stake. The King and Queen cannot be said to have yielded to a panic which circumstances might have justified, for they kept in their posts and protected with their unrivalled prestige these members of their household and chanceries whose close relatives had died in the flames. But the King and Queen must have been deeply impressed by a certain number of considerations: their leading class of dignitaries and civil servants was dangerously threatened both in its numbers and in its reliability, for this class was predominantly made up of men of *Converso* stock; the gradual evolution of the country towards a harmonious, if not altogether united, way of thinking, was gravely compromised by the failure of this mighty experiment; the obdurate attachment of possibly the majority of the *Converso* population to the way of living and believing of the "faithless" Jews could not be glossed over by any statesman in his senses. Assimilation, on the whole, had failed.

Nor can a parallel be drawn with present-day events—even though in point of actual cruelty and suffering inflicted there is little to choose between 1492 and 1938—for nowadays the dominant power jeers at agreement either with its own Jews or with any national or foreign general principle of humanity and peace; while, in the Spain of 1492, the "faith" was held to be the only possible truth for all men, who became equal, whatever their race, once they had professed it. The tragedy of the responsible and thinking spirits of those days—the King, the Queen, Talavera, Cisneros—was that they were ready to save the whole of the Jews of Spain in the faith of Christianity which they held as true, and that the Jews, whether public or secret, did not wish to be so saved.

This psychological situation was bound to lead to passion in the heart, since in the mind it led to a deadlock. Men who refused to see the light could not but be "depraved." "Depravity" was the word of the day. Every chronicler uses it. "Pestilence" is an equally significant expression of this emotional state which developed then against the Jews. Meantime, the old trouble—envy—still afflicted the humbler brethren of the Christian faith. By 1491, when Colón was in La Rábida skilfully negotiating through Fray Juan Pérez, strong pressure was already being exerted on the King and Queen for the expulsion of the Jews.

Such was the stormy background on which we must see the picture of Colón negotiating again with the King and Queen. Did they know who he was? The weight of evidence and probability is in favour of an affirmative. The King kept himself well informed of Genoese affairs; he was—in a more or less intermittent way—the suzerain of Savona, where the Colombos had lived for long. Italy was honeycombed with his agents and allies. Ferdinand must have secured all the information he wished about this family, and must therefore have known that they were of Catalan-Jewish origin. Nor should we exclude the possibility that this fact may have had a slowing effect on the leisurely rhythm of the negotiations.

It is, at any rate, significant that Colón should have made his name evolve from *Colombo* to *Colón* in exactly the way he did and which we may now follow according to official documents: he landed in Portugal as *Colombo*, and that is the name which Ruy de Pina, his first Portuguese chronicler, gives him; but, *in Portugal*, he seems to have gone straight over to *Colom* and *Colón*, for Barros, King John's historian, calls him *Colom*, while King John himself, in 1489, calls him *Colón*. And yet, in Castille, from 1485-86 down to 1492, *his name is always Colomo*. This is a curious retrogression in an evolution which was predetermined to end in *Colón* (as shown by King John's letter). It evinces a kind of caution lest *Colom* might prove dangerous in King Ferdinand's realms. When we know that both the Valencian Inquisition in 1461 and the Castillian Inquisition in 1489 convicted secret Jews by the name of Colom, *this otherwise inexplicable* action of the discoverer becomes clear. The first time *Colón* is allowed to see the light is when, already sure of his victory, the discoverer drafts his *Capitulations* and has himself styled Don Cristóbal Colón.

That the King and Queen were aware of much of this may be proved by one single observation: *they never mentioned his nationality*. In spite of the relatively high number of official documents and letters directly signed by them, or authorised by them, which we possess, not one is known in which Cristóbal Colón's origin is described. Now this is directly contrary to usage, for in those days the mention of "Venetian," "Florentine," "Frenchman," "Catalan," came as a matter of course immediately after the name of the person for whom the paper was drafted. (22) The most we read about Colón in official papers is *extranjero, foreigner*. Genoese, never. The rule is absolute.

Nor is this all, for we have positive proof that the King and Queen did not want to refer to the Genoese origin of the "stranger." Ruy González Puebla, ambassador of Ferdinand and Isabel in London, wrote to the King and Queen on June 23rd, 1498, referring to John Cabot as "another Genoese, like Colón." The King and Queen answered: "You speak of one like Colón who has proposed to the King of England an enterprise such as that of the Indies . . ." The word Genoese has evaporated. It was severely avoided so far as the King and Queen were concerned. It was never applied to Colón's brothers either. (23)

It should be noticed that neither Cristóbal nor Bartolomé were explicitly naturalised, though they tacitly became Castillian subjects. Diego is the only one who was ever naturalised by a legal act, a letter signed by the King and Queen on February 8th, 1504. (24) Nothing could have been more natural than to mention his country of origin in such an act. It is not mentioned. Moreover, the reason for this difference between Diego and his brothers is patent; it is, in fact, explicitly mentioned in the act, and at the head of the reasons adduced, which shows it was uppermost in the mind of its draftsman—possibly Don Diego himself: "so that you may have whatever ecclesiastical dignity and benefices which might be given you"; (25) for, as it is known, the King and Queen were adamant on the admission of foreigners to their Church. Yet this Churchman, in later years, when his brother was Admiral and Viceroy, was not granted a single ecclesiastical dignity either in Castille or in the Indies, a fact which would appear to point again to the Jewish origin of the family, for in later years Ferdinand and Isabel grew more cautious in the granting of sees to *Converso* ecclesiastics.

This circumstance, the Jewish origin of Colón, was therefore bound to be in everybody's mind when he came back to Santa Fé to negotiate with the Queen. The cosmographical matter was settled. The scheme was worth trying. What of the conditions? We know them. Colón had not abated one iota from them. He was to be knighted; he was to be a Don; he was to be Grand Admiral; he was to be Viceroy: these titles were to remain in his family in perpetuity: (26) he was to have ten per cent. on all transactions within his admiralty. These conditions must have created real stupor in those who were allowed to know them. Why, a starved beggar come from God knows where, ask the honours and privileges of the Admiral of Castille? The King and Queen would surely be struck first by the ludicrous disproportion between what was offered and what was asked. Yet, such is human nature, who knows but that the very magnitude of these demands may not have contributed to give weight and substance to the fabulous and nebulous offer? Withal, the privileges and honours asked by Colón were far too high and, moreover, dangerous. There must have been efforts towards some kind of bargain with him. He was adamant. The stiff-necked pride of his nature came out in all its steel-like rigidity. He was the Lord's agent, chosen not only to conquer a new world, so far existing only in his imagination, but also to stand up to this King and to this Queen who were oppressing half his nation and preparing to drive the other half into an inhuman exile. He had to hold his ground. He held it.

He looked like a beggar because he went about in poor thread-bare clothes. But he was not one. He was perhaps the proudest soul in that seemingly proud Court. Though, "seeing he was so much rejected and contradicted, afflicted and oppressed by so great a want, when perhaps by yielding on the privileges he demanded, by being content with less (when it seems as if he should have been content with anything), the King and Queen might have been willing to give him all he needed for his voyage, and for the rest, anything which in their judgment they should have thought fit to give him, he refused to soften on any one point, and with complete firmness he persevered in all that he had asked." (27)

And for the second time he was dismissed.

*
* *

Colón left Santa Fé—this time, as he thought, for good and all. His thoughts turned to England where his brother Bartolomé had been, or to France where he was then. But how could he go there, penniless as he was? And what had become of his brother?

All was lost again. 1492! Eight years of labour and patience, of hardship and humiliation; two sons; a woman who was "a load on his conscience"; and nothing but "the day and the night" as they say in that land which he meant to be his and which he was then preparing to leave. Again on the road. To France? To England?

His mental eyes must have then turned back to that bright and moving scene he had seen but a few days earlier—the rise of the Banner and the Cross over the Tower of Comares in the Alhambra —a sight beheld not merely by those who were present, not merely by the whole of Spain, but by all Christendom. The Cross and the Banner! Cristóbal Colón! Surely this and no other was the land for him. Where was he going, away from his destiny, from his mission? It was imperative that the land of the Cross and the Banner should be the land of Cristóbal Colón. Where was he going? Was this really the last of his Castillian quest?

While these thoughts turned in his head, as he rode away, early in January, three powerful friends took up for him the case he had abandoned: Deza; Cabrero; Santángel: *three Conversos*. Their intervention at the last moment, when Colón had already left Granada, is well established; (28) the evidence available suggests that their effort was combined and that Santángel was chosen to speak to the Queen. Don Luis de Santángel, "Escribano de Ración" of King Ferdinand of Aragon, a kind of Minister of the Budget, was, of course, a *Converso*. He was one of the most influential men in the kingdom, and his family one of the most powerful and respected in Aragon. It was in the house of his namesake cousin, Luis de Santángel, that the murder of the Inquisitor Pedro de Arbués had been discussed and prepared, barely six years earlier; and this cousin of his, as well as other members of his family, burnt, or otherwise punished, had been the victims of one of the most dramatic and sensational falls caused by the Inquisition. (29) Luis de Santángel himself had been prosecuted and sentenced to do public penance by the Inquisition in Saragossa, and it says much for the courage of the King and Queen that this fact did not in the least diminish his official position. He was even granted by Ferdinand a guarantee against inquisitional persecutions for himself and for his heirs. (30) It was this man who came to see the Queen on the day Colón left Granada for Córdoba with his mind set on a third exile.

Santángel made the Queen alter her decision. What did he say? The eloquent speeches made for him by the chroniclers need not detain us; they are pure fancy. (31) What did he actually say?

There is no doubt that he was the chief *Converso* at Court. No one was more powerful than he. If, as it is argued in these pages, the difficulty came from the exorbitant demands of Colón, the reasonable view is that Santángel limited himself to this point. "The plan," he would say, "is worth trying. On this you are all agreed. Why then haggle over privileges and honours? If he brings you the Indies, why not Admiral? If he does not bring them, no harm is done. Keep the paper secret till he is back." And then Santángel would suggest: "See the advantage of having this service performed by a new Christian. You will ease your situation. You will be able to point to him on the credit side, when my people have loaded your debit so heavily with their secret infidelity. Do not listen to your Visigothic grandees. Be sensible and reasonable. Let him have his conditions, since they are all subject to the success of his expedition. And if he succeeds, let him reap what he will deserve, since you will reap far more."

"But what about money?" the Queen would ask.

"I will lend you what you need. It is not much anyhow. And you can afford the interest."

Colón was crossing the Bridge of Pinos, (32) about eight miles out of Granada, when a Queen's *Alguazil* overtook his "beast" with a swifter horse. The Queen requested him to return. He hesitated for a while, for as long as he thought of the *Alguazil* as coming from the Queen; then he realised the *Alguazil* came from the Lord, and he returned to Santa Fé—and to immortality.

PART IV

THE VERY MAGNIFICENT LORD DON CRISTÓBAL COLÓN

CHAPTER XVI

WESTWARD

THE letter to the King and Queen with which Colón begins the diary of his first voyage contains the following words: "And thus, having expelled all the Jews from all your kingdoms and dominions, in the same month of January Your Highnesses commanded me that with a sufficient fleet I should go to the said parts of India; and for that purpose granted me great honours and ennobled me so that henceforth I should be styled Don and should be Grand Admiral of the Ocean Sea and Viceroy and Governor-General in perpetuity of the Islands and terra firma." (1)

These words have puzzled all historians. How could Colón be so inaccurate writing but a few months after the events? The Jews were expelled in August by a decree signed on March 31st. January had nothing to do with it. Yet these words in their very inaccuracy are one of the most revealing utterances of Colón.

Why bring in the Jews at all? He is going to speak about his voyage, possibly the only Castillian enterprise of the day which had nothing whatever to do with the Jewish question. What are the Jews and their expulsion doing in his caravel? Does not this unwarranted recall of the expulsion of the Jews suggest a sub-conscious obsession in his mind with the fate of his brethren? The obsession was indeed so strong that it led him to record as simultaneous events which took place at different dates; but these two events—the Jewish defeat and his own victory—were so closely intertwined in the soil of his being where his motives hid their roots, that he gave them both as occurring in January—in the month in which he won his victory over the King and Queen.

Hence that sentence so irrelevant and so much at variance with the outward facts, merely an unguarded expression of his inner thoughts: "Having expelled the Jews, you sent me to India and made me a grand Admiral. Having abased my race, you raised me."

There are other features which should be stressed in this letter. No contemporary, writing to the King and Queen in those days, would have mentioned the expulsion of the Jews without enlarging upon "the blessing which the monarchs conferred on the nation by so admirable a measure," or some such platitudinous mark of approval. Colón mentions the expulsion of the Jews dry and unadorned. Not a word on its merits. This silence is as good as a confession, and in those days it was dangerous enough. In Colón, it reveals not merely his Jewish race, but that self-absorption which led him at times to forget the world and to throw away years of carefully administered caution in one second of stiff pride or of absent-minded wandering.

Furthermore, a few lines earlier in the same letter, speaking of the Indians who lay in idolatry waiting for the Christians to come and enlighten them, Colón says of the King and Queen that they are "catholic Christian princes, lovers of the wholly Christian faith and propagators of it and enemies of the sect of Mahomet and all idolatries and heresies"; (2) again an admirable opportunity for having expressed the opinions which every other contemporary would have uttered there on the " Jewish Sect." But not a word. Does not his silence here suggest that, though a sincere Christian in his way, Colón felt the link which attached him to the persecuted race? He was too proud to approve. He kept silent, but his secret thought came out in a sentence which reflected the inner workings of his heart rather than the events outside.

By one of those caprices of history which makes it so dramatic, the Jewish question, which had been a permanent problem of Spanish life since the days of the Visigothic conquest, came to its final crisis not merely in his lifetime, not merely when his own scheme was in full swing, but at the very time it was launched. January saw the decision to send him to "India"; the Capitulations were signed on April 17th. The decision to expel the Jews was taken at about the same time; the royal decree of expulsion is dated March 31st. The two sets of events are closely intertwined, and we are to see that they will remain so till the very day of Colón's departure for his historical first voyage.

When Colón returned from the Bridge of the Pines, he had already won; all that remained was to register his victory in a written document. This document—the famous Capitulations of Santa Fé—was drafted by Fray Juan Pérez and by Juan de Coloma. (3) Yet another of the caprices of history: the two parties to the Capitulations are Colón and Coloma, and as Coloma was also the official who countersigned the edict of expulsion of the Jews seventeen days earlier, this near-namesake of Colón's may be said to have given official status to the two most important documents in the history of Spain.

He was not secretary for Castille, but for Aragon, a fact which shows that King Ferdinand was not averse to Colón's enterprise as, on the strength of Fernando Colón's assertions, it has been too readily believed. There is no doubt that most of the help which Colón received from the Court originated in the King's household rather than in the Queen's—Santángel, Cabrero and Coloma were all King's men. The first two were *Conversos.* As for Coloma, no proof seems to exist that he was or was not a member of this influential class. (4)

The Capitulations are in the form of a memorandum of agreement. (5) They are not in themselves a legal deed; but a record upon which legal deeds are to be executed later. They are sure to have originated on Colón's side, no doubt as the outcome of his many disappointments. His pride and assurance were more than enough to demand a guarantee that he was not returning in vain. By this time, his ground must have been well prepared and Coloma was easily persuaded to see a draft and sign it for the King and Queen.

It is addressed to the King and Queen, in the form of a series of paragraphs detailing the favours and honours granted to Colón, at the end of each of which there recurs the line:

"It pleases their Highnesses.—Juan de Coloma."

The Quixotic spirit of Colón is writ large all over these historic papers. The discoverer appears straight away as *Don* Cristóbal Colón, before anyone has authorised him so to style himself. The *first* condition registered is that their Highnesses are to make "the said Don Cristóbal Colón" their Admiral "in all the islands and continents which by his hand and industry might be discovered or conquered in the said ocean seas." Colón sets down with all precision the two points which he always raised in connection with this concession: that it should be extended to his heirs in perpetuity; and that his pre-eminences and prerogatives should be the same as those enjoyed by the Grand Admiral of Castille. He mentions this Admiral by name, Don Alonso Henríquez, one of the highest of Spanish magnates, actually belonging to King Ferdinand's family. In this relentless struggle for glory, honour and elevation to royal rank, may we not see his obsession and desire to avenge over King Ferdinand the humiliation of his race? "It pleases their Highnesses," coldly records Juan de Coloma.

The second condition of Don Quixote-Colón was that he should be Viceroy and Governor-General of all the islands and main-land to be discovered; here again he actually asks and obtains that "for the Government of each and any of them he shall nominate three persons for each post, out of which Your Highness will appoint one." This settled, he secures his tenth on all transactions, and then produces such an extraordinary demand that Juan de Coloma is shaken out of his equanimity and can only sign with a reservation: Colón is to administer Justice, either personally or through his representatives, in all trade affairs arising out of the commerce between Castille and the lands on which he may have such a right owing to his privilege as an admiral. This is an entirely medieval conception. The King and Queen were still trying hard to extirpate it from the minds of their grandees and bishops. (6) Colón, in many ways a thoroughly medieval mind, seeks to perpetuate in "the Indies" this feudal conception of justice. Nor is Coloma able to oppose a clear negative to this exorbitant demand. All he says is: "It pleases their Highnesses, if it pertains to the office of Admiral, as it was held by the said Admiral D. Alonso Henríquez and his predecessors in their districts, and if it be just." (7)

The document ends with a stipulation that Colón is to con-tribute one-eighth, if he so wishes, to all expeditions sent "to the said trade and business," and receive one-eighth of the profits.

There are two features in this singular document which have proved as fertile in controversy as any in Colón's life: one is the fact that the "Indies" are not mentioned in it. This is the stock argument of those who claim that Colón never meant to go to the Indies by the west. (8) This position is untenable, as has been shown in these pages. Colón did mean to go to the "Indies" by the west, even if he was vague about what those "Indies" were. The silence on this point is obviously due to the necessity of being discreet, for the King of Portugal was watching.

The second strange feature of the Capitulations is even more spectacular, yet not more substantial than the first. Its opening sentence registers "the things requested and which Your High-nesses give and grant Don Cristóbal Colón, as some satisfac-tion . . ." [How Colónish, that *some*! Exorbitant as his con-ditions were, they were only *some* satisfaction . . .] but for what? The document actually says "*for what he has discovered* in the ocean seas, and of the voyage which now, with the help of God, he is to undertake through those seas in the service of Your Highnesses." (9)

These words are so startling as to be almost unbelievable.

But the proof is conclusive that the original document signed by Coloma says "what he has discovered." (10) On the strength of these words, some Colombists have built up the tale of his pre-discovery of America. (11) They very aptly bring to bear on this point the repeated statements of Las Casas about Colón's assurance of discovering new land "as if he had it under lock and key." All this fairy-tale falls to the ground upon perusal of Colón's own diary of his first voyage, for it is obvious that he was surprised, puzzled, charmed and disappointed all in one by what he saw. (12) The real explanation of these words in the Capitulations is to be found in the Quixotic psychology of Colón. "He hugged his imagination" and would not part with it even if barefoot friars had begged him to, as Cervantes said of Don Quixote. He was so sure of his dream that he just gave it as a fact in the document in which he made the King and Queen pay so heavily for his "discovery." Just as he styled himself Don before the concession of this title, so he gave the "Indies" as discovered before leaving Palos to discover them.

The Capitulations of April 17th were made into a regular deed on April 30th. This deed is drafted by Juan de Coloma or in his offices. The discoverer is back to plain "Cristóbal Colón"; he goes to discover "certain islands and terra firma" which he has not discovered yet and which "it is hoped, with the help of God, to discover and conquer," and the titles (including the Don) and other privileges are explicitly adjourned to "after you shall have discovered and conquered the said islands and terra firma in the said Ocean Sea, or any of them." (13) The contrast between this official caution and the Quixotic-Colónish imagination cannot be more striking.

Colón may not have been then in a mood to notice it. He had won. Now he could navigate. Once on the open sea, with nothing but the unknown before him, he was in his element. Full of hope, he left Granada on May 12th. (14)

* *

One morning, twelve days before his departure, the sound of trumpets had brought him to the window in Santa Fé. (15) A King-at-Arms, two Alcaldes and two Alguazils were solemnly announcing to the people that the King and Queen gave three months' notice from that date, April 30th, to all the Jews and Jewesses of their Kingdoms who would refuse conversion, to leave the royal dominions, allowing them to take away their property by sea or land, except gold, silver, coin, or goods on the prohibited export list. (16) The stars had wished that to the very end the fate of Israel should be closely intertwined with his. On that very day, the man who had signed the decree expelling the Jews had put his signature to two all-important papers in the history of the discovery of America—by the first, Colón was granted the titles and dignities which had been stipulated in the Capitulations; by the second, the King and Queen reminded Diego Rodriguez Prieto, Alcalde Mayor of Palos, and "all other persons your companions and neighbours of the Borough of Palos," that they had been sentenced by the Council to serve the King and Queen with two caravels armed at their expense for two years, and commanded them to put the said caravels at the disposal of Cristóbal Colón to go to "certain parts of the Ocean Sea on some errands required by our service." (17)

Little wonder that Colón was later to link up in one sentence the expulsion of the Jews and the discovery of the Indies. With the royal order in his wallet he left for Palos, when the country was already astir with the economic and social effects of the uprooting of his old race from the soil in which it had thriven for so long.

While he travelled towards Palos, the little harbour which he was to immortalise, the wretched seed of Israel was preparing for its most tragic exodus. The decree of March 31st, 1492, was strictly understood in a religious, not in a racial sense. Yet though the number of *Conversos* was great, the unconverted Jews in the country were no less numerous, and the roots of all kinds, economic no doubt, but most of all spiritual, which they had struck in Spain, were as deep as might be expected considering they had lived in the Peninsula for about two thousand years. At the time when Colón was laying the foundations of his greatness, the Jews were liquidating their stake in the country as best they could, selling their houses and movable property, casting the last melancholy glance on the land in which they had been born and where they were to leave the ashes of their ancestors. "The Christians," says Bernáldez, "acquired their estates, very many, and very rich houses and lands for little money, and they [the Jews] went about begging to sell them and found no buyers, and they gave a house for an ass and a vineyard for a small cloth of wool or linen, for they were not allowed to take gold or silver out of the country; though in truth they did take away untold sums in gold and silver, and in particular many *cruzados* and ducats bitten out of shape which they swallowed and took away in their bellies, [. . .] and women especially swallowed more than men, for it happened that one person swallowed as many as thirty ducats." (18)

The heartrending scenes which were then to be seen in nearly the whole Peninsula can be easily imagined. They would be particularly tragic precisely in the zone which Colón was crossing on his way from Granada to Palos, for the Jews of Castille who flocked towards El Puerto and Cádiz were amongst the richest of Spain and they would present to the friendly observer a sight the more dismal and poignant as their fall was more precipitous. The haggard faces of the homeless, the oppressed, the persecuted, the betrayed, must have provided a background of tragedy and misery for the triumphant journey of the Quixotic discoverer. He may even have witnessed some of the preliminary migrations which were by then taking place towards the great exodus; moving sights in the extreme, even under the pen of the simple and bigoted Bernáldez: "Trusting the vain hopes of their blindness, they chose the hardships of the road and they left the land of their birth, small and big, old men and children, on foot and riding asses and other beasts and on carts, and they travelled to the ports from which they were to sail; and they went along the roads or across the fields with great hardship and risk, some falling, some rising, some dying, some being born, some falling sick, so that there was no Christian who did not feel grief for them, and wherever they went they were invited to be baptised, and some, in their plight, were converted and remained, but very few, and their Rabbis kept encouraging them, and they made the women and youngsters sing and play their tambourines to cheer the crowd." (19) The fiery imagination, the prophetic and missionary sense of Colón must have been deeply stirred both by the situation itself and by the Providential coincidence which dashed Israel to the ground when he was raised to his victory.

* *

The royal letters in his wallet, his faith in his own fortunes shining brighter than ever in his heart, Colón returned to Palos as a conqueror. On May 23rd, barely eleven days after his departure from Granada, he called a meeting of the authorities and citizens of Palos at the Church of St. George, and there solemnly read the letter of their Royal Highnesses (20) enjoining the citizens of Palos to put two armed caravels at the disposal of Cristóbal Colón. It is safe to surmise that he was proud and even overbearing. His authoritarian nature, long repressed by poverty and by lack of recognition, further heightened by the sights of persecution and misery which he must have felt deep down in his soul as an insult, had at last a magnificent opportunity to show itself. He brandished a royal order.

But he brandished it in vain. For the first time, he met that tough Spanish nature which in the presence of royal orders had coined a masterpiece of undisciplined evasion: "To be obeyed but not carried out." The royal order was duly respected by all, but nothing happened.

This must have been a deep disappointment for him in more ways than one: it delayed the achievement of his dreams at a time when the season for fair sailing was already well on; and, what was worse, it threatened to make him dependent on Pinzón and his brothers. Now, though the details of his relations with Pinzón are not yet fully known, it is generally admitted that before his last and successful journey to the Court, Colón must have come to some kind of contract, verbal or written, with the chief seaman of Palos; and all we know of Colón's doings at the time tends to show that he harboured the design of getting rid of Pinzón's protection or collaboration on the strength of his royal letters. His proud, independent and at the same time shy and distrustful character was bound to lead him to this attitude. He knew full well that a stranger such as he was would never command enough authority to recruit a crew foolhardy enough to follow him to Cipango across the Western seas; but, with his usual caution and foresight—a foresight, to be sure, theoretical rather than practical—he had obtained from Coloma an order suspending all criminal proceedings against the men who would accompany him on his voyage, an extraordinary measure which we know to have been adopted at his request from the text of the order itself: "and to take away the men he needs in three caravels he is taking, he says it is necessary to give a safe-conduct to those who would go with him, for otherwise they would refuse to go with him in that voyage." (21)

It would be difficult to find a more eloquent expression of Colón's will to power than this desperate provision. Anything rather than yield. Remembering, no doubt, the jeers and the doubts expressed to his face in Court and harbour whenever he gave vent to his hopes or half expressed his dreams, Colón is determined to return to Palos, armed from head to foot with royal provisions to meet all cases. This order enabling him to draw the crews, if necessary, from the prisons, explains the others, not only the royal letter of the same date, (22) by which all Andalucian authorities are requested to provide him at reasonable prices with all he might need for his fleet, but even the letter enjoining the men of Palos to give him two caravels.

The King and Queen had given ten days to the men of Palos for carrying out their order; the order was still "obeyed but not carried out." Colón then obtained an even more general order (23) addressed no longer to Palos but to all the authorities of the Andalucian coast, and not for two but for three caravels. On June 20th, Juan de Peñalosa is ordered by the King and Queen to have this order carried out, for they say: "It was presented in Moguer by Cristóbal Colón, and he demanded that it be carried out, and, though it was obeyed, it was not carried out." Colón's determination to crush opposition by sheer power is relentless. At all costs, even at the risk of having to conquer his Cipango and his golden spurs as the captain of a crew of cutthroats and thieves, he must be independent, and alone.

But the tough men of Palos saved him from the disaster which he was preparing for himself. It is a fair assumption that his decision to man his ships with criminals must have caused a real consternation in the hearts of the good monks of La Rábida, (24) where he was staying. Both Fray Antonio de Marchena and Fray Juan Pérez had staked their reputation on Colón and his expedition. It is unthinkable that they should not have intervened at this stage. Despite the royal letters, jeers and gibes went on at Palos in sailor's tavern and seaman's dwelling; (25) possibly stimulated—for such is human nature—by the Pinzón party, powerful as it was and, moreover, part and parcel of the pride of seamanship of the little harbour.

The upshot of it all was that Colón agreed to admit the Pinzón family to a friendly collaboration. From the days when Colón was still negotiating in Santa Fé, (26) Pinzón seems already to have been acting as the manager of the enterprise, providing ships, recruiting seamen and even paying out sums from his own pocket. This fact confirms both that Colón had entered into a contract with Pinzón and that the difficulties met with by Colón when back from Granada were due to the lone hand he tried to play then. At any rate, all obstacles vanished as soon as Colón accepted once more the co-operation of the man who could not only obey but carry out the orders of the King and Queen.

The reconciliation seems to have been complete, for Colón, whose eye never wandered away from *power*, and therefore (among other symbols and instruments of power) from money, wished to take a share of one-eighth in the expenses in order to put in a claim of one-eighth on the earnings, whereupon his generous rival came forward and handsomely advanced half a million maravedis. (27) From that moment on, the Pinzón family took a prominent part in the expedition. "Martín Alonso [Pinzón]," says one of the witnesses in the lawsuit, "put as much diligence in enlisting crews and in giving them courage as if the discovery were to be for him or for his children." "To some he said they would be raised above their poverty; to others that they would find there houses with tiles of gold; to some he offered good fortune, and for every man he had pleasant words and money; so that with this and the general trust in him, many people followed him from the towns." (28)

We seem to see the breezy sailor and to hear his warm, manly voice, arousing the enthusiasm of doubting, sceptical seamen along the shore of Palos harbour, in the speech attributed to him by one of the witnesses in the lawsuit: "Friends, come away, come away with us; you are all here crawling in misery; come away on this voyage, for, according to fame, we shall find gold-roofed houses and you shall all come back rich and happy."

This enthusiastic attitude of the chief sailor and citizen of Palos saved Colón from the most disastrous of the mistakes which his hot, headstrong, passionate nature was ready to commit—that of manning his ships with a handful of jailbirds. Though, on the strength of Colón's intentions and the royal letter which reveals them, the idea has gained some footing in history-books that he recruited his crew in the Spanish prisons, it is now certain that no man with a police record sailed with him. (29) The total crew (pilots, seamen and shipboys) amounted to ninety men; but there were on board another twenty or thirty persons, including "several officers of the King, who fancied to sail with him out of curiosity, as well as domestic servants and acquaintances of his." (30) There were no women, and, strange to say, no priests.

All this little world which was to swarm out of the Old Hive to the New Hive in the most momentous hour of the earth's history was packed up into three tiny caravels, which Colón owed also to the loyal co-operation of Pinzón rather than to the imperative but ineffective letters of the King and Queen. The caravels which the men of Palos were to deliver were discarded for reasons that are not clear. In their stead, Pinzón secured two local ships, the *Pinta*, which seems to have belonged to a local group, probably including Pinzón himself and certainly two men of her crew, presently to fight their way somewhat forcibly to the foreground of the story; and the *Niña*, believed to be the property of one Pero Alonso Niño, who acted as her pilot during the great

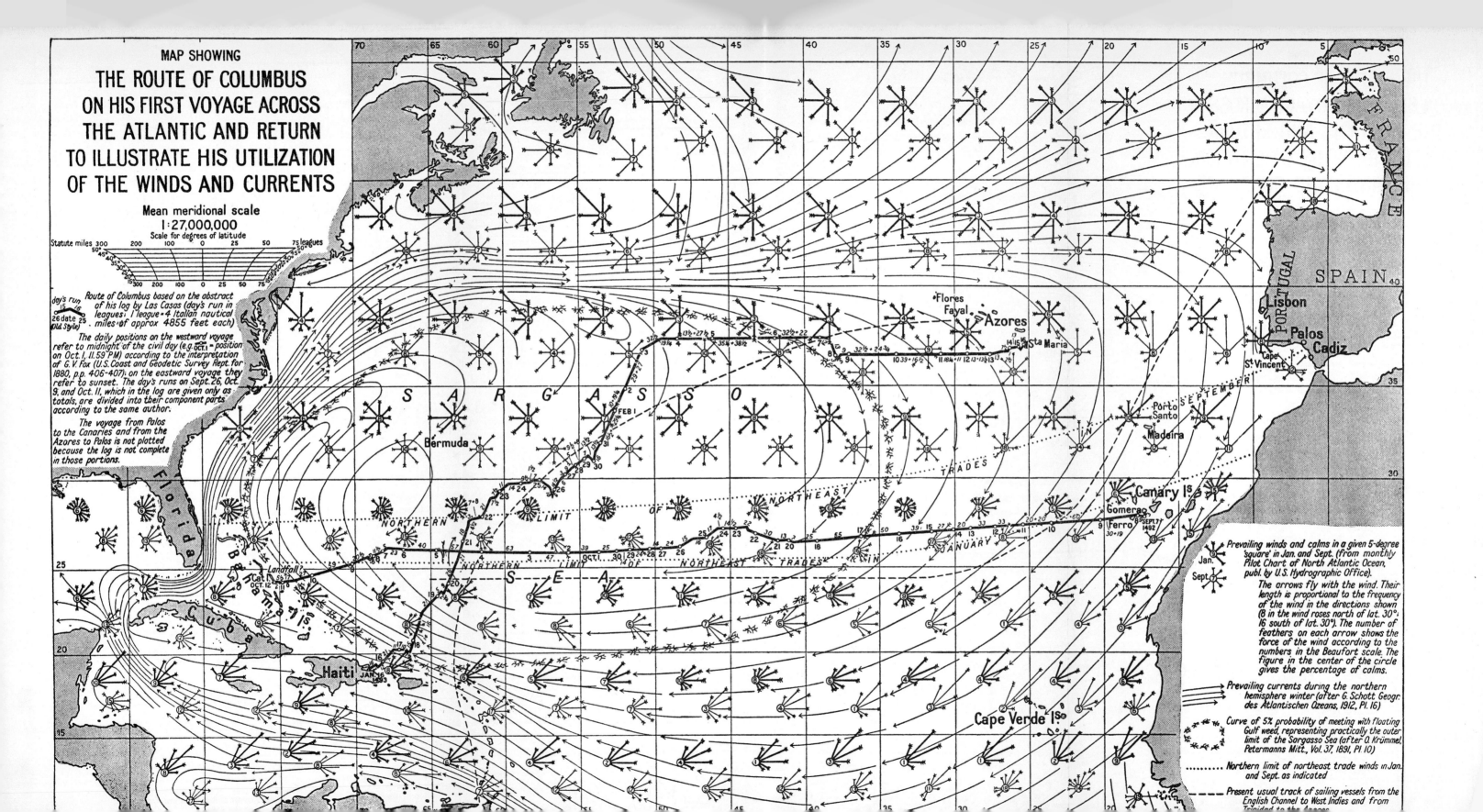

MAP SHOWING

THE ROUTE OF COLUMBUS
ON HIS FIRST VOYAGE ACROSS
THE ATLANTIC AND RETURN
TO ILLUSTRATE HIS UTILIZATION
OF THE WINDS AND CURRENTS

Mean meridional scale
1:27,000,000
Scale for degrees of latitude

Statute miles 300   200   100   0   25   50   75 leagues

Route of Columbus based on the abstract of his log by Las Casas (day's run in leagues; 1 league = 4 Italian nautical miles of approx 4855 feet each)

The daily positions on the westward voyage refer to midnight of the civil day (e.g. Oct.1 = position on Oct.1, 11.59 PM) according to the interpretation of G.V. Fox (U.S. Coast and Geodetic Survey Rept. for 1880, p.p. 406-407); on the eastward voyage they refer to sunset. The day's runs on Sept. 26, Oct. 9, and Oct. 11, which in the log are given only as totals, are divided into their component parts according to the same author.

The voyage from Palos to the Canaries and from the Azores to Palos is not plotted because the log is not complete in those portions.

SARGASSO SO SEA

NORTHERN LIMIT OF NORTHEAST TRADES

Prevailing winds and calms in a given 5-degree square in Jan. and Sept. (from monthly Pilot Chart of North Atlantic Ocean, publ. by U.S. Hydrographic Office).

The arrows fly with the wind. Their length is proportional to the frequency of the wind in the directions shown (8 in the wind roses north of lat. 30°, 16 south of lat. 30°). The number of feathers on each arrow shows the force of the wind according to the numbers in the Beaufort scale. The figure in the center of the circle gives the percentage of calms.

Prevailing currents during the northern hemisphere winter (after G. Schott Geogr. des Atlantischen Ozeans, 1912, Pl. 16)

Curve of 5% probability of meeting with floating Gulf weed, representing practically the outer limit of the Sargasso Sea (after O. Krümmel, Petermanns Mitt., Vol. 37, 1891, Pl. 10)

Northern limit of northeast trade winds in Jan. and Sept. as indicated

Present usual track of sailing vessels from the English Channel to West Indies and from Trinidad to the Azores

voyage. It is perhaps necessary to possess an inside knowledge of the Spanish language to taste the full flavour of these names, by no means saintly. *La Pinta*, the "Painted One"; *La Niña*, "The Girl," are names given by amorous seamen, not by continent Quixotes of the sea. The mood of the expedition in Palos, as suggested by these names, was therefore that of a full-blooded, irresponsible and gay adventure—not in the least the lean, tense and ambitious crusading spirit which animated Colón.

So that when the ascetic sea-knight heard that the third ship contracted for—provided, it would appear, by the combined financial efforts of the enterprise—was known as *La Gallega*, or worse still, *Marigalante*, i.e. "Frivolous Mary," he must have frowned hard. Colón never mentioned the name of his ship. On the strength of his chroniclers, who attribute the change of name to Colón himself, the ship has been re-christened *Santa María*. (31) But if the men "obeyed" their Admiral in this, they did not "carry out" his order, and *Holy Mary*, as she became for the Admiral, remained *Mary-Gallant* for the rest of the crew.

She was the biggest of the three, though she had to yield to the *Pinta* in point of swiftness. The seaworthiness of the three famous caravels may have been somewhat underestimated owing to the surprise and admiration which they won by the outstanding performance for which they became justly famous. To sail from the Canaries to the Antilles in thirty-four days is even in our time a remarkable feat for ships of that size. Over unknown seas and winds, it was a masterpiece of that happiest of combinations, daring, skill and luck. Caravel was the name given to a swift, long and narrow ship with one deck, a fender-beam at the prow, a flat poop, three masts, usually lateen (three-cornered) sails, and a few crossyards on the main- and fore-masts. No importance need be attached to the fact that Colón described the *Santa María* as a *nao*, a more mouth-filling word which expressed, no doubt, his sense of his own greatness rather than that of the ship itself. The flagship was just the biggest of three sister caravels. She measured 233 tons and had a big castle aft and a smaller one at the prow. She differed, however, from the lateen caravel in that her sails were square. She was about 117 feet long in all, with a length of deck of about 66 feet. The *Pinta* was about 51 feet long, and also square-sailed. The *Niña*, slightly less long than the *Pinta*, had but one castle (aft) and was lateen-sailed. The three ships were armed with the small artillery of those days, 4-inch *bombardas*, which, amidst much shaking, noise and black smoke, let off heavy balls of granite, and *espingardas* or *falconetes*, for lead projectiles of a smaller calibre. On all their sails a cross spread its arms in a pathetic, ever unanswered, gesture of universal peace. We may imagine the feverish sea-knight "hotter" than ever while the three sea-steeds were being harnessed, on which he was to cross the waves towards the unknown, yet certain, tangible Cipango of his imagination. The golden spurs, the glory of his name, raised at last from persecuted shame to the summit of achievement—wealth, splendour, victory—those were the heady wines of which he was to drink his fill on a now immediate morrow. Today, his relentless will-power, his ever-watching cautiousness and his universal mistrust were still required, more than ever required, while the last preparations were being made for the momentous voyage.

It is fair to surmise that he left most of the material equipment of the fleet to the wise, experienced and wealthy Pinzón. It was no ordinary expedition, for no one could say with certainty how long they would be away, or whether they would ever find any help or supplies anywhere until their return—if they ever did return. Food, water and wine must have been Pinzón's main capital investments after the ships themselves. According to Diego de Valera, (32) a good specialist in these matters, every man expected one pound of biscuits, one *azumbre* (rather more than two litres) of wine and two-thirds of a pound of meat or fish per day, though, he remarks, "They may do now and then with cheese, onions and vegetables and similar things with which ships must always be well provided, not forgetting oil and vinegar, which are things very necessary at sea." No concrete data exist as to the stores that were actually embarked, enough for one year or for six months being the more likely surmises. This would no doubt be the most valuable part of the cargo, and would require on the part of the managers the strict application of the measures of supervision for preventing leakage and token-embarkation (followed by the subsequent evaporation of the goods) which recur with ominous frequency in the legislation of the epoch.

The bottoms were ballasted with the heavy ammunition—stone and metal—required for the artillery. It can hardly have been a convenient cargo for such light ships across such heavy seas. The usual stores of lighting, heating, sailing and medical materials completed what might be described as the vital cargo. Over and above which, Colón saw to it that his ships conveyed "some grosse and sleight wares fit for commerce with barbarous people," (33) such as glass beads, mirrors, coloured bonnets, pins and needles to charm into Christian ways the simple heathens whom he expected to "discover." In this he was no doubt influenced by the history of recent discoveries along the African coasts and the tales of wonderful windfalls of gold conquered with shells and other treasures by Castillian and Portuguese sailors of fortune.

On the other hand, that double thought which inspired his discovery (*new* islands and *old* India, naked savages and over-dressed Grand Khan) prompted him to bring on board "one Luis de Torres who had been a Jew and knew Hebraic and Chaldean and even a little Arabic" (34) in the hope that he would be able to chat with the King of Cipango and to win him over to the Lord. But his main preoccupation would be, no doubt, with the higher staff of the expedition. A glance at the leaders suffices to show to what extent he had become indebted to the Pinzón group: while he personally took command of the *Santa María* as well as of the whole fleet, the *Pinta* was commanded by Martín Alonso Pinzón, and the *Niña* by Vicente Yáñez Pinzón, who was to prove in later years the greatest of the Spanish sailors of his time. Another of the Pinzón brothers, Francisco Martín, was the pilot of the *Pinta*. The master of the crew in the *Santa María* was the famous Juan de la Cosa, owner of the ship, a cosmographer of repute and the author of the most celebrated map of America. The little fleet was by no means lacking in seafaring skill and talent. As for the men, their Admiral himself paid them a handsome tribute: they were "good and seasoned seamen." (35)

All was now ready. After nearly six years of struggling, his dogged determination had won, with the help of that luck which, despite the classic dictum, is more apt to favour the persevering than the audacious. Over a million maravedis had been supplied by the Crown and advanced by Santángel; half a million by Colón himself, on a loan advanced by Pinzón. The considerable part given to this family in the management and command of the expedition leads to the surmise that they must have taken a share in the rest of the money raised.

If we put at 2000 maravedis a ton the price paid for the use of the caravels, and at about 500 the total tonnage of the fleet, this would account for one million; the upkeep for a year would amount to about 540,000; another half-million would suffice for the remaining expenses. (36) It is plain that without the help of the Pinzón family, of their prestige, enthusiasm and money, Colón would not have been, on August 2nd, casting a last glance of triumph and of hope on the three glorious ships.

* *

August 2nd! He was not to leave Spain till August 3rd. But he made everybody go on board on August 2nd.

August 2nd was the day of the great Jewish exodus. The melancholy human herds, limbs of mankind torn away from the body to which they had belonged, wandering desolate hither and thither in the Peninsula for the last three months, "now falling, now rising, now dying, now being born," now trudging along under the broiling sun of Castille, now moaning dejectedly by their century-old cemeteries which they were to abandon for ever, gathered at last in half a dozen ports to sail also—not to a new, fantastic world wrapped up in the glory of a fiery imagination, but to the same old, cruel, savage world which their ancestral memory knew only too well and had every reason to dread.

"Those who went to embark in El Puerto de Santa María and in Cádiz," says Bernáldez, "as soon as they saw the sea, shouted and yelled, men and women, grown-ups and children, asking mercy of the Lord in their prayers, and they thought they would see some marvels from God and that they would have a road opened for them across the sea; and as they remained there many days and saw nothing happen except misfortune, some wished they had never been born." (37)

All was over by August 2nd. Orders were given that the ships conveying the exiled Jews were to leave on that day. Hundreds of thousands left on that fateful date, some to rebuild their fortunes in other lands, others to suffer martyrdom at the hands of pirate or saracen. And on that date, which saw the affliction of Israel, Colón also chose to embark. He left the Spanish soil for his high mission on the same day the Jews left it for their second exodus.

On Friday, August 3rd, half an hour before sunrise, Colón gave the order to sail. One by one the three graceful ships let the fresh breeze of the dawn swell their sails on which the Cross opened its stretched out arms for ever; on the low shore, the whole population of the little harbour saw them gradually swallowed by the jaws of time and space; many a heart must have felt the pangs of anguish; many eyes must have wept. As the three caravels sailed down the Río Tinto, past the Island of Saltes, the first blushes of the dawn must have reddened their sails. The Straits which they were sailing were then ringing with the laments of the Wandering Race: while, still dark and mysterious under the vanishing veils of the fleeing night, a New World awaited them, as blissfully ignorant as they themselves were of the vast future which history was suddenly to open out before mankind.

CHAPTER XVII

THE DISCOVERY

ONCE on the sea, Colón was in his element. Scoffers, wiseacres, doubting Thomases, jeering and envious mediocrities, all the motley crowd of grandees, bishops, officials, courtiers and astrologers who had mortified him in his impatience for the last six years, were now left behind, swallowed out of sight in a grey horizon of flat oblivion like the hills and valleys of the vanished land. The billows of the ocean were less unfriendly. Threatening no doubt they were; but he was a sailor at the head of sailors. His boats were good; his men were good; his captains and pilots were excellent. Colón must at last have felt his own master. All he now had to face was the sea and that unknown which called out to him from the wilderness.

Sitting alone in the castle aft, on his way to the Canaries, he might well wonder at the extent of his victory. At his feet, below, the crowd of his sailors busy at the multifarious activities of a sailship, coming and going with the unsteady step of men tossed to and fro by the swell of the Atlantic, which gave a pendular rhythm to the cracking of the joints of the caravel carcass, to the grinding noise of the pulleys and to the screeching complaints of the distended ropes. There he was. The Captain. Beyond his prow, the *Niña* cut the water with a graceful swing which raised to right and left two diverging bands of white lace shining in the sun; while further ahead, opening the way, the *Pinta*, swiftest of the three adventurous sisters, could be seen rising and falling, all white-sail against a blue-grey sky.

There he was. The Captain. Soon he would be an Admiral —a real Admiral. Had he not been right in rejecting the advice of his well-meaning friends and in demanding all or nothing in the war of honours? Either he won or he did not. If he did not, he would have nothing in any case; if he won, his victory must be his and his the glory. This stubborn faith in his destiny had conquered the King and Queen before he had set sail. On May 8th his son Diego had been appointed a page to Prince Don Juan. Could a higher distinction have been dreamt of by any boy in the country, no matter how exalted his birth? Yet he,

197

Colón, an upstart come from nowhere, had conquered it for his son, merely by faith in his own self and by sheer refusal to abate one jot his own estimate of the value of his discovery-to-be. (1)

Not in vain had he chosen for his bastard son the name of the highest man in the land: Fernando. Don Quixote Colón, otherwise Don Cristóbal de Cipango, was now sure of his golden spurs. No glory was more splendid than his. He felt, to be sure, a worthy envoy to the high and gold-laden majesty of the Grand Khan, who, as was well known and as he had assured their Highnesses, was most anxious to become a Christian and had often "sent [embassies] to Rome asking for doctors in our holy faith to be instructed in it," which had not been done because "the holy Father had never seen to it." (2) This state of affairs was at last to cease. Colón had secured a letter from the King and Queen to the Grand Khan. There it was, in his wallet, together with his passport in good diplomatic Latin, signed also by the King and Queen. For the first time, a direct communication was sought between Christendom, personified in the great Catholic Monarchs of Castille-Aragon, and the Grand Khan, by the direct way of the west which he was to discover.

This thought was of a kind to heat up his inflammable imagination, well stocked with the rich materials of Marco Polo and Sir John Mandeville. How slow his caravels must have seemed to him, hour after hour, on his way to the Canaries, a known, dead piece of land, lying flat on the stone of knowledge, not like his Cipango, still alive in the sea of his imagination. How he must have wished that at least they should all have been able to keep pace with the swift *Pinta* ahead of him. The *Pinta*! Where was she? While he dreamt of her speed she had disappeared. And while he sought her on the horizon, thinking, fearing perhaps that she had run ahead to steal Cipango and its glory and golden spurs from him—for did not that Pinzón know all? . . . There was a rumour and a turmoil on board. *La Pinta*! Well. What is the matter with *La Pinta*? Here she is, close to the flagship. Pinzón is busy aft, but his younger brother Francisco Martín explains to the Admiral that the helm has suddenly snapped from its sockets on the beam and they will be a little time before they are ready to sail on.

This was his first incident. (3) He remembered that two sailors, part-owners of the caravel, had shown a marked disinclination to sail, as if they wished to go back on their word, and, suspicious as he was, he imagined at once that the "accident" must have been less casual than it might seem. Yet, he thought,

Pinzón was a man of energy and resource. (4) This was no doubt his sincere opinion. But after all, no human being can hold more than a certain amount of gratitude, and Colón owed so much to Pinzón that, in the interest of both, it would have been best if the debt had not been increased. Colón seems to have felt again, as he had felt in Palos, that the protection of Pinzón was somewhat irksome, (5) and to have begun then and there to load the loyal sailor of Palos with all the defects which were necessary to justify his suspicion, and later his open estrangement, from his right-hand man. As it happened, the helm of the *Pinta* broke again the next day, and Colón had a fresh occasion to test *in fact* the loyalty and "energy and resource" of Pinzón and to develop and ripen *in imagination* the mistrust and resentment which he felt towards his brilliant second.

Whatever the psychological solution, the *Pinta* had to be taken aground in the Great Canary, in sight of which they arrived on August 9th. Contrary winds and dead calm prevented them from reaching the island for three mortal days. (6) We can feel Colón's impatience to do something, to be on the move, to sail west, west, for he decided to let Pinzón stay in the Great Canary, repairing the *Pinta* and enquiring as to the possibility of replacing her, while he sailed on to La Gomera with the *Niña*, in search, he thought also, of another ship, but mainly of his own dream always ahead of his eager soul. In these comings and goings between the islands of the Canary group he lost nearly a month. Pinzón, like a practical man, attended to his repairs; Colón listened in La Gomera to the tales, which came naturally to him, like birds to their nest, about the island which could be seen at sunset—that ghostly island which arose in men's imaginations on every land of the ocean in those days. We may imagine how such stories would heighten his fever and his hurry. A ship in which Doña Beatriz de Bobadilla, lady of La Gomera, was expected any day, lured him into waiting another two days in the hope of buying her to replace the *Pinta*, though she only displaced forty tons. He sent a message to Pinzón instructing him to do exactly what the competent sailor was already doing, then, unable to wait any longer, put to sea, picked up his messenger on the way, arrived in the Great Canary on the 25th, hustled things on, had the *Niña's* sails altered from lateen, or three-cornered, to square (speed, more speed), returned to La Gomera to restock his fleet with food, water and firewood, and finally on Thursday, September 6th, he sailed resolutely west.

* * *

He was cautious at first, for he had been warned that the King of Portugal had sent three caravels to seize him, as he thought, "out of envy." (7) There is a curious air of unreality about those Portuguese caravels, as if they were but creations of his rich and fearful fancy. That the King of Portugal should go out of his way to thwart an enterprise so deliberately prepared and backed by the powerful King and Queen of Castille-Aragon does not sound very plausible; and that, having decided on so rash a course, he should have allowed his prey to escape him, is in the circumstances no less acceptable. It is more consonant with the character of the persons concerned that, the caravel coming from the Island of Hierro, mentioned by his biographers, having reported three Portuguese caravels—a perfectly normal, and even frequent, occurrence in those waters—Colón should have built up this romantic tale of persecution, feeling as he probably did somewhat uneasy in his conscience about the King of Portugal.

The wind—or rather the lack of it—made him waste Friday and most of Saturday, so that till the evening of the 8th he was not able to make much headway. At dawn on Sunday, September 9th, nine leagues off the Island of Hierro, they lost sight of land. The heart of many a simple sailor of the crew must have sunk. To be sure, it was not the first time that most of them had been out of sight of land, but they always knew where they were, and they always knew that they were either coming back to the coast that had just vanished, or going across to another friendly shore which would presently emerge from the horizon. But this deliberate departure away from Christendom, into a blank unknown, for a distance and a time which no one could fix with certainty, was more than most of them could stomach. That morning, many men looked dejected on board the flagship, and some of the mariners and boys wept.

This moment marks Colón's true original contribution to the history of navigation and discovery. He had made up his mind to sail dead west, away from land instead of along it; and to keep on his course till he had found out what he sought. Poor and simple men as they were, these sailors who were frightened by his resolution were representative of all contemporary seamanship. As Oviedo has truly said, sailing by the stars was taught in schools but no one had dared try it at sea—till Colón did.

Colón the great begins, then, on that Sunday, September 9th, when in the midst of faint-hearts at the sight of the last vanishing land, he provided the moral motive power to keep the fleet on its westward quest. True, he was not the only man on board capable of such a decision, as events were soon to show; but he was the originator and the leader of that bold enterprise which in its essence consisted in sailing resolutely ahead and away from the coast of the world then known.

Here again we meet with his peculiar style: resolution in his strategy; caution in his tactics. His heart was certainly set on sailing west as long as necessary; his avowed purpose was nevertheless limited, at least in appearance, by a skilfully conceived "instruction" (8) which he gave the fleet to the effect that after they had covered seven hundred leagues, they were not to navigate between midnight and daybreak. From the outset he had thus conveyed to his crews a tacit promise that land was to be expected then. Was it Toscanelli? Was it Esdras? Was it an intuition resulting from the many signs and portents then converging on observing minds and which only awaited an opinionated, stubborn and imaginative man to materialise, nay to incarnate and force themselves into history? Who can say? And how can we dissect a living man born in the midst of biblical faiths and legends, bred in the midst of cosmographical truths and errors, grown in the midst of sailing yarns and marvels, and analyse the vigorous impulse which led him across a sea of errors to the shore of truth?

He does not know Colón who does not realise this baffling complexity of his character. Ptolemy and Esdras have an equal value in his mind, a mind both medieval and modern, or better still, neither modern nor medieval. This immortal voyage, conceived with a prophetic imagination, is carried out with a seamanship and a spirit of observation admired by sailor and scientist alike. The choice of the 28th parallel, to which he remained obstinately faithful till nearly the end of the voyage, may have been dictated by the position in which he expected to find Cipango; but the fact is that, if he had tried to navigate further north, he would have met with disaster, since he would have stayed outside the zone of the trade winds. A contemporary American authority points out that on his way back, Colón sailed north-eastward till he reached the latitude of the Azores, and then, like a man who knows what he is doing, he pointed dead west. Why the Azores eastward and the Canaries westward? It so happens that by choosing these two different courses he got wide of contrary winds *both ways*. This would appear to suggest something more than mere luck. Such is the conclusion of this competent American authority, who claims that Colón discovered at once what Spanish seamen in the Pacific failed to do for over forty years—from 1520-21, the date of Magellan's expedition, till 1565, when Urdaneta discovered the west-to-east way. And he adds: "There were really three discoveries made by Columbus instead of one. His discovery of the two ocean routes was so overshadowed by the discovery of land that it has passed unnoticed." (9)

This is an arresting doctrine; but an examination of the routes adopted by Colón in *all* his voyages, and not merely in the first, destroys it altogether. The westward routes happened always to be favourable because Colón sought the south, where blacks and parrots come from; but his eastward voyages were all disastrous because he did not seek the trade-wind parallel, of the existence of which he had no notion. And this point of fact is confirmed by Oviedo, Las Casas and Fernando Colón, (10) who all explicitly say that the discovery of the trade winds was made *after* the Admiral's voyages. The conclusion to be drawn from the exceptionally complete data we possess is that Colón was extremely lucky on his first voyage, and that, while he proved good seamanship, he invented and discovered nothing in the field of winds and trade routes.

The conclusion cannot be so categorical with regard to another sensational discovery attributed to him. On September 13th, the journal, as preserved by Las Casas, reads that "the needles pointed north-west." Colón discovered the magnetic variation of the earth—"a memorable date in the annals of European nautical astronomy," (11) says Humboldt. The fact which to a comfortable scientific mind appeared later in a noble theoretical perspective, must have taken on quite a different aspect to empirical pilots and seamen meeting this unheard of phenomenon in mid-ocean. For think of it: they had left the familiar shores and ventured on the ocean immensity, trusting—not without straining their faith—on the needle. And now when all familiar marks were gone and nothing but the needle remained to keep them in their course, this safest and most reliable of sailor's friends played false! They all knew that needles pointed slightly east of the true pole: and now they saw them pointing west. On Monday the 17th "they found the needles deviating north-west quite a fourth of the wind, and the sailors were frightened and downcast and they would not say why." (12)

Colón met the situation with his usual assurance and resource. It is obvious that he did not know from the first how to explain the disturbing fact observed by his pilots. His views on it require separate treatment since they vary from time to time, and from scientific error to biblical fantasy. As shown in his remarks on September 30th, he began by believing that the fault lay with the Polar star, "for the needles always require truth," i.e. he interpreted the variation as a proof of the fact that "the [Polar] star moves like the others." This explanation, which was the first which occurred to him, had the advantage that it restored his men's confidence in the needle. He gave it out with the assurance of a dogma. It had the advantage that it could be "verified" by experience. "He instructed them to take the north again at daybreak, and they found the needles were true." (13)

The method may not have been above reproach in theory; it certainly was wise in practice. A caravel sailing the ocean for the first time in history is not the best school of astronomy that can be imagined. The men were reassured by the calm, self-possessed attitude of their leader in the face of happenings out of the common, and though the pilots—such men as Juan de la Cosa and Vicente Yáñez Pinzón—could not possibly have been taken in, they no doubt acquiesced tacitly in a technique which was probably not unknown to them.

Such is the background on which should be seen the device imagined by Colón to keep a double log of the ship's track so as to make the crews believe that the distance sailed was less than that actually covered. His declared purpose was to prevent "fear and dismay if the voyage proved long"; (14) to be sure, a double-edged weapon, since the fear and dismay of the crews would grow in proportion to time as well as in proportion to distance. But was this his real purpose? No doubts seem to have been raised on this point. Yet Colón's character, as well as several other utterances made later by him, point to an entirely different reason for his stratagem: *Colón wanted to keep the key of his discovery for himself.* By throwing doubt and confusion on his data, he wished to remain the indispensable guide and gatekeeper of his Cipango.

Nor could he do much more than throw doubt. His secret distances were not more accurate than those recorded publicly by the pilots of the other two ships. There was no special method, available only to him, whereby distances sailed could be more accurately reckoned than by the other pilots and masters. When he was asleep, moreover, he was bound to allow those who were awake to estimate the speed by the only way existing: the timing of the passage of a floating object between two set points on board ship gave the speed; this speed was kindly considered as constant as long as the speed of the wind, the course of the ship and the spread of sail were constant; and the result of all these approximates gave an equally approximate distance run. No special privilege attached to the Captain's estimate over those of the ship masters. The splendour of his historical name seems to have sufficed to impose the view that by some gift of his own, this very rough empirical method applied in his ship, even when he slept, gave better results than in those led by such first-rate sailors as the Pinzón brothers. Yet, all that happened was that when he was awake, he took charge of the measurements and he cut down the figures. The other pilots would soon notice that he was tricking them, or possibly think that there was some systematic error of observation in one or other of the three ships.

For the rest, the expedition went on smoothly enough, obsessed from the very outset by this expectation of land which lured the whole little swarm of men from the European hive. The King and Queen had given a tangible, material value to this expectation by promising a yearly grant of ten thousand maravedis for life to the first man who would see land; Colón had seemed to set a time-limit to it by his significant instructions not to sail by night after seven hundred leagues had been covered; every man on board started thinking of land as the goal and prize of his adventure, the repository of his wealth-to-come; but, as day followed day on the endless sea, land became for everyone the safe, solid element on which his life would be secure from wind and storm and liquid wilderness. At day-break and at sunset the three caravels drew together and tried to pierce the horizon, clearer and more transparent under the twilight. For the day, the ships dispersed by order of speeds: the *Pinta* usually ahead, the flagship usually in the rear, watching, watching. Birds were the greatest attraction, and their movements were closely noted and interpreted as good signs of coming land; all the happenings of the voyage have come to us clad in the highly imaginative language of the poet-admiral: "this night . . . they saw a marvellous nosegay of fire fall from the sky" (15) or else: "the air was most balmy; it was a great pleasure to taste the mornings; we lacked nothing but to hear nightingales." (16) On this very day they began to meet the Gulf weed of the *sargasso* Sea, "very green grass which seemed as if it had recently drifted away from land, which made every-body think that they were close to some island, but not of the mainland, 'for that,' says the Admiral, 'I reckon to be further on.'" (17) On such days, or when a bird known "never to fly more than twenty-five leagues from land" was seen, there was elation on board; the men would walk more briskly and climb to the masts with more alacrity; the boys would watch the passing fish more gaily, or dive playfully in the warm water, or try to hit a passing pelican; and at the prow or amidships, in their daily arguments and discussions, there would be a better spirit towards the lofty visionary who, silent and alone, in his upper cell, dreamt away his thoughts or assiduously wrote down his dreams. But night after night would fall, shrouding them in darkness and shutting them in within its negative vault, and lost in the awful silence of the empty black sea, the three little caravels, with no other company than that of their faint binnacle lights and the creaking noise of their own wooden bones shaken by the waves, had to pass through the agonies of ever-recurring doubts. In those long nights, the seaman kept awake by his night duty and his off-duty comrade kept awake by his wide-eyed anguish, would both brood over the many disappointments which bird and grass and other signs of land had already cost them. Would they ever see land at all, or were they doomed to sail for ever on and on till the endless sea had swallowed up even the very memory of them all? When this mood overcame them, the Admiral could always notice a more solemn and a warmer tone in their voices as, at sunset, following the tradition of Spanish seamen, they all sang together the "Salve Regina." For then, that Salve rising to the russet-coloured sky through rope and sail, from the weather-beaten ship full of weather-beaten sailors, implored a real personal hand to save a real crowd of repentant sinners. Gratefully, as do poor men, they accepted the humblest offerings of hope: "a live crab, which the Admiral kept, saying it was a sure sign of land, for they are never found beyond eighty leagues of land"; (18) a crowd of birds all flying westward, which made Pinzón rush forth shouting to the Admiral from his caravel that he expected to see land that very night; "showers without wind, a sure sign of land"; a "whale, which was a sign that they were close to land, for whales are always close to it."

This longing could not safely remain unsatisfied. Yet by then they had not sailed half—they had barely covered a third—of their voyage and night-fears were beginning to overcome day-hopes. Colón had chosen his course only too well. They had sailed in the wind since they had left La Gomera, and the men, anxious, no doubt, to express their vague fears in some concrete form, swore that there never would be a wind to carry them back to Spain. A contrary wind came to the help of the Captain; but next day (September 23rd) the men growled again, since after all it was their inner dissatisfaction they were venting, and said that the sea was so flat that there never would be enough wind to return, whereupon "the sea rose much without a wind, which astonished them, and here the Admiral says: 'So this high sea was very necessary to me, for this had not happened except at the time of the Jews, when they went out of Egypt with Moses who was leading them out of captivity.' " (19).

How present in his mind all this Jewish lore and how clear the subconscious link between his own person and that of the great Jewish patriarch! This phrase, which the simple-minded Las Casas reports verbatim, sheds a flood of light on those mysterious coincidences we noted between Colón's exodus and the exodus of his brethren expelled from Spain. Deep down in his subconscious being, he was not merely the sea-knight winning his golden spurs—he was the new Moses leading his persecuted people to a vicarious triumph.

Yet time went by and no land was to be seen. On September 25th that awful feeling which crawled about the ship—Doubt—seems to have infected Colón himself. He called Pinzón and asked him whether the chart which he had sent three days earlier to the *Pinta*, for Pinzón's inspection, did not justify his expectation of land there and then. Pinzón answered that it did and threw the chart back with a rope; the Captain with his pilot and mariners set to work on it. That very evening, at sunset, Pinzón, from the castle of his caravel, shouted joyfully that he had sighted land. Some climbed to the masts and rigging; others fell on their knees; some shouted and laughed, others wept and prayed. The Admiral ordered the course to be altered from West to South-West and sailed towards that hope for seventeen leagues—but when morning came, that "land" had vanished.

This time, the crew of the flagship felt deeply aggrieved. Their dismay was as deep as their hopes had risen high; their anger rose again as high as their disappointment had been deep. This stranger, this visionary, this lunatic, was sailing them into death. Something had to be done; and *what* no one needed to strain his imagination to know. The victim was self-designated; the edge of the caravel was not so high; the sea was deep and discreet. Let them but get rid of the foreigner and the voyage home could begin at once. He was the only obstacle. When they complained to him, he answered: "You waste your time in complaining, for I have come to the Indies and I shall sail on till I find them with the help of the Lord." (20)

Withal, he sought also the help of Pinzón, whom he informed of the conspiracy, bordering on mutiny, which threatened him in his ship. Pinzón's answer was characteristic: "Sir, hang half a dozen of them or throw them overboard, and if you dare not, my brothers and I will close upon them and do it, for a fleet which sailed mandated by such high Princes shall not return without good news." Whereupon Colón, who was less spirited before men than before nature, was content to reply: "Let us keep the peace with these gentlemen and sail on for a few days, and if by then we have not struck land we shall consider what we are to do." (21) We can perceive the different tone of voice and the typical difference in temper between the military, resolute, commanding Pinzón and the opinionated, stubborn but gentle and astute Colón. He knows he is in danger and he feels he cannot strangle it, as Pinzón would; so he knows he must set it to sleep. He puts off the ordeal and flatters " these gentlemen," "estos hidalgos." The combination of Pinzón's iron hand with Colón's velvet glove worked well: the "gentlemen" of the flagship were restrained by the thought that if they got rid of Colón, Pinzón would hang them and sail on with the rest; they were also stimulated and encouraged by Pinzón's decision. The danger blew over.

Pinzón again. We may read the effect of this increased hold of the seaman on the sea-knight in the way Colón reacted towards Pinzón's advice as to the course to be followed by the fleet. On October 6th Pinzón suggested that it should be altered from West to South-West. The Admiral was of a contrary opinion. Las Casas' transcription is worth quoting here because it illustrates Colón's mind and his attitude towards Pinzón. "Martín Alonso [Pinzón] said this because of the island of Cipango, and the Admiral saw that if they missed it they would not so easily find the [main]land and that it was best to go first to the mainland and then to the islands." (22) Now this "explanation" will not do. Cipango was for the Admiral as good as a mainland, and, as he was to show but a few days later, he obstinately sought it in the Caribbean Sea. The real trouble was that the suggestion came from Pinzón and this was unpalatable to his pride. He fought with his pride for the whole day and the best part of the next, which was a Sunday. In the morning, the Niña thought they had seen land; they hoisted a flag and shot a blank shot from their bombarda, as instructed by Colón; but when they had to confess their disappointment, Colón must have thought again of Pinzón's advice. He was perhaps missing Cipango by leaving it too far south. What was he to do? He glanced at the sky for inspiration, and the sky gave it. Flights of birds were passing, all south-westward. He bethought himself of the fact that most of the lands discovered by the Portuguese had been found by following the birds. He made up his mind to alter his course to South-West one hour before sunset. This happened on October 7th.

"All the night they heard birds passing." (23) This line vividly suggests their tense watch over the signs. On Thursday, the 11th, the crew of the *Pinta* picked up "a reed and a stick, and another stick carved, as it seemed, with iron tools and some grass which grows on land and a tablet of wood. They all breathed on seeing these signs and felt great joy." (24) The Captain shared the general satisfaction. After the "Salve Regina" had been sung, the night having fallen, under the faint light of the lanterns which picked out a man's face or arm here and there, leaving the rest in living darkness, he spoke to his men of the things that were at hand; he pointed out to them the favour which God had bestowed upon them in bringing them safely over and in sending them so many signs of land, and he urged them to watch with the utmost care, that night; he reminded them that they were not to navigate between midnight and daybreak after they had sailed 700 leagues, a reminder which he felt then safe to make; and he promised to the first man who would see land a velvet doublet over and above the ten thousand maravedis offered by the King and Queen. (25)

The mood was quite different now. Everyone felt that land was so near that it could not be missed. In the still night, the Admiral went up to his castle, to watch. Now his faith was at last to be vindicated. Esdras? Possibly. Toscanelli? Perhaps. Colón, certainly, for he had not committed himself to any definite theory or prophecy. He had merely *believed* that by sailing west, always west, he was sure to come across land—a land, the Grand Khan's land, the mainland, islands, he was not certain about that—but land. The caravels sailed on in the still night and that land was still unseen, unrevealed, undiscovered. Did it exist? asked one hundred sailors in the three wooden shells, sceptical to the last, believing to the last. Yes, he affirmed, alone in the dark, watching for it relentlessly.

Two hours before midnight, he saw a light on land; he did not dare affirm it was actually on land. He called Pedro Gutiérrez, a King's servant, who saw it, and then one Rodrigo Sánchez who did not see it.

"It was like a taper of wax which rose and fell, which few took for a sign of land." (26) Another short-lived illusion, perhaps. Time went by. The water flowed past the bulky flanks of his ship. Perchance he had forgotten his fickle light and wandered from his watch into a dream, when a gunshot shook him back into his bodily self. There was a turmoil ahead, in the *Pinta*. The flag had been hoisted. Two hours after midnight, a man, described as Rodrigo de Triana in the Diary, but whose real name seems to have been Juan Rodriguez Bermejo, had seen land from the prow of the *Pinta*. The Admiral ordered the ships to lie to. He was at last a real Admiral.

There were still two or three hours between Colón and reality, so, why not dream? The men now rested on the shore of certainty; some were excited and whiled away the night building up castles upon castles of idleness, lordship and prosperity; others snatched a well-deserved sleep from the dwindling hours of the remaining night. Colón could dream awake.

So he was right after all. At that hour of triumph, it must have seemed to him strange, almost unbelievable. The spring which he had kept obstinately taut against outside scepticism was set at rest. His soul must have felt relaxed for the first time in twelve years. Unharnessed, the Pegasus of his imagination must have experienced an instant of depression akin to scepticism. Land! And about where he said it would be! But was it land?

And then, on a vigorous return of his faith, Colón would ride the skies once more on his winged horse. He was close to Cipango. That was certain. He was sure of it, and so was Pinzón. Cipango was perhaps sleeping peacefully within a shot of his *bombardas*, sleeping in its luxurious beds of ivory, gold and ebony, under its roofs of golden tiles, in the splendour of its oriental luxury. Or perhaps Cathay? For if Esdras was right—and he could not go far wrong whom St. Augustine considered as a prophet—the earth was small and he might well have missed Cipango and sailed up to the mainland of the Grand Khan. Presently, tomorrow perhaps, he would be travelling in great state on a golden sedan chair over the thousand marble bridges of Quinsay, as the accredited ambassador of

Their Highnesses, and he would be introduced to the presence of the Grand Khan. . . . Or, perhaps, he was close to one of those innumerable islands which lie on the coast of the Indian Continent, and, as everyone knows, are so rich in gold that in some of them the streets are paved with the precious and lovely metal; in which case, he would take possession of the new-discovered territories in the name of the King and Queen and he would be their Viceroy and Governor-General, to the confusion and shame of those who had laughed at him in Portugal and Castille and who had persecuted and debased his people. He, the son of the weaver, he would reign over glorious lands; he would wear rich clothes and be obeyed by multitudes; true, his authority would be but delegated by the King and Queen, and he but a moon of those two suns; but they were far away and one never could tell how things might develop and how this mighty empire beyond the ocean, which was his, which he held in his hand, and which he had in his power to give to whomsoever he wished—or to keep for himself—— (27)

Here his dreams would vanish underground, to reappear again on the theme of gold, for gold is an excellent thing wherewith souls may be saved and Jerusalem may be liberated. He would deliver Jerusalem. He, Colón, would first become the Prince of the West and then the Liberator of the House of Sion. Else, why should the Lord have reserved for him this mighty discovery?

The night meanwhile was growing pale and dying away and, facing Colón's dreams, the dawn was gradually revealing and clarifying its own thoughts. The dawn was thinking of a lovely fresh sandy shore on which the surf beat gently, and round which tall, strange trees of vivid green rose to meet the vivid blue of the now luminous skies. Was he dreaming? Was he actually seeing the land which the Lord meant to be his, the Promised Land? There was a tense silence. The men drank in the exhilarating mixture of the safe, the strange and the unbelievable. All eyes, they forgot to speak. The land itself was silent, still asleep perhaps, surprised in its virgin bed by the intruding strangers. The caravels stole into the little cove on a silky water, which the morning light turned into liquid emerald. The land was still, quiet, living away its morning dream as it had done for centuries, blissfully ignorant of the unique significance of that fateful morning which closed for ever its age-long peace, within the undisturbed gardens of its soul. The caravels came closer and closer; crags, tall grass, trunks of unfamiliar trees, the rustling of birds . . . the island was beginning to give itself to the strangers, still half-asleep, half-adream. Suddenly, a parrot yelled. A few light-bodied men ran down to the shore and stared bewildered at the fantastic sails. The island's dream vanished—for ever. An age had died.

CHAPTER XVIII

THE DISCOVERY OF CIPANGO

THE Admiral went ashore with his two Captains and other leaders and officials of the fleet. He was wearing his most magnificent apparel and his right hand held firm and high the Royal Banner; while Pinzón and his brother Vicente Yáñez each carried a flag of the Green Cross on which the Cross was flanked with the crowned initials of Ferdinand and Isabel. The sea provided the white element, the land the brown, for that strange, incongruous meeting of man with man; in the centre Colón, the Pinzóns, Rodrigo de Escovedo, the fleet notary, and Rodrigo Sánchez de Segovia, its inspector, provided with paper and pen to write down the official minutes of the event; an armed guard; and their three banners; around them, a crowd of natives, young, beautiful and naked. What did these civilised men say to these savages? What symbolic gesture did they imagine to bridge over the gap which separated them? "The Admiral [. . .] asked them all [the Christians] to give faith and witness how he before them all took possession of the said island for the King and for the Queen, his sovereigns, with all the ceremonies required." It would be difficult to imagine a more tragically incongruous action between men and men. What could those natives make of it? Fortunately, the language barrier allowed them to misunderstand the strangers' ceremony as some magic or symbolic act, for otherwise an act of possession must have appeared to them utterly incomprehensible, devoid as they were of any sense of property. (1)

They watched with the earnestness of children to the very end, waiting patiently while the foreign magicians performed the most tedious and incomprehensible of their incantations—that of scratching white sheets of a material which looked like cotton cloth but was stiffer and more brittle, with the split point of a feather dipped in some mysterious black juice which one of them carried in a small horn hanging from his waist; a ceremony to which the pale strangers evidently attached great importance, for when all the sheets but one had been covered with black scratches, all their leaders successively scratched the last with the split-

212

pointed feather, some of them, the natives noticed, taking a wondrous time at it and showing their tongue between their teeth as their stiff fingers handled the magic feather.

The ceremony over, the natives mixed freely with their visitors. They were first conquered by the odd objects which with friendly gestures the foreigners put in their hands—red bonnets, glass beads, brass bells, the tinkling of which was truly delightful in its novelty; then amused by the childish pleasure which these heavy, bearded men took in such common and silly things as parrots, and puzzled by the interest and curiosity with which they watched, followed with their eyes, touched and tried to seize the small gold pendants which the vainer men of the tribe wore on their noses. As the newcomers seemed to enjoy the game, they freely exchanged cotton balls and parrots for glass beads and brass bells and also for curious little discs of silver and copper decorated with vague designs, and to which, apparently, the strangers attached considerable value.

Meanwhile, the islanders observed the caravel-dwellers and wondered at their appearance and ways. They were so strange! Their skin was pale and sickly and they were hairy like animals, save that some of them had no hair on their heads, as if it had all migrated to their chins, which made the youngsters of the tribe grin and laugh outright; others had wavy hair, not black, but all kinds of odd colours, tobacco, maize-straw, or silver, or gold. The leader struck them most of all, for his face was as white as cocoanut-milk, save that it was sun-speckled and at times took on a bright red tinge, while his eyes were the colour of the sky, possibly because he came from heaven.

But what puzzled the natives most were the heavy coverings which these unaccountable men wore: thick garments, some as thick as animals' skins, others thicker by far and as rigid as the back of the biggest turtle. A native wag whispered: "They are men with tails. That's why," and a ripple of laughter ran through the naked crowd. It was the standing joke in all the Antilles about the distant tribes which were known to go about covered with clothes. (2) But their fickle attention soon flitted to another curious feature of their guests: those sticks they wore hanging by their left legs, which were hollow, with another stick inside, flat, shiny and sharper than the sharpest fishbone! What could they be? One of the islanders was offered a stick of this kind by a laughing, good-humoured pale-face; he held it tight for an instant but at once let go—his hand was bleeding with a deep nasty cut. Quick as lightning, the word went round amongst the natives. Beware! They are dangerous beings. Their magic sticks draw blood. They may cause death. Beware! Beware!

Beware! The harm was done. The weapon, even handled in jest, had broken the primal trust. These new men were not like the usual kind. They might have been better, free from blood-sin and death. There was in the lofty brow and kind eyes of some of them a light that might have justified that hope. But, beware! It is *not* justified. The new men are no better than the fierce ones who come over now and then from Caniba and kill and wound us and eat those they take away. Beware! Beware!

* *

Colón was in Guanahani, known at present as Watling Island, one of the Lucayas, nowadays under the British flag. (3) Providence, fate or luck had decreed that everything in this discovery should conspire to dispose nature's truths in the shape of Colón's errors; not only was there a whole continent just at the spot where Colón's fanciful cosmography had placed "India" and "Cathay," but his course had led him to meet this continent at the only latitude where it is guarded by strings of islands, which was exactly what Colón, fed on Marco Polo, expected Cathay to be. Wandering from island to island in this sea-labyrinth, he "confirmed" his rooted conviction that he was off the coast of Asia and not far from Cipango. On November 14th Las Casas, transcribing his Journal, makes him say: "that he believes these islands to be the innumerable ones which are set down in the maps at the end of the Orient." (4) With that quixotic feature of his character which leads him to assert as a fact the fancy he happens to entertain at the time, he writes that gold "is born in this island, though owing to lack of time I could not fully prove it, and here also is born the gold which they wear hanging from their noses"; but he adds: "yet so as not to waste time I want to leave at once and see whether I can come across the Island of Cipango." (5)

For about a fortnight he wandered from island to island, christening them with Spanish names, in honour of saints or princes—Santa María de la Concepción, Fernandina, Isabela—wrapped in admiration before the beauty of the tropical landscape, which he often describes with poetical and subjective emotion rather than with actual sensibility for its own plastic qualities, seeking always the help of Spanish memories as points of reference. Gold remains—with Cipango—his chief obsession. This has been counted against him by modern authors, for, as everybody knows, no one is obsessed by gold nowadays. It is too easily forgotten that he had promised to discover lands of Oriental splendour (as seen through Western eyes), and that he had to "deliver the goods" or become the laughing-stock of Spain; that he was the head of an expedition organised by shareholders who expected a profit; and that then, as now, gold was the yardstick of success. Moreover, was he not by then Grand Admiral of the Ocean Sea, and should he not have a household and live like a prince of the Earth? He went about eagerly seeking every sign which might put him on the track of "the place where it is born," as he says with inimitable phrase. His "signs" were not all of equal prospecting value, witness this "observation" which we owe to Las Casas: "The Admiral argued from this heat of which he then suffered that in these Indies and in that region where he was, there must be gold." His hope rests always on the Lord: "And the Admiral believed that he was near the source and that our Lord would show him where gold is born." (6)

Yet, already at this early stage, we may discern his mind awakening to other possibilities of what we would nowadays call economic exploitation and political dominance—in one word, *Empire.* It is possible that his repeated disappointments on the matter of gold led him to seek compensation in the general wealth of the lands he had discovered. His early days in the Mediterranean, as a seaman, merchant and corsair—the three professions could easily melt into one in those days—had trained his eye to detect possibilities of profit and "development." "Your Highnesses may believe," he writes in his daily report on October 17th, "that this land is the best and most fertile and temperate and flat and good that can be found in the world." (7).

An episode which he sets down as having happened on November 25th may be quoted as symbolical of this healthy evolution of his attention from mere gold to real wealth. "He went to the river and saw in it stones which shone with gold-coloured spots on them, and he remembered that gold had been found close to the mouth of the Tagus, near the sea, and he thought that surely these stones had gold in them, and he ordered some to be gathered to take over to the King and Queen. While he was thus engaged" —i.e. gathering worthless stones, probably with some spots of mica or galena on them—"some shipboys shouted that they saw pinewoods. He looked towards the hill and he saw the pines, so tall and wonderful that he could not adequately describe their tallness and straightness [. . .], and he saw that out of them ships and great quantities of planks and masts might be made for the biggest ships of Spain. He saw oaks and *madroños* and a good river with all that was needed to set up water-sawmills." (8)

From this moment, the passages in his Diary which reflect his appreciation of the economic value of his discovery are too numerous for quotation; nor were his men less keen, for one brings him cinnamon, another musk, a third aloes, and he himself has many trees "bled" for musk-gum, and notes the abundance of cotton, shrewdly remarking that it would be better to sell it in the Grand Khan's cities than in Spain. (9) Colón extols the beauty of the land with a sound sense of the basic importance of land in all wealth: "for it is certain, my lord and my lady, that wherever such lands can be found there must needs be numberless things of profit." (10)

This economic trend of his mind was to appear in a less acceptable form when, quite early in the day, he betrayed an interest in the possibilities of slavery. His subconscious attitude towards the Indians was far less brotherly than his Christian professions might have led us to expect. The very first day he met them, he says in his Journal: "They must make good servants," and he records his intention to take six of them away to Spain to learn the language. Two days later, two days after the Cross had opened out its arms of ever-waiting, universal love over the virgin continent, Colón, the Messenger, the Chosen of the Lord, wrote down these words in his Diary: "These people are very simple in weapons, as Your Highnesses see from seven of them whom I ordered to be taken to bring them over so that they may learn the language and have them sent back, though Your Highnesses may, whenever you so wish, have them all sent to Castille or keep them all captives in the island, for with fifty armed men you will keep them all under your sway and will make them do all you may desire." (11)

Here is the beginning of the new slavery which the Christians introduced in America. Colón's idea was to triumph in the end, being more in harmony with the economic and psychological forces of the time than the Christian principles of Ferdinand and Isabel, as hereafter analysed. This fact should be given due weight in an estimate of Colón's idea of his mission as a propagator of the Gospel. He does not seem to be aware of the contradiction implied between his intention to enslave these native souls and his genuine—for it was genuine—desire to convert them to the law of Christ. The man who writes on November 6th urging the King and Queen to "propagate the holy Christian religion" by "converting such great peoples" writes on November 7th these revealing words, so utterly devoid of Christian spirit: "Yesterday a canoe came close to the ship with six [native] youths, five of whom came on board; I had them arrested and I am bringing them over. And thereafter I sent [men] to a house near the west river and they brought seven heads of women, some grown up, some girls and three children. This I did because the men will behave better in Spain having women of their country by them than without women." It would be difficult to find a starker utterance of utilitarian subjection of man by man than this passage of our otherwise sincere Christian. Its form is no less devoid of human feeling than its substance, and there is a sad inhumanity in the expression "heads of women" as one would say "heads of cattle." (12)

What was, then, the sense and the importance which Colón attached to the evangelisation of the Indies on which he writes so often and with so much insistence to the King and Queen? Two elements may be discerned in it; the first is a purely subjective feeling of a mission to fulfil—more directly associated in his mind with his Christian name *Christopher*, the Christ-bearer. This vision is egotistical, and though, logically, it assumes the existence of a place or people whither Christ is being borne, vitally, it needs no such people and no such place: the Christ-bearer sees himself carrying his precious burden, and the feeling of sacredness and importance which he derives from this mission suffices to balance his mental state. Such was to a considerable degree the subconscious attitude of Colón. He was meant to Christianise the continent, and that thought was enough for him without any elaboration of the consequences which it implied for *other human beings* whose presence he was far too egotistical to feel.

And, then, there was the political aspect of conversion, stronger in those days than in our own. Religion, civilisation, culture and civic life were then far less dissociated than they are in our time. Conversion, organisation, economic development and conquest were all one. By conversion, therefore, he meant as well a public, and even a political, action which was more specifically associated with his surname—Colón—i.e. colonisation or empire-building.

"He put up a big cross at the mouth of the harbour, [. . .] on a hill where it could be seen from everywhere, as a sign, he says, that Your Highnesses will hold this country as their own and mainly as a sign of Jesus Christ our Lord and in honour of Christianity," (13) says Las Casas. More than one of his utterances express this political conception of Christendom as a new order for the New World. There is a page in his Journal, quoted textually by Las Casas, under the date November 27th, which is typical in its inextricable mixture of religious, economic, political, military and health considerations. After extolling the profit to be expected from the lands and deploring the misunderstandings due to ignorance of the native language, he announces that he is going to have this language taught "to persons of my household," a delightful touch, be it said in passing, of his incurable megalomania; then he says: "and then the profit shall be known and we shall endeavour to turn all these peoples into Christians, which will be quickly done, for they have no sect and they are not idolatrous, and Your Highnesses will order cities and fortresses to be built in those parts and these lands will be converted." He then praises once more the fertility and wealth of the country, assures the King and Queen that there must still be many lands, cities and "innumerable people" about, which he proposes to discover before returning, and concludes: "I say that Christendom shall make good business with them, especially Spain, to which all must be subjected. And I say that Your Highnesses must not allow any foreigner to trade or set foot here, save Catholic Christians, for this was the end and the beginning of the enterprise, that it should lead to the increase and glory of the Christian religion, nor should any one come here who is not a good Christian." (14)

This page is all-important not only because it is a clear statement of the political aspect of Colón's religion, but also because it provides yet another indication—after so many—of his Jewish race. Despite its nationalist form, which may be, and probably is, due to cunning, this outline of a colonial empire is profoundly universalist in essence. No one should be—though some have been—misled by such phrases as: "Your Highness must not allow any foreigner to trade or set foot here." A careful reading of the whole text shows that Colón did not mean to close the Indies to anyone—*no matter his nationality*—who was a good Christian. This follows from two of his statements: the first is the saving clause which comes immediately after his apparent exclusion of all "foreigners"—*save Catholic Christians*; the second, his previous declaration to the effect that *Christendom shall make good business with them, especially Spain.* This is no nationalist conception, but one which opens the Indies to all men provided they be good Christians. Note that Colón speaks of *Spain*, not of Castille nor Aragon, and that in those days *Spain* meant the whole Peninsula. This is a second symptom which suggests

Judaism, though, this time, by no means exclusively. But there is a third one, exclusively Jewish. Colón speaks of *good* Christians, not of *old* Christians, thus leaving the field open to the *Converso* people, to which he has already given so many signs of belonging. This page is conceived by one whose subconscious attitude towards the problem of nationality is that no "good Christian" should be treated as a foreigner; read in the context of the day as analysed above, it is a further indication that Colón was of *Converso* descent.

* *
*

After a first period of mutual interest and friendly relations, the intercourse between the Christians and the natives became more precarious and fitful. There are few cases in which Colón shows himself more illogical and disappointing. He began well, by defending the interests of the natives against the sailors and ship-boys who tried to take advantage of their ignorance of European values. Yet, as he himself explains, he was not taking up their interests as such, but in order to make a good impression on them "so that the next time Your Highnesses send people here they should be well received," an idea which often recurs under his pen. On their way to Fernandina, they met an Indian from San Salvador, rowing hard in his small canoe. He was tired and came to the Admiral's ship. An inspection of the contents of a small basket he conveyed showed that he was going to give the Fernandina natives news of the Pale-faces just arrived in their world. The Admiral gave him bread, honey and wine and small presents, and conveyed him in the ship, leaving him close to the spot where he wanted to go "so that he gives a good report of us, and when Your Highnesses, so please the Lord, send more people here, they will be well received and [the natives] will give us all there is." (15)

Colón was therefore thinking as a statesman, not as a Christian; as *Colón*, not as *Christopher*.

Then he made his first capital blunder. He took away by force seven men of Guanahani. This tyrannical action, for all we know, may even have been wholly unnecessary, for enough men might have been tempted to follow him of their own accord. He does not seem to have even imagined that there was anything wrong with it, though, singularly enough, it was not merely un-Christian but unstatesmanlike as well; henceforth he had broken the bond of peace. The word must have spread like lightning. "Beware, beware. They are no better than the men of Caniba who come and eat us."

The situation soon became tragi-comic. As soon as the "Indians" saw the Spaniards anywhere they ran away for all they were worth, leaving their homes and possessions rather than meet the dreaded strangers whom they believed to have come from heaven, yet to be cannibals or little better. (16) Meanwhile, the Admiral was convinced that "Caniba is nothing else but the people of the Grand Khan [i.e. *Caniba*, ' the people of the Can '], which must be close by and will no doubt have ships and come to take them away as captives, and as they do not return [the others] think they have been eaten." (17) He repeats the statement many times and on many occasions, some of which lend some colour to his scepticism in the matter of cannibals, as when he was assured that the Caniba men "had but one eye and faces like dogs," and the Admiral thought they lied; (it did not occur to him that *Can* means *dog* in Spanish, an admirable opportunity for the crew's wag); or else when two natives were shown to him in whose bodies portions of flesh were missing and they gave him to understand that the cannibals had bitten them off and eaten them: "the Admiral did not believe it." (18)

It is therefore to the credit of his optimistic nature that just after one of these explanations on the identity of Caniba with the Great Khan, he should write: "Every day we understand these Indians better, and they us, though often they may have understood one thing for another." (19) Thanks to this happy understanding which reigned amongst them, Colón became more and more convinced that he was close to Cipango, for all the Indians spoke to him of a "great island" (they were two), one called Cuba and the other Bohio (*bohio* meaning house, he certainly misunderstood them and they meant Haiti), which fitted exactly with his Toscanelli, particularly as there were dozens of small islands in front and the mainland (Cathay, of course) behind. "And," says Las Casas, "from the words of the Indians, which he did not understand, he fancied they said there were sure to be there big merchant ships and places where great dealings were concluded." (20) Unable to restrain his impatience, he writes in his Journal on October 23rd: "I should like to leave today for the Island of Cuba, which must be Cipango, according to what these people tell me of its size and wealth." (21) He did sail that day and arrived in Cuba on Sunday the 28th. The exotic beauty of the Queen of Islands struck his poetic soul, and he declares that he had never seen anything so beautiful. Following his list of saints and princes, wherein he found the names for his discoveries, he christened the island *Juana*, after the heir to the throne. Then he wished to proceed with his quest. Where was he? And where was the gold? The second question hopelessly confused the first. It so happened that there was gold in the middle province of the island, and that, in the indigenous language, the word for *middle* was *nacan*. *Mid-Cuba* was therefore *Cubanacan*. *Can* again. The effect of this revelation was instantaneous. This land was not Cipango; it was the land of the Grand Khan. (22)

The misunderstanding multiplied itself *ad infinitum*, like the image of a person caught between two mirrors. The Indians fled on seeing the Spaniards, and the Spaniards, believing they fled because they mistook them for cannibals, whom the Spaniards mistook for the subjects of the Great Khan, shouted at the fleeing natives not to be afraid because they, the Spaniards, had nothing to do with the Great Khan. What the Indians made of these assurances, it is difficult to surmise.

Colón was very much elated. He fed on errors, and the more unreal a situation, the more able was his imagination to steer through it. Whenever he was squarely in the wrong, he adopted that language of passionate certitude which Cervantes was later to immortalise and which he seems to have borrowed for his Don Quixote de la Mancha from Don Cristóbal de Cipango. "It is certain that this [Cuba] is the mainland, and that I am before Zayto and Quinsay, one hundred leagues, little more, little less, from the one and from the other, as may be noticed in the sea which comes in a different way than it used to before, and yesterday while sailing north-westward I found it was cold." (23) He therefore decided to send a messenger forward to enquire about the King of the land, and in order to make it easier, he chose for this difficult message the *Converso* Luis de Torres, "who had been a Jew and knew Hebrew, Chaldean and even a little Arabic," so he was sure to misunderstand the Indians in more ways than a less tongue-gifted Spaniard would have done. Luis de Torres and one Rodrigo de Jerez left the fleet on November 2nd and ventured inland. They returned on the 5th. They did not find the Great Khan; they did not find the source of gold; but they found that which has since then raised more dreams than gold, and which wields more power over men than ever the Grand Khan did over his subjects. "The two Christians found on the road many persons going to their villages, women and men, with a brand in their hands to take their fumigations as they were used to do." Such was the way tobacco was discovered, "wherewith," comments Las Casas, fully half a century later, "the flesh is made numb and one almost gets inebriate, and they say they do not feel their tiredness. I know of Spaniards in this island who have acquired the habit. . . . I do not know what taste or profit they can possibly find in it." (24)

Tobacco was, to be sure, a most mighty potentate and a rich gold-mine, but it lacked the majesty of the Grand Khan. It left Colón cold and uninterested—such is our blindness to the kind acts of Fate. When Nature gave him gold in a new, unexpected form he did not recognise it and allowed it to be smoked away under his own nose without detecting its flavour. Disappointed, he was not discouraged, and he started on a patient exploration of the northern coast of the island which he took for part of the mainland of Asia. He was not merely reconnoitring "the mainland"; he was trying to find signs of Cipango. It was while the little fleet was engaged in this expedition that the *Pinta* sailed away and disappeared from sight. Martín Alonso Pinzón was also a keen believer in Cipango, and was to land before Colón in the island which, for Colón at any rate, was Cipango itself—even after he set foot on it; so that when, on November 21st, his eager and headstrong second let the east wind bear him away in his swifter caravel towards the precious goal of that long-sought enterprise, Colón must have felt his heart overcome with bitterness. He was a master in the art of suffering in silence, yet this time he waxed eloquent on the cupidity and insolence of Pinzón.

As usual with Colón's life, opinion is definitely split: some are *Colonites*, others *Pinzonites*. (25) And yet, though, as usual, the information available leaves enough gaps for argument and imagination to have free play, the conclusion is surely that both men were human, both ambitious, both eager to earn fame and renown and therefore both sure to commit every possible error against each other. All we know of Colón, particularly his own comments on the last voyage, goes to prove that he kept a jealous eye on any fact or move likely to admit anyone to share in his glory or profit as the discoverer and admiral. His sense of ownership with regard to the Indies was of the keenest. This was bound to be a thorn in the flesh of Martín Alonso, who had his own royal share of egotism. Colón's anxiety—a feeling which seems never to have left him—led him to fear that Martín Alonso's plan consisted in stealing a march on him and reaping the glory and benefit in Castille before the arrival of the slower flagship. But the evidence available today warrants the conclusion that Martín Alonso never thought of so dastardly an act. An accidental separation due to a change of course ordered by the Admiral when the

Pinta was not in a position to see the signals, Pinzón's own explanation, seems too easy a way out in view of the fact that the *Niña*, hardly less swift, was able to remain in touch with the flagship, and Las Casas (26) definitely says that the *Pinta*, sailing her own course eastwards, remained in sight of the fleet all Thursday and did not disappear till the night. The reasonable view is that Colón's egotism and overbearing ways were too much for the spirited and undisciplined Iberian, who sought relief in a kind of "holiday" combining business with pleasure, as is presently to be seen.

This view is borne out by the four facts we know for certain: (*a*) he sailed to Babeque, then to Haiti, or "Cipango" (later known as "Española"), where he knew Colón was also going, therefore he preceded Colón but did not run away from him; (*b*) he discovered a river, to which he gave his own name, seeking relief for the repression of his personality which Colón had made him endure; (*c*) he found much gold, bought it with trifles, in the usual "Christian" way, and gave half to the crew, keeping the other half for himself; (*d*) he sent messages to Colón and, receiving no answer, sailed out to meet him, while, being the swifter of the two, he need not have gone back to him at all.

Meanwhile Colón, who had returned to Cuba and had been delayed by contrary winds, arrived in Haiti on December 6th. He admired his new discovery even more than Cuba, and found it so much like Castille that he called it the Spanish Island, La Isla Española. (27) This is the second time we have occasion to observe the definite tendency of Colón to refer to *Spain* whenever he thinks politically: he may speak of the summer of Andalucía or of the valleys of Castille, but he speaks of the profit which *Spain* will have in the development of the Indies and calls the island *Española*. In his mind, this name meant to convey the excellences and beauties of Haiti, which seems to have struck him—as it did Las Casas—as the most beautiful of the Basket of Islands he had found on the Ocean.

The cultivated valleys, the splendid tropical woods, the beautiful natives "who, were they but dressed and kept from sun and air, would be almost as white as in Spain," the width, depth and natural defensive conditions of the harbours, the rivers, the fish, the birds, not forgetting the precious parrots, all they saw and experienced, kept the Christians in a state of enchantment. As for their leader, less and less *Christopher* and more and more *Colón*, he wrote to the King and Queen in his Journal: "This island and all the others are as much yours as Castille. . . . They [the natives] have no weapons and go about naked and are of no spirit for arms and very cowardly, for one thousand would not stand up to three, and so they are good to be ordered and to be made to work, sow and do all that is necessary, and to build towns and learn to be dressed and to take on our ways." (28) But time was soon to show that Colón had tragically underestimated the fighting spirit of the natives of Haiti, and this mistake was to become one of the causes of his downfall.

It was a mistake typical of our unfortunate West—that of imagining that kindness and ignorance (with the awe and uneasiness before the unknown which it raises in men) imply lack of courage and of resolution. There is no doubt that the natives of the Antilles, and particularly of Haiti, as described by Colón in terms which bear the stamp of truth, were a most intelligent and cultivated people who, within the limitations of their climate, had built up a notable civilisation. Both Las Casas and Colón refer to the high degree of cultivation of their lands; we are told of beautifully carved and sculptured canoes of mahogany, holding as many as one hundred and fifty persons, and of statues in the shape of women. Their manners are extolled by Colón: "All these lords are men of few words and of very delightful ways, and they convey their orders at most with a sign of the hand, whereupon they are wonderfully understood." (29) Nor should we imagine that their nakedness prevented them from cultivating the cosmetic arts; for in the finest of all, which, I take it, is hairdressing, they seem to have anticipated the perfection of our "hair stylists," as more than one lady of fashion will realise reading what Dr. Chanca has to report on the matter: "Their hair is cropped in many places, and in those places so much covered with curly locks that it could not be described. In fine, all that we in Spain might wish to do with a madman's head, here they will take it for a great favour." (30)

Colón, who had the civilised prejudice against nakedness, succeeded in making one of the local *caciques*, whom he decorates freely with the name of kings, wear a shirt and gloves, which in a land of naked people must have given his majesty a most kingly appearance. There is more than meets the eye in this interest in shirts evinced by the crafty Genoese, as will be revealed anon. Thus decorated, the *cacique* came to eat on board ship with the Admiral, who points out that "in his way of eating, in his neatness and beautiful cleanness he showed his lineage." (31) As for their moral culture, the portrait which Colón makes of them is so flattering that one is left wondering whether these natives of Haiti were not the only true Christians that ever existed. They gave all they had—gold as freely as water and as generously—much to the astonishment of the Admiral, who adds: "for it is easy to know when a thing is given with a heart eager to give"; and again: "he cannot believe that any man has ever seen people with such good hearts and ready to give away their own"; and finally, this judgment which the Bearer of Christ and the Seeker of Gold passes on the souls which he is to "convert": "they are peoples of love and without cupidity . . . they love their neighbour as themselves and have the softest and gentlest speech in the world." (32)

Meanwhile, Colón wandered about in search of gold. Much was liberally given him; much was bartered; there were signs, which did not escape his cautious eye, that "kings" and *caciques* began to look askance at this gold-hunting of the Christians; and an old native, with uncommon shrewdness, explained to the Admiral that there was great abundance of gold in many islands one hundred and more leagues away, thereby revealing the distance at which he wished to see the Christians, whom he tempted with "an island made all of gold and others in which there is so much of it that they gather it and pass it through sieves." (33)

What with gold-seeking and navigation, the Admiral-gold-prospector, conscientious to a fault, deprived himself of sleep, and one night when, in exceptionally calm conditions and "the sea like a plate," he had retired to rest, all the men went to sleep, leaving the helm to a boy—against the orders of their chief. The current ran the ship aground. The Admiral's story puts everybody in a bad light, including the master of the ship, who rowed away in the ship's boat with the men, instead of helping Colón to rescue her. As this master was the famous cosmographer Juan de la Cosa, and the ship happened to be his own property and there was not a vestige of danger—which, moreover, would not have been an acceptable explanation for Juan de la Cosa and his men—competent observers are not inclined to take Colón's story at its face value. (34)

This accident was crucial in the history of the discovery. First, Colón was able to observe the compassionate character of the natives, who sent their best help and were moved to tears by the sight of the beautiful ship lost; as well as their efficiency and discipline, for he testifies that all stores and valuables were removed and put away, and "he assures the King and Queen that nowhere in Castille could there have been so much attention in everything so that not one needle was missed." (35)

Then, the accident took place on Christmas Day, 1492, at midnight, and this fact could not but impress the missionary-visionary Christopher. After the first shock was over and the necessary action had been taken, he began to ponder over it and to consider it as a portent. The situation was serious. The *Pinta* had disappeared; the flagship was lost. *He had no room to bring the two crews back.* What was he to do? What else could he do but to leave behind those he could not carry? On this hard rock of necessity, he built up a castle of fancy and a cathedral of faith: he "realised that our Lord had made the ship run aground there to make him leave a settlement." And such was the birth of the first Christian settlement—or should we say settlement of Christians?—in the New World. It was named *Villa de la Navidad*—a fortress, which he provided with food for a year and abundant ammunition and stores, so that the natives should "obey with love and fear." As chiefs of Villa de la Navidad, he left Diego de Arana, his mistress's relation, and Pedro Gutiérrez, the King's butler, the only man, by the way, who had seen the light which had made Colón think he had seen land. And, having chosen the thirty-eight men who would remain under their orders, many of whom, he says, had volunteered, he made up his mind to return to Castille and report to the King and Queen. (36)

He was uneasy about Pinzón, lest the glory and benefit of his enterprise be stolen from him and possibly his foibles and mistakes brought to the fore. And "he had found what he was looking for." (37) What was he looking for? What had he found? Cipango. In his own rendering of the conversation with the "king" who had been so kind to him when his flagship had been lost, he writes that the king comforted him, for there was gold "in Cipango, which they call Civao." As in Cuba with Cubanacan, in Haiti a whole district called Civao or Cibao was at once read into Cipango by Don Quixote-Colón. It was exactly what he was looking for. One always finds in life what one brings to it. "He concluded that Cipango was in that island and that there is in it abundance of gold, spices, musk and rhubarb." (38) Thus comforted, Don Cristóbal de Cipango, Grand Admiral of the Ocean Sea, set sail for Castille on the *Niña* on Friday, January 4th, 1493.

CHAPTER XIX

HOME WITH THE NEWS

THE "fleet," reduced to its junior caravel, sailed at first somewhat leisurely along the coast, which Colón observed closely, with that conscientious eye for nature which he combined so strangely with his superb capacity for flying away from it. He left no bay unexplored, no hill uncharted, no bottom unsounded. (1) Two antagonistic forces seemed to be working in his mind at the time: fear lest Martín Alonso Pinzón had sailed away to Spain made him hasten eastwards; fear lest his second should be still in Española reaping a harvest of gold which would put him in the shade—for there is no sun like gold—acted like a break on his first impulse and made him linger while sailing east. This would appear to supply a plausible explanation for the curious, vacillating course which he kept from Friday the 4th till Sunday the 6th. On the 6th, " after midday, there rose a strong East wind, and he bid a sailor climb to the top of the mast to watch the sea-bottom, and he saw the caravel *Pinta* coming towards them, sailing before the East wind." (2) As there was no good anchorage near by, the Admiral decided to go back forty miles. He no doubt felt that he could not possibly sail on to Spain without having cleared up the situation. His worst fears were allayed. Martín Alonso was not betraying him, either by sailing ahead or by gold-hunting behind. He had had his holiday and returned to the fold. Yet Colón was full of bitter memories and of fiery and explosive passions.

The scene took place in the *Niña* and seems to have been stormy. Pinzón's explanations were coldly received; his offer of nine hundred pesos of gold haughtily rejected; his formal occupation of the valley he had discovered declared null and void; his naming of the river *Río de Martín Alonso* cancelled; and the four men and two girls whom he had kidnapped, to show the King and Queen what he could do, sent back home, for, writes Colón, "it is a service to Your Highnesses, since, though men and women, whether of this island in particular or of any other island, all belong to Your Highnesses, here, where

227

Your Highnesses have already made a settlement, we must honour and favour the natives in view of the abundance of gold, good land and spices in this island."

In short, there was only one "Colón," and any other man who tried to "colonise" was a poacher. Martín Alonso, who was a spirited man, and, moreover, on balance, in the wrong, must have found it very difficult to keep his temper, for Colón, who did not easily allow himself to be manœuvred into heroics, threatened to have him hanged from the cabin door, whereupon Martín Alonso was content to reply: "That is what I deserve for having raised you to the honour in which you stand."

But there was no hanging, and the quarrel was patched up to such an extent that the *River of Martín Alonso* became the *River of Grace*. Colón was not capable, like Magellan, of having one of his rebel captains stabbed by surprise and the others put to death by authority. He realised that his two captains were brothers and most of the sailors were their men; so he decided that his best policy was to dissemble and hasten back to get rid of them, for "that was not a good moment to apply punishment." This retreat, ultimately due to a certain lack of resolution in his character when confronted with strong personalities, did but embitter him further against Martín Alonso, whom he depicts in his papers under a most unfavourable light. (3)

It must have been a relief to the Admiral to return from all these human miseries, in which his spirit suffered all the more as he surely realised how his own character accounted for much that was bitter in them, to the sea, its problems, its beauty and its mysteries. "Yesterday, the Admiral says, [. . .] he saw three sirens, showing fully out of the sea, but they were not as beautiful as they are painted, and in some way they had man-shaped faces." (4) He was not tempted. He was by now in a hurry to return, and he longed for the day when, having shaken off the irksome company of the too popular, capable and independent Pinzóns, he would at last be master in his own house, for so he considered the Indies to be. Nothing could lure him now out of his homeward course. In vain did the Indies strew his path with the most alluring temptations: "an island in which there is more gold even than in this, and in which they gathered gold in nuggets bigger than beans, while in the Española they are no bigger than wheat grains"; and another one "inhabited only by women, which he knew from many persons."

He was now set.on "sailing with the utmost speed to bring the tidings to their Highnesses and get rid of the bad companions whom he had." (5)

He does not seem to have ever been quite sure about the wisdom of leaving forty Christians behind in so big an island as Española. More than once he seeks comfort in the thought that the scheme was meant by the Lord; then he stresses the weakness and cowardice of the natives; yet before leaving, he had a gun shot fired at the hull of the empty ship, and was much relieved to see how impressed the "king" was when the stone ball pierced the two sides of the wooden carcass and fell beyond in the water. This state of mind may explain why on January 12th, realising that he was still on the coast of Española-Cipango-Haiti, he should have been appalled—*espantado*. Was, then, this island so large, and therefore so populated? He was probably thinking of his men. The strong criticism and opposition which Martín Alonso expressed on hearing that the detachment had been left behind must have impressed him also, even if it only made him confirm his previous decision the more obstinately. On Sunday the 13th his men had a serious fray with a party of Indians somewhat fiercer and more painted than those they had met till then. One of them came to the caravel. "The Admiral thought he probably was one of the Caribbeans, who eat men." (6) There were as many as fifty-five more of them behind the trees, all naked and with hair as long as "women in Castille," and adorned with parrots' feathers. After a certain amount of barter, in order to disarm them by purchasing their bows and arrows with things no more dangerous than glass beads, the Christians saw the natives run away, then come back with more arrows and ropes, "they say," to tie the Christians with. The Christians thereupon fell on them, the Indians fled, having left many dead on the field. The Admiral, says Las Casas, "in part regretted it, in part did not, for so they will fear the Christians, for he thought them Caribbeans who eat men, and the boat he had left to the thirty-nine men in the fortress and city of *la Navidad* might meet with trouble here if it ever came." (7)

His lingering mood was strengthened at the time by astrological considerations. On that same day he was thinking of seeking a better harbour, there to await the outcome of "the conjunction of the Moon with the Sun which he expected on the 17th of the month and its [the moon's] opposition with Jupiter and conjunction with Mercury, and the sun's opposition with Jupiter, which is a cause of strong winds." (8) Under this exalted influence he seems to have tried an exploration of the Island of the Caribbeans or Cannibals, and of the Island of Matininó where women admitted no men; and even to have entertained the hope of carrying some "heads" of both types of human curiosities to Spain. But "he noticed that the crews began to feel downcast on his straying out of his course home owing to the great amount of water which the caravels were taking in, and they had no other remedy but that of God." So, on the 16th, he gave up his projected exploration and took up a straight course to Spain North-east-one-fourth-East. (9)

On his way back he thus deliberately chose a latitude further north than that which he had taken for his westward voyage—as far north as the Azores. This results from the plotting of his course made from the data provided by his Journal as well as from the fact that he changed from East-North-East to East precisely at dawn on Monday, February 4th, exactly the day after he observed that "the North star seemed very high, as at Cape St. Vincent," though "he was unable to take its height either with the astrolabe or the quadrant because of the wave." (10)

All this first part of the voyage was of the happiest. The sea was quiet and enjoyable, and although the weather cooled down as they reached more and more northern latitudes, the sailors must have had time to enjoy their dreams of affluence. Though the duty of freeing the caravels must have been heavy, there were no problems, no uncertainties, and every man had his little bag of gold nuggets and his parrot to whom he could, if he wished, teach his native tongue, including, no doubt, a fair amount of good Spanish swearing. As for the Admiral, since *revenge is a dish to be served cold*, he was granted the satisfaction of having to wait for the *Pinta*, which could not keep up pace with him because her mast was in a bad condition. This gave him an opportunity to write down that "if her captain, who is Martín Alonso Pinzón, had been as careful of securing a good mast in the Indies, where there were so many and so good, as he had been eager to sail away from him, thinking he would fill up his ship with gold, he would have had a good mast." (11) Colón, it is plain, had not shaken off his rancour.

On February 6th the pilots began to fancy themselves in or near the Azores. The Admiral believed—and rightly—that they were not there yet. A week later, when Vicente Yáñez and Roldán thought they had already left the Azores behind, they felt the first onslaught of the storm which was to try them so hard. Huge seas, frequent lightning, a strong wind. The two little caravels were tossed about by the billows like nutshells, and on the night of the 14th the danger was so great that Colón made up his mind to let the wind do as it pleased with his ship. So far as he could judge, Martín Alonso had come to the same decision. The two ships signalled each other the whole night, until the storm blotted them out of each other's view. This was the second time that Pinzón and Colón were separated, but this time both were the passive victims of the ocean which they had been the first to cross.

The morning was no better than the night. The wind blew more furiously and the sea rose more irate. The crew, broken with lack of sleep and with the exhausting labour of freeing the ship, began to wonder whether the cruel sea would not for ever swallow into oblivion the ship, the men, the gold and the parrots. Colón called them together, and with that spiritual democracy which men realise in the presence of death, proposed to them that they should draw lots for one of them to go as a pilgrim to Our Lady of Guadalupe with a five-pound wax taper. They brought chickpeas, one for each, and with a knife carved a cross on one of them. The Admiral put in his hand first. He drew the cross-marked pea. A second lot was drawn to send a man to St. Mary of Loreto, "in Ancona, land of the Pope, which is a house in which Our Lady has done and does many great miracles," and this time the crossed-pea was picked up by a sailor called Pedro de Villa, to whom the Admiral promised to give funds for his pilgrimage. (12) The storm did not abate its fury. A third effort was deemed necessary. A man was to spend a night in prayer in Santa Clara of Moguer, and to have a mass said, and this time the cross-marked chickpea fell again to the Admiral. Nor was this all; for the entire crew and their chief made a vow that they would all go together in their shirts on reaching land, to pray in the first church under the advocation of the Virgin which they should find.

Colón must have felt comforted and encouraged by this special deference with which he had been treated twice by the particular emanation of the Lord now known as the law of probabilities, materialised in the cross-marked chickpea. He was sure to think that the Lord had His eye on His humble gospel-bearer, and that since he, Colón, had been twice chosen to be the conveyer of the crew's gratitude to the Holy Virgin, there would be a cause for such gratitude and a man alive to convey it. He cannot have failed to have felt somewhat guilty in the circumstances, for the ship was far too light, the food having all been eaten and the water and wine drunk, while the Admiral, cruising in good weather amongst the islands, had omitted to have enough ballast taken on board ship.

His plight, as usual, made him brood over himself, his past, his future, his hopes, his fears. We may imagine him, as hour after hour he watches the fierce attack of the sea on the frail citadel where his whole fortune, life, dreams, float adrift at the mercy of winds and waves, clinging hard to the handrail while he argues his case and tries to placate the Lord or to guess His intentions. The very eagerness which he felt to convey such great tidings and to prove that he had been right made him fear the worst, and in the tiniest mosquito he saw a hindrance or an obstacle. He reproached himself for this lack of faith and of confidence in Divine Providence, from which he had received such a magnificent victory. He sincerely believed that all his actions were aimed at God's service and, since he had received from Him all that he had asked for, he felt confident that his work would be allowed to reach its natural fulfilment. Yet he felt weak and anguished before the storm, and thought of his two children who would be left fatherless, and as the King and Queen would not know of the great service which he had rendered them, they would not feel moved to come to their help. A thought tortured him particularly: that his discovery should remain unknown. He must have pondered over it for long, until he found comfort in action: he wrote, wrote hard. He wrote all the story of his voyage, and his discovery, on a parchment, good and strong, and added that anyone who should find it should deliver it to the King and Queen. He rolled the parchment inside a waxed cloth, tied it up, and put it in a cask which he threw into the sea. The sailors watched him and thought it was some kind of vow or devotion.

This was one of his whining moods. When he was led by his sensitive and self-centred nature to these states of mind, he revealed that *contractual* tendency which is typical of the Jewish attitude to life: he set out to square his accounts with Providence and with Fate. He took for granted that the Lord would help him because he had always served the Lord; he took for granted that the King and Queen would not be moved to help his children because they would not know he had discovered Cipango; he felt that Providence owed him his life and safe arrival in Spain, since he had worked so hard to organise and carry out this expedition.

This attitude naturally leads to a certain egotism. In the

moody reflections which the storm raises in him, Colón shows himself the most self-centred of men. Incredible as it may seem, not once does he think of the plight of the four-score men who are running the storm with him—forty in his caravel, forty in Martín Alonso's, swallowed by the night. Not once does he reflect that they also have their wives and children waiting for them since that day in August when, smiling through their tears, they waved their handkerchiefs while the little fleet sailed down the Odiel River towards Saltes and the sea.

He keeps his pity for himself. And, as usual in this state of mind, he exaggerates. He speaks of his two children "left fatherless and motherless in a foreign land" (13) when Diego was Prince Don Juan's page and Fernando lived in Córdoba with his mother, and neither was in a foreign land. Much ink has been wasted in the interpretation of this passage, on the assumption that it has to be treated like a cold statement of fact. But often, perhaps more often than not, Colón does not write facts; he writes emotions into the flame of which he throws facts as burning materials. When near at last to the goal, this peril thrown across his path filled his soul not only with fear but also with the feeling that he was being defrauded by Providence.

This mood did not, however, abate his determination or sap his vigour to withstand fatigue. From Wednesday the 13th till Sunday the 17th he did not sleep at all. On Friday and Saturday he fought with the wind which doggedly prevented him from coming near one or two of the islands—of the Azores he surmised—which he could see in the distance. It was not till Monday the 18th that, after many fruitless attempts, he succeeded in casting anchor. He sent the boat to enquire where they were. They had arrived in Santa María, the southernmost island of the Azores belonging to the King of Portugal.

The Admiral was very pleased with himself for having sailed straight where he wanted to sail—the Azores. He was indeed so pleased that he gave himself away: "He says," writes Las Casas, copying or paraphrasing his Journal, "that he feigned to have covered more distance [than he really had] in order to put the pilots and sailors who handled the charts off the track, so that he should remain the sole lord of the road to the Indies, as indeed he remains, for not one of them had noted down the way aright, so that no one can be sure of his way to the Indies." (14) This confession fully explains his trick of keeping a secret log which he covered up with yet another secret—that of the true motive for which he kept it. But, as it happens often in the life of secretive men, emotions will run away with discretion and truth will out.

The happy navigator and his crew were at first well received and presented with hens and fresh bread which must have tasted like heavenly manna to the famished crew. Then, mindful of their vow, they asked whether there was a house of prayer in honour of Our Lady, and they were pointed out a small house close to the sea, which was a hermitage. The rash Admiral sent half his men to fulfil the vow; they climbed the hill, all in their plain shirts, naked legs and feet, bowed head, towards the white little house which was for them the house of the Mother who had saved them. And even as they walked in their faith, treason round them was weaving a net to catch them. The Captain, one João de Castanheda, who said he knew Colón, fell on them with his armed men and threw them in prison.

Meanwhile, the Admiral, who was waiting for the boat to go to the hermitage with the other half of his crew, began to suspect that all was not well. He weighed anchor and sailed round the hill in time to see how a troop of armed horsemen alighted and entered his boat, to come, as he surmised, to take him prisoner as well. Castanheda stood in the boat and tried to induce Colón to join them, while Colón tried to induce Castanheda to enter the caravel, with the settled intention of holding him there till his companions had been set at liberty. Castanheda seems to have been a fool, but not to that extent. So Colón asked him "what innovation was that"? He explained to the Portuguese Captain that he was the Admiral of the Ocean Sea and Viceroy of the Indies, appointed by the King and Queen of Spain, and, if his men were not returned, he had enough people on board to sail to Seville and see that the Portuguese Captain was punished. Castanheda replied that he had no fear of the King or Queen of Spain, whereupon the Admiral took all the crew to witness that he promised never to leave the caravel till he had de-populated that island and taken one hundred Portuguese to Castille. (15)

This was grand. But what was he actually to do? There was no good harbour in either Santa María or San Miguel, the island near by, and despite his bragging, he had been left with no more than three men who knew anything about sailing. In his anxiety, for the weather was obstinately bad and the sea gave him no rest, he thought ruefully of the beautiful weather he had enjoyed in his Indies; he was struck by the fact that both on his way out and on his way back the weather had been admirable there and foul near the Eastern shores of the Ocean; this "observation" tallied with another one which he had made repeatedly in the Indies: that vegetation flourished to the very edge of the sea, which showed that they were free from storms. On these two "facts," based on so brief an experience, Colón's imagination took flight: "In conclusion, says the Admiral, the sacred theologians and the learned philosophers were right in saying that the Earthly Paradise is at the end of the Orient, for it is a most temperate place. And therefore, those lands he had now discovered are (says he) the end of the Orient." (16) This is the second step in the gradual building of the fantastic biblical-cosmographical construction which he was to put forward later.

But, meanwhile, he was far away from Paradise, with no anchorage, stormy weather, and only three seamen on board. What countenance could a Grand Admiral put before the King and Queen and all the world, arriving in Castille, if he did arrive at all, at the head of his smallest ship and twenty out of one hundred and twenty men? And how could anyone believe that he had discovered a world when he had been unable to rescue half his own crew from the puniest Portuguese island captain? There was nothing to do but to trust Providence, which had always paid so much attention to the affairs of Christ-bearer Colón; and this trust was justified, for, when the Admiral returned from San Miguel to Santa María the next day, his boat came to the caravel with two priests and a notary and five seamen, whom he received well, and the upshot of it all was that he showed his credentials, was believed, given back his men and allowed to depart in peace.

The weather, however, was not under the jurisdiction of the King of Portugal, still less of his local captain, and the Admiral tried in vain to take in ballast, so that on Sunday the 24th, even without ballast, seeing that the wind, though strong, was friendly and blew in the direction of Castille, he took his chance and sailed away. We can feel Pinzón away ahead pulling him west-ward against his better sense. The voyage was stormy all the way. The Admiral "was very grieved with so many tempests now that he was at the gate of home." (17) The wind broke through the sails on Sunday, March 3rd. He again called the crew together and drew lots for a pilgrim to go in his shirt to Santa María de la Cinta, in Huelva, and again the Lord chose him for the offering. The whole crew vowed that the first

Saturday after arrival they would observe a bread-and-water fast. Without sails "they ran the storm dry-masted in dire danger from the great tempest of the wind and sea which ate them both ways." (18)

In the midst of the most terrific storm, tossed from heaven to earth, in a night torn by lightning and drenched by rain, they realised they were near land; at great risk, he ordered the mainsail to be spread and let the fierce winds dash them closer to it. At dawn, on Monday the 4th, he recognised the Rock of Cintra. He made up his mind to seek shelter in the bay of the Tagus.

The wind drove him past Cascaes and he cast anchor further up towards Lisbon, while the whole town ran ashore astonished that the little ship had escaped the fury of the storm, which had been raging all over the west of Europe, causing great havoc everywhere. Later in the morning he sailed further upstream and anchored in Rastelo, a place worth mentioning if only because it witnessed one of the most quixotic scenes that ever were acted outside the immortal book. There happened to be at the time in Rastelo a ship of the Portuguese navy, "the best armed in artillery and weapons that ever was seen," commanded by a spirited man by the name of Alonso Daman. This Captain, on seeing the *Niña*, sent his boat with the Master Bartolomé Diaz to summon the newcomer to his ship and report to the officers of the King of Portugal. Colón took up his quixotic attitude with such felicity that this page of his Diary seems torn from Cervantes' book:

"The Admiral answered that he was Admiral of the King of Castille and that he did not give such reports to such persons, nor would he leave the ships or vessels wherein he might be [this from his one only caravel] except by necessity, not being able to withstand the force of arms. The ship-master answered that he should send the caravel-master; the Admiral said that he would send neither the master nor any other person, unless by force, for he thought it amounted to the same to send a person or to go himself, and that this was the custom of the Admirals of Castille, to die rather than give themselves or give men of theirs. The ship-master calmed down and said that since he was so determined it would be done as he wished, but he begged to be shown the letters of the King and Queen of Castille if he had them. The Admiral was pleased to show them, whereupon the master returned to the ship and reported to the Captain [. . .] who, with much ceremony, trumpets, drums and fifes, making much festivity of it, came to the caravel and spoke with the Admiral and offered to do all the Admiral would wish." (19)

Colón knew where he was. He knew that he had left Portugal seven years earlier because King John would not listen to him; that he had taken away the Toscanelli documents, which for the Portuguese Crown, deeply interested in discovery, were strictly secret; he knew that the word "Indies" had been proscribed from his letters of credence precisely not to awaken the suspicion of the King of Portugal; he "knew" that he had discovered Cipango and that, had it not been for the loss of the flagship and for the irksome company of the Pinzóns, he would have discovered Cathay also; he knew that, as soon as King John saw his "Indians," not black like Guiné men, but brown and comely like Easterners, the King would be vexed and would rue his past blindness. There was trouble ahead. A policy had to be hastily devised, for the storm which had forced him to seek refuge in Portugal had not allowed of such cogitations. There was only one policy—bluff. He was to stand up to the King, to make himself as big as possible—and, after all, he *was* big— and so to impress the King and keep him at arm's length.

There was method, therefore, in his quixotic madness, and his picturesque scene with Bartolomé Diaz may well have been due to a happy blend of two of the main features of his character —cautiousness and megalomania. He had written to King John, who was then in Val do Paraiso, near the monastery of Our Lady of Virtues, about nine leagues away, sheltering from a pestilence which was then prevalent in the region. Colón explained how the King and Queen had instructed him not to abstain from entering the harbours of the King of Portugal to ask for all he might need, for his money, and he begged the King to allow him to sail on to Lisbon, for evil people, bearing in mind that he brought back much gold, might commit some evil action while he was in that unpopulated port; he also explained that he did not come from Guiné but from the Indies. (20)

If we have to believe Barros, there was another reason why Colón was so anxious to go to Lisbon; "not so much to give pleasure to the King as to sadden him with his presence," (21) which in the circumstances it is but human to believe. The King, however, was too curious and possibly too anxious to be able to spare himself the ordeal of being the first to witness the glory of the man he had allowed to go, disappointed, from his Court to that of his rival. By this time the caravel had become a mecca for the curious and the idle, who flocked to admire the Indians and the popinjays.

King John seems to have recognised from the first the exalted position which Colón had assumed in Rastelo. On Friday, the 8th, the Grand Admiral of the Ocean Sea received the formal visit of Don Martin de Noronha—possibly a delicate allusion to the illustrious, ecclesiastical Portuguese connections of his deceased wife—with a letter from the King inviting him to come and see him, a request with which the Admiral complied to avoid suspicion, though by this time he seems to have had qualms as to the wisdom of the visit. (22)

King John was making things easy for him; he treated the Admiral with the honour due to his rank and instructed his officers to provide Colón free of charge with all he might need. But Colón may have wondered whether he was safe and whether the King and Queen would not look askance on this visit, made to their rival before they themselves were informed of the discovery. It was, however, too late to recede. The next day, March 9th, he went to see the King.

King John received him well, and whatever he thought of the event, he was gracious enough to leave on Colón an excellent impression, for the new-fangled Admiral saw himself treated as a grandee and bidden to sit down every time he was in the royal presence. The King expressed doubts as to the rights of Castille over those lands, and Colón diplomatically claimed ignorance of that side of the question. He stayed two days, and on Monday, after a visit to the Queen, who was in the monastery of Villafranca, he returned to the caravel.

Things, however, may not have been quite as simple as they seemed to Colón, and it may well be that while he drank the exhilarating wine of power and glory he was skirting more deadly dangers than storm or Indian had threatened him with. If his impression of the King was good, that which he made on the King and his Court was far less flattering, as recorded by the chief Portuguese historian of the period: The King "received him with friendliness, but was very sad when he saw that the natives who came with him were not curly-haired blacks and in their features as those of Guiné, but similar in figure, colour and hair to what he was told were those of India on which he had worked so hard. And as Colón told bigger greatness and things of that land than the land had, and this with a looseness of words, accusing and scolding the King for having rejected his offer, this way of speaking made some gentlemen so indignant that, having added their hate of his insolence to the sorrow they saw the King felt at the loss of that enterprise, they offered themselves to kill him, wherewith they would prevent his departure for Castille. For they really thought that his arrival would injure this kingdom and cause some worry to His Highness, owing to the conquest which had been granted him by the Pontiffs, from which conquest this Colón seemed to bring these people. Which offers the King rejected and even condemned as a Catholic prince, though he personally objected to the event itself, and instead, he honoured Colón and had the men he had brought from his new discovery dressed in red cloth, and with this bid him farewell." (23)

Colón seems, therefore, to have had a narrow escape. On Tuesday the 12th, when he was making ready to leave Llandra— where he had spent the night—he received an unexpected offer from King John to go to Castille by land. Was this an afterthought of the "Catholic Prince" who felt tempted to have Colón a little longer under his sway? Colón declined the offer, embarked and left Portugal the next day.

Two days later, at dawn on Friday, March 15th, the *Niña* passed the Saltes bar and at midday entered the little harbour of Palos in sight of an enthusiastic population. The anxiety which must have been felt by those whose men were in the *Pinta* was soon relieved. In the afternoon of the same day, Martín Alonso's ship, which had sought refuge in Bayona, a small harbour near Vigo, on the north-western coast of Spain, sailed up the Odiel. (24)

The joy could then be complete—save for those who thought of the forty men left in the new world. Though absorbed in his own triumph, there is little doubt that Colón was one of them.

CHAPTER XX

GLORY

LA RÁBIDA and the house of Martín Alonso Pinzón were for a time the headquarters of the now famous and victorious man. Though some estrangement remained between the Admiral and his impatient second, particularly owing to the settlement of the Villa de la Navidad, there was no open break between them. Pinzón, moreover, was gravely ill, a circumstance which would no doubt make Colón refrain from driving home any advantage, real or imaginary, which he might have. It seems certain that he stayed in Pinzón's house. (1)

Martín Alonso had written to the King and Queen from Bayona, as it was his right—and even his duty—to do. He can hardly have wished to claim for himself the discovery of the Indies, because there are at least two documents to prove that he acknowledged the Admiral's claim before knowing that the *Niña* had been saved from the waves. (2) His letter must have reached the King and Queen after that which Colón had sent them from Lisbon, amongst other reasons because in those days Lisbon had better roads and more facilities for sending a messenger than a small fishing-harbour in far-off Galicia. The sovereigns acknowledged his letter and bid him come to see them. But he died on March 20th and was buried in the monastery of La Rábida. With his death, Colón remained the only figure on the stage of the discovery. Vicente Yáñez Pinzón, Juan de la Cosa, were still to make their names; Colón's name was now safe: he was by now The Very Magnificent Lord Don Cristóbal Colón.

But in his character, fear was too predominant to allow caution ever to go to sleep. Colón was an "early-riser" in all that concerned self-defence and foresight. He knew how crucial the appearance of things is in this world of men. Presentation is half the battle of conviction. In our modern world, Colón would have made a superb Minister of Propaganda. As soon as the stay in the Azores had secured him some respite from the storm which had pursued him in mid-ocean, he wrote letters to the King and Queen. These letters are lost. They announced his discovery and put it, of course, under the light which he thought most

240

favourable, bearing in mind the interests and ideals of the two monarchs. This can be safely surmised from the tone of his Journal, preserved to us in the paraphrasing of Las Casas. Moreover, we possess one written at the same time, addressed to Luis de Santángel, and which he seems to have used rather as a circular letter for the information of all important men. In these writings Colón is anxious to establish a certain number of points which may justify the expedition and make of it so great a success for the present and so vast a hope for the future that the loss of the flagship may be forgotten and his name secured against possible attacks. These points are: (a) abundance of gold; (b) fertility and wealth of the islands; (c) proximity to "Cathay" and to the Grand Khan; (d) gentleness of the "Indians" and facility of the task of conversion to be undertaken.

He does not mention Cipango. Colón had the same mixture of faith and lack of faith which makes Don Quixote so subtle under his integrity; he is sure Española is Cipango, but he feels this faith far too tender to be exposed to the raw breath of scepticism. Yet in this same letter he dares venture opinions no less fantastic: speaking of Española, he declares that on the west side of it there remain two provinces which he has not explored, in one of which, known as Cibao, people are born with tails. He had not yet discovered the Indian joke; nor had Bernáldez, who rejects Colón's view, for a purely "scientific" reason, in the following words: "I do not think it can be there, to judge by how it is marked in the world-map in which I have read, and if it be there, it shall soon be known with the help of God." (3)

The King and Queen were delighted with the news. On March 30th, from Barcelona, where they happened to be at the time, they wrote to him, addressing him as "Don Cristóbal, our Admiral of the Ocean Sea and Viceroy and Governor of the Islands which have been discovered in the Indies"; they promised him more favours; and they at once evinced that haste which was going to dominate all their correspondence with him for the next six months: "We wish you to come soon and [. . .] that you should hasten your coming as much as possible so that everything may be seen to, and as you see that summer is with us and we must not let miss the [best] time to return, see whether something could not already be prepared in Seville or in other places for your return to the lands you have discovered. And write soon [. . .] so that we may be in a position to see to things while you are on your way here and back, so that when you return from here [Barcelona] all may be ready." (4)

The reason for this haste was patent: fear lest the King of Portugal should consider that the discovery was an act of poaching on his preserves and should act accordingly. This fear was justified: "King John," writes Barros, "was much put out at the news of the site and place of the discovery which Colón revealed to him, and truly thought that this discovered land belonged to him, and so he was told by the members of his council [. . .], over which business he held many councils, in which he decided to send there at once Dom Francisco Dalmeyda, son of the Count of Abrantes Dom Lopo, with a fleet." (5)

This was soon reported to the King and Queen by their faithful and powerful vassal the Duke of Medina-Sidonia, to whom the royal couple wrote on May 2nd, thanking him for his warning and adding that "they were dealing with the business with much care and diligence and intended to avail themselves of his services." They also begged him to see that "all the caravels of his estate were ready and equipped so that they should be available in case of need." (6)

But the King and Queen were not relying solely on their navy, confident as they were in its powers. They were also mobilising against King John their own diplomacy and the spiritual authority of the Pope. On May 3rd, Pope Alexander VI issued a bull granting them the Indies discovered or to be discovered in the same way in which the King of Portugal had been granted the lands discovered *in partibus Africae, Guineae et Minerae auri*, which hardly sounds like infallible geography; and the next day, another equally important bull divided all this no-man's-land of discoveries between the Peninsular Crowns by a line from Pole to Pole one hundred leagues from "any of the islands known as Azores and Cabo Verde," which again would appear to show that the Papacy was far less strict in these cosmographical matters than in matters of dogma.

Meanwhile, Ferdinand had sent an energetic protest to King John demanding that the fleet should not be dispatched and pointing out that the question of rights could always be discussed by their ambassadors. The King of Portugal agreed, but his ambassadors were slow to come, and the King and Queen did not abate their vigilance nor their eagerness to see Colón depart for their new empire. (7)

Colón's importance could not but increase in the light of this conflict. The scheme which had caused so much merriment in the two Courts was now so far vindicated that the two Courts were arming and feverishly watching each other for the spoils of it. He had become the man of the day. From the very first, four days after his landing, another "early-riser," the Duke of Medina-celi, wrote to the Cardinal of Spain with a plea to be allowed to send a few of his caravels to the Indies, as a reward for having introduced "Cristóbal Colomo" to the Court. (8) This letter is a sign of the interest—not all of it, presumably, evangelical—which the discovery had awakened in the country. On March 31st, Palm Sunday, Colón made a sensational entry into Seville, showing off his Indians, his gold and his popinjays; and after a brief stay, in which he devoted his time to the preparation of his second sally, he left for Barcelona. "The fame had begun to fly over Castille, that new lands had been discovered, known as the Indies, and so many peoples and so different, and things so new, and that the man who had discovered them came by such a road and brought with him men of such people; not only those in the townships through which he passed, but those from townships remote from his road came to see him, and the townships were emptied and the roads were filled to see him and come to receive him." (9)

It was just short of a year after his journey towards Palos. His triumphant progress through Castille and Aragon was a fit commemoration of the dismal progress of the expelled Jews. He can hardly have failed to think of it while he passed through the same roads and was acclaimed by the same people who one year earlier had watched the tragic exodus in sullen, sad or charitable silence.

Towards the end of April—possibly the same 31st which the previous year had been crucial in his history as well as in that of his Jewish brethren—he was received by the King and Queen with the utmost solemnity. The Queen felt in those days as if life was beginning afresh for her soul, just recovering from the anguish she had undergone while King Ferdinand fought with death as a result of an attempt to murder him. On Friday, December 7th, when Colón was navigating in the Indies, the King had been sitting in his Law Court in Barcelona as he was wont to do, "hearing the people from 8 to 12, and as he rose to go, he walked down the steps towards the square known as the King's Square, with many knights and citizens, who went each to his horse or mule, and the King stopped on the last step to speak to his treasurer, when that bad and treacherous man came towards him from behind, and as the King had finished speaking and he went down one more step to mount his mule [. . .] struck him with a sword or *alfange* as long as three palms, and with the point of the weapon cut a wound from the top of the head by the ear and the neck down to the shoulders." The Queen, writing to her confessor, said: "I had no heart to see the wound; it was four fingers deep and so long that my hand trembles to say it." But, she adds, "it spared all the strings and the neck bone and all that which would have been dangerous." (10)

During those three months the Queen, in her own words, "had tasted death." She was, despite her austere life, a pleasure-loving soul, and now that all was over, she sought relaxation in stately ceremony and in solemn music—in which she probably felt that along with her pleasure she served the pomp and power of the State. The reception granted to Colón was worthy of the best traditions of the Castillian Crown. The throne was set up in public. The King, still pale and thin, and the Queen received their Grand Admiral surrounded by all their Court, Prince John at the head of it. Colón must have then tasted the wine of glory at its best, and have felt like a true Admiral and a true Viceroy for the first time. He had organised his procession with his usual genius for presentation, and had deeply impressed the Court (which so thronged the streets that it hindered his progress towards the Palace) with a liberal display of all the treasures, parrots, Indians, golden masks, pearls and mother-o'-pearl and tropical fruit which he had brought over.

The King and Queen astounded their courtiers by granting him two singular honours so far reserved for the greatest of the great: they rose to greet him, and after the kissing of hands they offered him a stool. How far this unheard-of, coveted distinction, granted him in the presence of an envious Court, can be counted as one of the causes of his later troubles and ultimate downfall, it would be difficult to say. As for his speech, we may imagine it a comment and paraphrasing of his letters, no doubt warmed by the fire of his imagination and emboldened by the feeling of self-assurance and success which must have filled his heart in that glorious hour. Las Casas relates that the King and Queen were so much impressed by the story which their Admiral told them that they fell on their knees with tears of joy in their eyes, and that the singers of the Queen's Chapel "sang 'Te Deum Laudamus,' and the soprano wind instruments answered so that it seemed as if in that hour the delights of heaven had been opened and manifested and communicated themselves to them." (11)

By order of their Highnesses, the whole Court accompanied the Admiral to his lodgings that evening. The King and Queen were indeed impressed. More royal favours followed. The King bid the Admiral ride by his side, while the Prince rode on the other side, a privilege till then reserved to the royal blood.

This ascent cannot have been easy. The country was used to accepting that persons of humble extraction should reach the higher layers of the realm, for both brave soldiers and clever or saintly ecclesiastics rose rapidly in the State. The two ways of gaining heaven described by a famous poet of the century,(12) prayers and tears for the priest, and killing Moors for the knight, were also the two ladders up to worthy success. The discovery of the Indies could be fairly counted as good as the killing of a great quantity of Moors. But human nature being what it was, a society which, fairly democratic though it was, was nevertheless as keen a believer in the virtue of "blood" as any other in Europe at the time, must have found it difficult to reconcile itself to such a breathtaking ascent to the top of power and majesty on the part of one who, after all, was a Genoese adventurer of somewhat obscure origins.

There is no doubt that the King and Queen realised the position —which indeed was so natural that any fool could have predicted it—and that they were determined to make the Court and country "swallow" the new potentate. Their hand and will are visible behind the chief episode in this social ascent of Colón, as related by Las Casas. The Grand Cardinal of Spain, Don Pero González de Mendoza, brother of the Duke of the Infantado, "The Third King of Spain," "took him to his house to dine with him, and bid him sit on the most pre-eminent seat, next to him, and had him served in a covered dish and his food tested first for poison, and that time was the first that his food was tested and served in a covered dish, and henceforward he was served with the solemnity and greatness required by his dignified title of Admiral." (13)

What are the reasons for this remarkable behaviour on the part of the chief personage of the Spanish Court? "This munificent lord and great pontiff, seeing the merits and labours, and the fruit which was beginning to come therefrom, of the said first Admiral of these Indies, and how the grateful King and Queen had honoured and sublimated him, and how they had given orders that he should be honoured and venerated, he, first of all the grandees to do so," (14) invited him to his table. First of all the grandees to do so, though the King and Queen *had ordered* that he should be honoured, the Grand Cardinal, closest of all their subjects to the sovereigns' plans, wishes and designs, was told to give a lead to the Court. This shows how scrupulous Ferdinand and Isabel meant to be, and were, in the fulfilment of their obligations to Colón, and how generous in their interpretation of them. Withal, the episode has a strong symbolic value: *Colón's greatness was acknowledged by the ceremony of testing his food for poison.* Such is greatness amongst men that it carries with it the risk of poisoned food.

This determination of Ferdinand and Isabel to reward Colón up to and even beyond the limit of their commitments, dictated many a decision in that period of feverish work which extends between April and September, during which the second fleet was prepared and its Admiral's estate and greatness were firmly established. On May 20th, Colón is granted the right to wear a castle and a lion in his arms—a really exorbitant honour in those days, for the castle and the lion were the royal arms; on May 23rd, he is given a present of one thousand gold *doblas* (335,000 maravedis); on May 26th, he is granted the right to lodge with five of his servants wherever he goes, paying only for his food at current prices; on May 28th, the King and Queen solemnly confirm him in the titles, honours and privileges which had been agreed upon in the Capitulation of Santa Fé; on the same day he receives letters-patent appointing him Captain-General of the second fleet going to the Indies, and granting him authority to appoint any persons he might wish for the government of the Indies, pending the measures to be taken later for setting up the system defined in the Capitulations—that Colón should nominate three persons and the Crown choose one of them. (15) In short, with a commendable rapidity which should qualify the usual charges of cumbrousness and slowness raised against their administration, the King and Queen erected a magnificent personage before the Court and the world, and lavishly bestowed wealth, honour and power upon him.

How did he stand this difficult test—success? There are signs that he might have done it better. The first of them is that he profited by this period of honeymoon with the Crown to secure for himself the grant of ten thousand maravedis promised by the King and Queen to the first man who would see land. An *albalá*, or royal order, to that effect was signed by the King and Queen on May 23rd. Now it is obvious that he had not seen land and that he knew he hadn't, for otherwise he would have had the flag hoisted and the gun fired as he himself had instructed the three crews to do, as soon as land was sighted. But suppose he had. If ever there had been an obvious gesture to make in his career, this was it—to let the poor sailor who saw it from the *Pinta*, and who was obviously entitled to the prize, have the benefit of the doubt and receive the modest yearly grant which, for a man now at the summit of fortune, became a mere trifle. The claim was made and won by him when no clerk or official was in a position to resist him, and when he himself had every reason to believe that he would be the almost omnipotent lord of an almost unlimited world of islands, with a fabulous mainland behind. The disappointed sailor went over to Morocco and became a renegade. His faith, as is the case with most of us, apparently required works . . . by others. But how could he be expected to bear the burden of disappointment when his chief had broken down under that of success? The grant was made, but it is difficult to avoid the conclusion that the ungenerous Admiral was to pay heavily in later years for the ten thousand maravedis. Much of the disaffection, opposition, rebellion even, with which he was soon to meet might be traced to the effect produced in the humble folk by this inconsiderate action on his part.

* * *

Trouble began at once. The preparation of his second fleet proved a far longer and more arduous task than the impatient monarchs had expected. Ferdinand and Isabel had placed all "Indian" affairs in the hands of the Archdean of Seville, Don Juan de Fonseca, who, "though a cleric and an archdean, and later [. . .] bishop of Badajoz, then Palencia, then Burgos, which he was when he died, was very capable for worldly affairs, especially for assembling soldiers and for manning fleets, which is an occupation for Biscayans rather than for bishops, for which reason the King and Queen always entrusted him with the fleets which were armed in their lifetime." (16)

To this soldierly priest fell the task of organising the second fleet, in collaboration with Colón. Don Juan de Fonseca, "very capable for worldly affairs" indeed, obtained a yearly grant of two hundred thousand maravedis while he was to be engaged in this un-ecclesiastical occupation. The funds were to be taken out of a sum of fifteen thousand ducats of gold for the fleet expenses which had been entrusted to Francisco Pinelo, a *jurado* of the city of Seville, who acted as treasurer: Juan de Soria, the Prince's private secretary, was to be the chief comptroller and accountant.

The royal eye saw to everything. Lances are requisitioned in Granada, cuirasses, bows and shotguns in Málaga, powder and artillery ammunition are provided through Rodrigo Narváez, "*Mayordomo* of our artillery"; trusted men are appointed to receive the goods, notably the gold, at the other end, and also in Spain, to keep accounts, to administer justice in the Indies, to watch over the faith and conversion of the new royal subjects. But the frequent letters of the King and Queen reveal from the outset that all is not well with the urgent and mighty work.

Despite repeated royal orders for haste, the fleet never seems to be ready to start. On June 12th, a royal letter is sent to Colón in which he is begged to make haste; on July 25th, royal letters are sent both to Colón and to Don Juan de Fonseca, requesting them to make great haste in the departure of the fleet; on August 3rd, the King and Queen write to Gómez Tello, one of their "trusted men," allowing him to remain behind but requesting him to do all he can so that the fleet leaves as soon as possible; on the 4th, the indefatigable royal couple write to Francisco Pinelo, the acting treasurer of the fleet, pressing him "to put much attention and diligence in securing its prompt departure"; on August 18th, yet another royal request for haste to Don Juan de Fonseca, and a similar request to Colón; on September 5th, both men are again requested not to delay.

The preparation of a fleet of seventeen vessels manned in all— crew, soldiers, emigrants and other passengers—by one thousand to fifteen hundred persons can have been no easy matter. Despite the diligence and attention of Don Juan de Fonseca and his officials, and of Colón's own watchful and distrustful eye, we know from his later complaints that they were deceived more than once by the cunning of sundry self-seekers. The coopers gave them such poor barrels for their wine that much of this precious liquid flowed to waste in their ships, even as the wine of the skins which Don Quixote mistook for a giant; and the horsemen, having pranced before the eye of Colón, Fonseca, Soria and other over-seers on excellent Andalucian steeds, managed to smuggle skinny hacks in their places just before the ships' departure. There was, to be sure, a certain amount of inevitable delay. But we are led by the evidence to suspect that some of it must have come from the tension which set in between the men entrusted with the task of organising the expedition.

The tension arose, no doubt, out of the handling of things and people, but soon developed into a personal feud. The powers of the four persons chiefly concerned were not well defined. The royal letter of May 23rd was addressed jointly to the Admiral and the Archdean, giving them powers to buy ships and material and to enlist and pay the men; "All to be done and passed before Juan de Soria"; while Francisco Pinelo was to keep the funds and also the account of all moneys spent. Trouble arose between Colón and Juan de Soria; it is even possible to surmise that it arose also between Colón and Don Juan de Fonseca, without whose tacit or express acquiescence and sympathy the Prince's secretary would not have dared stand up to the Admiral as he did. Colón complained to the King and Queen, who most emphatically stood by him and wrote to that effect to him, to Fonseca and to Soria. (17) These royal letters are most instructive, for they reveal that the main trouble with Soria was a reluctance "to honour and respect the Admiral of the Indies as it should be done and as we wish it," which, the sovereigns explain, must be "according to the title we have given him"; the Soria episode was therefore part of the painful process of swallowing Colón's greatness on the part of a reluctant Court; nor can Fonseca himself be exonerated in this, for the King and Queen went out of their way to explain to him also, under cover of a message to Soria, how the Admiral should be respected. But, moreover, these letters also show that the trouble, on Colón's side, was a tendency to break away from all control and to assume independent and sovereign powers. This is patent in the royal letter to Colón, in which, and not in those to others, having said that they have given orders to have him treated "as is just and in accordance with the rank we have given you," they add: "you must see to it that he [Soria] signs everything that is spent, for he must keep the books for our Chief Accountants," (18) which plainly shows that Colón had tried to get rid of Soria's supervision.

The King and Queen were no doubt beginning to notice this tendency to rebel against all outside authority—and in the circumstances this amounted to rebellion against their own authority—on the part of this strange man whom they had made second to none in the land as a reward for his gift of an Empire. They were no ordinary monarchs. They were that man and that woman who had transfigured the Peninsula from a nest of anarchical kingdoms, dukedoms, earldoms, bishoprics and petty Moorish courts, into the strongest and most respected realm in Christendom. This had been achieved by sheer energy, faith and respect for their own royal functions and duties. The King and Queen who had tamed the Mendozas, Guzmáns and Manriques, could not be slow in detecting signs of indiscipline in a Colombo-Colón.

There is no doubt that in his intimate dreams he saw himself as a quasi-monarch of the Indies. The King and Queen heard with evident displeasure that he was taking over a personal bodyguard of *continos* (men in *continuous* service), a privilege then considered royal. (Bartolomé, the Admiral's brother, for instance, became a *contino* of the King and Queen.) In answer to Fonseca, who had imparted the news to them, Ferdinand and Isabel write: "As for the *continos* which you say the Admiral is taking over, you were right in telling him that he need not take any on this voyage, since every one of our men who is going must do whatever he may order in our name, and any separation of the men into his own and others might bring about many a drawback; but if he wishes to take over some whom he may call his own for his suite, he may take as many as ten squires out of the fifty who are going, and another twenty out of the other thousand persons who are going, and let them be paid as the others." (19)

The King and Queen were jealous of their own privileges, and probably anxious lest Colón were thinking of gradually setting up a separate establishment of his own which should enable him eventually to shake off the authority of Castille. At a closer range there was, moreover, another doubt in their minds: the Portuguese claim was still unanswered and undiscussed. King Ferdinand was playing for time, for he wanted to see the Castillian claim more firmly established by Colón's second expedition, and to get rid of the French threat on Roussillon; which he did in time to receive the Portuguese ambassadors with a free mind when they arrived in Barcelona on August 15th. This enabled him to keep the Portuguese ambassadors waiting and the matter open, until, as Barros says, (20) he was able to size up the discovery, a phrase which, in the Portuguese text, may be plainly read as a hint that the second expedition contained persons entrusted with the task of giving the King and Queen an independent account of the actual value of the discovery. It may be surmised that one of these persons must have been Antonio de Torres, since from the outset he was designated as the Captain of the return voyage of the fleet. This Antonio de Torres, "a notable person, wise and capable for such a post," (21) was a brother of the Aya of Prince Don Juan, and therefore close to the royal household. His appointment to so exceptional a post, at so early an hour, seems to suggest that he went in the expedition as a kind of second-in-command, and general watchman; for the King and Queen may have pondered over that visit of Colón's to the King of Portugal before he came to Spain. (22) Their lavish generosity to him may have had more than one cause, and behind the more luminous one of their natural gratitude and noble nature there may have lurked a less generous motive of fear. It is, at any rate, significant that they end their letter to Soria with this injunction: "We order you to see that he leaves with great satisfaction, for we wish it so and such is our pleasure, and we shall feel much wrath if it be not so." (23)

This second voyage seems to have been conceived on the basis of a memorandum prepared by Colón in April 1493. The Admiral is mostly concerned with a frank scheme of colonisation by Spaniards. There is a somewhat perfunctory reference to the conversion of the Indians, but the memorandum is accurately described in its first paragraph: "Obeying Your Highnesses' command, I will set down what occurs to me, save a better opinion, with a view to populating and developing the Española as well as the other Islands found or to be found." (24)

His suggestions are most sensible. Two thousand settlers are to be taken over on a voluntary basis; three or four *pueblos* or settlements are to be built; no one is to be allowed to dig or wash for gold save those who settle and build a house to dwell in the island; churchmen and worship implements are to be taken over; and, along with a number of measures for preventing leakage, gold-seeking is to be forbidden during certain periods of the year so that people can turn their minds to the land.

We are to find traces of these ideas of Colón in the instructions which he received from the King and the Queen on May 29th. (25) But, as was to be expected, the sovereigns had also ideas of their own. The mere fact that these instructions were deemed necessary is in itself significant. Colón was no longer leaving with a blank cheque, drawn, it is true, on a Blank Bank; he was leaving for an existing territory and more to come, "belonging" to the King and Queen; as "their" Admiral and Viceroy, and in strings firmly held by the most authoritarian monarchs of the age.

There are four kinds of ideas not always clearly separated in these instructions: religious welfare of the Indians; organisation of the expedition; commercial and accountancy arrangements; and political and constitutional rules. It is significant to find amongst the last the oath of allegiance to their Highnesses, to be taken by all the men taking part in the expedition, which was undoubtedly a discreet way of reminding Colón that all his men were royal men; the two following prescriptions speak for themselves:

> 12: That every time a sentence is carried out, the public crier is to say: "This is the justice which is rendered by the King and Queen, our sovereigns";

13: That all the decisions, orders and patents given out by the said Admiral, Viceroy and Governor, be written in the name of Don Fernando and Doña Isabel, King and Queen, etc., and signed by the said Don Cristóbal Colón. (26)

These two rules are a clear sign of the way the King and Queen were thinking. Taken together with the remaining provisions, they show, moreover, that this second expedition was clearly conceived as the first colonising effort of a series which was to occupy the best part of two centuries. The two lines of European invasion—spiritual and economic—are well represented in it. The instructions begin with an injunction to the Viceroy to work hard for the conversion of the Indians who are to be treated "very kindly and lovingly" ("muy bien y amorosamente"), under pain of severe punishment. A Benedictine friar of Catalan extraction, Father Bernardo Boil, or Buil, was put in charge of the spiritual welfare of the natives. He was seconded by a few lay brothers, though very learned, says Las Casas, one of whom was known as John the Red, "because he was so." (27)

The economic provisions were conceived on a reversal—perhaps subconscious and unnoted, but definite—of the original dreams of a gold-paved-and-roofed Cipango. Twenty peasants and a man knowing how to make *acequias* (28) were sent "to discover land," i.e. arable land; the horsemen were asked to take mares as spare mounts; (29) a number—which, as time was to show, was insufficient—of draft beasts, probably horses, was also embarked, as well as wheat, grain for sowing, vine plants and sugar-canes. Gold, to be sure, was not forgotten, but it was no longer the main nor even the predominant factor in the economic conception behind these instructions. Agriculture and trade were the paramount considerations, and if a rash critic would condemn the decision to keep a strict control on all men, things and goods going to the Indies, a wiser observer would realise that this order, taken on May 23rd, 1493, just over two months after the discovery had been made known to the world, was an elementary political precaution, pending the organisation of the new world, so suddenly thrown open to European enterprise.

The harbour chosen was no longer Palos, the resources of which were below the requirements of this more ambitious fleet, but Cádiz, next to Seville, the most important of the southern ports of Spain. There the ships were gradually assembled and equipped and the men congregated. This time it was not necessary for Colón to brandish an order of pardon for jailbirds, nor for Pinzón to make flaming harangues; recruits abounded and Colón must have been able to make a choice. Over and above his seventeen crews, he had on board a number of soldiers, both horse and foot, peasants, craftsmen of all kinds, a doctor and a surgeon, several priests, and a handful of *hidalgos* who went to the Indies in order to gain honour, or wealth, or both. He also had on board his brother, Giacomo, promptly transmogrified into Don Diego upon his arrival in Spain from his native looms. This in no way enhanced his colourless personality. But the majesty and power of Colón himself shone the more. He now travelled in great state, with a retinue of servants, a bodyguard of *continos*, almost a court of gentlemen. Would any man in his senses doubt now that he was a real Admiral? At last his dream had come true. He had risen to the acme of power and glory, next to none but the King and the Queen, and possibly the Cardinal of Spain. He had released from his suffering soul years of personal, and centuries of racial, humiliation. In his person, he had raised that people which Castille had expelled, to the summit of power over that Castille which had expelled it. He was, moreover, his own master in his own fleet. He had got rid of the detested Pinzóns. But did he know, that morning of September 24th, when he proudly gave the order to spread sails to his fleet of seventeen ships and caravels, did he know that there were men on board who were soon to make him home-sick for the loyalty of the three great sailors of Palos?

PART V

THE GRAND ADMIRAL OF THE OCEAN SEA

CHAPTER XXI

THE ADMIRAL'S SECOND VOYAGE

IF, sitting in his flagship castle, in the comfortable and even luxurious surroundings of his real cabin—a real admiral's cabin —Colón watched the trembling track left by the ship—slowest and last of his fleet—on the still waters of the Atlantic, his eye, though imaginative, would not yet see that other track, far vaster and more complex, which his discovery was opening in the mental seas of Europe. True, "Europe" was not then what it has become since, particularly in our century, the whole Continent in area, and its whole population in depth; true, "Europe" in its more conscious and responsible aspects was for practical purposes little more than the civilised crust of its civilised South-west; but in that Western and Southern area the news that Colón had discovered a new world was hailed with enthusiasm and emotion. His own report—the "circular" letter received by Santángel, Sánchez and others—was printed and published eight times within the year 1493—the first (in a Latin version) in Rome on April 29th. (1) But the most assiduous advertiser of the discovery was Peter Martyr, the Italian letter-writer, the confidant of the monarchs and grandees of Spain. His letters, addressed to men and women of high station in Spain and Italy, were channels for news and views similar, if not to our public press, to the printed "letters" more systematically circulated in our day by a few enterprising persons or societies. Those to whom they were addressed were free to treat them as confidential, but often handed them round to local groups, owing to their news value; and, thus multiplied by local Peter Martyrs, the news spread all over Europe in wider and wider circles, which no doubt diluted whatever truth it contained. Peter Martyr recorded the discovery of the Indies in a letter to Borromeo, dated in Barcelona, May 14th, 1493, the terms of which are now famous: "A few days later, one Christopher Colón returned from the Western Antipodes; he is a Ligurian who, sent by my Sovereigns, penetrated with just three ships into that province reported to be fabulous; he came back with tangible proofs, many precious things and notably gold which those regions generate naturally." (2)

Other letters follow this somewhat bald statement of the fact. They bear traces of conversations with the "Ligurian," for we meet with the now familiar details about the abundance of gold, the simplicity and nakedness of the natives and their readiness to be converted, and the beauty and strangeness of nature. The influence of the discoverer is indeed patent in some of these letters, such as that of September 13th, addressed to Cardinal Ascanio Sforza, and in which we hear that "after [three and thirty days of navigation] the explorers from the deck of the biggest ship, which conveyed Colón himself, announced land." (3) Colón was assiduously propagating his own view as to the first man to see the new world. It is therefore significant to find that in this letter Peter Martyr puts forward views which would appear to suggest a less enthusiastic estimate of the Indians than Colón had formed when he left Española. "The sense of mine and thine has sway over their lives as it has over ours, whence they seek to acquire luxury and wealth, which seems somewhat unnecessary for naked people." (4)

This "new world," as Peter Martyr was to call it for the first time in a letter to Borromeo on October 20th, 1494, was a constant source of wonder for the imagination of the wary men of Europe, alive to the fact that the East concealed immense fields of human life still closed to their curiosity and to their enterprise. The unlimited after-effects of the discovery were still unshaped and unrevealed in the bosom of time; but princes, geographers, philosophers and business-men, who had been watching the growing influx of Oriental goods, the slow penetration of Europe and Asia towards each other through the sands, physical and cultural, of Africa, felt at once, on hearing the news of Colón's discovery and its approximate location, that a new era was about to begin.

The obsession of Islam which had dominated Spain's history for seven centuries was, in a way, characteristic of the whole of Europe. The acme of European enterprise outside Europe had been reached in the crusades—South-eastwards, neither East, nor South, nor, least of all, West, blocked as it was by the ocean and by a veil of nothingness. Of recent date, the Portuguese had won the admiration of all Christendom by their navigating exploits along the coast of Africa and as far as the isles of Cabo Verde. But the veil still remained hanging over the ocean, and Christendom had never even imagined anything outside its own pale but Moors and Jews and the somewhat mythical and fabulous subjects of Prester John or of the Grand Khan.

Then came Colón and his first letters and conversations with the chief information officer of the age, Peter Martyr. Colón might talk of "Indians." Peter Martyr did not take it that way. He was not a quixotic man, capable of covering reality with a mask of his own dreaming. He had a quick, intuitive mind, and he grasped first the hard facts which were offered him—not merely by hearsay, since he could see the specimens of Indians in Colón's suite and was in a position to talk to them. The main point about these men was that they were *new*, i.e. they were neither Christians nor Jews nor Moors, nor, so far as he could judge, subjects of the fabulous *Grand Khan*. Nor were they blacks, either. This *inédit* character of the discovery was the feature which he was to emphasise in his letters; possibly not in a deliberate way, and yet in a way which can be quite clearly perceived even to this day in most of the letters he wrote. It was this sense of what had occurred which prompted him to coin the expression *New World* four years before it was to come to the pen of the discoverer himself. (5)

**
* **

Thus conveyed by the wings of fame, the news reached the Court of France, and in particular the house of Anne de Beaujeu, elder daughter of Louis XI, who had just two years earlier divested herself of the duties of Regent of the kingdom on behalf of her younger brother Charles VIII. There was a foreign gentleman in her household to whom the news was sure to be of the utmost interest, and so King Charles himself seems to have thought, for he asked this gentleman to come to the royal presence and hear it. The stranger was no other than Bartolomé Colón.

The future *Adelantado* of the Indies was then thirty-two. "He was a person of very good looks, tall, though not so tall as the Admiral, of good countenance, though somewhat forbidding, strong and courageous, very wise and cautious and cunning, of great experience for every kind of business. More wary and astute, so it seemed, and of less ingenuity than Cristóbal Colón; cunning and very shrewd in his dealings with men, singularly learned and experienced in sea-affairs. A great sailor and, to judge by the books and charts annotated by him, so proficient in that lore that the Admiral cannot have surpassed him much." (6)

His whereabouts between his Portuguese days and this summer of 1493 when he hears from the King—and from his brother also—that the Indies have been discovered, are one of the many mysteries of this most mysterious family. It seems well ascertained that he was in Portugal in December 1487, (7) for he was present when Bartholomeu Diaz returned from an expedition made famous by the discovery of the Cape of Good Hope, and he may even have taken part in this expedition himself. Moreover, as will be seen hereafter, he was in London in February 1488. Yet both Las Casas and Fernando Colón record that his arrival in England was delayed by "sea-thieves, Sterlings ('Esterlines') by nation. I know not their nation. This made him contract an illness and reduced him to extreme poverty, causing him to be a long time before he was able to arrive in England until God wished him to recover; and, somewhat restored by his industry and the work of his hands, for he made sea-charts," at last arrived in England. (8)

This story has given much trouble to historians of Colón. When did these melodramatic events take place? If Bartolomé was in Lisbon till December 1487 and in London in February 1488, it is obvious that they must have preceded the discovery of the Cape of Good Hope. Then, Bartolomé must have come back to Portugal *after* his adventure with the pirates. But Las Casas means to imply that the whole episode—sea-thieves, illness, poverty, recovery, arrival—took place on the way *from* Portugal to England. And there is no mention whatever of the country in which the years of illness and poverty were spent.

The story reads as if trouble and mishap had been accumulated on Bartolomé's head less by the hard hand of fate than by the liberal hand of imagination. Sea-thieves might have been enough; but illness and poverty as well! And these mythical "Esterlines," or Sterlings, too, of whom the honest chronicler cannot make head or tail. These lines of Las Casas leave the impression that the good bishop is innocently repeating a tale which the Colóns were interested in propagating, an impression strengthened by the fact that there is no room in Bartolomé Colón's life for so long an eclipse.

As if further to complicate matters, there is a statement by Bartolomé Colón himself, who roundly asserts that he was in Castille while his brother, the future Admiral, was endeavouring to get a hearing from a distracted and sceptical Court. It is no ordinary statement either, but an answer on oath to a *questionnaire* put to him by a Court of Law. The question put to him is:

"IX: Whether they [the witnesses] know and believe that what has been discovered in the land of Grace, known as Mainland, has been due to the industry which the said Admiral proved in opening the door and in making the first voyage in which he discovered the Indies. . . ."

To which, Don Bartolomé made the following answer:

"That he believes that which is contained in the said question because this witness went about with the said Admiral Don Cristóval Colón soliciting the King and Queen our Sovereigns, and because the said Admiral was the first who discovered these lands and Paria and no one had ever come till then; rather, when the said Admiral sought to achieve it, all made fun of the said Admiral and of this witness, saying that they wished to discover a new world. . . ." (9)

This statement cannot be easily disposed of. True, it raises as many problems as it solves, for if Don Bartolomé was in Castille in those early days, how is it no one speaks of him till 1493? Yet it is absolutely final. He went about with his brother soliciting the King and Queen, and with his brother he was the object of merriment and satire on the part of sceptics. These assertions are not only made on oath before a Court of Law, but also in the lifetime of many persons who were witnesses of, and even of some who took an active part in, the events to which they refer. The King himself, who was one of the parties to the suit before the court, was still alive and was to reign four more years. A prominent man like the Adelantado of the Indies could not possibly wander from truth on a point which concerned King Ferdinand so directly. There is no escape from the conclusion that Bartolomé Colón was in Castille with his brother at the time when the future Admiral was finding it difficult to be heard.

No one mentions him. True. But no one mentions Cristóbal either until he has come back from his discovery; and if the apostle, ten years older, obtains no attention, how could his acolyte, a young man of twenty-five as he was then, expect to be mentioned at all? Our feeling that Cristóbal was alone during those years is due to three facts only: (a) that the Duke of Medinaceli does not mention Bartolomé; (b) that Bartolomé obviously was not in La Rábida; (c) that Colón never speaks of his brother in the numerous passages of his writings in which he dwells on the days when he begged for caravels.

The first and the second facts are no proof whatever that Bartolomé was not in Castille; the third can easily be explained. To begin with, Cristóbal Colón was, we know, a most egotistical person, instinctively averse to sharing merits with anyone, and therefore, when emphasising his labours to see his scheme recognised, he would, of course, forget that his brother was helping him. But there must have been another reason, for his silence dovetails into the melodramatic yarn told us by Las Casas. The impression left jointly by these mythical "Sterlings" and the somewhat belated revelation of a stay in Castille made by Bartolomé in 1512 is that Bartolomé's first sojourn in the dominions of Ferdinand and Isabel must have been somewhat discreet. This younger brother cannot have been produced very liberally, and when, in 1512, he spoke of going about with his elder brother, he was not precisely lying, but he was possibly exaggerating. (10)

How and why, we do not know; but it is fairly safe to assert that Bartolomé Colón was in Castille during the first period of Colón's life there, and also to surmise that he supplied some of the sea-charts which Colón sold at the time for a living— for it was mostly Bartolomé who was the family draftsman. This, moreover, would provide a natural explanation for his voyage to England. By 1487 the affairs of Cristóbal Colón were deteriorating. He was receiving help from the Crown, but nothing definite seemed to be coming out of his endeavours in Castille. At this time he made the acquaintance of Beatriz Enríquez, and probably went to live with her. This would be the natural moment for his brother to leave him and try his powers of persuasion on King John of Portugal. It is even possible that the letter which we know Cristóbal wrote to King John, because the King mentions the fact in his answer, may have been conveyed to the King by Bartolomé himself. Then, the sequence of events takes a plausible aspect. Bartolomé is in Castille with Cristóbal until some time in 1487; he leaves for Portugal when his brother decides to go and live with Beatriz; he takes with him a letter for the King from the much-disappointed Cristóbal, trying to reconcile himself with King John and to enlist his help for the discovery; the King lets the matter lie dormant, and all this time Bartolomé hangs on in Lisbon and is present (December 1487) at the arrival of Bartholomeu Diaz back from his discovery of the Cape of Good Hope; this discovery itself reduces his scanty chances of success in Portugal, while filling him and his brother with a sense of urgency; he decides to leave for England, where we are to find him two months later, i.e. in February 1488; King John hears of this and, feeling perhaps that he has made a mistake, he writes honeyed words of invitation to Cristóbal in March 1488. This outline would, moreover, greatly help to clarify one other of the mysteries of the two brothers—that their books should be scribbled over with notes by *both* of them to an extent which so long a separation as that hitherto admitted would appear to render unlikely if not impossible.

One thing is certain. Bartolomé Colón was in London in February 1488. This is shown by the map which he made and dated there in order to explain his brother's scheme to King Henry VII. There is no trace of this map; but we owe to Las Casas the text of a few lines of Latin verse and prose which accompanied it and in which Bartolomé calls himself Bartholomeus Colombus de Terra Rubra and declares that Genoa was his fatherland. (11)

It does not in the least follow, of course, that the scheme was presented to King Henry in that month, nor even in that year. Despite the assertions of Colón, of his son Fernando and of his historiographer Las Casas to the contrary, it is evident that the proposal was either turned down straight away or indefinitely adjourned, until its success in Castille made any further consideration unnecessary. This follows from the facts and the dates on which they take place. For if Bartolomé had been successful in London he would not have gone over to try his powers on Charles VIII, in Paris, where the news that his brother had at last succeeded in persuading Ferdinand and Isabel found him. Bacon is non-committal between these two solutions, and his reference to Colón may be interpreted either way: "Before hee had obtayned a capitulation with the King for his brother, the enterprise by him was atchieved and the Western Indies by Providence were then reserved for the Crown of Castilia." (12) But Oviedo is more positive: "The King, being informed by his advisers and by the persons whom he entrusted with the examination of this, mocked at all that Colón said and held his words as hollow." (13)

Disappointed in England, Bartolomé came to France and settled there. Cristóbal wrote then to Bartolomé to come and serve the King and Queen, "for he would find honour and profit in it," (14) which shows that Bartolomé needed inducement to leave France. Finally, there is one more fact which does not seem to have attracted as much attention as it deserves: Bartolomé

Colón cannot have been so completely cut off from his brother as to remain seven months unaware of the fact that Cristóbal had struck a bargain with the King and Queen. Colón's plan was accepted in January 1492; he sailed in August 1492. It follows that, *if Bartolomé did not accompany his brother in his first expedition, the reason was that he chose it so.* He preferred a French sparrow in hand to one hundred parrots in Cipango's bushes. The view generally accepted—at any rate tacitly—that Bartolomé knew nothing of his brother until he came back as an admiral in 1493, is simply untenable. Nothing but the inertia of historians can explain that it should have held the field for so long, though in a quiet, unobtrusive way.

This time, however, the parrots were no longer in the bush, but in Colón's golden cages. So when King Charles told Bartolomé of the magnificent success of his brother, Bartolomé, "cunning and very shrewd in his dealings with men," kept silent about his brother's letter, for a King is a man for a' that and likes to be the only, or the first, one to have the news, since, as Las Casas says, "kings know the news before others"; (15) his reward was soon forthcoming, for the King gave him one hundred écus for his expenses and, thus reinforced, the cosmographer and commercial traveller for Don Cristóbal de Cipango and Co. left for Spain. The Admiral had gone. Now this is rather curious, because Don Cristóbal Colón had been in Spain no less than six months, and it is extremely unlikely that the news of the discovery should have taken as long as that to reach Bartolomé, even in those days. This again suggests that, even in the presence of the actual discovery, Bartolomé, despite Las Casas' narrative, did not at once fall to the idea of a Spanish career and that he must have hesitated for some time to leave Paris; which comes to confirm the general impression that Bartolomé had struck fairly strong roots on French soil. (May we, in passing, point out the peculiarly Jewish flavour of this facility to move from country to country, *and to settle in all*?) Evidently Bartolomé, who was far more of a realist and a man of affairs than his visionary brother, must have entertained some doubts about Christopher's scheme, and while willing to put it before this or that King, in case it came off, he must have thought that all these imaginations were not worth "a good plate of soup on a hot plate," as the French bourgeois says in a famous play.

When at last he made up his mind to go, the plate of soup was left behind in Paris and the imaginations had sailed again for Cipango and Cathay. Don Cristóbal had left instructions as to what his brother was to do and, in pursuance of them, Bartolomé left for Valladolid with his two nephews (now fourteen and six years of age), who were then appointed pages to Prince Don Juan, and he presented himself to the King and Queen, who ennobled him and gave him authority to style himself Don Bartolomé. But they did something which must have pleased him even more: they ordered him to arm three ships to go to Española, to put himself at the disposal of his brother the Admiral.

* *
*

The Admiral had left Cádiz at the head of a brilliant group of men. Cows, sheep, horses, gold-washers and farm-hands might well represent civil efforts—the age was nevertheless one in which the word *civil* meant *low*, and in that sense we meet with it more than once under the pen of Don Cristóbal de Cipango himself, a knight of the golden spur, who, therefore, had on board a good majority of gentlemen, i.e. men whose vocation was war. "All or most of them," says Las Casas, "took arms with them in order to fight if need be." (16)

First in rank, owing to his close relation to the Admiral, was his brother Don Diego Colón, "a person virtuous, very sane, peaceful, simple and of friendly disposition rather than cautious or evil-minded, who went about very quietly dressed, almost in clerical dress, and I do believe that he wished to be a bishop, or at any rate to obtain from the King and Queen that they should grant him a church income." (17) We may gather from this description that the Admiral would not feel very much strengthened by the presence of his youngest brother, who was not only lacking in spirit and in personal authority, but also far too young (twenty-five) to impress the forceful characters in the expedition.

Next to the two Colóns, the most important person on board was Antonio de Torres, a man in whom all seem to have put their trust—for we are to find him enjoying the confidence of Colón, of the King and Queen and of Colón's successor in the governorship, Ovando.

With him there came a number of members of the royal household. Las Casas, though a saintly friar, cannot resist the vanity of recording that his father, Pedro de las Casas, and his uncle, Francisco de Peñalosa, were among them—nor does he refrain from relating his uncle's glorious death. After serving three years in Española, Francisco de Peñalosa was sent by the

Queen, "who loved him well," to take a hand in the conquest of the Moors in Africa, then under Alonso de Lugo, Adelantado of Tenerife; a landing had been effected by the Adelantado, but so many infidels came upon them that the Spaniards ran back to the ships, whereupon Peñalosa, gathering twenty gentlemen round him, drew a round line on the ground and swore he would pierce with his spear any one of the twenty who would overstep it. They all died fighting and saved the rest.

Here is, then, at the beginning of the discovery, a man who acts in the style of Pizarro, one of the heroes of the conquest. This was the stuff of the Villalobos, Maldonados, Perafán de Riveras, Zúñigas, Coronels, Gallegos, Abarcas, Carvajales, who surrounded Colón and his pale satellite Diego; men born and bred in a hard climate, with centuries of civil war and religious war, inextricably mixed, behind them; used to looking after themselves and to getting into and out of difficulties without seeking anyone's helping hand; impatient of authority; hungry of adventure; contemptuous of comfort; rebellious to discipline; believing in God and the saints, but taking it all rather for granted and as *above-the-roof* matters, in the telling Spanish phrase; respectful of the Church, provided it did not pester them or expect them to take its sermons as rules of practical conduct; and always ready to justify their behaviour—however bad—by facing the grimmest consequences of it like men who knew no fear.

They were the surf of that wave of Spanish life which had been battering for centuries on the walls of Islam, until the last fortress had fallen; the wave which now, when the last resistance had gone, overflowed beyond the boundaries of Spain. The Spanish monarchies, strong though they were, had not yet evolved a national structure powerful enough to dam that wave and turn it to civic and political purposes. An old culture, the sap of Roman law and the blood of Christian charity, vivified their spirit perhaps more deeply than they themselves knew; but in their more vigorous reactions towards the drama of immediate life these men were, above all, hunters of danger and soldiers of fortune for the sake of fortune and of danger, not for that of either of the two ideals of Colón—the Banner of Empire and the Cross of the Gospel.

Chief amongst these were Alonso de Hojeda and Mosén Pedro Margarite. Hojeda came from the household of the Duke of Medinaceli. "He was short but very well proportioned and shaped; of beautiful countenance, the face beautiful and the eyes very big, one of the most agile men for running and turning round and for every other sport of strength to be found either in that fleet or in Spain. Every bodily perfection which a man can have seemed to have been congregated in him, save that he was small [. . .] though one of the bravest and always in Castille or here mixed in wars and challenges, for he was always the first to draw blood, he never was wounded in his life, nor ever a man drew blood from him, until about two years before his death when four Indians lying in wait for him wounded him by stratagem." (18)

As for Mosén Pedro Margarite, we know that Colón gave him the most difficult posts to hold and that he recommended him for promotion by the King and Queen, while Oviedo witnesses to his sense of loyalty to his men in the most trying circumstances, and to the conciliatory spirit wherewith he endeavoured to bridge over the differences which were soon to arise between Colón and Father Buil. (19)

And then there was a doctor on board, fortunately for us, for he took upon himself to write a diary of the voyage for the benefit of the Town Council of Seville. Dr. Chanca had volunteered to sail, and the King and Queen had written to him on May 23rd accepting his offer and going as far as to say that his presence would be of great profit to the health of those who were sailing to the Indies at their behest, which was going very far indeed. (20) Dr. Chanca seems to have been a jovial and sensible man, with a touch of that shrewdness bordering on scepticism which is found more frequently in orthodox, dogmatic, quixotic Spain than might at first be imagined. He proved of great service to the Admiral, not merely as a general practitioner in times of great strain for the health of the whole party, but also as a naturalist able to observe animals and plants with a competent eye and, in one case at least, as the man best qualified to unmask a dangerous enemy parading as a friend.

Five days were necessary to reach Gran Canaria; another five days to reach La Gomera; more time had to be spent there in stocking meat, firewood and water, and many more excellent things in which America abounds today, thanks to this thoughtful stay of the Admiral in one of the humblest of the Canaries, to wit: "heifers and goats and ewes and [. . .] eight sows at seventy maravedis apiece. From these eight sows have multiplied all the pigs which to this day have been and are in the

Indies, which have been and are numberless"; and "hens also, and this was the seed from which all that there is here of things of Castille has sprung, whether pips and seeds of oranges, limes, and melons, and all kinds of vegetables." (21)

Yet another day in going to the Island of Hierro, the westernmost and southernmost of the Canaries; so that the real crossing did not begin till October 13th, just one year and one day after the three caravels had seen land. The Admiral had given sealed instructions to the masters of the other sixteen ships, to be used only in case of emergency. This was his usual precaution now, to keep for himself the key of his discovery. This time he struck quite a different course, not west, but definitely southwest. His aim was to discover the Mainland. In so doing, he entered far further into the zone of the trade winds than he had done on his first voyage, and so on Sunday, November 3rd, after a crossing of twenty days out, a pilot of the flagship sighted land. There was great joy on board, and Dr. Chanca records that it was marvellous to hear the shouts and rejoicings, for they had all been sighing for land. They had a choice of two islands —Dominica and Marigalante; the anchorage was better in Marigalante, of which Colón took solemn and official possession, with the Royal Banner in his hand. Guadalupe was discovered the next day.

They were at last in the land of the Caniba, but Colón realised that these Caniba were not the subjects of the Grand Khan. Several captive women, who were delighted to be freed by the Pale-faces from the grim yoke of the Caniba natives, gave them a none too flattering picture of the life in the island. The Caniba kidnapped women and boys from neighbouring islands, for their own pleasure, and castrated the boys and ate them when they grew up. They also ate the children which they had by the foreign women, for they seem to have had a very high standard of racial purity.

The fleet wandered about pleasantly amongst the chain of islands which spread in a semicircle from Trinidad to Española, watching the natives, admiring the beauty of the evergreen autumn, observing harbours and hills, keeping the usual keen eye for gold, and now and then getting into trouble, as when one Diego Márquez, who was the captain of a ship, was lost with eight other men, having landed in Guadalupe without permission of the Admiral. Searching-parties were organised and trumpets sounded across the tropical woods, which must have echoed with mixed feelings noises so unusual and so much more powerful than their parrots' parliaments; but no answer came from the nine lost Christians; the fleet gave them up as eaten by the Cannibals, though, as Dr. Chanca points out, there were pilots amongst them who were able to come and go as far as Spain by the stars—but finally they reappeared in sight of the fleet, having struck the seashore in their wanderings and stuck to it for safety. The Admiral was content to punish the captain and leave it at that. Thus relieved of his anxiety, he discovered several islands, including Puerto Rico, which, though beautiful and big, can hardly have comforted Colón for his failure to find the elusive mainland, still behind the veil of mystery; and at last they arrived in Española. It is very probable that Colón would have discovered the mainland of South America on this second voyage, for he had started with a definite tendency to go south; but there was a disturbing force in his mind which diverted his course north-westwards: doubt— anxiety, perhaps—about La Navidad. This feeling, which the Admiral must have harboured even before starting from Spain— to judge by his actions—led him to hasten the voyage and to refrain from lingering amongst the enchanting sights which the ocean offered him always, new every day. No doubt he expressed it more cautiously to his crews and companion-leaders; but we find a trace of it in this remark of Dr. Chanca's: "Next morning, another island appeared, fairly large; we landed in none of these [islands] because we wanted to go and comfort the men that had been left in Española." And he adds: "And it did not please God, as will be seen anon." (22)

CHAPTER XXII

ADMIRAL *VERSUS* VICEROY

THEY were on a part of the island unfamiliar to those of them who had discovered it the year before, flat and low, so different from the northern coast that they had some doubts at first, not only on this score but also because the natives gave different names to each of the provinces of it, which, heard of through the haze of an imperfectly known language, made their own notions still vaguer. A caravel the Admiral had sent to sail round the whole island—you never can tell; suppose it were the mainland and instead of Cipango they had struck the coast of real Cathay?—had not come back these forty days. (1) Everything was new to their eyes and worth noticing, particularly animals and harbours and trees—and they noted it with a somewhat utilitarian eye and with a curious lack of sensibility for the beauty of the tropical landscape, due partly, no doubt, to the absence of persons with an artistic temperament in an expedition of men of action, but also to the fact that the century had not yet developed the sense of natural beauty which the discovery of America, amongst other factors, was precisely to foster in later days.

On they sailed towards La Navidad. In a small skirmish with a few cannibals, a Biscayan sailor was wounded. He died a few days later and was buried inland. Many of the men on board, being seamen, would be inclined to read some ill-omen into this event. The funeral boat, on landing, was surrounded with natives who, far from fleeing from the Christians, wanted all to be taken on board. The Spaniards would not have them, whereupon two of them, in a small canoe, came towards the fleet and ultimately made their way to the Admiral, to whom they explained that their "King" sent them to enquire who the strangers were, and to invite them to land, for there was much gold and food in the country which they could have. It is difficult to interpret this episode otherwise than as an attempt at trapping Colón on the part of some cunning islander. The Admiral seems to have been of this opinion, for "he gave them shirts and bonnets and other trifles" and excused himself because "he was going to Guacamari's land and could not tarry." (2)

270

This giving of shirts, however, was by no means a giving of trifles. Colón did not make his Indian friends don Spanish shirts out of prudishness, or even in the interests of the Catalan textile trade; his thoughts were deeper and more Machiavellian, as time was soon to reveal. Meanwhile, his mind was undoubtedly occupied with the situation which awaited him in Navidad, and if he lingered two days in "a harbour known as Monte-Cristi," this was "in order to study the aspect of the site, for the Admiral was not satisfied with the place where he had left his men as a site for a settlement." (3)

While surveying this site, some of them found two dead bodies, on the bank of the river. One of them had a knot round his neck, the other one round his foot. The superstitious amongst the Christians were vindicated. Superstitious men usually are, because human beings strew enough seeds of trouble on their path to make sure that no ill-omen will ever lack its crop of evil. The next day two more dead bodies were discovered, one of them bearded. "Some of ours," quietly says Dr. Chanca, "suspected more evil than good, and rightly so, for the Indians are all beardless." (4)

They were then about fifty miles from La Navidad, where they arrived on Wednesday, November 27th, at midnight. Eleven months away! Eleven months, not merely in another country but in another world. The Admiral, always a cautious navigator, remained outside the harbour till daylight. He seems to have carried cautiousness still further, because he did not cast anchor till the afternoon. While they were still distant from land, a canoe hurried towards them with five Indians who seemed to be most anxious to be received; but the Admiral was even more anxious to land, and did not wait for them. He had his *bombardas* shoot twice, hoping to get an answer from the *bombardas* he had left with Diego de Arana. There was no answer. This was truly ominous, the more so as no sign of life came from La Navidad.

During the night, while they all went about downcast, the same canoe which had tried to board them in the afternoon came close to one of the caravels. The Indians were taken to the flagship. They were anxious to see the Admiral and would not speak even to him until a light was brought and they were able to ascertain that they were in his presence. They brought gold-masks as presents for Colón and for Pinzón (whom they expected to find in the expedition); and when asked for news of the Christians, they answered that the Christians were all well though some had died of illness and others in the course of fights over feuds that had divided them. They volunteered the statement that Guacamari had not come because he was away, wounded in a leg; that he would come the next day; and that the two other kings, Caonabó and Mayrení, had attacked him and burnt out his settlement.

The news, so far, was mixed, and the Christians chose to take the good side of it; their spirits rose so high that when one of their own Indians told them that all the Navidad Christians had died, for he had it from the natives, he was not believed. The next day, while waiting for Guacamari, who did not come, the Admiral sent a landing-party, who reported that the settlement had been burnt out, that there were no Spaniards to be seen, and that the Indians, once so hospitable and eager to meet the Palefaces, avoided them and would not speak to them. Finally, one of Guacamari's relations explained that Caonabó and Mayrení had killed all the Christians and wounded Guacamari.

The first Spanish settlement in the New World had ended in disaster. Colón's first reaction was curious. He seems to have remained cool, in fact cold, at least outwardly; his orders were to search for any gold which the dead men might have buried— for he had instructed them to do so—and to look for a better place for a settlement. Any deeper effects of this tragedy which he may have felt at the time were carefully hidden behind that secretiveness which was one of his most typical features. He gave many—too many—reasons for his forbearance. The real one may well have been that he felt his own responsibility in the deed. Deeply mistrustful, he had left at the head of a settlement, which needed an outstanding chief, the man most personally connected with him, Diego de Arana. He was, more than once, to repeat this mistake, the exclusion of all but men bound to him by family ties.

Meanwhile, Guacamari did not appear. Many among Colón's men suspected him of treachery. Colón kept silent. The Indians unanimously accused Caonabó and Mayrení; yet would now and then drop hints as to the fondness of the Spaniards for native women. Eventually, Guacamari was found by some of Colón's captains, lying in his hammock, some twelve miles away from La Navidad. He explained to his visitors that he was wounded and could not go to see the Admiral, and he expressed the wish— no doubt merely diplomatic—that the Admiral should come and see him.

The Admiral went to visit the invalid "King." He did things well. Probably in order to influence the native prince with his power and magnificence, he took as a suite all his higher staff, all dressed in such a way that "they would have passed muster in an important city"; (5) he brought Guacamari presents, for he had already received some gold from the "King" and it was seemly that he should reciprocate. Guacamari told the story again, gave the Admiral more gold and other native jewels and tried in every way to be friendly. But, Dr. Chanca and a surgeon being present, the Admiral offered their services to the wounded King, who accepted them for lack of reason to refuse. He was bidden to come out into the light, and the surgeon and the doctor unbandaged his leg. "He had no more trouble in that leg than in the other," says Dr. Chanca, "though he pretended like a fox that it hurt very badly." Colón had now the proof of his treachery. But "the Admiral did not know what to do." (6)

The situation was no doubt difficult and possibly dangerous, yet in this, as in future cases, it seems that Colón did not show the qualities of decision and energy required in a true captain, and that he gave in too easily to his natural tendency to dissemble and procrastinate. Guacamari's brother came to the flagship the next day; he managed to speak to two Indian women who were on board and seems to have persuaded them to swim away in the night, which they did. The Admiral sent messengers to claim them back, but the Indian settlement was found empty and Guacamari had fled. This was not the kind of situation which a man like Hernán Cortés would have allowed to develop.

The itinerant temperament is a natural feature in sailors and explorers. Colón was, of course, in any case, a man much given to moving to and fro. But in particular, whenever he found himself in the presence of an unpleasant situation, he gave free vent to this natural proclivity. In these cases we are going to see him take refuge, if not in flight, at least in self-removal. A man of action would have felt that this spot where such grave matters had occurred demanded his presence until the position had been redressed; or, if the elements for action were not all available, he would have sought to secure them in the shortest possible time. Colón decided to start on a long voyage of exploration to seek a good site for another settlement. True, he might have thought it wise to begin by securing a base, and in so far as he did so, he may have been justified, for every man cannot have the temperament that made Cortés "burn" his ships. But one month looking for a site when Guacamari the accomplice and Caonabó the enemy were afield! And why so much time? Because "the Admiral decided that we should return up the coast towards the way he had come from Castille, because the news of gold came that way." (7) It is difficult to see how a leader who handled his men so could keep his authority over them for long.

Colón was always more at home at sea, where he was on the move, than on land, where he felt himself held up and stuck to hard facts. This feature is consonant with his imaginative temperament. The shifting sights, the changing situations, the very fluidity of the element on which he floated and of the element which drove him forth, the company of clouds, the free choice of all the winds of the compass—all that indeterminate environment was more akin to his fanciful soul than the hard-rock character of land and the heavy, solid problems which it raises. Yet all voyages must end, and after wandering a whole month Colón chose at last a good spot and gave orders to land, to the great relief of man, horses and cattle, not forgetting the eight sows.

On this spot, Colón founded the first town of the American continent, now in ruins through the neglect first of Spain and later of those who succeeded Spain in the land. He called it Isabela, in token of the special reverence he had for the Queen, and straight away built an army store-house, a church, a hospital and a strong-house for himself. The other leaders were invited to have houses built for themselves. And when the little town was beginning to take shape, it was visited by its first affliction— an epidemic. Little is known about it save that it affected nearly all the settlers. They attributed it to the overwork caused by the building up of Isabela and by the lack of adequate food. It may have been a mere wave of influenza, as we call it nowadays, without knowing much more about its real nature. Dr. Chanca was so much in demand that he claimed a rise in salary, which Colón transmitted to the King and Queen.

Meanwhile the Viceroy-Admiral was busy with two schemes: the exploration of Cibao in order to find out whether it really was Cipango, and also whether it contained gold; and the voyage of Antonio de Torres back to Spain to report to the King and Queen. The exploration of Cibao was entrusted to Hojeda, who, with fifteen men, went there and returned in fifteen days, bringing back cheerful news of Eldorados and friendly natives. This elated the Admiral so much that he forgot all about Cipango, and it enabled him to send a hopeful report, on this point at any rate, to the King and Queen through Antonio de Torres.

Colón had prepared his messenger carefully; he had appointed him *Alcaide* or Governor of the city of Isabela. The Admiral evidently thought that this man could be trusted to put his case to the King and Queen, yet, to make sure that his main points were not forgotten, he drafted a painstaking memorandum for his representative's guidance. The underlying tone of this document shows that Colón was not sure of his ground and that he was anxious to forestall possible criticisms of his enterprise. After a declaration of loyalty to the King and Queen, he devotes three long paragraphs to explaining why there has been as yet no outstanding success in the spice and gold line; he reaffirms the abundance of both in the island, but stresses the momentary difficulties—disease, lack of roads, Caonabó still at large. He then asks for Spanish food to be sent over, until the crops which have been sown are available and the animals brought and to be brought have multiplied. He goes on to suggest that numbers of cannibals should be sent to Spain to be converted and educated out of the habit; and then, by way of combining the two ideas, he proposes that a well-balanced trade might be organised if caravels were to come from Spain conveying cattle and to return with cargoes of cannibal slaves, which he believes would bring in substantial dues to the King and Queen.

This singular proposition was the only one which the King and Queen did not accept. (8) They withheld their opinion until a later time. Leaving for further discussion the attitude of Ferdinand and Isabel on slavery, the proposal made to them by the Admiral shows that Colón was already beginning to realise that there was less gold in Cipango and in the Indies than Marco Polo and Mandeville had led him to believe, and that it was necessary to look out for substitutes. Nor did this situation pass unnoticed at the Court. His gold was scanty; his "aloes" was not aloes; his "musk" was not musk; his "cinnamon" was not cinnamon. And when Antonio de Torres arrived with the news of the disaster of La Navidad, the rumour gained credence that Colón had not founded it in order to "populate," nor in pursuance of a special injunction of the Lord, but because he had no room for everybody on the way back after the loss of the flagship. "It was unavoidable to leave them behind," says Bernáldez, "for owing to the loss of the ship there was no way to convey them back, and this was not said here and it was said that they remained as the first settlers." (9)

The King and Queen might well ask themselves whether the enterprise was worth the trouble and expense. The splendid conquests—Mexico, Peru—were to be achieved in the next reign. What had they gained out of this discovery? Antonio de

Torres brought them news of a disastrous past, of a depressing present, of a disquieting future. The knights and gentlemen gone to discover an Eldorado humbly sought to be put on a list of salaries, as if discovery and conquest could be achieved by civil servants. Castille and its much depleted exchequer was to provide everything—animals, ships, salaries, pensions for the men's families; and in return Colón offered what? Cannibals as slaves.

So ran rumour in Spain. As for Isabela, there is little doubt that the Admiral felt himself criticised by those who surrounded him. Between this often taciturn, always secretive and cautious commander and the host of spirited soldiers and adventurers which he had taken over with him, there was an obvious temperamental discordance. He was, as will be seen by his actions, mistrustful of his principal companions (with the possible exception of Antonio de Torres), and mistrust naturally breeds mistrust. Moreover, some of them, at any rate, may have been and probably were self-seeking, undisciplined and ambitious. His first serious trouble broke out with the Chief Accountant of the fleet, one Bernal de Pisa, *Alguazil de Corte*, who had been given strict instructions to keep his eyes open and his pen sharp to report all that could be reported, to Juan de Soria. (10) As if he had carried over the Atlantic the spirit of Juan de Soria himself, Bernal de Pisa had written an "enquiry" on the Admiral's doings, which he had hidden inside a wooden buoy. The Admiral seems to have had a good intelligence service, for he found out the paper and put his Chief Accountant in prison while he punished several other conspirators, one of them probably with death, (11) if we are to give to Las Casas' somewhat enigmatic version the only interpretation which makes it intelligible. This firmness towards his own, possibly contrasted with his caution and forbearance towards Guacamari, was not of a kind to improve his position as a leader.

His next decision was not more fortunate. He had felt his curiosity whetted by Hojeda's report on Cibao, and he decided to go there himself. He had several men under him whom he might have left in charge during his absence. He left his young, parson-like brother Diego, of whose incapacity he was so much aware that he put by his side "persons who would advise and help him." (12) Having thus sown the seeds of trouble behind him, he started for Cibao on March 12th, 1494.

He had given Hojeda fifteen men, but he took with him a powerful army: "to put fear into them and show them that if they attempted anything, they [the Christians] were mighty enough to attack and hurt them; he made his men leave Isabela in war style, flags flying and trumpets sounding and guns shooting, which would leave the Indians fairly astounded, and he did so as he entered and left all native settlements on the way." It was a happy expedition in every way; after working hard to master a difficult pass, and to widen its narrow paths for their horses and trucks, the Spaniards set eyes on a valley "so fresh, so green, so clean, so colourful, so full of beauty, that they thought they had arrived in some region of Paradise, bathed and steeped in a deep and incomparable joy." (13)

The natives seem to have been worthy of the land, for they seemed to have little sense of mine and thine, despite Peter Martyr's opinion; they came to the strangers and freely took and gave whatever they fancied, or they withdrew to their huts and "shut" them by merely putting a few hollow canes across the entrance. The Admiral had these symbolic "doors" respected and gradually gained the confidence of the natives.

He reached Cibao. It was not Cipango. It was "Stony-land," for *Ciba* meant *stone* in the native language. But, in the numerous rivers of this dry, rocky land, his men found enough gold to justify, if not the Cipangish reputation which he himself had made for it, at least the construction of a good fortress and the settlement of a Spanish garrison. This he did near a "very merry river"; and as the object of it was to secure the control of the gold-mines which in the past had given rise to so much scepticism, he put this fortress under the advocation of St. Thomas, the patron of sceptics. Mosén Pedro Margarite was left at the head of it with fifty true men. (14)

When, on March 29th, he returned to Isabela, Colón found a deplorable situation. "Where there is no flour every mood is sour," (15) says a Spanish proverb. Hunger showed its lean face and big surly eyes everywhere. Most of the food brought over from Spain had become putrid under the hot, damp climate, and the native food did not agree with the Christians, used to good ham baptised with excellent wine. Colón had no flour, but he had wheat and a river; so he gave instructions to build a few mills; but his working men were thin and flabby with lack of food, and so this terrible man, this knight of the golden spur, had the daring to ask that the gentlemen and the Palatine men, "the dark-caped men," should help them. "They thought it as bad as death to have to work with their hands, particularly not eating," says Las Casas. (16) And as the Viceroy had to "add violence to command" to constrain everyone to work, this again increased in no small measure the disaffection which other actions of his, less justified perhaps than this one, had already spread amongst his followers.

The estrangement with Father Buil, which was to be one of the most dangerous features in his personal situation, seems to have begun then. Buil was, after all, the special representative of the Queen for spiritual affairs, and she was sure to have carefully selected him. He found Colón too severe in his punishment of the men and too sparing in their nourishment. The lack of adequate food for the sick was a frequent cause of suffering and death. "The Admiral," says Oviedo, "had several men hanged, particularly an Aragonese named Gaspar Ferriz, had others whipped and began to be severe and more rigorous than he was wont to be. [. . .] The Admiral was accused of being cruel, in the opinion of that friar [Buil] who, deputing as he was for the Pope, intervened; and as soon as Colón did something in matters of criminal justice, which the monk did not think just, he at once laid him under an interdict and had divine offices stopped. And thereupon the Admiral had rations stopped and [ordered] that Father Buil and his household should not be given food." This tragi-comic duel between the spiritual and the temporal power was bound to be detrimental to the moral authority of the Admiral-Viceroy. (17)

The general impression left by all these data is that, though Colón had a case, and a strong one, and though, no doubt, the "gentlemen" must have made it difficult for him, when they found the discovery to be less adventure and more hard work than they had expected, the sufferings endured by the expedition were terrible and death by hunger and want a dreadfully frequent occurrence. Legend is a transfigured image of history, and the legends current over Isabela very soon after were grim enough. The town was already depopulated in Las Casas' time, and those who had to go near it, notably for hunting pigs, which were by then abundant and had run wild, did so with fear and trembling, for it was known that one heard and *saw* voices of the desolate souls whose bodies had starved there. "It was also said [. . .] that one day one man or two were walking amidst those buildings of Isabela when, in a street, there suddenly appeared two rows or choruses of men, who seemed to be noble and Court people, well dressed, with swords girt and wrapped in travelling cloaks of the kind worn in Spain in those days, and when that person or those persons were wondering how such people so new and well dressed had landed there [. . .] on asking them whence they came, they answered silently by putting their hands to their hats to greet them and, when they took their hats off, their heads came off also and they remained headless, and then vanished: of which vision the man or men were left nearly dead and for many days pained and astonished." (18) This moving story provides a vivid proof of the impression left on the first settlers by the hardships endured in Isabela, and therefore of the loss of prestige and moral authority which the leader must have undergone then, whether the people entrusted to his care were entirely innocent or—what is more likely—partly responsible for the plight in which they all found themselves.

In the midst of these tribulations, Colón received news that the fortress of Santo Tomás was going to be attacked by Caonabó, while the natives in the whole district left their habitations empty and fled. He decided to send Hojeda with soldiers and stores of food and arms. Moreover, he made up his mind to get rid of hungry mouths and added to the expedition "all those who were not ill and who could walk" (19) so that they should explore the country and get used to the food of the land. It was Colón's intention that Hojeda should remain in Santo Tomás and that Margarite should go reconnoitring the country. Hojeda took with him sixteen horsemen, two hundred and fifty archers and one hundred and ten soldiers armed with shotguns (*espingardas*), as well as twenty officers. The instructions sent by Colón to Margarite make somewhat mixed reading: no swindling and no robbing of the Indians, but good treatment and payment for all supplies, even though the money was to be no better than beads and bells; if any Indian steal, punishment by cutting nose and ears, "for they are limbs that cannot be hidden," and so the island will be secure for "the natives will know that the good are well treated and the bad are punished." (This was no worse than the way similar crimes were punished in Spain or anywhere in Europe at the time.) Justice at home was to be equally severe, so that the troops were disciplined and were not allowed to disperse in twos and threes, which would be their undoing. And as Margarite was to move about the country, he was to erect tall crosses everywhere and to set up landmarks—in honour of God and of their Highnesses and to allow people to know where they were.

As for Caonabó, he must be caught alive. He must be flattered and befriended and told that the Christians are very numerous and more to come; then, but only then, do we realise the beauties of sartorial civilisation and Colón's generosity in the matter of shirts: "see that Cahonaboa [Colón's spelling of this King's name] comes to speak with you, so that he may be arrested more securely; and as he goes about naked, so that it would be difficult to seize him [. . .] see that he is offered a shirt and put it on him at once, and a cape and a girdle and put a cap on his head, and so you will be able to hold him and he will not be able to disengage himself." (20)

Colón was evidently in a more aggressive mood than when he had allowed Guacamari to escape after his treason or deceit. When Hojeda, following his instructions, had cut off an Indian's ear because of the theft of some clothes, put in chains a *cacique* and two other prominent natives who had complained of the punishment and sent them to him, the Viceroy suddenly turned ruthless and had the three prisoners beheaded in the centre of the square. Though Las Casas is seldom a safe witness, owing to his admirable, but unbalanced and passionate, bias in favour of the natives, it is difficult to see why he should have made up this incident which shows Colón punishing three innocent men, when he had allowed the guilty Guacamari to go scot-free. So that this, the first capital execution made by Christians in the New World, leaves the impression of a belated, impulsive outlet of energy on the part of a man who was not a complete master of his own mind and will.

CHAPTER XXIII

RETURN TO SPAIN IN SACKCLOTH AND ASHES

THE general situation could hardly be described as satisfactory. Isabela was hungry and dejected, more a hospital than a town of settlers and conquerors; Santo Tomás was threatened by an energetic enemy and boycotted by the surrounding population; the Spaniards were seething with disaffection; the Indians smarting under the execution of three of them; Antonio de Torres had gone with twelve caravels and would not be back for months. Any man of action would have stuck to his post. Colón was no man of action, but a dreamer, a wanderer, not merely in space but in mood, a man in search of his own soul.

He was moreover bitten by the desire to discover the mainland. This was, after all, his chief purpose. Settling was of course very important, and the King and Queen, who thought in terms of territory and empire, were entitled to some tangible results in the form of cities, provinces and revenues. But Colón was not a settler; he was an *unsettler*. He belonged to that type of man who is born to initiate things, to open them up, to sow; not to that type who develops and expands them, who reaps. He was not at home in the world of problems with which Isabela pestered him. "I shall be judged," he was to write later in his days of distress, "as a Captain who went forth conquering from Spain as far as the Indies, and not to govern town, city or village already settled, but to reduce to the obedience of their Highnesses savage and warlike peoples who live in mountains and in the wilderness." (1) It would be difficult better to express the *initiating* or *nascent* quality of his energy. He was all for discovery; once discovered, a land had no longer any allurements for him.

So he left Española on April 24th, with three caravels, the *Niña*, *San Juan* and *Cordera*. Repeating his previous mistake, though in a slightly attenuated form, he delegated his powers to a Council presided over by his brother Don Diego, and composed of Father Buil, Pero Hernandez Coronel, Alonso Sanchez Carvajal and Juan de Luxán, any one of whom would probably have had better claims to preside over the Council than the parson-like Don Diego. The next day he cast anchor in Navidad, and tried to get in touch with Guacamari, but the guilty *cacique* was not available; and having waited two days in vain, he sailed forth. He was anxious to explore Cuba, and to ascertain whether it was an island or, as he was inclined to think, the mainland, of course of Asia. On Tuesday the 29th, he saw the Cape of Bayatiquiri, easternmost point of Cuba, which in his first voyage he had named *Alpha and Omega*, meaning by it "beginning and end" of the East and the West. Such a name should have incited him to remain faithful to his main purpose—the mainland. But there was a Diego Colón on board who tempted him away from his duty.

This Diego Colón was an Indian. (2) The Spaniards often gave their own names to the non-Christians whom they baptised. It is well known that thousands of Jews bear to this day Spanish noble names which they received from their illustrious sponsors on the day of their conversion. Similarly, two of the Indians who arrived in Spain with Colón on the first caravel were christened Don Juan de Castilla and Don Fernando de Aragón, and lived at Court with the King and Queen. Assimilation was ever an almost instinctive line of action with the Spaniards. Colón had followed the fashion, and had given one of his Christian Indians the name and surname of his brother and of his son. Now, this Diego Colón, a Guanahani Indian of the first voyage, showed considerable interest in Jamaica, which, he assured his patron, was overflowing with gold. Who said gold?, Colón seems to have asked, and he changed his course from the mainland, still unfound, to the lovely and elusive metal. He discovered Jamaica on May 13th, 1494, and "thought it the most beautiful and graceful of all those he had as yet discovered." (3)

So here was Jamaica, the island full of gold; the island in which in years to come he was to taste the bitterest dregs of his intimate misery and to express his grief in unforgettable pages: here was Jamaica. But his acquaintance with the beautiful and "graceful" island was not to go beyond a first, rapid, superficial glance. After five days of cruising along its coast, one of which was marred by a fray with the natives, Colón heard the call of the West and returned to Cuba. He was this time determined to sail on and on for five or six hundred leagues till he had wrenched its secret from that mysterious land.

The ocean seemed to be keeping watch over it, for the little fleet met with every possible obstacle; a labyrinth of islands which the poet-discoverer named *The Queen's Garden*, and a series of storms which burst out every afternoon till the moon was out, and which more than once made the ships run aground. An Indian whom they met on the way assured them that Cuba was an island, but, as he also explained how the "king" of all that part and his people never spoke except by signs, his testimony may have been discounted.

Colón was then within about one hundred and fifty miles of the western end of the island. He could easily have reached it and gained a valuable piece of information which might have led him to Yucatán and to justify the discovery in the eyes of his unkindest critics with the splendour and wealth of Mexico. But it was not to be, and impressed, we are told, by the storms, the dangerous banks and islets and the low state of his stocks of food, he turned his back again on the sunny side of fate and set sail for Isabela on June 13th, 1494.

Yet, as events were to show, the scarcity of food cannot have been a weighty reason, for the fleet did not actually go to Isabela but went sailing about in a vacillating and leisurely way. The real explanation cannot be found in lack of food or in navigating difficulties, because Colón had shown before, and was to show later, that he could dare hunger and the waves. The real explanation was that he suddenly made up his mind that Cuba was the mainland. We know that for Colón, as for Don Quixote, outer reality only existed by permission of inner reality. What he thought, was. Now, on June 12th, just one day before he turned his back on the continent, Colón, exactly in the style of Don Quixote, made everybody aboard swear that Cuba was the mainland. Fernando Pérez de Luna, notary public of Isabela, acting notary of the fleet, was instructed by the Admiral to ask one by one all the pilots, masters and seamen, "to say whether they had any doubt that this land was the mainland at the beginning of the Indies, or the end for those who would wish to come to these parts from Spain by land; and that if they had any doubt or notion thereon, he begged them to say so, for he would soon remove it and would make them see that this is truly the mainland"; (4) and they were all made to swear and the notary threatened them with a penalty of ten thousand maravedis (or to receive a hundred lashes if they were shipboys) and to have their tongue cut off *every time* they should say the contrary thereafter; and they all swore and accepted everything he said, all including Juan de la Cosa, who was "master of making charts" and was sure to look upon this scene as sheer lunacy—just as those who listened to Don Quixote threatening with his spear any one who would not acknowledge Dulcinea as the foremost beauty in the world, were willing to acquiesce, and, leaving it at that, went about their business.

Thus satisfied that Cuba was the mainland, Colón sailed on leisurely. He stayed a while at the Isle of Pines, then sailed eastwards, and went round the southern coast of Jamaica; but, when, close to Española, he might have been expected to sail straight to Isabela, Colón was content to send nine men across country with news of the fleet, while he sailed on with his three ships, one might think aimlessly. He had not slept, he says, for thirty-two days, while the isles of the Queen's Garden and the storms conspired against his peace; he was probably beginning to feel the slackening effects of the illness which was to overcome him soon. He seems to have had in mind a punitive —or even an exterminating—expedition against the Cannibals. On his way thither (i.e. the present Puerto Rico) he discovered the islands which the natives called Amona, and the Spaniards, La Mona (the monkey), and soon after "he fell into a pestilential slumber which deprived him of all his senses and forces and he remained dead and they all thought he would not last one day." (5) The fleet, deprived of its commander, returned to Isabela, where it arrived on September 29th, 1494. It had been away five months and five days.

* *

"God squeezes but stifles not"; when the Admiral-Viceroy landed in Isabela he might well have remembered this Spanish proverb. He was laid up for long, he was actually ill five months; the colony was in a state of moral disintegration; but his brother, Don Bartolomé, was in Isabela, (6) feeling, no doubt, very much out of work. It was a far cry between Don Bartolomé and Don Diego, not only in point of age—for Don Diego was twenty-six and Don Bartolomé thirty-three—but in point of character, for the second brother was by far the most spirited and executive of the family.

Though unable to give continuous attention to the government of his island, Colón was still in a position to take an important decision, wise in its intention but most unwise in its form. He clearly felt that while he was unable to take up the government again, his safest substitute was his own brother; but he made the mistake of appointing him Adelantado. This was a serious step for, though in practice it meant little more than Governor and Commander-in-Chief by delegation, in name it meant the concession of a coveted title which carried with it a number of privileges. The unfortunate results of this rash measure were that "public opinion" in the island, which was already aroused against the Colóns, was lashed into a fury; and that later on, when the King and Queen were appraised of Bartolomé Colón's appointment, they looked upon it as an encroachment on their royal authority. (7)

The energy and resource of the new Adelantado were required to deal with a situation which went rapidly from bad to worse. The central region was in open revolt.

The events of this period are not clear. According to Las Casas, the Indians did not want to work; little food sufficed them and they wore no clothes; while the Spaniards ate more in one day than the Indians in one month and liked Indian women more than the Indian men would have wished; which all sounds true enough and human enough. Yet Oviedo's story is quite different and rings equally true. The men on Santo Tomás were reduced to a state of starvation and had to eat everything, down to lizards and snakes. One day a friendly Indian *cacique*, knowing that Margarite was ill, brought him two doves. Margarite called his men and put it to them that, as he was ill and as in any case there was not enough food in two doves for so many men, he proposed to eat them himself; he was approved by a crowd of hungry but sensible soldiers. Then, Margarite opened the window, let the doves fly into the vivid blue sky, and, to his astonished garrison, explained that he was not going to eat while his companions starved. (8)

This Margarite does not sound as bad as Colón's historiographers would make us believe. In conditions which are not clear, he left his post and sailed for Spain with Father Buil in the caravels which had brought Don Bartolomé over. He has been accused of all the misdemeanours committed by his garrison when they found themselves without a chief, and particularly of their dispersion in groups of twos and threes, which were often murdered by the natives. But this story may well be an invention due to the fact that, in his instructions to Margarite, Colón had warned him against that danger; moreover, even if Margarite had deserted his post, which, despite the definite assertions of Las Casas and Fernando Colón to that effect, it is difficult to believe, the responsibility for subsequent events lies with Don Diego Colón and his Council for not having appointed a successor.

The incident shows to what an extent the authority of the Viceroy had been weakened by events due partly to circumstances, partly to the character of his men, partly to his own character. The King and Queen, however, showed as yet no signs of cooling in their ardour for the discovery, and in their sympathy and confidence towards their Admiral and Viceroy. When Antonio de Torres arrived back in Isabela (September or October 1494) a letter was delivered to Colón in which their Highnesses thanked and congratulated him for all that he had done, "which for the most part has come true as if you had seen it before you spoke of it"; they very reasonably suggested that a regular service of one small caravel should be set up each way; they informed him of the agreement with Portugal concluded on June 5th in Tordesillas, whereby the limit of the two discoveries was set at a line three hundred and fifty leagues west of Cabo Verde; and they requested him to come and share in defining this line on the map, or, if his coming should give rise to grave objections, to send his brother in his stead. Torres also brought an order signed by the King and Queen on the same day, summoning all gentlemen, squires, officers and good-men to obey the Admiral in all he might command in their name. (9)

These letters may have helped him to recover. The winter, somewhat relieved on the Christian side by the food brought from Spain in Don Bartolomé's and Torres's caravels, was, however, agitated on the Indian side by the deep cleavage which had at last been revealed between the two civilisations. The Indians of Haiti—leaving aside for the moment what other Indians may have been—were a kind and intelligent race who lived happily in a state close to nature but by no means savage; though Oviedo's picture of them, particularly in sexual matters, is not flattering, in their attitude towards property at any rate, they might be described as Christians without Christ. The Spaniards were Europeans, i.e. men of action, bent on power, wealth and exchange. They were also, but in a totally different sense, Christians without Christ. The meeting of the two forms of mankind could not but end in tragedy. On March 24th, 1495, Colón with his brother Bartolomé, two hundred infantry and twenty horse, with twenty hounds specially trained, sallied forth from Isabela to have done with it. Two days later, he put to flight a huge army of natives estimated by Las Casas at one hundred thousand. There is ample room for reduction. The war of subjugation ("pacification," it is now called, for we have made some progress, in words) lasted for ten months, with a determination and a vigour which revealed a new influence—that of Don Bartolomé. In the course of it, Caonabó was taken prisoner by a stratagem less simple than the sartorial trick imagined by the Viceroy, yet based on similar principles. The natives did not know the use of shirts; they did not know the use of fetters either. So a set of fetters beautifully made in brass—a metal more esteemed by them than gold—was shown him by Hojeda. He was bidden to ride a horse—an animal which the common Indian dreaded and would not approach—and so Caonabó's men were kept at bay, and while on it, he was tempted to put on the dangerous present. He lost his liberty before his followers realised what was happening. In later days, when, chained in the hall of the Admiral's house, he saw Colón walk past, the proud chief would not move; but when little Hojeda went by, Caonabó would rise and bow low. When it was explained that Hojeda was but a subordinate officer of the great Chief, he would retort that the Admiral had not dared to come to arrest him, while Hojeda had, and therefore he bowed to Hojeda but not to the Admiral. (10)

Fortunately Antonio de Torres and his ships were available. Colón could send him back home to explain the position and overtake adverse reports. Trusting as he did, the brother of the Prince's Aya, who had already more than once proved so loyal to him, the Admiral decided also to send his brother Diego, whom he could spare better than Bartolomé. This, though not mentioned by either of his two historiographers, is proved by three documents referring to Don Diego, two of which bear the date May 5th, 1495, and the third, June 1st, 1495. These documents, signed by the King and Queen, reveal the scrupulous care with which the monarchs tried to be faithful to their Admiral and Viceroy. In the first they recommend the Bishop of Badajoz, Don Juan de Fonseca, to speak with the Admiral's brother who has just come from the Indies, to keep him satisfied in every possible way and to find out through him what can be done to please the Admiral himself; in the second the King and Queen order the Bishop to abstain from asking Don Diego Colón to give up some gold which he had brought from the Indies for himself, although legally Fonseca was entitled to do so; in the third, the King and Queen remind the Bishop of this order (which up to a point would justify the criticisms levelled against Fonseca by Colón's friends, for he seems to have been somewhat remiss in letting Don Diego benefit from the privilege granted him in this matter by the King and Queen), inform him that Don Diego, who had thought of going to Italy, has changed his mind owing to the war there, and express their pleasure at any decision which Don Diego may take about his movements, whether to go back to the Admiral, to remain in Castille, or to do whatever else he may wish. In fact the King and Queen are full of goodwill towards Don Diego, but, as the Admiral himself felt, they do not know very well what to do with him, nor do they seem to care. (11)

⁎

Enemies caught in a fight were, according to the ethics of the day, considered as slaves. Colón sent five hundred slaves to Castille along with Don Diego and his grievances, in the fleet of caravels commanded by Antonio de Torres. This again was not a very good move on Colón's part. His affairs were beginning to deteriorate at Court. Father Buil and Mosén Pedro Margarite were putting to the King and Queen, to Fonseca and to the other high officials of the Crown, a case which was bound to differ from Colón's own case. We cannot take at their face value the judgments passed on these two men by the two historiographers of the Admiral. They certainly had their own shortcomings and their more or less reasonable grievances; but Colón's record was by no means above criticism and their task must have been only too easy, well informed as they were on events in Española. In the circumstances, this cargo of human cattle consigned to Fonseca was bound to produce an unfavourable impression, both in itself, as an exhibition of human misery, and because it incarnated the Admiral's tendency to force the royal hand. His previous proposal on slavery was in suspense. Torres had brought him the non-committal and procrastinating answer of the King and Queen. This official, trusted by the Court, and undoubtedly familiar with its way of thinking, may have explained to him that from the political and religious standpoint of Castille slavery was only countenanced in the case of prisoners of war. Then Colón must have been tempted to rush matters by sending five hundred Indians taken in battle; his astute mind may have guessed that, though he might incur the displeasure of the Queen, he would conquer the suffrages of the five hundred officials and courtiers who would buy the slaves cheap. Nor were events to prove him altogether mistaken in this guess. (12)

Meanwhile, he tried all possible means of justifying himself at Court by securing more gold. As he was now master in the Island, he put a gold tax on the natives, which, according to Las Casas, was to be a Flanders bell full of gold every three months for every male over fourteen years living in the gold-mine district, and an *arroba* (about 25 pounds) of cotton for those dwelling in other regions. The payment of the tax was to be acknowledged by a brass medal to be worn by the tax-payer. This tax was a complete failure. The Indians countered with a refusal to sow the land and fled with their families to the mountain districts; many of them suffered hunger and death.

Such was the state of the island which Colón had dreamt of as a gold-roofed Cipango, when Juan de Aguado landed in it, sent by the King and Queen to see and report. His credentials were drafted in a way which might well give Colón food for thought and grounds for fear. They were not addressed to him. In fact, the Viceroy was ignored in this singular document: "The King and the Queen: Gentlemen and Squires and other persons who are in the Indies at our behest, we send you thither Juan Aguado, our Butler, who will speak to you on our behalf. We order you to have faith in him and to believe what he says." (13)

Aguado arrived in Isabela in October 1495, while the Admiral was still waging his war against the Indians. Aguado went ahead to meet him. The Indians were given to understand, or gathered, that this was a new Admiral come to supersede the old one. (It would be curious to know what they made of that word *Admiral*, so magical for Colón himself.) They were very much elated, for they probably thought that the new Admiral could not be worse for them than the old. Meanwhile the old and the new "admirals" came back to Isabela and started one of those stubborn campaigns of mutual defiance in which Spanish history is so rich. For five months they argued as to where and how the credentials of Aguado would be read and acknowledged by Colón. While the dispute went on, Aguado acquired abundant information on the discontent which prevailed in the colony against the Viceroy. Hunger was the worst grievance; there was little or no food; "just a plateful of wheat which they were given in the King's granary and which they had to grind in a handmill (many ate it boiled) and a slice of rancid bacon or of rotten cheese and I don't know how many beans or chickpeas, wine as if there were none in the world"; (14) the favourite oath was "so let God take me to Castille." This made, of course, first-rate ammunition for Juan Aguado.

The Very Magnificent Lord Don Cristóbal Colón felt a bitter

humiliation, seeing himself treated on equal terms by the King's butler, and even sometimes threatened by him with the royal displeasure and always criticised and challenged. "Neither the Admiral nor his decisions were as respected and obeyed as heretofore." (15) For a man of his pride and inordinate haughtiness, this crisis must have sunk him in deep tribulation. He decided to go to Castille as soon as possible. He felt his position at Court gravely shaken; and he saw his authority and prestige in "his own" Indies jeopardised by a "civil" servant of the King and Queen. His defensive move was characteristic of that stiff-necked *soberbia* (no English word can render this Spanish composite of pride, haughtiness and fullness of the self) which was his chief strength and his chief weakness. He knew he would be deeply humiliated; so he deliberately humbled himself. "As he was a very devout worshipper of St. Francis," says Las Casas, "he dressed in brown cloth, and I saw him in Seville, when he came back then, dressed almost like a friar of St. Francis." (16) The good bishop did not see deep enough. Colón was by no means a hypocrite or a dissembler in this. He was acting in all sincerity. But there were two deep-lying motives which prompted him to adopt this monastic garb: the first was a "mimetic" instinct, similar to that which makes some insects look like twigs or leaves; he was in outward danger—the displeasure of the Court; what better garb than that of a Franciscan? The second was an even deeper instinct: he was in inner danger— the fall from the heights of pride to the depths of humiliation; he determined that no one but himself should humble him; he, by his own free will, humbled himself down to the bottom of the ladder; henceforth, no man could abase him lower than he himself had done. He was proof against insults.

While the Viceroy and Admiral was learning hard at the school of grief and experience, nature rushed in and came to make bad matters worse. The island was shaken by that mighty and dreaded exhibition of nature's wrath and violence which the Indians knew as *hurricane*, (17) a word we have adopted from them. Isabela was a good harbour but somewhat exposed north-west; it experienced the full force of the storm, and the four ships which Aguado had brought over were all lost. There were no ships left to go to Spain. Colón had two caravels built, which, incidentally, shows that the colony had already at hand enough technical resources of men and material to build sea-worthy ships.

As the graceful frames rose gradually in his yards, he began his preparations for the voyage. He had several forts built and garrisoned in several parts of the island; he appointed his brother Bartolomé Governor and Captain-General, and Diego as his substitute and second-in-command; he therefore remained faithful to the shortsighted and self-centred policy of keeping the key posts in charge of men of his own kith and kin, which was bound to alienate from him the sympathy of the humiliated captains who had helped him in his work. To make matters worse, he left as Alcalde Mayor of Isabela and of the whole island, in charge of the administration of justice, one Francisco Roldán, a man of his household, "of good parts, though not learned," (18) which again could hardly be the best choice when there were so many men of higher standing in Isabela; and as time was to show, this appointment was to be disastrous for his cause. Then he began to select his return party. There was no lack of candidates. The King and Queen had ordered him to provide for the return of the sick and poor, and of all those whose wives or relations had complained to the royal chancery that the Admiral did not allow them to sail back home; many more importuned him to let them return. In all, the number of disenchanted settlers and conquered-conquerors amounted to over two hundred and twenty. There were also thirty Indians. The expedition left Isabela on Thursday, March 10th, 1496. Colón was on board one of the caravels and Aguado on the other. There was much water between the two fires.

As was his wont, he did not sail straight back, but lingered first amongst "his islands" like a collector who handles his treasures for the pleasure of seeing them shine in the light of day. On April 9th, he was still in Marigalante; the next day, in Guadalupe, where he was received in a warlike manner by an army of women; when he explained that all the Christians wanted was to buy some food, the women answered that the strangers were to apply to the other side of the island, where their husbands were tilling the land and they would see to it. The Admiral was, however, able to make a provision of popinjays, most valuable ones for propaganda purposes, for they were as big as cocks; and to send inland a party of forty men who brought him ten women and three boys; one of these women was the "Lady" of the district; that is what Las Casas calls her; Colón would have called her the "Queen." No ordinary woman. When the Christian—"a Canary-islander"—who ultimately caught her, ran after her, she "ran like a deer," and when she saw that he was overtaking her, "she turned on him like a mad dog and embracing him, felled him to the ground, and if other Christians had not come to his rescue, she would have strangled him." (19) To be sure, a most un-Christian behaviour on her part. However, the Admiral sent all the women back with presents, because he did not want to leave the Indians with a grievance, *since that island was on the way.* The "Lady" and her daughter apparently chose to remain in the caravel of their own free will, though Las Casas feels some doubts about the freedom of the will of those two Indian ladies in the hands of the Admiral.

On April 20th, the real crossing began. It was by no means fortunate. This time Colón followed the 22nd parallel, for in those days, as Las Casas explains, it was not yet known that the zone of favourable winds lies further north, on the 30th degree or higher up. Storms and contrary winds delayed their sailing, and as there were many persons on board they suffered from hunger, a kind of torment but too well known to many of them. They passed in sight of one of the Azores, but were not able to come to it. After fifty-two days at sea, the two first American ships to arrive in Europe cast anchor in Cádiz, on June 11th, 1496.

CHAPTER XXIV

THE ADMIRAL WINS AGAIN

COLON'S arrival in Cádiz must have aroused mixed feelings, including surprise and disappointment. Many, no doubt, had publicly feared and privately hoped that he had died. On April 9th the King and Queen wrote to Fonseca words which suggest that they, at any rate, had thought that their Admiral might be dead. "And because we fear that God may have disposed in some way of the Admiral of the Indies while on his way, since we have not heard from him for so long, we have decided to send thither Commander Diego Carrillo and another person of rank in charge, so that in the Admiral's absence, he may see to all the business over there, and even in his presence, he may put a remedy to all that might need it according to the information which we had from those who came thence." (1)

This letter, emanating as it did from the two persons who remained throughout his most thoughtful, considerate and loyal friends—the King and Queen—suggests the extent of the damage done to his prestige and reputation by his own doings as well as by his critics' reports.

Colón found in Cádiz Bay two caravels and a ship ready to leave with a load of food and livestock, and letters and dispatches for him. He sent the expedition off four days later with fresh instructions for his brother, and, after a brief respite, left for Seville. His train must have been less simple, and a good deal more puzzling to the crowds of the townships he crossed, than the triumphant procession of his first homecoming. There were the popinjays, and there were the Indians; there were the works of exotic art and craft, and there was the gold; there was in particular a gold necklace weighing six hundred castillians (i.e. 261,000 maravedis) which the wary Admiral made Caonabó's brother put on whenever he entered a town or village. (2) But at the head of all these exotic splendours, no longer a proud and magnificent Admiral, all silks and bright array, but a humble man with an unkempt beard, a drawn face, swollen eyes, white hair, "dressed in robes the colour of the frock of St. Francis

293

of the observance, and in cut very much the same, and a cord of St. Francis for devotion." (3)

This was the sight which struck the curious eye of the chronicler who noted it down—the curate of Palacios, Bernáldez, who on this occasion had Colón as his guest, together with Fonseca and "Don Diego," i.e. Caonabó's brother in Spanish Christian garb. During that stay in the good curate's house, Colón can hardly have improved his credit with Fonseca, the powerful ecclesiastic who was the chief administrator of Indian affairs in Spain. Bernáldez's *History* bears obvious traces of discussions between himself and the Admiral, which Fonseca must have heard with a silence full of contempt for the imaginative cosmographer who had discovered America by mistake. Colón explained once again how he had by now "ascertained" that Cuba (which he called Juana) was the mainland, and how, sailing that way, he hoped to find "the province and city of Cathay, which is in the dominions of the Grand Khan, [. . .] which is the richest province of the world and the most abundant in gold and silver and in all metals and silks; but they are all idolatrous and most shrewd people and necromancers and learned in all arts and knightly and thereof many marvels are written, as told by the noble English gentleman, John of Mandeville." To which Bernáldez, having no doubt first asked leave of the Bishop— for though he was the host, he was but a poor curate, albeit a good Christian and of sound judgment—argued that "much distance of time would be required to find that [Cathay], for the Grand Khan had been in the past Lord of the Tartars, and from Great Tartary, which is on the edge of Buxia and Bahia (and we may say that Great Tartary begins in Hungary, which are lands which lie when one looks from this Andalucía [in the direction] where the sun rises in the longest days of the year, in which direction merchants were wont to travel to those lands), but in the direction in which the Admiral looks for Cathay, it is my belief that with another twelve hundred leagues round the firmament of earth and sea, he will not get there." (4)

Don Juan de Fonseca was sure to share the sensible if ungrammatically expressed opinions of the chronicler-priest; but Don Cristóbal de Cipango was equally sure to look upon them as due either to ignorance or to malevolence, for not in vain had he sailed along three hundred and thirty-three leagues of "Juana" and made his crews and pilots swear that it was the mainland, just next door to Cathay.

No one knew better than he did how many winds there are

in the compass; and while he was thus full of south-west the King was looking north-east and the Queen north-west. Ferdinand was watching the King of France, who, out of spite for the help the Spanish Ferdinand had given his cousin, the Neapolitan Ferdinand, threatened Perpignan (then Spanish) from Narbonne. Most of that summer and autumn (1496) was spent in alarums and skirmishes and even in battles over the Roussillon. As for the Queen, she was busy with the naval arrangements in connection with the marriage of two of her children: the Infanta Juana, betrothed to Philip the Handsome of Burgundy, son of Emperor Maximilian; and Prince Juan, the heir to all the Spains—but Portugal—who was to wed Margaret, Philip's sister. A fleet of one hundred and thirty vessels, with an army of twenty-five thousand men, was to escort the Infanta to Flanders and to bring Princess Margaret to Spain. No lesser escort was needed in view of the war with France. The Admiral of Castille, who commanded it, could indeed look down upon the Admiral of the Indies who had landed in Cádiz, in Franciscan garb, at the head of two caravels; but though he had more ships, what were his dreams compared with those which the very Magnificent Lord of Cipango hid under his cowl?

The dispatch of such a fleet can have been no easy task for so painstaking and thorough a leader as Queen Isabel. And then, she was losing yet another daughter—this Juana in whom her eye, trained by dire experience, was probably beginning to detect the first signs of that mental instability which she had known in her own mother. The fleet left towards the end of September, and in October the Queen was back in Burgos, where she was able to turn her mind to the New World.

Colón was there, in his Franciscan robes, with his silvery beard and his sunken, reproachful eyes. He knew he would be gracefully received, for the King and Queen had put him at ease by sending him a letter of cordial welcome in the midst of their most agitated month of July. (5) But he knew that his critics were strong, and that some of them—Margarite and Buil in particular—had the ear of the King and Queen; he knew that the continual arrival in Castille of downcast, sick-looking ex-settlers was undermining the confidence of high and low in the soundness of his enterprise, and that, as Oviedo puts it, "some of those Spaniards who came in search of gold went back the colour of gold but without its shine"; (6) he knew that he had been accused by Father Buil of using his control of supplies, particularly of food, to exact complete obedience from all settlers high and low, for the King and Queen had ordered him somewhat curtly to distribute supplies to everyone, not excepting guilty parties, save if they had deserved death "which is as good as withholding food"; (7) he knew that the five hundred Indians had given much trouble to the King and Queen. This was a point on which he was by now informed by Fonseca. According to the Admiral's report, these Indians had been taken in battle and, in the light of the ethics of the times, they were fair prey for slavery. After the fall of Málaga—the one case in which the King and Queen had met with stubborn resistance and a rejection of all offers of good treatment on surrender—slaves were freely taken from the Moorish population. Pope Innocent VIII received one hundred Moors "well harnessed" and Queen Isabel sent thirty maids, "the most beautiful that could be found," to her cousin, the Queen of Naples, and thirty to the Queen of Portugal. Presents of slaves were given to a number of grandees and Court dignitaries, the list being headed by the Cardinal of Spain who received one hundred and twenty. (8)

This is the background which explains the first royal decision taken regarding Colón's five hundred Indians. In accordance with custom, Fonseca was instructed to have them sold. The royal order bears the date of April 12th, 1495. (9) But, possibly on the advice of Talavera or of Buil, a more cautious note is observed on the 16th, just four days later: "For we want to inform ourselves from learned men, theologians and canonists, whether with a good conscience these [Indians] can be sold by you or not, and this cannot be done until we see the letters which the Admiral must have written to know the cause why he sends them as captive." . . . (10) Fonseca is asked to receive no money in exchange for them until the matter has been investigated.

The Admiral knew only too well that his score was heavy. On his credit side, however, were: his success in the face of so much scepticism and opposition; the constancy of the royal favour; his own persuasive grace and fire; and also the fact that the King and Queen were seasoned statesmen and probably realised the difficulties of Colón's task better than most of their subjects seem to have done. He cannot have made a very good defence. His line of argument is to be gathered from his own summary of it at the head of his report on his third voyage. First, his usual recapitulation of the days of his struggle to be heard—surely a shrewd procedure, since it reminded the Queen how often he had been thought to be wrong by the Crown's best advisers, and how right events had proved him to be. This done, he went straight ahead to his favourite error: he had "discovered three hundred and thirty-three leagues of mainland, which was the end of the Orient" (his own fond delusions on Cuba, which he had explored); he had discovered seven hundred islands, which may be strictly true; it all depends on the minimum size of a rock one agrees to call an *island*; and he had pacified and conquered the island Española, with a sea-coast longer than that of Spain, which was inhabited by numberless people, all of whom paid tribute to the King and Queen. The Admiral was here combining the pleasure of imagination with the business of advocacy, for the numbers of Indians who were actually made to pay tribute amounted to very few and the tribute was not to be imposed for very long. But he felt himself threatened and could not afford to be mathematically correct, even if he had been able to, which he was not.

His self-assurance must have produced some effect; enough for him to feel that the moment had come to take account of his critics. Murmurs and contempt for the enterprise, he went on to say, were born of the fact that shiploads of gold had not begun to come from the outset, as if it were an easy thing, in a roadless country, with his men laid up and without the necessary basis for safety against attack from possibly treacherous Indians; as befits a Franciscan, albeit an honorary one, he then took this criticism as part payment for his sins and as part works for his salvation; then, as proof of his good faith, he showed his grains of gold, some like chickpeas, others as big as walnuts, and bigger, not forgetting the famous six-hundred-castillian chain; and he assured the King and Queen that there were excellent veins of gold and of copper in Española, as well as spices of all kinds.

But avaunt all this miserable accountancy and profit-taking! Are Your Highnesses tradesmen or the most glorious Princes in Christendom? Did not Solomon send ships from Jerusalem to the end of the Orient just to see Mount Sopora, which Your Highnesses now have in Española? (How superb he can be in his mastery of fanciful history and geography, this magnificent Don Cristóbal de Cipango!) Did not Alexander send messengers to see the way of living of the Island Taprobane; and Nero Caesar, did he not send persons to see the sources of the Nile? And when had Princes of Castille won lands outside their own till the Admiral of the Indies showed them the way? See next door the Kings of Portugal, how stoutly they have held to the discovery of Guiné and how they have spent gold and people there, nearly half their kingdom killed in it, and yet they persevered, though it has not given them any income till quite lately; and they dared also conquer Ceuta and Tangiers and Arcila and Alcazar in Africa, and constantly wage war on the Moors and all with great expense, just to behave like Princes and to serve God and increase their dominions. All those who attack this enterprise, do they bear in mind how much praise it has won in all Christendom for Your Highnesses, and how everyone, big and small, wants to receive a letter about it?

The King and Queen listened, won over by his ardour and eloquence, and as it often happened when they heard him, laughed heartily and good-humouredly to calm his excitement. (11) But they would, all the same, reflect on what he had said. The fact is that he had completely shifted his ground. He was no longer stressing the Eldorado which he was to put at their feet, gold-roofed Cipangos and marble-bridged Quinsays; he was, on the contrary, suggesting to them that they should spend gold and men in conquering lands for Castille, in emulation of the Kings of Portugal, for their own honour and glory and in the service of God. The King and Queen had every right—and duty—to think of their exchequer; this glory and service of God was all very well, but they had to supply salaries for five hundred persons in Española and they were not quite sure of the utility of it. During the previous year, they had tried to regulate the flow of people who might wish to go and "discover," or to settle in Española, without having to rely on a royal salary; settlers were assured their keep for a year, the full property of the houses built and of the lands tilled by them and one-third of the gold found by them; trade with Española was also opened under reasonable conditions; and "discovery" was allowed. An ingenious way was found for respecting Colón's rights of an eighth—the Admiral was expressly reserved the right to send one ship for every seven which should go to the Indies under this ordinance. (12)

The fact is that life in its tumultuous way was bringing to their attention a host of complex problems, personal, political, moral, all higgledy-piggledy, and all, as is the way with life, claiming imperious and urgent attention. There was first of all Colón's own character; his overbearing way; his failure to conquer the hearts of his men, and that kink in his manner which had made him break with Pinzón, with Fonseca, with Buil, with Margarite, with Aguado; that secret resentment which gave to his pride a diabolic stiffness and persistence and which made him in fact useless as an organiser of the discovered world; but, beneath this personal factor, there was a real situation which was living—in fact, being born—under their eyes and which was so *new* that they could not possibly see it in all its significance. Suddenly, when their realms were just beginning to take shape out of the anarchy of the previous reign, before they had had time to set up a civil service, which was not really organised until the reign of Philip II, a whole Empire swam into their ken. And so this able, well-meaning and straightforward couple was confronted with all the problems with which colonial life still baffles and tests modern nations. Discovery, sovereignty, safety, colonisation, matters of principle, of practice, religion, anthropology, navigation, cosmographical study, economic adjustment, choice of staff, all in a torrent of business, all mixed up and made acid and bitter by personal quarrels, and sublimated into biblical, cosmographical phantasmagorias by the wild imagination of their Grand Admiral.

Through the emotional clouds which he emitted, like a Jehovah amidst lightning strokes of indignant anger, the King and Queen began perhaps to perceive the real cause of the whole trouble: suddenly, a European nation, with the typical aggressive impulse of the white race, had invaded a virgin continent inhabited by a stay-at-home race; the two civilisations were clashing—not only in armed fights, mere symptoms of the situation, but in the whole range of their activities.

Colón was obsessed with the need of ensuring immediate results in wealth, preferably in gold. In this, he misinterpreted the true character of the King and Queen; there is ample evidence to show that, thankful as they were for the gold that came over and careful—as they surely had the right and the duty to be—to ensure that it was properly accounted for, (13) Ferdinand and Isabel never put any special stress on the material results of the discovery, and that most of the pleasure and gratification they manifested at its success came from the mere territorial acquisitions which it brought to their crown. But Colón, who was himself obsessed with gold, was convinced that gold was the only thing that would please the King and Queen and that would justify the discovery in their eyes.

**

Seen at a distance of over four centuries rich in colonial experience, the situation should have been understood with more insight and sympathy than it has received from historians and critics. There was a whole gamut of attitudes towards the issues raised by the discovery of this immense *res nullius* netted from the ocean by that fisher of islands who was Colón. First of all in spiritual rank was Las Casas. He stood uncompromisingly for the true Christian attitude: the Indies belonged to the Indians; it was their home as determined by God and all that was found in it, mineral, vegetable and animal, was their property. The Spaniards had no title whatever to be there, except the Gospel. For Las Casas, as for every European in those days, the Christian religion was truth and all the rest was error. But unlike most other Europeans, Las Casas *meant this truth to live*. His dilemma was inescapable: either the Christians behaved in the Indies like Christians or they had no business to be there at all. In many passages of his *History* he defines the policy which the Spaniards should have followed in the Indies as one of patience, service and evangelisation, for the ultimate benefit of the Indians themselves. "There is no legitimate reason for Spaniards to enter these realms and lands other than to spread news and knowledge of the one and true God and of Jesus Christ" (14)—he says boldly.

Whether such a policy would have succeeded or not depends on what is meant by success. It may be safely said that it would not have succeeded in the usual sense attached to this word in political life, for reasons which are to be seen hereafter. But those who criticise the Spanish Empire on the authority of Las Casas should bear in mind that the good bishop would have condemned in at least equally forcible terms every single colonial enterprise known to later history. His challenge is still unanswered by all collective life, whether colonial or metropolitan. It amounts to this: does the law of Christ work? No one knows, for though individuals have tried it, no *society* has.

The next in rank is the position of the King and Queen. For them, conquest was a title of sovereignty when the spoliated sovereign was not a Christian. This was as good as gospel truth in those days for all Christendom. (In later times, ethics have degenerated, since Christian princes spoliate other Christian princes without qualms of any kind.) (15) In the circumstances, Ferdinand and Isabel considered the Indians as their subjects *ipso facto*. They would not have taken the view which Las Casas was to take later: (16)—that the propagation of the Gospel was the *only* ground on which a Christian conscience could countenance the intrusion of Spaniards into the Indies. Yet, though princes entitled to sovereignty by conquest over pagans, Ferdinand and Isabel were fully conscious of their responsibility as Christian princes, and they explicitly accepted as their first duty towards their new subjects the enlightenment of the Indians and their conversion to the law of Christ. No fair-minded person having had direct access to the royal documents can entertain any doubts whatever on the earnest and well-meaning eagerness with which the King and Queen attended to the discharge of this duty.

But, of course, the Indies belonged to them and not to the Indians! They were anxious to see the natives well treated; to guard them against any spoliation or hardship; and to see that their liberty and their property were respected; but, just as Castille and Aragon, though split into thousands of land-owners, belonged to the King and Queen, so the Indies, though the Indians were not to be deprived of their personal property, belonged to the King and Queen. This was not even a claim on their part; it was an assumption which they had not stopped to analyse, owing to its sheer evidence.

What were they to do with their new territories? Obviously, to organise them first and then to develop them. So, they devise the best means for their government and defence, and they constantly urge Colón to let them have the best possible information of the kind we would nowadays call *scientific*—geographical situation, climate, flora and fauna, minerals, fisheries, land produce.

It is at this point that gold comes in. A sense of proportion is the virtue which strikes the reader most in the royal instructions and letters on the Indies. Gold is not for the King and Queen that ever-fascinating lure which we saw it was for Colón ever since his early days in Portugal, nor the tempting fiend which it became for many of the early Spanish settlers; it was just one metal more, one of the many products of the Indies, particularly welcome for their ever-needy exchequer, but by no means to be singled out of the general economy of their newly acquired realms. That is why the King and Queen were always ready—from the outset—to consider schemes for colonising the Indies with their Spanish subjects. They were not obsessed by Cipango and Cathay. It is not certain that they had read Marco Polo and it is doubtful whether they had ever heard of Sir John Mandeville. They were straightforward Spanish princes who were apt to think of new realms in terms of horses and cows, of wheat and oranges and silk, rather than to dream of them as Eldorados.

And then, there was Colón. Las Casas was an idealist; the King and Queen were realists; Colón was an unrealist. He had built for himself a vision of golden splendour and he felt it a moral obligation towards his own pride to make it materialise before the King and Queen. This was the tension which made him hasty in performance, impatient before obstacles, short and intolerant with men. He had been laughed at when he had vouched that he would sail to Cipango and Cathay, and he had confounded the scoffers and turned laughter into admiration; now he was to gain a similar triumph over those who had laughed about his promises of gold. This haste, this urge of personal vindication, was an irrelevant factor which strained his colonial policy and contributed largely to his downfall. But there were other factors for which he was by no means responsible. Are we to condemn him for his inability to handle the Indians with the technique of a contemporary anthropologist? He approached his tasks on the whole with honourable intentions and with an amount of freedom from prejudice, of intellectual detachment and of power of observation altogether unusual in his day and possibly also in ours. His limitations were for the most part due to his time and to the novelty and difficulty of his task. He tried at first the friendly way; but this way failed owing to his unwise decision to leave behind forty men in precarious conditions and, it would seem, of at least doubtful qualifications for a task so delicate as that of building the first psychological bridge between the old and the new world. When he returned on his second voyage and found Navidad destroyed and the forty men massacred, he realised that he would not be able to get the gold by friendly means; he then struck hard and subjugated the natives. But at this point, his real trouble began. *The natives would not work.* For the first time, the European came up against this conflict: he, born and bred in the belief that work is holy, used to seeing in man's wants the source of work, and in work the source of wealth, and in wealth the sign of civilisation, the civilised and hard-working European found that the native of warm lands has another answer for the problem of life—little or no work, few or no wants, and let the sun do the rest. What was Colón to do?

All administrators of African colonies know the answer: to lay a tax on the native. That is exactly what he did. But the tax yielded little, despite his assurances to the contrary to the King and Queen; and it was most difficult to collect it from a race of swift and slippery Indians who did not know the use of shirts. It was necessary to devise something else. Colón had no doubts whatever as to what the best solution was: slavery. It was a twofold solution; by exporting slaves one exported gold. "Gold is what yields gold," Pero Alonso Niño was to say later; by reducing the Indians to slavery the problem of their refusal to work was solved. True, this solution of *Colón* was difficult to reconcile with the mission entrusted by the Lord to *Christopher*; but Christopher Colón was a master in the art of reconciling irreconcilables. Most unrealists are. The King and Queen were realists and their conscience would have none of it. Colón then tried to turn the obstacle by beating the Indians in war. But this again was unsuccessful and Colón had to fall back on other schemes. The first of them was quite straightforward. Since the Indian would not work, Spaniards would be taken over and settled on the land. He asked for five hundred persons to be taken over on salaries, and the King and Queen cut the figure down to three hundred and thirty. (17) These settlers were to be forty squires, to be paid thirty maravedis a day plus twelve for their upkeep; thirty seamen, with equal emoluments; twenty shipboys at twenty maravedis a day and twelve for upkeep; twenty gold-washers paid like the squires; one hundred peons paid like the shipboys; twenty skilled workers of several trades, paid like the squires; fifty farm-workers and ten kitchen-gardeners, paid six thousand maravedis a year plus twelve a day for upkeep, and finally thirty women who were given no salary though they were to receive twelve maravedis for their upkeep. This contingent would form the nucleus of a colony of a frankly European character. The persons already residing in Española were to continue drawing their salaries as heretofore; the landworkers were to receive wheat for sowing and beasts—cows or mares—for tilling; and the gold in the island was to be turned into coin. The Indians were to pay the tax laid on them by the Viceroy and to wear a brass disc in sign of payment, and defaulters were to be punished "with some light penalty," put in, no doubt, by the hand of the Queen.

The Admiral had other ideas up his sleeve—a Franciscan sleeve is a roomy place—but he seems to have taken one thing at a time. The negotiation of this arrangement cannot have been very easy with so many critics, and even downright enemies, about. Moreover, the King and Queen were at the time deeply concerned with the fate of the fleet which was to bring their future daughter-in-law, Margaret of Austria, to Spain. The weather was persistently bad and the fleet did not arrive. The King and Queen had been waiting in Burgos where Colón was at the time negotiating his "colonial" agreement; one day he was told that the King and Queen had decided to go to Soria, giving up for the time being the hope of seeing the fleet arrive soon. The Court had left Burgos on a Saturday, the King and Queen having waited to leave on Monday. That night, Colón sent them a note saying that on a certain day the wind had begun to blow in the right direction; the fleet would wait for a day to be sure the good wind was steady; they would sail on Wednesday, and on Thursday or Friday they would be as far as the Isle of Wight (*Huict*, he calls it) and "if they do not call at Wight, they should be in Laredo [in Northern Spain] on Monday, or seamanship has lost its sense." The King and Queen listened to the old sailor, and on that Monday one of the ships which had not called at the Isle of Wight for lack of supplies, turned up at Laredo.

That Monday morning—or whenever the news was known at Court—brother Christopher, the Franciscan, must have needed his whole cowl to hide his pride. His stock went up by all the ease which the welcome news caused in the royal minds.

The Queen was most grateful: "I saw your letter and opinion on the voyage of the Archduchess, my very dear and beloved daughter"—she wrote to him on August 18th, 1496—"and it is very good and as of a learned man who has much experience of the matters of the sea. I am grateful to you and hold it a special obligation and service, both for your timeliness in sending it (as your warning and advice was most useful to us), as for having tendered it with the true goodwill and affection which have always been known in you; and so believe that all is received as coming from a special and faithful servant of mine." (18)

On March 19th, 1497, Prince Juan and Princess Margaret were married amidst festivities of the utmost splendour. They were both young and beautiful. The old Empire of Charlemagne was allied to the new Empire which Ferdinand and Isabel had partly built with their energy, partly acquired by the will of God. While the young couple enjoyed their brief and tragically terminated honeymoon, Colón worked hard at Court. On April 23rd, the Admiral pockets a number of valuable decisions duly signed by the two royal hands: the first checks the tendency in Spanish purveyors to share in the Indian Eldorado by increasing the price of goods delivered to its magnificent discoverer; the second grants the Admiral authority to recruit the three hundred and thirty persons whom he solicited; the third raises this number to five hundred, if the Admiral should deem it necessary; the fourth orders the Treasurer of the Indian Treasury to pay salaries and emoluments on the authority of documents bearing the signature of the Viceroy or of his representative; the fifth exempts from certain dues all goods to and from the Indies exported or imported by order of the King and Queen or of Don Cristóbal Colón; and finally, the whole system of arrangements as outlined above reappears signed by the royal hands in the form of instructions to the Admiral. At the head of these instructions, the King and Queen dictated the best and wisest of them and the most sinned against by all, including the Admiral: "First of all, that as soon as you arrive in the said islands, God willing, you shall endeavour with all diligence to encourage and draw the natives of the said Indies to peace and quiet, and to serve Us and be in our subjection willingly, and above all to have them converted to our Holy Catholic Faith." (19)

Having carried this first trench Colón, who was a master of Court strategy, pursued his advantage without respite. On the same date, April 23rd, all his titles and privileges as defined in the Capitulations of Santa Fé are explicitly confirmed by the King and Queen as an act of their "own absolute royal power"; on the same date also, he obtains a royal warrant to found an entail estate or *Mayorazgo*; on May 6th, the exemptions decreed on April 23rd are widely extended to include all kinds of goods and all kinds of taxes; on May 9th, the Chief Accountants are instructed to pay the Admiral any sums which he may have advanced on salaries to Spaniards in the Indies; on the 30th, he extorts one of those provisions which were sure to raise a bitter enmity against him in Court circles: on all transactions about expenses and profits arising out of the Indies, he is to have a representative as well as the King and Queen, yet another sign of that stiffnecked sense of equality with the crown which made him couch his agreement with Ferdinand and Isabel in the form of the Capitulations of Santa Fé; on June 2nd, he goes still further: having gained first a simple confirmation of all his privileges, he now brandishes the royal order of April 10th, 1495, in which the King and Queen, while opening wide access to the Indies, reserved Colón's rights by providing that he was to send one ship in eight, if he so wished; but the calculating Admiral does not agree at all: he argues—to be sure within his legal rights—that the Royal Order of April 10th, 1495, runs counter to his privileges and he obtains another order by which that of 1495 will be considered as null and void in so far as it goes against the Admiral's rights; on the same date, he obtains a favour in his long and stubborn dispute with the Crown over the interpretation of the Capitulations with regard to his profits: he argued that of all that came from the Indies, he was to receive one-eighth; from the remainder, costs would be deducted; and of the net result, a tenth was to be his; the Crown argued— more logically it would seem—that costs were to be deducted first; then Colón would have his tenth; and of the remainder, the eighth. The King and Queen, whose patience and generosity towards him seem to have been inexhaustible, struck a com- promise: he would pay nothing towards expenses and costs (he was supposed to pay one-eighth), save what he had spent in the first voyage; i.e. he would pay nothing for all that had been spent since then in voyages and administration; he would claim nothing beyond what he had had; and for the future, the first three years would be settled his way and the rest the Crown's way.

Yet, though he kept a close watch on his privileges and interests, he knew how to resist a dangerous temptation: the King and Queen offered him a tract of land fifty leagues from East to West and twenty-five from North to South in Española, with the title of Duke or Marquess, and he begged to be allowed to decline for fear of getting into trouble with the royal officials. This self-denial eased the way for a favour which he coveted—that a detailed study should be made of the privileges of the Admiral of Castille, in order to have them extended to him as Admiral of the Indies. The King and Queen had this done by Francisco de Soria, according to a Royal Order signed by them on April 23rd, 1497. (20)   A clear sign of his favour at Court was the appointment of his two sons as pages to the Queen, signed by Queen Isabel on the 18th and 19th of February, 1498, with a pension of 9700 maravedis for each. The Admiral saw to it that even after the death of Prince Juan his two sons were brought up at Court. He had perhaps already heard the proverb quoted by Oviedo: *He who has not been a page at Court always smells like a muleteer.*

On June 22nd, three royal charters reveal that his deeper thought had carried the day. Española was to be colonised by convicts. Time in Española was to count twice in serving the sentence of exile; ten years there to count as exile for life. Moreover, persons who had committed crimes would be reprieved if they consented to settle in Española. Heresy, lèse majesté, treason, sodomy and counterfeiting of coinage were excepted from the measure. On the same date, the Viceroy was given authority to grant and distribute land to persons who would bind themselves to at least four years' continuous residence and work on it. (21) Lest the stern moralist take too stiff a view of the provision which sent so many jailbirds to Española, oblivious of the fact that criminals are often the product of their environment, here is the matter-of-fact comment of Bishop Las Casas, who was at any rate an eyewitness of this experiment in colonisation: "I met several of these in this island, and even one who was earless [by the sword of the law], and I always knew him to be a very upright man." (22)

Colón had conquered all his critics and enemies. The King and Queen adopted his plan; they confirmed his privileges; they granted him new favours. As if further to settle the only points which remained on their Viceroy's score, by a kind of Bill of Indemnity, they granted Don Bartolomé the title of Adelantado of the Indies which the Admiral had made bold to give his brother of his own accord, by a patent abuse of his viceregal powers. (23) This royal grace implied a rebuke to the Viceroy, since the previous appointment was not even mentioned, and the King and Queen stood alone as the sole source and origin of the title; but even here, they found the most generous way of putting their indiscreet Admiral in his place and, though they made him yield to them in form, they yielded to him in substance.

Much elated with his success, Colón began to prepare for his third voyage. We may see a further mark of royal favour in the decision to replace Fonseca by Antonio de Torres at the head of Indian affairs. But, as it turned out, this decision worked against Colón, because Antonio de Torres was so exacting on the privileges and rights he was to be granted that the King and Queen went back to Fonseca and all papers had to be redrafted with much delay. (24) The King and Queen had ordered that six million maravedis should be paid over to the Admiral for the expenses consequent upon their agreement with him; but the Crown of Castille was always short of money, and that year, rich in royal weddings, had been a disastrous one for the royal exchequer, already heavily taxed by the French war. In September the Queen left for Alcántara with her elder daughter,

Isabel, widow of Prince John of Portugal, whom she had married in 1490, and lost in 1492. The princess was to try again to establish that link towards the union of all the Spains, which had been the steady, stubborn endeavour of the two royal houses which Fate successfully defeated. Queen Isabel delivered her daughter to her new fiancé, young King Manoel. She was anxious for the health of her son Prince Juan of Castille, sick of love, of too much sweet love: doctors had advised a temporary separation of the two youngsters; theologians had shaken their heads; the Queen had sided with theology against medicine, thinking that man should not separate what God had united. She was anxious, though. The King, whom she had left by the Prince's bedside, turned up at Alcántara, very self-controlled and affable. Queen Isabel asked how the Prince was. Ferdinand had not the courage to tell her that he was no longer. What was the gold of all the Cipangos of the world before this boy prince of nineteen whom his wife of eighteen had killed with love? A year later Isabel, Queen of Portugal, died giving birth to a boy, blissfully ignorant of the fact that he was solemnly called Don Miguel, and that for one year and seven months he incarnated the hopes of Iberian union. Then death took him also. "The first knife of grief"—writes Bernáldez with unusual power and emotion—"which pierced through the soul of Queen Doña Isabel, was the death of the Prince; the second, the death of her first-born daughter, Doña Isabel, Queen of Portugal; the third knife of grief was the death of Don Miguel, her grandson, and from these days the great and virtuous Queen Doña Isabel, so necessary to Castille, lived without pleasure, and her health and life were shortened." (25) So much for the great Queen. As for the great country she had built up, it was condemned by historic fate to an irrelevant empire in America, instead of a natural expansion in Africa; and to an irrelevant and ruinous union with Flanders instead of a natural union with Portugal.

CHAPTER XXV

LOVE AND DEATH IN CIPANGO

ONE day, in Isabela, an Aragonese youth named Miguel Díaz, being short of arguments during a quarrel with another Spaniard, drew his knife and wounded him. The wounds did not prove fatal, but Miguel Díaz, though a member of the Adelantado's household, thought it better "not to wait," as Oviedo puts it; and he was followed in his self-imposed exile by a few accomplices and friends. They kept to the coast and, having turned the easternmost point of Española, went forth, westward, until they came upon an Indian settlement, on the mouth of a most pleasant river.

On the banks of this river, Miguel Díaz spent delightful hours in the affectionate company of an Indian lady of quality—a *cacica*, says Oviedo—who eventually was baptised as Catalina and gave him two sons. But that was of course in due time. Meanwhile, the future Catalina, a living example of that wise French saying that *friendship confides its secrets but love lets them escape*, let her Aragonese lover know of the mines which lay seven leagues from the spot; we need not follow Oviedo to the point of attributing to her the desire and request to have the Spaniards migrate over from Isabela and settle in her lands. The lure of those mines was enough. "Thereupon this man, to please the *cacica*, and still more so because it seemed to him that if he brought news of a land so healthy and abundant the Adelantado, who was in a barren and sick country, would forgive him, and mainly because God wished it to be so [. . .]," crossed over to Isabela and, after careful soundings through friends, reported to Don Bartolomé, who received him well, forgave him and decided to go and see for himself. (1)

* *

It so happened that Don Bartolomé had received from his brother instructions which tallied admirably with the news Miguel Díaz had brought him. The ships which Colón had found in Cádiz ready to sail for Española arrived in Isabela at the beginning of July (1496). The Admiral, with the approval of the King and Queen, which he received in Cádiz, wrote to his brother, Don Bartolomé, to build a town on the south coast, closer than Isabela to the mines of San Cristóbal, which had by then been discovered. This pleased the Adelantado very much, for he was not a man to sit tight—and hungry—in Isabela when there was so much island still unexplored and so many Indians unsubdued. But, before starting on his expedition, Don Bartolomé dispatched the three ships back to Spain with three hundred Indians reduced to slavery. (2)

The Colóns were determined to push ahead with the slave trade, taking for the time being as a pretext the rebellious attitude and actions of the Indians, which, they knew, was a strong enough reason to appease the royal qualms. This business done, Don Bartolomé, leaving Don Diego in command at Isabela, left with the able-bodied men for the mines of San Cristóbal and the river where Miguel had known Indian love. It was a "very graceful river" indeed, then thickly populated on both banks. Having taken careful soundings of the harbour and found it excellent—so it was for the needs of the day—Don Bartolomé decided to found a city there. It was to be the oldest European-founded city in the American continent. He called it Santo Domingo. (3) The Admiral wished it to be called *Isabela-Nueva*, but in this, as in many other things of more import, the younger brother had his way. He was an executive man, more capable of ruthlessness than the Viceroy, with nearly as much fire, less air, far less water and more earth in his composition. He was quick in drawing the lineaments of the town, and he sent instructions to Don Diego to send everybody over except the sick, and the shipwrights who were building two caravels. Isabela was eventually deserted. (4) In Santo Domingo Don Bartolomé left twenty men cutting wood and beginning the construction of the fort, the first cell of the body of the future town, and this done, he set out with his able-bodied men for the "kingdom" of Xaraguá, of whose "King," Behechio, and particularly of the King's sister Anacaona, he had heard marvels.

This Anacaona was the widow of King Caonabó. She does not seem to have borne any grudge against the Spaniards for the loss of her husband, rather the reverse: "she was a very remarkable woman, very prudent, very gracious and courtly in her speech, ways and motions, and most friendly to the Christians." On his way to her, Don Bartolomé and his small battalion, after a march of about one hundred and twenty miles, came upon an "infinite army of Indians with their bows and arrows, ready for war, though stark naked, and please note what kind of a war they could wage with their bare bellies as shields." (5) Don Bartolomé sent a flag of truce to explain to Behechio that he came as a friend; and soon there was great rejoicing and merry-making on both sides. "There came numberless people and many lords and nobility [. . .] singing their songs and dancing their dances which they call *areitos*, a most merry and pleasant thing to see: there came out first thirty women, King Behechio's own, all stark naked, only their shames covered with cotton half-skirts, white and most elaborately decorated in the weaving, which they call *naguas* and which covered them from the waist to half-way down the leg; they carried green branches in their hands: they sang and danced and jumped moderately, as befits women, showing the greatest pleasure, rejoicing, festivity and mirth. They all came close to Don Bartolomé Colón, and kneeling down, with great reverence, offered him the green branches and palms which they carried in their hands; while all the rest, innumerable people, danced and rejoiced." In this guise Don Bartolomé was taken to the "Royal House" and given a banquet.

This was indeed the land of Arcady. The Adelantado might have taken a leaf out of the bishop's book, and reflected that this people could be carried along very far in the direction of friendliness, too far indeed, in some ways which may be guessed, when young, aggressive, wifeless Spaniards were treated to so generous an exhibition of feminine charms. Moreover, as if to correct the impression of effeteness which this first festival might have left on the Spaniards, the next day Behechio and his men offered the Pale-faces a native tournament in which two battalions fought with bows and arrows against each other with such eagerness that in a short while there were four dead and seven wounded on the field—"all in the midst of the greatest rejoicing, pleasure and mirth of the world, and paying no more attention to the dead and wounded than to a snap of the fingers in their faces." At Don Bartolomé's request, Behechio stopped the game, to spare men's lives. (6)

What kind of men were these? How could they combine so much nakedness with so much art, so much friendliness with such contempt for death? Don Bartolomé and his men were not men of our century. We would have understood the possibility of leaving them alone in the enjoyment of their naked life in their lavish island; asking at most a naval station and reserving the exclusive film rights for those suggestive dances. Don Bartolomé and his men belonged to a less balanced and more dogmatic age. It was necessary to have those people dressed and converted. It was also necessary to make them work. He lost no time in asking for a tribute. Behechio argued that he had no gold in his domains. Don Bartolomé was ready to accept payment in cotton. Thereupon Behechio agreed to have it sown in his "kingdom," not as a necessity for his subjects, for whom cotton skirts were not a garment but an ornament for dancing days, but to please the Paleface chief—possibly to get rid of him pending further decisions.

* *

When Don Bartolomé arrived back in Santo Domingo, his satisfaction at all these successes which he had achieved in Xaraguá was damped on finding the colony in mourning: during his absence no less than three hundred Christians had died of various complaints: not only, as Oviedo says, "because the food and bread of Spain is of a tougher digestion " and because the air of Spain was "thinner," and colder, but because the amorous Spaniards contracted a terrible disease in the arms of the Indian women: they called it *buas* or *bubas*, we call it syphilis. And it seems as if the sinister microbe had found a new virulence on discovering what, for it, was the new continent of the white race. (7) The Adelantado decided to disperse his men in the several settlements and forts, mainly to remedy the food shortage, "so that they should fight with their illness only and not with hunger as well." The measure does not seem to have been to the taste of the natives, who, led by a valiant *cacique*, known as Guarionex, engineered a general massacre of Spaniards. The garrison of Concepción was warned of the danger by friendly natives; they promptly sent a message to Don Bartolomé; the first stage of the courier was Bonao. The friendly Indian who was conveying the message knew that all the passes were watched by Guarionex's spies. He had hidden the letters inside a hollow stick. The Indians, who knew by then that "the letters of the Christians speak," were sure to keep them if they found them. The Indian courier met this difficulty with a shrewd stratagem; he feigned to be dumb and lame, and he passed all spies without any explanation more revealing than dumb-shows, leaning heavily on the stick which carried the message.

Through the loyalty of this man to the Spaniards and, conversely, his disloyalty to the Indians, for all coins have head and tail, Don Bartolomé was appraised of the situation. At once he was on the way, followed by his little band of still able-bodied men, and after a night of rest in Bonao he marched on to Concepción and in a surprise night attack fell on the Indians of Guarionex (fifteen thousand of them, says Las Casas) and defeated them hopelessly.

This victory enhanced the prestige of the Spaniards by as many points as there were Indians slain; presently, Behechio and his comely sister Anacaona sent word that the tribute was ready, and Don Bartolomé decided to go to Xaraguá in person to see for himself and to eat of the meat and fish of that fat land, for Isabela and Santo Domingo were still on short commons. Despite the historiographers' discretion on the point, it is difficult to shake off the impression that he went there drawn also by a metal more attractive. For, after all, he was thirty-five and handsome and victorious, and Anacaona, "most friendly to Spaniards," was a young Indian widow who went about dressed like Venus when she came out of the waves, and the flesh is weak (by which we mean that it is too strong for us) and it knows no racial barriers. So, when the dashing Adelantado arrived at the seat of "King" Behechio, the King in person went out to meet him, with Anacaona, of course, and thirty-two "lords," and they presented him with enough cotton to fill up a big house, and food for all his men. Don Bartolomé sent word to Isabela that the first caravel to be ready should be sent him to Xaraguá waters without fail, which greatly elated the hungry Christians, for whom the news meant a return cargo of good native bread. The princess was also elated, but for different reasons, and this is one of the blessings of joy, that though it be ever the same vivid flower, it can have so many roots; "she persuaded her Indian brother that they should go and see the Christian canoe. She had a small settlement halfway [from the King's city to the coast] where she wished all to stay the night; there she had a house full of a thousand things made of cotton, chairs, many vessels and domestic objects made of wood, wonderfully wrought, and this house was as her private room. This lady presented Don Bartolomé with many chairs, most beautiful," and many more things, including many *naguas*, the only feminine covering known to the island. Don Bartolomé, to be sure, must have been very much touched by this delicate hint, and the bishop says nothing on the events of that night, for the French novel had not yet reached its full development. We are told, however, that the next day the caravel arrived at Xaraguá, and though King Behechio and Queen Anacaona had each a richly decorated canoe, the royal lady, "as she was so courtly, would not go in the canoe but wished to go in the caravel's boat with Don

Bartolomé." A trip in the caravel round the bay gave further opportunities to the Pale-face Don Juan; he showed off the speed of his sails, and the noise of his guns, and had to laugh away the fear which the gunpowder had put in the heart of his Indian conquest. At last, in his caravel, full of Indian bread and other victuals for his hungry Christians, Don Bartolomé sailed from Xaraguá, "leaving the King and the Queen very joyful." (8)

It would appear that Don Bartolomé was not proof against the intoxication of success. Oviedo, usually a reliable chronicler and on the whole rather favourable than otherwise to the Colón clan, says so positively: "After the Adelantado had obtained these victories, it seemed as if his character had changed, for he proved very exacting towards the Christians from then on, to such an extent that some of them could not bear him." (9) The brothers Colón were suddenly confronted with a rebellion: its leader was Francisco Roldán, the member of the Viceroy's household who had been left as *Alcayde* of Isabela. But though there may have been personal reasons of pique and ambition on his part, Roldán would not by himself have had enough force in the island to put the power and authority of the Colóns in jeopardy for so long. Las Casas' narrative, unfavourable though it is to Roldán, provides valuable hints which permit a better estimate of the events than he himself gives. There was a kind of epidemic of discontent, due to hunger. The leaders of the colony do not seem to have directed its activities towards farming with sufficient energy and perseverance, for the newcomers were people who expected gold, land, houses and overlordship, but not to have to work. This deficiency in the first waves of immigration must have been due to a defective selection at home. It may have been inevitable in view of the lack of enthusiasm which the pitiful sight of the ex-settlers arriving back caused in the mother country—which, of course, closed a vicious circle, for they came back ill because there was no food because there were no farmers because they came back ill. . . . At any rate, the state of "public opinion" in Española was so precarious that when the caravel arrived from Xaraguá in Isabela full of cotton and Indian bread, Don Diego had her run aground for fear that the discontented crowd should seize her and sail away to Castille. This was Roldán's opportunity. He started a whispering campaign and soon put enough heart into the malcontents for them "to say aloud what they had been grumbling about in corners," namely, that the Colóns were making everybody work for them and treating the Indians infamously. Finally, Roldán led seventy or eighty men into open rebellion against the three Colóns, in the name of the King and as the liberator of the Indians.

As events were to show, Roldán had a good many allies amongst the gentlemen and knights of the colony, and notably Diego de Escobar, Pedro de Valdivieso and Adrian de Múxica, all three men of weight, whom Las Casas knew personally. Don Bartolomé tried to come to terms with the rebels but without success; then, in order to reconquer the good graces of the rank and file, he offered them one or more slaves each. It was no easy thing to christianise a new continent! In spite of this powerful inducement, Roldán's party grew bigger every day, and Don Bartolomé was beginning to doubt whether he would be able to deal with the rebellion and even to escape alive (for his death was the first item in Roldán's plan of action), when help was sent him by Providence in the shape of two caravels from Spain. This was good news indeed. It meant more food, and what food!—good Christian bread and meat and wine, all of tough digestion; it meant also ninety working men, rare birds in Española; it meant the collaboration, advice and support of the gentleman who came in charge of the ships, Pero Hernández Coronel, *Alguacil Mayor* (Chief Constable) of the island, "a prudent man and a man of authority"; and, as Don Bartolomé found to his great satisfaction, it meant the arrival of the royal letter appointing him Adelantado of the Indies. This royal letter was in itself worth more than all the rest. It restored Don Bartolomé's position and put the Roldanites in a dangerous situation, not merely as the enemies of a private individual and a foreigner, whose titles to authority they might challenge, but as rebels against the chief officer of the Crown in the absence of the Viceroy.

The Adelantado, however, though stronger in moral force, felt no stronger in striking power. With his usual acumen, he decided to send Coronel to Roldán. The embassy failed to bring about a return of the black sheep to the fold; but it impressed the rebels enough for them to adopt a Fabian attitude, and they decided to withdraw to Xaraguá, of whose hospitality and abundance they had heard golden stories.

The troubles of Don Bartolomé were not over, for at this point he was threatened with another Indian revolt. The origin of this second rising is not clear; it was probably due to a combination of three circumstances: the stimulus given to the prevailing discontent amongst the Indians by the internal feuds between the Spaniards and by the fact that Roldán appeared before them as the champion of "better treatment and no tribute for the Indians";

the fact that the Indians could again count on a leader, for the Adelantado had released Guarionex without conditions as a gesture of friendliness to the natives; and finally a subconscious— or even conscious—tendency in the Adelantado and in his men to find a war against the Indians necessary in order to justify another crop of slaves. "What is the news?" asked the men still on board ship when Las Casas arrived in Santo Domingo for the first time a few years later. "Good news. There is much gold and there is a war against the Indians, which means plenty of slaves." (10)

Whatever the reason, Don Bartolomé chose, or thought it necessary, to take the field on hearing that Guarionex had disappeared from La Vega. The Adelantado with his men pursued him to the hilly regions of Ciguay, the domain of another "king" known as Mayobanex, where Guarionex had sought refuge, whether to prepare a rebellion of his subjects or to avoid having to lead one, is not clear. A first skirmish with Mayobanex's vanguards was disastrous for the natives, who were unable to withstand the Christian cavalry even when it was represented by a mere handful of horsemen. The Adelantado, who seems throughout to have combined military decision with diplomatic shrewdness, sent some prisoners to Mayobanex to demand deliverance of Guarionex, but the proud *cacique* refused. Further efforts at peace, based always on the delivery of Guarionex, met with the same resolute resistance on the part of Mayobanex, even when his own men, impressed with the progress made by the Spaniards, would willingly have sacrificed their guest. Don Bartolomé tried again. His men were exhausted, eating but little and hunting the two native chiefs to and fro in the mountains of Ciguay. He sent away the faint-hearts, and with thirty men only he continued his relentless campaign. Two Indians, sent to Mayobanex with the usual message—give up Guarionex—were found dead on the way. But the small Spanish troop caught two of Mayobanex's Indians, who, under threats of torture, confessed where their chief was. Twelve Spaniards volunteered to take him prisoner. They stripped, painted themselves and hid their swords with palm-leaves, carrying them on their backs as they had seen the Indians do; and having found the *cacique* with his wife and children, they took him alive and brought him with his family to the Spanish chief. After starving for weeks in hiding, Guarionex gave himself up.

So ended this campaign against the last warlike *cacique* of Española. It had a pathetic epilogue. One of the prisoners, a sister or cousin of Mayobanex, a woman of signal beauty, was married to another "lord" who loved her deeply. This native lord came down to La Vega, threw himself at the Adelantado's feet and swore that if he got back his wife, he and his men would work for the Spaniards as slaves. Don Bartolomé was magnanimous. He let him have his wife without conditions, and along with the native beauty he freed also a number of other "lords" who should form a fit escort for her. A few days later, the grateful husband led to La Vega a peaceful army of four to five thousand field labourers, each with a *coa* on his shoulder, a stick hardened by fire with which they ploughed the land, and they tilled and sowed such an acreage of land as gave Don Bartolomé food worth thirty thousand Castillians—a fortune in those days.

Encouraged by this generous mood which they had called forth in the Adelantado, the Indians of Ciguay organised an expedition to La Vega in the hope of obtaining the release of Mayobanex. They came in numbers, all with humble offerings in their hands, bread, roast fish. (11) The Adelantado released the "Queen" and all her family and household, but kept Mayobanex. This firmness was no doubt a matter of policy. The *caciques* were the only —or at any rate the strongest—pieces in the political structure of the island. Once the most powerful ones had been destroyed, the others could be made to serve the new masters. The *caciques* were not unaware of the importance of religion in civil life. The poor hermit, Román Pane, who was instructed by the Viceroy to enquire into the religious ways of the natives, did find in spite of a "humility," of which he often boasts, and which kept him on the border between sanctity and stupidity, that the *cemis* or religious images which gave the natives their oracles, were connected by a hidden speaking-tube with another chamber in which the *cacique* could comfortably speak into a mouthpiece. The good friar was entitled to consider this arrangement as an infamous encouragement and abuse of superstition. And so it was. But men who were used to speaking in the name of God were bound to be considered by Don Cristóbal Colón as his natural rivals. (12)

Meanwhile Colón was in difficulties over the financing of his third voyage. The King and Queen had granted him six million maravedis. But it so happens that Pero Alonso Niño, whom he had found in Cádiz on his arrival and sent over to his brother Bartolomé with supplies and instructions, seems to have had but a vague notion of the harm which a witticism may do when uttered at the wrong moment; and when, casting anchor again in Cádiz on October 29th, 1496, with the three hundred slaves which the Adelantado was sending over, he referred to them as a cargo of gold—for gold is what yields gold—the King and Queen, taking him at his word, told Colón that the gold which Pero Alonso Niño had brought over would be more than enough to finance his expedition, and the six million went into the French war.

This Pero Alonso Niño must have been a light-hearted sort of pilot and captain, for, not content with the poor joke which he inflicted on the King, Queen and Admiral, he went to Moguer, his native town, and granted himself a two-months holiday without troubling to appear at Court until the end of December, with the letters from the Adelantado and the true report as to the nature of his "gold." The royal wrath was great, but of no avail to overtake the millions gone to turn the Frenchmen out of Roussillon, and Colón had to cast about for other expedients. Nearly three million were obtained from the Italian bankers, "Pantaleon Italian" and "Martin Centurion," to whom authority was given to export wheat to Genoa; this first instalment was not available till October 1497, but it enabled Colón to send off the first relief expedition commanded by Pero Hernández Coronel. (13) We possess some of the documents which were drafted in connection with this expedition, particularly a contract with a merchant Antón Marino, of Seville, and Inés Nuñes, his wife, for the supply of wine and meat, in which—eloquent witness of the persistent unity of the Roman Empire—this Spanish woman, writing in 1498, is made to say that she renounces "all the laws which Emperors Justinian and Valianus made in favour and help of women" and to agree that they will not be held valid for her in any dispute arising out of this contract. (14)

Colón was never happy in administrative details. His imaginative nature, his nascent energy and creative impulse, suffered agony in all these delays and complications. They invariably acted as a severe strain on his nerves and patience. For a man of his pride and dash, the compulsory association with an unsympathetic critic and collaborator such as Fonseca, with whom he was in double harness like a thoroughbred with an ox, must have been intolerable. All the preparations of the voyage had to be made alongside the wary and critical Bishop of Badajoz. Nor was this the worst feature of the situation, for a proud man may bear from a principal what he will not tolerate from underlings, and on Fonseca's staff there was an officer named Ximeno who seems to have exasperated the Admiral more than ever man did in his life. It so happened that this Ximeno was a *Converso*, and there is little doubt that this circumstance must have been a powerful factor in the psychological situation which developed. Colón was meeting with opposition in quarters in which he had a natural right to expect help. His anger was the stronger. The Admiral evidently nursed a cold accumulated fury against this man. He waited for the day he was to sail. Las Casas is positive on this point, which clearly establishes on Colón's part a pre-meditation of course of a purely passionate character. On deck, before leaving, he savagely attacked the Bishop's official, knocked him down and kicked him hard. Later on, in Española, suspecting —rightly—that this incident would tell heavily against him, he wrote to the King and Queen: "I entreat Your Highnesses to order the persons dealing with this business in Seville not to be averse to it and not to hinder it; I do not know what may have happened there about Ximeno, save that he is of a race in which they all help each other to the death, while I am away and an exiled foreigner; let Your Highnesses not turn me away, for You always helped me." No one with any knowledge of psychology would consider this text as an argument against the Jewish origin of Colón himself, but rather as a strong argument in favour. (15)

On Wednesday, May 30th, 1498, the Admiral sailed from San-lúcar de Barrameda at the head of six ships and two hundred men, not counting the sailors. Owing to the war with France, he avoided Cape St. Vincent, a place he knew well, because a French fleet was cruising there in the hope of combining business with pleasure, and went round to the Island of Porto Santo, which brought him memories of his youth over which he is absolutely silent in his Diary. He arrived on June 7th, a Thursday, and found it in great turmoil for fear that the approaching caravels should be French; having relieved the islanders by showing the Spanish ensign—which then was friendly and more than friendly to the Portuguese owing to the close relationship between the two royal families and to the fact that the King and Queen of Portugal were heirs presumptive to the Crown of Castille—he went ashore to hear mass, we hope, though he says nothing about it, for the soul of his Perestrello wife. On the following Sunday he was in Madeira. He was very well received, because, says Las Casas, he was very well known and had lived there—but mainly, no doubt, because he had discovered the Indies and was powerful, for otherwise, even though he had lived there, the Madeirans would not have cared a pin. This visit to his old haunts is most sugges-tive. He could not very well have paid it earlier, owing to the bad relations which had obtained between Castille and Portugal, nor in better conditions, for, though he had once come into the Azores, it had been under the compulsion of a storm. This call, *both* in Porto Santo and in Madeira, suggests that he wanted to show the islanders what the young man had become. The Magnificent Admiral tasted the wine of local glory for six days, and on Saturday the 16th he left for La Gomera, where he arrived on the following Tuesday. He found a French corsair in the harbour with some Castillian ships which he had captured. The corsair made a swift mental reckoning—six is to one as—— and without finishing the proportion, he spread sail and made off with one of the Castillian ships, in which six Frenchmen were watching over six Spaniards. Colón sent one of his swift sea-hounds after the fugitive; and the six Spaniards in the captive ship, seeing this relief in the offing, fell upon their guards, put them out of the way under deck and sailed back to La Gomera.

Well pleased with this episode, the Admiral started for his third voyage of discovery. He decided to split his forces. His brother needed encouragement and help; but *he* needed discovery and new glories. So he sent three ships straight to Santo Domingo, while he sailed more leisurely on his quest with the other three. As captains of the three ships trusted out of his sight, he appointed three men, two of whom were his relations—Alonso Sánchez de Carabajal, or Carvajal, who was one of his Española companions; Pedro de Arana, "a very honest man and most wise," brother of Beatriz Enríquez, his mistress and the mother of Don Fernando Colón; and Juan Antonio Colombo or Colón, his cousin, "a man most capable and prudent and of authority." His instructions were that each in turn should take command of the fleet every week and should be entitled to lead the fleet and to put up the lantern, i.e. the light aft which served the other ships as a guide. They were to sail to Dominica, thence to Santo Domingo bay; whenever they came in touch with Indians, even Cannibals, they were to give something in exchange for what they needed, and they would be sure the Indians would serve them well, while if they tried violent ways they would get nothing but trouble. Finally, he told them that he meant to sail south, through the Cabo Verde islands, past the Equator, then west, leaving Española north, to find out whether there were any islands and lands. "Let the Lord lead me and afford me a find in His service and in that of the King and Queen, and in honour of the Christians, for I do not think this road has ever been covered by anyone and that this sea is very unknown." (16)

CHAPTER XXVI

THE DISCOVERY OF THE EARTHLY PARADISE AND THE FIRST AMERICAN REVOLUTION

HAVING filled his hulls with water, firewood and other supplies, "particularly cheeses which are there plentiful and good," (1) Colón left La Gomera with one ship and two caravels on June 21st, 1498, sailing straight towards the Islands of Cabo Verde, "a misleading name," he says, "for they are dry enough and I saw not a green thing in them and everybody is ill and I dared not stop there." (2) He did, however, stop at the small Island of Buenavista, a name no less misleading than that of Cabo Verde, for it is most sterile, and there is close to it a smaller island where all the lepers of Portugal used to come to get rid of their disease by eating turtles and washing in their blood. He purchased some goat-meat in Buenavista and he tried in vain to buy some cattle in Santiago, the biggest island in the cluster, but his crews began to feel the unbearable heat of the place and he decided to sail away.

These hot regions excited his *Cipangish* imagination. He was puzzled, as an expert in undiscovered lands, by a statement of King John of Portugal (who had died the previous year), that "there was mainland in the south"; also by King John's insistence in throwing back two hundred and seventy miles the limit of his zone of discovery as defined by the Pope. Why? Colón believed that the King of Portugal was certain that within his zone he would find "famous lands and things." While he was thus brewing his dreams and fears, some of the local lights of the Island of Santiago came to see him. They cannot have had much to do there by way of distraction, and an Admiral of the Indies must have been for them a fairly interesting fowl to look at. Colón asked them about the slave trade, which was brisk in the island, and they said it was going strong, with much demand from Castille, Aragon, Portugal, Italy and Sicily, and that a man, even of the meanest, was worth eight thousand maravedis. (3) Their conversation naturally turned on islands, mainlands, and such like matters, and the Santiago gentry revealed to the Admiral that south-west of the Island of Fuego, twelve leagues away, an island could be seen (though probably not touched) and that King John had "a great inclination to send people to discover towards the south-west." Discover what?, it will be asked. But in those days that question was not put and the verb *to discover* needed no complement. Just to discover. This news must have raised the temperature of the Admiral by a few degrees, and he sailed away writing in his Diary: "May He who is three in one lead me, for the sake of His compassion and mercy to serve Him and to enable me to give some great joy to Your Highnesses and to all Christendom, as happened with the finding of the Indies, which resounded in all the world." (4)

We may imagine him sailing away in a hurry, lest the Portuguese caravels got there before him. There he was in mid-ocean, in the summer of 1498, nearly six years after his discovery of Guanahani, still wholly unaware of the real situation which his daring and his faith were to reveal to mankind, still in a world of Cipangos and Quinsays, of islands and mainlands, "in the Auster," or "towards the south-west," in a kind of no-man's sea or "far-west" of discoveries, ready to receive from the Holy Trinity another windfall like that of the Indies.

He sailed south, beyond the equinoctial line because, he said, below that line can be found more gold and valuable things. This was, of course, the "scientific" opinion of the day; Mosén Jaume Ferrer, an authority on cosmography, consulted by the King and Queen on all naval matters of scientific import, had written him in 1495 that "most valuable things come from very hot zones, the inhabitants of which are blacks or parrots, and therefore, until Your Lordship has found such people, you will not find abundance of such things." (5) The Admiral's care to show off his parrots and popinjays wherever he went in Spain turns out, after all, to rest, so to speak, on a scientific basis. He meant to say to the gaping crowds: Parrots—therefore, gold.

This, he might suspect, must have been the reason which prompted King John's interest in the Auster. It was necessary to find out the secret of King John. There might be gold in it. It is a fact that, while in his first voyage, under the influence of Toscanelli, of Esdras, or of both, he sailed dead west from La Gomera, all his other voyages are planned under an entirely different conception, for they all strike a course much further south. What was exactly this inspiration, it would be rash to say. Blacks and parrots, perhaps; perhaps a hankering towards the South Sea, which he seems to have sought *round* a land or peninsula pointing south, for he thought himself vaguely somewhere between Japan and the Philippines and he felt the Indian sea round Singapore; perhaps the "mainland in the Auster" in which King John believed and the Indians of Española also, though for entirely different reasons; perhaps all this, rolled up into one myth and obsession in his imagination; but most probable of all, as events were soon to show, what led him southwards every time was the hope of finding at last the true site of Paradise on Earth.

It was no easy matter and at first he may well have feared that he had reached the other place. On July 13th, he came upon such heat and ardour that he thought the ships would burn away and his men perish; the barrels burst open letting wine and water flow to waste, the wheat burnt like fire, the lard and salt-meat were roasted and rotted away. He was saved by rain and wind. But this experience made him change his course, which was a great pity for, had he kept on the one which he had followed till then from Cabo Verde, he would have seen land four or five days earlier than he actually did and, instead of arriving at yet another island, he would have discovered the mainland of King John's dreams at the mouth of the River Marañón.

Doggedly pursued by an adverse fate, he sails on, turning every day a little further away from that south-west which had been his first and his soundest intuition, until by the 28th or 29th he is on a course parallel to the mainland and in a direction which, but for Trinidad, would have taken him across the sea of the Antilles for days and days without letting him see land. He was suffering from gout and lack of sleep, but he kept in hand the command of the expedition with a capacity for physical suffering somewhat surprising in a man so given to speaking about it and even to laying stress on it. By the end of the month they ran short of water and he gave orders to alter the course straight north, towards Dominica, sailing hopelessly away from what was this time going to be his discovery. Towards midday, however, one of his servants, Alonso Pérez, went up to the top and saw land about fifteen leagues away to the west. He saw three summits. As it happens, Colón had made up his mind to christen the first land he discovered on this voyage *Trinidad*. So there was complete agreement between the land, the discoverer and Providence, and the island was named Trinidad, not in honour of this, but of the Holy Trinity.

There was great rejoicing on board, and the sailors sang

Salve Regina, "following the custom of mariners, at least of ours of Spain, when in grief or in joy." (6) Their first meeting with natives provides an excellent illustration of the misunderstandings that may arise between man and man. A canoe with twenty-five warlike young men on board came towards them and shouted, probably asking who they were. The Christians showed them shining objects, such as brass basins, to attract them and talk to them, but after two hours of unsuccessful efforts, Colón had some of his shipboys dance on deck, to the sound of a small drum; whereupon the twenty-five warriors levelled their bows at them and shot a volley of arrows at the strangers, no doubt interpreting this dance as a declaration of war.

The incident had no untoward consequences, but Colón had to rely on his unaided wits to explore the place. He sailed round Trinidad till he entered the Gulf of Paria from the north. It is an almost closed-in sea between the Island of Trinidad and the mainland; he saw the mainland in the distance, but took it for an island and called it *Isla Santa*, and later *Isla de Gracia*. Colón was very much pleased to find popinjays, though of a different kind, nearly as big as cocks, all red with a few blue and brown feathers on the wings; "they never speak," says Las Casas, "so they have nothing in them one can enjoy but their looks." (7) It did not occur to him that these birds kept silent in order perhaps not to reveal where the gold was; if that were the reason, they were more discreet than the inhabitants of the "Island of Grace," i.e. the coast of Venezuela, who gave all kinds of explanations to Colón's men, as to where to find not only gold but also pearls like those which some of them wore on their arms. These revelations were made to small reconnoitring parties which Colón sent on land; they were generally very cordially received and offered a kind of wine made of "maize, which is a seed which builds up an ear like a cob, of which I took some back and it is now abundant in Castille." (8) Thus was Indian corn found for the first time, both as a bread and as a wine. Colón was now, as usual, revelling in islands. The coast of the mainland opposite Trinidad is not altogether devoid of them, but there are in it so many bays and estuaries that Colón was inclined to see an island in every promontory. He was unwell, he was in a hurry, through lack of stores (for he wanted to save those he brought for Española) and probably also through subconscious uneasiness about events in Española and in Castille; and he was perhaps a little tired in his spirit, as revealed in his attitude, often negative, towards the native "kings": "they came in canoes to tell me their King begged me to land, and when they saw I did not take any notice of them, numbers of them came in canoes, many wearing gold ornaments on their necks, and some, pearls round their arms." (9) So, he did not land. And as if to mark the sarcasm and the irony of the situation with a final, unmistakable stroke, the words in which he explains why he sailed away from the true mainland repeat his erroneous belief that he had found the mainland when he sailed for days along the coast of Cuba! "I weighed anchor because I was in a hurry to restore my supplies . . . and also to restore myself, for I was ill, with my eyes sore for lack of sleep, for though during the voyage in which I discovered the mainland I was thirty-three days without sleeping and blind for so long, I did not suffer so much from my eyes nor did they burst and bleed as they have done now." (10)

Blind indeed he had been along the coast of Cuba and blind indeed he was now. But the eyes of his imagination remained wide open, and it was here, while in Paria, shut in with land all round, that he discovered the earthly Paradise. He had always noticed that the meridian one hundred leagues west of the Azores had special virtues (not in vain had Pope Alexander chosen it as the frontier between the Oceanic domains of the King of Portugal and those of the King of Castille): the needle changed its deviation from west to east on crossing it; and the air became softer and more temperate; he had been struck with the temperate climate of Trinidad, compared with that of Guiné; the men, moreover, were not black but almost white, and more civilised; finally, the Northern Star moved in such a way as to make him suspect that this hemisphere was different from the others. All these observations, some correct, others sweeping generalisations of a limited experience, led him to put forward the famous cosmographical conception which he had no doubt harboured for long, dropping now and then dark hints about its forthcoming revelation. "I always read," he says, "that the world, land and water, was spherical. . . . Now I observed so much divergence, that I began to hold different views about the world and I found that it was not round . . . but pear-shaped, round except where it has a nipple, for there it is taller, or as if one had a round ball and, on one side, it should be like a woman's breast, and this nipple part is the highest and closest to heaven, and it is under the equinoctial line, in this ocean sea, at the end of the Orient. I call end of the Orient where all land and islands end."

This, to be sure, was the discovery of a *new world*. It came to this: the meridian one hundred leagues west of the Azores divided the earth into two hemispheres; "Ptolemy and the other philosophers believed that it was spherical, believing that this hemisphere [the 'new'] was round just like the one yonder, where they were," and about this hemisphere he was good enough "to raise no difficulty and to grant that it was spherical as they say." But the other one, what did Ptolemy know about it, or anyone, "since no one had ever sent to *fetch* it till Your Highnesses now had it explored"? "To fetch it" is a delightful touch of his imaginative style.

Nor was this all, for it was a fact that the Gulf of Paria received huge amounts of fresh water which made its waters sweet fully forty miles into the sea; this suggested a most powerful river. The conclusion was obvious: "The Scriptures say that in the earthly Paradise grows the Tree of Life and from it flows a spring which gives birth to four rivers: Ganges in India, Tigris and Euphrates [. . .] and Nile, born in Ethiopia and flowing into the sea in Alexandria." These are big rivers, aren't they? So, whenever we find ourselves at the mouth of an even bigger one, we may expect to be on the track of Paradise. "I find nowhere writings of Latins or of Greeks which say for certain where the earthly Paradise actually is, nor have I seen it on a map, save when put there on the basis of authority and argument." As for him, he is far too scientifically minded—he really is, in spite of all this orgy of biblical imagination—to jump to conclusions; he points out that "no one can reach the earthly Paradise save by Divine Will"; "I believe that this water may come from there, even if it be far away"; and "all these are great signs of Paradise, for the site is in conformity with the opinion of great theologians, and all facts also point that way, for I never read or heard that so much fresh water could mix with salt water and penetrate so far into it, and in this, there is also some help from the soft temperance [of the climate], and if it does not flow from Paradise, the marvel is greater still, for I do not think there is known in the world a river so big and so deep." (11)

These words show Colón's mind at its truest: as an inextricable mixture of an empirical, truly scientific spirit of observation, and of a medieval faith in tradition and authority. He starts with observations, usually right, he ends with conclusions, often hopelessly wrong, because in his mind the light of nature is broken and deflected by all kinds of irrelevant notions. But it is a curious fact that, while he is in his empirical phase, Colón is most emphatically—though subconsciously—a believer in the superiority of facts over what he calls "arguments," i.e. opinions. So he writes that before the King and Queen had had it explored, "there was no certain knowledge of this hemisphere but only very slight and from argument,"(11) in a way which unmistakably is meant to suggest that knowledge "by argument" is not worth much. As was to be expected of such a mind, he did in the end gather and suspect that this was a very big land, for, whether that mighty flow of water came from Paradise or not, it was bound to come from a long river and therefore from a vast territory. "I believe," he writes to the King and Queen, "that this land which Your Highnesses have now had discovered is very large and that there are many more in the Auster, which have never been known." (12) So he says to the King and Queen; but let us now find out his reasons for this belief: "I am convinced that this is mainland, very large, unknown heretofore, and reason helps me greatly on account of this great river and sea, which is fresh, and then I draw help also from the saying of Esdras in Book IV, Chapter 6, which says that six parts of the earth are dry and one under water, a book approved of by St. Ambrose and St. Augustine." (13)

Similarly, with a power of observation which aroused the admiration of Humboldt, he discovers the movement of the sea waters from east to west and shrewdly remarks that they eat up the earth on the western edge of the ocean trough, hence the abundance of islands on that coast; but straight away he goes on to observe that "many precious things are born in them [in these islands] owing to the soft temperateness which comes to them from heaven, for they are on the top of the world." And lest there might be any doubts on this point, he remarks that when he came out of the Gulf of Paria through the Dragon's mouth, he found that his ships ran west so quickly that he made sixty-five leagues from mass-time to compline-time, with little wind, and this observation, probably correct (and due to the strong current there), leads him to the conclusion that "going towards the Auster one goes uphill [i.e. to the earth's nipple, or Paradise], and going towards the North, one goes downhill." (14)

He went downhill all the way to Española.

* *

He found it very far from Paradise indeed. Roldán had settled in Xaraguá with his seventy followers. He had set up a kind of independent kingdom in which he preached general protection and practised actual subjection of his Indian hosts. Servants and women were available, cheap and abundant, for the whole tribe of Spanish rebels. But Roldán seems to have had a certain amount of political acumen, for it was in his dominion of Xaraguá that, for the first time in Española, service from natives was secured by arrangement with the *caciques*; his rebellion was therefore something more substantial than a mere personal disloyalty towards the Adelantado. It embodied a different conception of the relations between Christians and Indians, one which avoided both the professions of wholesale Christianisation of the Indians and the practice of their wholesale exploitation through slavery. It was a popular revolt, and therefore empirical and immediate in its Indian policy, shorn of shame and of principles; the Indians were good fellows and they should not be taxed; their women were lovely and they should be at the Christian's discretion; and the men were idle and they should be made to work through the *cacique*.

This popular—we would nowadays say *democratic*—character of Roldán's rebellion is emphasised in a letter written to the Admiral by Miguel Ballester, his trusted Alcayde of Bonao, who more than once acted as an emissary and negotiator between Colón and the rebels. "And I take it as certain," he says, "that leaving aside the gentlemen and persons of quality which are with your Lordship, and the men of your own household, all of whom your Lordship will find most steadfast and ready to die in your service, on the common people I would not rely much." (15) It cannot be gainsaid, therefore, that Roldán was a leader of the common folk against the gentlemen round the Colóns. The Colóns and the gentlemen who surrounded them were thinking in bigger terms—not necessarily in better terms; in fact, so far as slavery was concerned, their policy was worse— but they were trying to set up a colony and to solve *problems* such as work, property, an adequate return to the King and Queen. The Roldanites were just living, expanding their *egos* to the new glorious dimensions afforded them by the new world suddenly opened out before their eager lives; they were spontaneous and free and anarchical, like forces of nature.

Colón brought workers from Spain; the workers turned into lords; Las Casas waxes indignant, thinking of the Indians they subjugated; Colón grew worried, thinking of the King and Queen, the "problem," the "plan," the revenue; but the exworkers were living like princes and cared precious little. And in the end they provided the institution which the "statesmen" had to adopt: the distribution of Indians amongst the settlers, as a compromise between the royal opposition to slavery and the settlers' determination to be served. This system, known as *repartimiento* and later *encomienda*, or *trust*, was to last for centuries and to provide an empirical solution for the chief social and economic problems of the Spanish empire—the adjustment of the economic relations between the two races.

As was to be expected, the people in revolt against the Colóns soon discovered their Jewish origin. We know that anti-semitism was always a democratic, and pro-semitism an aristocratic, attitude in Spain. It was therefore to be expected that in Española the "gentlemen and men of quality" would be with Colón and the people against him. We know that the Admiral was attacked as a *Converso* because he says so himself in a sentence the very obscurity of which is most suggestive; for Colón starts defending himself against the accusation before he has let out that he had been accused; and he at once counter-attacks: "But this would not be so if the author of the discovery had been a *Converso*, because *Conversos* are enemies of Your Highnesses and of Christians, but they spread that name and in such a way that all was lost; and these men who are with Roldán, who is now raising trouble against me, they say most of them are [*Conversos*]." (16) He is on the defensive. As Peter did Jesus, he denies Israel. (By 1498, the Inquisitors have become so powerful in Spain that one of them, Lucero, famous for his utter lack, not merely of religious sense but of the most elementary human decency, is persecuting Talavera's family, not daring to persecute the saintly archbishop himself.) But despite his denials, there are signs, as will be shown later, that the Spanish colony in Española remained convinced, that the Colóns were of Jewish extraction.

This handicap in his situation may have been one of the reasons which made him meet the rebellion with a policy so lacking in candour and in resolution. His brother Bartolomé, who had come out from Santo Domingo to meet him at sea, had put the situation before him. As soon as he landed (August 31st, 1498) he started a judicial enquiry, putting aside, at any rate formally, the proceedings of another enquiry which the Adelantado had initiated during his absence. The Admiral pursued a policy distinctly more conciliatory than Don Bartolomé. He was temperamentally more given to temporise and to put off the use of force, which, however, he usually wielded in subtler and slyer ways. While he was at work the three ships which he had sent on from La Gomera arrived in the harbour. They had first struck the island not far from Xaraguá, much to the satisfaction of Roldán; forty of the newcomers had gone over to him on being told that under the Admiral they would have to work hard, while under Roldán they would have Indians to do the work for them. Alonso Sánchez de Carvajal had remained with the rebels, by agreement with the other two captains, to try to bring them back to the fold. Colón did not like this arrangement at all and suspected Carvajal's loyalty, until this captain, "an honourable gentleman" says Las Casas, proved him wrong. As a first measure, calculated to reconquer some popularity, he had the public crier announce, on September 12th, that all settlers wishing to return to Spain would be allowed to do so and given ships and supplies for their return home. At this the rebels flagged, and most of their leaders came to Bonao to talk matters over with the Alcayde Miguel Ballester, a staunch upholder of the Admiral's authority.

On October 25th Colón wrote to Roldán an almost subservient letter. Roldán seems to have been tempted to come to terms, but was prevented by his rank and file. More adherents of the humbler folk "passed" over to his side from that of Colón. The Admiral sized up his forces and sounded their loyalty: the result was pitiful: seventy men at most whom he could count as loyal. He took two measures: a general amnesty for the past, with a promise of "humane and considerate justice" for the future (which would appear to justify the accusations of harsh treatment levelled against the three brothers by their Christian "subjects" in Española); and a special safe-conduct for Roldán and his friends to come and report to him. This safe-conduct is a curious piece. In it Colón gives Roldán his title of *Alcayde*, in spite of his rebellion. Roldán came to Santo Domingo and negotiated on equal terms with the man who should have put him in jail; then, like one who does not care overmuch, he left without concluding an arrangement. The Admiral sent one of his own men after him, to carry on the parley; this led to a rather exorbitant proposal from Roldán, which, however, the Admiral did not altogether reject. He sent Carvajal to the rebels, who were getting ready to attack the Fort of Concepción, then in the hands of one of Colón's men. On November 17th the agreement, on the basis of a return to Spain, within fifty days, of the rebels with their slaves and Indian women, was signed by Roldán, who had the insolence to add as a rider that his engagement not to recruit any more Spanish followers was subject to the Admiral signing the agreement within ten days. Colón signed within four, on the 21st. The rebels went to Xaraguá to prepare for their departure.

The Admiral was so anxious to see them go that he turned over to them two of the three ships he had made ready for Don Bartolomé, who was to explore the land of Paria. One of his trusted men was to go on this expedition to Spain, taking to the King and Queen secret letters in which Roldán was exposed and his instant imprisonment recommended. Carvajal went to Xaraguá. His report was not cheerful. The rebels, fearing the royal displeasure, were determined not to sail, and as the fifty days were over, they made the Admiral responsible for the breakdown of the arrangement. The Admiral wrote "with all modesty" to Roldán and to Adrian de Múxica, another rebel; he drew from them insolent replies. They asked for a caravel in order to send messengers to the King and Queen; Carvajal granted it; they demanded a written promise from the Admiral. Tired of their intransigence, Carvajal decided to send the two ships back to Santo Domingo and to return by land; whereupon Roldán changed his tactics, came out to meet him and, talking "under a shade," told him in secret that he would be ready to go and wind up this affair with the Admiral if he received a safe-conduct with the royal seal and another one signed by several of the men of quality close to the Admiral. Humiliating as they were for the Admiral, as well as for the men of quality concerned, the two papers were sent as Roldán wished; but, not content with this, the Admiral, eager to end the trouble, for fear of its effect at Court, left with most of his companions for Azúa, a harbour twenty-five leagues west of Santo Domingo, to meet Roldán half-way. The meeting ended in a complete surrender to the rebels, whose leader was appointed Alcalde Mayor, and who were explicitly granted the right to raise arms against Colón if he did not respect the terms of the agreement, while their rebellion was condoned in terms which implied an open and official condemnation of Don Bartolomé.

Dejected at his own surrender and humiliated daily by the insolent behaviour of Roldán, settled as Alcalde Mayor in Española, Colón thought of sailing for Spain with the Adelantado to fight his case there. But at this point a threatened Indian rebellion forced him to stay and he sent Ballester to Spain with letters and with the proceedings of the enquiry against Roldán, including a number of argumentative and casuistic reasons showing why the agreement signed by him as Viceroy was not valid, the general tenor of which may be gauged from one of these reasons to the effect that the document had been signed on a caravel, where he was not a Viceroy, but an Admiral. (17) He was evidently aware of his own weakness and incapacity. His faith, so precarious in its deepest roots, failed him at times altogether. The day after Christmas (1499), while fighting against a combination of Christian rebels and Indians, he passed through one of these crises: "I found myself in such extremity that, to fly from death, I left everything and went right out to sea, in a small caravel; then Our Lord came to my help, saying: *Oh man of little faith, have no fear. It is I. Have courage; be not dismayed, and fear not. I shall see to all. The seven years' limit for gold is not over; and in that as in everything else I will set things aright for thee.* And so He dispersed my enemies and showed me how I could fulfil my offers. Oh unhappy sinner, I, who made everything depend on worldly hopes!" (18)

He wrote to the King and Queen and asked for a learned man to administer justice, whose salary he would pay; he felt his forces failing him, and because "he was shrinking and his son Don Diego was growing in strength, becoming a man to be able to serve their Highnesses here," he asked leave to have him sent "so that he [the Admiral] should have some rest and Their Highnesses be better served." (19) Evidently fearing for his credit at Court, he added: "I do not know whether I am mistaken, but my opinion is that princes should favour their governors much as long as they hold them at their posts, for when out of favour all is lost." (20)

PART VI

FALL, DEATH AND TRANSFIGURATION

CHAPTER XXVII

THE FAILURE OF THE VICEROY

"GOLD is most excellent" but pearls are beautiful, and while gold is a most useful thing, pearls are exquisitely useless. They are the stones of Venus, like Venus, born of the sea, and no less miraculously, if we are to believe Las Casas. "In certain times of the year, when the oysters feel the inclination and appetite to conceive, they come out to the shore and open themselves out and wait for the dew from heaven, almost as if they waited and desired their husbands; they receive that dew from which they conceive and become pregnant, and the children they produce, which are the pearls, are such as may be the quality of the dew; if it be pure, the pearls will be born white; if turbid, they will be brown or dark [. . .] the earlier the dew, from dawn or morning, the whiter the pearls; the later the dew, from evening or night, the darker the pearls." (1) This would be one of the most remarkable cases of natural concordance known to man, if only it were true.

But even though their birth may not be quite so beautiful, pearls are one of the joys of sensuous life, and so it is not to be wondered at that, when Colón found them so rich and abundant in Paria, he should have been tempted to keep the discovery to himself a little while. This access of secretiveness was exposed by his enemies and the ugliest colours were put on it. There is no doubt that he did keep quiet about his new discovery and about some deal or arrangement he concluded thereon, because he is at pains to explain the matter—not very clearly, as was his wont— in his letter to the Aya of Prince Don Juan: "The pearls, I had them put together and fished by the people with whom I arranged to come back for them, and to my mind, by the bushel; if I did not write about it to Their Highnesses, the reason is that I should have liked to do the same with gold earlier." (2)

This secretiveness cannot have been deliberate nor due to any plot to retain the wealth of pearls, because the secret could not be kept from the crews; it was almost certainly an irrational reaction before the splendour of the find, a kind of secret joy in the sole possession of his treasure, which made him remiss in reporting it.

And in the end, even though he tarried, he wrote only too soon about them. On October 18th, 1498, Colón sent five ships to Spain. His news was mixed: Roldán's rebellion; the discovery of the coast of Paria and of a big river which might be one of the four rivers of Paradise; and pearls. Young Hojeda, very much out of work, was then in Seville, hanging about in the offices of Fonseca, where the papers and parcels of the Admiral were received. He heard of Roldán's rebellion and probably grinned; he heard of Paradise and probably smiled; he saw the pearls and probably gasped; and he saw Colón's map of the coast where the pearls came from and . . . he spoke to Fonseca. He was in Fonseca's good books. The bishop in charge of discoveries managed to let him have a letter authorising him to arm an expedition, on condition that he should not go near the preserves of either the King of Portugal or the Admiral of the Indies. This provision would have limited poor Hojeda to "discovering" in the moon, but for an ingenious limitation which the bishop appended to his own limitation of Hojeda's zone: he provided that Colón's own preserves should be understood as comprising all he had already found up to 1497. As Paria and its pearls were found in 1498, Hojeda was free to go and see what could be done there.

Fonseca seems to have acted in this with little regard for Colón's rights, aware of the precarious state of the Admiral's affairs at Court. His decision was to have far-reaching historical results; because, when Hojeda left Spain on May 20th, 1499, he had on board a Florentine clerk of the house of Juanoto Berardi, in Seville, whose name, and not that of Colón, was to be given to the continent. This clerk was Americo Vespucci. He was crossing the ocean for the first time.

Hojeda and his ships "discovered" for a number of weeks along the coast which they knew by Colón's chart, and when at last they ran short of supplies, with that coolness which was a typical feature of the leader, they set their course to Española where, on September 5th, 1498, they cast anchor in Yáquimo Bay.

When Colón heard of this he was deeply troubled. Uneasy as he was about his position in Spain, he may well have thought that this expedition came to supersede his authority, as another one was soon to do. The Adelantado was away inland. He felt that a show of authority was necessary; he struck on a bold idea which might have turned out disastrous for him but which, in fact, worked tolerably well: he sent Roldán, who sailed with two caravels and arrived close to Hojeda's quarters on September 29th, 1498. Roldán landed with a strong force, learned that Hojeda was inland with fifteen men, took up positions which cut the newcomer off from his ships and advanced to meet him. Hojeda explained what he had been doing—with some exaggeration—spoke of going to see the Admiral and hinted at some news which Colón would want to hear, albeit not good for him; but having shaken off Roldán, he sailed in the opposite direction and, instead of going to Santo Domingo, he cast anchor in Xaraguá in February 1500.

This district was the centre of the anti-Colonite faction. Hojeda soon perceived that feeling there was ripe for a rising. He knew enough about the state of affairs in Castille to be able to say that the King and Queen did not agree with the way in which Colón, and particularly his brother, dealt with the settlers, especially in the matter of salaries, which they did not pay. If we are to believe Las Casas, Hojeda declared himself ready to lead this revolt to Santo Domingo, though it is difficult to imagine him explaining his actions to the King and Queen afterwards. Roldán, sent by Colón with a force sufficient to impose respect, found the Xaraguá colony in civil war over the issue. By a mixture of daring and ruse he succeeded in getting rid of Hojeda and his ships, which sailed away and did not return; but, as a reward, the Xaraguá settlers wrested from him the right to take land for themselves, and he transferred to them an authority the Admiral had granted him to make use of the labour of the Indians while undertaking to have them instructed in the Christian religion. Thus every event in the island ended in a further step towards the practical enslavement of the natives.

But the undisciplined and spirited character of the Spaniard requires a firmer government than the unsteady rule which Colón, always wavering between weakness and violence, gave them. A Castillian nobleman, Don Hernando de Guevara, "very handsome, and of noble mien, and he seemed to be of a generous cast," (3) was ordered back to Spain by Colón because "he would not be quiet." He obeyed—*rara avis*—and left for Xaraguá, in the hope of sailing with Hojeda, but arrived too late for this purpose and was allowed by Roldán to settle somewhere close to his cousin Adrian de Múxica. This handsome young man proved unable to resist the charm of Anacaona's daughter, Higueymota, and promptly annexed her in the direct way in which Christians did these things in Española—and in many other places before and since—though Guevara took care, of course, to ask for a priest so as to have all the Sacraments administered to the lady, except, we gather, marriage. Roldán was wroth, whether because he had his own ideas on the young Indian beauty, or for reasons of higher statesmanship. This led to the usual warp and woof of parleys and fights, the upshot of it all being that Roldán sent Guevara in chains to the Admiral, along with many reams of legal paper in which his misdemeanours were told at length. Muxica thought it his duty to rise against an authority which put his cousin in jail, and managed to do so with enough followers in a surprisingly short time. The Admiral, who had then by his side but seven or eight members of his household and three squires on the royal salary list, took the field, fell on the rebels unawares and caught Múxica alive. His blood was up. He had so often yielded that this time he would not have done so for worlds. He sentenced Múxica to be hanged there and then. A tragi-comic scene ensued, mostly tragic, yet with a comic side to its grim earnestness and deadly end. A confessor had, of course, been provided. Múxica would not confess. He shouted that fear of death made him forget his sins—a pretty conceit for a man under a capital sentence. Tired of waiting, Colón ordered him to be thrown down from the tower, and it was done.

The "style" had changed since Roldán had been bought back. It is fairly clear from the trend of events in Las Casas' narrative that the chief inspiration in this change came from Don Bartolomé. Ruthlessness was the word. The Colóns were meeting with a situation which they had, in part at least, created, and one of the most disquieting features of it may have been the number of jailbirds whom they themselves had brought over in their eagerness to develop the land. Kept as workers under discipline, they might have made good, and some did. But most of them found themselves powerful magnates set over Indians, owners of land, yet without the character required to wield so much power. By the year 1500 the Colóns, sure of Roldán, were trying to reduce the Spanish colony by a rule of terror as demoralising as their previous phase of weakness had been. At this moment their power came suddenly to a dramatic end.

* *

Students of the relations between Ferdinand and Isabel on the one hand and Colón on the other sometimes miss the main point which makes them clear: Ferdinand and Isabel were good statesmen. They made mistakes, of course; but they were unusually good statesmen for all that. There was one craft about which they needed no lessons from anybody—statecraft. Now, it so happens that it was the craft in which Colón was particularly deficient. The history of Colón's credit with the King and Queen proves that while the two rulers of Spain always liked him and admired his discovery and thanked him for it in words, honours and wealth, there is one thing about which they grew cooler and cooler, and then more and more anxious—his capacity for ruling the lands he had discovered.

Trouble began from the outset with the disastrous decision to leave forty men in Isabela. It grew with the reports which Margarite and Fray Buil brought during the second voyage. Neither Ferdinand nor Isabel were squeamish about firmness in those in authority. They knew only too well the terrible severity of the measures they had found necessary to reduce their realms to order and discipline. Moreover, the times were not soft. But from all they had heard they were entitled to suspect that Colón, and more especially Bartolomé, were inclined to excessive severity whenever circumstances allowed them the use of force. Nor were they rash in coming to such conclusions. Despite the credit which they attached to Buil's and Margarite's opinions, they kept unabated their confidence in their Viceroy, and he left for his third journey with his powers undiminished.

But he was still at sea when they received the report of the unseemly scene which had scandalised Seville, when he savagely beat and kicked Fonseca's agent, Ximeno. This incident is bound to have had a deep effect on the King and Queen. They were too experienced to accept at once all they were told even by their most trusted men; reports came that the Colóns were harsh and violent, but who could tell? Now here was a clear case, seen by many, on Spanish land, in which the Admiral had let himself go in an unmistakable way to personal violence. Rumour and reports, then, were true. This man was not fit to govern. "In my opinion," says Las Casas, "this was the main cause, coming on top of other complaints which went to Spain from here [. . .], why the King and Queen, indignant, decided to withhold the government from him." (4)

While the after-effects of this incident were still fermenting at Court, the five ships sent by Colón in the autumn of that same year (1498) arrived in Spain. They can hardly have improved his credit. Following his policy of procuring funds by the sale of slaves and of procuring slaves by waging war, he had trumped up a case against some Indians in order to be able to fill up his ships with human gold; (5) and he enclosed a letter in which his plan for exploiting this human gold-mine is put before the King and Queen in terms which make one wonder whether they are due to unfathomable hypocrisy or to unfathomable incoherence: "In the name of the Holy Trinity, from here we can send as many slaves as can be sold, and brazil-wood, and if I am well informed, we might sell 4000 [slaves] which would certainly be worth twenty million and 4000 hundredweight of brazil-wood worth as much, with about six millions here for expenses [. . .] here all that is needed to secure that income is that ships should come frequently to take away the things I mentioned. I believe that sea-folk will soon take the bait, for these masters and sailors are sailing back all wealthy and intent on returning to carry away slaves at 1500 maravedis apiece and feed them, [hoping] to be refunded from the first money they may get out of them; and though they [the Indians] may die at first, it will not be always so, for the same happened with blacks and Canary-islanders at first, [. . .] and the one who may survive will not be sold by his owner for love or money." (6)

This slave-policy was contrary to the repeated decisions of the King and Queen in matters of slavery. Ferdinand and Isabel were not taken in by Colón's stratagem of presenting his slave-trade as legitimate war booty. The King and Queen were open to the idea of slavery as long as the men in question remained in an outlandish, exotic context. In a chart of discovery granted to Rodrigo de Bastidas (June 5th, 1500) they were to claim one-fourth on all precious metals and "pearls, precious stones, gems, slaves, blacks, parrots, which in these our realms [to be discovered] may be found and reputed as slaves, monsters or serpents. [. . .]" (7) But they proved by word and deed that they did not want their Indian "vassals" to be slaves. On June 20th they ordered Pedro de Torres, brother of Antonio and of Don Juan's Aya, and *contino* of their household, to set at liberty the Indians who had been brought over to Andalucía and sold by order of the Admiral, and these Indians, or at any rate the paltry twenty-one who survived the hardships inflicted on them by man and climate, sym-bolically enough went back to Española with the man who super-seded Colón as Governor. (8) This policy was sincerely applied, —at any rate by the King and Queen—as shown by the fact that in 1503 (December 20th) the Queen sent an order to the Governor of Española, because, "owing to the great liberty which the Indians enjoy, they avoid and shun all communication and commerce with the Christians, so that even when offered salaries, they refuse to work and go about vagrant," and she decides that they are to be made to work, but that the Governor is to see that they get a fair salary and are well treated "as free persons, which they are, and not as serfs." (9)

It is sheer prejudice or waste of time to read any hypocrisy in this royal order. The problem of labour at the frontier of two races was—and still is—baffling in the extreme. The Queen could not be expected to solve it. She gave it, not a hypocritical, but an inexperienced and possibly a naïve solution, considering the human raw material—very raw indeed—which she had to handle to build up her West Indian Empire. There can be no better proof of her sincerity than these words from her own testament, written under the shadow of death: "I entreat the King my lord most affectionately, and I charge and order the said Princess my daughter and the said Prince her husband, [. . .] that they do not consent nor give occasion for the Indian natives and inhabitants of the said Indies and mainland, won and to be won, to receive any injury in their persons and property; and I order that they may be well and justly treated. And if they have received any injury that it be remedied and seen to." (10)

The constancy of this royal tradition is confirmed by a stiff letter which King Ferdinand wrote on February 23rd, 1512, to Don Diego Colón, son and heir of the Admiral. He explains how in older days the Crown was not able to keep well informed of events in the Indies, but he adds: "Now, since, thanks to our Lord, I can handle the affairs of the Indies as those of Castille [. . .] the inhabitants and natives of that island must be considered as vassals and not as slaves, as they were held in past days." (11)

Enough has been said to show that the arrival of a cargo of Indians in Spain—six hundred of them, and two hundred for each master in payment of the freight—having crossed the ocean in the stifling hot hulls of the ships, under most inhuman conditions, must have produced a deplorable effect at Court, for it is difficult to see why Fonseca should keep silent about it.

Moreover, along with the famous pearls and the map of Paria, came the first reports of Roldán's rebellion, as told by the Admiral, but also as told by Roldán and, it is only reasonable to assume, as told by more than one detached and neutral observer. This revelation was no doubt crucial in the evolution of the royal attitude towards Colón. "Good enough for Admiral; not good for Viceroy," the King and Queen must have thought. His story, as summed up by Las Casas, (12) could hardly appeal as a coherent and vigorous report to the spirited monarchs; it was a tale of disorder, weakness and failure interspersed with whines and complaints, and suddenly a threat of violence which would confirm the King and Queen's worst fears as to Colón's incapacity to handle force. (13)

This dismal story tallied only too well with the complaints from Española against the three Colóns; they were accused of harshness and cruelty in the administration of the Spaniards who had gone on a salary list; of a refusal to provide supplies to those who displeased them; and of a selfish policy with regard to the grants of Indians for work. Many ex-settlers with claims against the Colóns gathered at Court and importuned King Ferdinand with their complaints, while hurling insults at Don Diego and Don Fernando, then pages to the Queen, if they happened to pass by: "There go the Admiral's sons, the mosquitoes of the man who found lands of vanity and deceit, which are the tomb and misery of the Castillians." (14)

Reluctantly, it would seem, if one is to judge by the slowness of the process, the King and Queen came to the conclusion that grave decisions had to be taken. They entered this road by gradual steps, the first of which was suggested by Colón himself. In his letter sent in October 1498, he asked for a learned man to administer justice out there. This seems to have been the first idea of Ferdinand and Isabel. They chose, says Oviedo, "a gentleman, an old member of the royal household, a man very honest and religious, named Francisco de Bobadilla, knight of the military order of Calatrava." Las Casas' report is no less flattering: "He must have been a simple and humble man by nature and character; I never heard him accused of any dishonest thing or anything savouring of cupidity, in those days when he was discussed daily ; on the contrary, all spoke well of him." "A great gentleman, and loved by all," writes Bernáldez. (15)

This was the man chosen by the King and Queen for a task which they knew to be delicate and which, as time was to show, they wished to see carried out with the utmost tact and deference towards Colón. The powers given him at first were strictly limited to a judicial enquiry into the rebellion against the Admiral and the punishment of the rebels. The Admiral was required to lend him all the help he might need. This provision is dated Madrid, March 21st, 1499.

Another batch of letters from Española, more disquieting than the first, led the King and Queen to take one step more, and a serious one this time for Colón: on May 21st, 1499, Bobadilla is appointed Governor and Chief Magistrate of Española, by letters patent in which no mention whatever is made of the two men who held three public functions of a similar character—Don Cristóbal, who was both Viceroy and Governor; and Don Bartolomé, who was Adelantado. The letters empower Bobadilla to decide whether any of the "gentlemen and other persons" in Española should be sent back to Spain, and set no restriction whatever on the persons who might be the object of such a decision; he is granted full powers to act forthwith in this sense, should he deem it necessary. On the same date, a royal letter addressed to "Don Cristóbal Colón, our Admiral of the Ocean Sea and of all the Islands and Mainland of the Indies," with a discreet omission of the other two titles of Viceroy and Governor, addressed also to "the brothers of the said Admiral" with no mention of the title of Adelantado, summons them and all other persons to surrender all forts, houses, ships, arms, munitions, supplies, houses, cattle and other things belonging to Their Highnesses to Francisco de Bobadilla. And on May 26th, Bobadilla is given a short letter of credence addressed to Colón, written in the most general terms, and asking Colón "to believe him and do what he says." (16)

These papers might be considered the legal armament of Bobadilla, ready and furbished in case it should be needed. Yet time went by and Bobadilla did not sail. The whole summer and the whole autumn of 1499 elapsed and the King and Queen waited for better news, resisting the pressure of Colón's critics who, no doubt, would urge them to strike, for, says Las Casas, "as they were sending [someone] to depose the Admiral from his State and Government, a big step to be sure, bearing in mind how much they owed him, and he deserved, for his great work, they wished to consider it carefully and were reluctant to do it." (17) The King and Queen settled for a time in Seville. It so happened that at this time the two caravels sent by Colón arrived in Seville. Ballester and Garcia Barrantes, entrusted by the Admiral with his papers and briefed by him to put his case to the King and Queen, must have had a difficult task. Colón's case was not good. His own way of putting it was deplorable, since in the letters which his two friends brought over, the King and Queen were asked to undo by force what he had done half in weakness, half in guile. The sights offered to the town by the caravels were by no means of a nature to improve the position; showy, ostentatious ex-settlers disembarked with slaves of their own, including young women pregnant or with little half-castes in their arms; slaves for sale—what remained, after the cruel crossing—completed the lamentable spectacle. The King and Queen must indeed have been "indignant" as Las Casas says. To crown it all, reports of disloyalty on Colón's part and of his readiness to hand over the island to a foreign nation thickened dangerously. It is difficult to form an opinion on this grave accusation, which seems to have centred round an alleged agreement with the Genoese. Reasons for accepting it are not lacking; here are some: first, the very persistence of the accusation, part of a handful *which happened all to be true*; then, the significant words of Oviedo, a well-informed and detached historian, who, writing shortly afterwards on the reasons for Colón's downfall, says: "the most true, that is to say, the gravest, remained hidden because the King and Queen preferred to see the Admiral amended rather than ill-treated"; (18) Colón's defiance against Bobadilla, even after he knew that the new Governor's powers came from the King and Queen; the King and Queen, who were in a position to be well informed, seem to have given credence to the accusation, for not only did they deprive him of the government of the Indies, but they insisted on the condition that any representatives of Colón there should in future be Spanish born; (19) finally, there is a curious statement in a document on the question of Indian labour, without date or signature, believed to have been sent to Cardinal Cisneros by a Jeromite father towards 1517; in the first paragraph of this document one reads the following bald affirmation, addressed, be it remembered, to the man who had been practically the Spanish Prime Minister for the last twenty years: "In the Indies [. . .] there have been and there are grave discords and damages, which began in the times of the Admiral Colón who discovered them, owing to the agreement he made with the Genoese, as a result of which Commander Bobadilla was sent as a governor." (20)

This set of facts and documents is most impressive; but there are strong reasons also for the view that even if Colón ever thought of such a thing, which is possible, he did not go so far as to meddle in disloyal actions. There is force in the argument which he himself put forward in self-defence, notably in his letter to the Prince's Aya: "Little as I know, I do not know of anyone who would believe me so poor-witted as not to realise that I could not keep these Indies, even if they were mine, without the backing of a Prince; if this be so, where could I find better help and security against being turned out of them, than in the King and Queen our sovereigns, who from nothing have raised me to so much honour and who are the most powerful princes of the world on land and sea?" (21)

And as a matter of fact, no other trace has been found of this alleged treason, either in Genoa or in Spain; though, of course, documents bearing on it may have disappeared with the whole proceedings of the Bobadilla enquiry, probably "mislaid" by officials of the Crown bought by Don Diego Colón soon after his father's death. (22) The matter must remain in suspense, one of the many unsolved mysteries of Colón's life, pending further documentary discoveries, if ever they should be forthcoming.

Yet, *justified or not*, this accusation is in itself a valuable indication of the way Colón struck his contemporaries. His magnificence, his pride, his tendency to exact privileges often exorbitant, even from monarchs the most jealous of their prerogatives which Spain had ever known; his exclusiveness within a narrow circle, limited almost to his blood relations, all this group of egotistical tendencies made up the natural stem on which his treason, whether real or imaginary, was grafted. It is this natural, this only too real stem which explains that in the end, genuinely alarmed, the King and Queen dispatched Bobadilla to supersede him.

CHAPTER XXVIII

RETURN HOME IN IRONS

ONE Sunday, August 23rd, 1500, Don Diego Colón, brother of the Admiral, saw two caravels cruising to and fro off the harbour of Santo Domingo, waiting for a favourable wind to come to port. It was seven or eight in the morning and he knew, like everybody else in town, that till ten or eleven the wind blowing off land would not change and enable the two sails to find rest and shelter. He was alone in the town, i.e. without either of his two brothers; Don Cristóbal was in Concepción, dealing somewhat summarily with his Christian adversaries; Don Bartolomé was in Xaraguá with Francisco Roldán, putting down the conspiracy which had disquieted that district as a sequel to the amorous adventure of Don Hernando de Guevara. Every now and then one or other of his military brothers sent poor clerical-minded Don Diego a batch of prisoners with strict injunctions to have them hanged without loss of time. And Don Diego, finding that one gallows was not enough, had erected two, one at each end of the town.

Don Diego was very curious to know who was coming in those caravels, and in particular whether his young nephew was in one of them, for the Colón clan was in need of reinforcements. Without waiting for the sea-wind, he sent out a canoe with three Christians—apart from the Indian oarsmen—one of whom was Cristóbal Rodriguez, nicknamed "The Tongue," because he was the first who had mastered the Indian language. The caravels were about four miles out. One of them answered to the not very elegant name of *La Gorda* (*The Fat One*); the other, no less modest, allowed itself to be called *La Antigua* (*The Ancient One*). When The Tongue and his companions were within speaking distance of *The Fat One*, Commander Bobadilla came out in person and explained that he was sent as an Enquirer into the rebellion. Andrés Martín, master of the ship, asked them for news of the island and The Tongue wagged to inform them that seven Spaniards had been hanged that week and five more were waiting to be hanged, including Don

346

Hernando de Guevara, Pedro Riquelme and others. The Commander (Bobadilla) asked if the Admiral and his brothers were in the town and The Tongue said that the Admiral was in Concepción and the Adelantado in Xaraguá, pursuing the rebels to arrest and hang them, for which purpose each had a confessor in his train. The Tongue then passed from the informative to the interrogative mood and asked the Enquirer what his name was and "who was he to say he was," and the Enquirer answered that his name was Francisco de Bobadilla—whereupon the canoe came back to Santo Domingo with The Tongue on board.

The town was agog; those on the salary list particularly, not having been paid, and suffering great need of food and clothes, were overjoyed. Presently the wind changed, the caravels sailed in and the first thing they saw were the two gallows "with two Christians still fresh hanged but a few days earlier. Everybody came and went, with bows and courtesies towards the Enquirer, but always cautiously till they saw what world came on top." (1) Bobadilla gave himself the whole day for reflection, and also no doubt to allow the Colóns time to take their own measures and be ready to receive him and hear what he had to say.

On Monday, August 24th, Bobadilla went to mass with all his men. There he met Don Diego, acting Governor, and Rodrigo Pérez, Alcalde Mayor. The mass over, Bobadilla, at the door of the church and in the presence of all these persons and of practically the whole town, had his Notary Public read the first of the royal letters patent, that in which he was appointed Enquirer into the rebellion. He went no further. This, of course, left Colón's authority intact. But on the strength of this first document alone, he summoned Don Diego to hand over all prisoners to him. Don Diego demurred. "The Admiral was away; he (Don Diego) had no powers; the letters patent which the Admiral had overruled those Bobadilla brought." Don Diego asked to have an official copy of Bobadilla's powers. Faced with this obstruction, Bobadilla, somewhat shrewdly, retorted that if Don Diego had no powers to hand over the prisoners, he could not have powers to demand a copy of his own. Had Don Diego handed over the prisoners there and then, Bobadilla might have struck a working agreement with the Viceroy and avoided graver events.

But next day, in view of Don Diego's refusal, Bobadilla thought it necessary to bring out his bigger gun. He went to mass again, and everybody else as well, " for," as Las Casas pawkily remarks, "in those days everybody felt great devotion to hear and see new happenings"; (2) and after mass, in front of the church, he made his Notary Public read the letters patent by which he was appointed Governor. Whereupon he took the oath and then summoned Don Diego Colón and Rodrigo Pérez to hand over the prisoners and the proceedings referring to them. He met with the same obstruction as on the preceding day, and so, without allowing the crowd to disperse, he had two more royal orders read, that in which all fortresses and arms were to be handed over to him; and another, signed a few days before his departure, in which he was instructed to pay those whose salaries were due, charging the amount to the sums held in the island on the royal account or on Colón's account, according to the cases concerned.

This last document brought out the best loyalty from many a hungry body and naked breast. Yet a third summons met with a third refusal on the part of Don Diego and his Alcalde Mayor. Thereupon Bobadilla, with his troops and many new-loyal volunteers, went to the fortress and after trying in vain to obtain by parley from its Alcalde or captain what Don Diego had refused him, broke in and took possession of the prisoners by force.

The Admiral heard of these events and, apparently thinking at first that it might well be such another adventure as that of Hojeda, instructed some of the friendly Indians to have troops ready for him, and came from Concepción to Bonao. While there, he received an "Alcalde with a stick"; the "stick" was the symbol of the judicial and military authority of the Alcaldes of Spain. This magistrate, whose "stick" came from Bobadilla, informed Colón verbally of the arrival of the new Governor and handed him copies of all the letters patent on which the new authority rested. Here, Bobadilla seems to have made his first mistake: he did not write to the Admiral, while he did write to Roldán, who was in Xaraguá.

Colón tried to compromise by explaining that he remained Viceroy and Governor-General, while Bobadilla came to administer justice and no more—his own initial idea. But Bobadilla sent him Father Juan de Trasierra and the King's Treasurer Velázquez, to show him the short letter of credence which could only be understood as a mark of complete and unlimited delegation of royal authority in favour of Bobadilla and over Colón. We have the Admiral's own statement as proof of the fact that, in spite of this paper, he tried to obstruct the new Governor:

"I published by word of mouth and by letters that Bobadilla could not use his provisions because mine were the stronger." (3) But we possess also another document bearing on this episode, which confirms the rebellious mood of Colón and adds a detail worth some attention. "They say," writes Peter Martyr, "that the new Governor has sent the King and Queen letters written by the Admiral in unknown characters, in which he warned and advised his brother the Adelantado, who was away, to come with armed forces to defend him against any affront in case the Governor intended to attack him by violence." (4) What unknown characters were these? No one seems to have raised that question. Neither Colón nor his brother knew any non-Latin language. It is not likely that they had made up a code *ad hoc*. Is it possible to surmise that they had—as a family tradition— some form of Hebrew cursive script? It is well known that in some Spanish-Jewish colonies newspapers are published in Spanish, though written in Jewish script, which justifies the assumption that the Colón family might have kept some knowledge of Hebrew script while knowing no Hebrew. Spanish, after Hebrew, was for a long time almost a ritual language with the Jews. Evidently a normal Jewish script would have been dangerous for Colón and his brother to use; but a more or less illegible cursive hand in Hebrew characters would have been quite safe, particularly as, even if recognised by some official of the Crown, such an official would be sure to keep quiet about a knowledge which would have been as dangerous for him to possess as for Colón.

These "unknown characters" (5) may therefore be added to the numerous suggestions, signs and peculiarities which, without actually providing proof, strengthen several other reasons of more substance and weight pointing to the conclusion that the Colóns were of Jewish origin.

Leaving aside this aspect of the question, the fact reported by Peter Martyr confirms the rebellious attitude which Colón had taken up from the first. After the visit of Father Trasierra and of Velázquez, he decided to come to Santo Domingo, rather belatedly, it would seem, for a Viceroy who knew that an important *official* change has taken place in his capital. On September 15th, 1500, Bobadilla formally notified Colón of the letters patent appointing him Governor. The Admiral answered that he had letters to the contrary from their Highnesses, and that therefore he "asked as a favour and demanded that the Commander should respect his letters." (6) Colón therefore stood on the ground that he was Governor by privilege and that the King and Queen could not deprive him of his position. He was in fact aiming at the King and Queen through their emissary. Bobadilla then struck hard: he arrested both Don Cristóbal and Don Diego Colón and put them in fetters. We possess only Las Casas' version on this step. It is a most scathing condemnation of Bobadilla's action. In the absence of any proof—which may have existed—that the step was necessary, it does seem at first singularly harsh. Yet there is something to be said for Bobadilla. He had evidently been told to keep his eyes open and to be ready for all emergencies. He had been given powers to seize, hold and send to Spain anyone, *without any exception whatsoever*, whom he thought necessary to get rid of, a provision which clearly shows that the King and Queen did envisage the possibility of Colón's arrest and exile from his fief; he had been warned to look out for signs of cruelty to Spaniards (not, as Las Casas rightly complains, towards Indians) on the part of the three brothers, and the first thing he saw *before landing* was the two gallows with the two "fresh" hanged men; and he knew that Colón had instructed his Indian allies to be ready to fall on Santo Domingo. This is a fairly formidable picture to have in one's mind when a mere Don Diego makes bold to resist the letters patent of the King and Queen. And if the irons do remain perhaps an unnecessary and harsh touch, the imprisonment of the three Colóns would appear, in the circumstances, entirely justified.

Having secured both the Admiral and his brother, the Governor bade the Admiral write to the Adelantado, who in Xaraguá "had sixteen Spaniards in a ditch or well, waiting to be hanged," (7) to suspend all action and to return. The Admiral did so, adding that the Adelantado should not worry about his being in prison because they would all go to Castille and the King and Queen would put a remedy to everything. Don Bartolomé arrived in Santo Domingo and was promptly sent to the fortress and put in irons like his brothers.

This was the time of bitterest humiliation for the three proud brothers. As usual in such cases, the ingratitude of the low souls showed its ugly face. No one would put the iron fetters on the Admiral's feet. Reverence and compassion prevented everyone present from moving. His own cook did it "and with as saucy a front as if he were serving him new and precious dishes." (8)

One day when Colón was in his jail, brooding over his misery, asking of the Lord what it all meant, Alonso de Vallejo, an *hidalgo*, a "straightforward person," stepped in and requested the Admiral to come with him to the caravel. The Admiral, "with aggrieved countenance and deep sadness, which plainly showed the vehemence of his fear, asked: 'Vallejo, where are you taking me?' 'Sir,' he answered, 'Your Lordship is now going to the ship, to embark.' The Admiral, in doubt, asked again: 'Vallejo, is it true?' Vallejo answered: 'By your Lordship's life, it is true, that you are going to embark.'"

And it had to be. For had not Don Quixote de la Mancha come home a prisoner in a wooden cage? How could Don Cristóbal de Cipango come home but in the jail in which reality encloses all those knights who do not respect it? Listen to these words which he wrote on board ship to the Aya, with his irons on his feet, and his crown of illusions on his head, these words in which one seems to hear the very voice of the knight of La Mancha: "I must be judged as a Captain who from long ago until today has carried his arms on his shoulders without laying them down for one hour; and by knights of conquest and usage, not of letters, save if they be Greeks or Romans, or other modern ones of which there are so many and so noble in Spain, for otherwise I receive a great affront." (9)

So one day of October 1500, just eight years from that day—also of October—when he had discovered Guanahani, Don Cristóbal de Cipango left for Spain in irons, like a criminal. "If I had stolen the Indies [. . .] and given them to the Moors, I could not meet with more enmity in Spain," (10) he wrote in his cabin. Alonso de Vallejo was in charge of the prisoners and of the voluminous papers in which their guilt was established by Bobadilla. This Vallejo belonged to the household of a Sevillian nobleman, Gonzalo Gómez de Cervantes, (11) who was an uncle of Bishop Fonseca, a circumstance which Las Casas, not unreasonably, considers as a sign of the personal interest which the bishop in charge of Indian affairs took in the proceedings. But if that be so, either Fonseca was not the inveterate enemy of Colón which a stubborn tradition maintains, or Vallejo showed a remarkable independence of judgment and behaviour, for both he and Andrés Martín, the master of the caravel, treated the prisoners with due deference and respect, and made every effort to allow them full freedom on board.

Colón, however, would not accept any favours. When Vallejo and Martín came to undo his irons, he opposed a firm refusal. He had been put in fetters by order of the King and Queen; nothing short of another royal order could deliver him. This attitude was, of course, in keeping with his usual style. When he had returned to Spain from his second voyage, he had appeared before the astonished Sevillians in Franciscan garb; now, he would appear before the astonished Gaditans dragging his iron chains—a fit payment for the chains of gold which he had hung round the necks of Castille and Aragon! That insolent cook and his garlic-smelling hands were but menial instruments: his irons had been locked round his ankles by the hands of Ferdinand and Isabel. Let those royal hands undo what they had done. He could afford to wait.

He had come to serve them and he had given such service as had never been seen or heard of. He had been made by the Lord the messenger of the new heaven and the new earth of which He spoke through St. John in the Apocalypse, and through Isaiah in the Old Testament; and the Lord had shown him the way thereto; he had wasted seven years trying to make the incredulous see this; he had spent nine years—or was it eight, they did seem nine!—in achieving most outstanding things and worthy of memory. And now, there was no man so low that he dare not insult him. St. Peter and the twelve apostles, burning in the Holy Spirit, had also fought down here and had also suffered similar hardships, but in the end they triumphed in victory. . . . Those pearls! . . . Those pearls! . . . He had sent them to cheer their hearts, so that they should see the splendour of the discovery; but neither pearls nor gold would make them see the light. The pearls just tempted them. That Hojeda. . . . And then Vicente Yáñez too. . . . And Adrián de Múxica! That one, anyhow, had found his condign punishment. . . .

The days followed the nights and the nights followed the days and the Admiral-in-irons revolved his meditations through his perennial sleeplessness, kept awake this time not by duty, as he so often had been on deck, but by grief. He, discoverer of Española, was exiled from that land, which was his and which he could have given to whomsoever he wished, by the authority of that King and that Queen to whom he had given them. He, who had unchained the shackles of the ocean, he crossed in chains that ocean which he had liberated. The slanders of the discontented had outweighed his services to the Crown. What if he had been remiss in paying their salaries? That could have been easily remedied. He had six hundred thousand maravedis untouched and his third on the gold mines, all available for the purpose.

This thought disquieted him, for there was nothing to be said for his policy of withholding salaries from those who were entitled to them. But he trusted that the King and Queen would believe that his errors had been committed in good faith. And in the end, God would judge them all. (12)

Colón was ever ready to rely on the Lord but never averse to lending the Lord a helping hand in all that concerned him personally. This time, the very depth and infamy of his position was—he knew—his best defence. Bobadilla had over-shot the mark and enabled Colón to surpass himself in the art and craft of humility, of which he was a past master. As a sign of humility, iron fetters were decidedly better than Franciscan clothes.

Towards the end of November they arrived in Cádiz. (13) Colón had remained in irons the whole way. These irons had become his pride, his glory, his most prized possession. He had them always with him and wished them to be buried with him. But meanwhile, they were going to be the instruments of his recovery. He had so far conquered Andrés Martín, the master of *La Gorda*, that with the help of this friendly sailor, he was able to send a servant of his with letters for his friends at Court, and in particular for the Aya of Prince Don Juan, in which he put his case along with many of the complaints and religious yearnings which had occupied his mind during the crossing. In this way he stole a march on Bobadilla and moved the King and Queen before they had been informed.

Ferdinand and Isabel were in Granada. When they heard that Colón was in prison, they were greatly shocked. They ordered him to be set free, and sent money—two thousand ducats, says Las Casas—to enable him and his brothers to come to Court on a footing worthy of their rank. The Colóns arrived in Granada on December 17th, 1500. When they found them-selves in the presence of the King and Queen, the Admiral stood speechless for a while, tongue-tied by his deep emotion; then he sank to his knees and burst into tears and sobs; the King and Queen made him stand up; he recovered on hearing the friendly tone of voice of Ferdinand and Isabel, and spoke at length to assure them of his loyalty and to explain that his errors had been committed in good faith. (14)

Don Bartolomé would neither weep nor kneel. He reminded the King and Queen that he was abroad when the discovery was made, and that he had been asked by his brother to come and work in Castille because he would rise in honour and gain; which, on his arrival, their Highnesses had confirmed to him by their letters; that he had given to this conquest seven years, during five of which he could swear he had not slept in a bed nor undressed, always with death by his side, and now, the service done, he was put in irons and deprived of his honour; and he asked to be paid his salary; he offered his services to the King and Queen if wanted, for otherwise he was in a position to provide for himself. (15)

The contrast between the two men could not be clearer. Don Bartolomé was an adventurer and nothing more. He had come to Spain from France because he thought there was money and honour in it. If he were wanted, he would stay; if he were not, he would go. He was not worried about his future. He was thirty-nine; he was able, strong and brave, and he knew enough of the Indies and of discovery in general to rise to the top wherever he went. His feet were on the ground, his head was on his shoulders, and he never allowed his dreams to rise higher than his straight, steely eyes. Don Cristóbal was not of so metallic a composition. There was more of the ocean and of the sky in his fluid and stormy soul. His head was in the clouds and even his feet were more at home on the rolling decks of caravels than on the tracks of mother earth or on the polished floors of princely houses. He saw visions and he heard voices. In his tense heart, he felt the unbearable pull of the imaginative passions—ambition, envy, resentment, vindictiveness, but above all, power, power over the world. This King and this Queen were his friends, but his friends from above. He loved them with a passionate hatred. He bowed before them, he knelt before them with infinite pride. While his body bent and fell at their feet, his soul rose triumphant over their heads in dreams of victory. He wept and sobbed, not from grief or repentance, but from sheer helplessness before their might, and while he sank, weak and dejected at their feet, his intimate demon, deep down under the storm, worked, dry-eyed and assiduous, to build his greatness anew on the solid foundations of the royal pity. Broken and insulted, the Admiral-Viceroy would rise again and conquer all his enemies.

This generous reception by the King and Queen has misled many a biographer of Colón into believing that Ferdinand and Isabel disapproved of Bobadilla's doings and disagreed with his findings. But there is abundant evidence to show that this was not the case. Courtesy, gratitude, the natural generosity of great potentates toward a subject who, after achieving outstanding deeds, had lapsed into grave errors, all these fairly obvious feelings would suffice to justify the affable attitude of the monarchs towards a man, moreover, of singular grace and appeal. But there was quite a distance between the heart and the brain of the two rulers of Castille-Aragon, and all these personal considerations did not in the least affect the royal *opinion* on Colón's rule in Española. It was definitely unfavourable.

There is no lack of documentary evidence to that effect: Bobadilla had confiscated the property of Colón and of his brothers in Española, a fact against which the Admiral and his son Fernando vehemently protest. But the King and Queen approve this measure in so far as it concerns the wealth acquired by them as Governors, and decide that this property must be retained, that the salaries owed by the Admiral must have a first claim on this sum, and that the remainder must go nine-tenths to the Crown, one-tenth to the brothers Colón. (16)

All the contemporary historians hold views on Bobadilla which are distinctly favourable. Oviedo says, that when "the King and Queen removed him from his post as Governor, they gave him permission to return to Spain, holding themselves well served by him during the time he had been here, for he had fulfilled his duties justly and as a good gentleman in all that pertained to his charge." (17) The Franciscan friars who accompanied him on his way out, and who came fresh from Spain and free from prejudice on local affairs—one of them was a Frenchman—all sided with him in their reading of the facts and are most eloquent in their advice to Cisneros against the return of any of the Colóns to Española. Father Deledeulle wrote to the Cardinal on October 12th, 1500, that "the Admiral and his brothers tried to revolt and to put themselves on the defensive, rallying Indians and Christians"; Father Juan de Robles begged the Cardinal, "for love of our Lord Jesus Christ [. . .], to work so that neither the Admiral nor anything belonging to him ever returns to this land"; Father Juan de Trasierra provides the most interesting comment: "For God's sake," he writes to the Cardinal, "since your reverence has been the occasion [. . .] for freeing this land from the sway of King Pharaoh, see that neither he nor any of his nation ever come to these islands." These lines are rich in news. They provide the information that Colón's disgrace originated with the powerful Cardinal-Prime Minister, a fact confirmed by a tale to be found at the end of Father Deledeulle's letter: "I report to your Lordship that the Admiral, speaking with my companion twenty leagues away from the harbour, told him amongst other things that though the Archbishop of Toledo had said that he would not return, he *would* return." Now Cisneros was not Fonseca. He bore no grudge against Colón; he was above ambition and vanity. And the fact that Colón had managed to bring this disinterested and public-spirited man round to so firm a decision against him would appear to confirm in a striking way the general impression that his removal from the Government of Española was a decision demanded from the reluctant monarchs by the failure of the Admiral as Governor-General of the discovered lands. (18)

But there are other proofs. The first is the policy thereafter followed by the King and Queen; for though they gave back to Colón all his honours and privileges, they did not allow him again either to govern in the Indies or to set foot in Española. Finally, there is a most outspoken statement of King Ferdinand himself in a letter, already quoted, to the Admiral's son and heir, Don Diego: "For when the Queen and I sent him [Ovando] as Governor of that island owing to the failure of your father in that charge which you now hold, it was all in revolt and lost and profitless." (19)

The matter can no longer be disputed. The fall of Colón was by no means an act of royal machiavellism, ingratitude or intrigue; it was an act of elementary prudence in the face of patent failure on the part of Colón and of his two brothers. This conclusion stands, even when due weight is given to the exceptional—indeed, the unique—difficulties of the task which confronted them, some of which, moreover, were of their own creating.

But there is one word in Father Trasierra's letter which must arrest the observant reader. "King Pharaoh," he calls the Admiral. *Faraones* was then in the island the nickname of the brothers Colón. No one seems to have been struck by this fact. The word has a special significance, particularly from the pen of a Franciscan friar. For we know that the Franciscan friars were the keenest advocates of anti-semitism, and that the chief anti-semitic pamphlet of the century, the *Coplas del Provincial*, was a Franciscan concoction. Now, if we turn to the famous *Coplas*, we find the following verse which is significant enough:

> " A tí frayle Bujarron,
> Alvaro Perez Orozco,
> En la nariz te conosco
> Por ser de los de Pharon."

" You, Friar Bujarron, Alvarez Perez Orozco,
I know by your nose that you are one of Pharaoh's people."

This means that *faraón* was Franciscan slang for Jew. The accusation of *Converso* levelled against him by the Colony had stuck. The Colóns were considered as *Conversos* by their contemporaries, and the fact would appear to be patent enough to be thus hinted at in a letter to the Cardinal and Prime Minister, who was soon to become Grand Inquisitor of Spain.

CHAPTER XXIX

THE ADMIRAL TURNS TO PROPHECY AND STARTS ON HIS FOURTH VOYAGE

COLÓN was not slow to realise that his creative career was blocked by the solid opposition of the three most powerful figures of Spain: the King, the Queen and the Cardinal. But he was not a man to remain idle in the possession and enjoyment of his privileges and revenues. It often happens that men's characters are judged and imagined mostly on what they do, while all the rich gamut of omissions, as suggestive of the form of character as shadows are of the physical form, is simply passed over. This is a crucial moment in the life of Colón and one which should be given its due weight, particularly by those who see in him a greedy and avaricious man. He was not greedy and he was not avaricious. He knew the value of wealth and he attached a great importance to it. He sought to acquire it and in its pursuit he made mistakes of tact and ethics owing to his eager and impatient character; but Colón was not essentially and ultimately attached to wealth; he wanted it as an instrument of power and glory; his ambition, though not saintly, was of a spiritual order; it was not saintly, because it was self-seeking; but it was spiritual, because it sought to fulfil itself on a plane higher than that of the flesh.

At this moment the King and Queen were confronted with a delicate problem: they had granted this upstart most exorbitant privileges; he was Viceroy and Governor-General of the Indies for life and the two posts were vested in his lineage; but, on the one hand, his discovery was revealing itself much vaster than ever he in his wildest dreams had dared to conceive; while, on the other, he was revealing himself a most imcompetent statesman to deal even with a tiny part of what, theoretically at least, was to be his vice-realm. It is silly and sentimental to accuse the King and Queen of breach of faith because they broke the Capitulations of Santa Fé, depriving Colón of his governorship; as if public affairs could be handled on the same principles of law as a sale of land. Ferdinand and Isabel could not have done better nor treated Colón more generously than they did, in view of the evidence before them. But precisely because of the necessity in

358

which they were of depriving him of his governorship, the King and Queen, who were anxious to please him otherwise, would have been ready to go very far in the way of favour and honours to the man who had given them an Empire. It is possible that their offer of a Marquisate with a vast strip of land in Española may have been made with this idea in mind. It is also possible—and it would be most in keeping with Colón's proud character—that his refusal may have been inspired less by the reason he gave than by his desire to keep his claims against the Crown intact—inner claims of glory and power, not merely outer claims of honour and wealth.

Colón was then forty-nine. If at this time of his life he had been willing to accept a position of golden idleness by the side of the King and Queen as the chief ornament of the Spanish Court, there is nothing that Ferdinand and Isabel would not have done to keep him out of the way of the Indies, honoured, pleased and harmless. But Colón was not made that way, and the fact that he did not accept this palatine retreat, as the Chief Exotic Popinjay in the Golden Cage of the Court, is never taken into account, because the mistakes that we do not make are never counted to our credit in our life. And yet it is significant enough that as soon as Colón realised that his Española days were over, he cast about for something else to do.

"About" is a manner of speaking. For a man such as Colón, reality is always in the inner world of his imagination. Colón looked inwards, into the vast world which he carried within, and he was not long in seeing there the other mission for which he thought himself chosen. He would liberate Jerusalem.

This was not a new idea with him. More than once, since that day in Baza when he had seen the embassy sent by the Great Sultan, he had mentioned it to the King and Queen and had even made them promise that the wealth of the Indies to be discovered should be devoted to the liberation of the House of Sion. He now came back to it with a new ardour. It was to be his outlet. While he rested in Granada, protected by the royal discretion against the legal effects of the papers sent by Bobadilla, he began to study the new plan.

He did not look up maps, nor did he trouble to gather information from merchants, sailors and ambassadors as to the strength of the Sultan's forces, the ports, the lines of supply. No, he read the prophets. And he set about at once to collect all the prophets who predicted that Jerusalem should be liberated, and by Spain. His main quest was always the matter of faith. Can we have faith in the enterprise? Yes? Then, let us do it. As he was soon to write to the King and Queen, sending them his Book of Prophecies: "St. Peter, when he jumped into the sea, walked on it as long as his faith was firm. He who would have as much faith as a grain of mustard seed would be obeyed by mountains. He who would have faith, let him ask and all shall be given him. Knock and it shall be opened unto you. No enterprise in the name of our Saviour must be feared if it be just and with a clean intention and in His holy service." So, why learn? Why pore over books? He had already said that, in the enterprise of the Indies, he had drawn no profit from "either reason, mathematics or world maps." Isaiah had foretold it and it was fulfilled. And now, he would apply the same method—prophecies—to the matter of Jerusalem, "in which enterprise, if there is faith, be sure of victory." (1)

This assurance in religious matters on the part of a layman, and in a letter to the King and Queen, must have struck them as most peculiar. But the doctrine on which it rested was more peculiar still; for Colón claimed that children and the innocent can reveal the spirit better than the learned, a truly evangelical doctrine, but one which did not savour of "Old Christian" orthodoxy—rather the reverse. This evangelical tendency towards essentials rather than forms and authority was characteristic of the *Converso* turn of mind. (2) The chief sentence in which Colón expounds this view in his letter to the King and Queen betrays the *Converso*; unorthodox, or, at any rate, bold in his orthodoxy, even in the way in which he brings in the Jews at once, as if subconsciously eager to break the monopoly of truth which the Christians believe they hold: "I say that the Holy Ghost works in Christians, Jews, Moors and all men of any other sect and not merely in the learned, but in the ignorant." (3) Far less bold statements than this were to lead *Conversos* to the stake during most of the sixteenth century. This view was revolutionary and a foretaste of the Reformation. Colón is, of course, unaware of the deep dogmatic and theological issues involved; he rushes in where angels will have their wings singed in the next generation. But he is already a protestant; and this particular flavour of his religious faith provides yet another indication of his Jewish origin.

Having put together the prophecies and texts which he considers relevant to the purpose, he writes to the King and Queen to urge them to take on this enterprise. His argument is relatively simple:

Both the Old and the New Testament foretell the end of the world. St. Augustine and others say the end will come during the seventh thousand of its years. Taking as a basis the reckoning made by Alfonso X, "which is held as the best," Colón believes that in 1501, when he is writing, the world is 6845 years old. It follows that the world has only 155 years to run. Now, our Redeemer said that before the end of the world all the prophecies would be fulfilled. But much remains to be done. That is why the Lord is hurrying the world on, as shown by the opening up of so many lands to the preaching of the Gospel. "The blessed Apostles quicken Me continually and with great haste." (4)

The central piece of this Book of Prophecies is the letter of Rabbi Samuel Jehudi, of Morocco, written in 1068, urging the Jews to be converted to the *law of Christianity*. It is preceded by a significant title: *Rabbi Samuel, in an Epistle or Letter translated from the Arabic into Castillian, sent by Rabbi Samuel of Israel, native of the city of Fis to Master Ysaach, Rabbi of the Synagogue of Morocco, who both were thereafter good and faithful Christians.* (5) What is this letter doing there? Is it not yet another of those subconscious returns of the Jew which occur so often in Colón? And does it not throw another sidelight on his urge to conquer Jerusalem, revealing his desire to rub out that *difference* by uniting Christians and Jews in one holy house? "And Jeremiah says again: *At that time they shall call Jerusalem the throne of the Lord: and all the nations shall be gathered unto it, to the name of the Lord, to Jerusalem; neither shall they walk any more after the imagination of their evil heart.*" (6) This seems to be a fixed idea with him. It recurs in at least two other passages in the book—a comment on St. John and a comment on Pope St. Gregory, in both of which, stress is laid on a church built by both Jews and Gentiles.

This document is followed by a number of quotations from the Bible, in which his prepossessed mind construes prophecies of the discovery of the Indies and of the liberation of Jerusalem. Isaiah is a frequent contributor: *And in that day there shall be a root of Jesse which shall stand for an ensign of the people: to it shall the Gentiles seek; and his rest shall be glorious. And it shall come to pass in that day that the Lord shall set His hand again the second time to recover the remnant of His people which shall be left, from Assyria, and from Egypt [. . .] and from the islands of the sea.* (7) And again: *Listen, O isles, unto Me, and hearken, ye people, from afar: [. . .] I will also give thee for a light to the Gentiles, that thou mayest be my salvation unto the end of the earth.* (8) *The Gentiles shall come unto Thee from the ends of the earth.* (9)

There is one item in this anthology of biblical texts and comments which deserves special attention. Colón is discussing Psalm II of David and reports that Rabbi Solomon, in his comments on this psalm, says that "our masters," i.e. Jewish rabbis, held it to apply to Christ. The whole discussion on which Colón enters here reveals a mind mainly centred on the *Converso* position —the man whose original faith has been Jewish and whose present faith is Christian. Thus, referring to Rabbi Solomon, he writes: "He calls heretics the *Conversos* from Judaism to the Catholic faith who reasoned against the others who had remained in their infidelity, on the basis of that psalm." And again: "Which is evident according to learned men converted from Judaism." (10)

It is always in this mental region that we find Colón: the border-line between the two faiths. The problem of the converted Jew, but also the problem of the Jew who remains unconverted. His mind is always watching the lost brethren, wondering whether they will ever follow him into the fold of the true faith, which he honestly and sincerely holds, yet with an inevitably Jewish flavour, with that sense of *promise*, of *mission*, and of *apocalyptical catastrophe* which the Jews took over and always take over into Christianity.

The Book of Prophecies was, in his mind, destined to be the material for a poem. This follows from a letter he wrote to Father Gorricio, requesting him to proceed with the work of selecting "authorities" as he has not the time to do it himself: "When I arrived, I began to select the authorities which seemed to me relevant [to Jerusalem] in order to come back to them later and put them in rhyme." (11) We may be certain that the poem would have been mediocre, if we are to judge by the samples of verse scattered in the Book of Prophecies. (12) Yet, at this time of his life, Colón had already developed a style truly magnificent when he was moved. This point will be discussed later. At any rate, the poem did not materialise because the would-be poet was called to other more pressing occupations.

It is not certain that the Book of Prophecies was ever actually submitted to the King and Queen. True, it contains the text of a letter to them. But this letter seems to be no more than a draft. It has no end and no date, and it goes no further than a vague advocacy of the enterprise which he had so much at heart. The letter lacks its spear-head, so to speak, and may never have reached the monarchs. The plan, moreover, does not seem to have materialised.

* *

The fact is that Colón was becoming restless for discovery. After all, Jerusalem for him was second-best to the Grand Khan. He knew that a crowd of "discoverers" was rushing through the gates of the ocean that he had burst open, and that all manner of strangers were intruding into his islands and mainland. He would have been inhumanly perfect if he had looked upon this spectacle without some bitterness. In 1499 Pero Alonso Niño and Cristóbal Guerra were allowed to cover very much the same ground as he had discovered on his third voyage. Hojeda had availed himself of Fonseca's protection to sail where he pleased —*pearlwards*, also. In June 1499 Rodrigo de Bastidas is granted a royal charter to go and "discover"; in July and August, capitulations are made with Alonso Vélez de Mendoza, to go with four ships to discover islands and mainland "outside that which has been discovered by Don Cristóbal Colón." Hojeda is given a second roving commission on July 28th, 1500, and a third one on June 8th, 1501, by his protector Fonseca. In the last of these, he is especially allowed to bring back thirty hundredweight of brazil-wood, ten being in compensation for a horse which the Admiral had taken from him "for the mares which are over there." The pearls brought by Niño, who had been Colón's flagship pilot on the first voyage, dazzled the Court. A number of clandestine expeditions no doubt sailed forth on their own, risking all for a plateful of pearls or a barrel of gold. On June 22nd, 1497, the King and Queen sign an ordinance directing their law officers to secure two ships armed and prepared by the Admiral for a voyage to the Indies, in which their shipmasters had sailed away without warning "to certain parts and voyages."

The foreigner is getting alive too, and Ferdinand's ambassadors in London are careful to warn the King of this suspect activity. "The King of England"—writes Ruy González de Puebla— "has sent five armed ships with another Genoese like Colón, in search of the Island of Brazil and the seven cities. They have supplies for a year. They are expected back in September. Considering the course they are taking, I find that what they are after is what Your Highnesses own." And the other ambassador, Pedro de Ayala, writes: "Those of Bristol have been arming two, three, four caravels, every year for the last seven years, in search of the Island of Brazil and the seven cities, owing to the phantasy of this Genoese. The King made up his mind to send him because last year he brought back an assurance that they had found land."

The "Genoese" here mentioned was no other than Cabot (this, incidentally, detracts from the value of many of the documents which describe Colón as a "Genoese," since Cabot was a Venetian). The King's answer to Puebla makes excellent reading, for it shows King Ferdinand's anxiety to keep Henry VII off his preserves. "As for what you say that one like Colón has come there to offer the King of England another enterprise like that of the Indies, without prejudice to Spain and Portugal, if he [Henry VII] fares as we have done in the matter of the Indies, he will have escaped unscathed. We believe this must be some agent of the King of France to divert the King of England from other business. See that the King of England is not deceived either in this or in similar ways, for the French will try to do it in every way they can. And these affairs are most unsafe and are better not undertaken nowadays [. . .] it is impossible to take a hand in this without injury to our interests or those ᶠ the King of Portugal." The anxiety revealed by this letter reappears in the instructions given to Hojeda in 1501: "to follow the coast which you discovered, and which, as it seems, runs east-west, because it goes towards the part in which the English are discovering, and to set up landmarks with the arms of Their Highnesses and other known signs which you may think fit, so that it be known that you have discovered that land, and to put a stop to [or forestall?] the discovery of the English in those parts." (13)

Everything we know of Colón's doings and character warrants the assumption that this news must have been poison to him. "They all made fun of my plan then; now even tailors wish to discover," (14) he was soon to write with a humour in which the trade of his own cousins in Genoa turns up unexpectedly, precisely when those cousins of his—tailors—had come to Spain to share in his glory. His possessive sense with regard to the Indies was so keen that he must have felt like a householder whose hearth and privacy are overrun by intruders and destroyers. This stay at Court can have been little else for him than a calvary of now patient, humble and entreating requests, now proud, ill-humoured and even exasperated demands that his rights be respected and his ocean given back to him. Fortunately, there were two factors in his favour. The first was that the King and Queen would on no account allow him to go back to Española and were therefore anxious to keep him busy elsewhere; (15) the second, that he struck on an idea which did appeal to the King and Queen—the search for a narrow passage across the new-discovered lands on to other seas.

Colón the forerunner of Magellan! The King and Queen could see nothing but advantages in this idea which would in any case keep Colón busy and, if successful, would put the quickest way to India under their control. They encouraged their Admiral to study the plan and promised their help towards its execution. Colón seized the opportunity to press forward his claims. He had by now obtained the withdrawal of Bobadilla. This well-meaning man had made a serious mistake in his administration—otherwise generally approved—of Española: he had granted the settlers freedom to collect gold for twenty years without having to refer to the Crown nor pay its dues. (16) This, along with the constant complaints of Colón and his brothers, seems to have brought the King and Queen to decide on a change. Their choice was Don Frey Nicolás de Ovando, a knight of the order of Alcántara. He was, says Las Casas, "a most wise man and worthy of governing many people, but not Indians [. . .], of average height, his beard very fair and red, he had and showed great authority; a lover of justice; he was most honest in his person and deeds, a very great enemy of cupidity and avarice, and not lacking in humility, which is the smalt of virtues: and not only did he show it in all his external acts, in his household, his table and attire, his public and private speech, in which he always maintained gravity and authority, but also in that when he was made a Chief Commander [of the Alcántara Order] he never allowed anyone to address him as 'Your Lordship.' " (17)

Ovando, appointed Governor on September 3rd, 1501, took over with him, as Alcalde Mayor, "a gentleman from Salamanca, a graduate, named Alonso Maldonado, a person very straight, wise, fond of doing justice and humane." (18) This description, from Las Casas' pen, would appear to suggest that Maldonado was a happy and a substantial improvement on Roldán. Thirty-two ships, two thousand five hundred men and twelve friars of St. Francis sailed with them from Sanlúcar, on February 13th, 1502; Antonio de Torres sailed as Captain-General of this large fleet. These changes were but a part of the process of reconstruction of his own fortunes in which Colón had been patiently engaged since he had landed in Cádiz. The King and Queen gave Ovando instructions to return to Colón and his brothers the personal property confiscated by Bobadilla; they instructed Ximeno to provide the Admiral with an account of the goods taken over to the Indies, so that he should be in a position to share one-eighth in the expenses and therefore to have one-eighth of the profit; and they authorised Colón to appoint a representative to check all commercial and gold-refining operations and to receive his tenth—a post of trust for which he chose Carvajal.

By October 1501, his affairs at Court were advanced enough for him to be able to leave for Seville to prepare his fourth expedition. He bought four ships of the kind he thought best for discovery—seventy to fifty *tonnels*, i.e. about sixty-three to forty-five tons—for he held that this tonnage was best for "discovery"; and he took over about one hundred and forty men. This deliberate choice on his part made his fourth expedition the most similar to his first in tonnage of ships and number of men, and would tend to show that the small size of his first expedition was not due merely to lack of backing and help. Amongst his companions he was taking over his brother Don Bartolomé, who sailed very much against his will; Don Diego he left behind, which was significant enough. But he took his son Fernando with him. The boy was just thirteen, but was unusually tall and brave for his age. The elder boy, Don Diego, then about twenty-one, was left behind to represent him and fight his battles at Court.

From Seville he wrote to the King and Queen: he wanted authority to call at some port of Española to get supplies and in case of emergency; he asked for two or three men knowing Arabic, "for he always was of opinion that, beyond this our mainland," says Las Casas, writing on American soil—"if he were to find a sea passage, he would find people of the Grand Khan." (19) He asked that his sons and brothers should be provided for. The King and Queen answered on March 14th, 1502, from Valencia de la Torre; they gave him full assurances about his family affairs and about his privileges; they were willing to give him his Arabic interpreters; but advised him not to tarry or waste time in looking for them; and they forbade him to go to Española on the way out, though they allowed him to call "in passing, and tarry little" on the way back. Finally, they urged him to leave as soon as possible. They gave him detailed instructions: most of them, the usual ones, now established by experience; but there are two new notes: one in which with much reiteration that his staff must obey him, he is told that he "must treat them as persons who go in our service," and the other, plainer still and final and blunt: "*and you must not bring back slaves.*" (20)

He sailed from Cádiz on May 9th, 1502.

* * *

"I was kept in Cádiz by the south-western until the Moors besieged Arcila," he writes from the Great Canary to Father Gorricio—"and thither, against it, I sailed to rescue." (21) But when he arrived before the city, the Moors had left, and the Admiral sent the Adelantado and the captains to offer his services to the Portuguese Commander, who was wounded, and who thanked him and offered to return the call in the company of some Portuguese gentlemen, amongst whom there were relations of Doña Felipa Muñiz, the wife of the Admiral. On May 20th the fleet was in the Canaries, and on the 25th they sailed forth. Colón struck a south-western course, and after a quick and happy crossing he cast anchor at the Matininó islands on June 15th. After three days' rest the Admiral fell into temptation and sailed straight for Santo Domingo. Ovando, with strict orders from the King and Queen, refused admittance, and Colón left for Puerto Hermoso, sixteen leagues west of Santo Domingo, where he sought shelter from a devastating storm.

His explanations are lamentable. One of his ships was "too spacious, and had not enough side to stand the sails"; (22) but it is obvious that, in his two crossings from Cádiz to Arcila and from Arcila to the Canaries, he had had plenty of time to find out that this one ship would not do. That the ship was dangerous was no doubt true, for he was anxious about it often enough during the rest of his stormy voyage. But all the facts point to the conclusion that he found this a convenient pretext to call at Española in the teeth of the repeated and insistent orders to the contrary from the King and Queen. Besides, he could easily have had the ship changed by sending one of his captains with her, while he waited in any of the islands available for the purpose.

The fact is that he found obedience irksome, and his inordinate pride revolted against the subjection to the King and Queen under which he remained. This state of mind, this inner, permanent revolt against the King and Queen, will become plain on reading his own description of the fourth voyage, given hereafter. Meanwhile, nature was preparing the most unexpected and spectacular satisfaction for his vindictive mind. The ships in which Ovando had sailed two months before him were in harbour waiting to leave for Spain. Bobadilla, Antonio de Torres and Roldán went on board the flagship with Guarionex in irons. There were on board one hundred thousand *Castillians* in gold for the Crown and as much again for private accounts. All was swallowed by a furious sea which destroyed twenty of the ships. Colón's enemies sank with the weight of gold they were conveying. (23)

Colón went on his way. After many dramatic vicissitudes, he found himself in Jamaica in July 1503. There, in deep agony of mind, but in great exaltation of spirit, he wrote to the King and Queen a letter so revealing, so vivid a portrait of the whole man, that this fourth voyage had better be read in his own vigorous, moving, and at times magnificent words.

CHAPTER XXX

COLÓN SPEAKS FOR HIMSELF (1)

MOST Serene, high and mighty Princes, King and Queen, our sovereigns: From Cádiz I went on to Canaria in four days, and hence to the Indies. (2) My intention was to hasten my voyage since I had my ships in good state, the people and the supplies [on board, or available] and my course was the Island of Jamaica; and in the Island of Dominica I wrote this; (3) up till then, the weather was all I could wish. That night when I entered there, I had a storm and a big one, and it has pursued me ever since. When I arrived close to Española, I sent the sack of letters and begged as a favour for a ship which I would pay for, for another one that I had was not seaworthy and did not hold the sails. They took the letters and for all I know they may have answered them. As for me, I was told not to come anywhere near land; the heart of my people sank for fear I should take them far away so that if they happened to be in any danger they would receive no help, rather might they receive an affront. Moreover, someone was pleased to say that the Commander [Bobadilla] would have the power to grant the lands which I would win. The storm was terrible, and during that night, it dismembered my ships; dragging each her way, with no hope but of death; each was certain the others were lost. Who was ever born, not excepting Job, who did not die in despair? [to think] that to save my life and my son's and brother's and friends', I should be barred access to the land and harbours which I, by the will of God, won for Spain with sweat of blood!

And I came back to the ships which the storm had taken away from me, leaving me by myself. Our Lord gave them back to me when He pleased. The unsafe ship (4) had tried to escape the storm as far as the Island La Gallega; she had lost her boat and most of the supplies; the one in which I sailed, marvellous bulky though she was, our Lord spared her for she did not lose a straw. In the unsafe one sailed my brother, and he, after God, was her saviour. And with this storm, really crawling, I arrived in Jamaica; there [the weather] shifted from strong sea to calm and to swift current, which led me to the Queen's Garden without ever seeing land. Thence, when I was able, I sailed towards the mainland, where I met with a wind and a terrible current against me; I fought against them for sixty days and in the end could not take more than seventy leagues out of them.

In all this time, I did not enter one single harbour, nor was I able to, nor was I left in peace by storms from the sky, rain, big thunder and lightning continuously, it seemed the end of the world. I arrived at Cape *Gracias a Dios* [Thanks to God] and from there our Lord gave me prosperous winds and currents. For eighty-eight days the frightful storm had not left me, so that I saw neither sun nor stars over the sea; the ships were split, the sails torn, the anchors, the rigging and the cables lost, as well as the boats and many supplies; the men very sick, all contrite and many having promised to enter a life of religion and none without vow of pilgrimage. Many times they had confessed each other. Other storms have been known but none which lasted so long and with so much frightfulness. Many felt downhearted often and often, whom we had thought courageous. The grief of the son I had on board wrenched my soul from me, the more so as I saw him so young, being thirteen, (5) in so great a hardship, and lasting so long; our Lord gave him so much courage that he quickened the others, and as for work, he did as much as if he had sailed eighty years, and he comforted me. I had fallen ill and had come many times to the point of death. From a small cabin I had had built on deck, I directed the course. My brother was in the worst ship and the most dangerous. Great was my grief and greater still because I had brought him over against his wish; for, such is my fate, that I have profited little by twenty years of service which I have served with so many hardships and dangers, for today I have not a tile in Castille; if I want to eat or sleep, I have no [place], save an inn or a tavern, and most times there is no wherewithal to pay for my share. Another sorrow wrenched my heart through my back, and this was Don Diego my son, whom I had left in Spain so orphan-like and so dispossessed of my honour and estate; even though I was certain that the King and Queen, being just and grateful, would return everything to him increased.

I arrived in Cariay (6) where I tarried to repair the ships and re-stock supplies and to give a respite to my men who were all very sick. I, who, as I said, had been so many times on the point of death, was told there of the gold-mines of Ciamba, which I was looking for. Two Indians took me to Carambaru, where people go about naked, with a gold mirror hanging from their necks, but they would neither sell nor barter it. They named many places on the sea-coast where they said there was gold, and mines, the last of which was Veragua, about twenty-five leagues away; I started with the intention of trying them all, and half-way there I learnt that there were mines two days on foot from where I was; I decided to send someone to see them on the eve of St. Simon and Judas, which day I had set for our departure: during that night there rose such a sea and such a wind that it was necessary to run wherever the wind wished, and the Indian guide to the mines still with me.

In all those places where I had been, I found that all I had heard did come true: this led me to believe what they say of the province of Ciguare, which they describe as lying nine walking days to the West by land: there, they say, there is infinite gold and the natives wear corals on their heads, bracelets made of it round their ankles and wrists, very thick, and with it they decorate and cover chairs, boxes and tables. They also say that women there wear necklaces hanging from the head down their backs. In all this, everybody in these parts is agreed and says so much that I would be content with one-tenth. They also know pepper. In Ciguare they deal in fairs and goods; so these people tell me and they showed me the way commerce takes place there. They also tell me that their ships have guns, bows and arrows, and there are horses in the land, and they are used to war, and they wear rich clothes and possess good things. They also say that the sea goes round Ciguare, and from there to the river Ganges there are ten days. It seems that these lands are in a similar situation towards Veragua as Tortosa is to Fuenterabía or Pisa to Venice. (7) When I left Carambaru and arrived in those places I spoke of, I found the same kind of customs amongst the people, save that the gold mirrors, those who had them, gave them for three bells, though they weighed as much as ten to fifteen ducats apiece. In all their habits they are like those of Española. Their gold gathering craft is different, though both are as nothing next to that of the Christians. All this I say is what I hear. What I know is that in '94 I sailed along the 24th degree to the West for nine hours [i.e. $135°$] and there can have been no mistake because there was an eclipse: the sun was in Libra and the moon in Aries. Moreover, all this which I know by word of mouth I had known it for long in writing. Ptolemy thought he had put Marinus right and now we find his [Marinus] writing very close to the truth. Ptolemy puts Catigara twelve lines [12×15—$180°$] from his occident, which is two and one-third degrees from Cape St. Vincent. Marinus limits the [dry] land to fifteen lines [$225°$]. Marinus puts down the Indus in Ethiopia more than $24°$ from the equator, and now that the Portuguese navigate it they find him right. Ptolemy says that the most southern land is the first zone and that it does not go further south than fifteen degrees and one-third. And the world is little; the dry of it is six parts and only the seventh is covered with water; experience has proved it and I wrote it in other letters and with adornment of Holy Scripture, with the site of earthly Paradise, which the Holy Church approves: I say that the world is not as big as the common folk say and that one degree of the equator is worth fifty-six miles and two-thirds; but this shall be touched with one's fingers. I leave this, for it is not my purpose to speak on this matter but to relate my hard and laborious voyage, though it is my noblest and most profitable one.

I say that on the eve of St. Simon and Judas I ran where the wind took me, without power to resist it. In a harbour, I spared myself ten days of great exposure to sea and sky; there I decided not to return to the mines and to leave them as won. I started, to proceed with my voyage, raining: I arrived in *Puerto de Bastimentos* [Supply Port], where I entered and not willingly; the storm and the current interned me there fourteen days, and then I left and not with good weather. When I had sailed fifteen leagues by force, the wind and the current shoved me back with great fury; on my way back to the harbour whence I came, I discovered the *Retreat*, where I withdrew with much danger and annoyance, and very tired, I, the ships and the men; I tarried there fifteen days, for so wished the cruel weather, and when I thought I had come to the end of it, I found I was beginning: there I changed my mind [and decided] to go back to the mines and do something while waiting for a weather for my voyage and to go to sea, and when I was four leagues away the storm returned and it tired me so much that I knew not [what to do] for my part. There my wound was reopened: nine days was I lost without hope of life; no eyes ever saw the sea so high, ugly, and turned to foam. The wind would not let us go ahead, nor did it allow us to run towards some cape. There it stopped me in that sea made into blood, boiling like a boiler on a hot fire. The sky had never been seen so terrible: one day with a night it burnt like an oven; and it threw forth such flames with its lightning that each time I looked up, lest it had taken away my masts and sails. They [lightning strokes] came with such terror-striking fury that we all thought they would melt my ships. In all this time, water never ceased falling from the sky, and not to be described as rain, but as a second deluge. The men were already so ground down that they wished to be dead to be free from so much martyrdom. The ships had already twice lost their boats, anchors, ropes, and they were open, without sails.

When Our Lord was pleased, I returned to *Puerto Gordo* [Fat Port] where I repaired everything as best I could. I went back again towards Veragua, proceeding with my voyage, though I was not fit for it. Winds and currents were still against me. I arrived almost where I had before, and there again, I met with winds and currents, and I returned again to the harbour, for, with such savage seas off a wild coast, I dared not wait for the opposition of Saturn, which most often brings storms and strong weather. This happened on Christmas day at mass time. I returned again where I had come from with so much fatigue; and after New Year's day I tried again, though by then, even with good weather, my ships were no longer seaworthy and the men were dead [tired] and sick. On Epiphany day I arrived in Veragua, breathless; there, the Lord granted me a river and a safe harbour, though at the mouth it was no more than ten hands deep; I entered with difficulty and the next day the bad weather began again, which, had it caught me out at sea, would have prevented me from entering owing to the shallows. It rained ceaselessly till February 14th, so that we were not able to land or to see to anything; and when I was already safe, on January 24th, suddenly the river came down very high and strong; it broke my cables and moorings and threatened to take away the ships, which, to be sure, were in a worse danger than ever. Our Lord saw to it, as He always has done. I do not know whether any man ever suffered worse martyrdom. On February 6th, raining, I sent seventy men inland; and within five leagues, they found many mines; the Indians who went with them led them to a very high hill, and there showed them all their eyes could reach in every direction, saying that in all of it there was gold, and that towards the west the mines stretched for twenty days, and they named the towns and villages and where there was much and not so much. Later on I learnt that the *Quibian*, who had provided these Indians, had instructed them to show [us] the mines which lay far away and which belonged to an enemy of his; and that within his own settlement it was possible for a man in one day to gather a load of gold; his Indian servants and [other] witnesses of this, I have with me. His settlement can be reached by the ships' boats. My brother came back with these men, and all brought gold which they had gathered in the four hours they stayed there. The quality is good, for not one of them had ever seen a mine, nor most of them, gold [and yet they recognised it]. Most of them were seamen and almost all shipboys. I had abundance of material and tools for building and of supplies. I founded a settlement and I gave many presents to Quibian, which is the name they give to the lord of that country; and I knew full well that our harmony would not last; [for] they [are] very rustic, ours very importune, and I took possession of land in his domains; as soon as he saw our affairs completed and our activity so much alive, he made up his mind to burn everything and to kill us all; it turned out the other way; he remained a prisoner with his wives, sons and servants; though his prison days were not many; the Quibian fled from [the custody of] an honest man to whom he had been entrusted with a good guard; and his sons from a shipmaster to whom they had been given for safe keeping.

In January the river mouth was closed up. In April the ships were all eaten up with shipworm and I could no longer keep them afloat. At this time the river opened up a channel, through which I made three of them come out, empty, with great difficulty. The boats came back for salt and water. The sea turned high and ugly and did not let them come out again: the Indians came in great numbers, together, and attacked them and killed them. My brother and the rest of the men were in a ship which had remained inside: I, very lonely outside, on so wild a coast, with high fever, in such a plight; all hope to escape was dead; I went up in that way as high as I could, with a frightened voice, weeping and in great haste, I called out to the war-masters of Your Highnesses, to all the four winds, for help; but they never answered me. Tired out, I went to sleep moaning: I heard a very compassionate voice, which said:

Oh fool, man slow to believe and to serve thy God, God of all! What more did He do for Moses or for David his servant? From thy birth, He always took great care of thee. When He saw thee of an age which satisfied Him, marvellously did He make thy name resound in the Earth. The Indies, which are part of the world, so rich, He gave them to thee as thine; thou gavest them to whomsoever thou didst please and He gave thee power to do so. Of the shackles of the Ocean Sea, which were bound with such strong chains, He gave thee the keys; and thou wast obeyed in so many lands and didst win such honoured renown amongst Christians! What more did He do for the people of Israel when He led them out of Egypt? Nor for David, whom from a shepherd He raised to be King of Judea? Turn thy face to Him and know thy error at last: His mercy is boundless: thy age shall not hinder great things: He has many very great mansions. Abraham was over a hundred when he begat Isaac, and Sarah, was she a girl? Thou callest out for uncertain help: answer, who has afflicted thee so much and so often, God or the world? The privileges and promises which God gives, He breaks them not, nor does He say, after He has received the service, that His intention was different and that it must be understood in another way, nor does He give martyrdom to anyone in order to lend some colour to sheer force: He sticks to the letter; all He promises, He fulfils and more: is this customary? I have said what thy Creator has done for thee and does for all. Now He will show some of the reward of this anxiety and danger which thou hast undergone serving others. I heard all half-asleep, but I had no answer for such truthful words, save to weep for my errors. He ended speaking, whoever he was, saying: *Fear not. Be trustful. All these tribulations are written on marble stone and not without cause.*

I got up when I was able and nine days later the weather calmed down, but not so much as to allow us to get the ships out of the river. I gathered together the men who were on land and all the others whom I was able to put together for we were not enough both to leave behind and to man the ships. I would have remained to maintain the settlement had I had a way to inform Your Highnesses. The fear that no ships would ever again call there made me decide otherwise, as well as the thought that, when we come back in strength, we shall be able to see to everything. I sailed in the name of the Holy Trinity on Easter night, with the ships rotten, eaten with worm, all in holes. There in Belén I left one, and many things besides. In Belpuerto, I did the same. Two only remained, in the same state as the others, boatless, empty of supplies, to cross seven thousand miles of sea with a son, a brother and so many men. Let those answer who are wont to find fault and to scold, saying, there in their safety: "Why did not you do this otherwise?"

I should like to see them on this voyage. I do believe that another voyage requiring different knowledge is awaiting them. For those of our faith there is none. (8)

On May 13th I arrived in Mango province, which is next to that of Cathay, and from there I sailed towards Española: I had two days of good weather, and thereafter it was against me. The way I took was chosen in order to leave aside many islands, so as not to get entangled in their banks. The wild sea overpowered me, and I had to go back without sails; I cast anchor in an island where at one blow I lost three anchors, and at midnight, when it seemed that the world melted away, the mooring cables of the other ship snapped, and she came upon me so that it was marvellous how we did not end in splinters; the anchor, and the way it stood fast, was, after Our Lord, what held me. After six days, with good weather again, I returned to my road; thus, with all rigging gone and the ships more perforated by worms than a honeycomb, the men most dejected and downcast, I went a little further than the previous time; then, the bad weather pushed me back again; I stopped at the same island, in a safer harbour; after eight days, I took to the road again and arrived in Jamaica at the end of June, always with head-winds and the ships much worse than ever; with three pumps, tubs and boilers, the whole crew could not conquer the water which came into the ship, nor is there any other cure for ship-worm. I took a road the closest possible to Española, which is twenty-eight leagues away, and I wished I had never begun. The other ship ran into port almost submerged. I struggled against the sea with the storm. My ship was submerged, for Our Lord brought me to land by a miracle. Who could believe what I am here writing? I say that I have not said one part in a hundred in this letter. Those who went with the Admiral may witness. If Your Highnesses are pleased to do me the favour of helping me with a ship of more than sixty-four [tons?], with two hundred hundredweight of biscuit and other supplies, that will suffice to take me and these men to Spain from Española. From Jamaica, as I said, it is less than twenty-eight leagues to Española. I would not go [to Española] though the ships might have gone. I said that I had orders from Your Highnesses not to land there. Whether these orders have been to the good, God knows. I am sending this letter by way and hands of Indians; it will be great wonder if it reaches you.

About my voyage: I say that there came one hundred and

fifty persons with me, including many [capable] enough as pilots and great mariners: none can give an accurate account of the way I went or came back: the reason is at hand: I left from the line of the port of Brazil: in Española the storm did not allow me to take the road I wished: we were made to run where the wind wished. On that day I fell ill; no one had sailed in those parts; the wind and the sea calmed down in a few days and the storm shifted to calm and strong currents. I went to shelter in an island known as *Las Bocas* [the Mouths] and thence to mainland. No one can give a true account of this, for no reason will suffice; for I ran with the current for so many days without seeing land. I followed the coast of the mainland which was all taken down by compass and art. No one can say under what part of the sky or when I left it [the mainland] to come to Española. The pilots thought they were going to the Island of San Juan [Puerto Rico] and it was in the land of Mango, four hundred leagues further west. Let them answer, if they can, what is the emplacement of Veragua. I say that they can give no other report or account than that they have gone to some lands where there is much gold and that they can certify that fact, but as for returning to them, they do not know the way; it would be necessary [for the pilots] to discover them as if for the first time. There is one account and one reason of astrology, and certain; he who knows it, finds it sufficient. Prophetic vision, I call this. The ships of the Indies, if they cannot sail save before the wind, that is not due to their shape being bad nor because the great currents which are found there are too strong; together with the wind, the currents prevent anybody from struggling with the bowline, for in one day the ships would lose what they had won in seven; nor do I except caravels, not even Portuguese lateen ones. This reason makes them refrain from sailing till they get a wind right aft and they will tarry six or eight months in harbour waiting for it, which is no wonder since in Spain it often happens also.

The people Pope Pius writes about, to judge by the situation and description [which he gives] have been found, but not the horses, gold poitrels and bits, nor is it to be wondered at, for there at the sea-shore they are not needed, there being none but fishermen; nor did I tarry [to find out] for I was in a hurry. In Cariay and in these lands of the region they are all great witches and very timorous. They would have given the world to be sure that I did not stay one hour. As soon as I arrived, they at once sent me two girls very much made up; the older would not yet be eleven nor the younger seven; both so free-mannered that whores could not outdo them: they brought witchcraft powders hidden: when they arrived, I had them adorned with our things and sent them back to land: on the hill there I saw a sepulchre as big as a house and carved, and in it the body uncovered and looking out. Of other crafts I heard and more excellent. Animals small and big there are many and very different from ours. Two pigs was I given as a present and an Irish dog dared not stand up to them. An archer had wounded an animal which looks like a polecat, save that it is much bigger and has a face like a man's; he had shot an arrow through its body from the chest to the tail, and because it was ferocious he cut off a leg and an arm from its body: the pig, on seeing this animal, was upset and ran away; I, seeing this, had the *begare* (that is the animal's name in its country) edged on to the pig; and just as it was on the point of death and the arrow still in its body, it threw its tail round the pig's neck and with the hand that it still had dragged the pig down by the head as it would have done an enemy. The novelty of the action and the beautiful hunting scene made me write this down. We took away many kinds of animals, but they all die of the bar. Hens very big and with feathers like wool I saw many. Lions, stag, deer, just as many, and also birds. When I was struggling over that sea, some men conceived a heresy that we were bewitched, and they still believe it. Other peoples whom I met ate men; the deformity of their faces said so. They say there are there great veins of copper; hatchets made of it and forges with all the outfit for silversmiths, and crucibles. They wear clothes, and in that province I saw big cotton sheets, wrought with very subtle craft; others very subtly painted in colours with brushes. They say that right inland, towards Cathay, there are [sheets] woven with gold. Of these lands and of what there is in them it is not so easy to be informed for lack of an interpreter. The peoples, though close together, have each their own language and to such an extent that they do not understand each other any more than we do those of Araby. I believe this to be so with these people of the seaboard but not inland.

When I discovered the Indies I said they were the biggest and richest dominion in the world. I spoke of the gold, pearls, precious stones, spices, commerce and fairs, and as everything did not turn up at once, I was put to shame. This lesson makes me now say no more than what I hear from the natives. Of one thing I dare speak because there are so many witnesses, that is that in this land of Veragua I have seen more signs of gold in the first two days than in Española in four years, and that the lands of the country cannot be more beautiful nor better tilled, nor the men more cowardly, and good harbour and beautiful river and easily defended against the world. All this is safety for the Christians and certainty of over-lordship with great hope of honour and growth for the Christian religion; and the way thereto will be as short as to Española because it will have to be with the wind. Your Highnesses are as much Lord and Lady of this as of Jerez or Toledo; when ships will go thither, they will be going home. From there they will draw gold. In other lands, to obtain what there is in them, gold has to be brought and left there, or else the ships will return empty, and while there one has to rely on savages for one's safety.

Of the other [point] which I do not mention, I have already explained why I held fast. Not that I stand adamant on all I may have said or written, nor [do I claim that] I am at the source [of knowledge? of gold?]. Genoese, Venetians and all those who possess pearls, precious stones and other valuable things, they all carry them to the end of the world to barter with them and turn them into gold: gold is most excellent: of gold is treasure made, and with it, he who has it does all he wants in the world, and can even lift souls up to Paradise. The lords of those lands of the region of Veragua, when they die, the gold they wear is buried with their bodies, so I am told: Solomon received at one time six hundred and sixty-six hundredweights of gold, over and above what merchants and mariners brought and what was paid [him] in Araby. With this gold, he made three hundred shields, and the stage which was to be erected over them he also made of gold and adorned with precious stones, and he made many more things of gold, and many vases and very big and rich in precious stones. Josephus in his Chronicle *De Antiquitatibus* writes it all down. In the *Paralipomenon* and in the *Book of Kings* it is all told. Josephus claims that this gold was found in Aurea: if that were so, I say that those mines in Aurea are the same and fit in with these ones in Veragua, which, as I said above, stretch over to the west twenty days and [both Aurea and Veragua] are at the same distance from the Pole and the Equator. Solomon bought all that, gold, stones and silver, [while] you can send there for it to be gathered if you wish. David in his testament left three thousand hundred-weights of gold of the Indies to Solomon, as a contribution to the building of the temple, and according to Josephus, it was the gold of these lands. Jerusalem and Mount Sion are to be rebuilt by Christian hands: whose hands, God by the mouth of the Prophet says in the fourteenth Psalm. (9) The Abbot Joachim said that this person would sally forth from Spain. St. Jerome showed the holy woman the way thereto. The Emperor of Cathay long ago sent for wise men who might instruct him in the law of Christ. Who will it be who will offer himself for this? If Our Lord takes me back to Spain, I bind myself to take him there safely.

These men who came with me have gone through incredible dangers and hardships. I entreat Your Highnesses, since they are poor, to have them paid soon, and grant them favours each according to his rank, for I warrant that, to my belief they are bringing Your Highnesses the best news that ever went to Spain. The gold of the Quibian of Veragua and of the other [Lords] of the territory, though according to my information it be much, I did not think it seemly nor in good service to Your Highnesses, to take it from them by way of robbery: an orderly behaviour will spare [us] all scandal and bad reputation and will [in the end] bring it all to the Treasury, so that not one grain remains [behind]. Had I had one month of good weather, I should have completed my voyage: owing to the state of the ships, I did not endeavour to wait for the good weather in order to leave, and for everything in His service I put my hope in Him who made me, and I will recover. I believe Your Highnesses will remember that I wanted to have the ships made in a different way: lack of time did not permit, but it is certain that I had found out what was wanted.

I think more of [having discovered] this business and these mines, with this harbour and dominion, than of anything else yet done in the Indies. This is not a son to be given out to a fostermother to be brought up. Española, Paria and other lands, I never remember them without weeping: I thought that their example might have been of use for this one; on the contrary; they are lying face downwards, though they die not; their illness is incurable or very long; he who brought them to that state, let him come out with the remedy if he can, or knows; for destroying, everyone is a master. Thanks and promotion were ever wont to be given to those who put their bodies in danger. It is not fair that the one who was so adverse to this business should now enjoy it—nor his sons. Those who went away from the Indies, shirking its hardships and speaking ill of them and me, have recovered their posts: thus was it ordered to be done of late in Veragua; a bad example and with no profit for the business nor for the justice of the world: this fear, with other cases, too many, which I saw full well, made me entreat Your Highnesses, before I had come to discover these islands and mainland, that they would allow me to govern them in their royal name: they were pleased: it was done by privilege and settlement, and with seal and oath, and I was made Viceroy, and Admiral and Governor-General of all; and Your Highnesses drew the limit, one hundred leagues from the Azores and Cabo Verde Islands, on a line from pole to pole, and over this and all that might be further discovered; and they gave me full powers; the deed says so at greater length.

The other most famous business (10) is calling out with its arms wide open: it has been a stranger till now. Seven years have I been in your royal Court; everyone who heard of this enterprise said it was mockery: now, even tailors apply for discovery. One would think they are going housebreaking and [yet] it is granted them, and all they make is with much damage to my honour and much loss to the business. It is good to give God His due and accept one's own. This is a just saying and on just things. The lands which here obey Your Highnesses are larger than all other Christian lands, and richer. After I, by divine will, had put them under your royal and high dominion and on the way to produce very big income, suddenly, while awaiting for ships to come to your high presence with victory and great news of gold, very sure and gay, I was arrested and thrown into a ship with two brothers, laden with irons, naked in body, with very bad treatment, having been neither summoned nor convicted by the law: who would believe that a poor foreigner could rise in such a place against Your Highness without a cause, without another Prince's arm, alone amidst your vassals and subjects, and with all my sons in your royal Court? I came to serve at twenty-eight, and now I have no hair on my person which is not white, and my body is ill, and all I had left is spent and taken from me and sold, and from my brothers all, even their clothes, without their being heard nor seen, much to my dishonour. I have to believe that this was not done by your royal orders. The return of my honour and [the reparation of my] damages and the punishment of the man who did it, will make your royal nobility resound; and as much to the one who stole my pearls and who made havoc in that admiralty. The greatest virtue, renown with example, will you gain if you do that, and Spain will conquer a glorious memory, for you will be remembered as grateful and just Princes. The intention, so pure, which I always had in the service of Your Highnesses and the affront so out of keeping [with it] allows not the soul to remain silent, though I should wish to do so: I beg Your Highnesses to forgive me.

I am as forlorn as I said: I have wept for others so far; let Heaven have mercy now and let the earth weep for me. In temporal matters, I have not even a dime for an alms; in spiritual matters, I fared here in the Indies as I have said; isolated in this grief, sick, waiting daily for death and beset by a million savages full of cruelty and enemies of ours, and so far away from the Holy Sacraments and the Holy Church, which will forget this soul if it leave the body here. Let those who have charity, truth and justice weep for me. I did not undertake this voyage to earn honour or wealth; this is true, for all hope of that was already dead. I came to Your Highnesses with a straight intention and an honest zeal and I do not lie. I humbly entreat Your Highnesses that, if God is pleased to take me out of here, I may be allowed to go to Rome and other pilgrimages. Whose life and high state may the Holy Trinity keep and increase.

In the Indies in the Island of Jamaica on July 7th, 1503.

CHAPTER XXXI

FAREWELL TO THE PROMISED LAND

As a self-portrait, the more faithful for being unpremeditated, this historical page stands unique in the annals of human psychology. All Colón is there, brave and weak, proud and humble, obstinate and shifting, good observer and hopeless dreamer, candid and dissimulating, generous and grasping, executive and vacillating, obsessed by his own swollen self and full of the sense of his prophetic mission, proud in his consciousness of divine protection. His style, involved and obscure, suddenly lights up with lightning-strokes of genius worthy of the mightiest poets or philosophers. His chief passion, that ambition to emulate and surpass the power of the King and Queen which tormented his humiliated soul, breaks through his cautious, prudent loyalty, and becomes almost insulting in its contemptuous irony towards the two crowned heads whose majesty tortures him. And, above it all, a breadth, a spaciousness of suffering, of tension, of aspirations, the vast scale of which is not unworthy of the Lord, that God of his, far closer to Jehovah than to Jesus, and of whom he manages to make an instrument of his diabolic passions.

It is not given to everyone with his poor words to build a ship majestical enough yet swift enough for the Lord to sail in her. Colón's style has this double quality without which divinity visits not the sons of men. It is great, but it is swift. It is, undoubtedly, the style of a great navigator; spontaneous and utterly unconscious; unaware of the issue of form, of expression, of way of saying, or of choice of words; but always—save when caught in whirls of caution and in involutions of secrecy— always carried forward by a spirit that blows unremittingly from sky-reaching heights. Statements of fact, of feeling, of observation, of hope, of theory, of fantasy, follow each other in his great letters like the waves of a sea:

"If my complaints of the world are new, its habit of ill-treating people is very old. One thousand onslaughts it has made on me, and all have I withstood until today, when neither ships nor warnings have availed me. With cruelty has it sent me to the bottom. The hope in Him that made us all, holds me: His help has ever been ready. Once before, and I being not much less low, He raised me with His divine arm, saying, '*Oh man of little faith, arise, for it is I. Fear not.*' " (1)

And as the waves of the tormented spirit pass, pursuing each other in their relentless flow, sudden flashes of sheer perfection catch the eye and keep it in wonder: "And with this storm, I had to crawl all the way to Jamaica." . . . "Now with my left arm shall I make him see" . . . "Where there is no love, everything ceases. . . ." "Another grief wrenched my heart through my back. . . ." "The other most famous business is calling out with its arms wide open." . . . (2)

This is the style of an imaginative man, of a man who *sees* things in sudden impacts of intuition, without much capacity to discriminate whether his visions are creations of his own fancy or images drunk in from the outside world. This phrase on the pearls he was supposed to have put aside is typical: "The pearls, I had collected and fished by the men, with whom I left an agreement to return to fetch them, and, as I understood, by the bushel." He begins with "The pearls," wholly out of grammar, i.e. out of logic, reason, but because that is what catches his passionate fancy; then, he puts his *order*, i.e. the first reaction after the visual fascination, being one of authority to get hold of the coveted treasure; then, *ayuntar*, put together, *collect*: "he had them collected"; the fishing of them does not come till afterwards! a truly superb case of imaginative and illogical style; finally, he comes to the irksome and bothersome process of contracts and established business which, in point of fact, no longer interests him, and ends with a vague vision of quantity.

This visual process is strengthened by the tendency to put everything in human terms which is both strongly Jewish and strongly Spanish: his plan for liberating Jerusalem suddenly becomes a Christ on the Cross for his hallucinated eyes and for his ears which hear it calling out in the wilderness: *The other most famous business is calling out, with its arms wide open.* This tendency to incarnate his passions and his dreams was bound to lead him to speak through the Lord's mouth whenever he wanted to utter his most proud and ambitious thoughts. Nothing more diabolically swollen with insolence and *soberbia*, to fall back on that Spanish word which fits him as to the manner born, than the words with which, through a divine voice heard by him in his agony, he castigates the King and Queen who had disappointed him and denied him his privileges:

"*Oh fool*," he makes the Lord say to him, "*man slow to believe and serve thy God* [. . .] *the Indies which are part of the world, so rich, He gave them to thee and thine: thou gavest them to whomsoever thou didst please, and He gave thee power to do so!* [. . .] *Thou callest out for uncertain help: Answer, who has afflicted thee so much and so often, God or the world? The privileges and promises which God gave us, He breaks them not, nor does He say, after He has received the service, that His intention was different and that it must be understood in another way, nor does He give martyrdom to anyone in order to lend colour to sheer force: He sticks to the letter; all He promises, He fulfils, and more: is this customary?*"

Yet, no black-magic Jehovah can ever soothe the soul and calm down its tempests. Despite his imprecations, curses and sarcasms, Colón remained thirsty and unsatisfied. His life was spent but his fire was unextinguished, nor had he had the power and the grace to transfigure it into light. This was the deep suffering which made him rise to the highest pitch of expression and write those unforgettable words which burst like burning lava through the rugged surface of his style: "Who was ever born, not excepting Job, who did not die in despair? . . ." "I have wept for others, so far; let Heaven have mercy now and let the earth weep for me!" (3)

* *

The agony of mind in which this letter was written was fully justified. Colón was in Jamaica, held up there, living in useless ships which he had run aground and with men of doubtful loyalty, Indians who gradually grew restive, and no hope of return. But then, why write this letter at all? The answer is that he had conceived the plan of trying to send a messenger across to Española in a canoe. It was a hopelessly bold plan, but his situation was equally hopeless. He called Diego Méndez, who had come as chief Notary of the fleet, "a person very wise, straight and of good speech." (4) This man had already proved his loyalty to Colón and his incredible pluck on various occasions. Colón led him gradually to the idea of, at any rate, discussing the plan. "Sir," answered Méndez, "the danger we are in, I see it right enough; for it is bigger than thoughts can think. To pass from this island to Española in as small a vessel as a canoe, I hold to be not only difficult but impossible; for one has to cross a gulf of forty leagues of sea and amongst islands, where the sea is more impetuous and restless, and I do not see who could venture into so plain a danger." Colón, however, had made up his mind that Diego Méndez should do it, and so, knowing his man, he just said nothing. Expectant silence brought out Méndez's *pundonor*. But his answer was both shrewd and humorous as well as brave: "Sir, many times have I put my life in danger to save yours and those of all these men who are here, and Our Lord has miraculously spared me; and yet, there has been no lack of gossips who say that your Lordship always trusts me with all the enterprises of honour which occur, while there are in the company others who would do it as well; and therefore, it seems to me that your Lordship might call them all and propose this business to them to see whether there is one amongst them who wishes to take it on, which I doubt; and when they have all stood back, I shall put my life to the death for your service, as I have done many times." (5)

The Admiral followed this advice, and as Diego Méndez had anticipated, no one would accept, for they all held it impossible. Then Diego Méndez declared himself ready to go, and thereupon, another man, a Genoese by the name of Bartolomé Fieschi, known by the Spaniards and even by Colón as *Flisco*, volunteered also. (6) A canoe was made ready, a few planks were nailed fore and aft, to keep the water from lapping in, and a mast and sail were raised on her frail frame; food and water for the two Christians and six Indians were taken on board up to the narrow limits of the space available, and the little expedition started towards the northernmost part of Jamaica to wait for a good wind. While there, however, the Indians decided to get rid of Méndez and his companion. The Christians realised it and thought it wiser to sail back, under cover of the night, to get a land escort which should enable them to wait in peace for the wind. We have to imagine the disappointment of Colón and his men, who had lost a whole fortnight of patience in their desperate plight. They were to be tried far more sorely. The Adelantado himself was sent with an adequate force and presently Méndez and his companions sailed boldly into the ocean, carrying with them letters to the King and Queen and to the Governor of Española.

It cannot have been a pleasure cruise under the tropical sun in July. The two "Spaniards" (as Las Casas calls them, fully aware that *Flisco* was a Genoese) had to keep night-watches, for they were not wholly certain of the loyalty of the Indians (it is extremely unlikely that the natives had volunteered); and they often took the oars; soon they all began to suffer from a tantalising thirst in the midst of that immense sheet of water; the Indians had drunk out their supply during the first two days; the two Christians gave them sparingly of their own barrels; and in the midst of all this physical suffering, worst of all, they were tortured by the fear of missing their first aim, the tiny Island of Navasa, eight leagues off Española, on their shortest route. No compass; no sea-chart; just a vague notion of the situation of lands and coasts in those new seas; a canoe almost without a keel to hold the sea; an improvised mast and sail; and summer in the tropics; this expedition should stand as one of the bravest deeds in the history of the sea. They had sailed for three days and three nights. That afternoon they had thrown overboard one of the Indians who had died of thirst, and some of the others lay lifeless, as it seemed, on the bottom of the canoe; the bravest of them were sad and downcast, expecting a similar fate every hour; now and then they damped their parched lips with sea-water, hoping to get relief, only to find their pain grown worse; they plucked up strength, however, and rowed hard in the hope of seeing Navasa, which they had expected to sight the previous evening; yet, the sun sank in the west, behind their aching backs, and the sea was as empty as a shroud. Their hearts were sinking in their dejected breasts when of a sudden the moon rose to the east; its luminous, round face was partly hidden by a black peak: Diego Méndez, who saw it first, knew that they were saved.

They landed in Navasa at dawn, after a crossing of four days. There was not a tree to be seen in the whole land, about two or three miles long; but in the hollows of the rocks they found enough rain-water to drink their fill and replenish their barrels; and some of the Indians drank themselves to death. They rested from dawn till sunset, and as soon as the day was over they started again. The next morning they landed in Española, on Cape San Miguel, the westernmost point of what is now Haiti. Méndez engaged six fresh Indians and, after two days' rest, started again along the coast, which he sailed in his primitive canoe for three hundred and twenty miles. In Azúa he was told that Ovando was in Xaraguá, and so, leaving his canoe to take care of itself, he went by land to Xaraguá, two hundred miles inland. He does not say how, but in those days the chances are ten to one that he walked.

Such devotion, pluck and perseverance might have melted a

heart of stone. But Ovando was a curious man and Las Casas does not seem to have fathomed his character. He was over-cautious through permanent fear and ruthless through too much foresight. He kept Méndez hanging on the whole summer and autumn, and did not allow him to proceed to Santo Domingo till the spring. Towards the end of May, 1504, the faithful Méndez was able to purchase a ship full of supplies and to send it to the Admiral; this done, he sailed for Spain as instructed by his chief.

He seems to have been a complex personality, by no means limited in his gifts to feats of daring. His will reveals that he was well read, and particularly fond of Erasmus: he left "*The Art of Dying Well*, by Erasmus, a Sermon of Erasmus in Castillian, Josephus' *De Bello Judaico*, *The Moral Philosophy* of Aristotle, the volumes which are known as *Lingua Erasmi*, *The Book of the Holy Land*, *The Colloquies* of Erasmus, a treaty on the quarrels of Peace, a book of contemplations on the Passion of Our Redeemer, a treatise on the vengeance of Agamemnon's death, and other small treatises." (7)

That *De Bello Judaico* in so small, if choice, a library, would suggest that Diego Méndez was also a *Converso*, a suggestion strengthened by his preference for Erasmus, an author much in favour with the *Conversos* in those days. (8) This factor would provide a natural explanation of his loyalty towards Colón. The loyalty does not seem to have been well rewarded, for in his will he complains of Don Diego Colón's ingratitude. But there is a paper in the famous lawsuit of the Colóns *v.* the Crown which would appear to suggest that neither Méndez nor Don Diego were averse to making money by exploiting the power which the law put into their hands. In a list of the "Innovations" which the Admiral, Don Diego, son and heir of Colón, introduced in Española, against the laws of King Ferdinand, we read that he made married men either return to Spain or bring their wives over, which sounds sensible enough; but, we are told that the Admiral punished those who demurred with severe penalties and then was willing to allow them to buy themselves out of the law: "in this way, Diego Méndez, Alguacil, by means of a letter of exemption which he obtained from the said Admiral, extorted two hundred pesos of gold from a number of married men in Cuba." (9)

* *

Meanwhile, week after week and month after month, Colón's

expedition lay in enforced idleness in Jamaica. Nothing is more dangerous than stagnant energy. Much of the energy of his men was being sapped by lack of adequate food and by disease. But Colón knew only too well that there was far too much health about for his safety, and the thought tormented him while he lay tied to his bed by a severe attack of gout. Presently, the rumours and criticisms of discontent found expression and leadership in Francisco de Porras, captain of one of the ships. On January 2nd, 1504, nearly six months after Diego Méndez had left them in quest of help, Porras went up to the castle aft of his ship and insolently shouted to the Admiral: "It seems to us here, Sir, that you do not want to go to Castille and that you will have us here, lost." The Admiral realised what was coming and, hiding his shame and humiliation, expostulated quietly with the rebel leader, but Porras cut him short bluntly, saying that no more speeches were needed, and, turning his back on the Admiral, answered: "I am going to Castille with those who wish to follow me." (10)

"And I with him!" "And I with him!", roared the conspirators behind. The Admiral rushed out of his cabin, tottering, for he could hardly walk, and the Adelantado, in his impulsive way, seized a spear; but their faithful servants held them back, and the rebels seized ten canoes which the Admiral had brought and "took to sea with as much elation and joy as if they were landing in Seville." (11) Their idea was evidently to emulate Diego Méndez's exploit, but though they tried twice, twice they failed in disastrous conditions, with much sacrifice of Indians; and they had finally to return to the island which held them all in thraldom.

While they were doing their best to keep body and soul together, the Admiral left with the sick, the wounded, the faithful and the weak, saw the tide of native good will which had kept him and his people alive, gradually ebb. By a careful administration of his reserves of trifles and a scrupulous purchase by barter of all they consumed, he had, so far, managed to ensure regular visits from natives ready to provide them with food and other necessaries of life. But whether because familiarity breeds contempt, or because the rebels worked the natives up against their former chief, the Indians began to break away from their allegiance and their services became less regular and reliable. Colón had every reason to be alarmed. He extricated himself from this dangerous pass by an ingenious stratagem which has become famous. He had on board a copy of the Astronomic

Calendar of Johannes Müller, known as *Regiomontanus*, in which he read that there was to be a total eclipse of the moon on February 29th (1504—a leap year). He had the Indian Caciques called for that very evening for an important communication, and addressed them in grave tones as one who is used to speaking for the Lord. A unique scene in the annals of the world. The dark bulk of the ship lying idle, as gouty and creeky as its chief mariner; the heavy, warm, tropical water lapping its sides; standing on the castle aft, the tall, wan, Pale-face chief, looking sad and grave; and, some on the shore near by in the tall grass, some on the ship, the natives, in twos and threes, living statues, lithe and slim, reflecting the faint light of dusk on their shiny muscles and on their bare, well-modelled backs. An Indian of the ship, who had picked up enough of their language to be able to convey to them some sort of a meaning which he gathered from the Christian's words, stood by Colón.

The Pale-face chief spoke to them about the great God whom he served, pointing to the sky where He was supposed to dwell. He warned them that great calamities would overcome them if they did not continue their peaceful commerce with the Spaniards, whom this great God protected, and foretold that, as a sign of His displeasure, the Lord would that very evening take away the moon from their sky. The interpreter looks up. He fears to have misunderstood. Take the moon away from the sky? This must be a joke. He grins, showing his white teeth. But Colón is glum and sad and has not even noted the Indian's hesitation. The interpreter looks now at him, now at the natives, and at last, not knowing what to make of it, he passes the puzzle on to the Jamaicans. They are nonplussed at first, wonder, grin, some of them chuckle, others discuss the matter. The excitement is not yet over when the moon rises in the east. Great elation greets the lovely orb, for all, even those who had grinned and chuckled, had feared deep down that the Pale-face chief might be right. The Pale-face chief is solemn and silent. The Spaniards who surround him are also silent; some of them smile. Suddenly the Pale-face chief, who has a glass half full of sand before him, lifts up his hand and points to the moon. All eyes look up. The orb is no longer an orb. It has a slight indentation at the lower edge. Astonishment opens wide the eyes of the natives. And soon the shadow grew over the moon's face, as if she were slipping out of sight through a slit in heaven; astonishment became fear, and fear became panic. Amidst tears and yells the natives asked to be forgiven and promised steady loyalty to the mighty Pale-face. Colón withdrew "to talk to God" till the eclipse was nearly over, and showed his face again as the moon's face reappeared and brought back peace to a distracted patch of mankind.

This settled the Indians for a while, but not the Spaniards. For month after month, their eyes sore with looking at the stubborn horizon, waited in vain for the caravel which Diego Méndez had instructions to send. All kinds of opinions flourished: they had been murdered by Indians; they had capsized; they did not care and had gone away for ever without bothering about them. One Bernal, a chemist, engineered a second rebellion and, when the rebels were going to strike, suddenly a small caravel appeared on the horizon. Their hopes rose high, but were soon to fall lower than ever. It was not Méndez's ship, but just a scout sent by Ovando to find out what the position was. To make sure that the caravel would not become too friendly with the Admiral's party, Ovando, in mortal dread of Colón's influence in Española, had sent in command one Diego de Escobar, who had been of Roldán's party and was on frigid terms with Colón. Escobar allowed no mixing of the crews, and kept at a considerable distance from the Admiral's ships. All he brought as supplies, after a whole year of hunger, was a barrel of wine and one ham. But he brought something worth many barrels of wine and many hams; the assurance that Méndez had arrived and that, therefore, rescue was at hand.

The Admiral gave Escobar a letter for Ovando. It was a civil, almost a humble letter. No reproach, no complaint. Thanks, assurances of constancy and fidelity; requests for help. The small caravel vanished again. Again alone. Again those long, long days of waiting, with dawns of hope and sunsets of dismay and nights of despair. The Admiral had sent a message to the Porras rebels, hoping to win them back by persuasion. He was anxious not to have to return to Spain again complaining of another Roldán. But the Porras group were adamant and countered the news of the caravel by arguing that so curious a ship, suddenly come, suddenly gone, never approached nor boarded by anyone, was surely due to some necromancy in which they held the Admiral to be an adept. (A hint again, be it noticed, of the Jewish colours under which he was seen everywhere.) Nothing daunted by these other-worldly powers, the rebels started an offensive; the Adelantado then took the field; he had with him fewer men and less exercised, and moreover "Palace people, more delicate," says Las Casas, allowing us to catch another glimpse of the popular character of the rebellions which Colón always managed to provoke, and of the courtly character of those who remained loyal to him. Nevertheless, the Adelantado won; for when their first onslaught failed, "they turned their backs, being low people and traitors." Porras was taken prisoner.(12) This final victory of Don Bartolomé took place on Sunday, May 20th, 1504, nearly a year after Méndez had left for Española. The next day the defeated crowd sent a petition to the Admiral, swearing oath upon oath of fidelity on pain of being left to die without confession, buried in unconsecrated ground like heretics, and denied absolution by Holy Father, Cardinals, Archbishops, Bishops or priests. The Admiral was magnanimous, but he kept Porras in irons. As for the rest, he let them roam on the island, rather than have them too close to the faithful herd.

Then the ships arrived, two of them. They were in charge of Diego de Salcedo, the very man to whom Colón had given the monopoly of soap in his dominions. Salcedo told Colón that Ovando did not despatch the rescue ships till the colony began to criticise him and preachers to refer in their sermons to his remissness. But all is well that ends well, and the stay in Jamaica, disastrous in so many ways, ended on June 28th, 1504, when the Admiral and his company left for Española. The crossing, which Méndez had done in four days, took him over three weeks, but he did not go to Navasa; he stopped in Beata Island, not far from Yáquimo, and there, on August 3rd, he wrote Ovando a letter more than courteous, courtly and even subservient, in which he declares that he cannot understand why he is suspected, nor of what. Contrary winds detained him there till the 13th, when he at last arrived in Santo Domingo, the city which his brother had founded.

The Governor received him with great show of honour and reverence, and invited him as his guest. But the Admiral was bitter in his comments on the deeds under these gestures. Porras was set free and the events of Jamaica were taken from his jurisdiction, an act which he resented as a breach of the privileges of the Admiral of the Indies. In every other way the proud Viceroy felt his interests and prerogatives set at nought by the sly, contemptuous Governor of the very lands he had discovered. Sick at heart and humiliated by this situation, the Admiral sailed for Spain on September 12th, 1504, eight years less one month from the day on which he had set eyes on the new world.

He was not to see it again.

CHAPTER XXXII

DEATH AND TRANSFIGURATION

On November 7th Colón landed in Sanlúcar de Barrameda, at the mouth of the Guadalquivir. He was never to sail again, save when fever and delirium made him dream he was still in the castle aft, fighting with nature and men, his body shaken by wind and wave, and his soul by hope and fear. He could hardly move; gout-ridden, he was conveyed to Seville, there to wait till the weather-beaten caravel of his body was repaired to sail on to the dangerous seas of the Spanish Court. His state of health made it impossible to attempt a journey northward to the bitterly cold tablelands of Castille, for they were in the raw of winter and, as he quaintly wrote to his son Diego, "the cold weather has so much enmity with this my ailment that I fear I might remain on the way." (1)

He had hopes, however—higher than his state warranted—and more than once he suggests an immediate departure. "My departure will be soon," (2) he writes on November 21st. But meanwhile he remains in Seville, with the Adelantado, himself afflicted with gum- and toothache. (3) In his enforced rest, unable even to write except by night, (4) he broods over his grievances, the injustices he has undergone, his privileges violated, his income curtailed or even destroyed. He writes to Father Gorricio: "I can say no more how great is my desire to see you and to impart to you something which is not for the pen"; (5) to his son, letter after letter, sending advice, money, information, tips on how to bargain for his rights: "I swear—and let this be for you only—that the loss to me on the rights granted me by their Highnesses [on the Indian revenues] amounts to ten millions a year, and that they can never be replaced. See how much their Highnesses must have lost, and they do not mind." (6)

His industry is unremitting, and he keeps eyes, ears and imagination on the task of recovering his goods—moral and material. There was some progress at first, for on November 21st he writes to his son Diego: "I was pleased to hear [the news

393

brought by] your letter and what our Lord the King has said and you will kiss his hand for it." (7) But on December 1st, his letter contains a sentence which no doubt expressed deep concern: "May the Holy Trinity give health to our Lady the Queen, so that what has been done may be finally settled." (8) A curious utterance, in which Colón, with that carelessness which now and then breaks the well-guarded armour of his caution, gives away the subconscious egotism which he hides under his love for Queen Isabel. When he wrote these words, the Queen was dead. In June 1504, the first news of the grave estrangement between Philip the Handsome and Doña Juana of Castille, and the first symptoms of mental derangement which this state of things had produced in the young princess, had burst on the Spanish Court like a thunderbolt. Ferdinand and Isabel were deeply affected and fell ill, but while Ferdinand recovered, Isabel, so heavily tried already, was unable to rise again. Her state went from bad to worse, and on Wednesday, November 26th, 1504, she died at Medina del Campo.

Her last wishes on the Indians have been already discussed: two other points in her testament deserve mention here; one because it admirably conveys the grace and gravity singularly intertwined in her mind, the other because it throws light on her attitude towards the Jewish question. "I beg the King my Lord, that he be pleased to use my jewels and belongings, or those which he may like best; so that, seeing them, he may have a more continuous remembrance of the singular love which I always felt for his lordship; and even so that he may ever bear in mind that he is to die and that I am awaiting him in the other life; and with this memory he may live more saintly and justly." (9)

The other provision refers to Andrés Cabrera, first Marquis of Moya. In her will the Queen had cancelled many favours and privileges granted during her lifetime "out of necessity and importunity"; but she makes one single exception; after extolling the services of Cabrera and his wife, she begs her successors to respect and increase their privileges. This was in 1504; the Inquisition, in the full force of its severity, had been purging Spain from doubtful *Conversos* for over fourteen years, but the Queen remained faithful to her *Converso* friend. For her there was no trace of racial barrier. A converted Jew was her brother in Christianity.

This seems also to have been the opinion of the King. Colón had at first entertained hopes that the Queen, before her death, would have restored him his power. "Here," he writes to his son on December 13th, "it is much rumoured that the Queen, who is with God, has left in her will that I be restored in the possession of the Indies"; a phrase in which, again, his grasp on words reveals the deep subconscious sense of ownership which *possessed* him: "restored in the possession of the Indies." Nothing less. Just over a week later he asks for daily letters to feed his insatiable impatience, and adds: "it is necessary to find out whether the Queen, who is with God, said something about me in her will." (10) But these hopes came to nothing, and Colón had to concentrate on winning Ferdinand's sympathy. Then, his repeated advice to his son Diego is to seek the help of, to rely on, always to consult with Deza and Cabrero: Deza, bishop of Palencia till January 1505, Archbishop of Seville thereafter, Inquisitor-General of Spain since Torquemada's death, was a Jew; Cabrero, chief Chamberlain to the King, was also a Jew. "You are to inform the Bishop of Palencia of this, with all the trust I put in him and also the Chamberlain"; "and it is necessary to hurry the bishop of Palencia, who was the cause why the King and Queen had the Indies and I remained in Castille, for I was on my way abroad; and also the Chamberlain." "With a courier who must arrive there today I wrote at length and I sent you a letter for the Chamberlain." (11) These two men had stood by him throughout, from his arrival in Castille, during the period of struggle, during victory, through his downfall, and now also during the last years of his earthly fight. Not in vain had he said, when thrown off his guard by Ximeno, that *Conversos* were "a lineage of men who help each other through life and death." His active correspondence reveals again that deeply Jewish co-operative sense within the narrower circle of the family: "Take great heed of your brother," he writes to his son Diego, "he has good natural parts and is already growing out of his youth. Ten brothers would not be too many. I never found better friends, right and left, than my brothers." (12)

In this parting advice we begin to perceive the voice of the man approaching death; but the fight goes on in his relentless mind, full of grievances and rights invaded. He is worried about three bishops who are to be appointed in the Indies; he wants to be consulted and heard on this. (13) He is still keen on all that means political and economic power over his islands of the Ocean Sea. Nor was he grasping or exorbitant in this. Was he not, after all, the real creator of all that empire? And yet, here he was in Seville, sick and alone, living on borrowed money, having spent all he had found available in Santo Domingo in bringing back to Spain the crews and soldiers who had gone out with him on his fourth voyage. (14) His Memoir of December 3rd is full of suggestions as to what should be done to save the Indies and the gold which is being stored without adequate measures against theft and leakage. He bewails his loss and writes to his son to be very exacting, "since His Highness says in his letter that he will give me all that belongs to me"; so he claims his third, his eighth, and his tenth; "for," he adds in his confidential way to his son, "there is always time to come down to what the person [the King] will be pleased to give." (15)

But time went by and he had not moved from Seville. Transportation was a difficult matter. He had thought of some kind of invalid conveyance, when he imagined he would be able to travel north in spite of the winter. The Chapter of the Cathedral of Seville had granted him the use of a magnificent litter which had been made two years earlier to transport the body of the Grand Cardinal of Spain from Tendilla to Seville. This solemn and somewhat forbidding conveyance was, however, unnecessary. On December 21st Colón wrote to his son Diego: "If, without troubling anyone, it were possible to get a licence to ride a mule, I should endeavour to leave some time after January." (16) The key to these words may be read in Bernáldez: "In the year 1494, the King and the Queen having seen that from all their realms of Castille and of Leon, they could hardly put together ten or twelve thousand horsemen for the war against the Moors, while there were more than one hundred thousand who rode mules, promulgated a law with very severe penalties forbidding anyone, knight, duke, earl or any other dignity, esquire or labourer, old or young, to ride a mule with bit and saddle, under pain of the mule being killed, save the clergy in orders and women [. . .] And the King himself gave such an example in this that he never rode a mule, but always a horse." (17) Colón was the victim of this royal provision which draws the highest praise from the public-spirited Bernáldez (particularly as he, being a cleric in holy orders, could ride a mule any time he pleased). The poor invalid refers to the matter again in his letter of December 29th and even goes one step further: "The mule licence, if it could be had without too much trouble, would be welcome—and a good mule also." (18) Don Diego was busy on this as on everything else, so busy indeed that, considering the proverbial slowness of officialdom, it should be counted to his credit that he obtained a royal licence on February 23rd, 1505, on account of ill health and old age (*ancianidad*). (19) Nevertheless, Colón did not move from Seville till May, probably owing to his fear of the cold weather. He was not only sick with gout; he was sick with humiliation and disappointment, as he was to write to the King: "I believe that the anxiety over the delays on this my business is that which most of all keeps me thus an invalid." (20) The fact is that, despite his utterances to the contrary, sincere and heartfelt though they were, he had never been able to detach himself from the wheel of desire on which he was being broken. These utterances of his, which look like renunciations of desire, should be read rather as revelations of the ambition and the hunger which remained unsatisfied in his tormented heart. "The Lord knows," he wrote, during his third voyage, "that I do not bear these hardships to hoard up or find out treasures for me, for, to be sure, I know that all is vain which is done down in this life, save that which is honour and service of God, not gathering up riches and *soberbias*, nor many other things we use in this world on which we are more bent than on those things which can save us." (21)

That word *soberbia* under his pen! And the word *riches*, the two poles of his ambition, denounced by himself in this revealing paragraph, and in that visual, illogical style of his, which makes him say *hoard up* before he says *find*, just as he had written *collected* before he wrote *fished* in the case of the pearls, because his passionate nature went straight for the full object of his desire and saw the fruit before the tree.

No, he was not detached in his innermost being. His experience had made his mind accept the fatal renunciation. He was sincere when, in his Jamaica letter, he wrote to the King and Queen: "I did not undertake this voyage to earn honour and wealth; this is true, for all hope of that is already dead"; but he could only be sincere because he did not know himself. Two years later, in May 1505, he presented King Ferdinand, then in Segovia, note after note demanding full restoration of what, with a strange mixture of the impulses of *riches* and *soberbia*, he calls "the capital of my honour," i.e. "the government and possession [again *soberbia* and riches] of the Indies." (22)

The King received him well and listened to him with affability. He very reasonably suggested that there should be someone in charge of the Admiral's affairs so that they should be promptly despatched; and the Admiral, after the usual courtly answer: "let it be whomsoever Your Highness orders," promptly added: "Who better than the Archbishop of Seville, since, with the Chamberlain, he had been the cause of Your Highness having the Indies?" Colón had lost no time in promoting his *Converso* friend to deal with his affairs. (23)

The King, who by an inveterate tradition based on Las Casas and on Fernando Colón, is misrepresented as inimical to the Admiral, granted his request on the spot and the matter was referred to Deza, who ruled that, in what concerned the estate and income of the Admiral, lawyers should be consulted, but not in the matter of government. This answer does honour to the common sense of the Archbishop. Colón, led by his *soberbia*, which made him see himself as the equal of the King, wanted to have the whole matter of his privileges treated as a legal dispute; the King and all sane men around him, were willing to submit any material dispute to lawyers or arbiters, but did not admit that public questions such as the government of the Indies could ever be a subject of dispute, legal or otherwise, between the King and any one of his subjects. (24) That is why Colón was so enraged by the attitude of King Ferdinand. He, of all people! The one man in the world whom he so profoundly desired to humiliate! He fell ill with disappointment and suppressed passion, and from his bed he wrote these revealing words to the Archbishop of Seville: "And since it looks as if his Highness were not pleased to fulfil what he promised on his honour and signature, together with the Queen (may she be in Holy glory), I believe that to fight on the contrary line, for me, who am a ploughman, would be like whipping the winds, and that it will be best, since I have done all I could, that I should let God our Lord do, Whom I have always found very propitious and ready for my needs." (25)

Colón was not in this a good interpreter of the Lord's intentions, for if there is one thing in which He does not differ at all from any of His creatures, it is in that He puts His interests above all else; and Colón was not altogether unaware of this fact, for every now and then he grew worried about it. "I say again, under oath"—he wrote during his third voyage—"that I have put more diligence in serving Your Highness than in winning Paradise." (26) And, coming back to the Indians and to the treatment they were undergoing since Christianity had been preached to them, he evidently tried to extricate himself from the difficult position into which he had sunk owing to his

eagerness to make the Indies pay: "he says"—Las Casas records
—"that the Indians of this Island Española are its wealth [. . .]
and he says more; that though he had sent many to Castille,
and had had them sold, it was all with the purpose of having
them sent back and recovered and to instruct the others, after
they had been taught our holy faith and our ways, arts and
crafts"; (27) a statement utterly at variance with his letters and
with his practice on slavery.

His uneasy conscience was adding to the heavy load which
he was then carrying. The Colón clan, led by the old, stubborn
Admiral and represented at Court by young Don Diego, were
fighting step by step to obtain their reinstatement as the *de facto*
rulers of the Indies. King Ferdinand was, of course, determined
to grant nothing of the kind. The amount of silly, sentimental
comment which this attitude of King Ferdinand has elicited,
from Las Casas down to modern authors, is incredible. Yet
the facts are clear, though they may not be plain without some
accurate study of the documents. (28) Colón held a contract and
a letter of privilege. The contract was the document known as
the Capitulations of Santa Fé. It granted him the title and
prerogatives of Admiral of the Ocean Sea and of the islands and
mainland for himself and his successors, and the titles of Viceroy
and Governor-General of the *lands discovered in his first voyage
only, and only for life.* This contract was subject to the laws of
Castille, and therefore the King and Queen reserved the right to
suspend Colón in any or all of these functions if the interest of
the State demanded it. The letter of privilege was signed on
April 30th; it made the titles of Viceroy and Governor-General
hereditary. Furthermore, on May 23rd, 1493, in the full elation
of discovery, Colón obtained from the King and Queen that the
area over which the three titles would apply should be the same
as was granted to Castille by Pope Alexander VI.

This was, then, the position. Colón was Admiral, Viceroy
and Governor-General of the Indies by contract; his heirs
would be Admirals by contract; but they could only be Viceroys
and Governors-General by privilege. The reluctance of the
Crown to create so immense a fief at so great a distance, in
favour of a family of foreign origin, was so natural that had
Ferdinand shown no signs of it, the fact would have laid him open
to the charge of incapacity. With a contractual sense which is
typically Jewish, and, be it noticed, with a lack of political acumen
which is typically un-Italian, Colón and his heir insisted on the
fulfilment of the promised word. Ferdinand was scrupulous and

even generous in the way he interpreted his royal obligations to Colón, whenever they did not conflict with his higher duties to the State. He had Colón sounded as to a spontaneous renunciation of his privileges in exchange for a fief in Spain— *Carrión de los Condes*; (29) but Colón was adamant, and even furious. He must have his Indian fief. Yet Ferdinand's attitude was clear. Within thirteen days of Colón's death he signed a letter to Ovando instructing him to hand over all the gold and other property of Don Cristóbal "to Don Diego, his son and heir in the Admiralty," and in this very letter the King speaks of Don Diego as the *Admiral of the Indies*; (30) this shows that the King was not withholding any *rights* he had granted, but only such *privileges* as he thought dangerous to maintain.

The pride and intractability of the Colón clan may be perceived in all their insolence towards the King as soon as, the old Admiral gone, the less cautious Don Diego gave vent to them petulantly in terms which throw much light on Colón's own intransigence: "I am determined," wrote Don Diego to one of the Duke of Alba's agents, "to accept no compromise on my honour, nor to sell it, for neither can I do it, nor do I wish to incur my father's malediction, nor can his Highness do otherwise than grant me what is my right [. . .] I shall not consider any compromise, and they need not be spoken on, for I laugh at what his Highness promises me and cannot give, for within ten years I trust God I shall have bought as much in Castille out of my [Indian] income, which will be much safer than what his Highness promises. [. . .] I beg his Lordship [the Duke of Alba] to write to his Highness very insistently, begging him to do me justice in accordance with my privileges and confirmations, signed by his Royal name, and that this be done right soon, with no more delays as in the past, and without talking to me about compromises, which do not suit me [. . .] Also that he writes to Don Fernando [the Duke's brother], my lord, that he hasten my business [. . .] and that he listen not to his Highness when he speaks to him on compromises." (31)

In the circumstances, it says much for Ferdinand's magnanimity that, in reply to this insolent young man's demands, he should be content to answer: "See, Admiral, if it were for you only, I would willingly trust you, but I cannot trust your sons and successors." (32)

Time was to prove the King right in Don Diego's own successor, utterly unworthy of governing not only the Indies but even his own miserable self. The King therefore acted throughout with a truly wise balance of motives in which the interests of the State prevailed over his genuine desire to be generous towards the Colóns, but, within this zone of freedom limited by his royal responsibility, King Ferdinand was always courteous, kind and even liberal to the man who had discovered the Indies. There is much to be said for this man also. Bedridden in Segovia or in Salamanca, later in Valladolid, he saw the dreams of greatness which his discovery had made gloriously real, gradually vanish again under forces which he could not be expected to gauge with a detached, historical spirit. He was a hot soul; not a cool mind. He suffered and imagined and suffered again. He did not think. And we may well believe that Don Diego was literally accurate in saying that any compromise on his part would have called out from the deep the malediction of his unyielding father. The man who had left Granada for exile and poverty rather than abate one iota of his exorbitant demands when the Indies were but a laughed-at dream, would surely be adamant to the death on the same privileges now that the Indies were a coveted reality.

* * *

Towards the beginning of 1506 (January 8th), Juana, now Queen of Castille and Leon, and her husband Philip, who ranks as Philip I in Spanish royal chronology, sailed from Flanders towards their realms. A storm threatened the safety of their fleet and they actually lost one ship "in which there came certain pages and much linen and many jewels." (33) They sought shelter in Weymouth; King Henry VII received them royally, and "Queen Doña Juana found great comfort with the Princess of England, Doña Catalina, her sister." (34) They stayed in England several weeks and finally landed in Coruña on April 28th, 1506. Colón, though bedridden, was not slow to present his respects . . . and his claims and hopes to the new sovereigns of Castille, in a letter which was the last he was to write. It is, as often happens with his letters, a most revealing document, for never did a secretive man give himself away more transparently in what he wrote: "I trust Your Highnesses will believe that at no time did I so desire the health of my person as since I learnt that Your Highnesses were coming hither by sea, in order to come and serve them and show them the experience and knowledge of navigation which I have. The Lord wished it so; therefore I humbly beg Your Highnesses to count me in the account of your loyal vassals and servants and to be certain that, though this ailment does at present ruthlessly belabour me, I shall still be able to serve them with service the equal of which has never been seen. These contrary times and other anguishes in which I have been put against so much reason, have led me to a great extremity; for which cause I have not been able to come forward to Your Highnesses, nor my son either. Very humbly I beg Your Highnesses to receive my intention and good will, as of one who hopes to be restored in my honour and state, as my writs promise to do. May the Holy Trinity protect and increase the very high and Royal State of Your Highnesses." (34)

The Adelantado took this letter to the young King and Queen. They were another Spain, and a transitory and unhappy one, a brief episode between the creative era of Ferdinand and Isabel and the imperial era of Charles V. Philip was to die within a few months, and his death was finally to destroy the unsteady balance of mind of his ardent and jealous wife. Colón could not find much attention in that Court, led then by young Philip in a spirit of petulant rivalry against King Ferdinand.

His own ailment grew from bad to worse. On May 19th, 1506, he dictated his will before the notary (*escribano*) Pedro de Hinojedo, and Bartolomé Flisco or Fieschi. It confirms in every way the features of his now familiar character. He begins by confirming the will and the deed of entail which he had made in 1502; he reappoints as heir his son Don Diego, and enjoins him not to reduce but rather to increase the entail and, with it and his person, to serve the King and Queen and the Christian religion; he recalls his right to the third, the eighth and the tenth, because when he came to serve the King and Queen he had given them the Indies, as a thing which was his; then, on the assumption that a regular income will accrue to his heirs on that basis, he proceeds to distribute it. Obsessed by the idea of continuity, he enjoins Don Fernando to keep his own income as an entail also; and, reversing the flow of his family interests from the future to the past, he orders Don Diego to keep a chapel in which three chaplains will say three masses a day—one in honour of the Holy Trinity, one in honour of the Conception of Our Lady, and one for the soul of his father, mother and wife. He orders his son Diego "to watch over the welfare of Beatriz Enríquez, Don Fernando's mother, and see that she is in a position to live as befits a person who is so much on my conscience. And let this be done as a relief to my conscience for it weighs much on my soul. The reason of it, it is not licit for me to write here." (35)

The *mayorazgo* or entail of 1498, though apocryphal, must be based on the paper of 1502 which has disappeared—precisely to allow the apocryphal one to be put in its stead—and therefore, those provisions which are not controversial, in particular those which have no money significance, are probably genuine. Such is the case with the provision about his signature, one of the most singular features in the whole document: "Don Diego, my son, or anyone who may inherit this entail, after having inherited and obtained possession of it, shall sign my signature which I now use, which is an X, with an S above, and an M, with a Roman A above, and above it an S, and then, a Greek Y, with an S above it, with their strokes and commas as I do now and as will be seen by my signatures and by the one hereafter. And he will write [sign] nothing but *The Admiral*, even though the King might give him, or he might win, other titles." (36)

This signature has been one of the favourite grounds for mystery-hunters, and the readings of it range from the over-ingenious to the half-witted. None is satisfactory, (37) and all forget a point which, though trifling in appearance, is all-important in reality: *Colón always writes his three S's between dots.* He never dots any other letter of his signature. There is not the slightest doubt that the letter S had a special significance for him. We find mysterious, solitary S's as marginal notes to some passages of the books he read, and particularly—which is worth noticing in view of all that has been said about his Catalan-Jewish origin—on the margin of the chapters of d'Ailly, dealing with Judea and with Majorca. (38)

The next thing to be noticed in this signature is its strictly geometrical character. Colón's wish in this has not been better respected than in other cases, such as that of his name; for, even in so scholarly a publication as the *Raccolta Colombiana*, the arrangement willed by Colón and always strictly adhered to by him, is typographically destroyed and his letter-pattern printed:

$$\cdot S \cdot$$
$$\cdot S \cdot A \cdot S \cdot$$
$$XMY$$

instead of:

$$\cdot S \cdot$$
$$\cdot S \cdot A \cdot S \cdot$$
$$X \ M \ Y$$

with the letters X S, M A S, and Y S in strict vertical arrangement. The first thing that strikes the eye in this signature is
its triangular character. It inevitably leads the mind to the
Cabbala. Thus does Colón himself, by strict adherence to a
most unusual practice, lead the least prepossessed observer to
the chief occult science of the Jews. This in itself should suffice
to add further material to the abundant hints already provided
of Colón's Jewish origin; but it so happens that a Cabbalistic
interpretation of the triangular arrangement, and particularly of
the dotted S's, translates this signature into the shield of David,
double triangle or hexagram. (39)

And so the old sailor would be coming back to his original
faith as he felt the approach of death. All was ready for his
departure. His dreams fulfilled, and proved vain. His struggles
resisted and beaten off like breakers by the immovable wall of
the Spanish royal State. The liberation of Jerusalem, still
calling out, with its arms wide open, would have to wait and
wait again for another man to attempt it. What could an old
Admiral do who would have raised ten thousand horse and
one hundred thousand foot to free the Holy City, (40) when the
gold which he would have put to so good a usage was being
squandered away in enriching "civil" people with no sense of
high endeavour and chivalrous enterprise? What could he do
but die?

On Thursday, May 20th, 1506, day of the Ascension, Cristóbal
Colón left Valladolid for his last voyage, that from which there
is no return.

* *

Now was the hour of truth. Now he would see the Lord and
tell Him how the world had made him suffer injustice upon
injustice; now he would at last expose that King who had denied
him his rights and privileges; now——

There was in front of him a gigantic Cristóbal Colón woven
with rays of transparent light. He was dressed in magnificent
garments as an Admiral of the Ocean Sea and wore golden spurs
which shone like diamonds. Pearls upon pearls studded his
sea-coloured mantle and he had a sword of lightning. Colón
was drinking in the vision, when it suddenly transfigured itself
into a brother of St. Francis, bearded, saintly and aggrieved,
but just as transparent, luminous and resplendent as the Admiral
of the Indies which had vanished: and no sooner had he
recognised himself in this new figure, when lo, a third Colón of

light was before his astonished eyes, leaning heavily on a table of burning ether, eyes sunken, tears of Veragua pearls falling from them, fetters of fire riveted round his luminous ankles. . . . And then, the glorious Admiral again, and the Franciscan brother, and the prisoner, following each other in quicker and quicker succession until the three visions were together before his eyes, all three perfectly distinct and clear and transparent, yet melted into each other, and no longer three, but one. "In the name of the Holy Trinity," thought Colón by sheer habit of mind. Then the visions spoke:

Let the dead bury the dead and let the earth be earthly. Why grieve? You did your best. You were not asked to do more. Shall a man rise above his crown or a tree catch birds beyond its top? You thought that you mattered, and that is why you suffered so much agony when days went by and you were not amongst the powerful. But you mattered not. What mattered was the Great Design, the union of Continent and Continent, the discovery of the earth by the earth, and of man by man. The time had come when mankind, which had lived for centuries with its hands joined upwards in a yearning, vertical gesture, the shape of its cathedral windows, had to lower its arms, disjoin its hands and make them active in horizontal, tumultuous and creative activities. Worship of the unknowable was to be superseded by the discovery of the knowable; the sons of men were to be given at last the full possession of their planet. An era had to begin in which man was first to seek the surface of the planet, then to fathom its depths, then the depths of infinite space and of that other infinite which is in the microcosm. Man had to discover man, the better to know himself. The cannibals had to create Caliban in the genius of Shakespeare; the new world had to bring forth the *Novum Organum* in the genius of Bacon; the naked Arcadians of Guanahani had to arouse Rousseau's imagination into chanting the beauties of natural man and to usher in the French Revolution, the rights of man and the gospel of Karl Marx. The time had come for a world to die and for another world to be born. The New World that was to be discovered was not merely the American Continent, but that world which the discovery of the American Continent was to bring forth in the minds of men. Someone was needed to open the way, to lead. And the first act could only be an act of faith—the discovery of a continent by one who had no reason whatever to believe in the existence of that continent. That lost world had to be found and someone had to find it; but this was bound to be the greatest day in human history, and had it been entrusted to a man who knew what he was doing, he would have been dangerous to men. This task had to be given to a man whose vision flew over the waters of reality like those birds which you heard pass over your tired sails the night before the discovery; and he had to be given an illusion so identical with reality that he would sail towards his dream with as much certainty as if he had been there before and had locked it up in his chest. What if he led for the wrong reason, since he led to the right place? Mankind may know where it is going even when its leaders do not. You did not matter at all. Between Europe and America, you were but a bridge of aching flesh. You did not discover America, which is what mankind was after; you discovered the Indies, which do not exist save in your imagination; and because you would bend to yourself that joy, the spirit denied you access to the knowledge of what you were doing—and the continent does not bear your name.

The vision vanished.

Colón died a second time. And he lives for evermore.

NOTES

I. ACKNOWLEDGEMENTS

Apart from the help and advice which has been given me generously on concrete points and which I mention when dealing with the points in question, I wish to express my thanks on more general grounds to the *Administrateur* of the Bibliothèque Nationale of Paris, Monsieur Julien Cain and to his collaborators, Monsieur de la Roncière and Monsieur du Bus; to the Director and staff of the London Library for their courtesy and advice; and, above all, to the authorities and staff of the British Museum for their proverbial hospitality—above praise and, I dare say, above gratitude. I may perhaps be allowed to single out in this connection my friend Dr. Henry Thomas, an indispensable pilot for all who venture on the oceans of Spanish science dammed within the walls of the venerable house.

II. SPELLING OF SPANISH NAMES

The position with regard to Spanish names in English-speaking countries is far from satisfactory. I am afraid it is even worse than that of English names in Spanish-speaking countries, though this is a hard saying. I will deal first with the name of *Columbus* and later with other Spanish names.

A. *Columbus.*—The reasons why I have decided to use the form *Colón* throughout the book are to be found in the text. It is no capricious choice. It was the name he chose and he wanted no other name, as shown in his will. His contemporaries knew him as *Colón, Colomo* or *Colom* in Spanish and *Colonus* in Latin. Peter Martyr, an Italian contemporary who knew him personally, latinises his name into *Colonus.*

One always hesitates to criticise such an admirable institution as the British Museum, but in this matter of Colón's name its case is perhaps the worst. Had the B.M. catalogued it under *Columbus,* wrong and unnecessarily cumbrous as that name is, it would have been after all in accordance with English-speaking custom. But no. It is catalogued under COLOMBO, which is the name Colón deliberately gave up. Now, Colombo, born a Genoese, would not be known to history and would not be catalogued at all in the B.M. if he had not become Colón, under which name he performed his life work. He founded a family of Spaniards with that particular name, and his name as a Spaniard and as a world historical figure is and was *Colón.* Furthermore, the B.M., having taken this wrong decision, is fatally led to such absurdities as cataloguing under *Colombo* persons who never bore that name, i.e. the two sons of the Admiral. It is evident that the natural moment to pass from *Colombo* to *Colón* is when dealing with the great man himself and not arbitrarily, as it is done now, with Don Luis Colón, the Admiral's grandson.

B. Other Spanish names.—The English-speaking peoples have a perfect right to use English names to designate Spanish persons or places, but not that of treating good Spanish names with the contempt for the Spanish language which they now evince.

Isabella is neither English nor Spanish. The Spanish is *Isabel.* The towns and islands named *Isabela* by Colón were feminised adjectives such as *Fernandina* from Ferdinand and *Juana* from Juan (Island being a feminine substantive). English and American authors may, if they so wish, call *Santo Domingo St. Dominic,* or even *St.*

410

Domingo. But *San Domingo* is just as bad as if Spanish-speaking people insisted in writing *Washingtom* or *Westmunster*. It reveals sheer indifference due to ignorance.

I know *Castile* is the usual English form for what Bacon gracefully calls *Castilia*, a more accurate and, in my humble opinion, more English form than *Castile*, which is little better than incorrect French. I have chosen *Castille*, because, while it deviates less from current usage than *Castilia* (which I would have preferred), it respects the two L's of the etymology. Moreover, Sevilla does give Seville and not Sevile.

I have accented names in order to enable the reader to pronounce them our way—if he so desires.

III. BIBLIOGRAPHY

There is a sea of books on Colón. None but those actually used are mentioned in the following list. The list has been compiled in alphabetic order following the abbreviations generally used in the notes.

Alba. Maria del Rosario Falcó y Ossorio : *Autógrafos de Cristóbal Colón.* Madrid, 1892.

Alba-Nuevos. *Nuevos Autógrafos de Colón y Relaciones de Ultramar, los publica la Duquesa de Berwick y de Alba, Condesa de Siruela.* Madrid, 1902.

Alfonso X. Alfonso X: *Crónica de España. Las quatro partes enteras de la Crónica de España que mandó componer el Serenissimo Rey don Alonso llamado el Sabio,* edited by Florian Docâpo cronista del Emperador. Zamora, 1541.

Altolaguirre. Angel de Altolaguirre y Duvale :
1. *¿Colón Español?* Madrid, 1923.
2. *Cristóbal Colón y Pablo del Pozzo Toscanelli.* Madrid, 1903.
3. *La Real Confirmación del Mayorazgo fundado por Don Cristóbal Colón.* Madrid, 1926.

A.R. José Fernández Amador de los Rios : *Historia, social, politica y religiosa de los Judíos de España y Portugal.* Madrid, 1875.

Asensio. José Maria Asensio: *Cristóbal Colón. Su Vida. Sus Viajes. Sus Descubrimientos.* Barcelona, 1891.

Bacon. Sir Francis Bacon, Lord Verulam: *The Historie of the Raigne of King Henry The Seuenth, written by the Right Honourable Francis, Lord Verulam, Viscount St. Alban.* London, 1622.

Baer. Fritz Baer: *Die Juden im christlichen Spanien.* Berlin, 1936.

Barros. Joâm de Barros: *Da Asia. Dos fectos que os Portugueses fizeram no descubrimento e conquista dos mares e terras do Oriente.* Lisboa, MDLII.

412

Bataillon. Marcel Bataillon: *Érasme et l'Espagne, Recherches sur l'histoire spirituelle du XVIe siècle.* Paris, 1937.

Beltrán. R. Beltrán y Rózpide:
Cristóbal Colón y Cristoforo Colombo. Madrid, 1921.
¿Cristóbal Colón Genovés?. Madrid, 1925.

Bensabat. Moses Bensabat Amzalak: *Uma Interpretaçao da assinatura de Cristobam Colombo.* Lisboa, 1927.

Bernáldez. Andrés Bernáldez: *Historia de los Reyes Católicos Don Fernando y Doña Isabel, escrita por el bachiller Andrés Bernáldez, cura de los Palacios y Capellán del Arzobispo de Sevilla, Don Diego Deza,* edición de la Sociedad de Bibliófilos Andaluces. Sevilla, MDCCCLXX.

Brasil. Carlos Malheiro Dias, Ernesto de Vasconcelos, Roque Gameiro: *História da Colonizaçao Portuguesa do Brasil.* Lisboa, MCMXXI.

Buron. Pierre d'Ailly: *Ymago Mundi,* edited by Edmond Buron, Maisonneuve frères. Paris, 1930.

Carreras. R. Carreras i Valls: *Los Catalanes, Juan Cabot y Cristóbal Colón.* 1931.

C.D.I.A.I. *Colección de Documentos Inéditos relativos al descubrimiento, conquista y colonización de las posesiones españolas en América y Occeania [sic], sacados en su mayor parte del Real Archivo de Indias,* bajo la dirección de los Sres. D. Joaquin F. Pacheco y D. Francisco de Cárdenas . . . y D. Luis Torres de Mendoza, en 42 volumenes. Madrid, 1864-84.
Segunda Edición publicada por la Real Academia de la Historia. Madrid, 1885-1900.

C.D.I.H.E. *Colección de Documentos Inéditos para la Historia de España por el Marqués de la Fuensanta del Valle y D. José Rayón.* Madrid, 1875.

Coplas. *Coplas del Provincial—Revue Hispanique.* 1894.

d'Ailly. See Buron.

David. Maurice David: *Who was Columbus?.* The New York Research Publishing Company, 1933.

Duro. — Cesáreo Fernández Duro:
  Pinzón en el Descubrimiento de las Indias. Madrid, 1892.
  Colón y Pinzón, Real Academia de la Historia. Madrid, 1896.

F.C. — *Historie del S. D. Fernando Colombo, Nelle quale s'ha particulare e vera relatione dell'Ammiraglio D. Christoforo Colombo, suo padre, Nuovamente di lingua spanuola tradotte nell'Italiana* dal S. Alfonso Ulloa. Venise, 1571. The history of his father was written by Fernando Colón in Spanish. His MS. was one of the bases for Las Casas' own history of the Indies in so far as it relates to Colón. But this original Spanish MS. is lost, and the first time the history sees the light is in the above Italian translation, which is, therefore, to be read bearing in mind this unfortunate circumstance.
  When quoted in Spanish:
  Historia del Almirante Don Cristóbal Colón, escrita por Don Fernando Colón, su hijo. Madrid, 1892.

Genoa. — Città di Genova: *Colombo.* MCMXXXII.

Gómara. — Francisco López de Gómara: *La Historia General de las Indias.* Edition of Antwerp, 1554.

Harrisse. — Henry Harrisse:
  Jean et Sebastian Cabot. Paris, 1882.
  Christophe Colomb, son origine, sa vie. Paris, 1884.

Humboldt. — F. H. A. von Humboldt: *Examen critique de l'Histoire de la Geographie et des progrès de l'Astronomie Nautique aux quinzième et seizième siècles.* Paris, 1836.

Jane. — Cecil Jane:
  Voyages of Christopher Columbus. 1930.
  The Administration of the Colons in Española. XXI International Congress of Americanists, 1924.

Kayserling. — Dr. M. Kayserling: *Christopher Columbus and the participation of the Jews in the Spanish and Portuguese discoveries,* translated from the author's MS. by Charles Gross, Ph.D. New York, 1894.

Las Casas. — Bartolomé de las Casas: *Historia de las Indias.* Volumes 62, 63, 64 of *C.D.I.H.E.*

Lollis. Cesare de Lollis: *Qui a découvert l'Amerique?*. Revue des Revues. Paris, January 1898.

Navarrete. Martín Fernández de Navarrete: *Colección de los Viajes y Descubrimientos que hicieron por mar los Españoles*. Imprenta Real. Madrid, 1825.

Nunn. George E. Nunn: *Geographical Conceptions of Columbus*. American Geographical Society. New York, 1924.

Oviedo. Gonzalo Fernández de Oviedo:
Coronica de las Indias. La hystoria general de agora nuevamente impressa, corregida y aumentada. Partes I y II, Juan de Junta. Salamanca, 1547. F. Fernández de Córdoba. Valladolid, 1557. Another edition (Real Academia de la Historia) por Don José Amador de los Rios. Madrid, 1851-55.

Pina. Ruy de Pina: *Cronica d'El Rey D. Joâo II. Colleçâo de Livros Ineditos de Historia Portuguesa.* Academia Real das Sciencias de Lisboa. Vol. II. Lisboa, 1792.

Pleitos. *Pleitos de Colón — C.D.I.H.E.*, Segunda Serie, Volumenes 7 y 8.

Pulgar-Claros. Hernando del Pulgar: *Claros Varones de Castilla y Letras.* Madrid, en la Imprenta Real de la Gazeta, con las licencias necesarias, 1775.

Pulgar-Crónica. Hernando del Pulgar: *Crónica de los Señores Reyes Católicos Don Fernando y Doña Isabel de Castilla y de Aragón, escrita por su cronista Hernando del Pulgar, cotexada con antiguos manuscritos y aumentada de varias ilustraciones y enmiendas.* Valencia, en la imprenta de Benito Monfort, 1780.

Raccolta. Reale Commissione Colombiana: *Raccolta di Documenti*, pubblicati dalla R.C.C. nel Quarto Centenario dalla Scoperta dell'America. Roma. Ministero della Pubblica Istruzione, 1892.

Ribeiro. Patrocinio Ribeiro: *A Nacionalidade Portuguesa de Cristovam Colombo.* Lisboa, 1927.

Sigüenza. Fray José de Sigüenza: *Historia de la Orden de San Jerónimo*, edited by D. Juan Catalina Garcia. Madrid, 1909.

Thacher. John Boyd Thacher: *Christopher Columbus: His life, his works, his remains.* New York, 1903.

Ulloa.   Luis de Ulloa:
Christophe Colomb Catalan. Paris, 1927.

Ulloa-Pr.De.   *El predescubrimiento hispano-catalán de América en 1473.* Paris, 1928.

Valera-Epístolas. Mosén Diego de Valera:
Epístolas y otros varios Tratados de Mosén Diego de Valera. Sociedad de Bibliófilos Españoles. Madrid, 1878.

Valera-Crónica.   *La Crónica de los Reyes Católicos.* Revista de Filología Española. Madrid, 1925.

Vignaud-Toscanelli.   Henry Vignaud:
Toscanelli and Columbus. London, 1902.

Vignaud.   *Histoire Critique de la grande entreprise de Christophe Colomb.* Paris, H. Welter, 1911.

Vignaud-Études.   *Études Critiques sur la vie de Colomb.* Paris, 1905.

IV. NOTES TO THE CHAPTERS

CHAPTER I

1 " Porque, cristianísimos, y muy altos, y muy excelentes, y muy poderosos Príncipes, Rey y Reina de las Españas y de las islas de la mar, nuestros Señores, este presente año de 1492, despues de vuestras Altezas haber dado fin á la guerra de los moros que reinaban en Europa, y haber acabado la guerra en la muy grande ciudad de Granada, adonde este presente año á dos dias del mes de Enero por fuerza de armas vide poner las banderas Reales de vuestras Altezas en las torres de Alfambra. . . ."—Cristóbal Colón : Journal of First Journey, *Navarrete*, vol. I, p. 1.
" En las partes donde llegaba Don Cristóbal Colón ponia las armas de Dios e del Rey, conviene a saber, la Cruz por Dios y una bandera por nombre de S.A."—Statement of witness in *Pleitos*.

2 The description of the surrender of Granada is based on *Pulgar-Crónica*, pt. III, ch. CXXXIII.

3 " ' Señor, pues este Rey Moro vos viene á facer reverencia, y es vuestro vasallo, cosa razonable es que como á vuestro súbdito le déis la mano á besar.' "
" ' Diéragela por cierto, si estoviera libre en su reyno : é no gela daré, porque está preso en el mio.' "—*Pulgar-Crónica*, pt. III, ch. XXIII.

4 " Esta Reyna era de mediana estatura, bien compuesta en su persona y en la proporción de sus miembros, muy blanca é rubia ; los ojos entre verdes é azules, el mirar gracioso é honesto, las faciones del rostro bien puestas, la cara muy fermosa é alegre. Era mesurada en la continencia é movimientos de su persona, no bebia vino : era muy buena muger, é placíale tener cerca de sí mugeres ancianas que fuesen buenas é de linage. Criaba en su palacio doncellas nobles, fijas de los Grandes de su Reynos, lo que no leemos en Crónica que ficiese otro tanto otra Reyna ninguna. [. . .] Amaba mucho al Rey su marido, é celábalo fuera de toda medida. Era muger muy aguda é discreta, lo qual vemos pocas é rara veces concurrir en una persona, fablaba muy bien, y era de tan excelente ingenio, que en comun de tantos é tan árduos negocios como tenia en la governacion de sus Reynos, se dió al trabajo de aprender las letras latinas : é alcanzó en tiempo de un año saber en ellas tanto, que entendia qualquier fabla ó escriptura latina. Era católica é devota, facia limosnas secretas en lugares debidos, honraba las casas de oracion, visitaba con voluntad los monasterios é casas de religion, en especial aquellas do conocia que guardaban vida honesta, dotábalas magnificamente. Aborrecia estrañamente sortílegos é adevinos, é todas personas de semejantes artes é invenciones.
" Placíale la conversacion de personas religiosas é de vida honesta, con los quales muchas veces habia sus consejos particulares : é como quier que oia el parecer de aquellos, é de los otros letrados que cerca della eran, pero por la mayor parte seguia las cosas por su arbitrio. Pareció ser bien fortunada en las cosas que comenzaba. Era muy inclinada á facer justicia, tanto que le era imputado seguir mas la via de rigor que de la piedad : y esto facia por remediar á la gran corrupcion de crímines que falló en el Reyno quando subcedió en él. Queria que sus cartas é mandamientos fuesen complidas con diligencia. Esta Reyna fué la que extirpó

417

é quitó la heregía que habia en los Reynos de Castilla é de Aragon, de algunos cristianos de linage de los judios que tornaban á judaizar, é fizo que viviesen como buenos cristianos. En el proveer de la Iglesias que vacaron en su tiempo ovo respeto tan recto, que pospuesta toda aficion siempre suplicó al Papa por hombres generosos é grandes letrados é de vida honesta : lo que no se lee que con tanta diligencia oviese guardado ningun Rey de los pasados. Honraba los Perlados é Grandes de sus Reynos en las fablas y en los asientos, guardando á cada uno su preeminencia, segun la calidad de su persona é dignidad.

"Era muger de gran corazón, encubria la ira, é disimulábala : é por esto que della se conocia, ansi los Grandes del Reyno como todos los otros temian de caer en su indinacion. De su inclinacion era verdadera, é queria mantener su palabra : como quiera que en los movimientos de las guerras é otros grandes fechos que en sus Reynos acaeciéron en aquellos tiempos, é algunas mudanzas fechas por algunas personas, la ficiéron algunas veces variar. Era muy trabajadora por su persona, segun se verá adelante por los actos desta Crónica. Era firme en sus propósitos, de los quales se retraia con gran dificultad. Érale imputado que no era franca ; porque no daba vasallos de su patrimonio á los que en aquellos tiempos la sirvieron. Verdad es que con tanta diligencia guardaba lo de la corona real, que pocas mercedes de villas é tierras le vimos en nuestros tiempos facer, porque falló muchos dellas enagenadas. Pero quan estrechamente se habia en la conservacion de las tierras, tan franca é liberal era en la distribucion de los gastos continos, é mercedes de grandes quantías que facia. Decia ella, que á los Reyes convenia conservar las tierras, porque enagenándolas perdian las rentas de que deben facer mercedes para ser amados, é diminuian su poder para ser temidos. Era muger cerimoniosa en sus vestidos, é arreos, y en el servicio de su persona : é queria servirse de homes grandes é nobles, é con grande acatamiento é humillacion. No se lee de ningun Rey de los pasados, que tan grandes homes toviese por oficiales como tovo. É como quiera que por esta condicion le era imputado algun vicio, diciendo tener pompa demasiada, pero entendemos que ninguna cerimonia en esta vida se puede facer tan por estremo á los Reyes, que mucho mas no requiera el estado real : el qual ansi como es uno é superior en los Reynos, ansi debe mucho estremarse, é resplandecer sobre todos los otros estados, pues tiene autoridad divina en la tierra. Por la solicitud desta Reyna se comenzó, é por su diligencia se continó la guerra contra los Moros fasta que se ganó todo el Reyno de Granada. E decimos verdad ante Dios, que supimos é conocimos de algunos grandes señores é capitanes de sus Reynos, que cansando perdian toda su esperanza para poderse ganar, considerando la dificultad grande que habia en poderla continar : é por la gran constancia desta Reyna, é por sus trabajos é diligencias que continamente fizo en las provisiones, é por las otras fuerzas que con gran fatiga de espiritu puso, dió fin á esta conquista, que movida por la voluntad divina pareció haber comenzado, segun que adelante en esta Crónica parecerá."

This pórtrait of Queen Isabel will be found in *Pulgar-Crónica*, pt. II, ch. IV.

5 "El Rey D. Fernando V de este nombre, nació en Aragon a dos días de Marzo del año del nacimiento de Nuestro Redentor a mil y cuatro cientos y cincuenta y dos, en una villa que llaman Sos : viernes nació a las diez horas del día, estando su planeta e signo en muy alto triunfo de bien aventuranza, segun dijeron los astrólogos."—*Bernáldez*, ch. VIII, vol. I, p. 29.

6 "Este Rey era home de mediana estatura, bien proporcionado en sus miembros, en las faciones de su rostro bien compuesto, los ojos rientes, los cabellos prietos é llanos, é hombre bien complisionado. Tenía la fabla igual, ni presurosa ni mucho espaciosa. Era de buen entendimiento, é muy templado en su comer é bever, y en los movimientos de su persona ; porque ni la ira ni el placer facia en él alteracion. Cavalgaba muy bien á caballo,

en silla de la guisa é de la gineta : justaba sueltamente é con tanta destreza, que ninguno en todos sus reynos lo facia mejor. Era gran cazador de aves, é home de buen esfuerzo, é gran trabajador en las guerras. De su natural condicion era inclinado á facer justicia, é tambien era piadoso, é compadecíase de los miserables que veia en alguna angustia. E habia una gracia singular, que qualquier que con él fablase, luego le amaba é le deseaba servir, porque tenia la comunicacion amigable. Era ansimesmo remitido á consejo, en especial de la Reyna su muger, porque conocia su gran suficiencia : desde su niñez fué criado en guerras, do pasó muchos trabajos é peligros de su persona. E porque todas sus rentas gastaba en las cosas de la guerra, y estaba en continas necesidades, no podemos decir que era franco. Home era de verdad, como quiera que las necesidades grandes en que le pusiéron las guerras, le facian algunas veces variar. Placíale jugar todos juegos, de pelota é axedrez é tablas, y en esto gastaba algun tiempo mas de lo que debia ; é como quiera que amaba mucho á la Reyna su muger, pero dábase á otras mugeres. Era hombre muy tratable con todos, especialmente con sus servidores continos. Este Rey conquistó é ganó el reyno de Granada, segun que adelante en esta Crónica será visto."—*Pulgar-Crónica*, pt. II, ch. III.

7 " E cada una tierra de las del mundo et a cada provincia honró Dios en señas guisas, et dió su don ; mas entre todas las tierras que ell honró mas, España la de occidente fué ; ca a esta abastó él de todas aquellas cosas que homme suel cobdiciar. Ca desde que los godos andidieron por las tierras de la una part et de la otra provándolas por guerras et por batallas et conquiriendo muchos logares en las provincias de Asia et de Europa, asi como dixiemos, probando muchas moradas en cada logar et catando bien et escogiendo entre todas las tierras el mas provechoso logar, fallaron que España era el meior de todos, et muchol preciaron más que a ninguno de los otros, ca entre todas las tierras del mundo España ha una estremanza de abondamiento de bondad más que otra tierra ninguna. . . .
" España es abondada de mieses, deleitosa de fructas, viciosa de pescados, sabrosa de leche et de todas las cosas que se della facen ; lena de venados et de caza, cubierta de ganados, lozana de caballos, provechosa de mulos, segura et bastida de castiellos, alegre por buenos vinos, folgada de abondamiento de pan ; rica de metales, de plomo, de estaño, de argent vivo, de fierro, de arambre, de plata, de oro, de piedras preciosas, de toda manera de piedra marmol, de sales de mar et de salinas de tierra et de sal en peñas, et dotros mineros muchos : azul, almagra, greda, alumbre et otros muchos de cuantos se fallan en otras tierras ; briosa de sirgo et de cuanto se face dél, dulce de miel et de azucar, alumbrada de cera, complida de olio, alegre de azafrán.
" España sobre todas es engeñosa, atrevuda et mucho esforzada en lid, ligera en afan, leal al señor, afincada en estudio, palaciana en palabra, complida de todo bien ; non ha tierra en el mundo que la semeje en abondanza, nin se equale ninguna a ella en fortalezas et pocas ha en el mundo tan grandes como ella. España sobre todas es adelantada en grandez et mas que todas preciadas por lealtad. ¡ Ay España ! non ha lengua nin engeño que pueda contar tu bien. . . .
" Pues este regno tan noble, tan rico, tan poderoso, tan honrrado, fué derramado et astragado en una arremesa por desavenencia de los de la tierra que tornaron sus espadas en si mismos unos contra otros, asi como si les minguasen enemigos ; et perdieron y todos, ca todas las cibdades de España fueron presas de los moros et crebantadas et destroidas de mano de sus enemigos.—*Alfonso X*, fol. ccii verso.

8 " Una de las cosas que los Reyes comarcanos vos an envidia, es tener en vuestros confines gente con quien, no solo podeis tener guerra justa, mas guerra santa, en que entendais é hagais exercer la Caballería de vuestros

Reynos ; que no piense Vuestra Alteza ser pequeño proveímiento."—
Letter to the Queen (1482), *Pulgar-Claros*, p. 150.

9 " La venida de la Reyna al real fué con placer comun de todos ; especialmente porque como las gentes estaban enojadas, deseaban ver cosas nuevas,
é creían que su venida traeria tal novedad, que el cerco que habia durado
seis meses con grandes trabajos é peligros, habria algun buen fin."—
Pulgar-Crónica, pt. III, ch. CXXII.

". . . fué por cierto caso digno de admiracion ver la súbita mutacion
que en su propósito se vido. E porque fuimos presentes é lo vimos,
testificamos verdad delante Dios que lo sabe, é delante los homes que
lo veyéron : que despues que esta Reyna entró en el real, paresció que
todos los rigores de las peleas, todos los espiritus crueles, todas las intenciones
enemigas é contrarias cesáron, é paresció que amansáron."—*Pulgar-Crónica*,
pt. III, ch. CXXII.

10 " El viernes que los Moros partieron de Illora para Granada, partieron
del Real el Marqués-Duque de Cádiz e el Adelantado de Andalucía con
gran caballería a recibir la Reyna Doña Isabel, a la Peña de los Enamorados,
que venía a ver el Real, e a ver parte de la victoria e buena ventura del
Rey su Marido, la cual traía consigo, dejando le gente que la fué a recibir,
hasta cuarenta cabalgaduras, en que había fasta diez mugeres, e recibimiento que le fué fecho fué muy singular, en que salieron al camino
los primeros el Duque del Infantadgo, que había venido de Castilla
a la guerra en persona muy poderoso e muy pomposo, e el Pendón de
Sevilla e su gente, e el Prior de San Juan, fasta una legua y media del
Real ; e púsose una batalla a la mano izquierda del camino por donde
ella venía, todos bien aderezados como para pelear ; e como la Reyna
llegó, fizo reverencia al Pendón de Sevilla, e mandolo pasar a la mano
derecha, e como la recibieron salió toda la gente delante con mucha alegría
corriendo a todo correr, de que su alteza ovo muy gran placer : e luego
vinieron todas las batallas, e las vanderas del Real e la facer recibimiento,
e todas las banderas se abajaban cuando la Reyna pasaba ; e luego llegó
el Rey con muchos Grandes de Castilla a la recibir, e antes que se abrazasen
se hicieron cada tres reverencias, en que la Reyna se destocó, e quedó
en una cofia el rostro descubierto, e llegó el Rey, se fué a la Infanta su
fija e abrazóla e besóla en la boca, e santiguóla ; venia la Reyna en una
mula Castaña en una silla andas, guarnecida de plata dorada, traía un
paño de carmesí de pelo, e las falsas riendas e cabezada de la mula eran
rasas, labradas de seda de letras de oro entretallada y las orladuras bordadas
de oro ; e traía un brial de terciopelo e debajo unas faldetas de brocado
e un capuz de grana, vestido guarnecido Morisco, e un sombrero negro
guarnecido de brocado al rededor de la copa e ruedo ; e la Infanta venía
en otra mula Castaña guarnecida de plata blanca, e por orladura bordada
de oro, e ella vestida de un brial de brocado negro e un capuz negro
guarnecido de la guarnición de la Reyna.

" El Rey tenía vestido un jubón de demesin, de pelo, e un quisote de
seda rasa amarillo, y encima un sayo de brocado y unas corazas de brocado
vestidas, e una espada morisca ceñida muy rica, e una toca e, un sombrero,
y en cuerpo en un caballo castaño muy jaezado, e los atavios de los Grandes
eran muy maravillosos e muy ricos, e de diversas maneras, así de guerra
como de fiesta que sería muy luengo de escribir : e llegó el Conde de
Inglaterra luego en pos del Rey a facer recibimiento a la Reyna e a la
Infanta muy pomposo, en estraña manera a la postre de todos armado
en blanco a la guisa, encima de un caballo castaño con los paramentos,
fasta el suelo de seda azul, y las orladuras, tan anchas como una mano,
de seda rasa blanca, e todos los paramentos estrellados de oro enforrados
en ceptí morado ; e él traía sobre las armas una ropeta francesa de brocado
negro raso, un sombrero blanco francés con un plumaje, e traía en su

brazo izquierdo un broquelete redondo a bandas de oro, e una cimera muy pomposa fecha de tan nueva manera, que a todos parecía bien, e traía consigo cinco caballos encubertados con sus pages encima todos vestidos de seda e brocado, e venían con él ciertos gentiles hombres de los suyos muy ataviados, e ansi llegó a facer reverencia al Rey, e anduvo un rato festejando a todos encima de su caballo, e saltando a un lado e otro muy concertadamente, mirándole todos los Grandes e toda la gente, e a todos pareció bien e desto Sus Altezas ovieron mucho placer, e ansí vinieron fasta las tiendas reales donde los Señores reyes, e su fija fueron bien aposentados, e las damas y señores que las acompañaban en este viaje."—*Bernáldez*, ch. LXXX.

11 *Valera-Crónica*, ch. LXX.

12 *Pulgar-Crónica*, pt. III, ch. LVIII.

13 " E luego demandó los cautivos cristianos que en Málaga estaban, e fizo poner una tienda cerca de la puerta de Granada, donde él e la Reina e la Infanta, su fija, los recibieron, y fueron entre hombres y mujeres los que alli los moros les trajeron fasta seiscientas personas ; [. . .] E llegando donde sus Altezas estaban, todos se humillaban e caian por el suelo, e les querian besar los pies, e ellos no lo consentian, más dábanles las manos e cuantos los veían, daban loores a Dios, e lloraban con ellos con alegria ; los cuales salieron tan flacos y amarillos con la gran hambre, que querian perecer todos con los hierros y adovones a los pies e los cuellos, e barbas muy cumplidas [. . .] E luego el Rey les mandó dar de comer e de beber e les mandó desherrar, e los mandaron vestir e dar limosnas para despensa de cada uno donde quisiese ir, y asi fué fecho y cumplido. E en estos cautivos había personas de grandes rescates que estaban rescatados ; e habia personas que habia diez, e quince e veinte años que estaban cautivos, e otros menos."—*Bernáldez*, ch. LXXXV, vol. I, pp. 249-50.

14 *Pulgar-Crónica*, pt. III, ch. LIV.

15 *Valera-Epístolas*.

16 *Valera-Epístolas*.

CHAPTER II

1 There are no portraits of Colón of which it may be said that they reproduce the features of the original as observed by an artist. Thacher devotes an exhaustive study to those which claim to represent the Admiral, and the *Raccolta* has by no means neglected the subject. The oldest, which might conceivably originate in some direct observation of Colón's features, suggest features usually associated with the Jewish type, particularly in the hair, nose, lower lip and general impression of the face.

 Colón is traditionally represented beardless. This is a stubborn tradition, and may be based on some hearsay grounded on fact. But it is certain that at some time of his life he let his beard grow (" y vistiose de pardo como frayle y dexóse crecer la barua").—*Oviedo*, bk. II, ch. XIII, fol. xix verso).

2 " LLegado, pues, ya el tiempo [. . .] cuando por estas partes de la tierra (sembrada la simiente o palabra de la vida) se había de coger el ubérrimo fruto [. . .] escogió el divino y sumo maestro entre los hijos de Adan que en estos nuestros tiempos habia en la tierra, aquel ilustre y grande Colón, conviene a saber, de nombre y de obra poblador primero, para de su virtud, ingenio, industria, trabajos, saber y prudencia, confiar una de las más egregias divinas hazañas que por el siglo presente quiso en su mundo hacer ; y porque de costumbre tiene la suma y divinal Providencia de proveer a todas las cosas, segun la natural condicion de cada una [. . .] y como este fuese tan

alto y tan arduo y divino negocio [. . .] por ende a este su ministro y apostol primero destas Indias, creedera cosa es haberle Dios esmaltado de tales calidades naturales y adquisitas [. . .] Fué, pues, este varón escogido de nación genovés de algun lugar de la provincia de Genova ; cual fuese, donde nació o que nombre tuvo el tal lugar, no consta la verdad dello más de que se solia llamar antes que llegase al estado que llego, Cristóbal Columbo de Terra-rubia, y lo, mismo su hermano Bartolomé Colón [. . .] Una historia portuguesa que escribio un Juan de Barros, portugués, que llamó 'Asia' en el lib. III, cap. 2. de la primera década, haciendo minción deste descubrimiento no dice sino que, según todos afirman, este Cristóbal era genovés de nación. Sus padres fueron personas notables, en algun tiempo ricos, cuyo trato o manera de vivir debió ser por mercaderías por la mar, segun él mismo da a entender en una carta suya ; otro tiempo debieron ser pobres por las guerras y parcialidades que siempre hubo y nunca faltan, por la mayor parte, en Lombardía. El linaje de suyo dicen que fué generoso procedido aquel Colon de quien Cornelio Tacito trata en el lib. XII al principio, diciendo que trujo a Roma preso a Mitridates, por lo cual le fueron dadas insignias consulares y otros privilegios por el pueblo romano en agradecimiento de sus servicios. Y es de saber, que antiguamente el primer sobrenombre de su linage, dicen, que fué Colón, despues, el tiempo andando, se llamaron Colombos los sucesores del susodicho Colón romano o capitán de los romanos ; y destos Colombos hace mención Antonio Sabelico en el lib. VIII de la década 10., folio 168, donde trata de dos ilustres varones genoveses que se llamaban Colombos, como abajo se dirá. Pero este ilustre hombre, dejado el apellido introducido, por la costumbre, quiso llamarse Colón, restituyendose al vocablo antiguo, no tanto acaso, segun es de creer, cuanto por voluntad divina que para obrar lo que su nombre y sobrenombre significaba lo elegía. Suele la divinal Providencia ordenar, que se pongan nombres y sobrenombres a las personas que señala para se servir conformes a los oficios que les determina cometer, segun asaz parece por muchas partes de la Sagrada Escritura ; y el filosofo en el IV de la *Metafísica*, dice : 'que los nombres deben convenir con las propiedades y oficios de las cosas.' Llamose, pues, por nombre Cristóbal, conviene a saber *Christum ferens*, que quiere decir traedor o llevador de Cristo, y ansi se firma él algunas veces ; como en la verdad él haya sido el primero que abrió las puertas de este mar Océano, por dende entró y él metió a estas tierras tan remotas y reinos hasta entonces tan incógnitos a nuestro Salvador Jesucristo [. . .] Tuvo por sobrenombre Colón, que quiere decir poblador de nuevo, el cual sobrenombre le convino en cuanto por su industria y trabajos fué causa que descubriendo estas gentes, infinitas ánimas dellas mediante la predicación del Evangelio [. . .] hayan ido y vayan cada dia a poblar de nuevo aquella triunfante ciudad del cielo. Tambien le convino, porque de España trajo el primero gente (si ella fuera cual debía ser) para hacer colonias, que son nuevas poblaciones traidas de fuera, que puestas y asentadas entre los naturales habitadores [. . .] constituyeran una nueva [. . .] cristiana Iglesia y felice república. Lo que pertenecía a su exterior persona y corporal disposición, fué de alto cuerpo, más que mediano ; el rostro luengo y autorizado ; la nariz aguileña ; los ojos garzos ; la barba y cabellos, cuando era mozo, rubios, puesto que muy presto con los trabajos se le tornaron canos ; era gracioso y alegre bien hablado, y segun dice la susodicha Historia portuguesa, elocuente y glorioso en sus negocios ; era grave en moderación, con los extraños afable, con los de su casa suave y placentero, [. . .] y discreta conversacion, y ansi podia provocar los que le viesen facilmente a su amor. Finalmente, representaba en su persona y aspecto venerable, persona de gran estado y autoridad y digna de toda reverencia ; era sobrio y moderado en el comer, beber, vestir y calzar ; solia comunmente decir, que hablase con alegría en familiar locucion, o indignado, cuando reprendía o se enojaba de alguno : *Do vos a Dios ¿ no os parece esto y esto ?* En las cosas de la religion cristiana, sin duda era católico y de mucha devoción ; cuasi en cada cosa que había o decía, o quería comenzar a hacer, siempre anteponía : [. . .] *Jesus cum Maria sit nobis in via* ; [. . .] su juramento era algunas veces : ' juro a San Fernando ' ; cuando alguna cosa de gran importancia en sus cartas quería con juramento afirmar, mayormente escribiendo a los Reyes, decía : ' hago juramento que es verdad esto.' Ayunaba los ayunos de la Iglesia observantísimamente ; confesaba muchas veces y comulgaba ; rezaba todas las horas canónicas como los eclesiásticos o religiosos ; enemicísimo de blasfemias y juramentos ; era devotísimo de Nuestra Señora y del seráfico Padre San Francisco ; pareció ser muy agradecido a Dios por los beneficios que de la divinal mano recibía, por lo cual, cuasi por proverbio, cada hora traía que le había hecho Dios grandes mercedes, como a David. Cuando algun oro o cosas preciosas le traían, entraba en su oratorio e hincaba las rodillas, convidando a los circunstantes y decia : ' demos gracias a nuestro Señor que de descubrir tantos bienes nos hizo dignos ' ; celosísimo era en gran manera del honor divino ; cupido y deseoso de la conversión destas gentes, y que por todas partes se sembrase y ampliase la fe de Jesucristo, y singularmente aficionado y devoto de que Dios le hiciese digno de que pudiese ayudar en algo para ganar el Santo Sepulcro ; y con esta devoción y la confianza que tuvo de que Dios le había de ayudar en el descubrimiento de este Orbe que prometía, suplicó a la Serenisima reina Doña Isabel, que hiciese voto de gastar todas las riquezas que por su descubrimiento para los Reyes resultasen en ganar la tierra y casa santa de Jerusalem, y ansí la Reina lo hizo, como abajo se tocará. Fué varón de grande ánimo, esforzado e altos pensamientos, inclinado naturalmente a lo que se puede colegir de su vida y hechos y escrituras y conversación, a acometer hechos y obras egregias y señaladas ; paciente y muy sufrido (como abajo más parecerá) perdonador de las injurias, y que no quería otra cosa, según del se cuenta, sino que conociesen los que le ofendían sus errores, y se le reconciliasen los delincuentes ; constantísimo y adornado de longanimidad en los trabajos y adversidades que le ocurrieron siempre, las cuales fueron increibles e infinitas, teniendo siempre gran confianza de la Providencia divina, y verdaderamente, a lo que del yo entendí, y de mi mismo padre, que con el fué cuando tornó con gente a poblar esta isla española el año de 93, y de otras personas que le acompañaron y que le sirvieron, entrañable fidelidad y devoción tuvo y guardó siempre a los Reyes."—*Las Casas*, bk. I, ch. II, vol. 62, pp. 41-45. The venerable Bishop is somewhat given to verbosity. The passages suppressed are either irrelevant or superfluous.

3   Bernáldez, ch. CXVIII, vol. I, p. 357 : "En el nombre de Dios Todopoderoso, ovo un hombre de tierra de Genova, mercader de libros de estampa, . . . que llamaban Cristóbal Colón, hombre de muy alto injenio, sin saber muchas letras, muy diestro de la arte de la Cosmographia, e del repartir del mundo."

4   *Pleitos*, vol. II, pp. 191-4. Here is the Spanish text : ". . . un fraile que se llamaba frey Juan Pérez, ques ya dyfunto, quiso fablar con el dicho don Cristóbal Colón e viendole despusycion de otra tierra o reyno ajeno a su lengua, le pregunto que quien era e donde venia, e aquel dicho Cristóbal Colón le dixo quel venia de la corte de su Alteza. . . ."

5   " Trato y conversacion he tenido con gente sabia, eclesiasticos e seglares, latinos y griegos, judios y moros y con otros muchos de otras setas," says Colón himself in his letter to the King and Queen prefacing his Book of Prophecies.—*Navarrete*, vol. II, p. 262.

6   " Como si dentro de una cámara con su propia llave, lo tuviera. . . ."— *Las Casas*, bk. I, ch. CV, vol. 62.

7   This letter is of so extraordinary a character that it came to be considered apocryphal by many scholars on the strength of Navarrete's version of it.

But on the publication of a photographic reproduction of it from the Archives of the Duke of Veragua, all doubts have been dispelled. Here is the text:

" Xpoual Colon. Nos Dom Joham per graça de Deus Rey de Portugall e dos Algarues daaquê e dallê mar em Africa Senhor de Guinee vos enuyamos muyto saludar. Vymos a carta que nos screpuestes e a booa vontade e afeiçam que por ella mostraees teerdes a nosso serviço vos agardeçemos muyto. E quanto a vossa vynda ca certo assy pollo que apontaes como por outros respeitos para que vossa industria e boo engenho nos sera necessareo nos a desejamos e prazer nos ha muyto de vyrdes porque em o que a vos toca se dara tal forma de que vos devaaes seer contente. E porque por tal ventura teerees alguu rreçeo de nossas justiças por razam dalguñas cousas a que sejaees obligado Nos per esta nossa carta vos seguramos polla vynda stada e tornada que non sejaaes preso reteudo acusado citado nę demandado por nenhuña cousa ora que seja civil ora crime de qualquer qualidade. E pella meesma mandamos a todas nosas justiças que ho cumpram asy e por tanto vos Rogamos e encomendamos que vossa vynda seja loguo e para ysso nô tenhaaes pejo alguu e agradeceruohemos e teeremos muyto em serviço scripta em avis a XX dias de março de 1488. El Rey.

" A Christouon Collon noso especial amigo em Sevilha."

Translation :

" Cristóbal Colón. We, Don Joham, by the grace of God King of Portugal and of the Algarbes of this and of the other side of the sea in Africa, Lord of Guinea, send you greetings. We have seen the letter which you wrote to Us and We are very grateful for the good will and affection which you show towards our service in it. And as for your coming, certain it is that both because of what you point out as for other plans for which your industry and good mind will be necessary to Us, We wish it, and shall have much pleasure in your coming for in what concerns you We shall arrange matters so as to please you. And since you might perhaps harbour certain distrust towards Our justices owing to obligations which you may have, We by this letter guarantee you that during your coming, stay and return you shall not be arrested, held up, accused, remanded or made to answer for any thing, whether civil or criminal of any kind. And We hereby instruct our justices accordingly and therefore We request and recommend you to hasten your coming, and have no fear about it and We shall be grateful and hold it as a great service. Written in Avis on March 20th, 1488. The King."

See *Vignaud-Études*, p. 677, the text and facsimile, as well as, in the preceding pages, a discussion of the authenticity and import of this royal letter.

8   Such is, for instance, the trend of Ulloa, a Peruvian author, presumably of Basque descent, but of strong Catalan and anti-Castillian feelings :

" The great official *Raccolta*, which does great honour to Italian science, inserts two hundred documents and more, bearing on Domenico Colombo, the supposed-to-be father of Colón, and on Domenico's children. This mass seems overwhelming. Yet, out of this imposing mass of papers only fourteen bear on Cristoforo Colombo or on the brothers Giacomo and Bartolomeo attributed to him. Of these fourteen pages, there are seven the originals or even legalised copies of which have never been known [. . .]. Out of the remaining seven, of which we are assured that originals or legalised copies exist, only one, dated September 10th, 1489, contains the names of Bartolomeo and Giacomo Colombo. This Bartolomeo, as well as his two brothers, if the document be genuine, were still minors, subject to paternal authority, for Domenico stands as their ' father and legitimate administrator.' At that date, the real Colón was in Córdoba, and the real

Bartolomé, according to the ' genoists ' themselves, was in London, where he had drawn the world-map."—*Ulloa-C.C.*, p. 349.

For a rejection of the Genoa case on the ground that such a family may have existed but was not that of Colón, see Ricardo Bertrán y Rózpide, *Cristóbal Colón y Cristóforo Columbo*, Madrid, 1921 ; and *Cristóbal Colón ¿genovés?*, by the same author, Madrid, 1925.

No time need be spent on the work of García de la Riega, whose claims to make of Colón a Gallegan Jew are based on a document which Spanish—in fact, Gallegan—scholars proved later to be a forgery.

9 This is Vignaud's line. The admirable industry and ingenuity of this devoted historiographer of Colón's life and deeds are marred by an obvious anti-Colón bias as well as by a deplorable lack of subtlety in the interpretation of the available *paper* data in terms of actual life.

This is also, curiously enough, the line taken by Colombo's countrymen. Thus : " Is it not more reasonable to relegate these extraordinary events to the realm of fancy and to the particular state of mind in which Columbus, when his ephemeral hours of triumph gave place to adversity, had taken refuge ? "—*Genoa*, p. 21. Such a " solution " of the problem of Colón is far too easy and far too lacking in respect for Colón himself.

CHAPTER III

1 " *Johannes de Columbo de Moconexi, habitator in villa Quinti,* promisit et solempniter convenit Guiermo de Balbante de Alamania, textori pannorum, presenti, facere et curare ita et taliter cum effectu, quod *Dominicus eius filius,* hic presens et consentiens, etatis annorum XI in circa, stabit et perseverabit cum dicto Guiermo pro famulo et discipullo, causa adiscendi artem suam, usque ad annos sex proxime venturos."—*Genoa*, p. 104. (State Notarial Archives, Genoa. Deed of the notary Quilico di Albenga (single file, No. 68), attested in Genoa on February 21st, 1429.)

2 On the lease of the house in Vico dell'Olivella see deed in *Genoa*, p. 122 :

" . . . *unius domus posite Ianue, in carubeo de Olivella,* cui coheret ab uno latere domus Petri de Croza de Rapallo, ab alio latere domus Bertore de Valetariis, quas conducunt a predicto monasterio, antea via publica seu carrubeus, retro quintana. . . ."

3 On Domenico's appointment to the wardership of the tower and gate of Sant'Andrea, *Genoa*, p. 124 :

" Illustris et excelsus dominus Janus de Campofregoso, Dei gratia Januensium Dux, *elegit ad custodiam turris et porte Olivele dilectum suum Dominicum de Columbo,* usque ad prefati illustris domini Ducis beneplacitum, cum pagis et obventionibus consuetis, omni prorsus exceptione remota."

4 On his salary as tower-keeper and the appointment of his successor, *Genoa*, p. 126 :

" (Die VII decembris 1450.)

" De mandato illustris et excelsi domini domini Ducis Januensium et magnifici Consilii dominorum Antianorum, vos venerandum Officium Monete Communis *solvite Dominico Columbo, custodi turris et porte Olivelle,* libras viginti unam januinorum, pro suo et sociorum stipendio trium mensium, sive . . . L. XXI.—

" MCCCCLI, die VII januarii.

" De mandato ut supra, vos venerandum Offitium Monete Communis *solvite Dominico Columbo, custodi turris Olivelle,* libras viginti unam januinorum, pro suo et sotii stipendio trium mensium incohactorum prima die presentis mensis, sive . . . L. XXI.—

"(MCCCCLI, die XVI aprilis.)

"De mandato ut supra, vos venerandum Officium Monete Communis *solvite Dominico Columbo, custodi turris Olivelle* libras viginti unam januinorum, pro suo et socii stipendio trium mensium sive ... L. XXI.—

"Die XXV septembris (MCCCCLI).

"Illustris et excelsus dominus Dux Januensium etc., elegit et constituit in custodem et pro custode turris et porte Olivelle dilectum suum Augustinum de Boliascho, pro mensibus tredecim proximis tantum, cum stipendio, prerogativis et emolumentis consuetis, que precessores sui soliti sunt habere et percipere. Ex quo mandat eum Augustinum admitti et teneri in custodem dicte turris ut supra, *statim finitis mensibus tredecim diu concessis Dominico Columbo nunc custodi dicte turris ut supra. ...*"

5 On Domenico's brother, Antonio, appointed lighthouse-keeper, *Genoa*, p. 128:

"(1449, die XI. a februarij.)

"De mandato illustris et excelsi domini domini Ducis Januensium et magnifici Consilij dominorum Antianorum, vos Venerandum Officium Monete Communis *solvite Antino Columbo custodi turris Capitis Fari* pro suo stipendio mensium duorum libras viginti unam, sive ... L. XXI.—"

6 Deed, Colombo's mother, *Genoa*, p. 150:

"*Sozana filia quondam Jacobi de Fontanarubea de Bezagno et uxor Dominici de Columbo de Ianua, ac Christoforus et Iohannes Pelegrinus filii dictorum Dominici et Sozane jugalium. ...*

"...sciens et perfectam scientiam habens dictum Dominicum de Columbo, virum ipsius Suzane et patrem ipsorum Christofori et Johannis Pellegrini, vendidisse et alienasse et seu vendere et alienare velle *quandam domum ipsius Dominici sitam in civitate Janue, in contrata porte Olivelle. ...*

"... ipsa Suzana per se et suos heredes annuivit et consensit, ac annuit et consentit dicte venditioni. ...

"Insuper iidem Christoforus et Johannes Pelegrinus filii dictorum Dominici et Suzane jugalium, ibidem presentes et audientes ac intelligentes, et scientes premissa omnia contenta in presenti suprascripto instrumento annuerunt et consenserunt ac annuunt et consentiunt dicte venditioni. ...

"*Actum Saone, in contracta sancti Iulliani, in apotecha domus habitationis ipsorum Dominici et Suzane. ...*"

7 Lease of another house, *Genoa*, p. 130:

"... Spectabilis dominus Jacobus de Flisco, quondam domini Ectoris, frater et procurator reverendi domini domini cardinalis de Flisco, commendatarii monasterii Sancti Stephani ordinis Sancti Benedicti ... in presentia etc. ... Locaverunt et *titulo locationis dederunt et concesserunt Dominico Columbo textori pannorum lane*, presenti, pro (se) et heredibus suis natis etc. *quoddam solum sive terram super quod seu quam edificium vel domum, positum in burgo Sancti Stephani, in carubeo recto ; cui coheret ante carubeus, ab uno latere domus Joannis de Palavania*, ab alio latere domus Antonii Bondi, super solo dicti monasterii. ..."

8 Domenico sent to Savona by the woolweavers, *Genoa*, p. 142:

"Cristoforus de Pentema et Antonius de Recroso, consules magistrorum artis textorum pannorum lane civitatis Ianue, et Guiliermus de Pentema. ... Antonius de Garibaldo, Bertonus de Sarnio, *Dominicus de Columbo* ... et Baptista Zenogius, *suis nominibus et nomine et vice aliorum magistrorum dicte artis textorum pannorum lane civitatis Ianue* ac hominum artis predicte, ... habentes noticiam et certam scientiam de quodam publico instrumento pactorum compositionis, ordiniationum ac decretorum et omnium aliorum indicto instrumento contentorum celebrato in civitate Saone hoc anno, die ultima februarii, et scripto manu Antonii de Rimere ... notarii saonensis, per et inter Antonium de Garibaldo et Dominicum de Columbo, magistros textores pannorum lane civitatis Ianue, suis nominibus et nomine et vice aliorum hominum dicte artis . . . dictum instrumentum confirmaverunt, approbaverunt, ratificaverunt ac omnia et singula in eo contenta."

9 Lawsuit with del Porto, *Genoa*, p. 164 :

" . . . *condemnamus et condemnatos esse pronunciamus dictos Dominicum et Christoforum, et quemlibet eorum in solidum, ad dandum et solvendum dicto Ieronimo de Portu libras triginta quinque monete currentis, infra annum unum proxime venturum*, omni contradicione cessante." (*Genoa*, p. 164.)

10 Domenico a publican, *Genoa*, p. 144 :

" *Dominicus de Columbo civis Ianue, quondam Johannis de Quinto, testor pannorum et tabernarius*. . . ."

11 Cristoforo's birth, *Genoa*, p. 170 :

" . . . *Cristofforus de Columbo filius Dominici maior annis decem novem* . . . confessus fuit et in veritate publice recognovit Petro Belexio de Portu Mauricio, filio Francisci, presenti, se eidem dare et solvere debere libras quadraginta octo, soldos tresdecim et denarios sex Janue. . . . Actum Janue, in Fossatello, ad bancum Lazarii Ragii notarii, *anno Dominice Nativitatis MCCCCLXX, inditione tercia iuxta morem Janue, die mercurii, ultima octobris*."

12 *Genoa*, p. 148. The deed says explicitly : " *Dominicus Columbus lanerius, habitator Saone, et Christoforus, eius filius*. . . ."

This does not prevent the drafters of this volume on behalf of Genoa from describing it, a few pages earlier, in the following inaccurate terms : " IV : In August 1472, Domenico Colombo and his son Christopher are described as woolworkers in Savona " (p. 141). Yet so far as Christopher is concerned, the deed says neither " woolworker " nor " in Savona."

13 Giacomo an apprentice, *Genoa*, p. 112 :

" *Iacobus de Columbo Dominici, civis Ianue*, sponte etc. dedit et locavit se pro famulo et discipulo cum Luchino Cadamartori, praesenti etc. per menses vigintiduos, ad addiscendam artem textorum pannorum. . . ." (*Genoa*, p. 112.)

14 Return to Genoa, *Genoa*, p. 154 :

" . . . *Dominicus Columbus quondam Iohannis olim textor pannorum, civis Ianue*, sponte et excerta scientia locavit et locat Iohanni Baptiste de Villa . . . *quandam appotecam cum domo in ea supraposita, sita Ianue in burgo Sancti Stephani, in carrubeo recto*. . . ."

15 Christophoro witnesses deed in company with a tailor, *Genoa*, p. 134 :

" † die XX marcii (MCCCCLXXII).—Cum nihil sit cercius morte . . . id circo prudens vir Nicolaus de Monleono quondam Iohannis . . . de se bonisque suis disposuit prout infra . . . *Actum Saone, in contracta palacii causarum Communis Saone, in apotheca ipsius Nicolai testatoris*, quam titulo locationis conducit a Iohanne de Uxilia ; presentibus Iohanne Vigna sartore, . . . Bernardo Sambaldo sartore, *Christoforo de Columbo lanerio de Ianua* et Dominico Vigna sartore, civibus Saone, testibus ad hec vocatis et rogatis ore proprio ipsius testatoris etc."

16 The deed is known as the Assereto document, from the name of the Italian scholar who discovered it. It will be found in *Genoa*, p. 136 :

" . . . Christofforus Columbus de ordine dicti Pauli missus fuit ad insulam Almadere et ibi incaparavit seu emit summam sucharorum supradictam. . . . Noverint universi et singuli presens publicum instrumentum testimoniale inspecturi quod constitutus in presentia mei notarij et testium infrascriptorum ad hec specialiter vocatorum et rogatorum *Cristoforus Columbus civis Janue*, requisitus hic in testem et pro teste recepi et examinati. . . . Qui quidem Cristoforus testis predictus, . . . testificando dixit se tantum scire de contentis in titulo, videlicet quod *veritas fuit et ext quod cum anno proxime preterito de mense julii ipse testis et dictus Paulus essent in loco Ulisbone,* transmissus fuit ipse testis per eundem Paulum ad insulam Amaderie. . . . *Interrogatus si est de proximo recessurus, respondit: sic, die crastino de mane pro Ulisboa.* Interrogatus quottannis est, quantum habet in bonis et quam partem vellet obtinere, *respondit quod est etatis annorum viginti septem vel circa,* . . . et vellet obtinere jus habentem."

17 Christoforo's father witnesses a will in company with a shoemaker, *Genoa,* p. 158:

" . . . Carlotina quondam domini Bartholomei de Vernacia et uxor Carloti Pisurni . . . testari cupiens . . . de se bonisque statuit, disposuit et ordinavit ut infra. . . . *Actum Ianue in burgo Sancti Stephani, videlicet prope portam Arcus . . . presentibus Dominico de Columbo olim textore pannorum lane,* quondam Iohannis, Marcho de Borzono callegario, quondam Iohannis, . . . civibus et habitatoribus Ianue, testibus ad premissa vocatis specialiterque rogatis." (*Genoa,* p. 158.)

18 Litigation with Cheesemonger, *Genoa,* p. 114:

" . . . Cum verum sit, ut partes asserunt et fatentur infrascripte, quod Iacobus Bavarelus formaiarius alis consecutus fuerit quoddam extimum in quadam domo cum appoteca sub ea, viridario, puteo et vacuo eidem domui contiguis, positis Ianue in contrata porte Sancti Andree, sub confinibus contentis et descriptis in dicto extimo, tanquam in bonis *Dominici de Columbo* quantum pro libris ducentis quinquaginta ianuinorum monete currentis . . . et quod contra dictum extimum per *dictum Dominicum, tanquam patrem et legiptimum administratorem Christofori, Bartholomei et Iacobi filiorum ipsius Dominici, ac filiorum et heredum quondam Suzane eorum matris, olim uxoris dicti quondam Dominici,* fuerit ellevata canela, et super hoc diu fuerit litigatum per et inter dictas partes, et iam facte multe et diverse expense."

19 1501, Genoese citizens swear that the three Colombos have been absent from Genoa, *Genoa,* p. 176:

" Qui Monetus et Manuel sicut supra, iussi et citati, constituti ubi supra, prius delato iuramento, et interrogati de infrascriptis, eorum et cuiuslibet ipsorum iuramento, dixerunt et dicunt coniunctim vel divisim, ac omni validiore modo, via, *dictos Christophorum, Bartolomeum et Iacobum de Columbis, filios et heredes dicti quondam Dominici eorum patris, iam diu fore a civitate et posse Saonae absentes, ultra Pisas et Niciam de Proventia, et in partibus Ispaniae commorantes, ut notorium fuit et est.* . . ."

20 The quotation from Gallo will be found in *Thacher,* vol. I, p. 190. The English version quoted in the text is based on Thacher's, but differs from his in one or two cases in which he seems to have overlooked not unimportant points. The work of Gallo was published in Milan, *Rerum Italicarum Scriptores,* by Ludovico Antonio Muratori, 1723-51.

21 For the text of Seranega's record see *Thacher,* vol. I, p. 195.

22 *Thacher,* vol. I, p. 202, gives an excellent reproduction of the title-page of the *Polyglot Psalter,* as well as of the pages in which the marginal comment on Christoforo Colombo begins.

CHAPTER IV

1 Colón never said that he came from Genoa. The deed of entail of 1497-98 cannot be accepted as authentic. It is obviously one of the documents fabricated either in the interests of the Genoese school or in those of the litigants in the lawsuit to which the disputes between Colón's heirs gave rise in the sixteenth century. This is not the place to enlarge upon the arguments which can be raised against this famous deed, beyond saying that it turns up in most suspicious circumstances and conditions in the

course of a lawsuit. But it is a curious fact that this document is considered as genuine by the Genoese school and as a forgery by those who do not believe that Colón was born in Genoa, evidently under the impression that it establishes the Genoese case. Yet if Colón mentioned Genoa in 1498, how is it that a man with a family sense so strong that he appears in history surrounded by two brothers, two sons and two nephews, does not mention his own father, who was still alive and in need of help ? And why does he insist that his heirs must be " de los de Colón " and not at all *Colombos* ? And why does he want the estate to maintain " in Genoa a person of our lineage who keeps there a house and a wife [. . .] and take foot and root there," when there lived his own Colombo cousins whom he does not mention—for he never mentioned any of his relations who remained in his native town ?

If this document were proved to be authentic, Colón would have been proved to be Genoese, but his identity with the wool-weaving family would have been destroyed unless the whole structure be conceived as a deliberate attempt by Colón to break altogether with his Genoese family while affirming his connection with Genoa. Thus read, the document would make sense, but would not speak much in favour of Colón's shrewdness and intelligence.

There are, moreover, other difficulties. No reference exists in the papers of Colón or of those of his two sons to this 1497-98 entail, while in a letter to Father Gorricio, his trusted friend and adviser, dated May 24th, 1501, i.e. when Colón was thinking of writing the 1502 will (which is lost), he asks his friend for a certified copy of " a provision which is there [in the Monastery of Las Cuevas] authorising me to establish an entail-estate " (" una probisiô q̃ ala esta por q̃ pueda yo hazer mayorazgo "), a sentence which Colón would certainly have drafted otherwise, had he already established an entail-estate and therefore already made use of this " provision " which he obviously unearths in 1501 for the first time.

Nevertheless, the Entail Deed cannot be a complete invention. It must have been fabricated on the basis of the will of 1502 which has disappeared without trace. And most of its executive clauses are probably—but only probably—correct.

For another view on this curious document see Altolaguirre, *La Real Confirmación del Mayorazgo fundado por Don Cristóbal Colón*, Madrid, 1926.

A well-known forgery which can have had no other object than that of " strengthening " the Genoa case is the famous *Military Codicil* in which Colón describes the Genoese Republic as his most beloved fatherland (see *Navarrete*, vol. II, p. 305). It should therefore be noticed that of the *only* two documents in which Colón speaks of himself as a citizen of Genoa, one is a proved forgery and the other one can inspire no confidence whatsoever, to say the least.

There is another paper of Colón which may be interpreted as a declaration of allegiance to Genoa—his letter to the Bank of San Georgio, which begins with the words : " Though the body be here, the heart is over there continuously." Yet it should be pointed out :

    (1) That this is all he says about Genoa, writing to the Bank of San Georgio, which was in many ways to the Republic what the Bank of England is to Great Britain, an institution second only to the government in official dignity.

    (2) That he writes these words in Spanish, like the rest of the letter.

Moreover, the authenticity of the letter is disputed, notably by Ulloa (*loc. cit.*), who, unfortunately, does not provide the proof of his opinion. Suspicions may be entertained on the following points :

    (*a*) The phrase " la escuridad del gobierno " does not ring contemporary.

(b) No trace exists of the legacy to the Bank of one-tenth of the whole income to be derived from America, which the letter mentions, though Giustiniani, in his *Castigatissimi Annali* (Genoa, 1537), says : " Et Colôbo nella morte sua fece come bon patriota, p. que lasso per testamêto all'ufficio di S. Georgio la decima parte delle sue entrate in perpetuo, ben que l'ufficio predetto (nô so p. qual cagione) no si ha fatto côto di questo legato ne ha datto opera habberlo."

(c) The letter says (April 2, 1502) :

" y porque yo soy mortal, yo deso a Don Diego my fijo que de la renta toda que se oviere que os acuda ali con el diezmo de toda ella cada un año para siempre. . . ."

Yet, a few days earlier (end March 1502), Colón writes to his son :

" Io te mando y encargo que tu lo debas tomar mucho a devocion de dar el decimo de todos los dineros que tuvieres que sean de rentas, que sean de qualquiera otra guisa el diezmo de ella, luego, sin dilacion de ora, dadlo por servicio de Nuestro Señor a pobres necesitados, y parientes antes que a otrós : e si no estuvieren adó estuvieres, apartalos para se los enviar."

Is it credible :

(1) That Colón should take two decisions quite different as to what was to be done with the tenth of all his income, both with reference to Don Diego, and within a few days ;

(2) And that he should not mention the more important of the two in his memorandum to his own son ?

The argument given in *Raccolta* (pt. I, vol. II, p. lxxvii) to the effect that the memorandum to Don Diego was not the appropriate place to deal with this business, which was rather of a testamentary character, turns against *Raccolta*, for practically every item in such a memorandum *is* of a testamentary character, as, for instance, the paragraph on Beatriz Enriquez.

The text of the letter is to be found in *Raccolta*, *loc. cit.*, p. 171 ; the memorandum to D. Diego on the previous page.

A forged letter, difficult to distinguish from the original, has been seen and is discussed by *Harrisse*.

2   ". . . como aquella Iglesia era una de las mas principales de sus Reynos, é tenia tierras cercanas á la tierra de los Moros ; é que no era razon que fuese de ella proveida persona estrangera, é no natural de Castilla. . . ."— *Pulgar-Crónica*, ch. XXXVIII, p. 238.

3   The relevant passages of Peter Martyr are to be found in the opening chapter of *Thacher*, vol. I. Trivigiano's Libretto is photographically reprinted by *Thacher* (vol. II, p. 456).

4   " Digo que Cristobal Colón, segun yo he sabido de hombres de su nascion fue natural de la provincia de Liguria, que es en Italia, en la cual cae la cibdad e señoria de Genova ; unos dicen que de Savona, e otros que de un pequeño lugar o villaje dicho Nervi que es a la parte del levante y en la costa de la mar, a dos leguas de la misma cibdad de Genova, y por mas cierto se tiene que fue natural de un lugar dicho Cugureo."—*Oviedo*, bk. II, ch. II.

5   ". . . y casi algunos, que de cierta manera quieren obscurecer su fama, dicen que fuá de Nervi ; otros de Cugureo ; otros de Bugiasco, lugarcillos pequeños cerca de Genova y situados en su ribera ; otros que quieren exaltarle más, dicen era de Saona, y otros genovés, y algunos tambien, saltando mas sobre el viento, le hacen natural de Placencia, donde hay personas muy honradas de su familia, y sepulturas con armas, y epitafios de los Colombos. . . ."—*F.C.*, ch. I.

6 ". . . El cual dicho Almirante Don Christobal Colón, de maravillosa y honrada memoria, natural de la provincia de Milan, estando en Valladolid el año de 1506, en el mes de mayo, murió en senectute bona, inventor de las Indias, de edad de 70 años poco mas o menos."—*Bernáldez*, ch. CXXXI, vol. II, p. 82.

For a complete discussion of all the dates suggested see *Vignaud-Études*, p. 214.

7 " Yo he andado veinte y tres años en la mar, sin salir della tiempo que se haya de contar."—Diario, *Navarrete*, vol. I, p. 101.

8 " De muy pequeña edad entré la mar navegando y lo he continuado hasta hoy ; la misma arte inclina a quien la prosigue a desear saber los secretos de este mundo ; ya pasan de cuarenta años que yo voy en este uso. Todo lo que hasta hoy se navega he andado."—Quoted by *Las Casas*, bk. I, ch. III, vol. 62, p. 47.

9 " Yo vine a servir de veinte y ocho años."—*Navarrete*, vol. I, p. 311. The explanation of this sentence as a printing error or a slip of the pen is rejected, with what appears to be good arguments, by Beltrán y Rózpide, *loc. cit.*

10 " Despues que yo vine a les servir que son siete años agora a 20 dias de Enero este mismo mes."—Diario, *Navarrete*, vol. I, p. 137.

11 " Ya son diez y siete años que yo vine a servir estos principes con la impresa de las Indias."—Letter 1500, *Navarrete*, vol. III, p. 254.

12 " Che comincio a navigar di quatordici anni."—*F.C.*, ch. IV.

13 For a negative answer to this question, i.e. for a rejection of the Genoa hypothesis on the ground of date of birth incompatibility, see *Cristóbal Colón y Cristoforo Colombo*, by Ricardo Beltrán y Rózpide, Madrid, 1921.

14 Bartolomeo's age. No direct documents exist. The deed of August 7th, 1473, already mentioned (*Genoa*, p. 150), does not mention him, though it mentions Christoforo and Pellegrino. He was therefore a minor. Another deed, registered at Savona, in which his father gives him a procuration on June 16th, 1489, has been lost (see *Vignaud-Études*, p. 115).

" Cinquenta años o mas."—*Pleitos*, Madrid, 1892, vol. I, p. 182.

15 *F.C.*, ch. II. The point, however, is not crucial.

16 Diego's age. This is the case with *Ulloa-C.C.*, p. 95 *et seq.* His argument that, being a Churchman, Diego must have been the elder brother, runs counter to the accepted tradition of a country of soldiers in which the Church took second best . . . and bastards.

I do not discuss Ulloa's other argument that *Giacomo* would never give *Diego* because he himself accepts that Jaume (Catalan for Giacomo) would, and in fact did, give Diego. So, if Jaume, why not Giacomo ? On the other hand, the *normal* Spanish rendering of Giacomo is Jácome. There is a witness in *Pleitos*, vol. I, p. 101, by the name of *Jácome Ginovés*. If, therefore, *Giacomo* Colombo became Diego, *after* Colón had named his son *Diego* in Castillian and not *Giacomo* nor *Diogo* (which is Portuguese for Diego), it strengthens the views put forward in the following chapter on the existence of a Castillian-Jewish tradition in the family, to which the whole group of *Colombos* returned on coming back to the Peninsula.

Giacomo, born 1468. See above, note 13, ch. III. The letter of Diego Colón to King Ferdinand will be found in Duchess of Alba, *Nuevos Autógrafos*, p. 20. Here is the relevant passage :

" verdad es que Hernando de Vega ha servido y sirve mucho a vuestra altesa ; pero el servicio quel almyrante, my hermano a vuetra altesa y a la corona real y el reyno hiso, bien cabia en my, siendo su hermano viejo y pobre y enfermo. . . ."

17 See *Vignaud-Études*, p. 506, where Colón's life as a seaman before 1473 is entirely wiped out as an invention. If Christoforo Colombo remained in Genoa-Savona till 1473, he *cannot* have been Cristóbal Colón, as shown by the language difficulty.

18 See note 12 of ch. III above.

19 " A mi acaeció que el Rey Reynel, que Dios tiene, me envió a Tunez para prender la galeaza Fernandina, y estando ya sobre la isla de San Pedro, en Cerdeña, me dijo una Saetia que estaban con la dicha galeaza dos naos y una carraca ; por lo cual se alteró la gente que iba conmigo y determinaron de no seguir el viaje, salvo de se volver a Marsella por otra nao y mas gente. Yo, visto que no podia sin algun arte forzar su voluntad, otorgué su demanda, y mudando el cebo del aguja, di la vela al tiempo que anochecía, y, otro dia al salir del sol, estabamos dentro del cabo de Carthagine, teniendo todos ellos por cierto que ibamos a Marsella."

20 Ulloa (*loc. cit.*), led by his strong Catalanist bias, paints this struggle as an effort of the Catalans to liberate themselves from a Castillian dynasty. It was nothing of the kind, as proved by the fact that, to get rid of King Juan, the Catalans offered the throne to the King of Castille himself, Henry IV. Things are not as simple in life as our mind makes them out to be later. There was much that was merely personal in the trouble between Catalonia and the King of Aragon.

21 Vignaud (*Études*, pp. 313-27) rejects this episode of King René as an invention of Colón. His arguments fall under two headings :

(a) " Colón, a Genoese, could not fight against Genoa, since René was then the enemy of Genoa, after the massacre of Frenchmen by the Genoese on July 17, 1461, precisely the year when young Colombo went to sea." This prejudges the issue. We do not know yet what was Colón's real attitude towards Genoa. The time has not come to discuss that yet, so this argument must remain in abeyance.

(b) " Technically, the trick played on his men by Colón is impossible." It is not. Vignaud himself in quoting authorities can go no further than to say that it required exceptionally favourable conditions.

CHAPTER V

1 Particularly in First Voyage, November 12th.—*Navarrete*, vol. I, pp. 54-5.

2 Colón's studies in Pavia University are one of the " facts " only to be found in Fernando Colón (*Historie*, ch. III, fol. 7 verso), and in *Las Casas* (bk. I, ch. III, vol. 62, p. 46).

An ingenious explanation has been supplied by Desimoni (*Quistioni Colombiani. Raccolta*, pp. 29-30) : " The woolworkers of Genoa kept a school for their children in Vico di Pavia " (quoted by *Vignaud-Études*, p. 294).

3 ". . . a este mi deseo hallé a Nuestro Señor muy propicio, y hube dél para ello espiritu de inteligencia. En la marineria me hizo abundoso, de astrologia me dió lo que abastaba, y ansi de geometria y aritmética, e ingenio en el anima y manos para dibujar esta esfera, y en ella las ciudades, rios y montañas, islas y puertos todo en su proprio sitio. En este tiempo he yo visto y puesto estudio en ver todas escrituras, cosmografía, historias, crónicas y filosofía y de otras artes. . . ."

To this *Las Casas* adds a marginal note :

" Dice *abastaba* porque tratando con hombres doctos en astrologia, alcanzó dellos lo que habia menester para perfeccioner lo que sabía de la marineria, no porque estudiase astrología. . . ."—*Las Casas*, bk. I, ch. III, vol. 62, p. 47.

4 ". . . o dicto Almirante [. . .] no recontamento das suas cousas, excedia sempre os termos da verdade. . . ."—*Pina*, p. 178.

5 " Como fuese [. . .] Cristóbal Colón tan dedicado a las cosas y ejercicio de la mar, y en aquel tiempo anduviese por ella un famoso varon, el mayor de los corsarios que en aquellos tiempos habia, de su nombre y linaje, que se llamaba Columbo Junior, a diferencia de otro que habia sido nombrado y señalado antes, y aqueste Junior trajese grande armada por la mar contra infieles y Venecianos y otros enemigos de su nación, Cristóbal Colón determinó ir e andar con él, en cuya compañia estuvo y anduvo mucho tiempo. Este Columbo Junior teniendo nuevas que cuatro galeazas de venecianos eran pasadas a Flandes, esperolas a la vuelta entre Lisbona y el Cabo de San Vicente para asirse con ellas a las manos . . ."
" [. . .] escogieron padecer antes la muerte del agua que la del fuego . . ."
" . . . el Cristóbal Colón era muy gran nadador, y pudo haber un remo que a ratos le sostenía mientras descansaba, y ansi anduvo hasta llegar a tierra, que estaría poco mas de dos leguas de donde y adonde habian ido a parar las naos con su ciega y desatinada batalla."—*Las Casas*, bk. I, ch. IV, vol. 62, pp. 51-2.
On the battle of St. Vincent and the two Colombo Corsairs see *Vignaud-Études*, pp. 333 and 165. His treatment is, as usual, painstaking and thorough. As regards the two Colombos it is, moreover, convincing. But as for the part taken by Colón, it is obviously prejudiced by a rigid *Genoese—woolweaver* point of view which leads him against all evidence to an obviously wrong conclusion, as pointed out in the text, i.e. that Colón fought for the Genoese and *against* Guillaume Colón : see below, note 9.

6 For the discovery of Ruy de Pina's and of Palencia's narrative see *Vignaud*, *loc. cit.*

7 Ulloa points out the passage in Diego de Valera's *Epistolas*, I, VII and VIII, pp. 29 and 32. The clearest passage is in Diego de Valera's *Crónica*, ch. XXI, p. 77 : " Del caso acaescido al capitan de la flota francesa llamado Colón en el cabo de Santa Maria que es a treynta y seis leguas de la cibdad de Cadiz." It was first found by Altolaguirre in an anonymous MS. at the Escorial. He refers to it, without knowing its actual author, in his pamphlet ¿ *Colón Español?*

8 Cristóbal Colón in a letter to the Aya of Prince Don Juan.
This utterance of Colón's is known through his son Fernando, and therefore in the Italian translation which, the Spanish original being lost, has to be quoted, even though with little guarantee of its fidelity to the original :
" Io non sono il primo ammiraglio della mia famiglia, metammi pure il nome, che vorranno, che in ultimo David, re sapientissimo, fu guardiano di pecore, le poi fu fatto re di Gierusalemme, e io servo son di quello istesso Signore che mise lui in tale stato."—*Raccolta*, pt. I, vol. II, p. 275.
The authenticity of this letter has been disputed by Tiraboschi, and the sin of making it up laid, along with many others, on Don Fernando. De Lollis has dealt with the subject and gives good arguments for considering it authentic. His psychological defence of Colón's claim that he was not the first admiral of his family is not convincing. But there again, how do we know ?—*Raccolta*, pt. I, vol. II, p. clxviii.

9 There are two more arguments : one is that, as Italian scholars have proved, Colón's name is not to be found in the list of the Genoese crews ; the other one is most aptly provided by Ulloa, who returns against Vignaud an argument rashly adduced on his side by Vignaud himself : Colón bequeathed certain sums of money to some Genoese gentlemen : they happen to be interested parties in the expedition which came to grief off St. Vincent in 1476. Vignaud tries to build up on this his case that Colón was on the Genoese side. Ulloa points out that the legacies were

left by Colón with the explicit proviso that they were to be paid so that " no one knows who gives the money " (" Hasele de dar en tal forma que no se sepa quien lo manda dar "), which does prove that the legacies represented conscience money, evidently from the Genoese corsair to the Genoese shipowners whose property he had attacked.

10 *Descubrimento das Ilhas de Castella per Collombo*, Pina, ch. LXVI, p. 177.

11 " Bien que el cuerpo ande aca, el coraçon está alí de continuo."—*Raccolta,* pt. I, vol. II, p. 171. See also note 1 to ch. IV.

12 The story that Colón offered his enterprise to Genoa was put into circulation by Peter Martyr, but it is generally held today that such an offer never took place—nor that to Venice either. See *Vignaud*, vol. I, pp. 413 *et seq.*

13 Diego did think of going to Italy ; as shown, amongst other documents, by the letter of the King and Queen to the Bishop of Badajoz, June 1st, 1495.—*Navarrete*, vol. II, p. 175.

14 " del ambra es cierto nascere in india soto tierra he yo me ho fato cauare in molti monti in la isola de feyti vel de ophir vel de cipango a la quale habio posto nome Spagnola y ne ho trovato pieca grande como el capo ma no tota chiara y parda y otra negra y vene assay."—*Raccolta*, pt. III, vol. I, table E. CL.

15 The annotated book is : *Historia di C. Plinio Secondo traducta di lingua latina in fiorentina* per Christoforo Laudius fiorentino, Venezia, 1489.

16 On Father Gorricio's nationality see *Raccolta*, pt. I, vol. II, p. xxvii. See Father Gorricio's letter to Colón on The Book of Prophecies in *Raccolta*, pt. I, vol. II, p. 75.

17 See letter from C. C. to Bartolomé Colón in *Raccolta*, pt. I, vol. II.

18 Thus Lollis in *Raccolta*.

19 Thus Vignaud.

20 Here is the text of the relevant part of the note :
" Esta es la coenta de la criacion del mondo segondo los Judios : Vivio Adam CXXX años y entonces [. . .] desde nació abraam fasta que foe destruido la segunda casa 1088 años y desde la destruccion de la 2ª casa segundo los judios fasta agora sciendo el año del nacimiento de nuestro Señor de 1481 son 1413 años y desde el comienço del mundo fasta esta era de 1481 son 5241 años [. . .] mundo [. . .] 5244."—*Historia Pie II, Apostilla*, 858.

21 Cesare Lollis, " *Qui a découvert l'Amérique ?* " : *Revue des Revues*, Paris, January 1898. Lollis points out Colón's tendency to give to the nominative plural of substantives the Spanish ending *as* or *os* ; and above all, the use of the peculiar Spanish impersonal " hay " rendered as " habet " in the following :
" ab ostro Hircani in Oceano septentrionalem versus orientem habet profundus nives."

22 This is, I regret to say, the explanation of Don Ramón Menéndez Pidal, with which I deal below (note 3, ch. VI).

23 The idea that Colón was a Jew has been mooted several times already. Don Vicente Paredes, a Spanish scholar, held that he was a Jew from Extremadura, of the famous *Converso* family of Santa María. García de la Riega made him a Gallegan Jew. They overlook the fact that the Discoverer was born in Genoa.
I am indebted for advice and suggestions on this point to the following gentlemen : President Morgenstern and Professor Marcus, of the Hebrew Union College, Cincinnati, Ohio ; Mr. Leon Huhner, of

New York; Dr. Cecil Roth, of London; and Professor W. J. Martin, of Liverpool. Dr. Roth has been good enough to communicate to me the following list of Italian Jewish Colóns, Colombos or *Jonas* (Hebrew form of Colombo):

Colón. Joseph ben Samuel.
Joshua. Turin. 17th/18th century.
Elijah. Bologna. 16th century.
Shemariah Jedidish. Fossano. 17th century (according to a personal MS. of Dr. Roth's).
Jonà. Joshua Hayim. Casale. 17th century.
Michael Solomon. Pontestura (Turin). 1770.
Solomon. Ivrea (Modena). 19th century.
Solomon ben Joseph. 1631.
Salvador (i.e. Joshua). Pinerolo. 18th century.
Simeon. Casale. 1670.
Colombo. Name of the last Cabbalist Rabbi of Leghorn. Died *circa* 1921.

CHAPTER VI

1 " Adonde pudiera yo tener mejor arrimo [. . .] que en el Rey e Reina nuestros Señores, que de nada me han puesto en tanta honra . . . ? "—Letter to Doña Juana de la Torre, Aya of Prince Don Juan, *Navarrete*, vol. I, p. 272.
" . . . y para ello me hicieron grandes mercedes, y me anoblecieron que dende adelante yo me llamase Don. . . ."—*Navarrete*, vol. I, p. 2.
Ulloa has overlooked this patent fact.—*Ulloa-Pr.De.*, p. 46.

2 " [Colom] se auia hecho natural vassallo de aquella tierra por su matrimonio."—*Oviedo*, bk. II, ch. IV, folio v verso.
" Teniendose por natural de estos reinos [Portugal and Castille] que eran patria de sus hijos."—*F.C.*, ch. XI.

3 " Viendole despusicyon de otra tierra o reyno ageno a su lengua."—*Pleitos*.
" Parece ser natural de otra lengua porque no penetra del todo la significación de los vocablos de la lengua castellana ni del modo de hablar de ella."
This word " parece " might in those days merely mean " shows " ; but the following quotations do seem to justify the assumption that Las Casas meant to be non-committal :
" En las cosas de la religion cristiana, sin duda era católico y de mucha devocion."—*Las Casas*, bk. I, ch. II, vol. 62, p. 44.
" Dicho queda el origen y patria y linaje y padres y persona exterior y costumbres y conversación [. . .] y tambien de lo que se conocia de cristiandad de Cristóbal Colón. . . ."—*Las Casas*, bk. I, ch. III, vol. 62, p. 46.
" El cual viendose muy debilitado como cristiano, cierto, que era, rescibió con mucha devoción todos los sanctos sacramentos."—*Las Casas*, bk. III, ch. XXXVIII, vol. 64, p. 194.
Don Ramón Menéndez Pidal has kindly sent me his MS. of a note which he prepared at my request on this point of Colón's language. It is, as was to be expected of the chief Spanish philological authority, a masterly study of Colón's language. But I am afraid I cannot accept the conclusions which the eminent philologist carries over from his special to the general field. His points against the Jewish hypothesis seem to me lacking in force :

(1) That Las Casas often refers to Cristóbal Colón's defective knowledge of the language of Castille. The answer is twofold :
(a) Las Casas says the same of Miguel Ballester : " Esta es su

carta, y bien parece que era Catalan, porque hablaba imperfecta-mente. . . ."—Vol. 63, p. 334.

(b) C. C. admittedly used an awkward form of Spanish, full of Portuguese, Catalan and Italian influences. But the more imperfect his Castillian is found to be, the more inevitable becomes the Jewish hypothesis ; for how else can we explain that a man should use an imperfectly known language as his ONLY written mode of expression, even for his own personal and intimate use ? The imperfections of his Castillian were those of a stock language which had degenerated by exile ; not those of a newly acquired tongue.

(2) That C. C.'s Castillian does not resemble some samples of Jewish Castillian which are known. There is no such thing as a Standard Jewish Castillian ; this is too patent to be elaborated.

(3) The usual " official " Genoese " facts," which Don Ramón Menéndez Pidal gives as fully ascertained without venturing to criticise them, but which cannot be accepted—for instance, that he fought on the Genoese side at St. Vincent, a " fact " based on an argument which begs the question ; and that C. C. resided in Genoa–Savona till August 1475, which is not true, as the Genoese documents themselves prove when they are read carefully (see our ch. III).

I understand that Don R. M. Pidal's note is to be published by the Revue Hispanique.

4 " bien que el Almirante, conforme a la patria donde fué a vivir y a empezar su nuevo estado, limó el vocablo para conformarle con el antiguo y dis-tinguir los que procedieron de él, de los demás que eran parientes colaterales, y así se llamó Colón, esta consideración me mueve a creer que así como la mayor parte de sus cosas fueron obradas con algún misterio, así en lo que toca a la variedad de semejante nombre y sobrenombre, no deja de haber algún misterio."—F.C., ch. I.

5 For the evolution Colombo—Colomo—Colom—Colón see in particular the opening chapters of Ulloa-Pr.De. His Catalan bias must be discarded. It constantly leads him into error. For instance, he imagines that there was a conspiracy on the part of King Ferdinand, in whom he sees an anti-Catalan fiend, to castillianise Colom into Colón, oblivious of the importance which the discoverer himself attached to the meaning of " Colón," as explained by both Don Fernando and Las Casas. But when his bias is not at play he is a valuable investigator, and his views on the Catalan origin of Colón are undoubtedly important.

6 " quod de domo Thome Colom et Elionoris, eius uxoris, Johannis Colom, eorum filii et Aldonce eius uxoris, pelleriorum, civium Valencia, neofitorum, fuit extractum corpus Clare, vidue, mortue, uxoris Gabrielis de Vilanova neofiti, quondam civitatis Xative."

See Baer, p. 444. Yet the same Baer says : " Ich kann auf ihnen [Colón] auch keine zweifelfrei jüdischen namen entdecken."—Vol. II, p. 307.

On the Amsterdam Coloms see Ulloa-Pr.De., note 72.

7 See the discussion of the blazon from the point of view of a Catalan ancestry of Colón in Ulloa-Pr.De., pp. 44 et seq. I owe a note on this study to M. van de Putt, the specialist on Catalan heraldry. He is non-committal on Ulloa's case, yet sanguine on Colón's Catalan origins.

8 According to these Catalan specialists, the crest in Colón's arms is described as a world of gules crossed with a cross of gold, surmounted by a cross of gules or a field of gold. These, they claim, are the arms of a Catalan family of Monrós which has been found allied to one of the Coloms, and whose arms fit the crest adopted by Colón for his scutcheon ; moreover, what

is more striking, the name Monrós, made up of two Catalan words *Mon Ros*, means Red World.

Now, Las Casas and Don Fernando tell us that in their youth both Bartolomé and Cristóbal used to sign themselves Columbus de Terra Rubra, i.e. Colom of the Red-Earth, or Colom-Monrós. It matters but little whether further study shows that the Colón family were or were not actually connected with the Colom-Monrós; the point remains that they made some vague and discreet claim to be related to them by actually borrowing their crest and signing themselves Terra-rubra. The Terrarossa of the *Genoites* appears to me as a somewhat shadowy afterthought to prove an already proved case. On Columbus de Terrarubra see *F.C.*, ch. X.

9 On the circular of the Consuls of Barcelona see *Ulloa-Pr.De.*, p. 301.

10 " Mais il ne faut pas oublier que les travaux des marins catalans furent, pour l'Afrique Occidentale, ce que ceux des marins Normands-Scandinaves avaient été pour le Nord du Nouveau Continent. Les uns et les autres ont précédé les découvertes qui ont illustré les noms de Dom Henri et d'Isabelle de Castille. L'île de Majorque, depuis le treizième siècle, était devenue le foyer des connaissances scientifiques dans l'art difficile du navigateur. Nous savons par le *Fenix de las Maravillas del orbe* de Raimond Lulle, que les Majorquins et les Catalans se servaient *de cartas de marear* bien avant 1286 ; qu'on fabriquait à Majorque des instruments, grossiers, sans doute, mais destinés à trouver le temps et la hauteur du pôle à bord des vaisseaux. De là, des lumières originairement puisées chez les Arabes se répandirent dans tout le basin de la Méditerranée. Les ordonnances royales d'Aragon prescrivirent, dés l'année 1359, que chaque galère devait être fournie, non seulement d'une, mais de deux cartes marines. Un navigateur Catalan, Don Jayme Ferrer, était parvenu dans le mois d'Août 1346 à l'embouchure du Rio de Ouro, cinq degrés au sud de ce fameux Cabo de Non, que l'Infant Dom Henri s'était flatté d'avoir fait doubler, pour la première fois, par des vaisseaux portugais, en 1419."—*Humboldt*, vol. I, p. 283.

11 " El verano y el invierno, los que andan continuo de Cádiz a Napoles ya saben cuando pasan por la costa de Catalunya, segund la sazon, el viento que han de hallar en ella y asy mismo cuando pasan por el golfo de Narbona. Estos que han de yr de Cádiz a Napoles, si es tiempo de ynvierno, van a vista de Cabo de Creo en Catalunya, por el Golfo de Narbona ; entonces vienta muy rezio y las vezes las naos conviene le obedezcan y corran por fuerza hasta berueria y por esto van mas al cabo creo, por sostener mas la bolina y cobrar los Pameges de Marsella, las Islas de eres y despues jamas se desabarcan de la costa hasta llegar donde quer.

" Si de Cádiz ovieren de yr a Napoles en tiempo de verano, navegan por la costa de berueria hasta cerdena ansy como esta de la otra costa de la tramotana, para estas navegaziones ay hombres señalados que se an dado tanto a ello que conoszen todos estos caminos y que tenporales pueden esperar segund la sazon del año en que fueren vulgarmente a estos tales llamamos pylotos ques tanto como en la tierra adalid que bien que uno sepa muy bien el camino daquy a fuent rabia para levar una hueste no lo sabe daqui a lisbona. Esto mismo acaesze en la mar que unos son pylotos de Flandes y otros de Levante cada uno de la tierra donde mas usa."—Letter to the King and Queen, February 6th, 1502, *Raccolta*, pt. I, vol. III, table A. XIc, pp. 10-11.

12 On the Cresques family see *A.R.*, vol. II, p. 202.

13 " No soy el primer Almirante de mi familia ; pónganme el nombre que quisieren, que al fin David, Rey muy sabio, guardó ovejas y despues fué hecho Rey de Jerusalem ; y yo soy siervo de aquel mismo Señor que puso a David en este estado."—*F.C.*, ch. II.

CHAPTER VII

1 " Bem vistes a repartição, que fiz das outras espadas que dei a vossos irmãos, e esta terceira guardei para vós, a qual eu tenho que assi como vós sois forte, assi e ela. E porque a um de vossos irmãos encomendei os povos, e a outro as donas e donzelas, a vós quero encomendar todolos senhores, cavaleiros fidalgos e escudeiros dêstes reinos, os quais vos encomendo que hajais em vosso especial encargo. . . . Eu vos dou esta espada com a minha benção, com a qual vos encomendo e rogo que queirais ser cavaleiro."—*Brasil*, vol. I, p. 29.

2 In his *As Relaçoes do descobrimento da Guiné e das ilhas Açores, Madeira e Cabo Verde*. Quoted in *Brasil*, vol. I, p 4.

3 This point—who arrived first in Lisbon, Christoforo or Bartolomeo ?— is by no means settled. Fernando Colón's definite statement that Christoforo came first is important. Nothing, therefore, can be built on this obscure detail of the biography of the two brothers.

4 ". . . creo por los libros y cartas de marear notados y glosados de su letra, que debían ser suyos o del Almirante que era en aquella facultad tan docto que no le hacia el Almirante mucha ventaja [. . .]. Era muy buen escribano, mejor que el Almirante porque en mi poder están muchas cosas de las manos de ambos."—*Las Casas*, bk. I, ch. CI, vol. 63, p. 80.

5 " Côtra parecer de muytos : sem achar alguum sinal pera satisfaçam daquelles que auiam este negocio por cousa sem fructo e muy perigosa a todolos que andauam nesta carreira, por este comû prouerbio que traciã os mareantes : Quem passar o cábo de nam, ou tornare ou nam. E era tam assentado o temor desta passagem no coraçam de todos, por herderam esta opiniã de seus auóos que cô muyto trabalho acháua o infante quê nisso o quisesse servir, però que jà o descobrimento da ylha da Madeira désse alguû animo aos navegantes. Porque diziam muytos, que como se avia de passar huû cabo que os mareantes de Espanha posseram por termo y fina da navegaçam daquellas partes : como homeês que sabiam, nam se poder navegar o már que estáva alem delle, assy por as grandes correntes como por ser muy aparcellado & cô tanto fervor das aguagées que sorvia os navios [. . .] nam sabemos [. . .] que fructo elle espera deste seu descobrimento, senam perdicam de quanta gête vay, em os navios, pera ficarem muytos orfaos & viuuas no reyno [. . .]. Porque sempre ahy ouue reyes & principes em Espanha desejosos de grandes impresas [. . .] nã vemos nem lemos em suas chronicas q̂ mandassem descobrir esta terra, tendoa por tâ vezinha."—*Barros*, dec. I, bk. I, ch. IV. Note the use of Espanha, Spain, for the whole peninsula.

6 See these concessions in *Brasil*, vol. I, p. lxxxv, footnote.

7 ". . . porque acerca dos homeês lhe ficasse nome de primeiro côquistador e descubridor da gente ydolatra. . . ."—*Barros*, dec. I, bk. I, ch. II.

8 " Et ultra illum Sinum est Grolandia, que est versus insulam Tyle magis ad Orientem. Et ita tenet totam illam plagam septrionalem usque at terram incognitam. De quibus Tholomeus nullam facit mentionem, et creditur de illis non habuisse noticiam [. . .]. In his regionibus septentrionalibus sunt gentes diverse, inter quas Unipedes et Pigmei ; item griffones sunt in oriente, velut vide in tabula."—Quoted by *Buron*, vol. III, p. 756.

9 No mention is made of the roundness of the earth in the queries which occupied people's minds just before the discovery, because no one doubted then that it was round, as everybody knows, except would-be historians with an axe to grind.

10 " Mito ergo sue maiestati cartam, manibus meis factam, in qua designantur litora vestra et insule ex-quibus incipeatis iter facere versus occasum semper, et loca ad que deneatis pervenire, et quantum a polo, vel a linea equinoctiali debeatis declinare, et per quantum spacium scilicet per quot miliaria debeatis pervenire ad loca fertilissima omnium aromatum et gemarum et non miremini si voco occidentales quia navigantibus ad occidentem semper ille partes invenientur per subterraneas navigaciones. Si enim per terram et per superiora itinera ad orientem semper reperirentur."

My summary of Toscanelli's letter follows the anlysis given by Alto-laguirre, which in my opinion is unanswerable.

On Toscanelli's correspondence there are three views :

(1) The old line : all is genuine ;
(2) Vignaud's line : all is forgery ;
(3) Altolaguirre's line : the letter from Toscanelli to the Canon of Lisbon is genuine ; the letters to Colón are apocryphal.

My view comes nearest to Altolaguirre. But I believe that he has not given a satisfactory explanation of the story and I have attempted to fill up this gap, though at a later stage.

11 Becario's map is of 1435. Andrea Bianco's of 1436. See this point well discussed in *Brasil*, vol. I, p. lxviii.

12 " E porque em a dita carta declara de ylhas despovoadas e que o dito Fernam Telles [. . .] mande povoar e poderia ser que em elle as assy mandando buscar, seus navyos ou jente achariam as Sete Cidades ou algunas outras ylhas poboadas, que ao presente nom sou navegadas [. . .] eu declaro per esta mynha carta [. . .] que me praz que aja em ellas todo aquello senhorio e sopreolidade e poder em os moradores [. . .] que para os moradores das outras ylhas dey."—*Brasil*, vol. I, p. cx.

CHAPTER VIII

1 " hómem expęrto, eloquente & bom latino & muy glorioso em seus negocios."
—*Barros*, dec. I, bk. III, ch. XI, fol. 37.

2 True, the oldest dated edition of Seneca's tragedies is that printed in Lyons in 1491, but Colón may have read undated ones, or, more likely, a folio palimpsest of the early fifteenth century. He is sure to have copied this text for personal use. The passage quoted occurs in line 371 of set II, and is said by the chorus. Here is Colón's translation :

" Vernąn los tardos años del mundo ciertos tp̄os en los cuales el mar occeano afloxera los atamîtos de las cosas y se abrirá una grande tierra y um nuebo marinero como aquel que fue guya de Jason que obo nôbre tiphi descobrira nuebo mûdo y estonces nô sera la ysla tille la postrera de las tierras."

3 The chief denier of the voyage to Thile is, of course, Vignaud. For Vignaud, the life of Colón is quite easy. Everything that does not suit his view of Colón is false. The elimination of early assertions of Colón's on this criterion leads, of course, to later eliminations : until nothing remains at all of what Colón said of himself.

4 " En unas anotaciones que hizo de como todas las cinco zonas son habitables, probándolo por experiencia de sus navegaciones, dice ansi : ' Yo navegué el año de cuatrocientos y setenta y siete, en el mes de Febrero, ultra Tile, isla cien leguas, cuya parte austral dista del equinocial 73° y no 63°, como algunos dicen, y no está dentro de la linea que incluye el occidente, como dice Tolomeo, sino mucho mas occidental, y a esta isla, que es tan grande como Inglaterra, van los ingleses con mercaderias, especialmente los de Bristol, y al tiempo que yo a ella fui no estaba congelado el mar, aunque

habia grandisimas mareas, tanto que en algunas partes dos veces el dia subia 25 brazas o descendia otras tantas en altura.' "—*Las Casas*, bk. I, ch. II, vol. 62, p. 48.

5 " [Homi]nes de Catayo versus oriens venierunt. [Nos] vidimus multa notabilia et [spe]cialiter in Galvei Ibernie virum et [uxo]rem in duobus lignis arreptis ex mirabili [pers]ona."—*Raccolta*, pt. I, vol. II, p. 292, note 10.

6 Negro. See the vicissitudes of this Portuguese-Jewish family in *Amador de los Rios*, notably pp. 280 and 456 of vol. II.

7 On the marriage of Colón, Vignaud is excellent (*Études*, p. 439). The passages from F. Colón and Las Casas will be found there.

8 There is a small chapter (XLII) in Ruy de Pina's *Chronicle of John II*, dedicated to the removal of the Convent of the Saints which took place in 1490, September 5th, by order of the King ; which is in itself a sign of its importance. The beginning of the following chapter recalls the birth of the bastard Prince Jorge, whom King John had by Don'Ana, the future Mother Superior.

9 The description of Colón is in *Oviedo*. Here is the Spanish text :
". . . de buena estatura & aspecto ; mas alto que mediano y de rezios miembros, los ojos biuos y las otras partes del rostro de buena proporciô : el cabello muy bermejo : & la cara algo encendida & pecoso, bien hablado, cauto de gran ingenio & gentil latino : doctissimo Cosmographo : gracioso cuando queria : & yracundo cuando se enojaba."—*Oviedo*, bk. II, ch. II, fol. ii, verso i.

10 " Andando y viniendo dias conoció la suegra ser Cristóbal Colón inclinado a cosas de la mar y de cosmografía, [. . .] ansi que entendido por la suegra su inclinación, contóle cómo su marido Perestrello habia sido tambien persona que tuvo inclinación a las cosas de la mar, y que habia ido por mandado del Infante Don Enrique de Portugal, en compañía de otros dos caballeros a poblar la isla del Puerto Santo, que pocos dias habia que era descubierta, y al cabo a él sólo cupo la total población della y en ella le hizo mercedes el dicho Infante y como entonces andaba muy hirviendo la práctica y ejercicio de los descubrimientos de la costa de Guinea y de las islas que habia por el mar oceano, y esperaba el dicho Bartolomé Perestrello desde aquella descubrir otras, como se descubrieron [. . .] debia tener instrumentos y escrituras y pinturas convenientes a la navegación, las cuales dió la suegra al dicho Cristóbal Colón, con la vista y leyenda de las cuales mucho se alegró."—*Las Casas*, bk. I, ch. IV, vol. 62, p. 53.

11 ". . . saltou com elles tamanho temporal com força de ventos contrarios à sua viàgem, que perderam a esperaça das vidas. [. . .] E como os marinheiros naquelle tempo nam eram costumados a se emgolfar tanto no peguo do mar, e toda sua navegáçam era per singraduras sempre a vista de terra, [. . .] andauan todos tam [. . .] fora de seu juizo [. . .] que nam sabiam julgar en que paragem eram. Mas [. . .] o tempo cessou, & posto que os ventos lhe fizeram perder a viagem que leuauam segundo o regimento do infante, nâ os desuiou de sua boa fortuna : descobrindo a ilha a que agora chamamos Porto Sancto. [. . .] Cô a cual nova sem ir mais auante se tornaram ao reyno, de que o infante recebeo o mayor prazer. [. . .] E acrecêtou a mais a este seu prazer, dizere aquelles dous cavaleiros a huu dos quaes chamauâ Joam Goçaluez Zarco dalcunha, e ao outro Tristam Vaz, que vinham tan contentes dos ares, sitio e fresquidam da terra, que se querian lá tornar á povoalla. [. . .] E nâ sómente elles & os outros da sua côpanhia que a viram, mas ainda muytos polo que della ouuiam, e tambien por comprazer ao infante se offereceram a elle cô este proposito de a pouoar : âtre os quaes foi hûa pessoa notauel

chamado Bertolameu Perestrello, que era fidalgo da casa do infante Dom Joam seu irmão [. . .] logo cô muita diligencia [Dom Enrique] mâdou armar tres nauios, huû dos quaes deu a Bertolameu Perestrello e os outros dous a Joam Goçaluez & a Tristan Vaz primeiros descobridores : indo muy apercebidos de todalas sementes & plantas & outras cousas como quem esperaba de pouoar e assentar naterra. Antre as quaes era hûa coelha que Bertolameu Perestrello leauaua prenhe metida em hûa gayola q̃ pelo mar acertou de parir, de que todos ouueram muyto prazer : & teueram por bô pronostico, pois ja pelo caminho começavam dar fructo as semêtes que leuauam, & aquella coelha lhe daua esperança de grande multiplicaçam que auiam de ter naterra. E certo que esta esperâça da multiplicaçam da coelha ôs nam enganou, mas foy con mais pesar que prazer de todos : porque chegados a ilha & solta a coelha cô seu fructo, en breue tempo, multiplicou en tanta maneira, que nam semeauam ou plantauam cousa que logo nam fosse royda. O que foy em tanto crecimento per espaço de dous annos, que aly esteueram, q̃ quasi importunados daquella praga, começou de auorrecer a todos o trabalho e modo de vida que aly tinham : dôde Bertolameu Perestrello determinou de se vir pera o reino, ou per qualq̃r outra necessidade q̃ peraisso teue."—*Barros*, dec. I, bk. I, fol. 6.

12 In particular, Vignaud, who seems to have a negative bias in his mind even when it is unnecessary and unwarranted.

13 " ansi que fuese a vivir Cristóbal Colón a la dicha isla de Puerto Santo [. . .] por ventura por sola esta causa de querer navegar, dejar alli su mujer, y porque alli en aquella isla y en la de Madera, que está junta, y que tambien se habia descubierto entonces, comenzaba a haber gran concurso de navios sobre su población y vecindad, y frecuentes nuevas se tenian cada dia de los descubrimientos que de nuevo se habian."— *Las Casas*, bk. I, ch. IV, vol. 62, p. 54.

14 *The Geographical Conceptions of Columbus.* A critical consideration of four problems, by George E. Nunn, American Geographical Society, New York, 1924. As will be shown later, Nunn exaggerates the knowledge of Colón in the matters of what are now called the " trade routes." But enough remains to justify my argument.

15 He navigated twenty-three years. See note 7 to ch. IV.

16 " De todas partes y por muchas maneras daba Dios motivos y causas a Cristóbal Colón para que no dudase de acometer tan grande hazaña."— *Las Casas*, bk. I, ch. XIII, vol. 62, p. 97.

17 Colón told this in books now lost, but which Las Casas read. See ch. XIII, quoted above.

18 Vignaud throws doubts on Pero Correa's story, i.e. on the fact that Correa did inform Colón as told by Las Casas and D. Fernando. There is little weight in Vignaud's objections.

19 " Cosas eran todas ciertamente para que él, que tan solicito ya vivia desta negociacion, se abrazase ya con ella, y señales con las cuales parece que Dios lo movia con empellones."—*Las Casas*, bk. I, ch. XIII, vol. 62, p. 101.

CHAPTER IX

1 On Colón's books see *Libros y autógrafos de D. Cristóbal Colón*, by Don Simon de la Rosa, Seville 1891 ; or *Raccolta*. Those that have been preserved are :

    Historia rerum ubique gestarum, by Enea Silvio Piccolomini (Pope Pius II) : Venice, 1477.

Ymago Mundi, by Cardinal Petrus de Alliaco or Pierre d'Ailly :
  believed to have been printed in Louvain between 1480 and 1483.
De consuetudinibus et conditionibus orientalium regionum, by Marco Polo :
  believed to have been printed in Antwerp in 1485.
Historia Naturalis, by C. Plinius : Venice, 1489.
Vidas de los Ilustres Varones of Plutarch, translated into Castillian
  by Alonso de Palencia : Seville, 1497.
Almanach Perpetuum of Abraham Zacuto : printed in Leirea in 1496.
Concordiae Biblia Cardinalis S.P., an MS. of the fifteenth century.

Three more books are believed to have been his :

Sumula Confessionis, by St. Antone of Florence : Venice, 1486.
Philosophia Naturalis of Albertus Magnus : Venice, 1496.
The Tragedies of Seneca, palimpsest of the fifteenth century.

He has certainly known and used the *Catholicon* of John of Genoa,
and the *Etymologies* of St. Isidorus of Seville. It was in the first that he
found this strange etymology for Germany, which he notes in passing,
on the margin of d'Ailly : " Germania, quasi gerens immania."

A detailed, comparative study of the marginal notes written by Colón
on his *Historia* of Pope Pius II and on his *Ymago Mundi*, made by *Buron*
in his introduction to d'Ailly (pp. 23 *et seq.*), proves conclusively that Colón
read his d'Ailly already in print in 1481. Moreover, as we are certain that
d'Ailly's book was well known in MS. in Portugal before it appeared in
print, d'Ailly's influence on Colón's plans is obvious and well established.

2 " in germania habet cristalum et gemmis alique. . . ."—Note 187, Text
of d'Ailly and of Colón, *Buron*, vol. I, p. 316. (D'Ailly's text not complete
in *Raccolta*.)

3 " [gignit] ytalia gemmas et coralum."—Note 211, *Buron*, vol. I, p. 329.

4 " [Y] gemarum metalorum ditissima."—Note 225-6, *Buron*, vol. I, p. 338.

5 " copia metalorum et lapis sagates et margarite."—Note 305, *Buron*,
vol. II, p. 383.

6 " tesalia fuit patria achiles [. . .] et solidi auri ibi primo facti sunt."—
Note 199, *Buron*, vol. I, p. 325.

7 " fl. pactulus."
" pactulus fl. qui arenas aureas trahit."—Note 430-31, *Buron*, vol. II, p. 475.

8 " vbi nascitur avis fenix."—Note 95, *Buron*, vol. I, p. 274. (There is a
misprint in this note.)

9 " Abeston lapidem qui semel acensus numquam extinguitur."—Note 207,
Buron, vol. I, p. 326.

10 " Lithie in plerisque locis auri et gemmis afluant."
" habet smaragdis et purissimum cristalum."—Note 150, *Buron*, vol. I,
p. 302.
The phrase on griffins is suppressed in C. C.'s marginal note.
It is also suppressed in the text of d'Ailly given by *Raccolta*, which
deprives this passage of its value !—*Raccolta*, pt. I, vol. II, p. 386.

11 " Vbi est fons que friget calore diei et calet frigore noctis."
" Vbi nascitur ferras et simie et dracones ac strucios et olin elephantis
plena."—Note 257, *Buron*, vol. II, p. 358.

12 ". . . dracones ex quorum celebro gemme extrahitur . . ."—Note 260,
Buron, vol. II, p. 360.
" de more et vita trogoditorum et situ eius multa miranda."—Note 262,
Buron, vol. II, p. 362.

13 " In qua ortu fingût fabule draconê peruigilem aurea mala seruantê."—
Buron, vol. II, p. 39.

14 " Crise & argire insule in indico oceano site sunt adeo fecunde copia metallorum ut pleriq : eas auream superficiem e argenteam habere dixerunt." —*Buron*, vol. II, p. 39.

15 " Vbi habuerunt nomen ventos et de proprietate eorum pestilencia que ex corupto aere nascitur ;
    Auster pestilentiam gignit.
    Aquilon repelit."
Notes 473-4, *Buron*, vol. II, pp. 491-2.

16 " tunc fit tempestates quando nec plena hiems nec plena estas."
" Vegetius docet quibus mensibus tutius sit nauigandi."—Note 475, *Buron*, vol. II, p. 494.

17 " Tagum fl. cartago ispanie ex qua ortus procedit. auriferis arenis copiosus." —Note 470, *Buron*, vol. II, p. 488.

18 " iherico ci. iheremie insignis orta. Multa loca iudeorum distinte scripta."— Note 446, *Buron*, vol. II, p. 479.

19 " Omnes nactiones habuerunt astronomiam a principio a Judeis."— *Raccolta*, pt. I, vol. III, p. 86, No. 639 ; or vol. II, p. 422.

20 " nec david nec Salomonne nec alij posederunt nisi a dan vsque Bersabe videlicet 160 miliaria."
" A Ioppe vsque Bethleem idest 66 miliaria qua propter parum possessum fuit a Iudeis."
" fl. yordan."
" hec est terminus terre promisionis."—Notes 113-15, *Buron*, vol. I, p. 284.

21 " hec aut terra variarum opum diues est frugibus fertilis aquis illustris opima balsamis."
" ubi propter hoc existauerût iudei eâ promissâ prophetibus terrâ fluêtes lacte & melle."
" In medio Hierosolima quasi umbilicus totius regionis ut de terra Iudee possit îtelligi ' operatus est salutem in medio terre.' "
" Comodo possumus intelligere operatus est salutem in medio terre."— Note 106, *Buron*, vol. I, p. 280.

22 " Vnde patet q̃ si cause speciales bone habitationis conuenirent seù côcurrerêt cû generali. videlicet q̃ terra esset bene fertilis. & bene situata ad Solê et cû bono aspectu celi tunc talis regio esset optime têperata. & verisimile ê q̃ paradis' terrestris talis sit. & forte etiâ ê locus quê actores vocât insulas fortunatas."
" paradisus terrestris forte est locus quem actores vocant insulas fortunatas." —Note 47, *Buron*, vol. I, p. 240.

23 " vnde gentilium error est propter soli fecûditatem eas esse paradisum."
" error gentilium dicentes quod fortunate insule erant paradisum propter soli fecunditatem."—Note 313, *Buron*, vol. II, p. 388.

24 " Fons est in paradiso ortum deliciarum irrigans & in quattuor flumina diuisus."
" fons est in paradiso."—Note 397, *Buron*, vol. II, p. 458 *et seq.*

25 " Paradisus est locus amenissimus in oriente longo terre et maris tractu a nostro habitabili segregatus."—Note 398, *loc. cit.*
" adeo altus ut usque ad lunarem globum attingat ubi aque diluui non parvenſt ; non tamen est intelligendum que secundum veritatem attingat circulum lune. S₃ loquendo yperbolice eius altitudo respectu terre inferioris incomparabilis insinuat. Et qua attingit usque ad aerem quietum supra istum turbulentum ubi finis est et terminus exalaciorum et vaporum humidorum quorum fluxus et progressus lunari corpori apropincuati."— *Loc. cit.*

" Eufrates fluuius ê etiâ Mesopotamie de paradiso exoriês copiosissimus gemmis."
"eufrates, fl. copiosissimus gemmis."—Note 418, *Buron*, vol. I, p. 468.

26 " Licet autem locus vltra tropicum Capricorni secundum aliquos sit optime habitationis. quia secundû Aristotilem Auerroim libro celi & mûdi ibi est superior & nobilior pars in mundo. propter quod est aliquorû opinio ꝗ ibi sit paradisus terrestris. tamen non inuenimus apud aliquê actorem terram illâ describi."—*Buron*, vol. I, p. 232.
" ultra tropico capricorni est optime habitacionis quia ibi est superior et nobilior pars in mundo paradisus terrestris."—*Buron*, vol. I, p. 232.

27 " Quis mouetur ad orientem vel occidentem habet novum meredianum."—Note 6, *Buron*, vol. I, p. 176.

28 " medietas dicitur emisperium."
" mons olimpus vbi fiunt stelle comate . . ."—Notes 7-8, *Buron*, vol. I, p. 184.

29 " quolibet ciuitati potest asignari proprium oriens et occidens respectu sui orizontis."—Note 55, *Buron*, vol. I, p. 250.

30 " per hunc modum inuentum fuit mensura terre."—*Buron*, vol. I, p. 188.

31 " tabule toletane ponunt versum occidens longe plus quam ptholomeus super capite s. vicencij."—Note 56, *Buron*, vol. I, p. 250.

32 " Nota quod arbis ciuitas est in fine primi climatis iuxta insula merois . . ."
" hec .ci. distat ab equinociali gradus 18. et ab occidente gradus 62. vide in ptholomeo et in quator cartis nostre."—Note 660, *Buron*, vol. III, p. 602.
This reference to his four maps might suggest that the note was written during this second period in which he was reduced to earning his living by drawing maps, i.e. towards 1490.

33 The view of Vignaud on Toscanelli and Columbus seems to me wrong. The letter and map *have* existed. This flows inevitably from Altolaguirre's discussion, and since the letter and map existed and Toscanelli's scheme is practically identical with Colón's, it follows that they were known to Colón. Moreover, how could he *not* have known them, living as he did in the same circles and moved as he was by so strong a passion for the very problem with which they dealt ?

34 " terra est rotunda sperica."—Note 480, *Buron*, vol. II, p. 522.

35 " aqua et terra simul facet corpus rotundus."—Note 8.
" Eclipsis lune causatur propter umbram terre."—Note 9, *Buron*, vol. I, p. 185.

36 " A fine occidentis usque ad finem indie per terram est multo plus quam medietas terre videlicet gradus 180."—Note 486, *Buron*, vol. II, p. 526.
" Quantitas terre multo maior est quam vulgus philosophorum estimat."—Note 489, *Buron*, vol. II, p. 526.

37 ". . . A fine occidentis, .s. portugalie vsque ad finem orientis .s. indie supra terram est valde longi."—Note 374, *Buron*, vol. II, p. 436.

38 " finem ispanie et principium indie non multum distat [. . .] expertum est quod hoc mare est nauigabile in paucis diebus ventus conueniens."—Note 677, *Buron*, vol. III, p. 660.
Same idea expressed in Note 43, *Buron*, vol. I, p. 236 : " finis terre habitabilis versus oriens et finis terre habitabilis versus occidens sunt satis prope et inter medium est paruum mare."

39 " Nota quod si taprobana est ut superius distaret a vero occidente ad zepheris gradus 58. quare bene dicimus quod inter hispaniam et indiam est paruum mare."—Note 37, *Buron*, vol. I, p. 232.

40 The point is discussed by Vignaud (*Toscanelli and Columbus*) in chs. VIII, IX and X, and in *Altolaguirre*. I incline to Altolaguirre's conclusions. See a justification of Colón's error on this in *Nunn*.

41 His real name was Ahmet ben Kebir. The observation of Vignaud (*loc. cit.*, p. 84) that Alfragamus's $56\frac{2}{3}$ miles were equivalent to Columbus's, is, I believe, successfully answered by Altolaguirre (*loc. cit.*, ch. III).

42 This fact leads Vignaud to doubt that the voyage to La Mina, where Colón is supposed to have measured the degree, ever took place.

Nunn, however, has proved that, in the circumstances, Colón was bound to make the mistake he made, and that therefore there is no reason to doubt his word.—*Nunn*, ch. I.

43 Like Toscanelli, he did not profess to know how wide the Western way was in itself, but he did try to calculate it on the basis of the West-to-East-by-land distance as known to him. Now, this land-distance he took from Marinus—$225°$; he realised that Ptolemy had corrected Marinus down to $180°$, yet observed that there was all the " Ultra-Ganges India," all the Asiatic continent beyond India proper, to add to Ptolemy's (and Marinus') length, and in this way he went back to $225°$; but these $225°$ were in reality a translation into degrees of the actual width of the Continent in leagues, i.e. 16,000 ; and as Ptolemy made out the degree to be $62\frac{1}{2}$ miles, Colón had to correct Ptolemy by reducing his degrees from $62\frac{1}{2}$ miles to $56\frac{2}{3}$ miles, and therefore the 16,000 miles of Asia and Europe covered for him not $225°$ but $282°$.

See all this calculation in *Nunn*.

44 See *Buron*, vol. I, p. 208.

45 The actual words of Esdras will be found in *Apocrypha*, II, 6, verses 42 and 47 (*The Apocrypha according to the Authorised Version*, University Press, Oxford) :

" 42 : Upon the third day thou didst command that the waters should be gathered in the seventh part of the earth : six parts hast thou dried up, and kept them, to the intent that of these some being planted of God and tilled might serve thee."

" 47 : Upon the fifth day thou saidst unto the seventh part, where the waters were gathered, that it should bring forth living creatures, fowls, and fishes : and so it came to pass."

46 " Ya dise que para la hesecuçion de la ynpresa de las Indias no me aprovechó rasón, ni matemática ny mapamundos ; llenamente se cunplió lo que diso Ysaýas."—*Raccolta*, pt. I, vol. II, p. 82.

47 " et medietas terre non est coperta aquis et quarta pars terre sub equinoxiali oposita ipsius in qua sumus est consimilis dispoxicionis ipsius et ideo debet esse utraque discoperta aquis et consimiliter habitacionis."—Note 487, *Buron*, vol. II, p. 526.

48 " habitacio est vsque ad illum locum vbi extremi mundi cardines sunt, vbi sunt dies per. 6. menses ; ibi est gens beatisima quae non moritur nisi sacietate vite."—Note 485, *Buron*, vol. II, p. 524.

49 Authors do not all agree that Colón's degree was $56\frac{2}{3}$ from the first. An easy calculation will show that, even if at the beginning of his career Colón accepted Ptolemy's standard of $62\frac{1}{2}$ (at the equator), his " 51 degrees " at the parallel of the Canary Islands would amount to about 2754 miles, still by far the shortest estimate ever made for crossing ever imagined, and one which therefore would lead him to expect islands at about 688 leagues, which is exactly where he did expect them.

50 ". . . insula taprobane que habet decem civitationes ; abque reliquis insulis plurimis."—Note 68, *Buron*, vol. I, p. 260.

" inter montes istos sunt insule innumerabiles inter quas sunt que plene margaritis et lapidibus preciosis."—Note 69, *Buron*, vol. I, p. 260 ; and *Raccolta*, pt. I, vol. III, p. 381.

51 ". . . elephantes ingentes Monoceron bestiam. Psitacum auem. Ebenû quoĝ lignû. & plures species aromaticas."
" taprobana habet gemmis et elephantis."
" mittit & ebur lapides preciosos plurimos. Ibi sunt & montes aurei quos adire propter drachones & griffes ac immêsorum hominum monstra impossibile est."—Notes 70 and 72, *Buron*, vol. I, p. 260.
" india multas res habet et species aromaticas et lapides preciosos plurimos et montes aurei."—Note 72, *Buron*, vol. I, p. 260.

52 " frons indie descendit vsque ad tropicum capricorni."—Note 74, *Buron*, vol. I, p. 262.
" debet intellegi quod frons indie que est versus . . . nos idest hispanie se extendit a borea vsque in tropico capri."—Note 75, *Buron*, vol. I, p. 262.

It should be pointed out that the tone and substance of these notes on India unmistakably show that they were written at an early date, during the time when Colón was ruminating his scheme. No difficulty need be raised on account of his mention of Spain in Note 75, for, as has been pointed out, Spain in those days meant the whole peninsula.

CHAPTER X

1 " Foy El Rey Dom Joham homem de corpo, mais grande que pequeno, mui bem feito, e em todos seus membros mui proporcionado : teve o rostro mais comprido que redondo, e de barba en boa conveniencia povoado. Teve es cabellos da cabeça castanhos, e corredios ; e porem, em hidade de trinta e sete annos na cabeça e na barba era ja mui caâo, de que mostraba receber grande contentamento, pola muita autoridade que a sua Divinidade Real suas caâs acrecentaban : e os olhos de perfeita vista, e aas veces mostrava nos brancos delles hûas veas, e magoas de sangue, com que nas cousas de sanha, quando era della tocado, lhe fazian o aspeito mui temeroso. E porem nas cousas d'honra, prazer e gasalhado, mui alegre e de mui Real, e excelente graça : ho nariz teve un poco comprido, e derribado algû tanto, sem fealdade. Era en todo mui alvo, salvo no rostro que era coorado em boa maneira. [. . .] Foi Princepe de maravilhoso engenho, e subida agudeza. [. . .] Foi de mui viva e experta memoria e teve o juizio craro e profundo, e porem suas sentenzas e fallas que inventaba, e dezia, tinhan sempre na envençam maís de verdade, agudeza e autoridade, que de doçura, nem elegancia nas palavras, cuya pronunciaçam foi vagarosa, entoda algû tanto pelos narizes que lhe tiraba graça. Foi Rey de mui alto esforçado e sofrido coraçam, que lhe fazia sospirar por grandes e estranhas empresas ; polo qual com quanto seu corpo pessoalmente en seus Reynos andasse polos bem reger como fazia, porem seu esprito sempre andava fora delles, com desejo de os acrecentar."—*Pina*, ch. LXXXII, p. 193.

2 " Dios nuestro señor milagrosamente me embió acá porque yo sirviese á Vuestra Alteza. dixe milagrosamente porque fuy aportar à Portugal a donde el rey de alli entendia en el descubrir mas que otro, él le atajó la vista, oydo y todos los sentidos, que en catorze años no le pude hacer entender lo que yo dixe."—Letter to the King, May 1505, *Raccolta*, pt. I, vol. II, p. 255.

3 The " 14 months " explanation is d'Avezac, quoted by *Vignaud*, vol. I, p. 364. The solution which consists in throwing over Colón as a liar comes, of course, from *Vignaud, loc. cit.*

4 This was Bacon's opinion. See below, note 12, ch. XXI.

5 A fact which has been overlooked by those who would accuse Colón of inaccuracy on the ground that John II was not King when, on Colón's

reckoning, he would have begun to put his plans before him. Here, again, Colón is found correct.

6 " Con este fuego vine a Vuestra saltezas . . ."—Letter of March 1502, *Raccolta*, pt. I, vol. II, p. 79.

7 *Barros*, dec. I, bk. III, ch. XI.

8 ". . . y como cada dia mas y con mayor vehemencia de imaginación pensase . . ."—*Las Casas*, bk. I, ch. IV, vol. 62, p. 54.
  " Esta autoridad y otras semejantes de este autor fueron las que movieron mas al Almirante para creer su imaginación."—*F.C.*, ch. VII.

9 The first who, to my knowledge, struck on this parallel between Don Quixote and Colón was Jacob Wassermann, in a book unfortunately marred by a total incomprehension of Ferdinand and Isabel. Wassermann also seems inclined to sympathise with those who think that Colón was Jewish ; but he did not go into the matter at all.

10 " En este tiempo he yo visto y puesto estudio en ver de todas escrituras : cosmografia, ystorias, cronicas, y fylosofia, y de otras artes, a que me abrió Nuestro Señor el entendimiento con mano palpable a que era hasedero navegar de aqui a las Yndias, y me abrió la voluntad para la hexecuçion d'ello ; y con este fuego vine a Vuestras Altezas."— Letter to the King and Queen, March 23rd, 1503, *Raccolta*, pt. I, vol. II, p. 79.
  So contagious was his ardent nature that Las Casas, in transcribing this letter, writes : " me abrasó la voluntad," i.e. " He consumed my will with fire," instead of " me abrió la voluntad," " He opened up my will."— *Las Casas*, bk. I, ch. III, vol. 62, p. 46.

11 True, Vignaud maintains that the Portuguese did not think of India when they talked of " India," but of Ethiopia and Prester John (*Vignaud*, vol. I, ch. IV), but his opinion is untenable, and has, I think, been successfully dealt with not only by *Altolaguirre* (*loc. cit.*) but by the Portuguese themselves (*Brasil*).

12 ". . . concebida en su corazon certisima confianza de hallar lo que pretendia, como si este orbe tuviera metido en su arca . . ."—*Las Casas*, bk. I, ch. XXVIII, vol. 62, p. 217.

13 " pero porque segun tengo entendido, que cuando determinó buscar un principe cristiano que le ayudase e hiciese espaldas, ya él tenía certidumbre que habia de descubrir tierras y gentes en ellas, como si en ellas personalmente hubiera estado (de lo cual cierto yo no dudo) . . ."—*Las Casas*, bk. I, ch. V, vol. 62, p. 55.

14 See below, note 17, ch. XV.

15 Vignaud, for instance, who is never more wrong-headed than when he denies that Colón meant to go to the Indies by the West. Of course he did—amongst other things.

16 " Cristóbal Colón no las llamó Indias por que hubiesen sido por otros vistas ni descubiertas, sino porque eran la parte oriental de la India Ultra-Gange, la cual, siguiendo siempre al oriente, venía a ser a nosotros occidental, como sea el mundo redondo [. . .] y por ser estas tierras lo oriental ignoto de la India, y no tener nombre particular, atribuyóle aquel nombre que tenía la mas propincua tierra, llamándolas Indias occidentales, mayormente que, como él supiese que a todos era manifiesta la riqueza y grande fama de la India, queria provocar con aquel nombre a los Reyes Católicos, que estaban dudosos de su empresa, diciendoles que iba a buscar y hallar las Indias por la via del occidente."—*Las Casas*, bk. II, ch. V, vol. 63, p. 57.

17 ". . . las grandes ciudades del Gran Can que se descubrirán sin duda . . ."— First Voyage, November 12th, *Navarrete*, vol. I, p. 54.

18 " plus medietatis quarte terre in qua sumus est nobis ignotum nec sunt .ci. a philosophis comprense."—Note 367, *Buron*, vol. II, p. 426.

19 " Mercería de Flandes, como son cascabeles, bacinetas de laton, hoja del mismo laton, sartas de cuentas, vidrio de diversos colores, espejuelos, tiseras, cuchillos, agujas, alfileres, camisas de lienzo, paño basto de colores, bonetejos colorados y otras cosas semejantes, que todas son de poco precio y valor, aunque para entre gente dellas ignorante de mucha estima."— *Las Casas*, bk. I, ch. XXVIII, vol. 62, p. 218.

20 " Propuso su negocio ante el rey de Portugal, y lo que se ofrecia a hacer esa lo siguiente : Que por la via del Poniente, hacia Auster o Mediodia, descubriria grandes tierras, islas y tierra firme, felicísimas, riquísimas de oro y plata y perlas y piedras preciosas y gentes infinitas ; y que por aquel camino entendía topar con tierra de la India, y con la grande isla de Cipango y los reinos del Gran Can."—*Las Casas*, bk. I, ch. XXVIII, vol. 62, p. 218.

21 " Primeramente, que le honrasen armándole caballero de espuelas doradas y que se pudiese llamar D. Cristóbal Colón ; él y sus sucesores. Lo segundo que le diesen titulo de Almirante Mayor del Mar Oceano, con todas las preeminencias o prerogativas, privilegios, derechos, rentas e inmunidades que tenían los almirantes de Castilla. Lo tercero que fuese su Viso-Rey y gobernador perpetuo, de todas las islas y tierras firmes que él descubriese por su persona o por su industria fuesen descubiertas. Lo cuarto que le diesen la decima parte de las rentas que el rey hubiese de todas las cosas que fuesen oro, plata, perlas, piedras preciosas, metales, especería, y de otras cualesquiera cosas provechosas, y mercaderías de cualquier especie, nombre y manera que fuesen que se comprasen, trocasen, hallasen, ganasen, dentro de su Almirantazgo. Lo quinto, que en todos los navios que se armasen para el dicho trato y negociacion, cada y cuanto y cuantas veces se armasen, que pudiese Cristóbal Colón, si quisiese contribuir y pagar la ochava parte, y que del provecho que dello saliese llevase tambien la ochava parte, y otras cosas que abajo aparecerán."—*Las Casas*, bk. I, ch. XXVIII, vol. 62, p. 218.

22 See *Brasil*, p. 30.

23 " Christoval Colom fue el primero que en España enseño a nauegar el amplissimo mar oceano por las alturas de los grados del sol y norte : & lo puso por obra : porque hasta el, aunque se leyese en las escuelas tal arte, pocos (o mejor diciendo, ninguno) se atreuian a lo experimentar en los mares."—*Oviedo*, bk. II, ch. III, fol. iii verso.

24 " todo lo que fasta oy se navega todo lo he andado."—Letter to the King and Queen, March 23rd, 1502, *Raccolta*, pt. I, vol. II, p. 79.

25 " El Rey, porque via ser este Christovâ Colom homem falador e glorioso em monstrar suas habilidades, & mais fantastico & de imaginaçôes com sua ilha cypango, que cẹrto no q̃ dizia dáualhe pouco crẹdito. Comtudo, a força de suas importunaçôes, mandou q' estiụésse cô Dô Diogo Ortiz, bispo de Cepta & com Mestre Rodrigo & Mestre Josope, a quem ele cometia estas cousas da cosmographia e seus descobrimentos : & todos ouueram por vaidáde as paráulas de Christouam Colom, por todo ser fundádo em imaginaçoes e cousas da jlha Cypango de Marco Paulo."—*Barros*, dec. I, bk. III, ch. XI, fol. 37 verso.

26 As shown by Vignaud (vol. I, p. 383 footnote). He seems, however, to be mistaken in believing that the three men made up a permanent " Committee of Mathematicians." Cf. *Brasil*.

Vignaud does, in my opinion, make a good case for his account of what happened with Colón's proposals in Portugal as against Las Casas and Fernando Colón. I have followed his narrative in all essentials.

27 Las Casas (bk. I, ch. XXVIII, vol. 62) and Fernando Colón (ch. XI) actually say King John did send such a caravel. I believe Vignaud is right in his scepticism on this point (vol. I, p. 394). It was an obvious case of fear and suspiciousness, from which Colón often suffered.

28 " Y porque convenía estar desocupado del cuidado y obligación de la mujer, para negocio en que Dios le había de ocupar toda la vida, plúgole de se la llevar. . . ."—*Las Casas*, bk. I, ch. XXVIII, vol. 62, p. 222.
" era Colom casado en aquel Reyno : & se auia hecho natural vassallo de aquella tierra por su matrimonio."—*Oviedo*, bk. II, ch. IV, fol. v verso.

29 Fernando de Rojas, the *Converso* author of *The Tragi-Comedy of Calisto and Melibea*, a masterpiece of Shakespearian excellence.

30 " francos & anglos non sunt habiles ad sciendum astrologiam."—Note 57, *Buron*, vol. I, p. 246.

31 My reading of the Toscanelli episode will now be plain. Curiously enough, Vignaud, who accuses Colón of all kinds of untruths, of which he is innocent, refuses to see that the author of the forgery of Toscanelli's letter is Colón himself. In my view, this results inevitably from the comparison of the Italian and Latin texts known through Fernando Colón and Las Casas with the Latin text discovered by Mr. Harrisse in the blank page of Pius II's *History*. Altolaguirre had already observed that the data which might be most useful for a navigator had been omitted and the crucial figure for the distance across the water misplaced with an obviously deliberate intention. This analysis of Altolaguirre should suffice to establish that the origin of the forgery is Colón himself.
There are other indications, and notably the word *populatissima*, an Italianism which Vignaud reproaches to the Spanish text and which occurs frequently in Colón's Spanish.
Finally, the version I have given provides an explanation for a still unexplained fact. Why did Colón run away from Portugal ? The fact is certain (cf. *Vignaud*, vol. I, p. 399), but no one has provided a plausible explanation. A man who has stolen an important document must run away. Secrecy in all that pertained to discovery was a policy already well established under King John. Colón could not leave Portugal leaving that document behind ; he could not show it without proving himself a thief. He made up the correspondence with Toscanelli (who was by then dead and would not deny it), and though such an invention would not have cut much ice in Lisbon, it certainly would in Seville, where he was in a position to give plausible reasons for keeping its existence secret from the Portuguese.

CHAPTER XI

1 See the discussion of this point in *A.R.*, vol. I, ch. I.

2 " Dificil será abrir la historia de la Peninsula Ibérica, ya civil, ya política, ya religiosa, ora científica, ora literariamente considerada, sin tropezar en cada página con algun hecho o nombre memorable, relativo a la nación hebrea."—*A.R.*, vol. I, p. 1.

3 *A.R.*, vol. I, p. 39.

4 Conclusion No. 2 may be extended even to the Church, over which some Jews came to hold considerable power by holding high functions of State. Here is an example :
" Don Samuel Levi, tesorero mayor del rey, y Velasco García, alcalde del rey, ambos oidores de su audiencia, por mandado del rey dieron sentencia en favor del obispo y cabildo de la catedral de Córdoba para que no pagasen

yantar al despensero del Monarca. Sevilla 1357, Sept. 18."—Rafael Ramirez de Arellano, *Historia de Córdoba*, vol. IV (*Ciudad Real*, 1920), quoted in *Die Juden im christlichen Spanien*, by Fritz Baer, Berlin, p. 180.

5 *A.R.*, vol. I, p. 106.

6 *A.R.*, vol. I, p. 5. See ch. XXIX, p. 361 of the present work.

7 " Dialogi latè dignissimi in quibus impiae judaeorum opiniones [. . .] confutantur."—*A.R.*, vol. I, p. 5 note.

8 *El Puñal de la Fé*, by Fray Reimundo Martin de Subirats ; *Puñal de los Judios*, by Fray Pedro de Barcelona : *A.R.*, *loc. cit.*

9 " E todo esto fué cobdicía de robar, segun paresció, mas que devoción."— Pero Lopez de Ayala, *Crónica de Enrique III*, dec. I, ch. XXXX (quoted by *A.R.*, vol. II, p. 38).

10 *A.R.*, vol. II, p. 404.

11 *A.R.*, vol. II, p. 496.

12 *A.R.*, vol. III, p. 56.

13 *A.R.*, vol. III, p. 131.

14 *Fortalitium Fidei*. *A.R.*, vol. III, p. 137, refers to an edition printed in 1494.

15 " Yo creo, que si se hiciera en este nuestro tiempo una verdadera inquisición, serian innumerables los entregados al fuego, de cuantos realmente se hallara que judaizan : los cuales, si no fueren aqui mas cruelmente castigados que los judíos públicos, habrán de ser quemados en el fuego eterno."—Quoted by *A.R.*, vol. III, p. 141.

16 I hope I will be forgiven for this neologism. *Hieronymites* is a pedantic mouthful and misrepresents the lively part taken by this order in the life of Spain in those days.

17 *Zelus Christi contra judaeos et Sarracenos*. *A.R.*, vol. III, p. 106 : " Ex ruina eorum constituitur et construitur vera et catholica spes christiana."

18 *A.R.*, vol. III, p. 237.

19 " La primera vez que confesso a la Reyna passo una cosa digna de saberse. Acostumbraua a estar ella y el confessor puestos de rodillas arrimados a un sitio o vanquillo ; llegó Fray Hernando, y sentóse en el vanquillo para oyrla de confessión ; dixole la Reyna : Entrambos hemos de estar de rodillas. Respondió el nuevo Confessor : No señora, sino yo he de estar sentado y vuestra alteza de rodillas, porque este es el Tribunal de Dios, y hago aqui sus vezes. Calló la Reina y passo por ello como Santa. Y dizen que dixo despues : este es el confessor que yo buscaba."— *Sigüenza*, vol. II, p. 295.

20 There are several letters of the Queen to her confessor. They are to be found in *Sigüenza*, vol. III, p. 320 *et seq.*

21 " y con esto pasaron obra de dos años e no valio nada, que cada uno hacia lo acostumbrado ; e mudar de costumbre es apartar de muerte."—*Bernáldez*, ch. XLII, vol. I, p. 125.

22 " esta heregia ovo [. . .] su impinación e lozanía de muy gran riqueza y vanagloria de muchos sabios e doctos, e obispos, e canonigos, e frailes, e abades, e sabios, e contadores, e secretarios, e factores de Reyes et de grandes Señores [. . .]. Habeis de saber, que las costumbres de la gente comun de ellos ante la Inquisición, ni mas ni menos que era de los propios hediondos judios, y esto causaba la continua conversacion que con ellos tenian ; ansi eran tragones y comilones, que nunca perdian el comer a costumbre judaica de manjarejos, e olletas de afinos, manjarejos de cebollas e ajos, e fritos

con aceite, y la carne guisaban con aceite, e lo echaban en lugar de tocino e de grosura por escusar el tocino y el aceite con la carne es cosa que hace muy mal oler el resuello ; y ansi sus casas e puertas hedian muy mal a aquellos manjarejos ; y ellos ese mesmo tenian el olor de los judios por causa de los manjares y de no ser baptizados."—*Bernáldez*, ch. XLIII, vol. I, p. 124 *et seq.*

23 Text in *Kayserling*, p. 27.

This author has no sense of historical aloofness and impartiality. Thus, on p. 44 he speaks of the " outrageous " persecutions of the Inquisition against Fray Hernando de Talavera, and on p. 45 he speaks of " Diego de Deza, a learned theologian of Jewish descent [. . .] much esteemed." But he omits the fact, which can hardly have escaped his notice, that the Inquisitor who authorised the persecutions against the saintly Talavera was Diego de Deza.

This strong bias, noticeable time and again in his otherwise scholarly book, adds weight to his assertion on the prevalence of " judaising " amongst *Conversos*.

24 *Pulgar-Crónica*, ch. LXXVII, p. 136.

See also the account which he gives of the new Christians who were found judaising in Toledo, and which he gives quietly in his usual way, yet obviously convinced that the findings of the Inquisition in the matter were true.—*Loc. cit.*, ch. LIV, p. 269.

25 " El prior del Prado [. . .] fué contrario al dicho oficio de la Inquisición."— Zurita, note to ch. XL of D. de Valera's MS. chronicle.

26 *A.R.*, vol. III, p. 40.

27 *Pulgar-Crónica*, ch. CIII, p. 176-9.

28 *A.R.*, vol. II, p. 220.

29 ". . . la mala costumbre de España que los trata peor a los que se conuierten destas sectas que antes que se conuiertan, porque apenas les saben dezir su propio nombre, de donde se sigue que rehusan muchos recibir una Fe que en los que la professan se vee tan poca caridad."—*Sigüenza*, vol. II, p. 305.

30 See *Erasme et l'Espagne*, by Marcel Bataillon, Paris.

31 Thus *Kayserling* : " his [King Ferdinand's] chief object was to secure the wealth of the Marranos."

32 " un regidor Juan de Córdoba [. . .] mandó que fuesen todos [a quien habia hecho daños y males] satisfechos de su hazienda e lo que cobró mandólo repartir a los pobres."—*Valera*, ch. XL, p. 122.

33 " E los guarecieron los señores e los Reyes siempre por los grandes provechos que de ellos habian."—*Bernáldez*, ch. XLIII, vol. I, p. 124.

34 *Revue Hispanique*, vols. 4 and 5.

35 Here again Kayserling shows his bias : he mentions the punishment but not the conspiracy (p. 34).

36 Cases such as Alonso de Espina, who, though a *Converso*, condemned both faithful and faithless Jews, are the exception which confirms the rule ; they represent the new Christian who has realised that the specific feature of old Christians is precisely not to distinguish between Jew and Jew.

37 " sed hanc istorum prophetiam Iudei reprobi non acipiunt ; acceperunt autem qui ex eis innumerabiles evangelio crediderunt. tunc enim vere Israel divisus est in duo, divisione illa que per Samuelem prophetam Sauli regi est immutabilis prenunciata. [. . .] Esdram etiam Iudei reprobi in actoritatem canonicam receptos novissimos habent."—Note 856 to *Historia* of Pliny, *Raccolta*, pt. I, vol. II, p. 366.

CHAPTER XII

1 See above, note 3 to ch. VI.

2 Let no person whose faith and convictions have not been tested by danger throw the first stone.

3 For La Rábida, Vignaud (vol. I, p. 485) seems to me a reliable guide. I have, on the whole, based my narrative on his scholarly and well-argued conclusions of fact ; not so in matters of *motive*.

4 *Duro*, p. 19.

5 " e se iba derecho de esta villa a la villa de Huelva para fallar y verse con su cuñado, casado con una hermana de su mujer [. . .] e que habia nombre Muliar."—Dr. García Fernandez in *Navarrete*, vol. III, p. 561.

6 No proof has been given that this friar was ever the Queen's confessor. The error, if it is one, as it probably is, may come from the fact that he had been *contador*, accountant, before he became a friar. And as the two professions do not go well together, he was *voce populi* promoted confessor from *contador*.

7 *Las Casas*, bk. I, ch. XIII, vol. 62, p. 100. He writes Deteine, instead of de Teive.
". . . y a la vuelta descubrieron la Isla de las Flores, guiandose por muchas aves que vian volar hacia ella, porque cognoscieron que eran aves de tierra y no de la mar, y ansi juzgaron que debian de ir a dormir a alguna tierra."

8 *Las Casas*, bk. I, ch. XIII, vol. 62, p. 98.

9 " Sirvió a su Rey todo el tiempo de su vida con tanta obediencia que la perseverancia que tovo en su servicio fué a otros exemple de lealtad.
" Fué hombre vencido del amor de las mugeres y él fué amado de ellas."— *Pulgar-Claros*, pp. 65-6.

10 This follows from two statements of Colón. The first, to be found in the diary of his first voyage (August 9th, 1492), to the effect that :
" Dice aqui el Almirante que se acuerda que estando en Portugal el año de 1484 vino uno de la isla de la Madera al Rey à le pedir una carabela para ir á esta tierra que via, el cual juraba que cada año la via, y siempre de una manera . . ."—*Navarrete*, vol. I, p. 5.
This Madeirean has been identified as Domingo de Arco, granted his privilege on June 30th. Vignaud (vol. I, p. 405) concludes that therefore Colón was still in Lisbon *at that date*, which does not follow inevitably, for Colón does not speak of *granting*, but of *asking*, and the way he mentions the fact rather suggests that he had left Lisbon before June 30th. The second statement of Colón is that, already quoted (see note 10 to ch. IV), from which it follows that he entered the King's service on January 20th, 1486, and as we know he did because the Duke of Medinaceli handed him and his dreams over to the King and Queen, the sequence is proved.
As a consequence, Colón stayed with the Duke from some late date in 1484 till January 1486. This amply suffices to justify the Duke's statement that he kept him two years, particularly since he is making that statement to ask for compensation, which would subconsciously lead him to overstate his case.

11 ". . . un marinero tuerto dijo al dicho Cristobal Colón, estando en el Puerto de Sancta Maria, que, en un viaje que habia hecho a Irlanda vido aquella tierra que los otros haber por allí conocian, e imaginaban que era Tartaria, que daba vuelta por el Occidente."—*Las Casas*, bk. I, ch. XIII, vol. 62, p. 100.

12 " [El Duque] mandó dar todo lo que Colón decia que era menester, hasta 3 o 4,000 ducados con que hiciese tres navios o carabelas, proveidas de comida para un año y para mas y de rescates y gente marinera, y todo lo

que mas pareciese que era necesario ; mandando con extrema solicitud se pusieren los navios, en aquel rio del Puerto de Santa María, en astillero, sin que se alzase mano dellos hasta acabarlos."—*Las Casas*, bk. I, ch. XXX, vol. I, p. 137.

13 " Y aquel fué el primer día que de todo en todo conoció y creyó ser caballero andante verdadero, y no fantástico, viéndose tratar del mismo modo que él había leido se trataban los tales caballeros en los pasados siglos."—*D.Q.*, vol. II, ch. XXXI.

". . . mandóle llamar y, haciendole el tratamiento que, segun la nobleza y benignidad suya y la autorizada persona y graciosa presencia del Cristóbal Colón merecia, informóse del muy particularmente . . ."—*Las Casas*, bk. I, ch. XXX, vol. I, p. 236.

14 " En el nombre de Jesuchristo Salvador y Redemptor del Mundo, en quince días del mes de Abril, año del nacimiento de Nuestro Redemptor de mil cuatrocientos ochenta y cinco, sacó el inclito y famoso Rey Don Fernando su hueste muy grande, e muy maravillosa, y muy fermosa, de Castilla para ir a facer guerra a los moros."—*Bernáldez*, ch. LXXV, vol. I, p. 201.

15 *Bernáldez, loc. cit.* ; *Pulgar-Crónica*, ch. XLI, p. 241.

16 *Pulgar-Crónica*, beginning of ch. XLVII, p. 259.

17 " e llovió tan recio, e tantas aguas que nunca los que eran nacidos estonces vieron ni tantas aguas, ni tantas avenidas en tan poco tiempo . . ." " e sacaron los monjes en barcos."—*Bernáldez*, ch. LXXVIII, vol. I, p. 215.

18 The text will be found in *Navarrete*, vol. II, No. XIV, pp. 20-1, or in *Vignaud*, vol. I, p. 528.

". . . como vi que era esta empresa para la Reina, nuestra Señora, escrebilo a su Alteza desde Rota, y respondiome que gelo enviase ; yo gelo envié entonces [. . .] su Alteza lo recibió y lo dio en cargo a Alonso de Quintanilla."

19 " Porque la tierra del Andalucia estaba fatigada [. . .] el Rey y la Reyna acordaron de la dejar folgar el invierno e venir al reyno de Toledo."—*Pulgar-Crónica*, ch. LIII, p. 266.

20 " El Rey y la Reyna desde Madrid a 20 de Enero escribieron al dean y cabildo dando las gracias de lo mucho que en esta calamidad habian socorrido al pueblo."—Zúñiga, *Anales Eclesiásticos*, 1486, vol. III, p. 135, ed. 1776. Quoted by *Vignaud*, vol. I, p. 553 footnote.

Vignaud gives it as possible that the King and Queen were in Córdoba as late as November 1485. This is most unlikely, for the Queen gave birth to the Infanta Catalina (the future Catherine of Aragon) in Alcalá on December 15th.

21 " Notable varon y deseoso del accresçentamiento y servicio de sus reyes." " mandauale dar de comer y lo necessario por una compassibilidad de su pobreza."

" por su respecto & intercession [of Quintanilla's] fue [Colón] conoçido del reueverêdisimo & ilustre cardenal de españa arçobispo de Toledo dô Pero gonçalez d'mendoça."—*Oviedo*, bk. II, ch. IV, fol. v verso.

22 ". . . todo lo que se cogia de la Cruzada e subsidio de la clerecia e de las penas que se ponian a los que habian judaizado, e se reconciliaban a la iglesia, e de las otras sus rentas ordinarias, e de todas las partes que podian haber dineros, mandaban destribuirlo en las cosas de la guerra."—*Pulgar-Crónica*, ch. XL, p. 241.

23 " embiaron a pedir prestados a algunas personas singulares."—*Pulgar-Crónica*, ch. LXIV, p. 283.

24 *A.R.*, vol. III, pp. 295-6. See also an entry of half a million maravedis,

dated 1484, to Don Isag Abrahan, " por otro tanto que prestó a sus Altezas para los gastos de la guerra."—*Navarrete*, vol. II, p. 5.

25 Zúñiga says : " Los Reyes vinieron de Madrid en Córdoba 2 de Mayo " (*Anales*, 1486, p. 135). Zurita says : " A veinte y ocho del mes de Abril " (vol. IV, bk. XX, ch. LXVII, fol. 346 R). Both quoted by *Vignaud*, vol. I, p. 566.

26 " Asi que Christobal Colón se vino a la corte del Rey Don Fernando y de la Reina Doña Isabel, y les hizo relacion de su imaginacion, a la cual [. . .] no daban mucho credito, y el les platico y dijo ser cierto lo que les decia, y les enseño el mapa mundo, de manera que les puso en deseo de saber de aquellas Tierras."—*Bernáldez*, ch. CXVIII, vol. I, p. 358.

CHAPTER XIII

1 " La gracia singular que [Dios] le concedió para el ministerio que le cometió."—*Las Casas*, bk. I, ch. III, vol. 62, p. 47.
   " y ansi podia procurar los que le viesen facilmente a su amor."—*Las Casas*, bk. I, ch. II, vol. 62, p. 44.

2 See above, note 10 to ch. VI.

3 On the collaboration of sea-power in the conquest of Seville see *Navarrete*, vol. I, p. xii.
   On Colón's habit of saying " by St. Ferdinand," see above, ch. II.

4 " barrio e alfondiga e forno e baño."—*Navarrete*, vol. II, p. 375.
   For a list of the explicit confirmations of the privileges of the Genoese see *Navarrete*, vol. I, p. cli.
   For the Catalan request to Alfonso X see *Navarrete*, vol. II, p. 375 footnote.

5 *Navarrete*, vol. I, p. xv.

6 *Navarrete*, vol. I, p. xix.

7 *Navarrete*, vol. I, p. xxi.
   For the use of artillery at sea see *Navarrete*, vol. I, p. cxviii.

8 *Navarrete*, vol. I, p. xxiv.
   For the text of this interesting law see *Navarrete*, vol. II, p. 378.

9 There is a good account of this episode of Spanish history in *Las Casas*, bk. I, vol. 62, ch. XVIII, where he reveals original documents of great interest.

10 " Eran preciadas porque en aquellas partidas caían muchos rayos del cielo, e creían aquellos bárbaros, que qualquier que traía una concha de aquellas era seguro de los rayos."—*Pulgar-Crónica*, ch. LXII, p. 115.
   " e una concha que no era estimada en precio alguno, acaeció valer por aquella causa en la ciudad de Sevilla y en aquellos puertos del Andalucía veinte reales de plata, por la gran requesta que de ellas había para llevar a aquella tierra."—*Pulgar-Crónica*, loc. cit., p. 114.
   " e acaeció haber de un viaje diez mil pesos de oro, que era cada peso valor de dos florines de Aragon."—*Pulgar-Crónica*, loc. cit., p. 114.

11 For an interesting episode of this sea-rivalry see *Valera-Crónica*, ch. XXII, p. 79.
   On an equally interesting case of collaboration between Castille and Portugal, thanks to the sea-power of Castille, see *Valera-Crónica*, ch. XXV, p. 86.

12 For the expedition to the Canaries see *Pulgar-Crónica*, ch. LXXVI, p. 135, who says it began in '78. *Bernáldez* gives more details and begins it in '79.— Vol. I, ch. XXXV, p. 100.
   ". . . a veinte y nueve dias del mes de julio, dia de Santa Marta, a medio

dia, fizo el sol un eclipse el mas espantoso que nunca los que fasta alli eran nacidos vieron, que se cubrió el sol de todo e se paró negro, e parecian las estrellas en el cielo como de noche [. . .] y nunca de aquel ora tornó el sol en su color, ni el dia esclareció como los dias de antes solía estar, e asi se puso muy calijinoso."—*Bernáldez*, vol. I, ch. XXXIV.

13 The Spanish text is as follows :
" y todas las islas que agora tienen descubiertas y cualesquier otras islas que se hallaren y conquirieren de las islas de Canaria para abajo contra Guinea. Porque todo lo que está hallado y se hallare y conquiriere e descubriere en los dichos terminos, allende de lo que ya es hallado, ocupado e descubierto, finca a los dichos reyes e principe de Portugal y sus reynos, tirando, solamente las islas de Canaria." Quoted by *Vignaud*, vol. I, p. 209 footnote.

14 Vignaud says of the decision of the King and Queen : " Cette décision était en réalité une fin de non recevoir." It is difficult to be more wrong-headed. Why should not the omnipotent King and Queen merely send him away empty-handed, as the King of Portugal had done ? Instead of which, they refer him to a Commission presided over by their overworked right-hand man : a signal proof that they had been impressed ; and this is actually recognised by Vignaud on his next page.
He is right, however, in his judgment on Talavera and in his condemnation of Las Casas and of Lafuente on this point.—*Vignaud*, vol. I, pp. 568-9-10.

15 On how overworked Hernando de Talavera was, see his biographer, Sigüenza, particularly ch. XXI, vol. II, p. 296.

16 Such as that of Pinilla (*Colón en España*) quoted by Vignaud (vol. I, p. 572), who sees in the appointment of this obvious Commission a Machiavellian scheme of Ferdinand ! The great King was somewhat Machiavellian, but not twenty-four hours a day, nor when it was unnecessary to be so.
Vignaud is generally good on the Commission and its work.

17 " [los Reyes] puesto que con benignidad y alegre rostro, acordaron de lo cometer a letrados, para que oyesen a Cristobal Colón mas particularmente y viesen la calidad del negocio y la prueba que daba para que fuese posible, confiriesen y tratasen de ello, y despues hiciesen a sus Altezas plenaria relacion."—*Las Casas*, bk. I, ch. XXIX, vol. 62, pp. 228-9.
The actual text has a comma after *daba* and no comma after *posible*, which makes it unintelligible.

18 " De cómo el rey don Fernando se partió de la ciudad de Cordoba, dexando allí a la reyna doña Isabel su muger, sábado por la mañana, bispera de pasqua de Sanctí Spiritus, a quinze dias del mes de mayo del año de Nuestro Redemptor de mill y quatroçientos y ochenta y seis años."—*Valera-Crónica*, ch. LXVI, p. 199.

19 " Y en Salamanca, a donde pasaron lo recio del invierno, a 30 de Noviembre." —Zúñiga, *sub anno* 1486. Enero 26. " Partieron los reyes, nuestros Señores, de Salamanca."—Cronicón de Valladolid. Both quoted by *Vignaud*, vol. I, p. 575.
There is a difficulty here : Maldonado (see below, note 29) says Talavera was then Prior of the Prado. But he had been made bishop of Avila in 1485 (see *Pulgar-Crónica*, ch. XXXVIII, p. 239—the friar's name is misprinted as Oropesa). The only suggestion is that Maldonado's memory was faulty.

20 " El principal que fué causa desta última despedida, se cree haber sido el susodicho Prior del Prado y los que le seguían, de creer es que no por otra causa sino porque otra cosa no alcanzaban ni entendían."—*Las Casas*, bk. I, ch. XXXI, vol. 62, p. 243.
" Coloro, che si redussero, non intenderano, quel che doverano."— *F.C.*, ch. XII, fol. 32 verso.

21 " La falta de las ciencias matemáticas, de noticia de las historias antiguas que los que tuvieron el negocio cometido tenían . . ."—*Las Casas*, bk. I, ch. XXIX, vol. 62, p. 232.

22 On Salamanca University as a centre of learning see *Vignaud*, vol. I, pp. 588 and 720, with the sources he quotes.

On Spain as a centre of astronomical learning : " Depuis deux cents ans les savants des Universités de la chrétienté allaient puiser en Espagne l'enseignement des lettres anciennes que les arabes avaient traduites ; ils y prenaient le goût des sciences mathématiques, astrologiques et philosophiques, non seulement dans Aristote mais même Averrhoés et les Orientaux."—*Buron*, vol. I, p. 35.

23 See below, note 29.

24 " pues como, Fray Hernando, que no aueys de querer obedecerme un dia de cuantos yo os obedesco a vos ? "—*Sigüenza*, ch. XXXII, vol. II, p. 298.

25 " ' V.S. me perdone, no alumbre un Prelado tan santo a un hombre tan descomedido y errado como yo.' ' Antes es oficio de Prelados alumbrar a los que yerran, y podia vuesa merced caer en essa escalera.'

" Tornáronse a juntar y a remeter las quentas, y hizose todo como él dezia."—*Sigüenza*, ch. XXXI, vol. II, p. 296.

26 " Puse en esto seis o siete años de grave pena."—Third Voyage, *Navarrete*, vol. I, p. 242.

" Siete años estuve yo en su Real Corte, que a cuantos se fabló de esta empresa todos a una dijeron que era burla."—Letter from Jamaica, July 7th, 1503, *Navarrete*, vol. I, p. 311.

" Comenzó a entrar en una terrible continua, penosa y prolija batalla, que por ventura no le fuera [tan] aspera ni tan horrible la de materiales y armas, cuanto la de informar a tantos que no le entendian, aunque presumian de le entender, responder, sufrir a muchos que no conocian ni hacian mucho caso de su persona, recibiendo algunos baldones de palabras que le afligian el alma."—*Las Casas*, bk. I, ch. XXIX, vol. 62, p. 227.

27 Vignaud has dealt effectively with these historical weeds.—Vol. I, pp. 579 and 588.

28 " siempre desque yo vine a Castilla, me ha favorecido y deseado mi honra."— Letter to his son, Diego, November 21st, 1504, Seville, *Navarrete*, vol. I, pp. 333-4.

It may be useful to point out at this juncture that the word *converso*, meaning originally an individual who was actually converted, took on a more general sense—that of the " class " or social group of Christian Jews—in which meaning, and only in it, can it be said to apply to such men as Pulgar or Deza.

29 " con el prior del Prado, que a la sazon hera, que despues fué arçobispo de Granada, e con otros sabios e letrados e marineros, platicaron con el dicho Almirante sobre su hida a las dichas yslas, e que todos ellos concordaron que hera imposible ser verdad lo que el dicho Almyrante decya, e que contra el parecer de los mas dellos, porfió el dicho Almyrante de yr el dicho viaje."—Statement made by Don Rodrigo Maldonado, governor of Salamanca, member of the Talavera Commission : *Pleitos*.

" Ellos juntos, muchas veces, propuesta [por] Cristobal Colón su empresa, dando razones y autoridades para que la tuviesen por posible, aunque callando las mas urgentes por que no le acaeciese lo que con el rey de Portugal. . . ."—*Las Casas*, bk. I, ch. XXIX, vol. 62, p. 229.

30 " 5 Mayo. di a Cristobal Colomo, extranjero, tres mil maravedis, que está aqui faciendo algunas cosas complideras al servicio de sus Altezas, por cédula a Alonso de Quintanilla, con mandamiento del obispo [de Palencia] Libro de Cuentas Francisco Gonzalez de Sevilla, Tesorero de la R.C.

" 27 Agosto. En 27 du dicho mes di a Cristobal Colomo cuatro mil maravedis para ir al Real, por mandado de sus Altezas por cedula de Obispo. Son siete mil maravedis con tres mil que se le mandaron dar para ayuda de su costa por otra partida de 3 de julio.

" 15 Oct. En ocho dias di a Cristobal Colomo cuatro mil maravedis que sus Altezas le mandaron dar para ayuda de su costa por cedula del obispo."—*Navarrete*, vol. II, p. 4.

CHAPTER XIV

1 16 June 1488. " Di a Cristobal Colomo tres mil maravedis por cedula de sus Altezas."—*Navarrete*, vol. II, p. 5.

2 " Toda esta dilacion no se pasaba sin grandes trabajos y angustias y amarguras de Cristobal Colón [. . .] porque via que se le pasaba la vida en valde, segun los dias que serle [ian] necesarios para tan soberana y diuturna obra esperaba hacer ; y sobre todas [las causas] ver cuanto de su verdad y persona se dudaba, lo cual, a los de animo generoso, es cierto ser, tanto como la muerte, penoso y detestable."—*Las Casas*, bk. I, ch. XXIX, vol. 62, p. 231.

3 See Book of Prophecies, *Raccolta*, pt. I, vol. II, p. 140.

4 Vignaud is brilliant in the demolishing part of his treatment of this episode, and, as usual, unable to build anything sensible once he has cleared the ground. My *facts* are based on his thorough and clear analysis. My conclusions are my own. *Vignaud*, ch. IV, vol. I, p. 601 *et seq.*

5 " Digo e mando a Diego, mi fijo, o a quien heredare que pague todas las debdas que dexo aqui en un memorial, por la forma que allí dize, a mas las otras que juntamente parescera que yo deva, y le mando que aya encomendada a Beatriz Enríquez, madre de don Fernando, mi hijo, que la probea que pueda bibir honestamente, como persona a quien yo soy en tanto cargo y esto se faga por mi descargo de la conçiençia, por que esto pesa mucho para mi anima. La razon d'ello no es liçito de la escribir aqui."—*Raccolta*, pt. I, vol. II, p. 264.

6 " Por quanto el Almirante mi señor me dexo encomendado a Beatriz Enríquez vecina que fue de [Córdoba] por ciertos cargos en que le hera. . . ." —Don Diego Colón's Will, September 8th, 1523, *Raccolta*, No. CXV.

7 " A Beatriz Enríquez hayas encomendada por amor de mi, atento como teniades a tu madre : haya ella de ti diez mil maravedis cada año allende de los otros que tiene en las carneceria[s] de Cordoba (*atento* certainly a mistake for *atanto*)."—*Raccolta*, pt. I, vol. II, p. 169.

8 They will be seen discussed in *Vignaud*. He adds one himself (vol. I, p. 637).

9 " No creían dar Dios galardon por virginidad y castidad."—*Bernáldez*, ch. XLIII, vol. I, p. 127.

10 " Don Juan de Torquemada Cardenal de Sant Sixto [. . .] sus agüelos, fueron del linaje de los judios convertidos a nuestra Santa Fe catolica."— *Pulgar-Claros*, ch. V, p. 80.

This is stoutly denied by Hernando del Castillo, Historiador de la Sagrada Religion de Predicadores (see *Pulgar-Claros*, p. 243). But :

    (1) Pulgar is contemporary and a *Converso* himself; while
    (2) Castillo writes much later,
    (3) is biassed,
    (4) mentions in Torquemada's pedigree a woman Tovar, and this name was that of a notorious *Converso* about fifty years later.

(See Bataillon's *Erasme et l'Espagne*, pp. 191-4, and others.)

As for the Inquisitor-General, Baer, in his *Die Juden im christlichen Spanien*, gives him as an old Christian.

11 This suggestion meets all the facts summed up in the text.

Point 3 has been dealt with in the text. Point 4 flows from 3.

Point 5: By 1523, the Jewish-*Converso* connection was positively dangerous. Diego had to be discreet. An even stronger argument: Diego had married into the most exalted house of Alba. It was not " nice " to recall such things.

Point 6: Fernando, who was a hopeless snob, may have kept silent over his mother on both grounds—illegitimacy and *Converso* blood.

Point 7: Colón loved her because, though she had given herself out of marriage, she was clean. He felt at liberty to give posts to her relations because it was still possible to do so without danger, and because it was necessary for him to be surrounded with *sure* men, who were almost of his family.

12 ". . . en el mes de mayo [. . .] el Rey Don Fernando sacó su hueste por la via de Murcia, estando él e la Reina, su mujer allí."—*Bernáldez*, ch. LXXXIX, vol. I, p. 260.

13 ". . . un marinero que se llamó Pedro de Velasco, gallego, dijo al Cristobal Colón en Murcia, que yendo aquel viaje de Irlanda fueron navegando y metiendose tanto al Norueste, que vieron tierra hacia el Poniente de Ibernia . . ."—*Las Casas*, bk. I, ch. XIII, vol. 62, p. 101.

14 This flows from the King's own answer (see text above, note 7 to ch. II). " *o que apontaes* " in King John's answer does suggest that Colón had expressed a wish to clear himself of something, for the second reason the King gives for Colón's return is " other matters in which your industry and skill may be necessary to Us," and therefore the first, " what you indicate," did not refer to anything Colón might do in the future. It was some *past* affair. A confirmation of this point of view is given in the text.

15 *Pina*, chs. XVII and XVIII, pp. 55-7.

16 This point has been much discussed. I believe Vignaud is right, vol. I, p. 653).

17 " & alli anduuo vn tiempo con mucha necessidad & pobreza sin ser entendido de los que le oyan [. . .] y aun teniase por vano cuanto dezia. Y turole quasi siete Años esta importunacion haziendo muchos offrescimientos de grandes riquezas y estados para la corona Real de Castilla. Pero como traya la capa rayda (o pobre) tenianle por fabuloso soñador y que todo quanto dezia & hablaua, assi por no ser conocido y Estranjero y no tener quien le favoreciese, como por ser tan grandes y no oydas las cosas que se proferia de dar acabadas."—*Oviedo*, bk. II, ch. IV, fol. v.

18 The incident is vividly recorded in *Bernáldez*, bk. I, ch. LXXXIV, vol. I, p. 239.

19 See above, ch. XI, note 34 and text to which it refers. Coplas 13, 14 of the edition made in the reign of Charles V. They are not to be found in the original.

> " A ti, Padre Fray andr[es]
> Que te llamas de Cabre[ra]
> Por quien dijo el de la [?]
> Ojos de cabra tenès.
> Tu padre bien sé quien [es]
> Pedro Lopez de Madr [id]
> En Cuenca rabi daui[d]
> arrendador malar [?]."

Foulché-Delbosc reads "madr[e]," which is obviously wrong, on reasons both of sense and rhyme.

20 On Luis de Santángel see *A.R.*, ch. VI. On Cabrero see *Kayserling*, ch. III, p. 30; ch. V, pp. 59 and 72. On Gabriel Sánchez see *Baer*, ch. II, pp. 610-14.

21 " Estaba este insigne varon en Castilla y Andalucía y lo mas del tiempo en Sevilla."—Zúñiga, *Anales*, vol. III, p. 144. Quoted by *Vignaud*, vol. I, p. 681.

22 " Concejos, Justicias, Regidores, Caballeros, Escuderos, Oficiales, é Homes-Buenos de todas las Ciudades, é Villas, é Lugares de los nuestros Reinos é Señorios : Cristóbal Colomo ha de venir à esta nuestra Corte, à entender en algunas cosas cumplideras à nuestro servicio. Por ende Nos vos mandamos que cuando por esas dichas Ciudades, é Villas, é Logares ó por alguna dellas se acaesciere, le aposentedes é dedes buenas posadas en que pose él é los suyos sin dineros, que non sean mesones ; é los mantenimientos á los precios que entre vosotros valieren por sus dineros."—*Navarrete*, vol. II, p. 6.

23 They are discussed and dismissed in *Vignaud*, vol. I, p. 681.

24 The narrative in the text is based almost exclusively on *Pulgar-Crónica*, ch. CXII, pp. 349-50.

25 "... a el sería forzado de tratar a los cristianos de su señorío en la manera que el Rey e la Reyna de Castilla trataban a los moros que eran de su ley y estaban so su amparo."—*Pulgar, loc. cit.*
" los moros, que eran de su ley y estaban so su amparo conservan sus personas en toda libertad, e poseen sus bienes libremente é los consienten vivir en su ley con toda esencion, sin les facer premia."—*Pulgar, loc. cit.*

26 See end of ch. VI above ; and Letter to the Aya of Prince Don Juan, *Navarrete*, vol. I, p. 265.

27 See *A.R.*, vol. III, p. 97.

28 " protesté a vuestras Altezas que toda la ganancia desta mi empresa se gastase en la conquista de Jerusalem, y vuestras Altezas se rieron y dijeron que les placia y que sin esto tenian aquella gana."—First Voyage, December 26th (end), *Navarrete*, vol. I, p. 117.

CHAPTER XV

1 *Pulgar-Crónica*, ch. CXXVIII, pp. 367-8, and ch. CXXIX, p. 368.

2 I am aware that Las Casas' narrative points the other way (bk. I, ch. XXIX, vol. 62, p. 232). But things do get mixed up in the perspective of time, particularly in the good bishop's memory.

3 " fueron dellos juzgadas sus promesas y ofertas por imposibles y vanas y de toda repulsa dignas . . ." because " no era cosa que a la autoridad de sus personas reales convenia ponerse a favorecer negocio tan flacamente fundado y que tan incierto e imposible a cualquiera persona letrad[a], por indoct[a] que fuese, podia parecer, porque perderían los dineros que en ello gastasen y derogarían su autoridad real sin algun fruto."—*Las Casas*, bk. I, ch. XXIX, vol. 62, p. 231.

4 " Finalmente los reyes mandaron dar respuesta a Cristóbal Colón, despidiendole por aquella sazon aunque no del todo quitandole la esperanza de tornar a la materia, cuando mas desocupadas sus Altezas se viesen [of the Granada wars] que el tiempo andando se podria ofrecer mas oportuna ocasion."—*Las Casas*, bk. I, ch. XXIX, vol. 62, p. 231.

5 " faltandole ya las cosas para su sustentacion necesarias, perdida toda esperanza de hallar remedio en Castilla."—*Las Casas*, bk. I, ch. XXIX, vol. 62, p. 234.

6 Vignaud (vol. II, p. 12) makes him go first to the Duke de Medinaceli for a second visit. For once, on these points of fact, he is wrong. There is neither need nor proof for such a visit. Vignaud makes it up to explain

the mention of " two years " in the Duke's letter to the Cardinal. I have explained away that difficulty. See above, note 10 to ch. XII.

7 That there were two friars has been finally proved by *Vignaud* (vol. I, p. 500).

8 " nos parece que sería bien que llevásedes con vos un buen estrologo, y nos parescia que seria bueno para esto Fray Antonio de Marchena, porque es buen estrologo y siempre nos pareció que se conformaba con vuestro parecer."—Letter from Barcelona, September 5th, 1493, *Navarrete*, vol. II, p. 109.

Marchena is thought by some authors to have been a Portuguese, cf. *Vignaud* (vol. I, p. 506 footnote). On the same page we find : " On suppose qu'il avait appartenu auparavant au couvent de franciscains qui se trouvait a Marchena, d'où lui serait venu son nom." This would not be in accordance with Franciscan practice. His name was almost certainly not Marchena, but perhaps he came from Marchena, and, following the Franciscan practice, he hid his identity behind his birthplace name. His astrological proclivities create *a presumption* that he might be a *Converso*. In the trial of Pedro Serrano (1487-90), quoted by *Baer*, pp. 476-7, there occurs a mention of " Frey Diego de Marchena, que fué quemado por apóstata en Guadalupe."

9 " Ya saben Vuestras Altezas que anduve siete años en Su Corte ymportun- andoles por esto. nunca en todo este tiempo se halló piloto ni marinero ni philosopho ni de otra sçiençia que todos no dixessen que mi empresa era falsa ; que nunca yo hallé ayuda de nadie, salvó de fray Antonio de Marchena, despues de aquella de Dios eterno."—*Las Casas*, bk. I, ch. XXXII, vol. 62, p. 250 ; *Raccolta*, pt. I, vol. II, p. 41.

" Todos los que habian entendido en ello y oido esta plática, todos a una mano lo tenian a burla, salvo dos frailes que siempre fueron constantes." —Third Voyage, *Navarrete*, vol. I, p. 242.

10 On Pinzón the best guide is Cesáreo Fernandez Duro : *Pinzón en el Descubrimiento de las Indias*, Madrid, 1892 ; and *Colón y Pinzón*, Madrid, 1896.

11 Statement before the Law Court : " A la onzena pregunta, dixo que la sabe, porque este testigo es fijo del dicho Martin Alonço Pinçon y estava estante en Roma con mercaderia de su padre, e que fue dicho su padre a Roma aquel dicho año antes que fuese a descobryr e aquel dicho Martin Alonço Pinçon padre de este testigo estando un dia en la libreria del Papa alyende de otras muchas veces que habia estado por razon de mucho conocimiento que tenia con un familiar criado del papa que era grande cosmografo y tenia muchas y largas escripturas y ally les enseño platicando muchas vezes al dicho su padre y este testigo con el susodicho criado del papa en las [. . .] alli fue informado el dicho su padre y este testigo destas terras questavan por descobryr y juntamente con mucha industria e saber que en las cosas de la mar el thenya dijo muchas vezes a este testigo como ayudava y queria armar dos navios e yr a descobrir estas tierras, e que sabe por lo que dicho tiene e paso asy e lo vido a vista de ojos."—*Pleitos*, vol. II, pp. 228-31 ; or *Vignaud*, vol. II, p. 608.

12 " y visto lo susodicho por el dicho Almirante se fizo tanto su amigo de su padre deste testigo que fizo concierto con él e le rogó que fuese en su compañía."—*Vignaud, loc. cit.*, p. 609.

13 See García Fernández's statement to the Court, quoted by *Vignaud* (vol. I, p. 601). I agree with Vignaud that this writer mixes up into one only visit the events of 1485-86 and those of 1491 : " En seguridad de esperanza fasta que su Alteza le escribiese."

14 " La Reyna nuestra señora [. . .] enbió veynte mil maravedis, en florynes, los quales traxo Diego Prieto, vecino desta villa, e los dichos con una carta a este testigo para que los diese a Cristobal Colón para que se vistiese

onestamente e mercase una bestezuela e paresciese ante Su Alteza."—Statement by G. Fernández, *loc. cit.*

15 This is the obvious result of an examination of the data collected by Vignaud (vol. II, p. 56). But he sees neither this conclusion nor the all important consequence which it entails.

16 " le descubrió en puridad su corazón."—*Gómara*, ch. XV.

17 Two other explanations have been given :

(1) Colón revealed to Fray Juan Pérez that he had already been in the Indies. This is Ulloa's view (*Pr. De.*, ch. III). It is maintained, it must be owned, with an impressive wealth of observations, every one of which can, however, be resolved without having recourse to his somewhat fantastic identification of Colón with Johannes Skolvus, the Dane (or Pole) who *pre-discovered* America. See below, note 12 to ch. XVI.

(2) He revealed to Pérez that an unknown pilot had told him of his discovery of America, then died in his house. This yarn has circulated amongst many chroniclers, including Las Casas (ch. XIV). Vignaud is fascinated by it. It is, in my opinion, untenable. See *Vignaud*, vol. I, p. 513.

18 "Tampoco pude saber cuanto ni en qué ni como le favoreciese."—*Las Casas*, end of ch. XXXII, vol. 62, p. 250.

19 This interpretation of Fray Juan Pérez's success flows from the set of events happening at the time in Castille ; it is singularly strengthened by the fact that it provides a fitting explanation to another set of events so far left in the air—the Toscanelli correspondence. We do know for a fact that Toscanelli's letter to the Lisbon canon was copied by Colón on a blank page of one of his personal books, and we do know that two letters purported to be by Toscanelli and addressed to him have been published by his personal biographers and proved to be apocryphal by modern research. But we did not know why this forgery had been perpetrated. If, as seems to be the case, it must be attributed to Fernando Colón, the explanation would be that, finding the copy of the genuine letter in his father's book and knowing the importance it had in determining his father's course, he should have wished to legitimise the acquisition of this important document.

20 *Bernáldez*, ch. C, vol. I, p. 290.

21 " le puso Santa-fé, porque su deseo e el de la Reina su mujer, era siempre en acrecentamiento e favor de la Santa Fé Cathólica de Jesuchristo."—*Bernáldez, loc. cit.*, p. 293.

22 Cf. : " Lo que se asentó por mandado del Rey e de la Reina nuestros señores, con Juanoto Berardi Florentin. . . ."—*Navarrete*, vol. II, p. 159.

23 See note 13, ch. XXIX.

24 *Navarrete*, vol. II, p. 300.

25 " para que podais haber é hayais cualesquier dignidades é beneficios Eclesiásticos que vos fueren dados."—*Loc. cit.*

26 See *Las Casas*, bk. I, ch. XXIX, vol. 62, p. 232.

27 " viendose con tanta repulsa y contradiccion afligido y apretado de tan gran necesidad, que quizá aflojando en las mercedes que pedia, contentandose con menos y que parece que con cualquiera cosa debiera de contentarse, los Reyes se movieron a darle lo que era menester para su viaje, y en lo demás lo que buenamente pareciera que debiera darsele, se le diera, no quiso blandear en cosa alguna, sino con toda entereza perseverar en lo que una vez habia pedido."—*Las Casas*, bk. I, ch. XXXI, vol. 62, p. 244.

28 See notes 11 and 23 of ch. XXXII.

29 See *A.R.*, vol. III, pp. 435-6.

30 See *Kayserling*, p. 147.

31 See, for instance, *Las Casas*, bk. I, ch. XXXII, vol. 62, p. 247. As for Isabel's jewels and so forth, the fairy-tale is no longer worth exposing.

32 This Bridge has become a Gate for some non-Spanish authors (including *Vignaud*, vol. II, p. 90) because in those days *puente*, bridge, was feminine and they misread La Puerta for La Puente.

CHAPTER XVI

1 " Así que despues de haber echado fuera todos los judíos de todos vuestros reinos y señoríos, en el mismo mes de Enero mandaron vuestras Altezas à mí que con armada suficiente me fuese à las dichas partidas de India ; y para ello me hicieron grandes mercedes, y me anoblecieron que dende en adelante yo me llamase Don, y fuese Almirante mayor de la mar océana é Visorey y Gobernador perpetuo de todas las Islas y Tierra firme. . . ."— *Navarrete*, vol. I, p. 2.

2 ". . . vuestras Altezas, como católicos cristianos y Príncipes amadores de la santa fé cristiana y acrecentadores della, y enemigos de la secta de Mahoma y de todas idolatrías y heregías. . . ."—*Navarrete*, vol. I, p. 2.

3 This fact is proved by the first paragraph of the *Memorial del Almirante sobre agravios que recibió, Alba-Nuevos*, Madrid, 1902, p. 25. There is, moreover, in Colón's own hand a covering note on a copy of the Capitulations, in which he actually says that it was made (" fizieron") by frey Juan Pérez e mosen Coloma.—*Loc. cit.*, p. 29.

4 A Coloma Sanchís is the subject of a curious story in the trial of Violante Nartesa : August 8th, 1509. She declares that in past days there came many Jews to her mother's house, one of which, Coloma Sanchis, very learned, went later to Naples, where he became a great favourite of King Ferdinand (of Naples) before whom he performed miracles. One day he produced a Crucifix before the King, and on the King asking why it was covered with thorns, the Crucifix answered that " the Jew had written it for him and his (the Jew's) name is Rabi Ysayas."—*Baer*, vol. II, p. 542.

5 See text in *Navarrete*, vol. II, p. 7.

6 See in *Pulgar-Crónica*, ch. LIII, p. 267, a dispute between Queen Isabel and the Grand Cardinal because the Queen administered justice through her own magistrates while residing in Alcalá, a town the Cardinal claimed as " his," since he was Archbishop of Toledo.

7 " Place a sus Altezas, si pertenece al dicho oficio de Almirante, segun que lo tenía el dicho Almirante D. Alonso Henriquez, y los otros sus antecesores en sus distritos, y siendo justo. Juan de Coloma."—*Loc. cit.*

8 Chief exponent of this theory is Vignaud. This obsession warps most of his observations on Colón. No precise page need be given, for it permeates his whole work.

9 " Las cosas suplicadas é que vuestras Altezas dan y otorgan ă D. Cristóbal Colón, en alguna satisfación de lo que ha descubierto en las mares Océanas, y del viaje que agora, con el ayuda de Dios, ha de hacer por ellas en servicio de vuestras Altezas. . . ."—*Navarrete*, vol. II, p. 7.

10 Navarrete, nonplussed, altered them to " is to discover "—" ha de descubrir."—Vol. II, p. 7.

11 See notably Ulloa (*Pr.De.*), who argues it with great cogency.

12 There are other arguments against the pre-discovery hypothesis, such as the nautical impossibility of the voyage suggested by *Ulloa,* as will be seen by comparing what he imagines to have happened with the chart of roads and currents given by *Nunn,* to be found p. 192 of the present volume.

13 " e se espera que, con la ayuda de Dios, se descubrirán e ganarán algunas de las dichas Islas e Tierra Firme."—*Navarrete,* vol. II, p. 9.

" despues que hayades descubierto e ganado las dichas Islas e Tierra Firme en la dicha mar oceana o cualesquier dellas."—*Loc. cit.*

There are other important differences between the Capitulations and the deed of April 30th. They are discussed in ch. XXXII.

14 See his own letter—Prologue to the First Voyage, *Navarrete,* vol. I, p. 2.

15 *Cronicón de Valladolid* in *Documentos Inéditos para la Historia de España,* ch. XIII, p. 192. Quoted by *Kayserling,* p. 85 note.

16 " E assi mismo damos liçençia e facultad a los dichos judios e judias que puedan sacar fuera de los dichos nuestros Reynos e señorios sus bienes e faciendas por mar e por tierra, en tanto que non seya oro nin plata, nin moneda amonedada, nin las otras cosas vedadas por las leyes de nuestros reynos, salvo mercaderias que non seyan cosas vedadas o encobiertas."— *A.R.,* vol. III, p. 603.

The Jews were allowed to take away " cambios," i.e. commercial paper equivalent to foreign currency. See Zurita, *Anales de Aragon,* bk. I, ch. VI, vol. V. Quoted by *A.R.,* vol. III, p. 307 note.

17 " A vos Diego Rodriguez Prieto, é á todas las otras personas, vuestros compañeros e otros vecinos de la Villa de Palos, e a cada uno de vos, [. . .] Bien sabedes como por algunas cosas fechas e cometidas por vosotros en deservicio nuestro [. . .] fuisteis condenados a que fueredes obligados a Nos servir doce meses con dos carabelas armadas [. . .] e agora por cuanto nos habemos mandado a Cristóbal Colón que vaya con tres carabelas de armada, [. . .] para ciertas partes de la mar Océana sobre algunas cosas que cumplen a nuestro servicio. . . ."—*Navarrete,* vol. II, p. 11.

18 " ca ovieron los christianos sus faciendas muy muchas e muy ricas casas y heredamientos por pocos dineros, y andaban rogando con ellas, y no hallaban quien se las comprase, e daban una casa por un asno, y una viña por un poco paño o lienzo, porque no podian sacar oro ni plata ; empero es verdad que sacaron infinito oro e plata escondidamente, y en especial muchos cruzados e ducados abollados con los dientes que los tragaban e sacaban en los vientres, e en los pasos donde habian de ser buscados, e en los puertos de la Tierra e de la mar, y en especial las mujeres tragaban mas, ea a persona le acontecia tragar treinta ducados de una vez."—*Bernáldez,* ch. CX, vol. I, p. 338.

19 " confiando en las vanas esperanzas de su ceguedad, se metieron al trabajo del camino, y salieron de las tierras de sus nacimientos, chicos e grandes, viejos e niños, a pie y caballeros en asnos, y otras bestias, y en carretas, y continuaron sus viajes cada uno a los puertos que habian de ir ; e iban por los caminos y campos por donde iban con muchos trabajos y fortunas, unos cayendo, otros levantando, otros moriendo, otros naciendo, otros enfermando, que no habia christiano que no oviese dolor de ellos, y siempre por do iban los convidaban al baptismo, y algunos con la cuyta se convertian e quedaban, pero muy pocos, y los Rabies los iban esforzando y facian cantar a las mujeres y mancebos y tañer panderos y adufos para alegrar a la gente . . ."—*Bernáldez,* ch. CXII, vol. I, p. 342.

20 See official record of proceedings, *Navarrete,* vol. II, p. 13. Text of letter, *Navarrete,* vol. II, p. 11.

21 " e para llevar la gente que ha menester en tres caravelas que lleva, diz que es necesario dar seguro a las personas que con el fuesen, porque de

otra manera no querrian ir con él a dicho viaje . . ."—*Navarrete*, vol. II, p. 15.

22 *Navarrete*, vol. II, p. 14.

23 This follows from the *sobrecarta* given to Juan de Peñalosa, enjoining him to have the first one carried out. Navarrete, imagining, no doubt, that this *sobrecarta* refers to the original letter (the Palos two caravels letter) prints it (vol. III, p. 480) under the double date April 30th/June 20th. But he is obviously mistaken, as the text shows :
". . . fue presentada por el dicho Cristóbal Colón en la villa de Moguer e requería que la compliesen ; e como quier que la obedecieron, non la han cumplido."

24 That he was staying at La Rábida is well established by *Vignaud*, vol. II, p. 143, note 256.

25 This is proved by many a witness in the lawsuit.

26 As deposed by the witness Alonso Gallego quoted by *Vignaud*, vol. II, p. 144, note 258.

27 *Las Casas*, bk. I, ch. XXXIV, vol. 62, p. 256.

28 " Martín Alonso traía tanta diligencia en allegar gente e animalla, como si para el e para sus hijos hobiera de ser lo que se descubriese. A unos decía que saldrían de miseria ; a otros que hallarían casas con tejas de oro ; a quien brindaba con buena ventura, teniendo para cada cual halago y dinero ; e con esto e con llevar confianza en él se fue mucha gente de las villas."—Statements of several witnesses quoted by Duro, *Pinzón-Duro*, p. 44.
" Amigos, andad acá ; ios con nosotros esta jornada, que andais acá misereando ; ios esta jornada, que segun fama habemos de fallar las casas con tejas de oro, e todos verneis ricos e de buena ventura."—Statement of Fernàn Yàñez de Montilla, pp. 95-255, quoted by Duro, *Colón y Pinzón*, R.A.H. 287.

29 " On peut regarder comme certain qu'aucun criminel ne fit partie de l'equipage des trois navires."—*Vignaud*, vol. II, p. 167.

30 " algunos criados del Rey que se aficionaros a ir con él por curiosidad y otros criados y cognoscientes suyos."—*Las Casas*, bk. I, ch. XXXIV, vol. 62, p. 260.

31 See the discussion of the flagship name in *Vignaud*, vol. II, p. 156. Herrera (dec. I, bk. I, ch. IX) and Fernando Colón (ch. XV) popularised the name Santa María. There may be a confusion between this flagship and that of the second expedition which *was* a *Marigalante*.

32 " A cada onbre, por dia, una libra de viscocho e vn açumbre de vino, e de carne o pescado a tres onbres dos libras ; como quiera que algunas veces puedan pasar con queso e cebollas e legumbres, e semejantes cosas de que los navios deuen yr siempre mucho fornecidos, no olvidando el azeite e vinagre, que son dos cosas mucho nescesarias en la mar." Diego de Valera. Memorial de lo que convernia para el armada para guardar el Estrecho.—*Epístolas*, p. 80.

33 See below, note 12 to ch. XXI.

34 " un Luis de Torres que había sido Judio y sabía diz que hebraico y caldeo y aun algo de arabigo."—Journal of First Voyage, November 2nd, *Navarrete*, vol. I, p. 47.

35 " Buenos y cursados hombres de mar."—*Las Casas*, bk. I, ch. XXXIV, vol. 62.

36 See contract between the King and Queen and Juanoto Berardi in *Navarrete*, vol. II, p. 160, for the freight of 2000 per ton and the estimates ("Relacion

del Costo") for an Armada fitted out in July 1493 (*Navarrete*, vol. II, p. 82) for the cost of maintenance of a crew of 125 men.

37 " Los que fueron a embarcar por el Puerto de Santa Maria e Cadiz, ansi como vieron la mar, daban muy grandes gritos e voces, honbres y mujeres, grandes y chicos, en sus oraciones demandando a Dios misericordia y pensaban ver algunas maravillas de Dios y que se les habia de abrir camino por la mar y desque estuvieron allí muchos dias y no vieron sobre sí sino mucha fortuna, algunos no quisieron ser nacidos."—*Bernáldez*, ch. CXII, vol. I, p. 342.

CHAPTER XVII

1 See Albalá, signed by the Queen only, in *Navarrete*, vol. II, p. 17. The boy was granted 9400 maravedis for his keep and clothing (" vestuario e mantenimiento ").

2 " Como muchas veces él y sus antecesores habian enviado a Roma a pedir doctores en nuestra santa fe porque le enseñasen en ella y que nunca el Santo Padre lo habia proveido."—Preface to First Voyage, *Navarrete*, vol. I, p. 1.

3 " desencasose o saltó de sus hebillas el gobernario a la carabela *Pinta* [. . . y segun se sospechó por industria de unos marineros, Gómez Rascón y Cristóbal Quintero, cuya era la caravela, porque les pesaba ir a aquel viaje y iban contra su voluntad ; y dice Cristóbal Colón que antes que partiese habia tomado en ciertas grisquetas o reveses a los dichos Gómez Rascón y Cristóbal Quintero."—*Las Casas*, bk. I, ch. XXXV, vol. 62, p. 264.

4 " Perdía alguna de la mucha pena que tenía por cognoscer que Martin Alonso era persona esforzada y de buen ingenio."—*Las Casas, loc. cit.*

5 There is a trace of this subconscious working up of Colón's mind in Fernando Colón's remarks on this incident : " Dal qual disordine e disaventura, avvenuta a quella Caravella in perder due volte il timone nel principio del suo camino, chi fosse stato superstitioso havria potuto congietturar la disubidienza e contumacia ch' ella uso' poi contra l' Ammiraglio, allontanandosi due altre volte da lui per malignita di detto Pinzone."—*F.C.*, ch. XVI, p. 39.

6 The narrative of the story of the fleet in the Canaries is based—not uncritically—on *F.C.*, ch. XV.

7 See Diary in *Navarrete*, vol. I, p. 7, September 6th.

8 The instructions prepared by Colón in the Canaries have been lost. This particular article, the first, is known through *F.C.*, ch. XXI, and *Las Casas*, bk. I, ch. XXXIX, vol. 62, p. 287 : " pues habiendo puesto en el primer capitulo la instrucción que dió a cada capitan de cada navio, partiendo de las Canarias, conviene a saber, que habiendo navegado 700 leguas hacia el Poniente, sin haber descubierto tierra, no navegasen mas de hasta media noche, lo cual no habian hasta entonces guardado y él lo habia disimulado por no darles mas pena, por el ansia que llevaban de ver tierra."

9 See a discussion of this point in *Nunn*, pp. 31-53. The quotation given in the text is from p. 52.

10 " Esta navegación no pudo facilmente y luego en aquellos tiempos alcanzarse, la cual solamente la experiencia ha mostrado, asi que, por esta falta hizosele mas largo al Almirante su viaje."—*Las Casas*, bk. I, ch. CXI, vol. 63, p. 127.
　　" . . . prosiguio su viaje navegando por el grado 22, cuando mas o cuando menos, segun los vientos requerian, porque entonces no se tenia

experiencia de meterse bien hacia el Norte para hallar los vientos vendabales. . . ."—*F.C.*, ch. LXIII, vol. II, p. 27.
See also *Oviedo*, fol. xii verso and xiii.

11 " Epoque memorable dans les fastes de l'astronomie nautique des Européens." . . . " C'est donc à tort que, sur le témoignage de Sanuto, on a attribué cette découverte importante à Sébastien Cabot."—*Humboldt*, vol. III, p. 31.

12 " tomaron los pilotos el Norte marcándolo y hallaron que las agujas noruesteaban una gran cuarta, y temían los marineros y estaban penados y no decian de qué."—*Navarrete*, vol. I, p. 9.

13 " Mandó que tornasen a tomar el norte en amaneciendo y hallaron que estaban buenas las agujas ; la causa fué porque la estrella que parece hace movimiento y no las agujas."—*Navarrete*, vol. I, p. 9.

14 " Porque si el viaje fuese luengo no se espantase ni desmayase la gente."—Journal, Sunday, September 9th, *Navarrete*, vol. I, p. 7.
This remark should have sufficed to prove Vignaud wrong when he claims that Colón was sailing to a definite spot about 750 leagues from the Canaries. Colón's fixity was in his will, not in his ideas.

15 " esta noche . . . vieron caer del cielo un maravilloso ramo de fuego en la mar."—September 15th, *Navarrete*, vol. I, p. 8.

16 " hallaron aires temperantisimos, que era placer grande el gusto de las mañanas, que no faltaba sino oir ruiseñores."—September 16th, *Navarrete*, vol. I, p. 9.

17 " yerba muy verde, que poco habia, segun le parecía, que se había despegado de tierra, por lo cual todos juzgaban que estaban cerca de alguna isla, pero no de tierra firme, segun el Almirante, que dice : *porque la tierra firme hago mas adelante.*"—September 16th, *Navarrete*, vol. I, p. 9.

18 " hallaron un cangrejo vivo, el cual guardó el Almirante, y dice que aquellas fueron señales ciertas de tierra, porque no se hallan ochenta leguas de tierra."—Monday, September 17th, *Navarrete*, vol. I, p. 10.

19 " alzóse mucho la mar y sin viento, que los asombraba, por lo cual, dice aqui el Almirante : *asi que muy necesario me fué la mar alta, que no pareció salvo el tiempo de los judios cuando salieron de Egypto contra Moysen que los sacaba de captiverio.*"—September 23rd, *Navarrete*, vol. I, p. 12.

20 " y añadía que por demás era quejarse, porque él habia venido a las Indias, y que asi lo habia de proseguir hasta hallarlas con el ayuda de nuestro Señor."—Wednesday, March 10th, *Navarrete*, vol. I, p. 19.

21 " ' Señor, ahorque Vuesa merced media docena de ellos o échelos a la mar, y si no se atreve, yo y mis hermanos barloaremos sobre ellos y lo haremos, que armada que salió con mandado de tan altos principes no habrá de volver atrás sin buenas nuevas.'
" Martín Alonso, con estos hidalgos hayamosnos bien, y andemos otros dias, e si en estos no hallaremos tierra, daremos otra orden en lo que debemos hacer."
The incident must be studied in *Duro*, pp. 293 *et seq.* The quotations, from the statement of Hernán Pérez Mateos, one of the pilots, is in p. 303.

22 The Spanish text as punctuated in *Navarrete* (vol. I, p. 17) is utterly unintelligible. The following is the correct punctuation :
" Esta noche, dijo Martín Alonso que seria bien navegar a la cuarta del Oueste, y a la parte del Sudueste ; y al Almirante pareció que no. Decía esto Martín Alonso por la isla de Cipango, y el almirante via que si la erraban que no pudieran tan presto tomar tierra, y que era mejor una vez ir a la tierra firme y despues a las islas."

23 " Toda la noche oyeron pasar pájaros."—October 9th, *Navarrete*, vol. I, p. 18.

24 " una caña y un palo y tomaron otro palillo labrado a lo que parecia con hierro, y un pedazo de caña y otra yerba que nace en tierra y una tablilla. Con estas señales respiraron y alegraronse todos."—*Navarrete*, vol. I, p. 19.

25 See *F.C.*, ch. XXI.

26 " era como una candelilla de cera que se alzaba y levantaba, lo cual a pocos pareciera ser indicio de tierra."—*Navarrete*, vol. I, p. 20.

Navarrete (vol. III, p. 611) discusses this point and shows, in my opinion conclusively, that Colón did not see land and knew he had not, though he claimed he did and was awarded the prize.

27 See ch. XXX of this book.

CHAPTER XVIII

1 " El Almirante llamó [. . .] y dijo que le dieran fe y testimonio como el por ante todos tomaba, como de hecho tomó, posesion de la dicha isla por el Rey y por la Reina sus señores, haciendo las protestaciones que se requerian."—October 11th, *Navarrete*, vol. I, p. 20. As to the sense of property shown by the Indians, see October 13th, *Navarrete*, vol. I, p. 23 : " y por la gana de haber de nuestras cosas, y temiendo que no se les ha de dar sin que den algo y no lo tienen toman lo que pueden y se echan luego a nadar ; mas todo lo que tienen lo dan por cualquier cosa que les den."

Navarrete's text says *teniendo*, a misprint for *temiendo*.

2 " Allí dijeron al Almirante que adelante de allí era *Magon*, donde todas las gentes tenian rabo, como las bestias o alimañas, y que a esta causa los hallarian vestidos, lo cual no era ansí mas parece que entre ellos hay este crédito de oidas, y los simples dellos lo creen ser ansí con su simpleza, y los discretos creo yo que no lo creerán, porque parece que ello fue dicho primeramente por burla faciendo escarnio de los que andaban vestidos [. . .] y ansí los de esta provincia de Ornophay como ellos todos andan desnudos, hombres y mujeres, facen escarnio de los que oyen decir que andan vestidos, y el Almirante supo ser burla, que si algunos donde ellos decian andan vestidos, tampoco tienen rabo como ellos dijeron."—*Bernáldez*, ch. CXXVIII, vol. II, p. 58.

All the concrete incidents, such as the fact that the Indians wounded themselves with the Christians' swords, are to be found in the Journal of the First Voyage, October 13th–14th. As for the Indians thinking of the Europeans as no better than the cannibals, see *Navarrete*, vol. I, p. 63, where Colón, sceptical about the existence of cannibalism in the Indies, gives as his argument that the Indians of Guanahani thought the same of the Christians at the beginning.

3 There is an excellent discussion of this point in *Thacher*, vol. I, pp. 587-98 (chs. LVIII and LIX). May I take this opportunity to suggest that the name of the island which saw the greatest event in history should not be that of an English privateer but either *Guanahani* or *San Salvador* ? The British Government owe that mark of respect to culture and history.

4 " y dice que cree que estas islas son aquellas innumerables que en los mapamundos en fin de Oriente se ponen."—*Navarrete*, vol. I, p. 58.

5 " Aqui nace en esta isla, mas por el poco tiempo no pude dar asi del todo fe, y tambien aqui nace el oro que traen colgado a la nariz ; mas por no perder tiempo quiero ir a ver si puedo topar a la isla de Cipango."—Saturday, October 13th, *Navarrete*, vol. I, p. 23.

Compare with *Don Quixote* : " You must know, Sancho, that it is a very easy matter for such (enchanters) to make us seem what they please ; and this malignant one, who persecutes me, envious of the glory he saw I was likely to acquire in this battle, has transformed the hostile squadrons into flocks of sheep. Now, Sancho, do one thing, for my sake, to undeceive yourself, and see the truth of what I tell you : get upon your ass, and follow them fair and softly, and you will find that, when they are got a little farther off, they will return to their first form, and, ceasing to be sheep, will become men, as straight as men can be, as I described them at first. [. . .] But do not go now ; for I want your help and assistance. . . ." —Pt. I, ch. XVIII.

6 " Por este calor que allí el Almirante dice que padecía, arguye que en estas Indias, y por alli donde andaba, debia de haber mucho oro."— November 21st, *Navarrete*, vol. I, p. 62.
   " Y creia el Almirante questaba muy cerca de la fuente y que nuestro Señor le habia de mostrar donde nasce el oro."—December 17th, *Navarrete*, vol. I, p. 95.

7 " Crean vuestras Altezas que es esta tierra la mejor e mas fertil, y temperada, y llana, y buena que haya en el mundo."—October 17th, *Navarrete*, vol. I, p. 32.

8 " Fue al rio y vió en él unas piedras relucir con unas manchas en ellas de color de oro, y acordose que en el rio Tejo, que al pie del junto a la mar se halló oro, y parecióle que cierto debia tener oro, y mandó coger ciertas de aquellas piedras para llevar a los Reyes. Estando así dan voces los mozos grumetes, diciendo que vían pinares. Miró por la sierra, y vidolos tan grandes y tan maravillosos que no podia encarecer su altura y derechura como husos gordos y delgados, donde conosció que se podían hacer navíos e infinita tablazon y masteles para los mayores navios de España. Vido robles y madroños, y un buen rio y aparejo para hacer sierras de agua."— November 25th, *Navarrete*, vol. I, p. 65.

9 See Journal, November 12th, *Navarrete*, vol. I, p. 54.

10 " Es cierto, Señores principes, que donde hay tales tierras que debe haber infinitas cosas de provecho."—November 27th, *Navarrete*, vol. I, p. 70.

11 " Ellos deben ser buenos servidores."—*Navarrete*, vol. I, p. 22.
   " esta gente es muy simplice en armas, como verán vuestras Altezas de siete que yo hice tomar para les llevar y deprender nuestra fabla y volvellos, salvo que vuestras Altezas cuando mandaren puedenlos todos llevar a Castilla, o tenellos en la misma isla captivos, porque con cincuenta hombres los terná todos sojuzgados, y les hará hacer todo lo que quisiese."— Sunday, October 14th, *Navarrete*, vol. I, p. 24.

12 " ayer vino a bordo de la nao una almadia con seis mancebos, y los cinco entraron en la nao ; estos mande detener e los traigo. Y despues envié a una casa, que es de la parte del rio del Poniente, y trujeron siete cabezas de mugeres entre chicas grandes y tres niños. Esto hice porque mejor se comportan los hombres en España habiendo mugeres de su tierra que sin ellas."—*Navarrete*, vol. I, p. 55.
   " Heads," however, is also found in Dr. Chanca's narrative (*Navarrete*, vol. I, p. 205) : " trajo este capitán [. . .] diez cabezas entre mochachos y mujeres " ; and even in a royal letter signed by Ferdinand and Isabel, which shows incidentally how closely the King and Queen watched and repressed every attempt at slavery : ". . . Asimismo el dicho Juanoto dice que el Almirante Don Cristóbal Colón le envió nueve cabezas de Indios para que los diese á algunas personas para que aprendiesen la lengua ; y pues estas nueve cabezas no son para vender salvo para aprender la lengua, vos mandamos que ge las fagais entregar luego para que faga dellos lo quel dicho Almirante le escribio. . . ."—*Navarrete*, vol. II, p. 177.

13 " Puso una gran cruz a la entrada del puerto [. . .] en un alto muy vistoso en señal de Jesucristo nuestro señor y honra de la christiandad."— *Navarrete*, vol. I, p. 86.

14 " y despues se sabrán los beneficios, y se trabajará de hacer todos estos pueblos cristianos porque de ligero se hará, porque ellos no tienen secta ninguna ni son idólatras, y vuestras Altezas mandarán hacer en estas partes ciudad e fortaleza, y se convertirán estas tierras [. . .] digo que terná la cristiandad negociacion en ellas, cuanto mas la España a quien debe estar sujeto todo. Y digo que vuestras Altezas no deben consentir que aquí trate ni faga pie ningun extranjero, salvo catolicos cristianos, pues esto fué el fin y el comienzo del propósito que fuese por acrecentamiento y gloria de la Religion cristiana, ni venir a estas partes ninguno que no sea buen cristiano."—*Navarrete*, vol. I, p. 71.
　　There is an equally good text for the purpose in *Navarrete*, vol. I, p. 54.

15 " porque otra vez cuando vuestras Altezas aquí tornen a enviar no hagan mala compañia."—October 15th, *Navarrete*, vol. I, p. 27.
　　" por que dé buenas nuevas de nosotros, y cuando vuestras Altezas, placiendo a nuestro Señor, envien acá, aquellos que vinieren reciban honra y nos den de todo lo que hobiere."—*Las Casas*, bk. I, ch. XLII, vol. 62, p. 307.
　　Also Journal, October 15th, *Navarrete*, vol. I, p. 28.

16 See end of November 26th (*Navarrete*, vol. I, p. 68) and December 13th (vol. I, p. 88) for this tendency of the natives to take the Spaniards for cannibals.
　　There is another passage of his Diary in which he excuses this habit of kidnapping Indians by the impossibility of *explaining* to them why they are taken away.

17 " y asi torno a decir, como otras veces dije, que *Caniba* no es otra cosa sino la gente del gran Can, que debe ser aquí muy vecino, y tenia navios y venian a captivarlos, y como no vuelven creen que se los han comido."— December 11th, *Navarrete*, vol. I, p. 86.

18 " y decian que no tenian sino un ojo y la cara de perro, y creia el Almirante que mentían."—November 26th, *Navarrete*, vol. I, p. 68.
　　" mostraronles dos hombres que les faltaban algunos pedazos de carne de su cuerpo, y hicieronles entender que los canibales los habian comido a bocados : el Almirante no lo creyó."—November 17th, *Navarrete*, vol. I, p. 94.

19 " Cada dia entendemos mas a estos indios y ellos a nosotros, puesto que muchas veces hayan entendido uno por otro."—Journal, December 11th, *Navarrete*, vol. I, p. 86.

20 This situation is candidly described by *Las Casas*, bk. I, ch. XLIV, vol. 62, p. 314 *et seq.*, from which the quotation is taken : " y de las palabras de los dichos indios que no entendia, se le figuraba que decian haber allí naos grandes de mercaderes y de lugares de muchos tratos."

21 " Quisiera hoy partir para la Isla de Cuba, que creo que debe ser Cipango, segun las señas que dan esta gente de la grandeza della y riqueza."— *Navarrete*, vol. I, p. 38.

22 *Las Casas*, bk. I, ch. XLIV, vol. 62, p. 323.

23 " Y es cierto questa es la tierra firme y que estoy ante *Zayto* y *Guinsay*, cien leguas poco mas o menos lejos de lo uno y de lo otro, y bien se amuestra por la mar que viene de otra suerte que fasta aquí no ha venido, y ayer que iba al Norueste fallé que hacia frio."—November 1st, *Navarrete*, vol. I, p. 46.
　　There is a typical case of misunderstanding as related above on the same date, p. 45.

24 " Hallaron los dos cristianos por el camino mucha gente que atravesaba a sus pueblos, mugeres y hombres con un tizon en la mano, yerbas para tomar su sahumerio que acostumbraban. con el cual se adormecen las carnes y cuasi emborracha, y asi diz que, no sienten el cansancio. Españoles cognosci yo en esta isla española que los acostumbraron a tomar."
" . . . No sé que sabor o provecho hallaban en ellos."—Both texts in *Navarrete*, vol. I, p. 51.

25 For the Colonites see most of the classic biographers, notably Roselly de Lorgues. For the Pinzonites, Vignaud and particularly Duro. An interesting case of a Colonite author is *Asensio*, bk. II, ch. V, vol. I, p. 339.

26 Bk. I, ch. XLVII, vol. 62, p. 345.

27 " hay unas vegas las mas hermosas del mundo y cuasi semejantes a las tierras de Castilla, antes estas tienen ventaja, por lo cual puso nombre a lo dicha isla la Isla Española."—Journal, December 9th, *Navarrete*, vol. I, p. 84.

28 " . . . que si vestidos anduviesen y se guardasen del sol y del aire, serian cuasi tan blancos como en España."—December 16th, *Navarrete*, vol. I, p. 92.
" Y crean questa isla y todas las otras son asi suyas como Castilla. [. . .] Ellos no tienen armas, y son todos desnudos y de ningun ingenio en las armas y muy cobardes, que mil no aguardarian a tres, y asi son buenos para les mandar, y les hacer todo lo otro que fuese menester, y que hagan villas y se enseñen a andar vestidos y a nuestras costumbres."—December 16th, *Navarrete*, vol. I, pp. 93-4.

29 " todos estos señores son de pocas palabras y muy lindas costumbres y su mando es lo mas con hacer señas con la mano, y luego es entendido a maravilla."—*Navarrete*, vol. I, p. 110.

30 " . . . las cabezas rapadas en logares, é en logares con vedijas de tantas maneras que no se podria escrebir. En conclusion que todo lo que allá en nuestra España quieran hacer en la cabeza de un loco, acá el mejor de ellos vos lo terná en mucha merced. . . ."—*Navarrete*, vol. I, p. 221.

31 " En su comer, con su honestidad y hermosa manera de limpieza se mostraba bien ser de linaje."—*Navarrete*, vol. I, p. 114.

32 " y facil cosa es cognoscer cuando se da una cosa con muy deseoso corazón de dar."
" no puedo creer que hombre haya visto gente de tan buenos corazones y francos para dar."—*Navarrete*, vol. I, p. 102.
" son de gente de amor y sin cudicia [. . .] aman a sus prójimos como asi mismos y tienen una habla la mas dulce del mundo y mansa."—*Navarrete*, vol. I, p. 113.

33 " supo el Almirante de un hombre viejo que habia muchas islas comarcanas a cien leguas, unas en las cuales nace muy mucho oro hasta decirle que habia isla que era todo oro, y en las otras que hay tanta cantidad que lo cojen y ciernen como con cedazos."—*Navarrete*, vol. I, p. 98.

34 Thus Duro, *Colón y Pinzón*.
A proof of Juan de la Cosa's competence and authority will be found in the letter addressed by Queen Isabel to the officers of the *Casa de Contratación* :
" Y aunque este partido es mejor y mas provechoso quel que diz que se ofresce a facer el dicho Juan de la Cosa, yo seria mas servida quel dicho Juan de la Cosa ficiese este viaje poniendose en lo justo porque creo que lo sabrá facer mejor que otro alguno [. . .] sé que es hombre que sabrá bien lo que aconsejare."—*C.D.I.H.E.*, vol. 13, p. 496.

35 " Certifica el Almirante a los Reyes que en ninguna parte de Castilla tan buen recaudo en todas las cosas se pudiera poner sin faltar una agujeta."—*Navarrete*, vol. I, p. 113.

36 " conoscio que nuestro Señor habia hecho encallar alli la nao porque hiciese alli asiento."—*Navarrete*, vol. I, p. 115.
" porque con amor y temor le obedezcan."—*Navarrete*, vol. I, p. 116.
" mucha gente desta que va aqui me habian rogado y hecho rogar que les quisiese dar licencia para quedarse."—*Navarrete*, vol. I, pp. 115-16.

37 " partiría a su viaje sin mas detenerse en cosa alguna, pues habia hallado lo que buscaba, porque no quiere mas enojo con aquel Martín Alonso hasta que sus Altezas supiesen las nuevas de su viaje y de lo que ha hecho."—*Navarrete*, vol. I, p. 130.

38 " en Cipango a que ellos llaman Civao."—*Navarrete*, vol. I, p. 114.
" Concluye que Cipango estaba en aquella isla y que hay mucho oro y especiería y almáciga y ruibarbo. . . ."—*Navarrete*, vol. I, p. 124.

CHAPTER XIX

1 " Andaría en todo aquel día treinta y dos millas, que son ocho leguas. Dentro de las cuales notó y marcó nueve puertos muy señalados, [. . .] y cinco rios grandes, porque iba siempre junto con tierra para verlo bien todo."—Journal of First Voyage, November 26th, *Navarrete*, vol. I, p. 67.

2 " Despues de medio dia ventó Leste recio, y mandó subir a un marinero al tope del mastel para mirar los bajos, y vido venir la carabela *Pinta* con Leste a popa."—*Navarrete*, vol. I, p. 126.

3 To form a balanced opinion of this episode, and in general of the relations between Colón and Pinzón, Duro is indispensable, though his pro-Pinzón tendency may need watching. *Navarrete* (January 6th-10th), Duro (p. 311 *et seq.*) and the witness statements in the Probanzas in *Navarrete*, vol. III, are safer than Las Casas, Fernando Colón, or even Oviedo. The quotations follow :
" es servicio de vuestras Altezas, porque hombres y mujeres son todos de vuestras Altezas, asi desta isla en especial como de las otras. Mas aqui donde tienen ya asiento vuestras Altezas, se debe hacer honra y favor a los pueblos, pues que en esta isla hay tanto oro y buenas tierras y especeria."—Journal, January 10th, *Navarrete*, vol. I, p. 131.
" eso merezco yo por haberos puesto en la honra en que estais."—Statement of Francisco Medel, quoted by *Duro*, p. 315.
" no era tiempo de entender en castigo."—Journal, January 8th, *Navarrete*, vol. I, p. 128.

4 " El dia pasado [. . .] el Almirante [. . .] vido tres serenas que salieron bien alto de la mar, pero no eran tan hermosas como las pintan, que en alguna manera tenian forma de hombre en la cara."—January 9th, *Navarrete*, vol. I, p. 130.

5 " otra isla grande en que hay muy mayor cantidad de oro que en esta en tanto grado que cogian los pedazos mayores que habas, y en la isla Española se cogian los pedazos de oro de las minas como granos de trigo."—Journal, January 6th, *Navarrete*, vol. I, p. 127.
" una isla adonde no habia sino solas mujeres, y esto diz que de muchas personas le sabia."—Journal, January 6th, *Navarrete*, vol. I, p. 127.
" sino venirse a mas andar por llevalles las nuevas y por quitarse de la mala compañia que tenia."—Journal, January 8th, *Navarrete*, vol. I, p. 129.

6 " Juzgó el Almirante que debia ser de los caribes que comen los hombres."—*Navarrete*, vol. I, p. 134.

7 " por una parte le habia pesado y por otra nó, porque hayan miedo a los cristianos, porque sin duda la gente de allí es diz que de mal hacer, y que creia que eran los de *Carib*, y que comiesen los hombres, y porque viniendo por allí la barca que dejó a los treinta y nueve hombres en la fortaleza y

Villa de la Navidad, tengan miedo de hacerles mal."—*Navarrete*, vol. I, p. 138.

8 " queria ver en que paraba la conjunción de la Luna con el Sol, que esperaba a 17 deste mes, y la oposición della con Jupiter y conjunción con Mercurio, y el sol en oposito con Jupiter, que es causa de grandes vientos."— *Navarrete*, vol. I, p. 133.

9 " notó en la gente que comenzó a entristecerse por desviarse del camino derecho, por la mucha agua que hacian ambas carabelas, y no tenian algun remedio salvo el de Dios ; hobo de dejar el camino que creia que llevaba de la isla y volvio al derecho de España, Nordeste cuarta del Leste."— *Navarrete*, vol. I, p. 139.

10 " Parecióle la estrella del Norte muy alta, como en el cabo de San Vicente ; no pudo tomar el altura con el astrolabio ni cuadrante, porque la ola no le dió lugar."—Sunday, February 3rd, *Navarrete*, vol. I, p. 146.

11 " si el capitán della, ques Martín Alonso Pinzón, tuviera tanto cuidado de procurarse de un buen mastil en las Indias, donde tantos y tales había, como fué cudicioso de se apartar dél, pensando de hinchir el navio de oro, él lo pusiera bueno."—Journal, January 23rd, *Navarrete*, vol. I, p. 143.

12 " Echóse otra vez la suerte para enviar romero a Santa María de Loreto, que está en la marca de Ancona, tierra del Papa, ques casa donde Nuestra Señora ha hecho y hace muchos y grandes milagros, y cayó la suerte a un marinero del Puerto de Santa María que se llamaba Pedro de Villa, y el Almirante le prometió de le dar dinero para las costas."
The remaining details, like the quotation copied above, are all to be found in the Journal, February 14th, *Navarrete*, vol. I, pp. 149-53.

13 " le daba gran pena dos hijos que tenía en Córdoba al estudio que los dejaba huérfanos de padre y madre en tierra extraña."
This quotation will be found in *Navarrete*, vol. I, p. 152, as well as Las Casas' version of Colón's meditations during the storm.

14 " Y diz que fingió haber andado mas camino por desatinar a los pilotos y marineros que carteaban, por quedar él Señor de aquella derrota de las Indias, como de hecho queda, porque ninguno de todos ellos traía su camino cierto, por lo cual ninguno puede estar seguro de su derrota para las Indias."—*Navarrete*, vol. I, p. 154.

15 " y tornó el Almirante a llamar al Capitán y a todos ellos, y les dió su fe, y prometió, como quien era, de no descender ni salir de la carabela hasta que llevase un ciento de portugueses a Castilla, y despoblar toda aquella isla."—Journal, February 19th, *Navarrete*, vol. I, p. 157.

16 " concluyendo dice el Almirante, que bien dijeron los sacros teológos y los sabios filósofos, quel paraiso terrenal está al fin del Oriente, porque es lugar temperadísimo. Así que aquellas tierras que agora él habia descubierto, es (dice él) el fin del Oriente."—February 21st, *Navarrete*, vol. I, p. 158.

17 " Estaba muy penado con tanta tormenta agora questaba a la puerta de casa."—Journal, Wednesday, February 27th, *Navarrete*, vol. I, p. 160.

18 " anduvieron a árbol seco por la gran tempestad del viento y la mar que de dos partes los comia."—Sunday, March 3rd, *Navarrete*, vol. I, p. 161.

19 " y la mas bien artillada de artilleria y armas, que diz que nunca nao se vido.
" Respondió el Almirante quel era Almirante de los Reyes de Castilla, y que no daba él tales cuentas á tales personas, ni saldria de las naos ni navios donde estuviese si no fuese por fuerza de no poder sufrir las armas. Respondió el Patron que enviase al Maestre de la carabela ; dijo el Almirante que ni al Maestre ni á otra persona si no fuese por fuerza, porque en tanto tenia él dar persona que fuese como ir él, y questa era la costumbre de los Almirantes de los Reyes de Castilla de antes morir

que se dar ni dar gente suya. El Patron se moderó y dijo que pues estaba en aquella determinacion, que fuese como él quisiese ; pero que le rogaba que le mandase mostrar las cartas de los Reyes de Castilla si las tenia. Al Almirante plugó de mostrárselas, y luego se volvió á la nao, é hizo relacion al Capitan [. . .] el cual con mucha orden con atabales y trompetas y añafiles, haciendo gran fiesta vino á la carabela, y habló con el Almirante, y le ofreció de hacer todo lo que le mandase."—*Navarrete*, vol. I, p. 162.

20 " estando el rey o anno de quatrocentos nouenta & tres a seis de márço en Val do parayso junto do mosteiro de nóssa senhora das Virtudes termo de Santarem, por razam da peste que andaua per aquella comarca."— *Barros*, dec. I, bk. III, ch. XI, fol. 36 verso.

   " Luego escribió el Almirante al Rey de Portugal, questaba nueve leguas de allí, de como los Reyes de Castilla le habian mandado que no dejase de entrar en los puertos de su Alteza á pedir lo que hobiese menester por sus dineros, y quel Rey le mandase dar lugar para ir con la carabela á la ciudad de Lisboa, porque algunos ruines pensando que traia mucho oro, estando en puerto despoblado, se pusiesen á cometer alguna ruindad, y tambien porque supiese que no venia de Guinea sino de las Indias."—*Navarrete*, vol. I, p. 162.

21 " nâ tanto por aprazer a el Rey quanto por ô magoar com sua vista."— *Barros, loc. cit.*

   Duro (cf. *Pinzón en el Descubrimiento de America*, p. 115) thinks this the *only* reason, for, in his view, the storm being due to South and later South-East wind (cf. C. Colón's letter to Santángel), the natural and *safe* thing to do was to go to Galicia, which is what Pinzón did.

22 He says as much in his Journal on that date.—*Navarrete*, vol. I, p. 163.

23 " pero que ô recebeo com gasalhado, ficou muy triste quando vio a gente da terra que com elle vinha nam ser negra de cabello reuolto & do vulto como a de Guiné, mas conforme en aspecto, cor & cabello como lhe diziam ser a da India, sóbre que elle tanto trabalhaba. E porque Colom falaua mayores grandezas & cousas da terra do que nella auia, & isto com hûa soltura de palauras, acusando e reprehendo a el rey em nam aceptar sua offerta : indinou tâto esta maneira de falar à alguûs fidalgos que, ajuntando este auorrecimiento de sua soltura, com a magoa q̃ viam tẹr a el rey de perder aquella empresa, offerecerâ se delles que ô queriam matar, & com isto se euitaria jr este hômem a Castella. Ca verdadeiramente lhe parecia q̃ a vinda delle auia de prejudicar a este reyno & causar algum desassosego a sua alteza, por razam da conquista que lhe era côcedida pelos summos pontifices : da cual conquista parecia que este Colom trazia aquella gête. As quàes offertas el rey nam aceptou, ante âs reprehendeo como principe cathólico, posto q̃ deste feito de si mesmo teuesse escandalo : & em lugar disso fez merce a Colom & mandou dar de vestir de grâ a aos hómeês que trazia daquella nouo descobrimento, & com isto ô espedio."—*Barros*, dec. I, bk. III, ch. XI, fol. 37 recto.

24 The arrival of the *Pinta* on the same day completes a remarkable set of coincidences :

   The fleet left Palos on a Friday, August 3rd, 1492.
   It saw land on a Friday, October 12th, 1492.
   It left for Spain on a Friday, January 4th, 1493.
   It arrived in Spain on a Friday, March 15th, 1493.

CHAPTER XX

1 It would be difficult to find a more flagrant case of the havoc which presumptions can play in history than the way this episode of Colón's life is treated by many authors. There is no reason to assume that Colón enter-

tained any special grievances against Pinzón owing to his second separation, and the situation arisen out of the first had already been patched up. Yet historians will take a melodramatic view of the arrival of the *Pinta*. In my opinion, Colón must have been very much elated at seeing his second caravel arrive—after him. The most reasonable view is taken by Duro in his *Pinzón*, even though he evinces a certain anti-Colonite bias.

2 Juan de Aragon, a Moguer sailor, states before the Court that " un Martín Alonso Pinzón dijo a este testigo y a los demás que D. Cristóbal Colón y Juan Niño y sus hermanos y parientes habian descubierto las Indias." Pero Enríquez of Palos stated that " while in Bayona he saw the Indians who came from Guanahani and they told him that the Admiral had discovered the Indies " : " e este testigo vido los Indios que traian de la Isla de Guanahani, e le dijeron que el Almirante habia descubierto las islas."— *Pleitos*.

3 " me quedan de la parte de poniente las provincias que yo no he andado, la una de las cuales llaman Cibau, a donde nace la gente con cola."— Letter to Santángel, *Navarrete*, vol. I, p. 171.
   " De la parte del poniente de la isla Juana quedaron las provincias que Colón no anduvo, a la una llaman los Indios, Naan, donde dice que nacen los hombres con la cola, empero yo no creo que sea alli, segun se señala en el mapa-mundi en lo que ho he leido, y si es alli, no tardará mucho en se ver con la ayuda de Dios."—*Bernáldez*, ch. CXVIII, vol. I, p. 366.

4 " deseamos que vuestra venida fuese luego, por ende, por servicio nuestro, que dedes la mayor prisa que pudieredes en vuestra venida, porque con tiempo se provea todo lo que es menester, y porque, como vedes, el verano es entrado, y no se pase el tiempo para la ida allá, ved si algo se puede avanzar en Sevilla o en otras partes para vuestra tornada a la tierra que habeis hallado. Y escribidnos luego [. . .] porque luego se provea como se haga, en tanto que acá vos venis y tornais ; de manera que cuando volvieredes de acá, esté todo aparejado."—*Las Casas*, bk. I, ch. LXXVII, vol. 62, p. 475.

5 " El rey Dom Joam com a noua do sitio & lugar que lhe Colom disse da terra deste seu descobrimento, ficou muy confuso : & creo verdaderamente ĝ esta terra descubérta lhe pertencia, & assi lho dauan a entender as pesóas de sen conselho [. . .] sobre o qual negocio teue muytos conselhos : em que assentou demandar logo a dom Frâcisco Dalmeyda fillo do conde de Abrantes Dom Lopo com hũa armada a esta parte."—*Barros*, bk. II, ch. xj, fol. 37 verso.

6 " Nos entendemos luego en el proveimiento dello con mucho recabdo e diligencia y en ello nos entendemos servir de vos [. . .] que estén puestas y aparejadas todas las carabelas de vuestra tierra porque nos podamos servir dellas en lo que menester fuere."—*Navarrete*, vol. II, p. 23.

7 See the Papal bulls in *Navarrete*, vol. II, pp. 23 and 28 ; the sense of the King's message to Portugal in *Barros*, bk. III, ch. xj, p. 37 ; and the answer of King John and slowness of his ambassadors in the letters of the King and Queen to Colón, *Navarrete*, vol. II, p. 76 (June 12th) and p. 78 (July 27th).

8 It will be found in *Navarrete*, vol. II, p. 20. See also ch. XII of the present book.

9 " Tomó comienzo la fama a volar por Castilla, que se habian descubierto tierras que se llamaban las Indias, y gentes tantas y tan diversas, y cosas novisimas, y que por tal camino venia el que las descubrió, y traia consigo de aquella gente ; no solamente de los pueblos por donde pasaba salia el mundo a lo ver, pero muchos de los pueblos, del camino por donde venia, remotos, se vaciaban, y se hinchian los caminos para irlo a ver, y adelantarse a los pueblos a recibirlo."—*Las Casas*, bk. I, ch. LXXVIII, vol. 62, p. 477.

10 " estando el rey un viernes [. . .] en la casa del juzgado, asentado en juicio, juzgando y oyendo al pueblo, en lo cual habia estado desde las ocho horas hasta las doce, e desque se levantó del juicio descendió por unas gradas abajo fasta una plaza que dicen Plaza del Rey, con muchos caballeros y ciudadanos con él. Los cuales todos cada uno se fué a cabalgar en sus caballos e mulos, y el Rey se paró en la mas cerca de las gradas abajo, cerca del suelo, a departir con su tesorero, y allegóse cerca de él, por detrás aquel dañado y traidor hombre, y asi, como el Rey acabó de departir con el tesorero, abajó un paso para cabalgar en su mula [. . .] y el traidor que tiraba el golpo con un alfanje o espada, cortanchano de fasta tres palmas [. . .] alcanzolo con la punta de aquel muerón una cuchillada desde encima de la cabeza por cerca de la oreja, el pescuezo ayuso fasta los hombros."—*Bernáldez*, ch. CXVI, vol. I, p. 352.

" Yo no tuve corazon para verla tan larga y tan honda, que de honda entraua cuatro dedos y de larga cosa que me tiembla el corazon en dezirlo.

" Mas hizolo Dios con tanta misericordia que parece se midio el lugar por donde podia ser sin peligro. Y saluo todas las cuerdas y el hueso de la nuca y todo lo peligroso."—*Sigüenza*, vol. II, p. 323.

11 " cantan 'Te Deum Laudamus' y responden los menestriles altos, por manera que parecia que en aquella hora se abrian y manifestaban y comunicaban con los celestiales deleites."—*Las Casas*, bk. I, ch. LXXVIII, vol. 62, p. 479.

12

" El vivir que es perdurable
no se gana con estados
mundanales,
ni con vida deleytable,
en que moran los pecados
infernales ;
mas los buenos Religiosos
gananlo con oraciones
y con lloros ;
los Caballeros famosos
con trabajos y aflicciones
contra Moros."

JORGE MANRIQUE.

13 " le llevó un dia saliendo de Palacio a comer consigo, y sentole a la mesa en el lugar mas preeminente y mas propincuo a si, e mandó que le sirviesen el manjar cubierto e le hicieren salva ; y aquella fué la primera vez que al dicho almirante se le hizo salva, y le sirvieron cubierto como a señor, y desde allí adelante se sirvió con la solemnidad y fausto que requeria su digno titulo de almirante."—*Las Casas*, bk. I, ch. LXXX, vol. 62, p. 491.

14 " Este munificentisimo señor y gran Pontifice ; viendo los merecimientos y trabajos, y el fruto que dellos comenzaba a salir del dicho primer Almirante destas Indias, y como los gratisimos Reyes le habian honrado y sublimado, honraban y sublimaban, y mandado honrar y venerar tanto, él, primero que otro Grande . . ."—*Las Casas, loc. cit.*

15 All these documents are to be found in *Navarrete*, vol. II. On the actual meaning of the letter confirming his privileges, see also ch. XXXII hereafter.

16 " aunque eclesiástico y Arcidiano, despues deste cargo que le dieron los Reyes de las Indias, fué Obispo de Badajoz y Palencia, y al cabo de Burgos, en el cual murió, era muy capaz para mundanos negocios, señaladamente para congregar gente de guerra para armadas por la mar, que era mas oficio de vizcainos que de Obispos, por lo cual siempre los Reyes le encomendaron las armadas que por la mar hicieron mientras vivieron."— *Las Casas*, bk. I, ch. LXXVIII, vol. 62, p. 478.

17 Cf. their letters to Cristóbal Colón, August 4th, 1493 (*Navarrete*, vol. II, p. 89) ; to Fonseca, same date (*Navarrete*, vol. II, p. 92) ; and to Juan de Soria, August 5th (*Navarrete*, vol. II, p. 93), in which the following words must be noted :
"non mirais e acatais al Almirante de las Indias como es razon y nosotros lo queremos de que habemos habido mucho enojo, y porque nos queremos que el Almirante sea honrado y acatado segun el titulo que le dimos."

18 " porque él y todos queremos que vos acaten y honren como es razon y segun el estado que nos habemos dado [. . .] vos dad lugar quel haya de firmar en todo lo que se gastare pues ha de tener la cuenta dello en nombre de nuestros contadores mayores."—*Navarrete*, vol. II, pp. 89-90.

19 " y cuanto a los continos que decis que toma el Almirante de las Indias, bien fué lo que le dijisteis que para este viaje no ha menester tomar continos algunos, pues todos los que allí van por nuestro mandado han de facer lo quel en nuestro nombre les mandare, y facer apartamiento de suyos e ajenos podía traer mucho inconveniente ; pero si para su acompañamiento quisiere llevar algunos que lleven nombre de suyos, bien pode llevar fasta diez Escuderose n cuenta de los cincuenta escuderos que han de ir, e otras veinte personas en cuenta de las mil personas que han de ir, y a estas se pague su sueldo como a las otras."—*Navarrete*, vol. II, pp. 91-2.

20 " & como atencam del rey Dom fernando era dilatar este caso te lhe virem, outros nauios que tinha enuiado a estas islas que descobrira Colom, pera que Segundo a calidade da cousa assy fazer a estima della."—*Barros*, bk. III, ch. xj, fol. 37.
Barros says the Ambassadors arrived in June, but the King and Queen, writing to Cristóbal Colón on August 18th, say that the Portuguese Ambassadors " vinieron tres dias ha."—*Navarrete*, vol. II, p. 96.

21 Cf. *Las Casas*, bk. I, ch. LXXXII, vol. 62, p. 497, where the words quoted will be found : " persona notable, prudente y habil para tal cargo."

22 " Yo creo que se acordará vuestra merced cuando la tormenta sin velas me echó en Lisbona, que fui acusado falsamente que habia ido ya* allá al Rey para darle las Indias. Despues supieron Sus Altezas al contrario, y que todo fué con malicia."—*Navarrete*, vol. I, p. 272.

23 " Nos vos mandamos que procureis como vaya con mucho contentamiento, porque así lo queremos e nos place e de lo contrario habremos mucho enojo."—August 18th, *Navarrete*, vol. II, p. 95.

24 It will be found in *Raccolta*, pt. I, vol. I, p. 136.
The original is dateless, but the arguments put forward by de Lollis in favour of 1493, i.e. as a memorandum towards the preparation of the second voyage, are excellent. The first para. of the memorandum runs : " Obedesçiendo lo que Vuestras Altezas me mandaron, diré lo que me ocurre para la poblaçion y negoçiaçion asy de la Ysla Española como de las otras asy halladas como por hallar, sometiendome a mejor parescer."

25 They will be found in *Navarrete*, vol. II, p. 66.

26 " 12 Item : que cualquier Justicia que se hobiere de facer diga el pregon : Esta es la justicia que mandan facer el Rey é la Reina nuestros Señores.
" 13 Item : Que todas las provisiones, é mandamientos, patentes que el dicho Almirante, Visorey, é Gobernador hobiere de dar, vayan escritas por D. Fernando é Doña Isabel, Rey é Reina, &c., é firmadas del dicho D. Cristóbal Colón, como Visorey, é sobreescriptas é firmadas del Escribano que toviere, en la forma que lo acostumbran los otros Escribanos que firman Cartas de los otros Visoreyes, é selladas en las espaldas con el sello de sus Altezas, como lo acostumbran facer los otros Visoreyes que ponen sus Altezas en sus Reinos."—*Navarrete*, vol. II, p. 70.

* ya misprint for yo.

27 *Las Casas*, bk. I, ch. LXXXI, vol. 62, p. 494.

28 *Acequia*=a kind of dyke used for irrigation purposes.

29 Letters to Fernando de Zafra, May 23rd, *Navarrete*, vol. II, pp. 39 and 41.

CHAPTER XXI

1 Two more in Rome, one in Basle, three in Paris and one in Antwerp. See *Vignaud*, vol. II, p. 242.

2 " Post paucos inde dies rediit ab antipodus occiduis Christophorus quidam Colonus vir ligur, qui a meis Regibus ad hanc prouintiam tria vix impetrauerat nauigia, quia fabulosa que dicebat arbitrabuntur, rediit, preciosarum multarum rerum, sed auri precipue que suapte natura, regiones ille generant, argumenta tulit."—See text in *Thacher*, vol. I, p. 54.
　　Note that P. Martyr, writing in Latin, says *Colonus*, and not *Columbus*.

3 " Terram post hec, e cauea grandioris nauis, qua Colonus ipse vehebatur, speculatores proclamant."—Text, *Thacher*, vol. I, p. 57.

4 " acsi meum ac tuum, veluti inter nos, inter eos versaretur, lautiqz apparatus ac pecuniarum cumuli desiderarentur, qua nanqz: re indigere nudos homines, putabis."—*Thacher, loc. cit.*

5 " ningunos principes de España jamás ganaron tierra alguna fuera della, salvo agora que vuestra Altezas tienen acá otro mundo."—Journal of Third Voyage, August 1498, *Navarrete*, vol. I, p. 263.

6 " Era persona de muy buena disposicion ; alto de cuerpo, aunque no tanto como el Almirante, de buen gesto, puesto que algo severo, de buenas fuerzas y muy esforzado, muy sabio y prudente y recatado, y mucha experiencia y general en todo negocio."—*Las Casas*, bk. I, ch. CI, vol. 63, p. 80.
　　" Mas recatado y astuto, a lo que parecia, y de menos simplicidad, que Cristóbal Colón ; latino y muy entendido en cosas de hombres."—*Las Casas*, bk. I, ch. XXIX, vol. 62, p. 224.
　　" gran marinero, y creo, por los libros y cartas de marear glosados y notados de su letra [. . .] que era en aquella facultad tan docto, que no le hacia el Almirante mucha ventaja."—*Las Casas*, bk. I, ch. CI, vol. 63, p. 80.
　　I have interpreted *latino* as *ladino*, "cunning," for it suits better the place it occupies in the character-sketch and the character it describes.

7 On this point Vignaud (vol. I, pp. 437-55) seems to me to be correct.

8 " Se partió para Inglaterra, y en el camino quiso Dios a él tambien tentarle y ejercitarle, porque hobo de caer en poder de ladrones corsarios de la mar, de nación Esterlines, no se que nacion fueron. Esto fué causa que enfermase y viniese a mucha pobreza, y estuviese mucho tiempo sin poder llegar a Inglaterra, hasta tanto que quiso Dios sanarle ; y reformado algo por su industria y trabajo de sus manos, haciendo cartas de marear, llegó a Inglaterra. . . ."—*Las Casas*, bk. I, ch. XXIX, vol. 62, p. 224.

9 " IX. Yten : sy saben e creen que lo que se ha descubierto en la tierra de Gracia a que llaman Fyrme, a seydo por la yndustria que dió el dicho almyrante en abryr la puerta e hazer el prymero viaje en que descubrió las yndias. . . ."
　　" A la novena pregunta dixo, que cree lo contenido en la dicha pregunta porque este testigo andovo con el dicho almyrante don Cristoval Colon solicitando con El Rey y la Reyna nuestros señores, e porque el dicho almyrante fue el primero que descubrió estas tierras, e Paria, e nunca otro avya venydo hasta estonces, antes el tiempo quel dicho almyrante lo

solicitava fazian burla del dicho almyrante e deste testigo diziendo que querian descobrir otro mundo nuevo. . . ."—*Pleitos*, vol. 7, p. 185.

It is a remarkable fact that Vignaud, who knew this statement, does not discuss it and merely ignores it.

10 A Spanish historian claims that Bartolomé left Portugal for England with Count Penamacer, one of the prominent members of the Braganza family who conspired against King John (S. de la Rosa, *Solución de todos los problemas relativos a Cristóbal Colón* : Congress of Americanists, 1901) ; to which Vignaud objects that according to Rui de Pina (*Chronica*, ch. XXXIV) Penamacer did not go first to England but to Seville. This would appear to confirm my analysis and to supply an explanation for it. But it does not go beyond conjecture. And Bartolomé's return to Portugal in 1488 makes it unlikely.

11 　　　" Terrarum quicumque, cupis feliciter oras
　　　　Noscere, cuncta decens docte pictura docebit.
　　　　Quam Strabo affirmat, Ptolemaeus, Plinius atque
　　　　Isidorus : non una tamen sententia quisque,
　　　　Pingitur hic etiam nuper sulcata carinis.
　　　　Hispanis zona illa, prius incognita genti,
　　　　Torrida, quae tandem nunc est notissima multis.

　　　　Pro auctore, sive pictore : Janua cui patriae est nomen cui Bartholomeus Columbus de Terra Rubra, opus edidit istud, Londonijs anno Dni 1480, atque insuper anno octavo decimaquae ; die cum tertia mensis Febr."—Text copied from *Vignaud*, vol. I, p. 456.

12 " Somewhat before this time also, there fell out a memorable Accident. There was one SEBASTIAN GABATO, a *Venetian*, dwelling in Bristow, a man seene and expert in *Cosmographie* and *Nauigation*. This Man seeing the Successe, and emulating perhaps the enterprise of CHRISTOPHERUS COLVMBVS in that fortunate discouerie towards the *Southwest*, which had beene by him made some six yeares before ; conceited with himselfe, that *Lands* might likewise bee discouered towards the Northwest. And surely it may bee hee had more firme and pregnant coniectures of it, then COLVMBVS had of this at the first. In the two great *Islands* of the *Old* and *New World*, beeing (in the shape and making of them) broad towards the *North*, and pointed towards the *South*, it is likely, that the discouerie first beganne where the *Lands* did nearest meet. And there had beene before that time a discouerie of some *Lands*, which they tooke to bee *Islands*, and were indeed the *Continent* of *America*, towards the *Northwest*. And it may bee, that some Relation of this nature comming afterwards to the knowledge of COLVMBVS, and by him suppressed (desirous rather to make his enterprise the *Child* of his *Science* and *Fortune*, then the *Follower* of a former *Discouerie*), did give him better assurance, that all was not *Sea*, from the *West* of *Europe* and *Africke* vnto *Asia*, then either SENECA's *Prophesie*, or PLATO's *Antiquities*, on the nature of the *Tides*, and *Landwinds*, and the like, which were the *Coniectures* that were given out, whereupon hee should have relyed. Though I am not ignorant, that it was likewise laid vnto the casuall and *wind-beeten Discouerie* (a little before) of a *Spanish Pilot*, who died in the house of COLVMBVS. But this Gabato bearing the King in hand, that hee would find out an *Island* endued with rich Commodities, procured him to man and victuall a Ship at *Bristow*, for the discouerie of that *Island*. With whom ventured also three small shippes of *London-Merchants*, fraught with some grosse and sleight wares, fit for commerce with barbarous people. Hee sayled (as hee affirmed at his Return, and made a Card thereof) very far Westwards, with a Quarter of the North, on the *North-Side* of *Tierra de Labrador*, vntil hee came to the latitude of Sixtie Seuen Degrees and a halfe, finding the

Seas still open. It is certain also, that the Kings Fortune had a tender of that Great Empire of the West-Indies. Neither was it a refusall on the Kings part, but a *Delay* by accident that put by so great an *Acquest*. For CHRISTOPHERUS COLVMBVS refused by the King of Portugall (who would not embrace at once both *East* and *West*), imployed his Brother BARTHOLOMEVS COLVMBVS vnto King Henry, to negotiate for his Discouerie. And it so fortuned, that hee was taken by *Pirates at Sea*, by which accidental impediment hee was long ere hee came to the King. So long that before hee had obtayned a Capitulation with the King for his Brother, the Enterprise by him was atchieved, and so the *West Indies* by *Prouidence* were then reserved for the *Crown* of *Castilia*."—The Historie of the Raigne of King Henry The Seuenth, written By the Right Honourable Francis, Lord *Verulam*, Viscount *St. Alban*, London 1622, pp. 186-8.

13 " informado el Rey de sus consejeros y personas a quien él cometió la examinacion desto, burlo de quåto Colom dezia, tuuo por vanas sus palabras."—*Oviedo*, bk. II, ch. IV, fol. v.

14 " Dice que viviendo con Madama de Borbón, el Almirante su hermano, le escribió que viniese a servir a vuestra Alteza, porque seria honrado y acrecentado."—Extracto de un expediente formado a petición de Don Bartolomé Colón, *Colección de Documentos Inéditos para la Historia de España*, vol. XVI, Madrid, 1850, p. 559.

15 " los Reyes sabian primero la nuevas que otro."—*Las Casas*, bk. I, ch. CI, vol. 63, p. 79.

16 " toda la mayor parte iba con sus armas para pelear ofreciendo caso."— Bk. I, ch. XXXII, vol. 62, p. 497, whence come the facts about the gentle-men on board, save in what concerns Mosen Pedro Margarite, for whom my source is *Oviedo*.

17 " persona virtuosa, muy cuerda, pacifica y mas simple y bien acondicionada que recatada ni maliciosa, y que andaba muy honestamente vestido, cuasi en hábito de clérigo, y bien creo que penso ser obispo y el Almirante le procuró, al menos que le diesen los Reyes renta por la Iglesia."—*Las Casas, loc. cit.*

18 " era pequeño de cuerpo, pero muy bien proporcionado y muy bien dispuesto, hermoso de gesto, la cara hermosa y los ojos muy grandes, de los mas sueltos hombres en correr y hacer vueltas y en todas las otras cosas de fuerzas, que venian en la flota y que quedaban en España. Todas las perfecciones que un hombre podia tener corporales, parecia que se habian juntado en él, sino ser pequeño [. . .] siendo de los mas esforzados, y que así en Castilla. [. . .] viendose en muchos ruidos y desafios como despues aca. [. . .] y que él siempre era el primero que habia de hacer sangre. [. . .] nunca jamás en su vida fué herido ni le sacó hombre sangre hasta obra de dos años antes que muriese que le aguardaron cuatro indios. [. . .] y con gran industria le hirieron."—*Las Casas, loc. cit.*

19 Cf. Colón's memorandum of January 30th, 1494, *Navarrete*, vol. I, p. 234. " Mosen Pedro Margarite & los otros caballeros entendia en hazerlos amigos. . . ."—*Oviedo*, bk. II, ch. XIII, fol. xix verso.

20 " e aprovechareis mucho a la salud de los que por nuestra mandado allá van."—*Navarrete*, vol. II, p. 54.

21 " como becerras, y cabras, y ovejas y [. . .] ocho puercas a 70 maravedis la pieza. Destas ocho puercas se han multiplicado todos los puercos que, hasta hoy, ha habido y hay en todas estas Indias que han sido y son infinitos ; metieron gallinas tambien y esta fue la simiente de donde, todo lo que hoy hay aca de las cosas de Castilla, ha salido, lo mismo de las pepitas y simientes de naranjas, limones y cidras, melones y de toda hortaliza. . . ."— *Las Casas*, bk. I, ch. LXXXIII, vol. 63, p. 3.

22 " Luego a la mañana paresció otra isla harto grande : á ninguna destas no llegamos por consolar los que habían dejado en la Española, e no plogo a Dios segun que abajo parecerá."—*Navarrete*, vol. I, p. 206.

CHAPTER XXII

1 Dr. Chanca, *Navarrete*, vol. I, p. 210.

2 This episode will be found in Dr. Chanca, *Navarrete*, vol. I, p. 211 : " El Almirante les mandó dar sendas camisas e bonetes e otras cosillas e les dijo que porque iba a donde estaba Guacamari non se podria detener."
This *cacique* is called Guacanagari by Las Casas.

3 " No cesamos de andar nuestro camino fasta llegar a un puerto llamado Monte-Cristi, donde estuvimos dos dias para ver la disposicion de la tierra, porque no habia parecido bien al Almirante el logar donde habia dejado la gente para hacer asiento."—Dr. Chanca, *Navarrete*, vol. I, p. 211.

4 " Algunos de los nuestros sospecharon mas mal que bien, e con razon, porque los indios son todos desbarbados."—*Navarrete*, vol. I, p. 212.

5 " Fué el Almirante a tierra e toda la gente de pro con él, tan ataviados que en una ciudad prencipal parecieran bien."—*Navarrete*, vol. I, p. 217.

6 " no tenia mas mal en aquella que en la otra, aunque él hacia del raposo que le dolia mucho. [. . .] El Almirante no sabia que se hacer."— *Navarrete*, vol. I, p. 218.
For Colón's reasons for leniency towards Guacamari see *Las Casas*, bk. I, ch. LXXXVI, vol. 63, pp. 14-15.

7 Dr. Chanca says : " Acordó el Almirante nos tornásemos por la costa arriba por do habiamos venido de Castilla, porque la nueva del oro era fasta allí. Fuenos el tiempo contrario, que mayor pena nos fué tornar treinta leguas atrás que venir desde Castilla, que con el tiempo contrario e la largueza del camino ya eran tres meses pasados cuando decendimos en tierra."— *Navarrete*, vol. I, p. 219.
If he means, and he can hardly mean anything else, that when they landed in what was to be *Isabela* they had been over three months on board ship since they sailed from Cádiz (September 25th), this would date the foundation of Isabela some time after December 25th. The doctor says later (p. 221) : " el dia que yo salí a dormir en tierra fué el primero dia del Señor "—which I suppose means December 25th. Therefore, Colón took just short of a month in finding—plus the time he took in founding— Isabela, before he could turn his attention to Caonabó and Guacamari.

8 The instructions to Antonio de Torres and the royal answers are to be found in *Navarrete*, vol. I, p. 225.

9 " fué forzoso [. . .] dejarlos porque, como se perdió el navio, no habia en que viniesen, y esto se calló acá y se dijo que no quedaban sino por comienzo de pobladores."—*Bernáldez*, ch. CXVIII, vol. I, p. 367.

10 See these instructions in *Navarrete*, vol. II, p. 74. These are dated June 7th, 1493.

11 " de donde colijo que algun testigo debiera en aquellos de haber ejecutado." —*Las Casas*, bk. I, ch. XC, vol. 63, p. 28.

12 " personas que en ella [la gobernacion] le aconsejasen y le ayudasen."— *Las Casas*, bk. I, ch. XC, vol. 63, p. 28.

13 " por poner temor en la tierra, y mostrar que si algo intentasen eran poderosos para ofenderlos y dañarlos los cristianos, a la salida de la Isabela,

mandó salir la gente en forma de guerra, con las banderas tendidas, y con sus trompetas, y quizá disparando espingardas, con las cuales quedarian los indios harto asombrados, y asi hacia en cada pueblo al entrar y al salir."— *Las Casas*, bk. I, ch. XC, vol. 63, p. 28.

" tan fresca, tan verde, tan descombrada, tan pintada, toda tan llena de hermosura, que ansi como la vieron, les pareció que habian llegado a alguna region del Paraiso, bañados y regalados todos en entrañable y no comparable alegria."—*Las Casas*, bk. I, ch. XC, vol. 63, p. 29.

14 Las Casas says that the garrison was raised to three hundred. But he probably refers to the expedition sent with Hojeda, part of which was meant to reconnoitre the island. See below, note 20.

15 " Donde no hay harina todo es mohina."

16 " era necesario que tambien ayudasen los hidalgos y gente del Palacio, o de capa prieta, que tambien hambre y miseria padecia, y a los unos y a los otros se les hacia a par de muerte ir a trabajar con sus manos, en especial no comiendo [. . .] añadir al mando la violencia."—*Las Casas*, bk. I, ch. XCII, vol. 63, pp. 40-41.

17 ". . . el almirante ahorcó á algunos, y en espeçial á un Gaspar Ferriz, é á otros açotó ; é començó á se mostrar severo é con mas riguridad de la que solia. [. . .] El almirante era culpado de crudo en la opinión de aquel religioso, el qual, como tenia las veçes del Papa, ybale a la mano ; é assi como Colom haçia alguna cosa que al frayle no le paresçiesse justa, en las cosas de la justiçia criminal, luego ponia entredicho y haçia cessar el ofiçio divino. Y en esta hora el almirante mandaba cessar la raçion, y que no se le diesse de comer al fray Buyl ni a los de su casa. . . ."—*Oviedo*, bk. II, ch. XIII.

Las Casas denies this, but Oviedo appears to be right, since we have documentary proof that Colón was forbidden by the King and Queen to withhold supplies as a method for enforcing his authority.

18 " Dijose tambien publicamente y entre la gente comun al menos se platicaba y afirmaba que una vez yendo de dia un hombre o dos por aquellos edificios de la Isabela, en una calle aparecieron dos rengleras, a manera de dos coros de hombres que parecian todos comc de gente noble y del Palacio, bien vestidos, ceñidas sus espadas, y rebozados con tocas de camino de las que entonces en España se usaban, y estando admirados aquel o aquellos, a quien esta vision parecia como habian venido allí a aportar gente tan nueva y ataviada, sin haberse sabido en esta isla dellos nada, saludándoles y preguntándoles cuando y de donde venian, respondieron callando solamente, echando mano a los sombreros para los resaludar, quitaron juntamente con los sombreros las cabezas de sus cuerpos, quedando descabezados, y luego desaparecieron ; de la cual vision y turbación quedaron los que los vieron cuasi muertos, y por muchos dias penados y asombrados."—*Las Casas*, bk. I, ch. XCII, vol. 63, p. 43.

19 " toda la gente que no estaba enferma y la que podia andar."—*Las Casas*, bk. I, ch. XCII, vol. 63, p. 44.

20 " que Cahonaboa vaya a hablar con vos, porque mas segura se haga su prision ; e porque él anda desnudo e seria malo de detenerle, e si una vez se soltase e se fuyese, no se podria asi haber a las manos por la dispusicion de la tierra, estando en vistas con él, hacedle dar una camisa y vestirsela luego, y un capus, y ceñidle un cinto, y ponelle una toca por donde le podeis tener e no se vos suelte."—April 9th, 1494, *Navarrete*, vol. II, p. 110.

C. C. sends him 16 horse, 250 foot archers and 110 musketeers (*espingarderos*) with 20 officers (p. 111). Las Casas is therefore misinformed in saying that Colón sent only seventy soldiers. He may, on the other hand, be right in thinking that most of them could just walk.

CHAPTER XXIII

1 " Seré juzgado como a capitan que fué a conquistar de España fasta las Indias, y non a gobernar Cibdad, ni villa, ni Pueblo puesto en regimiento salvo a poner so el señorio de S.A. gente salvaje, belicosa y que viven por sierras y montes."—Towards end of 1500, *Navarrete*, vol. II, p. 254.

2 On Diego Colón the Indian see *Las Casas*, bk. I, ch. XCIV, vol. 63, p. 51.

3 " Desque la vido [. . .] le pareció la mas hermosa y graciosa de cuantas hasta entonces habia descubierto."—*Loc. cit.*, p. 52.

4 " que dijesen si tenian dubda alguna que esta tierra no fuese la tierra firme al comienzo de las Indias y fin a quien en estas partes quisiera venir de España por tierra ; e que si alguna dubda o sabiduría dello toviese que les rogaba que lo dijesen porque luego les quitaria la dubda, y les faria ver que esto es cierto y qués la tierra firme. Y yo así lo cumpli [. . .] y les puse pena de diez mil maravedis por cada vez que lo que dijese cada uno que despues en ningun tiempo el contrario dijese de lo que agora diría, e cortada la lengua ; e si fuese grumete o persona de tal suerte, que le daria ciento azotes y le cortarian la lengua."—*Navarrete*, vol. II, p. 145.

5 "súpitamente le dió una modorra pestilencial, que total mente le quitó el uso de los sentidos y todas las fuerzas, y quedó muerto, y no pensaron que un día durara."—*Las Casas*, bk. I, ch. XCIX, vol. 63, p. 70.
  " I believe it is certain that Colón suffered from foot-gout. If he was a Jew, this might provide yet another confirmation, for it is a very frequent ailment with that race. It was then more prevailing than now. In Spain, it was the most frequent of all diseases. Our Vives, who in his *Refectio Scholastica* describes and extols the marvels of a vegetarian diet and of pure water, died of gout (though he did follow his own doctrine), and he admirably describes the disease, with attacks similar to those we find in Colón. Colón's type, with his red face and easily reddening complexion and premature white hair, corresponds to the ' martial ' type, so called owing to its resemblance with Mars, sanguine and wearing a white helmet." —From a private letter to the Author by Dr. Gregorio Marañón, who is not only a distinguished historian but an authority on rheumatism. May I add that Vives was of *Converso* descent. (*A.R.*, vol. III.)

6 Thrice Las Casas says Bartolomé arrived on April 14th, 1494, which is an obvious impossibility, since the Admiral arrived on September 29th. As for Harrisse, having given his date of arrival—Midsummer Day 1494— he quotes Navarrete on a fleet organised in April 1495 as his authority for the number of caravels which Bartolomé brought over (vol. II, p. 60).

7 " acordó, como Visorey, pareciendole tener auctoridad para ello, de criarlo e investirlo de la dignidad ó oficio real de Adelantado de las Indias como él lo era Almirante ; pero los Reyes, sabido, no lo aprobaron, dando a entender al Almirante no pertenecer al oficio de Visorey criar tal dignidad, sino sólo á los Reyes."—*Las Casas*, bk. I, ch. CI, vol. 63, p. 80.

8 See *Oviedo*, bk. II, ch. XIII, fol. xviii verso.

9 " todo lo que al principio nos dijistes que se podria alcanzar, por la mayor parte todo ha salido cierto, como si lo hobierades visto antes que nos lo dijesedes."—Letter dated Segovia, August 16th, 1494, *Navarrete*, vol. II, p. 154.
  " A vos, los Caballeros, Escuderos, oficiales e Homes-Buenos."— *Navarrete, loc. cit.*

10 *Las Casas*, bk. I, ch. CII, vol. 63, p. 88.

11 There is no trace of the return voyage of Don Diego Colón, but he was there before his brother's departure for Spain on March 10th, 1496, since he was left by Colón as second in command."—*Navarrete*, vol. II, p. 174.

12 This episode provides a curious example of the aberrations to which the prejudice which would make of Spaniards specialists of cruelty may lead the most honest of historians. Harrisse (vol. II, p. 61) says :

"malgré les scrupules de la reine Isabelle, ils furent vendus comme esclaves à Seville. 'Aussi peu soignés que l'auraient été des carnassiers' ces infortunés ne tardèrent pas à périr tous de privations et de chagrins."

A footnote on his quotation provides his authority :

"Quinientas ánimas de indios e indias, todos de buena edad, dende doce años hasta treinta y cinco, poco mas o menos, los cuales todos se entregaron en Sevilla al Señor Don Juan de Fonseca, e vinieron ansi como andaban en su tierra, como nacieron, de lo cual no habian mas empacho que alimañas los cuales todas vendieron, y aprovecharon muy mal que murieron todos los mas, que los probó la tierra."—*Bernáldez*, ch. CXX, vol. II, p. 37.

It will be seen that Harrisse misunderstood Bernáldez to such an extent that his "translation" bears no relation to the original. What Bernáldez said was that : "they came [to Spain] as they went about in their country, as [naked] as they were born, and *they were no more embarrassed than animals.* . . ." Harrisse "translates" the underlined part as follows : "As little cared for [by the Spaniards] as if they had been wild beasts."

13 "El Rey e la Reina : Caballeros y escuderos, y otras personas que por nuestro mandado estais en las Indias, allá vos enviamos a Juan Aguado, nuestro Repostero, el cual de nuestra parte, os hablará. Nos vos mandamos que le dedes fe y creencia. De Madrid a nueve de Abril de mil cuatrocientos noventa y cinco años. Yo el Rey—Yo la Reina."—*Las Casas*, bk. I, ch. CVII, vol. 63, p. 109. The text in *Navarrete*, vol. II, p. 159, though copied from *Las Casas*, is, by an oversight, incomplete.

14 "una escudilla de trigo que lo habian de moler en una atahona de mano (y muchos lo comian cocido) y una tajada de tocino rancioso y de queso podrido, y no se cuantas habas o garbanzos, vino, como si no lo hobiera en el mundo.

"no se juraba otro juramento sino 'asi Dios me lleve a Castilla.'"—*Las Casas*, bk. I, ch. CVII, vol. 63, p. 115.

15 "Ya no era el Almirante ni sus justicias tan acatado y obedecido como de antes."—*Las Casas, loc. cit.*, p. 114.

16 "porque es muy devoto de Sant Francisco, vistiose de pardo, y yo le vide en Sevilla, al tiempo que llegó de acá, vestido cuasi como fraile de Sant Francisco."—*Las Casas*, bk. I, ch. CII, vol. 63, p. 89.

17 See *Las Casas*, bk. I, ch. CVIII, vol. 63, pp. 114-15.

18 "un escudero criado suyo, bien entendido aunque no letrado."—*Las Casas*, bk. I, ch. CXI, vol. 63, p. 124.

19 "La una era la señora del pueblo, y por ventura de toda la isla, que cuando la tomó un canario [. . .] corría tanto que no parecia sino un gamo, la cual, viendo que la alcanzaba, vuelve a él como un perro rabiando y abrázalo y da con él en el suelo, y si no acudieran cristianos, lo ahogara."—*Las Casas*, bk. I, ch. CXI, vol. 63, p. 126.

"por dejar no tan agraviados los vecinos de aquella isla porque, diz que, aquella isla estaba en el paso."—*Las Casas, loc. cit.*

CHAPTER XXIV

1 "y por que temiendo que algo ha Dios dispuesto del Almirante de las Indias en el camino que fue, pues que ha tanto tiempo que dél no sabemos, tenemos acordado de enviar allá el comendador Diego Carrillo, e a otra persona principal de recaudo para que, en ausencia del Almirante, provea en todo lo de allá, y aun en su presencia remedie en las cosas que conviniere

remediarse, segund la información que hobimos de los que de allá vinieron."
—April 9th, 1495, *Navarrete*, vol. II, p. 162.

2 *Bernáldez*, ch. CXXXI, vol. II, p. 78.

3 " vestido de unas ropas de color de hábito de fraile de San Francisco, de
la observancia, y en la hechura poco menos que hábito, e un cordon de
San Francisco por devocion."—*Bernáldez, loc. cit.*

4 " buscar la provincia y ciudad de Catayo, diciendo que le podia hallar por
allí, que es en el Señorio del Gran Kan, la cual se lee [. . .] que es la
mas rica provincia del mundo, y la mas abundosa de oro y plata, y de
todos metales y sedas ; pero son todos idólatras y gente muy agudisima y
nigromántica, y sabia en todas artes y caballerosa, e dellas escriben muchas
maravillas, segun cuenta el noble caballero inglés Juan de Mandavilla.

" Yo digo que habia menester muy grande distancia de tiempo para lo
hallar, porque el Gran Kan fué antiguamente Señor de los Tártaros ; y
desde la Gran Tartaria, que es en los confines de Buxia e Bahia, e podemos
decir que se comienza la Gran Tartaria desde Ungria, que son tierras que
están, mirando desde esta Andalucía, por el derecho a donde sale el sol en el
mes de los mayores dias del año, e por aquel derecho solian ir los mercaderes
en aquella tierra ; que por la banda que el Almirante buscaba el Catayo,
es mi creer que con otras mil e docientas leguas, andando el firmamento
de la mar e tierra, en derredor, no llegare allí y ansi se lo dije e hice entender
yo al año de 1496 que fué mi huesped, en presencia de Don Juan de
Fonseca."—*Bernáldez*, ch. CXXIII, vol. II, pp. 42-3.

5 " mucho placer habemos tenido de vuestra venida ende, la cual sea mucho
en buen hora. . . ."—Almazán, July 12th, 1496. See *Navarrete*, vol. II,
p. 179.

6 " aquellos primeros españoles que por acá vinieron [. . .] algunos de los
que venian en esta demanda de oro si allá volvian eran con la misma color
dél, pero no cô aql lustre."—*Oviedo*, bk. II, ch. XIII, fol. xviii.

7 " Nos vos mandamos . . . salvo si los tales delitos fueren tales por que
merezcan pena de muerte, que es igual el quitar los mantenimientos."—
June 1st, 1495, *Navarrete*, vol. II, p. 176.

8 " el rey e la reyna enbiaron al Sancto Padre Inocencio octavo cien moros
bien guarnecidos. [. . .] E la reyna enbio treynta esclavas donzellas, las
mas hermosas que allí se pudieron hallar, a la reyna de Napoles, su prima
e a la reyna de Portugal treynta. E mandaron dar el cardenal çiento y
veynte ; e al duque de. . . ."—*Valera-Crónica*, ch. LXXXVIII, p. 272.

9 *Navarrete*, vol. II, p. 158.

10 " porque Nos querriamos informarnos de letrados, Teologos e Canonistas
si con buena conciencia se pueden vender estos por solo vos o no ; y esto
no se puede facer fasta que veamos las cartas que el Almirante nos escriba
para saber la causa por que los envia aca por cativos."—The King and
Queen to the Bishop of Badajoz, April 16th, 1495, *Navarrete*, vol. II, p. 173.

11 All this scene is paraphrased, and at times actually quoted from Colón's
own account.—*Navarrete*, vol. I, pp. 242-5.

12 *Navarrete*, vol. II, p. 165.

13 " y vuestras Altezas me respondió con aquel corazon que sabe en todo el
mundo que tienen, y me dijo que no curase de nada de eso, porque su
voluntad era de proseguir esta empresa y sostenerla, aunque no fuese sino
piedras y peñas, y quel gasto que en ello se hacia que lo tenia en nada,
que en otras cosas no tan grandes gastaban mucho mas, y que le tenian
todo por muy bien gastado lo del pasado y lo que se gastase en adelante,
porque creian que nuestra santa fe seria acrecentada y su Real señorio
ensanchado. . . ."—*Navarrete*, vol. I, p. 263.

14 " No habiendo otra causa legitima para entrar cristianos en estos reinos y tierras, sino solo para dar les noticias y cognoscimiento de un solo y verdadero Dios y de Jesucristo, su hijo, universal Redentor."—*Las Casas*, bk. I, ch. CXIV, vol. 63, p. 142. See also the beginning of ch. CXIII, vol. 63, p. 134.

15 In seven centuries of internal strife the several kings of the Spanish Peninsula never fought a war for union (which would have meant the spoliation of a reigning prince), but only to resist disunion once it had been brought about by marriage and inheritance.

16 This view was elaborated into a theory of law by the great Franciscan Father Vitoria, professor of Salamanca during the reign of Charles V and a contemporary of Las Casas. It may be considered as the historical origin of the institution of Mandates by Wilson.

17 See documents CIII, CIV, CV and CVI in *Navarrete*, vol. II, pp. 181-8. The last of these four documents authorised Colón to increase the number of salaried settlers to five hundred on condition they are paid on local supplies. That is why I surmise that he began by asking for five hundred, for the scheme was originally his and he had a way of coming back to what he wanted till he got it.

18 " saben bien Vuestras Altezas lo que acontesio el año de nouenta y syete cuando estabâ en burgos en tal côgoxa por quel tiêpo perseveraba crudo y se sucediâ los estirones q. de enfadados e yban a soria y partida toda la corte un sabado quedarô V.A. para partir lunes de mañana y aun cierto proposito en aquella noche, en un escripto mio que envie a V.A. dezia tal dia comêzo a vêtar el viêto. El otro dia no partira la flota aguardâdo si el viêto se afirma. Partira el miercoles y el jueves o viernes sera tant avant como la ysla de huict y sy no se metê en ella serâ en laredo el lunes que viene o la razon de la marineria es toda perdida. este escripto mio con el deseo de la venida de la prinzesa movio a V.A. a mudar de proposito de no yr a Soria y espirmêtar la opiniô del marynero y el lunes remaneszio sobre laredo una nao que refuso de entrar en huit porque tenia pocos bastimentos."—Letter of Colón to the King and Queen, February 6th, 1502, *Raccolta*, pt. I, vol. III, p. 12.

Cristóbal Colón, Mi Almirante del Mar Oceano, e Visorey e Gobernador de las Islas de las Indias : Vi vuestra letra e la escritura e parescer vuestro para el viaje de la Archiduquesa, Mi Muy cara e Muy amada fija, el cual es muy bueno, e como de home sabio e que tiene mucha platica e experiencia en las cosas de la mar. Yo vos lo agradezco mucho, e tengo en especial cargo e servicio, asi por vuestro buen comedimiento en lo haber enviado en tiempo, que sin duda nos ha aprovechado mucho vuestro aviso e consejo, como por ser cierta de la voluntad e aficion conque lo decis, la cual siempre se ha conocido de vos, en todas las cosas de mi servicio ; e asi creed que se rescibe todo como, de mucho especial e fiel servidor mio. De Laredo a diez y ocho de Agosto de noventa y seis años. Yo la Reina."—*C.D.I.A.I.*, vol. 38, p. 357.

19 " Primeramente, que como seais en las dichas islas, Dios queriendo, procureis con toda diligencia de animar y atraer a los naturales de las dichas Indias a toda paz e quietud, e que nos hayan de servir e estar so nuestro Señorio e sujecion benignamente, e principalmente que se conviertan a nuestra Santa fe Catolica."—*Navarrete*, vol. II, p. 182.

The decisions outlined in the text are all inserted within pp. 180-90, vol. II.

20 For the order to Soria on the Admiral's privileges see *Navarrete*, vol. I, p. 355 ; and for the letters appointing the two boys pages to the Queen see *Navarrete*, vol. II, p. 220.

21 These documents are to be found in *Navarrete*, vol. II, pp. 190-216.

22 " Destos cognosci yo en esta isla a algunos, y aun alguno desorejado, y siempre le cognosci harto hombre de bien."—*Las Casas*, bk. I, ch. CXIII, vol. 63, p. 132.

23 On July 22nd, 1497, the title is given Don Bartolomé as a *favour* (" merced "). —*Navarrete*, vol. II, p. 217.

24 *Las Casas*, bk. I, ch. CXXVI, vol. 63, p. 197.

25 " El primero cuchillo de dolor que traspasó el ánima de la Reina Doña Isabel, fué la muerte del Principe, el segundo fué la muerte de Doña Isabel su primera hija, Reina de Portugal ; el tercero cuchillo de dolor fué la muerte de Don Miguel su nieto ; y desde estos tiempos vivió sin placer la inclita y muy virtuosisima y muy necesaria en Castilla Reina Doña Isabel y se acortó su vida y salud."—*Bernáldez*, ch. CLIV, vol. II, p. 137. Details on the royal weddings and Don Juan's death are from this and from the preceding chapter.

CHAPTER XXV

1 " E aquí tomó este Miguel Diaz amistad con una caçica, que se llamó despues Catalina, é ovo en ella dos fijos, andando el tiempo. Pero desde á poco que aqui se detuvo como aquella india prinçipal le quiso bien, tratóle como amigo que tenia parte en ella, é por su respecto a los demás, é dióle notiçia de las minas que están siete leguas de esta cibdad, é rogóle que fiçiesse que los christianos que estaban en la Isabela (que el mucho quisiesse) los llamasse é se viniessen á esta tierra que tan fértil y hermosa es, é de tan exçelente río é puerto ; é quella los sosternia é daria lo que oviessen menester. Entonçe este hombre, por complaçer á la caçica, é mas porque le paresçió, que llevando nueva de tan buena tierra é tan abundante, el adelantado por estar en parte tan estéril y enferma le per- donaria, é prinçipalmente porque Dios queria que assi fuesse. . . ."— *Oviedo*, bk. II, ch. XIII, p. 52.

2 The account of Las Casas is typical of the three attitudes analysed in our previous chapter : his own, uncompromisingly Christian ; Colón's, all for slavery ; and the King and Queen's, accepting slavery only as the punishment for rebellious subjects. Cf. *Las Casas*, bk. I, ch. CXIII, vol. 63, p. 135.

3 *Las Casas* (vol. 63, p. 136) says because he arrived on a Sunday (Domingo in Spanish) ; Fernando Colón (*F.C.*, ch. LXXII) because Domingo (Domenico) was his father's name ; however, all has been settled by the present President of the Dominican Republic, who has changed the his- torical and quatri-centennial name to Ciudad Trujillo, in honour of himself.

4 There is an interesting report on the ruins of Isabela, with a diagram, in *Thacher*, vol. II, p. 286.

5 " una muy notable mujer, muy prudente, muy graciosa y palanciana en sus hablas, y artes, y meneos, y amicisima de los cristianos."—*Las Casas*, bk. I, ch. CXIV, vol. 63, p. 140.
" un ejercito de infinitos indios con sus arcos y flechas, armados en son de guerra, puesto que desnudos en cueros ; y notad qué guerra pueden hacer con las barrigas desnudas por broqueles."—*Las Casas, loc. cit.*, p. 138.

6 " Salen infinitas gentes y muchos señores y nobleza [. . .] cantando sus cantares y haciendo sus bailes, que llamaban areitos, cosa mucho alegre y agradable para ver, cuando se ayuntaban muchos en numero especial- mente ; salieron delante treinta mujeres, las que tenia por mujeres el rey Behechio, todas desnudas en cueros, sólo cubiertas sus vergüenzas con unas medias faldillas de algodon, blancas y muy labradas, en la tejedura dellas, que llamaban naguas, que les cubrian desde la cintura hasta media pierna ; traian ramos verdes en las manos, cantaban y bailaban y saltaban

con moderación, como a mujeres convenía, mostrando grandísimo placer, regocijo, fiesta y alegria. Llegaronse todas ante Don Bartolomé Colón y, las rodillas hincadas en tierra, con gran reverencia, danle los ramos y palmas que traian en las manos ; toda la gente demas que era innumerable, hacen todos grandes bailes y alegrias, y, con toda esta fiesta y solemnidad [. . .] llevaron a Don Bartolomé Colón a la casa real [. . .] donde ya estaba la cena bien larga aparejada."—*Las Casas*, bk. I, ch. CXIV, vol. 63, pp. 138-9.

" cayeron en breve espacio cuatro dellos muertos y muchos bien heridos. Todo con todo el regocijo y placer y alegría del mundo, no haciendo mas caso de los heridos y muertos que si les dieran un papirote en la cara."—*Loc. cit.*, pp. 139-40.

7 " porque los bastimêtos y el pan de España son de mas rezia digestiô q̃ estas yerbas y malas viâdas q̃ aca gustarian ; y los aires mas delgados y frios q̃ los desta tierra. Padecieron [. . .] muy crueles dolores y passion del mal de las buas (porque el origen dellas son las Indias) y digo bien, las Indias : assi por la tierra donde tan natural es esta dolêcia, como por las indias mugeres destas partes."—*Oviedo*, bk. II, ch. XIII, fol. xviii verso.

8 " Sabido por la señora reina Anacaona, persuade al Rey, su hermano, que vayan a ver la canoa de los cristianos. [. . .] Tenia un lugarejo en medio del camino Anacaona, donde quisieron dormir aquella noche ; alli tenia esta Señora una casa llena de mil cosas de algodon, de sillas y muchas vasijas y cosas de servicio de casa, hecha[s] de madera, maravillosamente labradas, y era este lugar y casa como su recámara. Presentó esta señora a Don Bartolomé muchas sillas, las mas hermosas [. . .] y naguas de algodon [. . .] blanco a maravilla, cuantas quiso llevar y que mas le agradaban. [. . .] tenian el Rey e la Reyna su hermana sendas canoas muy grandes y muy pintadas y aparejadas, pero la señora como era tan palanciana, no quiso ir en la canoa, sino con Don Bartolomé en la barca. [. . .] Dejó alegres al Rey y a la Reyna."—*Las Casas*, bk. I, ch. CXVI, vol. 63, pp. 148-9.

9 " Despues que estas victorias ovo el adelâtado, peciaq̃ ·· se le auia trocado la côdicion, porq̃ se mostró muy riguroso côlos x̃pianos de ali adelâte en tâta manera q̃ no le podiâ sofrir algunos."—*Oviedo*, bk. III, ch. II, fol. xxii verso.

10 " ' que nuevas hay en la tierra ? ' ' buenas, buenas, que hay mucho oro [. . .] y que hay guerra con los indios porque habria hartos esclavos.' "—*Las Casas*, bk. I, ch. CXXII, vol. 63, p. 178.

11 See *Las Casas*, bk. I, chs. CXX and CXXI, vol. 63, pp. 164-75.

12 See *F.C.*, ch. LXI.

13 See *Las Casas*, bk. I, ch. CXXIII. Also *Raccolta*, pt. I, vol. I, pp. cxx-cxxii. Lollis points out (p. cxx) that, contrary to what Navarrete suggests, Coronel was still in Seville on February 17th, the date when Colón acknowledges receipt of the money he obtained to finance this first expedition. (The document to which he refers is not, as he is made to say by his printer, No. XIII, but No. XII, of *Raccolta*.) This finally disposes of Asensio (vol. II, p. 240), who gives February 3rd as the date of Coronel's arrival in Española.

14 " yo la dicha Ynes Nuñes renunçio las leyes que fizieron los enperadores Justiniano e Valiano, que son en favor e ayuda de las mugeres, que me non valan en esta razon en juisio ni fuera dél, en tiempo alguno ni por ninguna manera."—January 1498, *Raccolta*, pt. I, vol. I, p. 296.

15 " y aguardó el dia que se hizo a la vela [. . .] arrebatólo el Almirante, y dále muchas coces o remesones, por manera que lo trató mal . . .

" Tambien suplico a Vuestras Altezas, que manden a las personas que entienden en Sevilla en esta negociacion que no le sean contrarios, y no la impidan ; yo no sé lo que alli pasaria Ximeno, salvo que es de generacion que se ayudan a muerte y vida, e yo ausente y invidiado extranjero : no me desechen vuestras Altezas, pues que siempre me sostuvieron."—*Las Casas*, bk. I, ch. CXXVI, vol. 63, pp. 199-200.

16 " hombre muy honrado y bien cuerdo—hombre muy capaz y prudente y de autoridad."—*Las Casas*, bk. I, ch. CXXX, vol. 63, pp. 221-2.

" Nuestro Señor me guie y me depare cosa que sea su servicio y del Rey y la Reina, nuestros señores, y honra de los cristianos que creo que este camino jamás lo haya hecho nadie y sea esta mar muy incognita."—*as Casas*, bk. I, ch. CXXX, vol. 63, p. 222.

CHAPTER XXVI

1 " quesos en especial, los cuales hay allí muchos y buenos."—*Las Casas*, bk. I, ch. CXXX, vol. 63, p. 222.

2 " falso nombre porque son atan secas que no vi cosa verde en ellas, y toda la gente enferma que no osé detenerme en ellas."—Report on his Third Voyage, *Navarrete*, vol. I, p. 242.

3 *Las Casas*, quoting a letter of C. C. to the King and Queen.—Bk. I, ch. CLI, vol. 63, p. 323.

4 " Aquel que es trino y uno me guie, por su piedad y misericordia, en que yo le sirva, y a Vuestras Altezas dé algun placer grande y a toda la Cristiandad, asi como fue de la fallada de las Indias, que sonó en todo el mundo."—*Las Casas, loc. cit.*, p. 225.

5 " La mayor parte de las cosas buenas vienen de region muy caliente, donde los moradores de allí son negros o loros, y por ende, segun mi juicio, fasta que vuestra senioria falle la gente tal no fallará abundancia de las dichas cosas."—Jaume Ferrer de Blanes to Colón (Burgos, August 5th, 1495), *Navarrete*, vol. II, p. 105.

6 " segun la costumbre de los marineros, al menos los nuestros de España, que con tribulaciones y alegrias suelen decirla."—*Las Casas*, bk. I, ch. CXXXII, vol. 63, p. 229.

7 " hay una especie de papagayos [. . .] muy grandes, poco menos que gallos, todos colorados, con algunas plumas en las alas, azules y algunas prietas ; estos jamás hablan ; no tienen otra cosa de que se goce dellos, sino de la vista ; en lo demás son desgraciados."—*Las Casas*, bk. I, vol. 63, p. 236.

8 " maiz, que es una simiente que hace una espiga como una mazorca, de que llevé yo allí y hay ya mucho en Castilla."—Third Voyage, *Navarrete*, vol. I, p. 251.

9 " vinieron en canoas a la nao a rogarme, de parte de su Rey, que descendiese en tierra, e cuando vieron que no curé dellos, vinieron a la nao infinitisimos y muchos traian piezas de oro al pescuezo, y algunos atados a los brazos algunas perlas."—Diary, Third Voyage, *Navarrete*, vol. I, p. 251.

10 " levanté las anclas porque andaba mucho de priesa por remediar los mantenimientos [. . .] y tambien por remediarme a mi que habia adolescido por el desvelar de los ojos, que bien quel viaje que yo fuí a descubrir la tierra firme estuviera treinta y tres dias sin concebir sueño, y estoviere tanto tiempo sin vista, non se me dañaron los ojos, ni se me rompieron de sangre y con tantos dolores como agora."—Diary, *Navarrete*, vol. I, pp. 251-2.

11 " Yo siempre lei que el mundo, tierra é agua era esférico [. . .] Agora ví tanta disformidad, como ya dije, y por esto me puse á tener esto del mundo, y fallé que no era redondo en la forma que escriben ; salvo que es de la forma de una pera que sea toda muy redonda, salvo allí donde

tiene el pezon que allí tiene mas alto, ó como quien tiene una pelota muy redonda, y en un lugar della fuese como una teta de muger allí puesta, y que esta parte deste pezon sea la mas alta é mas propinca al cielo, y sea debajo la línea equinocial, y en esta mar Océana en fin del Oriente : llamo yo fin de Oriente, adonde acaba toda la tierra é islas. . . ."

" Tolomeo y los otros sabios que escribieron de este mundo, creyeron que era esférico, creyendo queste hemisferio que fuese redondo como aquel de allá donde ellos estaban [. . .] no hago yo que hay ninguna dificultad, salvo que sea esférico redondo como ellos dicen : . . ."

". . . porque deste hemisferio non se hobiese noticia cierta, salvo muy liviana y por argumento, porque nadie nunca lo ha andado ni enviado a buscar, hasta agora que vuestras Altezas le mandaron explorar é descubrir la mar y la tierra."

" La Sacra Escriptura testifica que nuestro Señor hizo al Paraiso terrenal, y en él puso el Arbol de la vida, y del sale una fuente de donde resultan en este mundo cuatro rios principales : Ganges en India, Tigris y Eufrates [. . .] y el Nilo que nace en Etiopia y va en la mar en Alejandria. Yo no hallo ni jamas he hallado escriptura de Latinos ni de Griegos que certificadamente diga el sitio en este mundo del Paraiso terrenal, ni visto en ningun mapamundo, salvo, situado con autoridad de argumento. . . ."

" y creo que pueda salir de allí esa agua, bien que sea lejos. [. . .] Grandes indicios son estos del Paraiso terrenal, porquel sitio es conforme á la opinion de estos santos é sanos teólogos, y asimismo las señales son muy conformes, que yo jamas leí ni oí que tanta cantidad de agua dulce fuese así adentro é vecina con la salada ; y en ello ayuda asimismo la suavísima temperancia, y si de allí del Paraiso no sale, parece aun mayor maravilla, porque no creo que se sepa en el mundo de rio tan grande y tan fondo."—*Navarrete*, vol. I, pp. 255-6, 258-9.

12 " creo que esta tierra que agora mandaron descubrir vuestras Altezas sea grandisima y haya otras muchas en el Austro de que jamas se hobo noticia."—Third Voyage, *Navarrete*, vol. I, p. 259.

13 " yo estoy creido que esta es tierra firme grandisima, de que hasta hoy no se ha sabido, y la razon me ayuda grandemente, por esto deste tan grande rio y mar, que es dulce, y despues me ayuda el decir de Esdras en el libro IV, cap. 6° que dice que las seis partes del mundo son de tierra enjuta, y la una de agua, el cual libro aprueba Sant Ambrosio en su Examenon y Sant Agustin." Quoted by *Las Casas*, bk. I, ch. CXXXIX, vol. 63, p. 264.

14 " y aqui en ellas todas nascen cosas preciosas por la suave temperancia que les procede del cielo por estar hacia el mas alto del mundo.

" yendo al Austro se va mas alto y andando hacia el septentrion, como entonces, se va descendiendo."—Diario, Third Voyage, *Navarrete*, vol. I, p. 260.

15 " y yo cierto, creo, que despues de los hidalgos y hombres de pró que vuestra señoria tiene junto con sus criados, que aquellos que los terná vuestra señoria muy ciertos para morir en su servicio, y la otra gente de comun yo pornia mucha duda."—*Las Casas*, bk. I, ch. CLIII, vol. 63, p. 333.

16 " De todo esto me acusaban contra toda justicia, como ya dije, todo esto era porque Vuestras Altezas me aborreciesen a mi y al negocio ; mas no fuera así si el autor del descubrir dello fuera converso, porque conversos, enemigos son de la prosperidad de Vuestras Altezas y de los cristianos ; mas echaron esta fama y tuvieron forma que llegase a se perder del todo ; y estos que son con este Roldán, que agora me da guerra, dicen que los mas son dellos."—*Las Casas*, bk. I, ch. CLXIII, vol. 63, p. 384.

17 *Las Casas*, bk. I, ch. CLX, vol. 63, p. 368.

18 ". . . y llegué a tal estremo, que por huir la muerte, dejándolo todo me metí en el mar, en una caravela pequeña ; entonces me socorrió Nuestro Señor, diciéndome : ' Oh hombre de poca fe, no tengas miedo, yo soy. esfuerza, no desmayes ni temas : yo proveeré en todo ; los siete años del término del oro no son pasados, y en ello y en lo otro te daré remedio. y así derramó mis enemigos y me mostró como podía llenar mis ofertas : Oh infeliz pecador, yo que lo hacía pender todo de la esperanza del mundo.' " —*F.C.*, vol. II, p. 120 ; and *Navarrete*, vol. I, p. 274.

19 " iba descreciendo y su hijo Don Diego Colón crecia en fuerza, haciendose hombre para poder acá servirles, que le hiciesen merced le mandar que viniese acá a ayudarle, para que él descansase algo y sus Altezas fuesen mejor servidos."—*Las Casas, loc. cit.*

20 " yo no sé si yerro, mas mi parecer es que los Principes deben hacer mucho favor a sus gobernadores en cuanto los tienen en el cargo, porque con disfavor todo se pierde."—*Las Casas*, bk. I, ch. CLXI, vol. 63, p. 137.

CHAPTER XXVII

1 " En ciertos tiempos del año, cuando tienen la inclinación y apetito de concebir, sálense a la playa y ábrense, y allí esperan el rocio del cielo, cuasi como si esperasen y deseasen su marido ; reciben aquel rocio del cual conciben y se empreñan, y tales producen sus hijos, que son las perlas o margaritas, cual fuese la calidad del rocio ; si puro fuese, nascen las perlas blancas, si fuese turbio, salen pardas o escuras [. . .] cuanto mas el rocio fuese del alba o de la mañana, tanto mas blancas salen ellas, y cuanto mas a la tarde o noche llegaren a recibirlo, tanto mas serán escuras." —*Las Casas*, bk. I, ch. CXXXVI, vol. 63, p. 246.

2 " Las perlas mandé yo ayuntar y pescar a la gente con quien quedó el concierto de mi vuelta por ellas ; y, a mi comprender a medida de fanega ; si yo non lo escribi a SS. Altezas, fué porque así quisiera haber fecho del oro antes."—*Navarrete*, vol. I, p. 267.

3 " muy gentil hombre y de autoridad y parecia bien ser de generosa casta [. . .] por no andar muy quieto. . . ."—*Las Casas*, bk. I, ch. CLXX, vol. 63, p. 431.

4 " a mi parecer, por esta causa principalmente, sobre otras quejas que fueron de acá [. . .] los Reyes indignados proveyeron de quitarle la Gobernacion."—*Las Casas*, bk. I, ch. CXXVI, vol. 63, p. 199.

5 See *Las Casas*, bk. I, end of ch. CLI, vol. 63, p. 325.

6 " De acá se pueden, con el nombre de la Santisima Trinidad, enviar todos los esclavos que se pudiesen vender, y brasil, de los cuales, si la información que yo tengo es cierta, me dicen que se podrán vender 4000, y que, a poco valer, valdrán 20 cuentos y 4000 quintales de brasil, que pueden valer otro tanto, y el gasto puede ser aqui seis cuentos [. . .] acá no falta para haber la renta que encima dije, salvo que vengan navíos muchos para llevar estas cosas que dije y yo creo que presto será la gente de la mar cebados en ello, que agora los Maestres y marineros (de los cinco navíos habia de decir), van todos ricos y con intención de volver luego y llevar los esclavos a 1500 maravedís la pieza, y darles de comer, y la paga sea de los mesmos, de los primeros dineros que dellos salieren ; y bien que mueran agora, así no será siempre desta manera, que así hacian los negros y los canarios á la primera, y aún aventajen estos (quiere decir que los indios hacen ventaja a los negros), que uno escape no lo venderá su dueño por dinero que le den, etc."—*Las Casas*, bk. I, ch. CLI, vol. 63, pp. 323-4. (The brackets are interpolations of Las Casas.)

7 " perlas e piedras preciosas e joyas e esclavos e negros e loros que en estos nuestros Reinos sean habidos e reputados por esclavos e monstruos e serpientes. . . ."—*Navarrete*, vol. II, p. 245.

A similar claim is inserted in a chart of discovery granted to Alonso Vélez de Mendoza, July 20th, 1500.—*Navarrete*, vol. II, p. 247.

8 *Navarrete*, vol. II, p. 246. Comments of *Las Casas*, bk. I, ch. CLXXVII, vol. 63, p. 474.

9 " a causa de la mucha libertad que los Indios tienen huyen y se apartan de la conversación y comunicación de los cristianos ; por manera que aun queriendoles pagar sus jornales, no quieren trabajar, y andan vaga-mundos [. . .] lo cual hagan e cumplan como personas libres que son y no como siervos."—*Navarrete*, vol. II, p. 299.

Las Casas devotes several pages to exposing those who deceived the Queen into believing that such an order was necessary, but the Queen's sincerity is evident.

10 " Suplico al Rey mi Señor muy afectuosamente, e encargo y mando a la dicha Princesa mi hija, y al dicho Principe su marido, que [. . .] non consientan ni den lugar que los indios vecinos y moradores de las dichas Indias y tierra firme, ganadas y por ganar, resciban agravio alguno en sus personas y bienes ; mas mando que sean bien y justamente tratados. Y si algun agravio han rescibido, lo remedien y provean." Quoted by *Asensio*, vol. II, p. 562.

The measures taken by King Ferdinand to carry out this last wish of the Queen will be seen in *C.D.I.A.I.*, vol. I, p. 255, together with the measures taken by his own secretary to render them ineffective and make a fortune out of their violation.

11 " Agora que, gracias a Nuestro Señor, las cosas desas partes las entiendo yo como las de Castilla [. . .] los vecinos y naturales desa ysla deven estar como vasallos y no como esclavos, segun los tovieron en tienpos pasados."—*Pleitos*, vol. I, p. 324.

12 *Las Casas*, bk. I, ch. CLV, vol. 63.

13 So says *Las Casas*, *loc. cit.*, p. 343.

14 " Mirá los hijos del Almirante, de los mosquitillos de aquel que ha hallado tierras de vanidad y engaño para sepulcro y miseria de los castellanos."— *F.C.*, ch. LXXXV.

15 " un cauallero, antiguo criado de la casa real, hôbre muy onesto y religioso llamado Frâcisco de bouadilla, cauallero de la ordê militar d' Calatraua."— *Oviedo*, bk. III, ch. VI, fol. xxvi.

" Y en la verdad, Bobadilla debia ser de su condicion y naturaleza, hombre llano y humilde ; nunca oi dél, por aquellos tiempos que cada dia dél se hablaba, cosa deshonesta ni que supiese a cudicia, antes todos decian bien dél. . . ."—*Las Casas*, bk. III, ch. VI, vol. 64, p. 33.

" Gran caballero y amado de todos."—*Bernáldez*, ch. CXCVI, vol. II, p. 253.

16 These documents are to be found in *Navarrete*, vol. II, pp. 235-40. The enumeration of the forts, etc., to be handed over to Bobadilla is as follows :

" fortalezas y casas, y navios, y armas y pertrechos y mantenimientos y caballos y ganados y otras cualesquier cosas que Nos tenemos en las dichas islas."

17 " que como enviasen á deponer al Almirante de su estado, quitándole la gobernacion, cosa, cierto, muy grande para quien tanto se le debia y les habia merecido, y con tan immensos trabajos, querian muy bien mirallo, y hacíaseles de mal efectuallo."—*Las Casas*, bk. I, ch. CLXXVII, vol. 63, p. 473.

18 " pero las mas verdaderas quedabâse ocultas ; porĝ el rey & la reyna quisierô mas verle emêdado que maltratado."—*Oviedo*, bk. III, ch. VI, fol. xxvi.

19 See letter of the Queen to Ovando, then Governor, on November 27th, 1503.—*C.D.I.A.I.*, vol. XXXIX.

This fear may have been the origin of the exclusion of foreigners from the Indies.

20 " Digo que en las islas de las Indias [. . .] ha habido, & hay grandes desconciertos e daños, los cuales comenzaron en tiempo del Almirante Colón, que las descubrió, sobre el concierto que hizo con los Ginoveses, de donde se siguió que fué por Gobernador de las islas el comendador Bobadilla."—*C.D.I.A.I.*, vol. I, p. 247.

This document is not quoted, to my knowledge, by any of the critics who have discussed this aspect of Colón's life.

21 " Bien que yo sepa poco : no sé quien me tenga por tan torpe que yo no conozca que aunque las Indias fuesen mias, que yo no me pudiera sostener sin ayuda de Príncipe. Si esto es así adónde pudiera yo tener mejor arrimo y seguridad de no ser echado dellas del todo que en el Rey é Reina nuestros Señores que de nada me han puesto en tanta honra y son los mas altos Príncipes por la mar y por la tierra del mundo ? "—*Navarrete*, vol. I, p. 272.

22 This point is ably put by *Altolaguirre, loc. cit.*

CHAPTER XXVIII

1 " en las cuales estaban dos hombres cristianos ahorcados, frescos de pocos dias ; iban y venian gentes a los de los navios, hacian sus comedimientos y reverencia al pesquisidor Bobadilla, preguntaban y respondian, pero todos siempre con recatamiento hasta ver qué mundo sucedía."—*Las Casas*, bk. I, ch. CLXXVIII, vol. 63, p. 479.

The facts on which my narrative of Bobadilla's arrival is based are given by Las Casas, *loc. cit.* They completely destroy Fernando Colón's narrative and restore Bobadilla's action to its true features. They also put the Colóns' case as what it was—unfortunately very bad—for Las Casas can on no account be dismissed as an adversary of the Colóns.

2 " en estos dias era grande la devocion que todos tenian de ver y oir novedades."—*Las Casas*, bk. I, ch. CLXXXIX, vol. 63, p. 483.

3 " Publiqué por palabra y por cartas que él no podia usar de sus provisiones, porque las mias eran las mas fuertes."—Letter to the Aya, *Navarrete*, vol. I, p. 270.

4 Dec. I, bk. VII, ch. IV. Quoted by *Altolaguirre*, 2, p. 328.

5 My first acquaintance with the problem of the Jewish origin of Colón was in New York in 1935, when Mr. Maurice David asked to see me about it. He explained to me the reasons why he believed Colón to be a Spanish Jew. Unacquainted as I then was with the subject, I was able to see at once that a number of Mr. David's arguments were plainly based either on misapprehensions or on insufficient knowledge of the Spanish history and language. But I was deeply struck by one argument, which, in my opinion, has an undoubted human value. Mr. Maurice David explained that he was the son and the grandson of rabbis, and he assured me that, as soon as he saw the monogram which appears on the left-top corner of all but one of the letters addressed by C. C. to his son Diego, he recognised it as identical with that which his father and grandfather always scribbled on the same spot in all their letters, i.e. an old Hebrew Greeting or

benediction frequently used amongst religious Jews ; the combination of the two letters *beth* and *hai* standing for Boruch Hashem.

Mr. David takes up this argument in his book (p. 66), unfortunately without adducing his own personal experience ; he shows that no letters addressed to other persons bear that sign ; while it is to be found in all but one which—its context implies—might have to be shown to the King and Queen. The arguments against him are :

(1) Though he says : " Any handwriting expert can confirm this," the majority of Hebrew-script experts I have consulted are not of his opinion and the minority are just non-committal.

(2) The sign may be a library sign, for all the letters *with* the sign come from the library of Veragua, and the only letter *without* it comes from that of Alba.

(3) The letters to his son, just like the others, are all headed by a +, which would be illogical on Mr. David's hypothesis.

On the other hand :

(1) There is the spontaneous recognition of the sign by Mr. David as a familiar monogram used by his rabbinical ancestors.

(2) Mr. J. Leveen, of the British Museum, points out to me a Hai-beth sign or monogram which is certainly " on its way " to become like the sign on C. C.'s letters (Oriental 9165, fol. 36*a*).

(3) True that, with peculiar devilry, luck has distributed C. C.'s letters to Diego in such a way that the *only* one which reads as if it might have to be shown is in the Alba's library, while the secret ones are in the Veragua's library, but the " library " explanation will not do because :

(*a*) The sign does *not* occur in *any* other letter of the many from C. C.'s hand in the Veragua's library, but only in those to his son.

(*b*) There is at least one letter in which the pen that traced the sign started again to write the first word without leaving the paper (December 29th, 1504, *Raccolta*, Table XXXV).

(*c*) The darkness and thickness of the sign are not constant and vary with those of the letters themselves.

(4) The use of this sign may have been an old family habit which had lost its religious significance and was used by Colón as the mere equivalent for " secret and confidential." Thus the only document, not a letter, in which it is found, is a memorandum addressed " para ty muy caro fijo " (see *Thacher*, vol. III, p. 330).

I feel that the value of this sign has been underestimated, but as I am not competent to argue the point, I have made no use of it in the text.

6 " El Señor Almirante respondia que el tiene cartas de sus Altezas en contrario desta ; por ende, que pide por merced al Señor comendador e requiere le guarde las dichas cartas que tiene de sus Altezas e que a la paga desto ques cosa de cuenta, que esté presto de estar a ella e della."— *Autografos de Colón*, Duquesa de *Alba*.

7 " Tenia el adelantado ya en Xaraguá y Francisco Roldán presos [. . .] diez y seis metidos en un hoyo o pozo, para los ahorcar."—*Las Casas*, bk. I, ch. CLXXXI, vol. 63, p. 496.

8 " no se hallaba presente quien por su reverencia y de compasion se los echase sino fué un cocinero suyo descognoscido y desvergonzado, el cual con tan deslavada frente se los echó como si le sirviera con algunos platos de nuevos y preciosos manjares."—*Las Casas*, bk. I, ch. CLXXXI, vol. 63, p. 497.

9 " Y así llegando Alonso de Vallejo, un hidalgo, persona honrada, [. . .] a sacalle y llevalle al navío, preguntóle con rostro doloroso y profunda tristeza, que mostraba bien la vehemencia de su temor : ' Vallejo, ¿donde me llevais ?' respondió Vallejo : ' por vida de vuestra señoria, á se embarcar';

repitió, dudando el Almirante: ' Vallejo ¿ es verdad ? ' responde Vallejo :
' por vida de vuestra señoria, que es verdad que se va a embarcar.' Con
la cual palabra se conhortó, y cuasi de muerte a vida resucitó."—*Las Casas*,
bk. I, ch. CLXXXI, vol. 63, p. 499.

" Yo debo ser juzgado como Capitan que de tanto tiempo fasta hoy trae
las armas á cuestas sin las dejar una hora, y de Caballeros de conquistas
y del uso, y no de letras, salvo si fuesen de Griegos ó de Romanos, ó de
otros modernos de que hay tantos y tan nobles en España, ca de otra guisa
rescibo grande agravio. . . ."—*Navarrete*, vol. I, p. 274.

10 " Si yo robara las Indias [. . .] y las diera a los moros, no pudieran en
España amostrarme mayor enemiga."—Letter to the Aya, *Navarrete*,
vol. I, p. 266.

11 He was *Corregidor* of Jerez, and there is a letter of the King and Queen
appointing him to prepare a fleet to sail for Africa and the Canary Islands.
July 12th, 1501, *C.D.I.A.I.*, vol. 38, p. 491.
On August 17th, 1501, he is given authority to send to Española any
married or unmarried men who wish to go and settle there.—*C.D.I.A.I.*,
vol. 38, p. 509.

12 This meditation is a summary and paraphrase of Colón's letter to the
Aya of Prince D. Juan, written on board ship, as reported by *Las Casas*,
bk. I, vol. 63, p. 501 ; *Navarrete*, vol. I, pp. 265-76.

13 20th or 25th, says *Las Casas*, at the beginning of ch. CLXXXII, bk. I,
vol. 63, p. 501.
" Estos grillos guardó mucho el Almirante, y mandó que con sus huesos
se enterrasen, en testimonio de lo quel mundo suele dar a los que en el
viven por pago."—*Las Casas*, bk. I, ch. CLXXXI, vol. 63, p. 496.

14 *Las Casas, loc. cit.*, vol. 63, p. 512.

15 *C.D.I.H.E.*, vol. 16, pp. 528 and 559.

16 See Royal *cédula*, September 27th, 1501, in *Navarrete*, vol. II, p. 275.
This royal decision does imply that Colón was believed to keep gold by
without accounting for it to the Treasury. There is a curious hint of this
in an " Inventory of the gold and jewels received by the Admiral [. . .] since
March 10th, 1495 " (" Relacion del Oro y Joyas que recibió el Almirante
despues que el Receptor Sebastian de Olaño partió de la Isla Española
para Castilla, desde 10 de Marzo de 1495 "). The last paragraph reads :
" Recibió mas el Señor Almirante, de Molina, que le habia dado un
cacique por cierto rescate, un espejo grande de oro, y mas once granos de
oro, los cuales no se pesaron porque no quiso el Señor Almirante, y serán
de peso de diez pesos de oro y otros mas y otros menos."—*C.D.I.A.I.*,
vol. 10, p. 9.

17 " los reyes catolicos le remouierô del cargo & le dierô licêcia q̃ se fuesse
a españa teniêdose por muy servidos d'l eñl tpo q̃ aca estuuo, porq̃ auia
retamête como buê cauall'o hecho su officio en todo lo q̃ toco a su cargo."—
Oviedo, bk. III, ch. VII, fol. xxviii.

18 " el s. comendador escryve a vuestra s. como el almjrante e sus ermanos
se quisyeron alçar e ponerse en defensa juntado yndjos y xpyanos.
" hago saber a vuestra s. como el almjrante fablando al mj compañero
20 leguas adelante del puerto, entre çiertas razôs dixo que aunquel arçobjspo
de toledo avya djcho que no bolverya aca que el se bolverya.
" rogamos por amor de nuestro Señor ihux [. . .] que trabajeys como
el almirante ni cosa suya buelva mas aesta tierra.
" por amor de dios que pues Vuestra rreᵃ a sido ocasion [. . .] que
salyese esta tierra de poderyo del Rey faraon, que faga que él ni nenguno
de su nacion venga en estas islas." Quoted by *Asensio*, vol. II, pp. 393-5.
Asensio argues in favour of Colón that these monks had been indoctrin-

ated by Bobadilla, but they were independent men, the most independent in the island from the civil authority, and they wrote long enough after their arrival to have been well informed.

19 " quando la Reina que santa gloria aya e yo lo enbiamos por gobernador a esa ysla e a causa del mal recaudo que vuestro padre se dió en ese cargo que vos agora teneis, estaba toda alçada y perdida y sin ningun provecho."— *Pleitos*, vol. I, p. 44.

20 Copla No. 22, *Revue Hispanique*, vol. 5, p. 258.

CHAPTER XXIX

1 " san Pedro, quando saltó en la mar, andovo sobr'ella en cuanto la fee fué firme. quien toviere tanta fee, como un grano de paniso, le obedeçerán las montañas ; quien toviere fee, demande, que todo se le dará. pusad y abriros han. no deve nadie de temer a tomar qualquier ynpresa en nonbre de Nuestro Salvador, seyendo justa, y con sana yntinçión para su santo serviçio."

" Ya dije que para la esecución de la impresa de las Indias no me aprovechó razon ni matemática ni mapamundos : llenamente se cumplió lo que dijo Isaías, y esto es lo que deseo de escrebir aquí por le reducir á V.A. á memoria, y porque se alegren del otro que yo le dije de Jerusalen por las mesmas autoridades, de la cual impresa si fe hay tenga por muy cierto la victoria."—Letter to the King and Queen in Book of Prophecies : *Navarrete*, vol. II, p. 265.

2 There is an abundant and convincing wealth of documents to prove this in Bataillon's *Erasme et l'Espagne*.

3 " Digo que el Espiritu Santo obra en cristianos, judios, moros, y en todos otros de toda seta, y no solamente en los sabios, mas en los inorantes."— *Navarrete*, vol. II, p. 263.

4 " aquellos bienaventurados Apóstoles [. . .] de contino sin cesar un momento me avivan con gran priesa."—*Navarrete, loc cit.*

5 " En una epistola o carta trasladada de aravigo en rromançe, la cual embió el rrabi samuel de Israel natural de la cîbdad de Fis, a maestre Ysaach, rrabi de la Synagoga de Marrucos etc, los quales despues fueron buenos e fieles Christianos."—*Raccolta*, pt. I, vol. II, p. 94.

6 Jeremiah iii. 17, actually quoted by Rabbi Samuel and copied by Colón in his Book of Prophecies : " et fiet unum ovile, idest una Ecclesia ex Iudeis et gentilibus collecta " ; *Raccolta*, pt. I, vol. II, p. 143.

7 " In die illa radix Iesse, qui stat in signum populorum, ipsum gentes deprecabuntur, et erit sepulchrum eius gloriosum. et erit in die illa : adiiciet Dominus secundo manum sua ad possidendum residuum populi sui, quod relinquetur ab Assyriis, et ab Egypto [. . .] et ab insulis maris."— Isaiah xi. 10, 11, 12.

8 " Audite, insule, et a[t]tendite, populi, de longe : [. . .] dedi enim te in lucem gentium, ut sis salus mea usque ad extremum terre."—Isaiah xlix. 1 and 6 ; *Raccolta*, pt. I, vol. II, p. 114.

9 " te gentes venient ab extremis terre."—Jeremiah xvi. 19.

10 " vocat autem hereticos conversos de iudaysmo ad fidem catholicam, qui contra alios permanentes in perfidia arguebant de hoc psalmo. " sic patet secundum homines litteratos de judaysmo conversos."— *Raccolta*, pt. I, vol. II, p. 147.

11 " Quando vine, començé a sacar las auctoridades, que me parescia que

haçian al caso [de Jerusalén] para despues tornarlas a rrever, y las poner en rrima."—September 13th, 1501 (Granada), *Raccolta*, pt. I, vol. II, p. 75.

12 There is a note of Cesare de Lollis to the first of these verses in which he shows that they are believed to be by Don Fernando Colón in an MS. (Add. 13.984 British Museum).

13 " El Rey de Inglaterra embio cinco naos armadas con otro genoves ccmo Colón a buscar la Isla de Brasil y las siete ciudades.* Fueron proveydos por un año. Dicen que seran venidos para el setiembre. Vista la derrota que llevan allo que lo que buscan es lo que Vuestras Altezas poseen."— July 25th, 1498 : Letter of Ruy González de Puebla to the King and Queen.

" Los de Bristol ha siete años que cada año an armado dos, tres, cuatro caravelas para ir a buscar la isla del Brasil y las siete ciudades con la fantasia deste Ginoves. El rey determino de le embiar porque el año passado le truxo certenidad que havian hallado tierra."—July 25th, 1498 : Letter of Pedro de Ayala to the King and Queen.

" Quanto a lo que desis que alla es ydo uno como Colón para poner al Rey de Ynglaterra en otro negocio como el de las Yndias syn perjuysio de españa ni de portogal sy asy le acude a el como a nosotros lo de las Yndias bien librado estara crehemos que esto sera echadiso del Rey de françia por poner en esto al Rey de Ynglaterra para le apartar de otros negocios mirad que procureis que en esto ny en lo semejante no Resciba engaño el Rey de Ynglaterra que por cuantas partes pudieren trabajaran los franceses de gelo hazer. y estas cosas semejantes son cosas muy ynçiertas y tales que para agora no conviene entender en ellas y tambien mirad que aquellas [. . . blank in text] no se puede entender en esto syn perjuisio nuestro o del Rey de Portogal."—Letter by the King Ferdinand to Ruy González de Puebla, dated by Harrisse March 28th, 1496, I believe by mistake, for it obviously answers Puebla's letter of July 25th, 1498. *Harrisse*, p. 314.

" Que vaes e sigais aquella costa que descobristes, que se corre Leste-ueste, segun paresce, por razón que va hacia la parte donde se ha sabido que descobrian los ingleses, e vais poniendo las marcas con las armas de Sus Altezas, o con otras señales que sean conocidas, cual vos paresciere, porque se conozca como vos habes descobierto aquella tierra, para que atajes el descobrir de los ingleses por aquella via."—*C.D.I.A.I.*, vol. 38, p. 470.

On Hojeda's horse see *loc. cit.*, p. 466.

On Bastidas and Alonso Vélez de Mendoza see *Navarrete*, vol. II.

On P. Alonso Niño and Guerra see *Thacher*, vol. II.

14 " todos a una dijeron que era burla : agora, fasta los sastres suplican por descubrir."—*Navarrete*, vol. I, p. 311.

15 On the first part cf. *F.C.*, ch. LXXXVII : " Ma tornando al Ammiraglio, dico, che in Granata, si come a' Re Catolici piacque di mandare alla Spagnuola il detto comendatore, cosi stimarono ben fatto, che si dovesse mandar l'Ammiraglio ad alcum viaggio [. . .] que egli si occupasse."

On the second part cf. *Las Casas*, bk. II, ch. IV, vol. 64, p. 22 : " Item que aunque ya era viejo y muy cansado de tan immensos trabajos, todavia tenia proposito de gastar la vida que le quedaba en descubrir, por su servicio, muchas otras tierras mas de las que había descubierto, y que creía hallar estrecho de mar en el paraje del puerto del Retrete, que agora es el Nombre de Dios."

16 *Navarrete*, vol. II, p. 273.

17 " Este caballero era varon prudentísimo y digno de gobernar mucha gente, pero no indios, porque, con su gobernacion, inestimables daños, como

---

* The text printed in *Harrisse* says "vicinidades," which is obviously a misprint.

abajo parecerá, les hizo. Era mediano de cuerpo, y la barba muy rubia ó bermeja, tenia y mostraba grande autoridad, amigo de justicia ; era honestísimo en su persona en obras y palabras, de cudicia y avaricia muy grande enemigo, y no pareció faltarle humildad, que es esmalte de las virtudes ; y, dejando que lo mostraba en todos sus actos exteriores, en el regimiento de su casa, en su comer y vestir, hablas familiares y públicas, guardando siempre su gravedad y autoridad, mostrólo asimismo, en que despues que le trajeron la Encomienda mayor, nunca jamàs consintió que le dijese alguno señoría."—*Las Casas*, bk. II, ch. III, vol. 64, p. 17.

18 " Trujo consigo por Alcalde Mayor un caballero de Salamanca y licenciado, llamado Alonso Maldonado, persona muy honrada, prudente y amigo de hacer justicia y humano. . . ."—*Las Casas, loc. cit.*, p. 18.

19 " Pidio asi mismo que pudiese llevar dos o tres hombres que supiesen arábigo, porque siempre tuvo opinion, que pasada esta nuestra tierra firme si estrecho de mar hallase, que habia de topar gente del Gran Khan."— *Las Casas*, bk. II, ch. IV, vol. 64, p. 24.

20 " a los cuales habeis de tratar como a personas que nos van a servir en semejante jornada—y no habeis de traer esclavos."—*Navarrete*, vol. I, pp. 280-81.

21 " El vendabal me detuvo en Cádiz fasta que los Moros cercaron a Arcila, y con él sali al socorro, y fui al puerto."—*Navarrete*, vol. I, p. 331.

22 " llevaba uno de los cuatro navios muy espacioso asi porque era mal velero como porque le faltaba costado para sostener las velas."—*Las Casas*, bk. II, ch. V, vol. 64, p. 29.

23 Both Las Casas and Fernando Colón say that the Admiral foretold the storm and said so to Ovando, who did not believe him. It is unbelievable that the Admiral should not have said so in his letter to the King and Queen in which he refers to this storm.

CHAPTER XXX

1 Text in *Navarrete*, vol. I, pp. 296-312.

2 This sentence ends with the words " where he wrote " (" donde escribia "), which obviously is a scribe's interpolation.

3 He may refer to the beginning of the letter. But the bulk of it was written in Jamaica.

4 *Navarrete* writes the word *Sospechoso* with a capital S, which suggests a name. It probably meant " the ship one could not trust, not being seaworthy."

5 This was Don Fernando, who was to be his future historian. He was then really fifteen. But Colón, when moved, always exaggerates in the direction of his emotion.

6 Possibly *Cathay*, though, in this letter at any rate, he several times writes *Catayo* for *Cathay*.

7 He means on opposite sides of the same peninsula.

8 This passage is very cryptic and obscure. It may be corrupt. But it may be one of those elliptic utterances of which Colón was so fond. I interpret it, tentatively, in this way : " Those who criticise me for my navigating errors will navigate soon to Hell. Those like me who have the faith, shall not have to make that voyage."

9 " Oh that the salvation of Israel were come out of Zion ! " . . .—Psalm xiv.

10 I believe he means the liberation of Jerusalem.

CHAPTER XXXI

1   " si mi queja del mundo es nueva, su uso de maltratar es de muy antiguo. Mil combates me ha dado, y a todos resistí fasta agora que no me aprovechó armas ni avisos. Con crueldad me tiene echado al fondo. La esperanza de aquel que crió a todos me sostiene : su socorro fué siempre muy presto. Otra vez, y no de lejos estando yo mas bajo, me levantó con su brazo divino, diciendo : *O hombre de poca fé, levantate que yo soy, no hayas miedo.*"— Letter to D. Juan's Aya, *Navarrete*, vol. I, p. 265.

2   " E con esta tormenta, asi a gatas, me llegué a Jamaica." . . . "mas yo le faré ver con el brazo izquierdo." . . . "a donde no hay amor todo lo otro cesa." . . . "otra lástima me arrancaba el corazon por las espaldas." . . . " El otro negocio famosisimo está con los brazos abiertos, llamando." . . . —*Navarrete*, vol. I, pp. 297 . . . 272 . . . 272 . . . 298 . . . 311.

3   Thacher, who, despite that noted absence of critical sense which was observed by Vignaud, is at times useful, is lamentable in his treatment of this letter. He wastes twelve pages on a photographic reproduction of an Italian translation on the ground that the original MS. is unknown and utterly disregards the Spanish original come to us through perfectly reliable channels. He is unable to realise that the style of this Spanish original is pure royal Colón, and that no translator, adaptator or commentator could possibly *create* such vigorous, gloriously ungrammatical twists and gems of expression. He actually speaks of " the Spanish *translation*"!! (vol. II, p. 686 note 2) ; and he crowns his incompetence with the following howler :

" In the Spanish, the phrase is ' y son en una distancia lejos del polo y de la linea,' which, of course, could not have been the meaning of Columbus, for this would make him say that these lands were situated in forty-five degrees from the Equator north, if it was an equal distance from the Pole."—Vol. II, p. 595 note 2.

His own translation is : " and are a long distance from the Pole and also from the line."

The Italian text is : " & sôno in vna distancia longe dal polo : & etiam dela linea."

Poor Thacher was the only one who did not see the point ! He misunderstands *both* the Italian and the Spanish. In both Colón's and his Italian translator's text, the word *una* means *the same, en una distancia, in vna distancia*, i.e. at the *same* distance, but not, as Thacher read the Spanish (God knows why he read the Italian otherwise, since it is identical), that Veragua and Aurea were at the same distance from the Pole and from the Equator, i.e. on the 45 parallel, but that, though both at different distances from the Pole and from the Equator, those two places, Veragua and Aurea, were on the same spot of the earth, since they were in his (Colón's) mind one and the same place.

Enough has been said to show that Thacher was not in a position to handle Spanish texts.

4   Diego Méndez de Segura, que habia venido por escribano mayor de aquella flota, persona bien prudente y honrada."—*Las Casas*, bk. II, ch. XXX, vol. 64, p. 155.

5   " Señor : el peligro en que estamos bien lo veo, que es muy mayor de lo que se puede pensar. El pasar de esta Isla a la Isla Española en tan poca vasija como es la canoa, no solamente lo tengo por dificultoso, sino por imposible : porque haber de atravesar un golfo de cuarenta leguas de mar y entre islas donde la mar es mas impetuosa y de menos reposo, no se quien se ose aventurar á peligro tan notorio.

" Señor : muchas veces he puesto mi vida a peligro de muerte por salvar la vuestra y de todos estos que aqui estan, y nuestro Señor milagrosamente me ha guardado la vida ; y con todo no han faltado murmuradores que dicen que vuestra Señoria me acomete a mi todas las cosas de honra, habiendo en la compañia otros que las harian tan bien como yo : y por tanto pareceme a mi que vuestra Señoria los haga llamar a todos y los proponga este negocio, para ver si entre todos ellos habrá alguno que lo quiera emprender, lo cual yo dudo ; y cuando todos se echen de fuera, yo pondre mi vida a muerte por vuestro servicio, como muchas veces lo he hecho."—*Navarrete*, vol. I, p. 322.

6 *Las Casas* (*loc. cit.*) speaks of two canoes, one in which Flisco sailed and the other one for Méndez ; but Méndez's narrative is clear. There was one canoe, in which he put " mantenimientos para mi y *para un cristiano y para seis indios, que eramos ocho personas.*"—*Navarrete*, vol. I, p. 383.

7 " Los libros que de acá os envio son los siguientes : Arte de bien morir de Erasmo. Un sermon de Erasmo en romance. Josefo de Bello Judaico. La Filosofia moral de Aristóteles. Los libros que se dicen Lingua Erasmi. El libro de la Tierra santa. Los coloquios de Erasmo. Un tratado de las querellas de la Paz. Un libro de Contemplaciones de la Pasion de nuestro Redentor. Un tratado de la venganza de la muerte de Agamenon y otros tratadillos."—*Navarrete*, vol. I, p. 328.

8 Cf. *Erasme et l'Espagne*, by Bataillon.

9 " Yten el dicho almirante ha procurado e procura que todos los casados que están en estas partes, que tienen sus mugeres en castilla, se vayan a ella o las traygan, poniendo para ello muchas penas de perdimiento de vienes, lo qual solamente ha a provechado e aprovecha para poner a los tales casados en muchas necesidades e gastos, cohechándolos e llevándoles mucha suma de pesos de oro porque se sobresea lo susodicho ; y desta manera diego Méndez, alguacil, por una cedula de sobresimiento que alcanzó del dicho almirante, llevó a ciertos casados que estavan en la ysla de cuba doscientos pesos de oro, e asy se han llevado e lleva otras muchas cantidades sin que el fin para el que se manda e procura aya efecto ny se cumpla ny ejecute."—*Pleitos*, vol. II, p. 373.

10 " parecenos, Señor que no quereis ir a Castilla, y que nos quereis tener aqui perdidos.
" yo me boy a Castilla con los que seguirme quisieren."—*Las Casas*, bk. II, vol. 64, pp. 163-4.

11 " se embarcaron con tanto regocijo y alegria como sí ya desembarcaran en Sevilla."—*Las Casas*, vol. 64, p. 165.

12 " como ellos eran muchos mas y mas sanos, y ejercitados mas en trabajos, por ser marineros, y cognosciesen los que iban con el Adelantado ser muchos menos, y gente de palacio, mas delicada. . . ."
" por manera que fueron todos desbaratados, y, como gente vil y traidores, volvieron las espaldas."—*Las Casas*, vol. 64, p. 178.

CHAPTER XXXII

1 " cierto estoy con gran temor, porque el frio tiene tanta inimistad con esta mi enfermedad que habré de quedar en el camino."—Letter, November 21st, 1505, *Navarrete*, vol. I, p. 334.

2 " Mi partida para allí será breve."—*Navarrete*, vol. I, p. 336.

3 " Tu tio ha estado muy malo y está de las quijadas y de los dientes."—Seville, November 28th, 1505, *Navarrete*, vol. I, p. 337.

4 " Mi mal no consiente que escriba salvo de noche, porque el día me priva las fuerzas de las manos."—Letter to his son Diego, Seville, December 1st, 1505, *Navarrete*, vol. I, p. 340.

5 " Yo non sey ya que diga a mi deseo de veros y comunicar algo que non es de pendula."—January 4th, 1505, *Navarrete*, vol. I, p. 333.

6 " Yo fago juramento, y esto sea para tí solo, que de las mercedes que sus Altezas me tienen fechas, en mi parte me alcanza el daño diez cuentos cada año, y que jamás se pueden rehacer. Ved que parte será o es lo que toca a sus Altezas, y no lo sienten."—Letter to Don Diego, Seville, November 21st, 1504, *Navarrete*, vol. I, p. 334.

7 " Plugome mucho de oir tu carta, y de lo que el Rey nuestro Señor dijo ; por el cual le besarás las reales manos."—*Navarrete*, vol. I, p. 334.

8 " Plega a la Santa Trinidad de dar salud a la Reina nuestra Señora, porque con ella se asiente lo que ya va levantado."—*Navarrete*, vol. I, p. 338.

9 " Suplico al Rey mi Señor que se quiera servir de todas las joyas e cosas, o de los que a su señoria mas agradaren ; porque viéndolas pueda haber mas continua memoria del singular amor que a su Señoria siempre tuve : e aun por que siempre se acuerde que ha de morir, e que le espero en el otro siglo ; e con esta memoria pueda mas santa e justamente vivir."—Quoted by *Asensio*, vol. II, p. 579.

10 " acá mucho se suena que la Reyna, que Dios tiene, ha desado que yo sea restituydo en la posesión de las Yndias."—December 13th, 1504, *Raccolta*, pt. I, vol. II, p. 243.
" Acá si posible fuese, querría cada dia cartas. . . . es de trabajar de saber si la reyna, que Dios tiene, dexó dicho algo en su testamento de my."—December 21st, 1504, *Raccolta*, pt. I, vol. II, p. 244.

11 " el Señor obispo de Palencia es de dar parte desto con de la tanta confiança que en su Merced tengo, y ansí el Señor Camarero."—December 1st, 1504, *Raccolta*, pt. I, vol. II, p. 237.
" es de dar priesa al Señor Obispo de Palencia, el que fué causa que sus Altezas oviesen las Yndias, y que yo quedase en Castilla, que ya estaba yo de camino para fuera, y ansí el Señor Camarero de su Alteza."—December 21st, 1504, *Raccolta*, pt. I, vol. II, p. 244.
" Con un correo que ha de llegar allá oy te escrivy largo y te embié una carta para el señor camarero."—January 18th, 1505, *Raccolta*, pt. I, vol. II, p. 251.

12 " de tu hermano haz mucha cuenta, él tiene buen natural, y ya desa las moçedades diez hermanos non te serían demasiados, nunca yo fallé mayor amigo, a diestro y sinistro, que mis hermanos."—December 1st, 1504, *Raccolta*, pt. I, vol. II, p. 237.

13 " Acá se diz que se ordena de enbiar o fazer tres o quatro obispos de las Yndias, y que al Señor obispo de Palençia está remetido esto. despues de me encomendado en su merçed, dile que creo que será servicio de sus Altezas que yo fable con él, primero que concluyan esto."—December 1st, 1504, *Raccolta*, pt. I, vol. II, p. 237.
" Yo he oydo que están para elejir tres obispos para enbiar a la Española. si plaz a su Alteza de me oyr, antes que esto concluyan, que diré con que Dios Nuestro Señor sea bien servido, y su Alteza y contento."—Memorial para Don Diego, December 3rd, 1504, *Raccolta*, pt. I, vol. II, p. 241.

14 " bibo de enprestado, mis dineros que allá ove, alí los gasté en traher esa gente que fué conmigo acá a sus casas."—December 1st, 1504, *Raccolta*, pt. I, vol. II, p. 236.

15 " Yo he de haber el tercio, ochavo y diezmo. porque despues habrá sienpre lugar de abasar a lo que la persona quisiese, pues su Alteza diz en su carta que me quêr dar todo lo que me pertenece."—Letter, December 13th, 1504, *Raccolta*, pt. I, vol. II, p. 243.

16 " Si, sin inportunar, se oviese licencia de andar en mula, yo trabajaria de partir para alla pasado henero."—*Raccolta*, pt. I, vol. II, p. 245.

17 " En el año de 1494, habiendo visto el Rey y la Reina que de todos sus reinos de Castilla y Leon par la guerra de los moros, a duras penas podian llegar diez o doce mil hombres de a caballo, y habia mas de cien mil encabalgados en mulas, proveyeron de una premática, con muy grandes penas, que ninguno, ni alguno caballero, Duque, ni Conde, ni otra dignidad, escudero, ni labrador, viejo ni mozo, no fuese osado de cabalgar en mula enfrenada y en silla, so pena de que se la matasen, salvo la clerecia de orden sacra y las mujeres [. . .] y el Rey mesmo dio tal ejemplo en esto que jamás cabalgaba en mula, salvo siempre à caballo."—*Bernáldez*, ch. CXXXIV, vol. II, p. 88.

18 " La liçencia de la mula, si sin trabajo de puede haver, folgaría della, y de una buena mula."—*Raccolta*, pt. I, vol. II, p. 249.

19 *Navarrete*, vol. II, p. 304.

20 " creo que la congoxa de la dilaçion d'este mi despacho sea aquello que mas me tenga asi tullido."—Later than May 1505, *Raccolta*, pt. I, vol. II, p. 256.

21 " Plega à Nuestro Señor de me librar dellos (de los ojos dice) que bien sabe que yo no llevo estas fatigas por atesorar ni fallar tesoros para mí, que, cierto, yo conozco que todo es vano cuanto acá en este siglo se hace, salvo aquello que es honra y servicio de Dios, lo cual, no es de ayuntar riquezas ni soberbias ni otras cosas muchas que usamos en este mundo, en las cuales más estamos inclinados que en las cosas que nos pueden salvar."—*Las Casas*, bk. II, vol. 64, pp. 308-9.

22 " La governacion y possesión en que yo estaba es el caudal de mi honrra."— *Raccolta*, pt. I, vol. II, p. 257.

23 " dijo el Almirante : ' sea la que vuestra Alteza mandase,' y añidió : ' quien lo puede mejor hacen que el Arzobispo de Sevilla, pues había sido causa con el camarero que su Alteza hobiese las Indias ? ' "—*Las Casas*, vol. 64, p. 188.

24 Las Casas completely misses the point. " Respondió el Rey al Almirante que lo dijese de su parte el Arzobispo ; el cual respondió que para lo que tocaba a la hacienda y rentas del Almirante, que se señalasen letrados, pero no para la gobernación ; quiso decir, segun yo entendí, porque no era menester ponello en disputa, pues era claro que se le debia."—*Las Casas*, vol. 64, p. 188.

25 " Y pues se parece que su Alteza no a por bien de cumplir lo que ha prometido por palabra y firma juntamente con la reyna, que aya sancta gloria, creo que combatir sobre el contrario para mi, que soy un arador, sea açotar el viento ; y que será bien, pues que yo e hecho lo que e podido, que agora dexe hacer a Dios Nuestro Señor, el qual e siempre fallado muy prospero y presto a mis necessidades."—*Raccolta*, pt. I, vol. II, p. 258. (*prospero* no doubt for *propicio*.)

26 " Torno a decir con juramento que yo he puesto mas diligencia a servir a Vuestras Altezas que no a ganar el Paraiso."—*Las Casas*, vol. 63, p. 256.

27 ". . . dice aqueste : ' que los indios de esta isla Española eran y son, dice él, la riqueza della, porque ellos son los que cavan y labran el pan. . . . y dice más, que bien que hobiese enviado a Castilla muchos dellos y se hobiesen vendido, pero que era con proposito, que, despues que fuesen instruidos en nuestra sancta fé y en nuestras costumbres y artes y oficios, los tornarian á cobrar, y los volver á su tierra para enseñar á los otros.'"— *Las Casas*, vol. 64, p. 190.

28 They will be found best explained by Altolaguirre in *Estudio Juridico de las Capitulaciones y Privilegios de Colón*, "Boletin de la Real Academia de la Historia," vol. XXXVIII, Madrid, 1901.

29 See *Las Casas*, vol. 64, p. 191.

30 " Don Diego Colón, su hijo e sucessor en el Almirantazgo . . ."
" Don Diego Colón, Almirante de las dichas Indias . . ."—June 2nd, 1506,
Navarrete, vol. II, p. 316.

31 " Yo estó determinado de no hacer partido ni venta de mi honra, porque
ni lo puedo hacer ni incurrir quiero en la maldicion de mi padre, ni su al.
es parte para mas que para darme mi justicia [. . .] e todos los partidos son
escusados para mi, e no conviene hablar en ellos, porque yo me rio de
lo que su A. me promete, ni puede dar, que de oy en diez años yo fio en
Dios terné comprado en Castilla otro tanto de mis propias rentas, que
será mas firme que lo que su a. promete. . . .
" Lo que suplico a su señoria es que escriba a su A. muy encargada-
mente, suplicándole me haga cumplimiento de justicia, conforme a mis
privillejos e confirmaciones que tengo firmadas de su Real nombre, y esto
sea luego, sin mas dilaciones de las pasadas, y syn hablarme en partidos,
que no me convienen. . . .
" Item que asi mismo escribe a Don Fernando, mi Señor, que dé mas
priesa en estos negocios de la que ha dado [. . .] e que no oya a su Alteza
cuando le hablase en cosas de partidos."—Instruccion del Almirante Don
Diego Colón para Jeronimo de Agüero. *Alba*.

32 " Mirad, Almirante, de vos bien lo confiaria yo, pero no lo hago sino por
vuestros hijos y sucesores."—*Las Casas*, bk. II, ch. XLVII, vol. 64, p. 237.

33 " e perdioseles una nao donde venian ciertos Pages, e mucha ropa e
joyas."—*Bernáldez*, ch. CCIV, vol. II, p. 278.

34 " e la Reyna Doña Juana ovo con la Princesa de Inglaterra Doña Catalina,
su hermana, mucha consolacion."—*Bernáldez, loc. cit.*
Asensio (vol. II, p. 601) gives Henry VIII as the host, advancing by
three years the accession to the throne of Catherine of Aragon's husband.
" Sereníssimos é muy altos poderosos príncipes rey y reyna nuestros
señores. Yo creo que Vuestras Altezas creerán que en ningún tiempo
tuve tanto deseo de la salud de mi persona, como he tenido después que
supe que Vuestras Altezas avían de passar acá por la mar, por venirle a
servir y ver la experiençia del conoçimiento que con el navegar tengo.
á Nuestro Señor a placido así. porende, muy humildemente supplico a
Vuestras Altezas que me cuenten en la cuenta de su real vasallo y servidor,
y tengan por cierto que, bien que esta enfermedad me trabaja así agora
sin piedad, que yo les puedo aun servir de serviçio que no se aya visto su
igual. estos revesados tiempos e otras angustias, en que yo e seido puesto
contra tanta razón, me han llegado a gran extremo. a esta causa no e ydo
a Vuestras Altezas, ni mi hijo. muy humildemente les supplico que
resçiban la intençión y voluntad, como de quien espera de ser buelto en
mi honrra y estado, como mis escripturas lo prometen.—La Sancta Trinidad
guarde y acreciente el muy alto y real estado de Vuestras Altezas."—April-
May, 1506, *Las Casas*, bk. II, ch. XXXVII ; *Raccolta*, pt. II, vol. I, p. 259.

35 " E le mando que haya encomendada à Beatriz Enríquez, madre de Don
Fernando, mi hijo, que la provea que pueda vivir honestamente, como
persona á quien yo soy en tanto cargo.
" Y esto se haga por mi descargo de la conciencia, porque esto pesa
mucho para mi ánima."—*Navarrete*, vol. II, p. 315.

36 " Don Diego, mi hijo, o cualquier otro que heredare este Mayorazgo,
despues de haber heredado y estado en posesion de ello, firme de mi firma,
la cual agora acostumbro, que es una X con una S encima, y una M con
una A romana encima, y encima della una S y despues una Y griega con
una S encima con sus rayas y virgulas, como yo agora fago, y se parecerá
por mis firmas, de las cuales se hallarán muchas, y por esta parecerá."—
Navarrete, vol. II, p. 229.

37 Thus Maurice David in his *Who was Columbus?* explains this signature as a Kaddish for the alleviation of Colón's Jewish conscience. He is, I believe, mistaken, as can be easily shown, for his interpretation implies the integration of the last line of the signature "X.p.o. FERENS" into the Kaddish, to make it say:
　　　" Shadai, Shadai, Adonoy, Shadai Yehdra, molai,
　　　　chesed, Nanthai o'vou pesha, chatuo."
But for Colón the signature had one fixed and compulsory part, and one variable:　　· S ·
　　　· S · A · S ·　was fixed; but below that, which was always the
　　　　X M Y
same, his signatures varied and he sometimes wrote, in block capitals, a disciplined and quiet X.p.o. FERENS, or else he flourished off a grandiloquent and tempestuous *El Almirante*, all crossed and recrossed by lines and waves and winds. This explanation, therefore, must be rejected. Professor Moses Bensabat Amzalak in *Una Interpretaçao da Assinatura de Cristovam Colombo*, Lisbon, 1927, by a kind of translating of the letters used by Colón into their nearest Hebrew equivalent, reads the signature *God of Hosts*, and *God holy and one*. That may be so. But it is not certain that Colón knew Hebrew, though there is a haunting similarity between the Hebrew character *áin* and the peculiar shape of Colón's Y which would correspond to it.

38 See *Buron*, vol. I, p. 284, and vol. II, p. 446. These notes are not to be found in *Raccolta*.

39 There is an interesting study on the cabbalistic interpretation of Colón's signature in a book otherwise not very useful by Patrocinio Ribeiro: *A Nacionalidade Portuguesa de Cristobam Colombo*, Lisbon, 1927. The study in question is by Dr. Barbosa Sueiro, p. 167 *et seq.*

40 ". . . escrebí al Rey y á la Reina mis Señores, que dende á siete años yo le pagaría cincuenta mil de pie y cinco mil de caballo en la conquista della, y dende á cinco años otros cincuenta mil de caballo é cien mil de pie para esto. . . ."—*Navarrete*, vol. II, p. 282.

GENERAL INDEX

SPECIAL INDEX ON CHRISTOPHER COLUMBUS

(ALSO COLOMBO, COLOM, COLOMO, COLÓN AND COLUMBO)

The Four
Voyages
of
Columbus

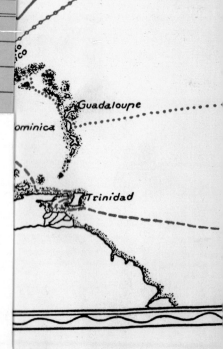

59294

59294   E
                        111
                        M172
Madariaga, S. de.
    Christopher Columbus.

DATE	ISSUED TO

Guadaloupe

ominica

Trinidad

CARLOW COLLEGE
Grace Library
Pittsburgh, Pennsylvania

Rep